RAFFAELLO

THE PAINTINGS • THE DRAWINGS

RAFFAELLO

THE PAINTINGS · THE DRAWINGS

ISTITUTO GEOGRAFICO DE AGOSTINI - NOVARA

This edition published for Costco Wholesale
by arrangement with De Agostini Rights Ltd. (MEB/OP)

© Istituto Geografico De Agostini

ISBN 0-7489-5302-7

MARIO SALMI

INTRODUCTION

pages 6-7

I

LUISA BECHERUCCI

RAPHAEL AND PAINTING

pages 9-198

II

ALESSANDRO MARABOTTINI

RAPHAEL'S COLLABORATORS

pages 199-302

III

ANNA FORLANI TEMPESTI

THE DRAWINGS

pages 303-428

Medallion of Pope Paul II for the Consistory of 1466 (recto and verso). Medagliere, Vatican.

INTRODUCTION

Raphael's name, like that of Michelangelo, has always been the object of universal acclaim.

The name of the latter evokes admiration for his superhuman genius and for his art, in which the suffering of a long and lonely life finds sublime expression. Raphael's praises on the other hand (and here we do not speak of Urbino, where he is the tutelary deity and where every year they commemorate him like a patron saint) are sung with the spontaneous sympathy of the human heart and he has acquired immense popularity. Thus, to define exceptional female beauty with special emphasis, popular language uses the phrase " as beautiful as a Madonna by Raphael." It is a phrase that would seem banal if it were not so accurate in referring to a lofty idealized beauty that rises above any comparison with earthly beauty.

Still, in the admiration for Raphael there has sometimes been disagreement, prompted by partisan attitudes or due to changes in taste. For example, while the Master was still alive, the frescoes in the Loggia of the Farnesina with the "Hellenistic fable" of Cupid and Psyche unveiled in 1518 were defined by a partisan of Michelangelo as a "shameful thing." In the same century Giorgio Vasari, himself an admirer of Raphael, (in one of those comparative scales of value which is impossible for us to understand) placed him second to Buonarroti. We may add that the appreciation for our painter, which during the following two centuries was unconditional, met with reservations among the Purists (1843), who expressed a negative judgment of his work done after the Disputa del Sacramento, that is, during the last eight years of his activity. Shortly thereafter the English Pre-Raphaelite movement turned its interest backward in time from the fifteenth century to the thirteenth, exalting the Primitives and considering the Renaissance, represented by Raphael's art, a period of deterioration. Still, in spite of certain parentheses, the fame of the Master has not suffered any serious injury and his art has today an objective and complete critical evaluation, beyond and above narrow-minded opinions. Parallel to the already-mentioned aesthetic currents during the second half of the last century, art historians began a complex task of literary research that has continued into this century alongside studies in other fields—iconology, formal criticism, and psychology. This continual study, which illustrates the inexhaustible interest in the Master, is also the premise for our own positive critical assessment. It is permissible, therefore, to ask ourselves why the art of Sanzio has stimulated such extensive historical interest as well as being so widely appreciated on a popular level.

Raphael, who has been defined as the poet of the classically attuned High Renaissance culture, worked within the context of Neo-Platonic idealism, as the artist himself explains in a letter written in 1514 to Baldassarre da Castiglione. In reference to the fresco of Galatea in the Farnesina, Raphael says that in order to paint " a beautiful woman I need to see a number of beauties, to be able to select the most beautiful," with the help, of course, of the distinguished writer who had praised the fresco. He continues by adding that, because of the lack of competent experts and of beautiful women, he uses a certain idea which comes to his mind, in order to arrive at eccellenza d'arte. He did not depend on references taken directly from reality—the points of departure for the classical-humanist, quattrocento tradition which had as its authoritative spokesman Leon Battista Alberti—but he availed himself of the idea " that dictates from within " and expressed it with marvelous spontaneity.

Raphael's classicism is not static: it has its mutations and, after the phase of graceful Hellenizing refinement, reaches a peak of solemn grandeur around 1515 in the Vatican tapestries. Then, especially in the altarpieces with more complex and dynamic compositions, it is directed towards the portrayal of human emotion in a new rapport between man and the divine. This was to find its greatest appreciation during the late Renaissance and the Baroque.

And later, when with an inexhaustible illustrative richness he composed designs for the Loggias in the Vatican, he combined a decoration of genius inspired by the Antique with those episodes from the Old and New Testaments that were completed with the collaboration of assistants in 1519. Thus we see a prodigiously assimilative spirit in the various stages of his life, which lasted only thirty-seven years. He maintained a constant fidelity to classical sources, though at the same time he was sensitive to the art of his contemporaries from Perugino to Pinturicchio and the Venetians, and from Leonardo to Michelangelo—an art that he creates anew within his own sensibility and within his own figurative language.

Concerning the sources, I would mention only two points here. The first one regards Raphael's participation in the decoration of the Piccolomini Library in the Cathedral of Siena. Scholarship today correctly agrees that Sanzio painted nothing there. But that imposing system of arcades that contain the salient episodes in the life of Pius II, with an architectural scheme taken over from Perugino's in the Crucifixion in Santa Maria Maddalena de' Pazzi in Florence, we believe was suggested to Pinturicchio by Raphael. This is confirmed by the certainty of Raphael's collaboration in designing the individual compositions. Then, the large medallion of Paul II for the Consistory of 1466, whose author is still unknown despite proposed attributions (Andrea di Niccolò from Viterbo, Piermatteo Orfini, and even Fioravante from Bologna), can offer us some insights.

The medallion with its clear design in very low relief is certainly not a masterpiece, but it contains two imposing compositions which have attracted our attention. The first, showing a Pope among the dignitaries of his court, high on a throne as he opens the Consistory (illustration at the left), seems a clear compositional precedent (notwithstanding the diverse shape of the scene) for two of the frescoes in the Library—that showing Aeneas Sylvius Piccolomini before Eugenius IV, and that with Pius II in the act of canonizing St. Catherine.

It is possible that the medallion was known to and inspired Pinturicchio, who had worked in the Borgia Rooms in the Vatican. However, the other side bears another composition still more interesting for us. Christ within a mandorla composed of angels' heads appears flanked by two rows of patriarchs and apostles, while below we see a rather confused representation of the Last Judgment and an altar with the Virgin and St. John the Baptist, and the symbols of the Passion. The compositional scheme, the details of the Christ within the mandorla, and the presence of the altar make one think that for his Disputa del Sacramento Raphael had recourse to this medallion, as well as (for the upper part of the famous painting) to Ghirlandaio's fresco with Christ in Glory in the main chapel of Santa Maria Novella and that with the Judgment by Fra Bartolommeo in the Museum of San Marco in Florence. This, moreover, may have been the case even though the subject was indicated by Julius II. One can, therefore, form the hypothesis that the design of the two previously mentioned Sienese frescoes was by Raphael.

This reference is only to demonstrate how inexhaustible studies can be when they deal with an art such as we are considering.

It may be said that in the past, for over three centuries, the interest in Raphael was concerned exclusively with his pictorial work. Luckily his lasting fame stimulated collectors to search for whatever could document his activity: frescoes and panel pictures, with sacred and profane subjects, among which some memorable portraits; and the drawings which are found in conspicuous numbers (more than four hundred) in both Italian and other collections. And if they, too, bear witness to his artistic genius, often they serve also as a precious documentation for the origins of various single works. From about 1514-15 the Master, weighed down with numerous commissions, turned to his assistants, whose presence often can be proved. Still, contrary to what has been claimed, the pupils did not overshadow Raphael's personality, even if some of them like Giulio Romano and Perin del Vaga expressed themselves in their own language after his death.

The Master did not exhaust his artistic energies merely in painting. He was also an architect who was appreciated in his own time, though later forgotten because of the overwhelming admiration for his painting, until in the late nineteenth century a serious literary examination brought fundamental contributions to the knowledge of this second aspect of Raphael's art, which developed from Bramante in his Roman period but expressed itself with the originality of genius. We must add that Raphael, appointed by Leo X to oversee the monuments of Rome, contributed on the one hand to the protection of the city's antiquities and on the other to their study and description, carried out with a systematic exactitude unknown to the artists of the Early Renaissance who had enthusiastically drawn them.

MARIO SALMI

RAPHAEL AND PAINTING

by Luisa Becherucci

The paintings

Raphael has been considered ever since his own time as the painter par excellence, almost the incarnation of painting itself, surpassing such masters as Leonardo, Titian and Correggio. He was not always loved, and even sometimes harshly attacked, but even his denigrators gave him credit for his greatness. His reputation has been unaffected by this comparison with other artists and has remained triumphant despite changes in taste and ideals over the centuries. It is symptomatic that even today, at a moment when artistic expression seems to reject the direction he followed, there is a new interest in Raphael, a reflowering of studies that explain his development. Even the writings of non-specialists detect in the Olympian, detached, " divine " Raphael, reflections of our own anxieties and uncertainties. They recognize in his " man," who had been considered an almost superhuman model, a current image of man today, disturbed by doubts, contradictions and uncertainties. The crowds in the museums still flock to the work of Raphael with an enthusiasm that has endured over the years and the centuries, and today these crowds come from all continents, from cultures that are quite different from his, and still they understand and appreciate him, as if he really had spoken for all men.

If one scans the vast body of literature on Raphael (and it would require years to gain a critical command of it), one sees the never-ceasing popularity, the continued interest in the artist, whether in agreement or in contrast, as if each artistic period had sought its legitimacy in a comparison with Raphael. According to Vasari, and especially according to those artists who came after Raphael and worked in his idiom, albeit with highly individualized accents, the Renaissance placed him at the apex of its conquests in painting, second only to Michelangelo, but superior to all others, the ancient and the modern, superior to reality itself (to which he wished to remain faithful) so that " . . . nature was conquered by his colors." For centuries the ways of appreciation have not changed, as the words that express them have not changed: facility, naturalness, sweetness, grace, perfection, ideal beauty—words repeated to such an extent that they have become meaningless. The relationship between Raphael and his critics remained for a long time that between a divinity and its faithful, whether worshipers or qlasphemers. He always appeared in a different dimension, it was possible to be a believer or a rebel, but it was impossible to erase his great presence from the horizon of painting. Only in the nineteenth century was a new approach initiated. Beyond the miracle one can perceive the fullness of the historical facts and their complexity. Raphael arrived at the summit by a difficult path, and it is this which must be traced to appreciate his conquest. The nineteenth-century monographs by Quatremère de Quincy, Passavant and Cavalcaselle sought to assemble all the biographical facts and the circumstances of his activity—which had been outlined solely by Vasari—in order to illuminate his experience as a whole, that of a man coping with practical problems and that of the artist. These monographs relate a human drama, giving substance to the unclear image that emerged from preceding acritical biographies. The new titles, " poet of a culture," " poet of a civilization," refer above all to his intellectual dominion over that culture, by means of which he was able to give it direction, as a protagonist, and at the same time to celebrate it as a poet. L'âge d'or, the klassische Kunst, can be considered the apogee of the Renaissance and can be analyzed and defined through the art of Raphael, who was able to bring into balanced synthesis the ceaseless questions of Leonardo and Michelangelo. It was, to be sure, a brief apogee, which ended with his death. And we can see in Raphael's work the beginning of the decline. Not even the most penetrating and as yet unsurpassed study of Raphael's lyricism—that by Ortolani—is completely free of this concept, that is, of the idea of an apex that was so high that the first to reach it could not remain there for very long. Without the poetic intuition which was its justification, the language created by Raphael becomes in the others habit or *maniera* (even though *bella maniera*), it was defenseless in the face of a slow and subtle corruption which little by little altered and emptied it until the new naturalism of the Seicento finally brought about its complete depreciation.

Today we ask if this historical reconstruction is true. Must we really see in Raphael the illusion of perfection which is in fact the beginning of its decadence? Is it correct to consider the Renaissance, of which Raphael was undoubtedly the most profound interpreter, as only an illusionary endeavor of sublimation, a figurative creation of Neo-platonism?

The answers to such questions are the task of current research on Raphael and on the Renaissance. The younger critics turn to Raphael as to the highest consciousness of the Renaissance, to one who, although dominant in every field of art, preferred to work in painting because he saw in it not a medium limited by its technical possibilities, but a "mode," newly invented, with contributions from all the arts, for expressing the true discovery of the Renaissance, that of a universe not alluded to in metaphors and symbols but taken in its dynamics, in an inevitable play of relationships, in a perpetual genesis of forms, in a dramatic process of which man is the conscience: the *moto che è causa di ogni vita*, which Alberti proposed as the theoretical foundation of a new *pictura* in which the entire expressive effort of a culture was concentrated. We turn to Raphael today, no longer as an inaccessible idol, but as a subject of research, in order to understand his free, responsible, and untiring search—to assimilate every experience, even that of intellectual harmony, of "ideal" beauty, merely to exhaust it and then freely to go beyond it. A painter, but as Alberti had defined one a century earlier, *l'ingegno scorgitore erudito* who, to his examination of reality, committed his intelligence as well as his lyric intuition. Raphael was the poet of a culture not because he glorified it, but because he had the courage to guide it, to lead it across the awesome threshold of a fullness of expression. He differed from Leonardo and from Michelangelo only in his serene faith that he could go forward without destroying or losing himself—this was the Renaissance faith in the *virtus* of man. Not man in precarious balance between the illusion of an apogee and the delusion of decadence, but man operating at the heart of a problem, slowly clarifying it by freeing it from the obscuring encrustations of outdated experiences. Not the mythical hero of a no less mythical "golden age" but one who had the power to serve and to surpass it. This is the justification, despite the apparent differences between our times and his, for a renewed study of Raphael. [1]

URBINO

This study is faced from the beginning with serious problems. In Raphael's activity, the youthful period lacks documentation and is still obscure. The documents are scarce and the known works are few and late. A pupil, however gifted, did not sign the works in which he collaborated with the master, even when the work was almost wholly his, and this was true of Raphael in Perugino's workshop, as we shall see. His first signed and dated work, the *Marriage of the Virgin* from Città di Castello (now in the Brera), is from 1504, when Raphael, born on April 6, 1483, was more than twenty years old. For an artist of known precocity and one who, as the son of a painter, Giovanni Santi, must have used paint brushes since infancy, twenty years is a long time; for Raphael these years must have been particularly intense, judging from the maturity expressed in that masterpiece.

The most recent studies have sought to trace Raphael's path toward that maturity, but the scarce documentation has helped little. There is the will of his father, who died in 1494, and the notarial deeds regarding family controversies between Santi's second wife, Bernardina di Parte, and his avaricious brother, Don Bartolomeo, who apparently contested the will. The judges ruled against Bartolomeo and his innocent ward, Raphael. Attempts are being made, using both internal and external evidence, to arrive at a plausible chronological order for the works reasonably considered as youthful. More than a century ago, Quatremère de Quincy and Passavant complained of the difficulties of comparing works dispersed in many countries, and since then the situation has not improved. Furthermore, the works have been altered by all kinds of damage, not the least being the so-called restorations. Little help comes from photographs which eliminate color from the work or alter it to such a point that incorrect deductions and hypotheses result. Thus we must conclude by recognizing the real value, once absurdly doubted, of the first biography of Raphael, that by Vasari, which drew on the direct testimony of friends and disciples and which was based on an acute capacity for artistic judgment of works that were then directly available. It is from Vasari that an integration of the documents and formulations of hypotheses on Raphael's youth can be derived.

Vasari tells us that it was Giovanni Santi who taught painting to his son, still a child. He had recognized his *bellissimo ingegno* and even used him as an assistant "in many works he executed in Urbino." But it is not from this statement that we can deduce, as some have attempted, the beginning of the early and decisive formation of Raphael in Urbino. The assistance was that expected of the youngest helpers in a workshop: grinding colors, tieing brushes and sharpening pencils. What the ten-year-old boy used to see, observing the creation of his father's paintings, was a correct symmetry of perspective and a diligent ability to render, in timid, formal ways, faces, fabrics and landscapes that appeared natural. These were the echoes, but not the substance, of what Santi may have learned from Melozzo and the Flemish and Italian decorators of the Ducal Palace in Urbino. That great Albertian concept of perspective, which, through Laurana and Piero della Francesca, had characterized the artistic tradition of Urbino, was too difficult for a young lad to grasp to retain as a lasting impression. His father's works could not have helped him in achieving this understanding, either; according to Vasari, Santi had the merit solely of recognizing his son's exceptional abilities and of starting him on the right road under the guidance of an excellent master, who was riding the crest of a wave of fame and commissions. Santi did this so that the lad's career would be more successful than his own, which had been on the fringe of pictorial activity in Urbino; there he had watched the ducal commissions go to Piero, Melozzo and the group of " foreigners " from Flanders, and then to Signorelli and perhaps even to Perugino. If one considers the plausibility of this reasoning, common to all disillusioned fathers of modest talent who see in their sons a chance for vicarious success, it is not difficult to believe Vasari when he tells us that " this good and loving father knew that his son could learn little from him, and arranged to place him with Pietro Perugino, who, he had been told, occupied the first place among painters of that time. Perhaps it was not only from what he had been told that Giovanni Santi knew Perugino's worth. Even though his work in Sinigaglia and in Fano was probably not begun until later, the Umbria where he was already well-known was just across the border from Montefeltro. More valid evidence of a knowledge that was also a critical acknowledgment, is given in the rhymed *Cronica*,[2] which Santi wrote in honor of Federico da Montefeltro shortly after his death in 1482 and which reflects the extent to which the mediocre painter carefully studied and understood the artistic situation of his time. The historical conditions are clearly presented: painting develops along the new direction of perspective, and its evolution is followed, with far-ranging vision, from Flanders to Florence to northern Italy. The work concludes with an exaltation of Mantegna, whom Duke Federico, the protagonist of the *Cronica*, stops to admire on his trip to Mantua. The identities of the greatest masters already seem to have been established by this contemporary, who certainly reflected the general opinion. And if one looks carefully, he will see that their listing is not casual; on the contrary, it seems to indicate a clear distinction of tendencies. After the brief mention of the principal Florentine painters, among whom he includes Piero della Francesca, Santi seems to dwell on the situation in Verrocchio's workshop, which, between 1470 and 1480, was the principal center of discussion and of experimentation of the new painting. He mentions Domenico Ghirlandaio, Botticelli, Filippino Lippi (who is specified to have been very young at the time), and Luca Signorelli, all artists who for more or less lengthy periods were active in or at least visitors to the workshop. Along with these he names Leonardo and Perugino, and if it seems ingenuous of him to have described them as *par d'anni e par d'amore*, placing two masters of such different stature on the same level, one should remember that what is evident to us today was not necessarily so for one who was judging them while they were young, around 1482. At that time Perugino had only recently achieved fame with his fresco in the Sistine Chapel. Leonardo, on the contrary, had outlined his entire future direction in the *Adoration of the Magi*, but he had not finished the work, which was put aside in the house of Giovanni Benci; the *Last Supper*, the *Mona Lisa* and the *Battle of Anghiari*

1 Leonardo, Adoration of the Magi (detail). Florence, Uffizi.

were still to come. By ranking these two artists together Santi may have indicated that he understood the significance of their artistic directions when they themselves had barely enunciated them—that he grasped their common intention to *ridurre in moto* the entire image, to animate everything, men and objects, that appeared in the space of the perspective with a play of infinitely varied intensities of light. The selection as master for his own son of the only one of the two artists who was available after Leonardo left to work in Milan was not accidental in Santi, but was dictated rather by a clear understanding of the new problems of painting, which he did not dare approach himself.

In his criticism, if not in his works, he indicated a program upon which Raphael later was to reflect and to which he remained faithful; the experience of his youth was essentially that of those two masters and was not the experience of a tradition, however illustrious, such as that of Urbino; it was rather the experience of the most current problems, as they were examined in Florence.

FLORENCE

It was not, therefore, when Raphael was twenty years old, an age when was already mature and author of a great masterpiece, that the decisive encounter took place which so vitally affected his style. His apprenticeship under Perugino, as Cavalcaselle has correctly stated, was not preceded by an apprenticeship in Urbino with his father and then with Timoteo Viti, pupil of Francia, who did not return to Urbino from Bologna until 1495. [3] From his purely manual work in his father's shop Raphael went directly in his early years to Perugino's shop, where he came into contact with the most progressive ideas in the artistic study then being carried on. After the discoveries in the field of perspective, this study was concerned with luminous and graphic dynamics in order to include the element of color in the totality of the image. It was necessary to refine the relationship of color in order to identify it with the infinite, ever-changing light, and render it able, as the play of light and shadow, to suggest the inevitable development of form in infinite movements of action, to attain that *dolcezza ne' colori unita*, that *bellezza nuova e più viva*. These were the new aspects of painting which Vasari in his preface to the " third age " of art indicates as elements of the conquest in expression achieved by Perugino and Leonardo.

It is that conquest which recent criticism has seen in Raphael from his early years, and it has been hypothesized that he had an earlier contact with Florence than that of 1504. Longhi, [4] proposing the necessity of a Florentine apprenticeship to give coherence to the confusing youthful career of the artist, indicated the possibility that he followed his master Perugino on his frequent trips from Perugia, which from 1495 was the center of his activity, to Florence, where he maintained his residence and where he saw to such important commissions as the polyptych for the Certosa of Pavia. Perhaps we may dare make a further step, although purely hypothetical, in this direction. It was primarily the extreme youth of Raphael at the time of his father's death on August 1, 1494, that led to the supposition that he was taken to Perugino's workshop in the following year, 1495, when the master was beginning in Perugia a work of great dimensions, the complex polyptych for the main altar of San Pietro. Thus, Vasari's account—that Giovanni Santi had gone to Perugia personally to propose to Perugino that he take on Raphael in his shop, and that there he had awaited the master's return from Rome, meanwhile obtaining occasional commissions—would be relegated to the realm of fiction. According to Vasari, he received Perugino's consent and then brought the very young lad from Urbino himself. With the exception of the romanticized report of a tearful farewell to his mother, impossible because Magia Ciarla had died in 1491, the very plausibility of the account makes it believable. This was not the flash of inspiration of Cimabue discovering the genius of Giotto that kindled the fantasy of the storyteller; this was the prosaic discussion of two mature men, both painters, deciding the lad's apprenticeship, weighing the factors pro and con, one of which may have been Raphael's youth. Giovanni Santi died in the summer of 1494 and it is possible that perhaps he knew he had some grave illness and, sensing that his days were numbered, he hastened to assure his son's future. The circumstances of Vasari's account confirm that in 1493 Perugino, who had worked in Rome on the decorations for the coronation of Alexander VI, was able to stop in Perugia on his return to Florence where he was to marry Chiara, daughter of the architect Luca Fancelli, in September of that year. [5] Raphael was then ten years old, but it was not an incongruous age for an assistant who had not been *a leggere* or *all'abaco*, that is, in a regular school, before being placed in a workshop. This must have been the case with Raphael, who was certainly *omo sanza lettere*, judging from his ungrammatical youthful writings. If he had been with Perugino since 1493 or 1494, not in Perugia, where the master did not return until 1495, but in Florence, we can imagine him in that household which had a young and beautiful mistress in Chiara, in a situation quite similar, for example, to that of young Vasari in the house of Andrea del Sarto: not merely a shopboy or a pupil, but rather a member of the family. And this would support our analysis of the continuous and coherent Florentine elements that appear in Raphael's early work.

This supposition is supported, in the first place, in the drawings. Although we have none that can be dated with certainty to a period before 1500, we can see (for example, in those for the altarpiece of San Niccolò in Città di Castello, which are by the eighteen-year-old Raphael) [6]

2 Perugino, Madonna Enthroned (detail). Florence, Uffizi.

the Peruginesque characteristic, a constant attempt to allude to forms almost lost in the atmospheric vibrations of light and to take on a completely new force of plastic definition, of the suggestion of motion, and of vast spatial scope. These are aspects derived from Florentine experiments, especially from those of Leonardo in the studies for the *Adoration of the Magi*. And, while it is unnecessary to repeat a point that is elaborated in another part of this volume, it can be deduced that Raphael, during his apprenticeship with Perugino, must have had access, in addition to the drawings of the master, to those left by Leonardo in Florence after his departure for Lombardy. From the youthful drawings by Raphael, other indications can also be derived, especially from the very beautiful drawing in Oxford which very old texts indicated as his self-portrait and which, even if that question is under discussion, is accepted as an autograph. [7] In this drawing the pencil line assumes the clarity of a pen, defining each lock of hair, and the light shines on the clearly defined planes of the face; this work has its exact counterpart not in the drawings of Perugino but in the splendid series of human faces executed in silver point that constitute the most stylistically significant nucleus of Lorenzo di Credi's work. It is sufficient to compare the Oxford drawing with those by Credi in the Louvre, in Cambridge, or in the Uffizi, or with the presumed self-portrait in London (Wright) [8] to see the complete agreement of method and intention, even though Lorenzo di Credi was never able to achieve such clarity of expression or to follow the sweet outline of the cheek with a line that reveals the form with the decisiveness of the chisel. And this indication is neither circumstantial nor isolated. There are others that indicate an early Florentine experience for Raphael. Later, the composition of the Ansidei Altarpiece repeats the formula not only of Verrocchiesque altarpiece in the Duono of Pistoia, which we know was executed by Lorenzo, but also of that of Santa Maria Maddalena dei Pazzi, now in the Louvre, which he executed for Filippo Mascalzoni between 1489   13

5 Nativity of the Virgin. Fano, Santa Maria Nuova.

3 Madonna with Child. Urbino, Casa Santi.

4 Resurrection. São Paulo (Brazil), Museum of Art.

and 1493. The echo of compositions by Lorenzo di Credi persists in Raphael up to the *Aldobrandini Madonna*, usually dated to the period of the Stanze, which is analogous to the *Madonna* by Lorenzo now in the Borghese Gallery and to the beautiful preparatory drawing in Darmstadt. [9] We shall see other such analogies in Raphael's portraits: even such an absolute masterpiece as *La Muta* echoes the portrait by Lorenzo now in the Pinacoteca in Forlì. And there are some portraits whose attributions are contested between Raphael and Lorenzo, such as that of a youth in the Uffizi, and another, famous one, supposedly by Perugino, in the same museum.

This striking image, whose exceptional power of characterization inspired its attribution to Raphael, but which today has been correctly restored to Lorenzo di Credi, links his name with that of Perugino, suggesting other considerations. It does not seem only a casual circumstance that the young face of Lorenzo was added by Perugino, as is now believed, to those of the onlookers in the *Giving of the Keys* in the Sistine Chapel of 1481. They were students together in the workshop of Verrocchio, and a relationship of collaboration and probably of friendship seems to have endured between them afterward; certain common activities suggest this, although there exists no documentary proof. Lorenzo's altarpiece for the church of Santa Maddalena precedes only slightly the celebrated fresco of the *Crucifixion* painted by Perugino in the nearby convent between November, 1493 and 1496, immediately after the return from Rome mentioned by Vasari. In the now deconsecrated church of Santa Chiara, the *Nativity* by Lorenzo di Credi (now in the Uffizi, undated but placed by Degenhart [10] between the fifteenth and sixteenth centuries), which has some Peruginesque elements, was a perfect companion piece, in form and dimensions, to Perugino's *Pietà*, dated 1495 (now in the Pitti). The previously mentioned portrait in the Uffizi seems almost to be a later answer by Credi to Perugino's portrait of *Francesco delle Opere*, of 1494; in his work Lorenzo seems to emulate the sturdy modeling achieved with the fully mastered pictorial means of the Flemish manner. Both painters seem at this point to have been intent upon acquiring a complete mastery of the technique of oil painting. Perugino borrowed from the warm impastos of Memling for the reverberations of sunset in his distant landscapes. Lorenzo, instead remained faithful to Hugo van der Goes, the great model of the Florentine painters for more than a decade, with the clear cool light of the winter horizons in the Portinari Altarpiece. Both, besides, were involved in the problem posed in Verrocchio's workshop of a new art of painting which would capture the " chromatic naturalism " of Flemish painting within the dramatic tension of the image typical of Florentine *gran disegno*.

Without drawing definite conclusions, which can only result from more detailed study, we limit ourselves to indicating that all the elements exist for the hypothesis of a contact, and perhaps also a collaboration, between Perugino, who in 1493 returned permanently to Florence, where he set up house, and Lorenzo di Credi, the heir to Verrocchio's workshop and all the *cose di arte* therein, which he defended tenaciously against the claims of relatives. A well-informed Vasari tells us that there were " drawings, reliefs, statues and other items "—that is, everything left there by Verrocchio and his illustrious disciples, Domenico Ghirlandaio, Botticelli and the young Filippino, and, foremost, Leonardo.

If this hypothesis of the possible beginning of Raphael's career in Florence can be verified, we will have a much more plausible background for that which his later development suggests— that is, his access to an extremely rich body of material for study, in which the *famulus* of Perugino could have attained not only the complete mastery of painting and drawing techniques but also the awareness of the problem that was to become relevant in all his painting. This problem, posed and assiduously elaborated by Florentine art, was one of a total animation, of an integral dynamics of the image that would capture and express the incessant transformation and evolution that the Renaissance discovered as it own sense of existence. The *storia* which Alberti[11] had theorized as the *somma opera del pittore* was this infinite play of relationships which always renewed themselves in an unceasing course through the infinite moments of time.

The final step had been taken in drawing by Leonardo. But understanding his new direction was not an easy task, even for those who had worked by his side. The unfinished *Adoration* remained an incomprehensible message until he himself, on his return from Milan to Florence, indicated the means of understanding it. And precisely in this interim period, the presence of a modest genius such as that of Lorenzo di Credi was important. He did not lack the tenacious will to interpret and to learn, and he worked with scrupulous integrity. We owe to him the mediation not of the problems, but of the solutions offered by young Leonardo to his contemporaries and especially to the very young. Presently, the first hypotheses are being stated regarding Leonardo's contact with Baccio del Fattorino, the future Fra Bartolomeo and Mariotto.[12] It seems possible to include Raphael in this group; he had just arrived in Florence, and he may have begun a study of Leonardo's drawings, under the artist's guidance. And this master, whom Vasari describes as patient and gentle, faithful to the point of devotion to the glorious traditions of Verrocchio's workshop, could have constituted for Raphael an alternative to Perugino's teaching: the alternative of a deeper consciousness of form, of bolder composition, of a surer graphic sense, and, ultimately, of a stronger sense of reality, to which Perugino's lyricism might be anchored. This was the basis of that *peruginismo critico* which Ortolani and Castelfranco [13] have seen in Raphael's later method, that which, since Vasari, has been recognized as the period during which he worked with Perugino in the years between the end of the fifteenth century and his return to Florence in 1504.

15

PERUGIA

These were the years of experience, the *Wanderjahre* of Fischel,[14] during which we see Raphael travel about in central Italy, wherever his work took him, always ready to relate occasional contacts to the coherence of his problems, almost in a deliberate selection. This coherence has its active agent in Perugino, with whom Raphael, once he mastered a sure technique and solid grasp of design, was able to collaborate, first in a secondary capacity, later almost as an equal and finally, it seems, assuming the entire responsibility for commissions given to the master, such as, according to recent critics, the *Coronation* for San Francesco in Perugia.

In these years between 1495 and the end of the century, Perugino completed the work for the convent of Santa Maria Maddalena in Florence and accepted almost contemporaneously commissions for the major conventual orders: in Perugia, the large polyptych for the Cassinese of San Pietro, and for the Carthusians of Pavia, the equally elaborate polyptych which he probably worked on in Florence. In the meantime, he was also active in Perugia on the frescoes in the Sala del Cambio. He therefore maintained two workshops, in Florence and in Perugia, and he had to organize his work on an almost industrial scale, using a host of collaborators; ultimately this had a negative effect on his art. Raphael's activity must have been a part of this collaboration; his participation soon became clearly recognizable and his individuality was affirmed, though not in opposition to the teachings of Perugino. On the contrary, he was completely in accord with Perugino's pictorial achievements, which at this time were at an apex. Perugino had not yet begun that decline which some art historians see in the works that came after the Albani Polyptych of 1491. The *Portrait of Francesco delle Opere*, dating from 1494, was his masterpiece, equal to Flemish art, with a chromatic construction of marvelous unity and with a profound orchestration of warm tones penetrated by light that loses itself in the distant echoes of a broad, undulating landscape, creating a subtle contemplative lyricism, a final echo of his master, Botticelli. The *Crucifixion* of Santa Maria Maddalena retains, even in the arid color of the fresco, these luminescent effects around the figures of the saints; this lyric chromatism is also found in the masterpiece of the Pavia altar frontal.

In this some have seen a collaboration by Raphael;[15] it is better regarded as an apex of Perugino's inventiveness that many have awakened inspiration still dormant in the spirit of the adolescent pupil. I believe that Cavalcaselle, in attributing to Raphael's presence the master's heightened inspiration in this moment, allowed himself to be somewhat carried away by his imagination.[16] There were in the life of Perugino (who, Vasari no less romantically relates, braided with his own hands the hair of his young wife) stimuli to that lyric abandon which was his most sincere quality, had he not succumbed to the obsession (also attested to by Vasari) of accumulating money, accepting all commissions, without scruple, and having them executed by his " company." But when he worked alone, and this seems to be the case of the Pavia altar frontal, he shows himself to be the best painter of the time. And if it is possible to date in these years (instead of considering them as coming after the *Giving of the Keys*, as is usual) the two splendid final frescoes on the walls of the Sistine Chapel, the *Baptism of Christ* and the *Life of Moses*, the portion not executed by Pinturicchio is evidence of the rich resonance even in formal rhythms, of the vigorous structural energy that the supposedly lazy dreamer was able to achieve.[17]

What criticism has not always been able to see was perceived by the ingenuous eyes of Raphael. In these years he followed the master on his journeys between Florence and Perugia, and while he continued to study the drawings of Leonardo, under the guidance of Lorenzo di Credi, he discovered the roots of that luminous penetration of form which had determined Perugino's new coloristic discovery. His imitation of the master to the point of identifying with him was not the result of the inertia of one among many helpers in Perugino's workshop. It was, rather, the result of a deep admiration, the recognition of an expressive power which he had first to imitate if he wished later to equal it. The rewards of this loyalty, which was

8 Portrait of Don Biagio Milanesi.   Florence, Uffizi.

9 Portrait of the monk Baldassarre.   Florence, Uffizi.

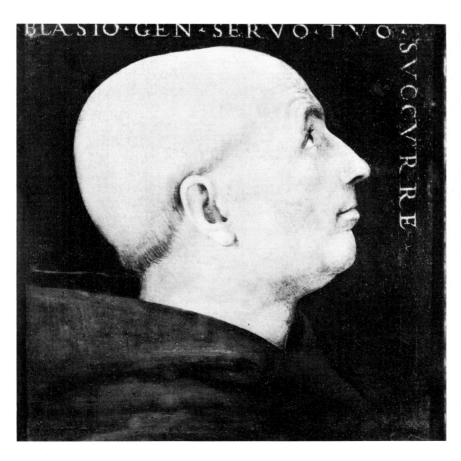

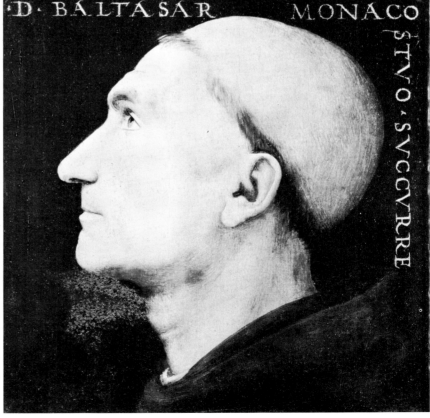

17

10 Fortitude and the Heroes of Antiquity: Lucius
Sicinius, Leonidas, Horatius Cocles. Detail
from the decoration of the Collegio del Cambio
in Perugia.

the beginning of a critical ascendancy, are evident in the work which Longhi [18] has correctly
referred to as the first collaboration of Raphael (which would thus represent his earliest-dated
activity), the predella of the altar frontal in Santa Maria Nuova in Fano, on which the date
1497 appears.

If it is compared with the work by Perugino and his assistants that is closest in time and
most analogous, that is, the predella of the polyptych of San Pietro in Perugia, begun in 1496,
the difference is amazing and demands the acknowledgement of the collaboration of a more
vigorous individual presence, which can legitimately be supposed to be that of Raphael. The
Stories from the Life of Christ on the predella in Perugia, though admirable for their fluent
composition, appear in comparison as inorganic and unsophisticated, almost as a persistence
of quattrocento particularism in the face of a compact rhythmic unity which already indicates a new era. This work no longer had the anecdotal aspect of the predella in which the
iconic symmetry of the altar frontals was diffused—the work " with small figures " which usually
was left to the first efforts of pupils. The small scenes in Fano have, rather, the structural
grandeur of the great altarpieces by Perugino; their concise pictorial unity had now become
the conscious end for the artist. One sees, for example, in the *Birth of the Virgin*, the deep

18

shadow in the portico, with elements that were never so robust and heavy in Perugino, become animated by the reflections, lights and shadows in the group of women around the child. Their wreath-like rhythm springs from the figure of the seated woman which appears to be a proof of Raphael's authorship because it repeats the fresco of the *Madonna* in his house in Urbino, which is considered to be by him.   And even if formal elements give preference to the old attribution to Giovanni Santi, its value as proof is not diminished: the memory of a familiar and beloved image which he inserts into a completely new concatenation of figures derived from drawings by Perugino.   These drawings were perhaps knowingly selected among those with the surest forms, those for the last frescoes of the Sistine Chapel, from which there are direct citations.   But this pupil (who according to Longhi and to us is certainly Raphael) makes the figures of his master live in wider spaces, filled with the sonorous echoes of great arches, pilasters and cornices on which the light is subtly differentiated, in a vital play in which the figures are caught in their palpitating animation; the play of light has its origins in the *Adoration* by Leonardo.   Twice, in the *Marriage of the Virgin* and in the *Presentation at the Temple*, the artist returns to the same theme: groups that move within the articulation of the columns of a portico, and twice he interprets it differently, once opening the arches onto a luminous sky, the second time filling them with shadow outlined by luminous columns. There is a deep thematic coherence, even when in the *Assumption* the *mandorla* in which the Virgin is framed appears precisely in the valley of light between two cliffs, and especially when in the *Annunciation* the infinite reverberations from corner to corner as far as the luminous abyss on the distant horizon and the slight movement of the angel alighting do not disturb the enchanted silence surrounding the praying Madonna.   The vacuous sentimental effusion of Perugino has become the ecstatic moment of the mystery which is accomplished.   The vague

11   The Prophets, detail from the decoration of the Collegio del Cambio in Perugia.

poetic intuitions become a powerful lyric inspiration which completely renews the language, transforming Perugino's litany into a metric clause in which the episode is musically expressed. It is in this way, from an interpretation that touches the profound in order to revitalize all conventions, that the soft cadences of Perugino will give birth to the great rhythms of classical language.

If the date 1497 (even if we advance it a bit for the execution of this secondary part) can be accepted for the Fano altarpiece, it would be a surprising announcement of a new era made by a fifteen-year-old adolescent. But the fact of this announcement has a coherence of development which makes it acceptable. It is precisely this elevation of accent which allows us to distinguish this exceptional collaborator in other Peruginesque works of the time. Such a distinction has been proposed by critics such as Cavalcaselle and Adolfo Venturi, while others, no less acute, such as Ortolani, have denied even the possibility. However, Fischel and Longhi, as we have seen, remained convinced and recently Wittkower has tempered his skepticism admitting at least the legitimacy of the attempt. We do not deny that it is not without risk that such a suggestion may be made. However, there are results which, though not without contrasts, have been justified to the degree that they are acceptable in their illuminating relation to the ascertained evolution of Raphael, which appeared in his youth to

13-15 Predella of the Oddi Altarpiece: Annunciation, Adoration of the Magi, Presentation in the Temple. Pinacoteca Vaticana.

21

16 Portrait of Verrocchio or Perugino. Florence, Uffizi.

be a realization of what in Perugino had been left in a potential state, and in deducing from them the figurative themes later destined to reappear in his greatest masterpieces.

Consider, for example, the case of that *Resurrection* which was ordered from Perugino on March 2, 1499, for San Francesco al Prato in Perugia and which is now in the Vatican Pinacoteca. Cavalcaselle saw in this work an extensive participation by Raphael, and supported his hypothesis with two drawings by Raphael in Oxford which were preparatory studies for figures in the painting. Later, critics preferred to relate those drawings to the *Resurrection* now in São Paulo, Brazil,[19] confirming their attribution to Raphael, and denying such an attribution to the Vatican *Resurrection*. Yet whatever value one wishes to give to these drawings, which could, with minor variations, have served for both works, it seems to us that Cavalcaselle's position is still valid. The altarpiece in São Paulo, evidently derived from the predella of the polyptych of San Pietro, as were many other works by Perugino's collaborators, should be carefully examined, also as regards its state of preservation, in order to place it without doubt in the catalogue of Raphael's works. In its lower portion depicting the episode of the sleeping soldiers, the Vatican *Resurrection* shows exaltation of inspiration and expression that justifies the attribution of the Fano predella. The prototype, in the polyptych of San Pietro, seems in comparison a feeble suggestion, even though it is one of the most valid Peruginesque creations in its presentation of the appearance of Christ, who seems to overturn in all directions both the sleeping and the awakened soldiers. In the Vatican painting, the sarcophagus, with the very bold foreshortening of the transversely placed cover, is a very powerful construction of abstract geometry, distinct planes, lines scrutinized singly by a light which analyzes and magically exalts them. This perfect form is precisely framed by the two converging curves of the forms of the sleeping soldiers; in these forms the rhythm of the composition is concluded, a perfect metrical clause, but not because of a puristic correspondence of beautiful and regular structures. The younger soldier, at the right, abandons himself within his perfect rhythmic pattern as if to a dream. His pure profile, that of a Leonardesque angel, stands out against the dark background with the whiteness of an apparition, like the hand which hangs, accenting the other, in a stupendous formal arrangement. Once again it was Leonardo, the poet of light, with his youthful *Annunciation*, who furnished the means for Raphael to take back to its origins an impulse that had become habit for Perugino. The theme of the dream is evident in the two figures in the foreground, in that in the background at the right, and gives birth in Raphael's mind to the lyric that was to appear many years later in the *Liberation of St. Peter*.

Little by little we recognize in Raphael's Peruginesque interpretations the delineation and development of his future language, which was particularly indebted to that persistent relationship with the Florentine tradition which was the basis of Perugino's own formation. Raphael was not satisfied merely to continue the solutions proposed by his teacher; he had to repeat, in an original manner, the experiences that determined them. We have seen that by now he was progressing with a knowledge of light of Leonardo. With equal diligence he experimented with chromatic problems: not only the technique of oil painting but that which it made possible—the distinction of values, the fusion of tones, a pictorial unity that was also a precise recognition of reality. All this is attested by his work on the altarpiece for the Convent of Vallombrosa, which Perugino probably began in Florence around 1500,[20] which date is written on it. It is an easily discernible collaboration: the style of the figures shows how the master distributed the work between two helpers, reserving for himself the central figure and the two figures of saints on the left. In our opinion, Raphael executed the figures of St. Benedict and St. Michael on the right and some of the figures of angels. The figure of the warrior archangel presents such close analogies with that in the polyptych of Pavia as to make evident immediately the model that the pupil chose to analyze in his work. It is this same analogy that reveals the differences as well. The figure in Pavia is a series of magical flashes and chromatic shadings, but the one in Vallombrosa is a confident play of forms, within the spatial restrictions of a single plane. The delicate head turns in a direction opposite to the ample mass of the chest as if the whole bust rotated on the vertical axis of the shield. There is a search for the "marvelous manner of movement" of Donatello's prototype. The movement is not a rhythmic abstraction; it has precise motivation. The right hand seizes and grasps the sword, ready to strike; the eyes, though in the dreamy gentleness of the face, really "see"; the hair seems to be blown by a light breeze. The most subtle resources of pictorial modeling serve to create this vital animation. The same animation differentiates the *St. Sebastian* in Brescia from Perugino's *Magdalene* in Florence (Pitti), of which Raphael's painting is an interpretation. The dreamy face that Perugino left in shadow is brought by Raphael to prominence in the clear light. This rediscovery of the vivid reality of all forms was the aim of a painterly discipline that had its origin in Perugino. It is believed that the two heads of monks now in the Uffizi, were part of the lost predella of the altarpiece for Vallombrosa, where, as in the polyptych of San Pietro, they may have been placed between the panels. These figures also suggest their attribution to Raphael because of their strong, essential plastic structure, the result of a vigorous modeling of chromatic impastos without recourse to shadows. The purity of form of those shaven heads, especially that of the monk Baldassarre, set in the neat frame of a fringe of hair, almost achieves geometric abstraction. The delicate poses of Perugino are far removed from this courageous approach to stark reality. But from him came the capacity to express it with the power of color, that forceful plasma

17-18 Standard for the church of the Trinità in Città di Castello: The Trinity with SS. Sebastian and Rocco, the Creation of Eve. Città di Castello, Pinacoteca Civica.

which, since the *Francesco delle Opere* of 1494, he had derived from Flemish art. This, too, was an experience that Raphael himself continued, not satisfying himself with the results. His portraits speak of it, as we shall see, and it is particularly evident in the masterly male portrait now in the Borghese Gallery, which was attributed to him in preference to Perugino and even to Holbein, because of the power of the characterization and the clear refusal of any pictorial flattery in order to give absolute evidence of the form. This identification of " form," in its geometric reality with the moral " form " of man, caught up in a ceaseless drama, was the basis of his approach, the " terrible " test of his experiences. It is the element that distinguishes him from Perugino even when, with fidelity and humility, he adheres to the teaching of his master.

This element induced Adolfo Venturi to essay the daring, but in our opinion fruitful, attempt to define Raphael's participation in the frescoes in the Udienza of the Collegio del Cambio in Perugia.[21] The entire decoration of the vault and walls, decided in 1496 (but the payments were made with a certain regularity only after 1499 and continued, after the painted date of 1500, up to 1507), was, of necessity, executed with the assistance of helpers, and it would have been unusual for the master not to employ the best of them in this work. The differences of quality and intention also attest to this; they are evident in certain parts of those allegories which, as in the earlier allegories in Palazzo Vecchio in Florence, presented famous personages of classical Antiquity and the Bible as models of virtue.

Although we cannot, in this study, enter into a detailed analysis, we shall note how from the monotonous series of Sages, Heroes and Virtues, there emerge figures much more structurally

23

and pictorially vivid. These include not only the figure of Fortitude, already singled out by Venturi, but also, in the zone below, the three warriors: Leonidas, Horatius Cocles, and especially Lucius Sicinius, a figure which reelaborates, but with greater espressive vigor, the Donatellian St. Michael in the Vallombrosa altarpiece. A similar collaboration for the Cambio is quite logical at this same time. And it could have lasted even later—when Raphael was departing from the master's style—in those sections datable between 1500 and the last payments made in 1507. In the fresco on the opposite wall which concludes the cycle with the Sibyls and Prophets, Venturi saw in "the bony profile of the Libyan Sibyl" an "acute sensitivity, rare even in Raphael's art," and noted the "slow and profound" gaze of the Cumean Sibyl and of Solomon. This animation of the "tired heroes of the aged Perugino" gives to the whole a passionate vehemence, as if a violent wind had shaken the symmetry of the other frescoes; it fills the placid sections with the whisper of rustling garments, with a movement of hands not in the style of a devotional allegory but in that of a real historical evocation of a great moment—when those who had predicted the coming of Christ see their

19 God the Father with the Virgin and Cherubs. Naples, Museo di Capodimonte (formerly at the top of the S. Niccolò Altarpiece in Città di Castello).

20 Altarpiece depicting S. Niccolò da Tolentino (copy). Città di Castello, Pinacoteca Civica.

prophesies realized in the *Nativity*, represented there in the fresco painted by Perugino. The old master was never again to achieve such animation. But it was to be achieved by his pupil, then about to leave the master for those directions which are announced in the first work that was completely his own: the *Coronation of the Virgin* for San Francesco in Perugia, now in the Vatican Pinacoteca.

This large altarpiece appears to have been executed for Alessandro di Simone degli Oddi and has, therefore, a *terminus ante quem* of 1503, the year in which, on August 10, immediately after the death of Alexander VI, the Oddi were deposed from the government of Perugia by Giovan Paolo Baglioni. Usually it is dated by scholars slightly earlier, when Raphael had already obtained and completed commissions on his own for Città di Castello. But Vasari mentioned it before these, and Wittkower,[22] following this indication, deduced for the *Coronation* an earlier date, around 1500, knowing full well that his proposal would give rise to a polemic among Raphael scholars. However it seems quite acceptable to us, even considering only the exterior circumstances, which also hint at the activity of Perugino's workshop in the Umbrian capital, which was almost his personal domain.

The painting has its iconographic source in the *Ascension* at the center of the polyptych of San Pietro, which Perugino finished before January 13, 1500, when the altar was consecrated. [23] The master derived from it the *Ascension* for the Duomo of Sansepolcro, executed in Florence, whence it was carried by hand to its destination in a year that is unspecified but which scholars tend to place at the beginning of the century. Many years later, in December of 1512, when he accepted a commission to do yet another version in the *Assumption* for the church in Santa Maria di Corciano in the territory of Perugia, he promised in the contract to remain faithful to the *Coronation* in San Francesco, that is, the one painted by Raphael. [24] It seems strange that a master still of the first rank would subordinate himself, by his own statement, to the work of a pupil, even one of the stature then attained by Raphael. If he did it almost as a guarantee of Raphael's participation, he would have named him, but instead he cites only the work. Besides, Perugino could consider it his own if, as it has reasonably been assumed, it was a commission given him as a result of the enthusiasm created by the large *macchina* of San Pietro and left by him, too busy with other work, to be executed by a pupil who was by then his equal. At this time Raphael must have been discussing the first works for Città di Castello, which he had obtained for himself. Here, instead, he does not emerge from anonymity and seems to regard the models of the master with the desire to follow the schemes even in the single figures. But almost against his will, he changes and animates all the Peruginesque elements through the filter of his own personality, now not only mature in his own ideas but also educated, in the tradition of Verrocchio and Leonardo (in which he was guided by Lorenzo di Credi), to a feeling for reality that was never achieved by Perugino. His preparatory drawings for this work fit well into the more lofty contemporary Florentine tradition. The line has the vigor of Leonardo in affirming the form in the most subtle relations with an ambience saturated by atmosphere and light. [25] It is precisely the presence of this true light which reveals, in infinite ways, every form, from the crystalline block of the sarcophagus to the excited apostles and the angels barely alighting and still moving as in flight, as if it were a magnificent high relief. Here we truly may think, as has been suggested, that the majestic altarpieces of the Della Robbia were more important in Raphael's formation than the devotional versions executed by Perugino. As always, Raphael's intelligence uncovered the most profoundly Renaissance sources in his work, and he proceeded from them. In the interpretation of the model new accents abound, in new pronouncements of a lyricism that slowly creates its expressive meter: the white hand of the Redeemer raised against an area of shadow, the abandon of the angel on the right, intent on obtaining the full sound of his instrument with the bright line of his bow, the thoughtful cherub curled up in the fold of a mantle and, finally, at the center, as the new statement of a time-wearied theme, the adoring face looking upward, concentrating all the light of the painting in its planes. The religious allegory is not an extraneous element, developed in a different sphere from which man operates; it is an aspect of the human soul in a moment of contemplation. In this, Raphael's Humanism, aligning itself with the highest Florentine conquest, from Giotto to Masaccio and Donatello, begins, from this time on, his celebration of man in *storia, la somma opera del pittore*, which was the designated aim of expression ever since Alberti.

The color itself seems to abandon the Peruginesque fusions for a more ringing sonority, moving easily among the boldest relationships to the point of a certain dissonant irridescence. Here, typical Florentine coloristic effects are superimposed on Perugino, poetically allusive of things beyond experience. The predella of the *Coronation* avails itself of the limpid chromatism to bring to light the structure, which is still Peruginesque. The light is almost broken up into its contrasting, vivid components around the very straightforward columns, in the limpidity of the openings in the half-ruined hut. Distinct tones, as in a bunch of flowers, play against each other among the marvelous architectural elements furnish the light with large areas for clear reflections. The quattrocento traditions of Florentine color also converge in the grand synthesis which is begun by this Florentine by adoption. They are confirmation of his formation in Florence, both initially and during the intervals between his periods of activity in Perugino's

21 Crucifixion with the Virgin, St. Jerome, St. Mary Magdalene, and St. John the Evangelist, called the "Mond Crucifixion." London, National Gallery.

studio. However, one who had so many expressive resources and such an impetus of fantasy must have inevitably felt himself a master and must have considered as chains the conventions which were imposed upon him. This work, in which the pictorial expression strains with all possible force against a scheme which was by then foreign to him and is able to add marvelous figurations to it, but not to eliminate it, seems fully to support Wittkower's hypothesis. It was the last work by Raphael in the anonymity of his collaboration with Perugino. Even though he never rebelled against his master—indeed he remained loyal to him and consented to help him—he began nonetheless to start out in his own direction. And the first steps are indicated by the commissions Raphael undertook for Città di Castello.

CITTÀ DI CASTELLO

According to Vasari, Raphael began this activity during the protracted absence of Perugino who, in fact, remained in Florence during the whole of 1498. [26] However, the first work that Raphael completed for Città di Castello seems to be later than 1499, the year of a pestilence, to which the votive standard for the church of the Trinità, today in the local Pinacoteca, can be linked. The execution of Raphael's work can be circumscribed between this date and that of the more important commission of a large altarpiece with the *Coronation of St. Nicholas of Tolentino* for the Augustinian church, which was contracted for on December 10, 1500. This time we are on firm ground because another document reports that the final payment was made September 13, 1501. In both, the name of the eighteen-year-old *magister Rafael Johannis Santi de Urbino*[27] precedes that of his older collaborator, Evangelista di Pian di Meleto, who is not called a master. These circumstances, carefully analyzed by Wittkower, have led to the very acceptable deduction that Raphael, who had already affirmed himself in such an important work as that of the *Coronation* in Perugia, was invited to work for Città di Castello and that, in order to be able to do this, while he was still under obligation to Perugino, he had recourse to the old workshop of Giovanni Santi in Urbino; this was still his legitimate property even though during his youthful absence his father's old companion, Evangelista di Pian di Meleto, had maintained its activity. For this reason he was mentioned first and given the title *magister* in the notarial documents. His work must have fully satisfied the most important citizens of Città di Castello since, after the altarpiece for the Augustinians, he was requested to do another, of no less importance, namely, the *Crucifixion* for the Gavari Chapel in San Domenico, now in the London National Gallery; the work is often called the *Mond Crucifixion*, from the name of its owner. Finally, concluding this phase of his activity gloriously, in 1504 he painted for the Albizzini Chapel in San Francesco his first great masterpiece, the *Marriage of the Virgin*, now in the Brera.

22-23 Predella of the Crucifixion: St. Jerome Revives Three Dead Men and The Miracle of St. Jerome. Lisbon, Museu Nacional de Arte Antiga, formerly in Richmond, Cook Collection.

This entire episode, the first truly autonomous one in Raphael's career, the real *gradus ad Parnassum* which gives full affirmation of his maturity, occurs in the shadow of Perugino. The figurative schemes elaborated in his workshop persist in the mind of his pupil, as the punctuation, the syntactical structure, the very alphabet of a language in which he can express himself. His direction is still that enunciated by Perugino—to give to these schemes univocally pictorial meanings, to proceed toward a total conquest of color. In this language the powerful poetic inspiration that develops and is clarified in Raphael's spirit is expressed; the artist, now eighteen years old, is at the end of his adolescence and on the threshold of a youthful maturity.

In the *Crucifixion of the Standard*, he freely chooses from among the master's themes, going back to the Peruginesque elegy in Santa Maria Maddalena dei Pazzi, but now the adoration of the two saints is framed by the high cliffs in the cool shade of a mountain valley, and we hardly know if it is prayer or profound emotion, a silent communing with nature. Now there are extreme pictorial refinements: the color passes from dark masses to unexpected brightness, to glaring dissonances reminiscent of Credi, uniting and animating the figures and the landscape, which is the real protagonist of this scene, as it was of the scene of the *Creation of Adam* on the reverse of the standard. It is the kind of landscape which, since the famous drawing of 1473, Leonardo had seen as a reduction to vibrant light of the infinite life of the plants and of the water which mirrors the sky. Here this light becomes one with the color. Perhaps it was also the same in the large altarpiece of St. Nicholas, which unfortunately was destroyed and which can only be reconstructed from the sketch of the whole in Lille, together with the eighteenth-century copy of the altarpiece in the Pinacoteca of Città di Castello and with the Angel in Brescia, the only original fragment surviving. The upper part with God the Father and the Madonna, preserved in the Capodimonte Museum (Naples), seems to be an early Manneristic alteration by Evangelista of the poetic language that Raphael was creating.

Notwithstanding the uneven aspects of parts that are barely suggested and others that are better defined, the drawing is sufficient to suggest the pictorial unity of the work from its very beginning and its genesis, like the predella in Fano, from a subtle quivering of reflections in the shadow of a large arch. The vision of God was to appear in this shadowy recess. A quick application of very fine lines indicates the knowing use of light which captures the energetic plasticity of the figures and the sure spatial mastery of their contrasts. These elements of form and movement explicitly declare their Florentine origin, even though they came through Signorelli, who originated the central theme of the group with a standing figure trampling another, boldly foreshortened. The Angel that survives from this work is evidence of the chromatic material used. Its pensive face, closed in an inner dignity, merits the adjective "classical."

That the painting of Città di Castello dates to a period of collaboration with Perugino is indicated by another drawing in Lille,[28] the first study from life for the head of God the Father. It is surrounded by sketches that refer to works and undertakings of the master and his workshop: studies of swans which recall the doves of Venus on the vault of the Cambio, two arcades that allude to a courtyard by Laurana in Urbino but have the pedimented window of the *Annunciation* in the Raineri house in Perugia.

The date of the *Gavari (Mond) Crucifixion*, presumably slightly earlier than 1503, the year of the construction of the altar on which it was placed, is verified by the increasingly unitary pictorial animation and the reduction of the landscape to a series of luminous bands up to the diffused brightness of the sky. To the Peruginesque unity of tone is added the variety of Florentine chromatic relationships. There is a central element of this pictorial emotion that transforms it into pure poetry. It is the face of Christ Crucified, which has no counterpart in Perugino's art. It is as if the design itself, with its evocative ability to define movement, became the painting, dissolving the neat chromatic layout in the cursory allusions of the brush stroke, in the shadow that slowly comes over the face, where the eyelids are already closed in death. And we may ask, considering this innovative pictorial power, whether Raphael did not already know what was being done at that time in Venice, and whether he had not already seen and studied in Montefeltro the altarpiece painted in Pesaro by Giovanni Bellini.

At the foot of the cross Raphael's signature appears for the first time, *Raphael Urbinas P.* He used the musical Latin of the scholars to celebrate himself as a master. And certainly his painting then included new accents which distinguish him from the mass of Perugino's followers. This expressive vigor appears also in the two fragments which are from the lost predella of this altarpiece, one formerly in Richmond (Cook Collection) and the other in the Lisbon Museum. Even in the photographs (we have not personally viewed the works) we can see the pictorial richness in the landscape depicted in deep tones, simplified in undulating expanses, behind the more lively movement of the light-toned figures, multicolored flashes in the half-light of dusk.

The *Marriage of the Virgin* (now in the Brera) in 1504 marked the end of this period of work in Città di Castello. It had been a fundamental phase in his art, which, in his first concrete individual affirmation, called upon all of his early experiences, both Peruginesque and Florentine, in order to give expression to his own poetry. In it was announced a new, mysterious rapport between man and nature in the ineffable moments when the passage from day to evening transforms the colors of the landscape. Raphael captured these transient moments— the quick animation of the miracles in the predella, as well as the slow agony in the *Gavari Crucifixion*—in the same manner. Over and above the elements of sentiment, however lyrically intense, the inspiration rises as on wings now that the center of the drama represented is no longer man, with his impulses and moments of abandon, but is the very creation of his intellect,

24 Detail from the Marriage of the Virgin. Milan, Brera.

the perfect harmony of form. The protagonist of the *Marriage* is the circular temple, a play of precise forms, arches, columns, and, on high, the hemispheric dome that contains the prism of the thousand faces, rising in a pure midday light out of the varicolored base of the crowded scene below. Critics have been severe in analyzing the work, which they have called uneven, with no link between the two elements that constitute the painting, the scene and the building. But all objections fall before the unity of this work, which has rarely been equaled. This figuration presupposes a high degree of knowledge, all the knowledge gained over two centuries in the efforts of the Renaissance. But Raphael freed it from the wearing traces of this effort; he stripped it of every intellectualism. The lad from the Marches, who came to Florence armed only with the skill in working with brushes and colors, saw those mature products of a most highly refined culture as he saw the flowers in the fields or the light of the sky, and he abandoned himself to them in a boundless admiration. The high point of their achievements was for him the starting point for transforming them poetically. It was not, as Cavalcaselle thought, Perugino rejuvenated by Raphael's presence. It was not only the master, but his art, and, even more, the tradition which fed it, to which Raphael gave a miraculous new youth. For him even the most sophisticated speculation became reality, a living nature. Around the sublime abstraction of the temple in the *Marriage* there is the teeming life of men and of the sky which lightens beyond the thin line of dark forests, beyond the vault of that immense dome, glimpsed through the frame formed by the two portals.

Perhaps for Raphael, as for the great initiators of the early quattrocento, perspective was the subject of his first systematic study. Usually the abused equation—perspective: Urbino (and the equation is easily deduced) Urbinesque perspective: Raphael—has caused other considerations to be neglected. In the first place, since Raphael had left Urbino in 1494 or 1495 at eleven or twelve years of age, he had neither the time nor the capacity to realize the significance of what evidence existed in Urbino of Alberti, Piero della Francesca and their refinements of perspective. And he spent little time in Urbino during the following years, which were taken up with his collaboration in Perugino's work in Umbria, where, on the other hand, there were no real incentives to these studies. These were, instead, the basis of the formation of 29 young artists in Florence, where the science of perspective had originated with Brunelleschi and where Albèrti had written a full exposition of it, precisely because it was considered to be the indispensable basis of painting and an essential study for painters. When Perugino was in his formative phase in Florence there were, according to the *Cronaca* of Benedetto Dei,[29] more than thirty teachers of perspective who were also architects or master woodworkers. The creation of perspective effects became art in the intarsias of the woodworker Francione's pupils, among whom were Giuliano da Maiano and Baccio Pontelli. Today there is an attempt to discover how much of the famous Urbinesque perspective was the result of the importation of these Florentine masters, who are responsible for the extraordinary perspective effects in the intarsias of the Studiolo of Duke Federico.

If, as I do, one proposes Florence as the site of young Raphael's first systematic study, to which he had been directed by a consummate master of perspective like Perugino, Vasari's almost casual allusion in his life of Fra Bartolomeo takes on a new importance; Vasari reports that Raphael, who came to Florence " to learn art," " taught . . . perspective " to the friar who, in turn, taught Raphael his color technique. Vasari, who was especially well-informed about this life, places this episode at the time of Raphael's Florentine sojourn in 1504.[30] But we may ask what need Fra Bartolomeo had to learn the elements of perspective at that time if he had already given a masterful demonstration of his command of these elements some years earlier, in 1499, in the Paradise in the *Last Judgment* of Santa Maria Nuova, constructing a very precise semicircle of figures, a motif that Raphael was to take up in the fresco in San Severo in Perugia and ultimately in the *Disputa*. There is a temptation to formulate a hypothesis which at this time can be no more than a suggestion for further study. Is it not possible that Vasari, confusing the dates, had relegated to 1504 events which had actually occured in 1499 and that Raphael, who in those years continually traveled between Florence and Perugia, had helped his friend, not yet a friar, in the difficult constructive theme of the fresco? This hypothesis would lead to others, all within the realm of possibility. That is, it would be supposed that Raphael and Baccio della Porta already knew each other, and this is possible through a common contact with Lorenzo di Credi. This presupposes what we have attempted to demonstrate, that is, that Raphael's artistic formation began in Florence. It is true that no other work by Fra Bartolomeo either presages or repeats that broad, splendid construction, while Raphael continued to use it even in his full maturity. We are not so intensely attached to a concept that is not ours. And Raphael, at sixteen years of age, could already have acquired such a mastery over perspective while working with Perugino as to be able to pass it on to his friend. One should not forget that Perugino was the son-in-law of Luca Fancelli, follower of Alberti, and through him could have had access, along with his pupil, to an incomparable body of material for study, comprising architectural and perspective drawings among which there may even have been some by Fancelli's own teacher, Leon Battista Alberti.

Returning to earth from the realm of speculation, we note that Raphael must have had a thorough experience in perspective in order to construct with such exactness the *Marriage of the Virgin*, and this experience must have included applied perspective, learned from architects, if he was able to give a unity of form of an almost emblematic harmony (and nonetheless feasible as a construction) to the purely fantastic temple in the *Giving of the Keys* or that of loosely conceived but noble forms in the other *Marriage*, the one commissioned from Perugino in April, 1499, for the Chapel of the Santo Anello in the Duomo of Perugia (now in the Caen Museum), which Raphael surely used as a model, but which he surpassed. In the temple in the *Marriage*, echoes of Urbino, and especially of Laurana's courtyard, which is Albertian in style, have been seen. The southern light that subtly differentiates and clearly defines the faces of the drum is correctly judged to be derived from Piero della Francesca. That which may have been fixed in the artist's memory since infancy only now became a conscious, meditated choice. This would have been possible in a formation that took place in Florence where, in the elaboration of perspective problems, there had evolved a method of learning by *ingegno scorgitore erudito*. This method, academic and not practical, must have been followed by Raphael in studying perspective as well as drawing. In Florence he had before him not only the theory of perspective but its great application as well, from Brunelleschi's dome to a series of buildings on the central plan, from Brunelleschi's chapels to the tribune built by Leon Battista Alberti[31] for the church of the Annunciata. In these perspective creations in Florentine architecture, Raphael saw *concinnitas* and *venustas*, Alberti's ideal principles, become the true substance of art, very different from Perugino's indefinite musical rhythms. He perceived a measured order in which his poetic emotion could be modulated and become song. This was to be, from that time on, the direction of his research, which became clear to him at the end of his activity in Città di Castello. The inscription *Raphael Urbinas* which he proudly painted on the temple's trabeation, with the date MDIIII in Roman numerals, was as a celebration of a new direction.

SIENA

On December 12 of the following year, 1505, Raphael, together with Berto di Giovanni, stipulated in Perugia the contract for the execution of the *Coronation* for the main altar of the convent church of Monteluce. Indicating the places where, in case they did not fulfill their obligations, he and his friend could be prosecuted, he listed seven cities: Assisi, Gubbio, Rome,

25 Marriage of the Virgin (detail). Milan, Brera.

Siena, Florence, Urbino and Venice. [32] The two minor Umbrian centers (Assisi and Gubbio)
may have referred only to Berto's activity, and we see Raphael indicate places that he may have
wished to see alongside the names of those where he actually worked. This is the only document
in which Venice appears in Raphael's career, and Rome must have then been only a great
hope. But for Siena, Urbino, and Florence, his sojourns can be proved or are at least probable
in the first years of the new century, years of definitive experiences and of new directions.
While the motivation of these travels was the practical one of seeking worthy, well-paid and
stable work that would allow him to free himself from the subjugation of Perugino's workshop,
Raphael took advantage of them to gain new experience. The document confirms the notice
in the history of the Convent of Monteluce which indicates that since 1503 the Abbess, Suor
Chiara de' Mansueti, had been seeking a talented master for the execution of the proposed
altarpiece, and that " the best master " had been indicated by the Franciscan Fathers and
by various towns people as " Master Raphael of Urbino."

The year 1503 was the date of the *Crucifixion* for Città di Castello. The great altarpieces
which he had executed in the preceding two or three years there and in Perugia had already
made Raphael's name known. But he had not yet obtained, besides these occasional commissions, an important commission that would occupy him for several years, nor had he an
illustrious patron of ample means, a base of security for the present and the future, such as his
master Perugino had in his workshop in Perugia, where he had a virtual monopoly on all
local commissions. Raphael had to remain connected with the workshop even though his self-
assurance, gained in the various commissions personally obtained, probably made him champ
at the bit. This eagerness seems to be reflected in his insistence on signing his name very clearly

on the works for Città di Castello. These occasional commissions, which were in any case about to terminate, were not sufficient to secure the future of the twenty-year-old artist. Meanwhile, the master left to him the task of completing the projects at the Cambio and those in the Perugian monasteries while Perugino renewed his relations with Pinturicchio, his former collaborator in the Sistine Chapel (and pupil, according to Vasari), who had never left the papal court and who may have kindled Perugino's hopes of new commissions in the Vatican palaces.

After 1500, having completed his work for the Bufalini Chapel in Santa Maria Aracoeli in Rome, Pinturicchio had returned to Umbria to work for the Baglioni at Spello.[33] But an important commission came to him from the papal court in Rome, one that regarded a great decorative project, similar to that in the apartment of Pope Alessandro Borgia, which he had completed in about 1498. Cardinal Francesco Piccolomini, a very important member of the Curia who shortly afterward became Pope Pius III, commissioned him in 1502 to do the fresco decorations of the Library of the Duomo of Siena, which was to be a monument to his illustrious ancestor, Aeneas Silvius, the Humanist Pope Pius II. There in an unspecified but long-standing tradition that associates Raphael's name with this undertaking.

Vasari tells us both in his life of Raphael and in that of Pinturicchio[34] that Raphael assisted

33

the renowned master in the preparation of the frescoes. However, his indications are not very precise, and they must be interpreted in order to obtain the exact sense. First, in 1550, Vasari says that " Raphael made the *cartoons* of *all the sketches of the scenes for* the Library," and that one of them was still in Siena. In the life of Raphael, he specifies that Pinturicchio " being on close terms with Raphael, arranged to have him come to Siena because he was a fine draftsman, so that he might do the *drawings and cartoons* for that work; Raphael was persuaded and transferred himself to Siena, and he did *some* of them." From this it seems possible to deduce that Raphael's collaboration was in the working phases of the drawings and, ultimately, the cartoons developed from the quick sketches of the various compositions by Pinturicchio. In the second edition of the *Lives*, in 1568, Vasari's indications are more precise: " *the sketches and cartoons of all the stories* which Pinturicchio made there were by the hand of Raphael of Urbino." One of these cartoons is still in Siena " and *some sketches* by Raphael's hand are in our book." This statement is, however, qualified in the life of Raphael: " he made *some of the drawings and cartoons* of that work."

It seems clear that Vasari's statements derive from two facts: a cartoon that he saw in Siena before 1550, and some drawings which came into his possession perhaps between 1550 and 1568, and which he believed to be Raphael's originals. What complicates the question then as now, is the apparent internal contradiction within the frescoes, which Vasari perceptively noted, that is, the ingenuous, lively, unorganized color patterns that were still essentially quattrocentesque, as was the taste for narrative and decorative details characteristic of Pinturicchio, as compared to the broad scope, the organic sense of perspective in the compositions that are beyond anything Pinturicchio had ever done or sought to do, in all of his vast opus. Hence the conclusion, more hinted at than expressly stated, is to attribute to the master the actual execution of the frescoes, but to credit Raphael with the entire concept, not just the elaboration of Pinturicchio's sketches. The two original drawings extant, in the Uffizi and in the Contini-Bonacossi Collection in Florence,[35] whether or not they are those which were once possessed by Vasari, lead us to persist in this reasoning. A full discussion of them is given in another part of this book and the external objection that the contract prescribed that Pinturicchio should execute the designs by his own hand may be disregarded, considering that within the organization of the workshops of the time, helpers were considered little more than tools of the trade, used by the master under his complete responsibility.

It seems, too, that Pinturicchio had relied too much on this system when there was an attempt to commission him to do the frescoes in the Duomo of Orvieto (before their execution was entrusted to Signorelli), while he was still working for Pope Alessandro Borgia. There are echoes of this fact in the documents in Orvieto and the terms of the contract for the Sienese commission perhaps were aimed at precluding a recurrence of the problem.

But such terms are made to remain on paper, and, if necessary, Pinturicchio could have eased his conscience with the thought of the absolute homogeneity of the finished work, in which scholars have excluded the possibility of even a single brush stroke by Raphael. It is that glaring and contrasting color which destroys the compact figurative coherence of the drawings, although—and this is the only indication in favor of Pinturicchio's authorship of the sketches— the narration has an anecdoctal character which Raphael had already overcome in the predella of the Vatican *Coronation*. We also see here an intention to impose a center of action that was not understood by the artist who painted the fresco. In the drawing for the *Departure of Aeneas Sylvius for the Council of Basel* the episode of the horses dominates, as in the Vatican predella; it is brought to the center and animated by a Leonardesque vigor, and the furious horses of the *Adoration of the Magi* return to the mind of the artist. But in the fresco a multitude of gesticulating figures suffocate this episode. These same figures interfere, in all the scenes in the Library, with the tranquil observation of the vast spatial perspectives; they keep us from appreciating the creative coherence of the disposition of the crowd below, in order to leave open the space above: open in loggias, vaults, high ceilings, or even vast clear skies, against which trees and monumental edifices are outlined. Here, the influence of Signorelli's work in Orvieto is evident in the placing of figures and edifices in the vast sky above the convulsive tangle of figures below. The question is whether it is the work of Pinturicchio, intent only on appropriating the motifs,

29 St. George and the Dragon. Paris, Louvre.

or Raphael, who was struggling to master the figurative problems that were paving the way in his mind for the *Marriage of the Virgin*? It is as difficult a question for us to answer as it was for Vasari. We can, however, contrary to diffident scholars, not only believe, but even consider it proved that Raphael collaborated with Pinturicchio perhaps in the whole enterprise; this is also suggested by the inscription on the Uffizi drawing, which indicates a series. Fischel has supposed,[36] not without reason, that Raphael inserted, almost as a timid signature, his self-portrait in the large *Coronation of Pius III* at the exterior of the Library. This was the last of the scenes, since the event represented suggests a date no earlier than 1503. In this grandiose historical allegory, there are derivations from Signorelli and original elements such as the group of horsemen or the white miters, so skilfully inserted in a harmonious rhythm of arches as to presage the grand figural themes of the Stanze, which would have been impossible for an artist like Pinturicchio.

Raphael must have suffered the humiliation of seeing the rich production of his imagination once again become lost in the anonymity of a collaboration that was a misunderstanding of his ideas. Although this cannot be materially demonstrated at this time, but is only suggested by a comparison between the drawings and their interpretation by Pinturicchio, it is sufficient to refute, in our opinion decisively, the oft-proposed hypothesis of a special attention by Raphael in his youth to Pinturicchio's art. This presumed dependence, if one reflects carefully, is almost always evoked to justify works which can only laboriously be attributed to Raphael, precisely for their trite decorative elements. It has also been deduced from the circumstances of the Peruginesque source common to both artists. The only historically ascertainable contact that of work for the Library in Siena—is evidence of a contrary situation. That is, that Raphael

was now becoming the master and Pinturicchio the pupil, and a pupil so bound to earlier traditions as to be unable even to understand what was new in Raphael's approach.

It could hardly have been otherwise, if we recall that Pinturicchio, slightly younger than Perugino, based his work on Perugino's style as it was at the time of the first Sistine Chapel frescoes, in 1481-82, when Perugino had not yet approached the great painterly problems of *Francesco delle Opere* or the Pavia polyptych—problems of the last decade of the century, when Raphael began his apprenticeship with him. Not in Siena, nor earlier, could Pinturicchio have taught Raphael anything; he could, perhaps, only offer him at Siena the occasion to contemplate compositional problems that bore fruit afterwards in the Stanze.

Nothing was lost on such a fervid and inventive artist as Raphael. Not even the aridity of a collaboration with masters whom he had, unknowingly, far surpassed and who, though in good faith, exploited his skills to their own advantage. Perhaps the summons to Raphael to participate in the Sienese project was due to a suggestion by Perugino. Vasari tells us that Pinturicchio was assisted in the work on the Library " by many assistants and workers, all from Perugino's school," as if Perugino had put at his disposal his entire group in Perugia, among them that " excellent draftsman," Raphael. But Perugino needed him in Siena because Pinturicchio's activity coincided in time with his own Sienese activity, mentioned in documents and by tradition, of which little has survived. There is, in fact, only the altarpiece with the *Crucifixion* in Sant'Agostino, which he contracted for with Mariano Chigi on August 4, 1502,[37] almost contemporaneously with Pinturicchio's contract for the Library. The predella of this work and the altarpieces for San Francesco are lost in their entirety. The altarpieces for San Francesco, one commissioned in 1506-08 by Gerolamo and Bernardino Vieri and another of the *Madonna*

37

32-33 Portraits of Elisabetta and Guidobaldo da Montefeltro. Florence, Uffizi.

with Saints on the altar of the Tondi family, were both destroyed in the fire of 1655. There is nothing extant of the extensive wall decorations that Giulio Mancini mentions in 1620 as executed by Perugino in the *Palazzo del Papa*, probably the Piccolomini Palace. It was a work of sufficient importance to justify calling to Siena assistants from Perugia, who were also employed by Pinturicchio. Raphael, too, must have been at the disposition of both masters, for in the *Crucifixion* there is at least one figure, that of St. Augustine kneeling at the left, which is distinctly different from those by Perugino in its formal and chromatic structure. How different this composition is from the *Crucifixion* by Raphael in Città di Castello; Raphael's work faithfully repeats the composition of Perugino's, but renders it organic, coherent and firmly architectonic.

There are sufficient indications for dating the Sienese episode between 1502 and 1503, during the same years as Raphael's activity in Città di Castello. It is nothing more than yet another paragraph of the collaboration with Perugino, certainly not a decisive moment of ascent. Only if it will be possible to make a further analysis of the frescoes in the Library, and exhaustively demonstrate the hypothesis of Raphael's participation in their creation, can a significant value in Sanzio's youthful development be seen in them.

The exterior consequences of the probable Sienese sojourn should not be overlooked. These may have included the first contacts with the Chigi, the Borghese and the Sergardi, who were to become great patrons of Raphael. Vasari's report that at Siena Raphael was given an indication of the great new ideas that were being announced in Florence is not unlikely. Raphael had been away from there for years while working on the altarpieces for Perugia and Città di Castello. These indications were, however, of a rather vague nature, because the commissions to Leonardo and Michelangelo of the battle scenes for the assembly hall in the Palazzo Vecchio came only later. In those years Michelangelo also was busy in Siena with a commission given him in 1501 by Cardinal Piccolomini for statues for the family altar in the Duomo, which were finished in 1504. At the same time, he worked on the *David*. And, according to Vasari, " he did not finish it (the Library) because his love for art drew him to Florence." More realistically, though without denying to Raphael his desire for such an experience, we may believe that the many projects undertaken by the Florentine Republic excited in him the hope of work that would finally permit him a complete and personal affirmation. The trip, or, rather, the return to Florence was not dictated by foolish enthusiasm. He prepared for it carefully. He did not have to present himself as a pupil, but as the " best master " of Perugia. He needed a guarantee in the form of an influential recommendation, and he seems to have sought it from the Duke of Urbino, when he returned there.

BOLOGNA

The circumstantial evidence mentioned up to this point has confirmed what Raphael himself declared in the document of 1505 in Perugia. Among the localities listed there, Siena and Florence appeared actually to have been sites of his activity. We have no way of evaluating his contacts with Venice, which is also named. Perugino did have such contacts, as some vague notices seem to indicate but they did not produce any concrete activity. For Raphael, on the other hand, there are not even such vague indications, unless one wishes to relate the uncertain indications of a stay at Bologna with an intentional journey toward Venice. His visit to Bologna would have occurred during his *Wanderjahre*, the years of travel around the beginning of the century, when the young man sought to anchor his life to a continuous and well-paid activity which would gain him a worthy position among the painters of the first rank.

The hypothesis of a Bolognese sojourn is based upon a controversial document: the letter sent from Rome on September 5, 1508 to Francesco Francia in Bologna, published for the first time in 1678 by Malvasia, who had found it.[38] It has been doubted by some, who consider it a seventeenth-century forgery, but Filippini and Adolfo Venturi have accepted it, also admitting some corrections in the form by a seventeenth-century publisher. The proof of its authenticity is precisely in the fact that its content is extremely circumstantial, with references that today seem obscure because they are related to earlier facts not of primary historical importance but relative to the private life of Francia and of Raphael, facts well-known to them but not to us. The letter appears to refer to a previous cordial and friendly encounter and to the expressions of esteem that Raphael addresses to the old master, thanking him for having sent his self-

34 St. George and the Dragon. Washington, National Gallery.

portrait; "It is very beautiful and so alive that it tricked me into thinking that I was with you, listening to your words..." He promised to send Francia his own self-portrait when he should find time to paint it. On that occasion he sent him a drawing of *quel Presepe*, a work which, judging from the tenor of the reference, seems to have been known to Francia, and which is supposed to have been painted by Raphael in Bologna, although it is not that in the Fantuzzi house which was mentioned by Malvasia. He asked Francia for the drawing for the fresco of the Story of Judith which the master had painted in the palace of his patron, Giovanni Bentivoglio. It must have been lost in 1508 when the palace was destroyed by the people after the expulsion of Bentivoglio from Bologna in 1506, and Sanzio seems to console his friend for this loss, affectionately concluding his letter, *Fatevi in tanto animo, valetevi della vostra solita prudenza, et assicuratevi che sento le vostre afflizioni come mie proprie; seguite d'amarmi come io vi amo di tutto cuore.* There was not only an exchange of letters between the two masters, one which Vasari wished to place later, romanticizing it in terms of Francia's dismay at the arrival in Bologna of the *St. Cecilia* in 1514,[39] but, rather, a friendship of long standing. Critical study has shown how Francia's attention, centered for years on Perugino's work, then tended toward that of Raphael. Difficult questions are raised. In one of Francia's masterpieces, the *Mystical Marriage of St. Cecilia* in the Oratory of San Giovanni in Monte, which he painted together with Costa, Tamaroccio and Chiodarolo between 1504 and 1506 for Giovanni Bentivoglio,[40] there are surprising similarities with the *Marriage* by Raphael. Re-elaborating his Peruginesque prototypes, Raphael had inverted the position of the two groups of men and women, enclosing them in a more harmoniously composed action. This Raphaelesque composition, the movement of the figures and especially that of the women, led by the beautiful one in profile, recurred in the *Mystical Marriage of St. Cecilia.* In which direction was the influence? It seems there is a priority for Raphael, whose work is dated 1504, while the only date that appears in the Bolognese Oratory, which seems to have been begun after 1504, is that of 1506, on a fresco by Costa. But how could Francia know a work that was executed in Città di Castello or in the workshop in Urbino? There were, it is true, drawings that may have been instrumental in circulating the ideas. But, until more reliable proof is presented, the question must remain open.

Besides, a direct contact between Raphael and the Bolognese work by Francia and Costa would serve to confirm something in Raphael's painting immediately following the years in Città di Castello, that is not explainable by Perugino's influence alone. This is especially the color, which is enriched by deep but vivid and contrasting tones in a relationship carried, within the pictorial unity, almost to the unreal. There is the gemlike, shining range of colors which Francia and Costa maintained from the Ferrarese tradition, even though they attempted to achieve the atmospheric fusion introduced in Bologna by Perugino's works, such as the *Madonna in Glory* which he painted for San Giovanni in Monte, in an unspecified period that was not long removed from the time of the Vallombrosa altarpiece (around the end of the fifteenth century or at the beginning of the sixteenth).

Bologna, too, seems a road already opened by Perugino, like all those attempted by Raphael during these first five years of the cinquecento. The obstinacy of the critics has precluded a correct interpretation of these Bolognese conditions in insisting on refering them to an initial formative period of Raphael, earlier than his apprenticeship with Perugino, that would have occurred in Urbino through Timoteo Viti, who had been in Francia's workshop until 1495. We believe, instead, however much has been said of a totally Florentine formation for Raphael, that Viti had no part in it and that his only active function in Raphael's life was limited, at this time, to an introduction to his master, from whom he had parted on cordial terms. The only fact upon which to base a more particularized research remains the chromatic and fanciful exaltation which, difficult to suggest as derived from Perugia and from Florence, appears in the works for Città di Castello, and is reaffirmed in those that followed when he returned to Urbino in 1504.

Filippini, the only critic to give the Bolognese episode of Raphael an historical dimension that later study has not always accepted, wished to date it specifically in 1506, the year of the triumphal visit of Julius II to Bologna, which had been restored to papal dominion with the expulsion of the Bentivoglio family. It was the year of Michelangelo's recall after his unworthy and exasperated flight from Rome; as did Michelangelo, so other artists, according to Filippini, could have converged on Bologna in the hope of obtaining papal commissions—and among these would have been Raphael—contributing to stimulating the local tradition, which persisted in the outdated fifteenth-century style of Francia and Costa.

There are indications in Raphael's works of a Bolognese experience before that year: indications not so much of a direct influence, but of certain derivations from an artistic ambience new to him. If the correspondence noted between the *Marriage* of Città di Castello and Francia's fresco in the Oratory of Santa Cecilia cannot produce sure conclusions, there seems to be a direct Bolognese influence in the *Via Crucis* at the center of the predella of the altarpiece of Sant'Antonio in Perugia, the so-called Pala Colonna now in New York; this work was certainly commissioned from Raphael before 1505 or 1506, the date scholars give to the last phases of its execution.[41] The forceful movement that pulls Christ and his executioners in the same direction, away from the Virgin fainting in the arms of the Holy Women, has its origin in the predella by Ercole de' Roberti (formerly in San Giovanni in Monte, and now in Dresden) and

35 Self-Portrait. Munich, Alte Pinakothek.

36 Self-Portrait (?). Hampton Court, Royal Gallery.

37 Madonna and Child with the Infant St. John, called the "Diotallevi Madonna." Berlin, Staatliche Museen.

perhaps in those great, similar works, the marvel of Bologna, the now-lost frescoes by Ercole in the Garganelli Chapel in San Pietro.

Similarly, Raphael's two famous small pictures with St. George, works executed in Urbino before 1506, as we shall see, seem to be an animated, fanciful transposition, almost as in the tone of Ariosto, of the *St. George*, now in the Galleria Corsini in Rome, painted by Francia in his youth.[42]   And in the Bovio Collection in Bologna there was a *Portrait of a Gentleman*, now in Vaduz (Liechtenstein), which was then attributed to Raphael and which has been restored to him after a long interlude of attribution to Francia. Filippini thought it was the portrait of Guidobaldo, Duke of Urbino; to us it seems to present a resemblance to a member of the Albizzini family who appears on the right between the attendants in the *Marriage* from Città di Castello. The same features: the long nose, the narrow and hard mouth, the lifeless gaze, recur twice in Raphael's characterization. The date, correctly proposed by Longhi as 1503-1504, would be still another reason for connecting the Bolognese circumstances with those of a later date, of Città di Castello, perhaps immediately after the collaboration with Pinturicchio and Perugino in Siena.

In this context, we can only refer to these indications as subject for further research. Nonetheless, they point to the first five years of the sixteenth century as a period of feverish acticity on

Raphael's part, entailing continuous travels among the cities of central Italy; Perugia, Città di Castello, Bologna, with brief stops in Urbino to reorganize the old workshop. There was no great distance separating these cities, although Umbria and Romagna are separated by the Apennines; but once the mountains were crossed in passing from Perugia to Urbino, the trip was pleasant. Similarly, the life of old Perugino was also a continuous traveling between Florence, Perugia, Siena and Città della Pieve. Any laziness in his young pupil was overcome by his anxiety to rapidly stabilize his career, seeking out work where he could find it. And at Bologna the Bentivoglio still ruled and gave important commissions to Costa and Francia.

To persist in this hypothesis, necessary for those years which are poorly documented but were already marked by mature masterpieces, which presuppose intense experiences, we see the contact with Francia and the more general one with the Bolognese ambience take the form at this time more of receiving than of giving: the attentiveness of a young genius to elements that were different from those of his development under Perugino and in Florence. The existence of these connections, of which there is nothing more than an indication, is indirectly supported by scholars, who in the past have almost constantly referred works to the school of Francia which today are given, although not unanimously, to Raphael. One such work is the portrait in Vaduz; then are those slightly later ones of the Dukes of Urbino and finally, passing from Viti to Aspertini, the one in Munich which Volpe has recognized, in an exhaustive demonstration of its validity, as a youthful self-portrait of Raphael. [43] It is the portrait of a twenty-year-old, although disastrous cleanings have removed all the the power of modeling, giving the face a smooth, almost infantile, rotundity. And while there are echoes of Florence in the arrangement

38 Madonna and Child, called the " Solly Madonna. " Berlin, Staatliche Museen.

which shows the influence of Credi and which recalls the *Noblewoman* now in Forlì, and there
are echoes of Perugino in the solid impastos derived from Flemish art, there is also a much more
lively chromatic emotion, a deeper feeling for the play of color and light, in the smooth columns
of jasper and in the broad meadows between the trees. They are like announcements of a new,
pungent, pictorial lyricism.

It is this announcement that makes the activities of Raphael between 1500 and 1504 in Città
di Castello, presumably in Bologna and finally in Urbino, so decisively important not only in
Raphael's development, but in the entire course of art.

At Bologna, if one considers the question, there were polarized wide experiences that then
came into contact with an entire pictorial culture, one which, on the other side of the Apennines,
had had a completely different development from that of Florence. In Florence, since the beginning of the quattrocento, problems of a new artistic expression had been posed. Art had
been the concern with images in which the Renaissance had proceeded through a new interpretation of reality. In Florence the problems and the methods of this search had been defined in art,
along with its critical conscience. The expression that the first theoretician of the Renaissance,
Leon Battista Alberti, had called *pictura* was quite unlike that which until then had been working with colors and brushes. The quality of color took a secondary place because of the newly
discovered espression, *disegno*, the means of capturing the thousand movements of the actions
of men, the incessant changes of all nature in the transformation of light in every moment of the
day. Every enticement was dissolved in this cold and tenacious attempt of dramatic historicity,
the feverish play of relationships that formed the monumental architecture of the medieval
world. The *moto che è causa di ogni vita*, the dynamic unity of the image, was for a century the
goal of this total expressive renewal which had occupied all the arts in the continuous proposal
of very bold experiences and in the continuous surpassing of them. Through the rational domi-
nation of space achieved with the new science of perspective (but at an extreme tension because
of the drama which moved it and which was captured in the design, at the end of the fifteenth
century artists arrived at the difficult problem of capturing the qualification of appearances

in an unending play of color in a changing light. This was the problem that Leonardo had confronted in trying to apply chromatic values to the chiaroscuro in his *Adoration*. All of his scientific speculations as well as his researches as an artist seeking a new form were employed in this task.

In his first Florentine experience Raphael had recognized the presence of this problem in Leonardo's design, which he carefully studied. But he had nothing to help him resolve the problem other than the color conventions of Perugino, who had exhausted his efforts in his use of the Flemish manner in the portrait of *Francesco delle Opere*. After, there was never more than a skillful use of this manner in his paintings. And Raphael could do no more than animate it with his extremely vivid light in the altarpiece of Vallombrosa and in the *Coronation* in Perugia, but without completely renewing it.

But in the contact with the transapennine culture, the world of color appeared to him more vast, its expressive possibilities seemed much greater. This was so because in the large region which extended from Venice, through Montefeltro, to the southernmost shores of the Adriatic, the Renaissance language enunciated by Donatello in Padua and by Alberti and Piero della Francesca especially in Urbino had had a profound elaboration precisely in the area of color. It was not the exasperated Florentine practice which went beyond any visual experience into the very essence of life, but the recognition of an essential value in this appearance of which it was useless to seek the reasons and laws and which could be dominated only by an abandonment to contemplation.

The significance of this point of view, intuitive and poetic, must have seemed immense to the young Raphael. But he was too involved with the Florentine problems not to perceive in this world the possibility of furthering his understanding of them. It was in the extreme acuity of

40 St. Sebastian. Bergamo, Accademia Carrara.

the chromatic relation that the tension of the image could achieve deep meanings. The beauty that the color hinted at, as to a world beyond the rational one, could allow for a poetic result in the laborious search by the Florentines for reality. This conquest could become inspiration. In transferring the problems of rational knowledge to the context of poetic intuition, he traced to their common origin the apparently divergent courses of two cultures. Both a tireless rational research and a contemplative abandon went to nourish the expression of his art. The diverse solutions of a single problem flowed together in an intuited synthesis of a new poetry. And Raphael would have proceeded in this intuition: the " poet of a culture," as he has been called, able, as Vasari says, " to make many manners into one," not by means of an eclectic alternation between solutions proposed by others, as some scholars have myopically maintained, but by the sovereign, total intuition of the search and the conquest of the Renaissance.

The attention which matured through acquaintance with the complex pictorial factors across the Apennines already appears in the works for Città di Castello. In the *Gavari Crucifixion* there are Venetian echoes from the paintings of the Pietà and the Crucifixion by Giovanni Bellini, whose works were diffused in the whole territory of Montefeltro, where he had worked for a long period and where he left one of his finest masterpieces, the Pesaro Altarpiece.[44] That Raphael had known and carefully studied them is indicated by the recurrence in a series of his drawings of direct citations from the central group of the *Coronation of the Virgin*. We can even suppose that Raphael derived the motive of the Vatican *Coronation* from it, and even in later years the influence persists and is elaborated, up to the point of providing the compositional impulse for the same scene at the center of the *Disputa*. Perhaps the congeniality of the poetic emotion in Bellini's painting urged Raphael, around 1505, toward Venice. It was a dream that apparently never was realized. But Bologna, and Francia and perhaps Lorenzo Costa as well, opened up to him the very different world of Ferrarese painting. The echoes of Ercole de' Roberti tell us how he moved from deductions to the prototypes themselves. And besides its impetuous compositional impetus, he captured its bold coloring, the vibrations of tones that were an exaltation of things dreamt rather than seen: of precious materials, and enameled glass, of the splendid pigments of the miniaturists. It was to be this strong colorism that was to restore vigor to the arid range of Perugino's color; it appeared if we are to attempt to suggest a date for it, between 1503 and 1504, in the *Madonna with Two Saints*, now in Berlin, whose compositional module ultimately goes back to the school of Francia. This same phenomenon of a chromatically strengthened Peruginesque style seems to us to link it with (perhaps as immediately preceding works, executed in Umbria, parallel to the late phase at Città di Castello) the *Diotallevi Madonna*, although it was finished at a later date, and the so-called *Solly Madonna*, both in Berlin. The large altarpieces for which he must have had the commissions around the

42 Deposition. Florence, Galleria dell'Accademia.

43 Madonna with Child and Two Infant Saints, called the "Terranuova Madonna." Berlin, Staatliche Museen.

year 1504, although he finished them later—the one for San Fiorenzo in Perugia, commissioned by the Ansidei and now in London, and the other for the nuns of Sant'Antonio, now in New York—which represent his last works for monasteries in Perugia, belong in terms of pictorial invention to this moment when the new experience intervenes to enliven the color, to derive from it new poetic accents which infuse new life in the residual conventions of his Peruginesque apprenticeship. In the stupendous landscape of the Ansidei Altarpiece, the bright light is exalted in infinite vibrations which, in the foreground, so acutely define the sharp geometry of the steps of the throne and animate the niche with a sudden flash of brightness. This is light which now penetrates the color, effecting a tonal unity; there is no longer the multicolored effect, derived from Credi, of the predella of the Vatican *Coronation*, but, in what is left of the predella of this altarpiece, the *John the Baptist Preaching* now in Pullborough (Mersey Collection), there is the luminous blending of deeper gradations, the pictorial interwearing of the figures in a continuity of action in which each participates wholeheartedly (observe the rapt attention which is the theme of an entire group of men and boys at the right and which culminates in the dreamy face of a youth, white with light on the dark background of a hill).

Raphael's expression became fully liberated of all conventions in the great works of the following years, those which were executed during the period that begins with his return to Urbino.

Raphael was already in the capital of Montefeltro on October 1, 1504, the date written on a letter with which the sister of Duke Guidobaldo, Giovanna Felicia, wife of Giovanni della Rovere, prefect of Rome and lord of Sinigaglia, recommends him to Pier Soderini, Gonfaloniere of the Florentine Republic.[45] The original letter is lost and its authenticity was doubted before Milanesi restored the wording altered by the copyists. Today it is universally accepted and marks a basic date in Raphael's biography because it testifies that the prestigious introduction was certainly sought by him and attests that Florence was then his desired destination.

Since 1501 Michelangelo had had the commission for the *David* which was to bring him fame, and on January 25, 1504, a commission of artists, among them Perugino, discussed the appropriate location for the completed masterpiece. During the autumn of 1503, Leonardo da Vinci obtained the commission for the *Battle of Anghiari* for the Sala del Consiglio in Palazzo Vecchio and about a year later the young Michelangelo was assigned to do a companion piece, the *Battle of Cascina*.[46] Raphael, still young and, since his work in Città di Castello, conscious of his own abilities, must have entertained the hope of making his way in the Florentine arena. For this reason, notwithstanding the fact that he already knew the ambience, he had to find a powerful introduction as a proved master to the head of the Signoria, who was now the patron of the arts. His was a bold hope that must remain undeclared: the letter speaks only of a trip for the purpose of study. It also reveals that there was not even a full realization at home of Raphael's value, though he was already considered " the best master " by the Abbess of Monteluce and by many in Perugia. For the Prefettessa, he was merely a " discreet and gentle lad " still not on the same level as his father (called *molto virtuoso*) who had worked for her in Sinigaglia. And " having good skill in practice, had thought to stay for some time in Florence in order to learn." However, if Soderini guessed the motive of this high recommendation with which Raphael presented himself, he must have prudently adhered to the letter's literal contents. Florence had a sufficient number of masters not to have to use beginners from outside. If Raphael, as can be assumed, although there is no proof, went to Florence in the autumn of 1504, it brought him no practical gain, nor did he remain there for long, for during the following year he was busy with the final commissions in Perugia and the new ones which came from the ascendant court of Urbino, to which Guidobaldo, after the tragic parenthesis of Cesare Borgia's usurpation, triumphantly returned in 1503.

This brief period and the one immediately following, up to the first sure Florentine date of

44 The Dream of the Knight. London, National Gallery.

1506 for the *Madonna del Prato* in Vienna, are difficult to reconstruct because there are no documents. The dates on the works in Perugia are uncertain, while the young artist's activity was intense and was guided by a desire for stability; he wished to be able to give mature direction to his art in order to conclude a long period of experimentation. One almost has the impression that he proceeded simultaneously in many directions, those traditional ones which appealed to provincial patrons and assured him employment, and those of new directions, which prodded his imagination without, however, finding opportunities to express themselves. This was the reason for his travels between Urbino, where he had his house and workshop; Perugia, where he had firmly taken command of Perugino's workshop; and Florence, which increasingly became the center of his studies. Hence the discontinuity of the works of these years, and the difficulty of tracing in them a coherent, continued evolution.

It seems that Raphael's attention, after his return to Florence, first converged on Leonardo, who had been living there since 1500, after the political vicissitudes and ultimate fall of his patron, Ludovico il Moro, had forced him to leave Milan. And he was the master from whom, without ever having him near, Raphael had learned his first and most decisive lessons. But now there were no longer in Florence only the paintings of Leonardo's youth or the drawings to study under the patient guidance of Lorenzo di Credi. There was, instead, the presence of the master himself, at the height of his creativity. It would be fascinating to think that Raphael had known the master personally and had heard in Leonardo's own words the explanation of the message in his works. But there is not even the smallest indication to support such a hypothesis. Indeed his drawings from these Florentine years, although they do not exclude the possibility that Raphael had access to the rooms where Leonardo worked, seem rather to indicate rapid visits followed by notes made from memory rather than slow and minute observation. For example, in the drawing (Louvre, 3882) [47] which evidently was inspired by the *Gioconda*, Raphael captures the general arrangement, but he varies the details and seems to completely ignore, or never have seen, the marvelous landscape. And this interpretation was to reappear later in Raphael's transposition of Leonardo's work in the portrait of *Maddalena Doni*. Besides, we do not know the various phases that the celebrated portrait by Leonardo had undergone before arriving at its final state. Anyway, if Raphael's drawing can be dated around the beginning of 1505, it could indicate that he still saw Leonardo in the mental context of his youthful study of the master's works, without appreciating the new pictorial problems presented in them. His attention does not turn to the subtle landscape but on the clear, ample, formal construction of the erect figure between two columns, similar to the composition of the *Mar-*

riage of the Virgin, in which the temple rises to dominate the representation. Raphael found again in the art of the mature Leonardo this reinforced formal structure, this concentration of rhythm that rejects the evanescent undulations of Perugino in favor of a concise harmonious construction of plastic elements. That which had been his implied criticism of the teaching of his master now found confirmation and became a directive for new study. The drawings that may be dated to the first stage of his return to Florence seem to confirm the purpose indicated in the Prefettessa's letter, that is, an intense study, especially in the realm of form. He could not as yet study from the cartoons for the *Battles* which were then being made and which were inaccessible to him, but he concentrated his research on the whole formal problem proposed in the works of a century of artistic activity which had given expression to Florence. There were the drawings from Donatello's *St. George*,[48] a reworking of the Peruginesque theme of Vallombrosa and of the Cambio, now approached directly, in its essentially sculptural nature; there were studies from Michelangelo's *David*, and others from drawings and paintings by Antonio Pallaiuolo. And, finally, there are drawings after ancient sculpture. A very beautiful drawing, made from the Leda that Leonardo was preparing for a lost painting of these Florentine years, indicates that the research was about to bear fruit. In it was understood the rhythm, the harmony that in Leonardo's mind was revealed as the inner law that gave unity to the continuous course and transformation of life. It is with this principle of a harmony beyond contingent experience that art was able to achieve, only by confronting the total experience of reality, a new direction. Concrete experience was exercised on elements, man and nature, which classical antiquity had not isolated; harmony was not an intellectual abstraction but was a discovery of the most intimate essence of existence. These were the paths on which Raphael traveled with greater understanding of Leonardo's synthesis than when he first came

46 Christ Blessing. Brescia, Pinacoteca Tosio-Martinengo.

51

to Florence. He was indeed the first to understand these problems, because he had studied them since they were first proposed. Once again he could take up his Leonardesque studies, looking at Leonardo's early works in the light of his understanding of the mature ones. And in this new critical illumination there was the entire Florentine tradition, from Donatello and Pollaiuolo, which Leonardo had so superbly interpreted.

This introduction of himself as a protagonist in the new culture, alongside Leonardo and Michelangelo, establishes the significance of Raphael's presence in Florence, even though he was left out of the principal artistic competitions and was not given the opportunity for such great manifestoes as the *Battle* scenes.

The extent to which Raphael's artistic scope was enlarged, determining an entirely different course for his artistic vision, is confirmed by a comparison between the Florentine drawings of this period and those of the immediately preceding years. We believe we can still use the notebook of drawings (copy in Venice) in which Passavant and Cavalcaselle thought they could trace the interior history of his youth.[49] Later criticism has correctly excluded Raphael's hand from it, hypothesizing either that of Pinturicchio or of Umbrian followers, or even that of a modern forger. In fact, the lack of an absolutely characteristic mark makes an attribution to Raphael impossible. But the evident gradual evolution within a span of time that goes from the interpretation of Perugino's drawings to sketches of works observed, such as the *Graces* in the Library of Siena or the " famous men " of the Ducal Library in Urbino, or the landscapes from which Cavalcaselle wished to reconstruct Raphael's travels in the territory of Montefeltro (they are more like fragments from Flemish pictures), up to original studies in preparation for his own works, has such precise coincidental relationship with the development of young Raphael that an absolute rejection of it creates perplexities. And we may ask if a new study would

47 Detail from the Ansidei Altarpiece: St. John the Baptist. London, National Gallery.

48 Madonna and Child Enthroned with St. John the Baptist and S. Nicola da Bari (Ansidei Altarpiece). London, National Gallery.

49 Predella of the Ansidei Altarpiece: St. John the Baptist Preaching. Pullborough (London), Mersey Collection.

50 Madonna and Child Enthroned with the Infant St. John, St. Peter, St. Catherine, St. Margaret (or Cecilia) and St. Paul (Colonna Altarpiece). New York, Metropolitan Museum.

51 Predella of the Colonna Altarpiece (central panel): The Way of the Cross. London, National Gallery.

52 Predella of the Colonna Altarpiece (left panel):
Agony in the Garden. New York, Metropolitan Museum.

not reveal an Urbinesque origin, a repertory at the disposition of the workshop for use in the rapid execution of various commissions. The study of Perugino's group of assistants, with its infinite repetitions and manipulations of the master's motifs, has raised the suspicion that such repertories existed in his industrialized organization. It was an organization that Raphael was to emulate when, in Rome, he had to undertake an immense series of works, impossible without a vast collaboration. Comparing that probable documentation of his youthful esperience with those Florentine drawings dated after 1504, it is almost surprising how, over a period of only a few years, his intellectual horizon changes and widens. In the first instance we are dealing

53 Predella of the Colonna Altarpiece (right panel):
Pietà. Boston, Isabella Stewart Gardner Museum.

55

with an amplification of a fully quattrocento expressive language, and in the second, with the construction, in his terms, in his syntax, in his highest expressive tone, of the language of a new culture, the newly "classic" one of the sixteenth century.

In these drawings there comes from Donatello, Pollaiuolo and ancient sculpture the knowledge that this intense movement of chiaroscuro which constituted the core of Florentine design, the tension of form that had been enunciated by Leonardo in the *Adoration*, had its origin in sculpture. In ancient sculpture was found the origin of that rhythm which, though repeated in a conventional pattern, in its best moments formed the enchantment of Perugino's art. Thus he turned to the study of sculpture in order to revise his own mastery of form because in it there was still grace, active effectiveness of gesture, a *gentilezza* that was also *naturalità*, the terms established by Ghiberti for the "new art" many years earlier.

Florence, where Raphael apparently in this first phase did not find the desired commissions, had a decisive importance in opening his vision to new horizons. Its fruit must have matured only gradually in his painting. Now, in 1505, he was still busy with commissions for the monasteries in Perugia and with some for the court re-established in Urbino. The latter was a highly cultured circle which was to be reflected a few years later in the figure of the ideal gentleman of the sixteenth century—educated in Classicism, in the Platonic cult of beauty, as a contrast to a subtle modern consciousness of the complexity of the human soul— namely the *Cortigiano* of Baldassarre Castiglione.

The Duchess Elisabetta Gonzaga, wife of Guidobaldo da Montefeltro, came from one of the most active centers of Renaissance culture, where Andrea Mantegna had for a long time

54 Self-Portrait. Florence, Uffizi.

55 Madonna and Child, called the " small Cowper Madonna." Washington, National Gallery.

dominated in art,[50] and where it seems that Raphael's father, Giovanni Santi, had spent a brief time. Perhaps it was from Urbino that there passed into the collection of the Gonzagas and from there, like so many works, into that of Charles I of England where they were found, those two small panels (now in the Louvre) of *St. Michael* and *St. George*. Once, monographs on Raphael began with these panels, but today they are considered somewhat later, and some relate them to Raphael's sojourn in Urbino in 1505. Due to the similarity in size and subject, they are considered part of the same diptych. Nevertheless, the identity of a stylistic moment is undeniable, one in which Raphael, not constrained by devotional schemes, takes advantage of the occasion offered by the heroic feats of two warrior saints to give free rein to the adventurous chromatic fantasy that had come to him in his recent contacts with Bologna. *St. Michael*, who descends perpendicularly to trample the monstrous demon underfoot, retraces the executioner of the Gavari predella of only a few years earlier (about 1503). But here there are no peaceful stretches of landscape at dusk; there is, instead, a teeming mass of small monstrous forms, of tiny ranks of Dante's damned, under a fiery sky. Had Raphael seen the *barde* with small scenes of hell which the goldsmith-painter Francia had, according to Vasari,[51] executed for the Duke of Urbino? This chromatic fantasy has more of Bologna and Ferrara than of Perugino. But in the *St. George*, more sure and coherent, although probably contemporaneous, the chromatic qualities become a poetic accent of a violent action evoked with enthusiasm, as in an octave from Ariosto. In the stupendous preparatory drawing, which is usually associated with the Florentine drawings from sculpture, the battle is quite differently

57

56 Madonna and Child with the Infant St. John, called the " Madonna del Cardellino." Florence, Uffizi.

savage in the simultaneous movements of the warrior and the dragon. Donatello's relief on Orsanmichele or the fierce horsemen, not yet those of the *Battle* but those of the *Adoration* by Leonardo, are closer to it. But the color does not yet have this force: it is only an imaginative transposition on a lyric key of the formal fury. This discordance between an imaginary color rich in effects and a drawing that surpasses it in dramatic power confirms the dating of this painting and its twin to this interim period between two different directions. For the other version of *St. George*, the one now in Washington, a later dating of 1506, suggested by its identification with a gift from Guidobaldo to the King of England, who on April 23, 1506, conferred on him the Order of the Garter,[52] is justified by the attenuating of this divergence. The relative drawing is less impetuous.

In the year or months in between, Raphael's intention must have been that of bringing his color, with its wealth of gradations, to operate in the broad rhythmic distention of Leonardo's new structures. But precisely this chromatic intensity, fortified by the acquaintance with trans-apennine painting, impeded him from understanding and following Leonardo in his invention of *sfumato*—the continuous vibrations of light which linked figures and landscapes, man and nature in a subtle relationship. In Raphael this fusion could be attained only if the color, which was an essential qualification of objects, did not lose any of its beauty. The ineffable life of light had to be a part of color, identifying itself with it to signify not only a cosmic harmony discovered by the intellect but one which the inexperienced eye could discover and which the spirit could detect in the contemplative abandon to the " natural beauty of the universe." This total sense of reality, in which poetic intuition was one with rational awareness, prevented his disassociating himself from his problems, his abandoning himself on the shoals of intellectualism, on which so much of the *bella maniera* was later to come to a standstill.

Along with the search for dramatically expressive form modeled in rhythms of perfect harmony, the attempt to build form in the living reality of color was proceeding. This dual and at the same time unique attempt had its beginning phases precisely in the Urbino period, which was punctuated by trips to Umbria and Florence, geographic episodes that had stylistic parallels, difficult to place in order because of the inherent incoherence of any such attempt. An infinite number of circumstances, even of a practical order, could have intervened, to intensify or retard the process, to produce the synthesis of the masterpiece alongside failures due to stylistic compromise, although from such a compromise, from the coexistence of different factors, there could emerge in a creative capacity such as Raphael's a tension of opposites, works of high level. Precisely from the various aspects of a study still unfinished, the brief period of 1505 and 1506 can be individualized. It is the year that appears, as mentioned above, on one of the Florentine Madonnas in which all divergences have been overcome. In this year, or in a period only slightly longer, there can be included, even though their chronological order is destined by the lack of documentation to remain in question, a series of works in which the common denominator is the actual presence of the problem which has not yet been resolved and which nonetheless nourishes the masterpiece.

There are circumstances which indicate Raphael's probable return to Florence in the last months of 1505. The determining factor seems once again to have been Perugino's activity.

57 Madonna and Child with the Infant St. John, called the " Madonna del Prato " or " del Belvedere." Vienna, Kunsthistorisches Museum.

59

On April 18, 1504, Filippino Lippi died, after having hardly begun the large *macchina* of the polyptych for the main altar of the Florentine church of the Servites, SS. Annunziata.[53] It was to have been comprised of two large altarpieces, the *Assumption*, facing the church, and the *Descent from the Cross*, facing the choir, surrounded by at least ten minor panels with figures of saints in a rich frame of carved and gilded wood, on which Baccio d'Agnolo had been working since 1500; it was a monumental complex isolated under the large arch between the church and the tribune, of the type that Perugino had executed for the church of San Pietro in Perugia. Filippino, according to Vasari, had been able only to begin the painting of the *Descent from the Cross*, from the top portion, at the time of his death. It seems that at the moment of the commission in 1503, Leonardo also had hoped to obtain it, and the friars, with the kind consent of Filippino, had acceded to his hope, giving him space in the convent so that he could work there. But Leonardo had done nothing and, at Filippino's death, he was too busy with the *Battle of Anghiari* to be called elsewhere. Thus the commission was entrusted to Perugino, expert at this type of work. It was his last work in Florence and brought him nothing but criticism in an artistic circle that was by then far too advanced to content itself with those old-fashioned motifs, repeated to the point of boredom in a work that had fallen to the level of craft.

It is possible that in undertaking it on August 5, 1505, Perugino called to Florence his collaborators from Perugia, as was his habit. To them, more than to the master, belongs the greater part of the paintings, dispersed since the break-up of the polyptych, begun in 1546. The painting of the *Assumption*, which was to have been at the center facing the church, seems to have been executed almost completely by assistants and is so flat and monotonous that when it was finished, it was decided to place it on the back, facing the choir, giving preeminence to the more vivid *Descent from the Cross*. It is this certain superiority of quality, which makes it stand out in the gray monotony of the entire complex, that made Gamba suspect the intervention of Raphael.

In the upper portion, where Filippino had left off, after having " finished," as Vasari specifies, not the dead Christ, but " the men who took him down from the Cross," Raphael's work may be recognized, while Perugino " executed the fainting Virgin and some other figures below." However, in fact, a very vivid articulation of movements and contrasts is present in the interweaving of men climbing or descending the two ladders as they support the inert body, and continues down to the groups of women scattered by the oblique fall of the Virgin. Only in the three other figures at the bottom, and especially in the Magdalene, do the quiet cadences of Perugino return. We do not know whether Filippino had designed the whole composition or whether he had at least left a cartoon, which is probable. Nevertheless, it must have been interpreted in a different manner by the two masters who, evidently, completed the work. Whoever worked on the group above obviously had to cover over Filippino's painting to give unity to the whole; there is no painterly diversity between the two groups of Christ and the bearers and the swooning Virgin, while one does exist between this whole section and the three other figures. Should one accept the hypothesis of Gamba and see Raphael and his old teacher working side by side again, as they did in the Vallombrosa altarpiece? The quick movement of clothing, draperies and ribbons in the group above reflects the figurative restlessness of the late Filippino, although the swooning Mary has its most clearly defined parallel in the predella of the altarpiece for Sant'Antonio which Raphael was still working on in Perugia in 1505, although it was completed later. The nude Christ has that fullness of chromatic modeling, that marblelike sculptural clarity, contrasting with the dark-toned chiaroscuro of the bearers, which recalls an authentic work by Raphael, the *Risen Christ* now in Brescia, dated to 1504 by Cavalcaselle on the basis of its Florentine elements.[54] A confirmation of this collaboration cannot be obtained until an analysis conducted with the new methods of scientific examination is effected on the *Descent from the Cross*. Stylistically it seems possible, and it would give coherence to the fragmentary nature of Raphael's activity during this year. It would be the first instance of work in Florence after the unfruitful recommendation of the Prefettessa the preceding year, and it would be a justification for the delays in the completion of the altarpieces in Perugia. It would also be an indication to refer those paintings that wavered between old and new experiences to Florence and to this period.

The *Christ* in Brescia, for which there are proposed datings that range from 1502 to 1508, seems to belong to this period because of the formal fullness, similar to classical marble, though modeled with a robust chromatic impasto that is penetrated with light in a bold relation to the clear sky. But above this harmoniously Apollonian torso is a gentle face, absorbed in a melancholy devotion that is still Peruginesque. There is the same confluence of forces and diverse intentions which, as has been said, become poetry in Raphael. This is what the so-called *Madonna del Duca di Terranuova*, now in Berlin, so full of parallels with the Ansidei Altarpiece and with the earliest portions of the Sant'Antonio altarpiece, seems to indicate to us, but it is so different from them in its subtly lyric sentiment which pervades and unifies the whole work. The forms enlarge themselves; they seem to seek a solemn classical measure filling the whole lower half of the painting with their mass. But in the vast, luminous sky overhead, as in the Città di Castello altarpieces, the white face of the Madonna stands out as she bends forward, fully absorbed in the quiet play of the Infant Christ and his little friends, in the sweet intimacy of a moment in which time itself seems to stand still. Only her hand, a glimmer of light, is slightly raised in the silence where the echo of the children's voices seems to fade like the cheeping

of drowsy birds. Still this spontaneous linking of simple acts succeeds in imposing a unified rhythm on an infinitely complex play of monumental structures. Leonardo, the Leonardo of the *Gioconda* and of the *St. Anne*, had revealed this ideal world of forms beyond any human measure, of rhythms beyond any earthly harmony. But Raphael alone succeeded in achieving the difficult conquest of the intellect in credibly actual terms of simple human sentiments. It is not the refinement to the point of ambiguity that links his figures to the enchantment of a landscape at dusk, but only their response to it with the innocence of their gestures, which are contained, and of their thoughtful and absorbed faces. The distant majesty of the icon becomes familiar and close; it is penetrated by human emotions. For this, Raphael, the hero of a culture which had reached the height of its intellectual conquest, was acknowledged as able to speak to all and in every age, even in our own anguished modern times.

In this manner he achieved the absolute poetry of that tiny masterpiece, the *Connestabile Madonna*, which is from this Florentine period even though it was destined for and perhaps also executed in Perugia. The compositional theme of the *Terranuova Madonna* is simplified to the extreme. Elaborated in various drawings, little by little, it passes from the play of the mother who hands an apple to the Child, to the concentrated attention of both on a little open book. The whole Florentine tradition that came through Leonardo had nourished the figure of the divine mother with a subtle human sense; Leonardo permeated the entire group of the *St. Anne* with it, searching, if we can believe Fra Pietro da Novellara,[55] to incorporate within it complex theological allusions. However, Raphael returned the Leonardesque suggestion to its first, basic inspiration; he liberated it from all intellectual implications. His sure mastery of design, of plastic

61

59 Portrait of Angelo Doni. Florence, Galleria Palatina.

qualities and structural rhythm, comes completely under the impact of the color, able to sculpture solidly the simple groups, but also able to reveal the vital play of soft flesh in the twilight that is reflected in a clear pool between low hills already covered with shadow.

Raphael's answer to the " intellectual poetry " of Leonardo is this rediscovered pristine poetical inspiration which presents the most complex figurative tradition as a natural fact, without revealing the effort involved. The only metrical support is the clear song of color. The theoretical speculation of Leonardo, the synthesis of a whole century's research, becomes in Raphael integral " painting."

At the end of this process we can place, although they were perhaps executed later (in 1506), those two famous small paintings which were once considered the beginning of Raphael's career, but which cannot be thought of as anything other than fully mature works, the *Dream of the Knight*, in London and the *Three Graces* in Chantilly.

Certain similarities with the knightly saints in Urbino should not delude us. They serve rather to further underscore the profound difference, which is one of figurative and poetic maturity. In the early work there was the ringing tone of the octave, but here, even in the knightly scene, there is the pungent elegy of the *Connestabile Madonna*. The patrons were neither Florentines nor Urbinese, but, as Panofsky correctly observes,[56] they were members of the Borghese family then living in Siena, where Raphael could have come into contact with them.

It is from a traditional family name, according to Panofsky, that Raphael may have derived his subject, the ancient allegory of Cicero's "Somnum Scipionis," to exalt a youth whose name was Scipione. This could also be an indication of a literary background acquired by Raphael in the highly cultural atmosphere of Florence. This moved ahead at an equal pace with the maturation of his figurative language. In the *Three Graces* there was all the experience of Leonardo's *Leda* in investing the continuous planes of classical sculpture with animating light. The origin is, in our opinion, undoubtedly in the fragmentary group in Siena, whether Raphael knew it firsthand or from a drawing by Federighi, who was in Siena in 1502, when the *Three Graces* was still in Rome. However, he had an impression that he translated into a drawing, which was faithfully copied in the Venetian notebook. Translating it into a painting, he added to the perfect formal harmony the light dissonance of the geometricized unclassical rhythm of the arms and the undulation of the bodies which reverts back through Perugino to the Venus by Botticelli. This immobile dance of perfect forms (the gold spheres seems to be their pure symbols) is performed on an expanse of brown earth, where silent waters reflect the bright light of the sky. Once again the music of form emerges from silent nature. Classical perfection is identified with this harmonious painting, and it indicates the direction of Raphael's later art, as well as the art of the sixteenth century.

60 Portrait of Maddalena Doni. Florence, Galleria Palatina.

With this evocative power Raphael could now undertake the most immediate kind of reality, that of portraiture. The portraits of members of the court in Urbino might suggest a return to that city during the first months of 1506, and they represent something quite different from the earlier ones in Vaduz and Munich. The masterpiece is the portrait of the young man in the Uffizi, in which the image of Francesco Maria della Rovere, the heir to the duchy, has been seen. He is apparently the same person who has been unquestionably identified in another portrait in the Uffizi (a frontal pose) as the Duke himself, Guidobaldo da Montefeltro.[57] A number of years separates the two portraits, and there are signs in the later one of the illness which caused the duke's death in 1508, when he was only thirty-six years old. In this work the light reveals the fine structure of the pallid face, where there is still a tense resistance to the consumption that erodes his body. He looks at the world indifferently through clear, glassy eyes. The form of the garment's folds is monumental and broad, and seems to imprison the figure, isolating it from the distant landscape. There is also a complementary opposition between the intense reds of the garment and the clear green of the landscape. Everything in this marvelous picture, which molds the solid new Florentine form in the gemlike chromatic material of Ferrara, converges in the sad reality of a drama. The man painted by Raphael is weighted down with the story of his life, distinguishable not only in his appearance, but captured in the implied interior drama, in which all formulas and expressive conventions are rejected. In the painting all that remains of Perugino's teaching is an echo of *Francesco delle Opere*, in which Perugino attempted to follow the direction of Flemish objective naturalism in order to achieve the char-

64   61 Deposition (detail). Rome, Galleria Borghese.

PLATE I An Angel. Pinacoteca Tosio-Martinengo, Brescia.

PLATE III Three Graces. Condé Museum, Chantilly.

PLATE IV Madonna and Child, called the " Granduca Madonna." Galleria Palatina, Florence.

PLATE V Madonna and Child with the Infant St. John, called " La Belle Jardinière. " Louvre, Paris.

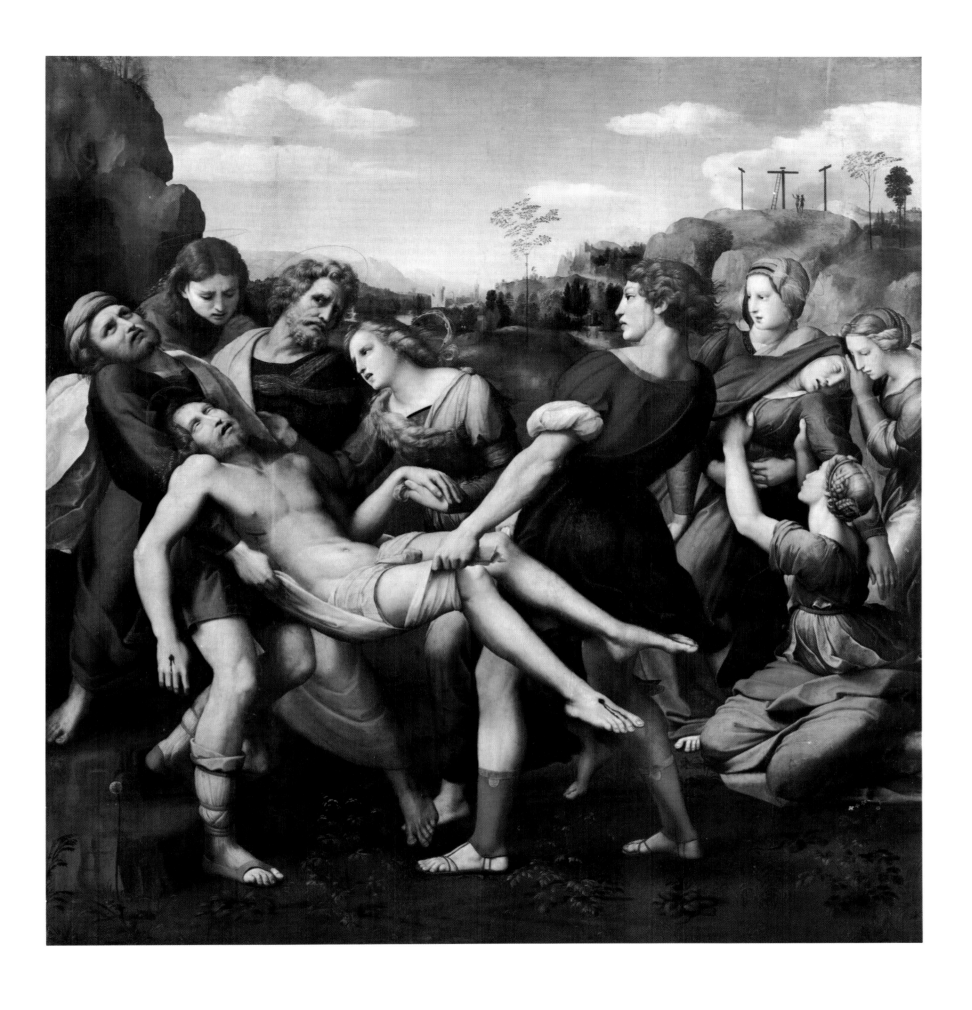

PLATE VI The Deposition. Borghese Gallery, Rome.

acteristics of a well-defined individuality by means of color. But in Raphael, reality is no longer
description; it is a probing into the essentials, to the point where the image becomes almost
emblematic. These portraits become projections of history on a level of great dignity, poetical
evocations that foreshadow the heroical figures of the Stanze.

The portrait of a youth, in Budapest, derives from the *Portrait of Guidobaldo*, and it seems
obviously to represent Pietro Bembo, who came to Urbino after a period as Venetian ambassador
in 1505, and remained there in following years, making frequent visits to Ferrara. There is the
long neck, as yet not hidden by the full beard, which is seen in youthful images on medals;
there are the bulging eyes, with the lively glance that Raphael was able to recapture years later
in the Doctor who had become Cardinal, when he painted him among the philosophers in the
School of Athens. This work would, thus, be the portrait of Bembo during his stay in Urbino that
Marcantonio Michiel reported as being in his house in Padua.[58]

Although the painting in Budapest has deteriorated because it has been cleaned too energeti-
cally, especially in the area of the face, the intelligent vitality, quite different from the exhaustion of Guidobaldo, is still seen and it accords well with the range of full reds in the doctoral
hat and in the clothing, in complementary contrast with the light green tones of the new spring
grass. It must have been the spring of 1506. While it does not achieve the deep dramatic
character of the *Guidobaldo*, there is here the essence of a figure historically alive. And we do
not know whether the desire of the artist to render his image faithfully in color was due to
Bembo's enthusiasm for the picture. Raphael's colors could quite coherently move from a major
tone to a minor one to achieve two different kinds of expressions, as musical variations on the
same theme.[59]

Perhaps slightly earlier is the *Portrait of the Duchess Elisabetta*, in the Uffizi, which we believe was painted by Raphael during his Urbino period from 1504-1506; the attribution of the work is still under discussion. The high quality and expressive intensity preclude placing it within the anonymity of any " school," but its proposed attribution to the school of Francia has a certain justification in the deep, rich impasto color, truly reminiscent of Ferrara and Bologna. It is precisely this element which makes us think of Raphael in 1505. The face is not a beautiful one, but the intense gaze from under the heavy lids is highly suggestive of a long, unhappy human drama. There is a strong chromatic relation between the golden tones of the skin and those of the sky at sunset; the relation is attenuated in the garments, although they are rich with decorations in gold. This makes us think that Raphael executed the face and then left the lower part to be finished by his workshop assistants while he was away from Urbino. In completing the review of Raphael's portraits in Urbino, we believe that it is possible to insert among them the youthful *Self-Portrait*, in Hampton Court, which Volpe has irrefutably restored to Raphael.[60] Were it not so damaged in its lower portion, it would perhaps repeat the ample structure, with the solid base of the wide sleeves and the hands resting on a windowsill, of the portraits of Guidobaldo and Bembo. He painted himself among the protagonists of aulic dignity and humanistic culture. He was no longer the " discreet and gentle youth " whom the sister of Guidobaldo recommended to the Florentine Gonfaloniere only in memory of his " very virtuous father." Now his portraits of the personages of the court could hang on the walls of the Ducal Palace alongside those of Federico and Battista Sforza by Piero della Francesca. And those who saw them might see the connecting link in the structural dignity and the vivid effects of the limpid light. Now, and not before, Raphael, in his full maturity as an artist, had arrived at the point of understanding the Renaissance message of the great master. Subordinating and unifying everything in light, he could understand now how the fifteenth-century master could attain

65 St. Catherine of Alexandria. London, National Gallery.

66

the essence of classicism. But the return to this classicism was a difficult one, which forced him
to free himself from certain cultural habits acquired in Florence. From this point, and not earlier,
we can speak of the action of an Urbinesque substratum, derived from Piero della Francesca,
in the renewed consciousness of a monumental exaltation of expression.

The works discussed up to now may be dated between 1505 and 1506 in a plausible evolutionary development in which stylistic indications concur with exterior data. Summarizing
them, we can deduce that after the summer of 1505, when Raphael and Perugino collaborated
on the *Deposition* in Florence's church of the Annunziata, he must have returned to Perugia.
We find him there between December 12 and 22, when he stipulated the contract for the altarpiece of the monastery of Monteluce and received the first payments for the work. And we have
seen from the contract that his range of activity was extended to include Perugia, Florence, Siena,
Urbino and, hopefully, Venice and Rome. Perhaps at that time Perugino hinted to him of still
another collaboration that would take the form of the Vatican commissions which may have
been under discussion then, although they were not executed until some time later. However,
the altarpiece for Monteluce was not executed until after Raphael's death, and then by his pupils.
Although, in Perugia, he had almost finished the Ansidei Altarpiece, he had only just begun
the central part of the altarpiece of Sant'Antonio. And perhaps the commissions for the *Deposition* for Atalanta Baglioni and that for the fresco of the Trinity for the Benedictines of San
Severo belong to this period, confirming the validity of the date, 1505, inscribed on the fresco
later, perhaps on the basis of a preceding contract of commission. The completion or the   67

execution of these works was delayed because Raphael's interest was straying further and further from the tradition established by Perugino in Umbria, and he limited his sojourns in Perugia, preferring to stay at Urbino and Florence. Nor can we be sure whether the works like the *Terranuova Madonna* and the *Connestabile Madonna* were executed in Florence or in Perugia, because the stylistic features that connect them to the Ansidei Altarpiece are Florentine.

There are external indications that during the spring of 1506 Raphael interrupted his fruitful, if not thoroughly enjoyed, activities in Perugia. Duke Guidobaldo da Montefeltro, after having spent a year in Rome with Pope Julius II who was his friend and who had appointed him *Capitano Generale* of the Church, returned to visit his duchy. In Rome the ambassador of the King of England had conferred on him the Order of the Garter and the honor was celebrated with a solemn religious ceremony held in Urbino on April 23, St. George's Day. In the following July, Count Baldassarre Castiglione left for London bearing a return gift to the King, the *St. George* by Raphael, now in Washington. Everything points to Raphael's return to the court, which now formed a magnificent circle around the Duke, where he took up again the position he had probably held a year earlier during the reign of the Duchess Elisabetta, for whom he had painted, it seems, the *St. Michael* and the first *St. George* and had at least begun the portrait now in the Uffizi. At the court in Urbino, in this festive period, the tedium of the Perugian commissions was dissipated. Once again Raphael was able to paint with fresh intuition the second *St. George* (that in Washington); in the portraits of the Duke and his friend Pietro Bembo he was able to measure the sum of his experience against human reality and meditate on the best approach, far from the feverish activity of Florentine art at that time.

There are no indications of a direct study by Raphael of the works by Piero della Francesca. The drawings, even those indirectly related to Raphael in the Venetian notebook, seem to show his interest in Urbino in Giusto di Gand, and in Berruguete, in the "famous men" of the Ducal

67 Portrait of a Woman, called "La Gravida." Florence, Galleria Palatina.

Library. Perhaps Piero seemed archaic to him, since he was surpassed in design by the Florentines. But it is not arbitrary to think that at precisely this moment, Piero's works in Urbino, the ducal portraits and the San Bernardino Altarpiece, might have revealed to Raphael what they had revealed to Giambellino and Venetian art a few years earlier. They could have shown him how, with light, the soul of unified perspective space, color alone could create the most historically expressive and classically harmonious form. At the same time, there was the Florentine experience combined with it to make up the " invented " color of Raphael, as it was used, for example, in the red of Guidobaldo's garments and the ivory of his pale face.

It is also quite possible that after such an experience in Urbino, he could, on his return to Florence in the same year, become a great portraitist, not yet of popes or cardinals or celebrities, but of the bourgeois leaders of Florentine society. It is in these portraits that we see with greater clarity the next phases of his evolution, in which the effort of research gives way to its fruits— the humanistic joy of presenting the central feature of all reality: man and his history. Perugino was still a master to the pupil, who was drawing away from him in other respects, in his portraits, especially the *Francesco delle Opere* with its solid, concise, chromatic structure. We have mentioned how Lorenzo di Credi responded in Perugino's portrait now in the Uffizi, which, for the presence of this influence has been attributed to Raphael. Raphael himself responded more directly in the portrait of an unidentified woman which is usually called *La Muta*, which is both a final affirmation and a definitive critique of Perugino's teaching. Here, once again in the Florentine ambience, he seems to recapitulate his long experience, from Verrocchio, to Perugino, Lorenzo di Credi and especially to Leonardo, but it is only in order to give it the mark of a new, free, authentic reality. The attribution to Raphael has been questioned when only the isolated features of the complex culture reflected in this work are considered. A thousand factors con-

70 Holy Family with the Lamb. Madrid, Prado.

69 Holy Family with the Palm. London,
Ellesmere Collection, Bridgewater House.

verge in it in a subtle pictorial articulation: the gold necklace casting its faint shadows, the
white puffs of the blouse against the emerald green of the dress, the rings rendered with Flemish
precision on the thin fingers. All these features of a painterly mastery that achieves an illusive
virtuosity are but marginal aspects of the essential expression of character. We are not dealing
here, as has been claimed, with an aristocratic woman of the court in Urbino. There is nothing
refined in this thin face and watchful eyes, in the wiry hands, hands that know how to work,
momentarily at rest to display the jewels that attest to the prosperity of the family. She is the
active mistress of a wealthy bourgeois household who regretfully has left her household activities
to pose; in his *Dialogo*, Leon Battista Alberti assigned her the task of administrating the
ménage. She sits observing the painter, almost annoyed at having to stay there while her
household is abandoned to servants or her inexperienced daughters. The young painter scru-
tinizes her in turn, looking beyond a certain hostility in her expression to discover her continuous
self-sacrifice. This is the drama that he is able to evoke in his meticulous rendering of her
face, hands and jewels in a subtle light in which nothing of the story, which is not hers alone,
is lost. Alongside the *Gioconda*, with her mysterious smile echoing a cosmic life, we can place
this unsmiling image which contains the profound mystery of an exclusively human life. She
is as inexorably silent as Guidobaldo in his premonition of death or as the hermits in the
Vallombrosa altarpiece.

Thus, in portraiture Raphael set out to compile in his sitters his " history. " This was not to
be a heroic projection or an emblematic allusion; rather, as at the beginnings of Masaccio and
Donatello's figurative Humanism, it was to be the reflection of life in its everyday aspects, revealing life's drama in the veiled drama of individuals. The wealthy bourgeois families of Florence,
whose members were from then on to be his patrons, became the subject of his study, more

70

congenial and accessible than the monastic clientele inherited from Perugino which commissioned him to do the conventional themes of altarpieces.

Among them were the Taddei, the Nasi, the "citizens" for whom Baccio d'Agnolo constructed houses and palaces. They may have been among the visitors to his workshop where, according to Vasari, the best artists of Florence came to exchange ideas.[61] Vasari mentions "many young Florentines and foreigners" as well as such recognized masters as "Andrea Sansovino, Filippino, il Maiano, il Cronaca, Antonio and Giuliano Sangalli, il Granaccio and, on a few rare occasions, Michelangelo," but "first among them was Raphael of Urbino, then a young man." If the presence of Filippino can be taken as referring to events before his death in 1504, the absence of Leonardo makes us think of a period after his departure in March of 1506, which is also the period when Raphael was most frequently in Florence. However, Baccio's workshop was active over a long period and there must have been many of those winter days when the evenings were longer and favored these indoor gatherings. In these discussions between private citizens and artists in the intimate atmosphere of the workshop, the atmosphere must have been quite different from that in the court of Urbino, where it was possible to discuss the subtle points of Platonism. Here more concrete matters would have been discussed by those men of affairs who for centuries had been the protagonists of local civic history, in which art was considered an aspect of practical action. At that time, around 1506, the shaky initiative of the Signoria in the decoration of the Sala del Consiglio, which Leonardo had abandoned to return to Milan and which Michelangelo took up again after his flight from Julius II's court, must have been discussed. The cartoons for the *Battle* scenes were beginning to be studied and were becoming a manifesto of the new art. We can guess that they were discussed and that they made all other art appear antiquated in form and composition. Lorenzo di Credi could have been the constant point of Raphael's contact with Perugino and also with Leonardo, who had been a member of Verrocchio's workshop when he was young. Aspects of Credi's portrait

71 Holy Family with the Infant St. John and St. Elizabeth, called the "Canigiani Holy Family." Munich, Alte Pinakothek.

71

of Perugino indicate the persistence of old working habits, but his participation in the meetings at Baccio d'Agnolo's may also indicate a shift to new problems. In 1506 Baccio saw to the elaboration in the forms of a revived classicism, with the architects that Vasari records in his workshop, of the large cornice for the dome of the Cathedral, which met with universal contempt, including that of Michelangelo, as did the Palazzo Bartolini years later, because it represented a break in the current tradition, something not more ornate but more formally complex in comparison to the simplicity of Brunelleschi's forms.

The movement toward new problems occurred, for Raphael, in directions already outlined by his own painting, and while he began his new experience with the *Battle* cartoons, he proceeded with his own development of portraits. Probably in the year 1506, the portraits of Agnolo and Maddalena Doni were executed. In them the residual elements from Perugino have been eliminated, and the direction is the one set forth by the portraits made in Urbino. The image of Maddalena is a fully conscious repetition of the expansive formal construction of the *Gioconda* but is justified by the physical appearance of the woman, her heavy body clumsy in her heavy silk dress. The colors of her garment become limpid areas of pink and deep blue. There is, as in *La Muta*, the same subtle search for real values in fabrics, jewels and flesh, which are the exterior manifestation of a character that is revealed as quite different. The facial expression is not, as has sometimes been claimed, characterized by an almost bovine apathy. On the contrary, if one looks carefully, one sees the beginning of a teasing smile. This wealthy bourgeois woman, in her holiday clothes, but with a few strands of hair straggling from under the elegant net, is much the same type as *La Muta*; both have the same kind of latent energy of the mistress of a busy and active household. So Monna Maddalena appears to us, not in a flattering light, but in a frank appraisal of her few graces and her active spirit. Her husband, Agnolo Doni, lover of art to the degree that he commissioned Michelangelo to work for him, but parsimonious to the point of arousing Michelangelo's anger over discussions of price, is caught in all his sharp intelligence in the other portrait, a superb construction of vivid reds and black contrasts. The structural system of the Urbino portraits is strengthened by the oblique placement of the sitter; the modeling of the face becomes more intense, and transparent shadows contribute to the revealing play of light. This mobile Leonardesque light is an intimate part of color, as in the pale lips that seem to move with each breath. The high point of this synthesis of color and light is found in the most beautiful of these portraits, only rarely surpassed by Raphael: the so-called *Gravida* in the Galleria Palatina. Here the formal expansion seem to avail itself of the physiological state of the woman depicted and even the subtle search of chromatic values is renounced, as where the jewel hanging from the necklace is hidden by the dress. The structure is reduced to simple masses of reddish and black tones and of intense white, emerging from the dark background in powerful, sculptural forms. The smooth flesh of the breast, the neck and the face, which seems enclosed in an abstract geometry, and the revealing play of light achieve such an intensity as to recall the *molte dolcezze*, which Ghiberti had seen a century earlier in the modeling of a classical statue, so subtle that sight alone could not discover their beauty, but " only the touch of the hand could find them. "

It was Leonardo who made these vibrations of form possible and available to sight, the essential sense for painting. They were part of his theory of painting which by then had perhaps already been elaborated, not only as a commentary on his own creations but as an enunciation of the future. Raphael was, however, the first to work within the new theory and to make it coincide with the palpitations of life, indeed, all life, not only that of his Madonnas, but that of ordinary people, caught in the affairs of everyday life but ennobled by their awareness and acceptance of their roles.

Even this extraordinary equilibrium, this description of the image resolved almost completely in color, this expressive achievement which would have sufficed for an entire artistic activity, was for Raphael merely a phase to go beyond in a never-ending search.

The undertaking of the large painted decorations for the Sala del Consiglio was virtually a failure but it had left the two *Battle* cartoons, which were in themselves manifestos of the new art. In 1506 they were made accessible to all [62] and they were feverishly studied precisely for their clear statements of the new language. They were the interpretations of two different artists who were exceptional individuals, treating the problem that Florentine art had faced for nearly a century. In the *Battle of Anghiari* Leonardo had fulfilled the promise that he had made in the *Adoration* of 1481, in capturing the expressive tension which charged an entire action with all its historical complexity. His forms were not only Donatellian, full of the dynamics of life, but also modulated in that ideal harmony which platonically oriented thought proposed as the internal cohesive law of the entire universe. Classical sculpture, which had furnished the means to a recovered " naturalism, " was also from the beginning of the Renaissance the unexcelled model of that ideal *gentilezza* which Ghiberti had seen as indivisibly connected with the new art. Now it was not the classical relief that was studied, but rather the large statue, the " colossus, " seen as a heroic, ideal projection of the human image. And the " stories " narrated in the *Battle* scenes, both by Leonardo and by Michelangelo, were no longer human events, but tensions of titanic magnitude beyond human dimensions. The same theme assumed an emblematic dimension; it was no longer a battle of an earthly scope, but seemed to propose the final themes of existence, the eternal conflict between life and death. The " battle " became a new interpretation of life as an unending conflict which was without respite. In order to express it in images, it was necessary to go far beyond the harmonious manipulation of forms which

72 Madonna and Child, called the "Madonna d'Orléans." Chantilly, Musée Condé.

had been the direction of art for decades in the artists' workshops of Florence. It was necessary to begin again according to the examples which the *Battle* cartoons had proposed. This was true even for those like Raphael who had already achieved their own syntheses in the expression of their artistic vision.

However, the grand compositions of the *Battle* cartoons remained strictly examples of design. They did not approach the full dimensions of color, as they had of form. Leonardo turned away from the problem, never to take it up again. Michelangelo continued to study it, but resolved it only later, in the vault of the Sistine Chapel. Along with the *Battle* cartoon, the Doni *tondo* of the *Holy Family* remained unique in Florence. Its chromatic quality achieved incredible acuteness, only because its dissonant contrasts contributed to the strained tensions of the design. The problem which faced the art of Florence was, therefore, a dual one: not only to achieve a formal heroic idealism, but also to effect its translation into painting. It was also a problem for Raphael to overcome the humanistic equilibrium of his portraits.

The enthusiastic engagement in a difficult adventure was not for Raphael. Instead, he began a slow figurative meditation that was reflected point by point, not in his portraits, but in the careful elaboration of single themes, especially the *Sacra Conversazione*, which had as its fulcrum the theme of the *Madonna and Child*.

It was a theme derived from the teaching of Perugino but quickly traced to its Leonardesque origins. And slowly his attention shifted to the solutions proposed by Michelangelo, and to his first impressions of Michelangelo's sculpture. We may consider the so-called *Northbrook Madonna*, now in London which is not far removed from the *Christ* in Brescia, as a transition between an as yet not exhausted echo of Perugino and a new desire for unity and fullness of form. We see, then, that the study takes a Leonardesque direction in the *Madonna del Granduca*, in which the plastic interlacing of the infant body between the mother's hands blends in a unitary harmony with the figure of the Mother, and a subtle motif of lightly caressing shadows envelops the whole image as if it were absorbed in a vague dream. It is Leonardo of the cartoon of *St. Anne* who gives a deeper tone of poetry to the idyll of the *Terranuova Madonna* or of the *Connestabile Madonna*. But the accent becomes stronger, in a more ample and complex play of forms, in the elaboration marked by the three Madonnas that pursue the same theme in order to give it even greater depth, the theme of the two children, Jesus and St. John, playing within the protecting circle of the maternal arms. It is not certain which is the first: perhaps it is the *Madonna del Prato*, now in Vienna, that bears the date 1506 and, moreover, recalls the Leonardesque *St. Anne* in the countenance that seems to enclose in its gentle shadows all the tenuous light of the sky that forms its background. The group is grandiose, sculptural, fixed in an immobility woven of infinite, harmoniously corresponding movements. Even in this idyll, there is a search for the heroic world of the *Battles*. And in the *Madonna del Cardellino*, in the Uffizi, it is the same Michelangelo of the *Madonna of Bruges*, which had already been finished in 1506, who provided the model for that perfect integration of the Child among the great masses of the Mother's knees so as to make of the whole group a single, closed, plastic knot. Finally, in the later one, the *Belle Jardinière*, in the Louvre, which bears the date of the following year, 1507, the great bulk is articulated in a livelier concatenation of movements without losing anything of its compactness. The Virgin wheels in space, foreshortened, the folds of her garments flutter in the wind, almost breaking up the precise pyramid, and the entire unitary cohesion seems to be entrusted to the taut interlacing of her hand, in the center, with the arm of the Infant St. John. Like the simple structures of the portraits, these laboriously achieved balances, marked by lively tensions, are also constructed by the sole force of color that has the firmness of marble. Yet it plays with the light in the subtle coloring of the flesh as in the flowers, grass, slender trees, and the hills receding into the brightness of the sky. The drawings that accompany and prepare these figurations, even to the minutest details and even in their most poignant emotional aspects, reflect Raphael's slow, assiduous meditation, in all its phases, on the figurative horizon that had been opened to him in the cartoons of the *Battles*. He does not set himself the heroic theme of struggle, but exalts the theme most congenial to his fantasy—the loving play of young mothers with their infants. Once more, as in the portraits, formal idealism is redeemed by a cordial adherence to life, the life of human beings, of plants, of landscapes, of all that which palpitates in the "natural beauty of the world." This is the solution that Raphael alone was able to give to the problem posed by the drawings of Leonardo and of Michelangelo, the proclamation of a new art of painting.

These three Madonnas, executed in the brief span of a year, from 1506 to 1507, are the focal point of Raphael's ideas of figuration, which, moreover, are presented intensely in his feverish artistic activity. At the same time he had to complete the Colonna altarpiece, which had been left unfinished in Perugia. It was a work begun with different intentions and, therefore, concluded half-heartedly, although there are some notes of a powerful lyricism, especially in the predella. It is this painting especially which gives us an indication, as Vasari has rightly stated, of how, in his search to adapt his color to the new complexities of drawing, he approached —and in our opinion not for the first time—Fra Bartolomeo who, around 1506, had taken up his brushes again and was painting the *Vision of St. Bernard*.

The saints that surround the Virgin in the Perugian altarpiece are almost the sign of a momentary disorientation that the friar helped him to resolve. In these figures the form is amplified, but in an emphatic way, overloading the draperies, as a concession to a fashion

73 Holy Family with the Beardless St. Joseph. Leningrad, Hermitage.

the reasons of which are not yet understood. It seems that the friar, in the exaggerated plastic excitement, which is also chromatic, of the *Vision of St. Bernard* may have given him a suggestion as to how to overcome the difficulty pictorially. It was the suggestion of that vividness of tones, of that irrational sharpening of relationships that Raphael was to remember and make use of later, in his own way. Fra Bartolomeo was also a great draftsman, capable of the most musical inventions of forms, with a fancifulness which had its roots in Filippino and which was made more forceful by the pretences of the new formal idealism. But even if he was one of the first Florentines to strive for pictorial renewal, his art was lacking in that profound sense of reality that allowed Raphael to give a very personal interpretation to all his cultural acquisitions. Even in his formal fullness Fra Bartolomeo always remained within a visionary, sometimes lyrical orbit, but he was never capable of concreteness, of a real figurative discovery. At times he was almost a forerunner of Baroque fantasies. For this reason, and rightly so, the estimation of the importance of his influence on Raphael, apart from the bond of brotherly friendship, has been diminished. Although he was able to anticipate some of Raphael's solutions regarding color, Fra Bartolomeo was quickly surpassed by Raphael, and the disciple became the master. Gamba[63] has noted that Fra Bartolomeo's great altarpieces follow and do not precede the *Madonna del Baldacchino*. If the aforementioned hypothesis that Raphael, an expert in perspective, had helped his friend in 1409 in the exact semicircular construction of the *Paradiso* in Santa Maria Nuova can be substantiated, it will also be necessary to discount the decisive influence of the friar that critics have always been prone to glimpse in the *Trinity with Saints*, executed by Raphael probably in 1507-1508, although it had been commissioned earlier for the

monastery of San Severo in Perugia. In the very beautiful drawing of the face of St. Placidus, there is a quick sketch from Leonardo's cartoon, a sign of quite different influences. Rather, the friar's influence is in the intense chiaroscuro masses that penetrate between the amplified plastic elements. But in the friar they were smoky shadows that obfuscated the limpid clearness of the color: in Raphael they are only deeper concentrations of chromatic quality directly penetrated by light.

Meanwhile, in 1507, Raphael was nearing completion of another of the Perugian commissions, the *Deposition*, commissioned by Atalanta Baglioni for the ancestral chapel in San Francesco; the work was undoubtedly commissioned some years before, when the memory of the frenzied slaughter that had robbed her of her son, Grifonetto, was still vivid. It was a work of lengthy elaboration, in which Raphael, as attested by his drawings, passed from the Peruginesque theme of the lament over the dead Christ to that of his transfer to the tomb, drawn with a greater dramatic tautness in the exertion of the bearers amid the convulsive desperation of the Apostles and the Holy Women, which culminates in the swooning of the Madonna. We have seen that Raphael derived this powerful play of forms from an etching by Mantegna, but the divergent tension of the bearers suggests the possibility that he was not unfamiliar with the *Deposition*, in London, which, despite certain dissensions among critics, could have been conceived only by Michelangelo's innovating fantasy. But the thought that evolves in progressive figurative accents from the drawings to the finished work reveals an interest in the frenzied struggles in the *Battles* that little by little becomes conviction and new inspiration. Raphael came gradually to understand their emblematic message, the revelation of a new

76 Madonna and Child with the Infant St. John, called the " Esterházy Madonna." Budapest, Museum of Fine Arts.

meaning, of an incessant drama of human action and of history. His language underwent renewal in this message, beyond the mysterious accord between figures and landscape, between man and nature, persisting even in the " heroic " amplification of his contemporary Madonnas. But the attempt is still incomplete. There is no reconciliation of the dissension between the disordered agitation and the contemplative calm of the landscape that spreads out, luminous beyond the shady gorge between the rocks where the drama comes to a close. It is a landscape that is lovingly presented in every one of its details, from the distant trees, slender as the crosses, black signs on limpid clouds, to the trembling in the foreground of blades of grass around the thread-like stem of a pappus, the soft luminous sphere that will dissolve at the first breath of wind. The elegy of this dulcet nature, in which there is a return of the pictorial lyricism of the *Connestabile Madonna* and of the *Three Graces*, prevails over these figures, studied in the drawings down to the very skeleton in order to ferret out and to express the whole structural tension. The momentary compromise is reconciled to a greater degree in the predella where in the chiaroscuro alone the harmonious unity of complex tensions, the mastery of the new language that Raphael is acquiring, appears more clearly. The synthesis is achieved once more in the *St. Catherine*, in London, where the same torsion of the bust is lyrically justified in the directing of the rapt look upward, and all the light of the marvelous landscape is gathered in the face, transfiguring it.

The evolution of this phase, between 1506 and 1507, consequently can be symbolized in Raphael's confrontation—with all the poetic capacity that he had achieved—with the new lesson of the *Battles*, and in his relationship with Leonardo and Michelangelo, not as pupil but as an interpreter, not as an imitator of their solutions but as a most perceptive critic of their formulation of problems. For to the heroic world of the *Battles*, he contrasts his own world, which rejects nothing of the more actual human meanings and dominates that intellectual effort in the humanistic conviction of the valid significance of life even in its most humble aspects, such as the trembling of a blade of grass or the smile of a child. To the hyperbole of form and movement, he contrasts the serene strength of his color, which can rise to lyrical heights while still drawing strength from the most basic substance of things. For him alone, the tragic surpassing of every harmony, the Michelangelesque sense of a " harsh chain " against which the expressive urgency chafes, dissolves in a resolution of the drama of form in the catharsis of color. Raphael alone understood what infinite differentiations, oppositions, dissonances, but also what harmonious concordances, are contained in the mysterious world of chromatic quality. He understood that the apparent quietude of diffused light is the result of chromatic tensions no less insistent than those which design creates in the play of forms. He avails himself of this without disassociating it; he does not intensify dissonances, he does not draw visionary unrealities from them, but he adapts their clamor to the symphonic, total orchestration of color, attribute of the universe. He too seeks the integral dynamic of the image, not beyond appearances in the metaphysics of the drawing, but in the contemplative abandonment to all that reality which reveals itself to the ingenuous eye of the poet. Thus, in the fullness of the Renaissance he penetrates into that ultra-rational world on the threshold of which Alberti's theory had come to a halt. He makes of it a total awareness, a poetic evocation of all historical actuality. The creation of the fullness of Renaissance artistic expression, the Albertian " pittura," was his alone, and his great teachers, later his competitors, could not claim it as theirs.

At the beginning of 1508 he was already proceeding with a sure step along the path of this conquest, although he was still working with the old themes. The past cannot be rejected all at once, especially when the taste of patrons is still anchored in it. Raphael's patrons were still the same ones: the monasteries of Umbria, the rich middle class of Florence, and still, occasionally, the court of Urbino. We know from a letter of Bembo[64] that in the winter of 1507 Raphael painted the *Agony in the Garden*, now lost, for the Duchess Elisabetta. We are not certain if we can gain an idea of this from the altarpiece of Sant'Antonio in which there is a similar scene, but one so damaged by restorations that the very beautiful theme is barely discernible: a figure in prayer, dominant against the clear sky over the figures of the Apostles asleep in the shadowy foreground. Raphael was in Urbino on October 5, 1507 to sign a document settling a financial dispute with a family named Cervasi. His self-portrait, now in the Uffizi, comes from Urbino and may belong to this phase. But its authenticity, incredibly, has sometimes been doubted because of an inability to recognize its evident very high quality through the damages inflicted by the old restorations. It is an extremely simple image. Abandoning the sharp, clear tones of the previous self-portraits of Munich and Hampton Court, the artist avails himself solely of a reduced range of blacks and greys and pale ivory flesh tones. But the result of this extreme modesty of means is a form of infinite complexity. The head and the neck rotate in slow opposition to the bust in profile, in which the intense, differentiated plasticity is hidden, unfortunately, by the crescendo of tones. The head rotates to turn on the viewer a poet's passionate gaze, justifying the profound structural tension with a real motive, as in the *St. Catherine*. Raphael asserts his sincerity in the anxiety of this phase of his intellectual research that is laboriously redeemed in a lyrical abandonment. I believe that the portrait of Guidobaldo, now in the Uffizi, extremely emaciated, on death's threshold, a pallid specter that rises from the somber shadow of the room, from the black of his garments, in a weak light, can be inserted into the context of this anxiety, which rejects all conspicuous chromatism for its intensity. This is a portrait which has deteriorated and which was, to a

78 Madonna and Child Enthroned with SS. Peter, Bruno (or Bernard), James and Augustine, called the "Madonna del Baldacchino." Florence, Galleria Palatina.

77 Madonna del Baldacchino (detail). Florence, Galleria Palatina.

great extent, executed by assistants in the Urbino workshop; but it was certainly conceived by Raphael in the same period of anxious melancholy reflected in his images, even in his own self-portrait in the Uffizi.

A letter of April 21, 1508, written from Florence to his uncle, Simone Ciarla,[65] refers to the duke's sad end, of which Raphael has learned "not... without tears." It also refers to an *Our Lady* painted for the "prefettessa" Giovanna della Rovere, sister of Guidobaldo. Would a more accurate, detailed research make it possible to identify it with that "small Cowper Madonna" now in Washington, that must have been executed for Urbino since the church of San Bernardino, where the dead duke must have been buried, is depicted in the background. The dating would seem to be 1507-1508, when the form was turning to the animated monumentality of the *Belle Jardinière*, to which the gemlike chromatic scale is adapted in order to intensify it further, as is the movement of the brush stroke in pursuit of an exteme evanescence. This is one of the signs of Raphael's pictorial evolution after the arduous experimentation of 1507.

It would be tedious to trace the phases of this evolution in the great number of works that he was able to execute now that he had such able Florentine assistants as Ridolfo del Ghirlandaio and the young Bugiardini, who turned to him with relief from the difficult study of the cartoons. The study of composition in progress posed ever new difficulties. It was extended to a greater number of figures, from the *Holy Family with the Lamb*, dated probably in 1507, with its persistent echo of Leonardo, to that in Leningrad and that known as the *Madonna of the Palm Tree*, in London, perhaps painted for Taddeo Taddei, Bembo's friend, who had given him hospitality. There is always an extremely skilful formal exercise, an ever more animated and harmonious entwining of movements in which the lively relationships are articulated. In the *Sacra Conversazione*, the holy figures do not give themselves up, motionless, to adoration,

77

79 The Trinity with S. Mauro, St. Placidus, St. Benedict, S. Romualdo, St. Benedict the Martyr, and St. John the Martyr. Perugia, church of the Monastery of San Severo.

but they participate in the same human life as the faithful. Thus we arrive at the brilliant achievement of the *Holy Family*, painted for Domenico Canigiani, where as many as five figures are arranged in a tight, intricate mass of forms that is brought back to the intellectualistic unity of the pyramid by the figure of St. Joseph standing over them, leaning on his staff. Yet it was necessary for the artist to pass through the straits of this intellectualism in order to incorporate and dominate the exasperated tensions of the Leonardesque combatants of the *Battle of Anghiari* and those of Michelangelo's bathers, but not for the purpose of imitating them, as is attested by the very diversity of themes, the very absence of those "nudes," the apex of Michelangelo's graphic skill, used even in the background of the Doni *Holy Family*. Raphael understood that that dynamic was not inherent in the theme, but arose from purely figurative intentions, and he could attempt it even in the elegy of his *Sacre Conversazioni*. It is the chromatic animation that progresses and is intensified in order to redeem the virtuosity in emotion that now, in order to rise to an ever higher pitch, includes the same irrationalities of Florentine color, the chromatic substratum of Fra Bartolomeo. For a moment it seems that Raphael's color too, though refining itself in the lightness of the brush stroke, is drawing away from any confirmation of reality. The portrait of the *Lady with the Unicorn*, in the Galleria Borghese, which so subtly evokes the golden texture of the hair, eludes the pictorial profundity of *La Muta*, whose scheme it repeats in the acid contrast between the gilded greens and carmine reds. Yet splendid, new poetic inventions are born as if by enchantment from this study, which is guided by the intellect. One such invention is the theme of the Child who capriciously seeks the mother's breast that we have seen evolve from the *Madonna of Orléans* to the *Colonna Madonna*, all linked to the Borghese portrait by the same subtleties and dissonances of color. The formal structure has still another variation in the *Bridgewater Madonna*, with that stupendous horizontal motion of the Child within the harmonious guidance of the Mother's parallel hands.

Finally there comes the felicitous moment in which the color is liberated; it no longer requires artificial relationships or unrealistic acuities for its joyous song. In the *Tempi Madonna* the suggestion of Fra Bartolomeo's *Vision* is taken up in order to liberate the expression of an ardent impulse of love from all structural calculations. Mother and Child clasp each other, cheek to cheek, in a triumph of color that follows the form, caught in a mounting impetus in which the lengthy thematic elaboration that had begun with the *Madonna del Granduca* is nullified. It is, in musical terms, like passing from a subdued "minor tone" to the sonorous fullness of the "major tone." Finally, it is in the *Niccolini Madonna*, now in Washington, dated with certainty to 1508, that the rise in tone avails itself also of a more meditated knowledge in order to recast all previous and actual experience in the fullness of form. This would have been the only Madonna, perhaps, that would have been able to stand comparison with the "terribile" (awesome) *Holy Family* of Michelangelo, because its intense chromatism is one with its intense sculptural quality; this was the only color that could have been used for the cartoons of the *Battles*.

But a similar opportunity was not granted to Raphael in Florence, even though this had been his constant hope. In the letter of April, 1508 to his uncle Ciarla he refers to a ducal recommendation to the *gonfaloniere* of Florence, who would have been useful to him "for a certain room to be decorated that is in the competency of his lordship to allocate," probably the Sala del Consiglio that had now been abandoned by Leonardo and Michelangelo. But his hopes must have been dashed once again and the only important commission that remained for him in Florence was that of the altarpiece for the altar of the Dei family in Santo Spirito, the *Madonna del Baldacchino*[66], which he had perhaps already received in 1506. He executed it in the hope of a handsome remuneration and of other assignments. In the letter to his uncle he says that he had already finished the cartoon. Now there was no longer any trace of the old Peruginesque conventions to which he still had to remain subject in Perugia. The whole structure of the altarpiece is entrusted to an animated play of forms, of impetuous angels, of Saints who turn to each other in a conversation that, in the inviting gesture of St. Augustine, now also includes the viewer; they move monumentally in the chromatically refined masses of their garments. In order to unify this almost Baroque tension Raphael found it necessary to recur to the architectural motif of the niche, as Botticelli had done in the St. Barnabas altarpiece, and as Piero della Francesca had in the one for Urbino, now in Brera. The fact that this motif was a totally figurative necessity refutes Riedl's thesis according to which this background was a later addition, as was the upper part of the niche. We must remember that even in the altarpieces for Perugia and in the one in Città di Castello, as the drawing attests, Raphael had always provided an architechtonic frame for the attendant Saints. The work that placed a definitive "classical" seal on even the most traditional iconic convention was, however, never finished. On September 5, 1508, Raphael was in Rome. From there he wrote to Francia, and we can read his exultation even in declaring himself overburdened with work. Something of a sudden and definitive character must have intervened to crown a long period of waiting that had begun in 1505. It was, indeed, something fateful; the great "pittura" that he had constructed in Florence, the goal of all the research of the Renaissance was to become the language of all and was to justify itself in a new, universal fullness of content. This was the task that awaited him in Rome.

The language

On January 13, 1509, in the presence of two witnesses, Pietro Busoraga of Florence and the goldsmith Cesarino Rossetti of Perugia, Raphael signed a receipt handed to him by the papal treasurer Giovanni Turroni. This receipt, acknowledging payment of two hundred ducats " ad bonum computum picturae camerae de medio eiusdem Sanctitatis testudinatae," has been considered proof that the work in the Stanza della Segnatura had already begun. It could, however, also signify the solemn formalizing of a contract, that the work was to begin only then, and that Raphael was being paid the first installment *(ad bonum computum)* for the actual execution. In the same year, on October 4, Pope Julius II, *motu proprio*, appointed Raphael to the office of Writer of Apostolic Briefs, thus assuring him a permanent stipend.[67] These are the only indications that during the year 1509 he carried out the work of the first Stanza, on two of whose walls are written the date of completion—1511, the eighth year of the pontificate of Julius II.

Before arriving at the phase of actual execution, coincident with the beginning of 1509, there must have been a preparatory phase consisting of two stages: the determination of the subject matter, which was of an unprecedented complexity and the designing, no less complex, of the figural representation, which saddled Raphael with problems much more arduous than any he had faced up to then. The Segnatura has elements from all of Raphael's earlier works, but they are resolved in the terms of a wholly new concept whose evolution can be followed through the course of execution of the great work. And it is precisely in it that the solution to the Renaissance's problem of a new expression, the Albertian " pictura," is articulated in a renewed dialectic and adapts itself to the loftiest meanings. It expresses that which in the Renaissance had not found expression in any other ambit of thought, neither literary nor philosophical, and becomes totally " language."

We can believe that Raphael dedicated to this preparation the first months of his stay in Rome, which began sometime between April 21, 1508, the date of his letter from Florence to his uncle, Simone Ciarla, and September 5, the date of his disputed letter from Rome to

80 The Vault of the Stanza della Segnatura.
Vatican.

81 Vault of the Stanza della Segnatura. Detail: Astronomy or First Movement.

82 Detail from the Vault of the Stanza della Segnatura: Apollo and Marsyas.

84 Detail from the Vault of the Stanza della Segnatura: Adam and Eve.

83 Detail from the Vault of the Stanza della Segnatura: The Judgment of Solomon.

Francia.[68] The authenticity of this letter can be confirmed precisely by its perfect integration into this phase of Raphael's activity.

When he wrote to his uncle, Raphael was still thinking of the coveted commission of the Signoria of Florence, but at the same time he referred to his desire to "satisfy" Giovanna della Rovere, sister of the dead Guidobaldo, because "now I shall have need of them," that is of the protection of the ruling house. It is therefore probable that the commission for the Stanze, where Julius II had for sometime been thinking of establishing his private apartments, was already in the making.[69] A decision must have been reached very quickly; the works in progress in Florence were left half finished. This happened to both the *Madonna del Baldacchino* and the small *Esterházy Madonna*, which is the most evolved of the Florentine compositions and which has Roman ruins in the background, as if the artist had brought it with him in his swift move from one city to the other. Certainly it was a hasty departure, which some critics assert was followed by a brief sojourn in Perugia in order to put the finishing touches on the Trinity fresco in the church of San Severo.

The cause of this sudden departure might have been, as Vasari states, a letter from Bramante, who had already powerfully asserted himself in the papal court, with the news that he "had induced the Pope to have certain apartments done, and that Raphael might have a chance of showing his powers there." But the Della Roveres, successors to the duchy of Urbino and kinsmen of Julius II, were also powerful at the papal court. It is better to agree with Cavalcaselle and to combine the two circumstances: recommendations from the Urbino court backed by Bramante.[70] Moreover, it is not unlikely that the Pope himself had heard about the rising young artist's fame when he passed through Urbino in 1506, during the successful military

85 Detail from the Vault of the Stanza della Segnatura: Justice.

86 Detail from the Vault of the Stanza della Segnatura: Poetry.

87 Detail from the Vault of the Stanza della
Segnatura: Theology.

88 Detail from the Vault of the Stanza della
Segnatura: Philosophy.

90 Detail from the Disputa del Sacramento: The Trinity with the Virgin and St. John the Baptist. Vatican, Stanza della Segnatura.

89 Detail from the Disputa del Sacramento: The Eucharist. Stanza della Segnatura.

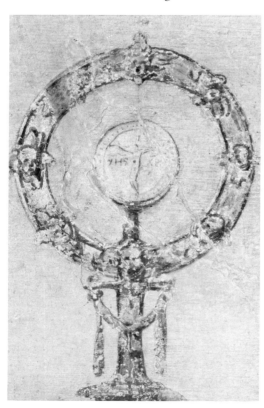

undertaking in Bologna. In Condivi[71] there is also an indication, albeit imprecise, of a suggestion coming from Michelangelo himself, who supposedly proposed Raphael for the decoration of the Sistine chapel, a task which was unwelcome to the older artist, but which he was obliged to assume between March and May, 1508.

So then, if in the following summer Raphael went to Rome there is no occasion for surprise when in September, writing to Francia, he describes himself as oppressed by "heavy and unceasing labors." He already seems to have been introduced to the personalities of the Curia: he knows the Datario (Msgr. Gozzadini of Bologna) and Cardinal Riario, and already says that he is "obligated to patrons," hence committed to produce works. It is logical for him to resume contact with Bologna, the city recently reconquered and therefore very dear to the Pope; from there he could obtain powerful prelatial support to consolidate his position in the papal court. Raphael's activity on behalf of his patrons in Bologna and, in general, of Emilia Romagna, continued unabated in the subsequent years. Indeed, it is precisely during these years, around 1508-1509, that the beginning of the Raphaelesque influence on Emilian painting can be discerned, even touching the young Correggio. In the letter to Francia there is a reference to the dispatch of a drawing for a Nativity scene, different from a previous one that Francia had praised (and which is attributed to Giovanni Bentivoglio, about 1506). If, as is maintained, the one to which Raphael refers is the one now in Oxford, published by Filippini,[72] the difference appears above all in the dawning of a new culture. The Madonna, who raises the veil of the cradle to show the Child to the shepherds, is positioned in an architectural framework that already has a sonority quite different from that of the Dei Altarpiece, showing a hint of the influence of Bramante. The sign is subtle as in the first ideas for the *Disputa;* it is as if Raphael, from his first work in Rome, became aware of other pictorial possibilities and

91 Detail from the Disputa del Sacramento: Angels. Stanza della Segnatura.

began to explore these avenues, preparing himself for the undertaking that, perhaps, had already been proposed to him—that is, to work alongside the masters already engaged in the decoration of the Vatican Stanze. Working there at that time were Signorelli,[73] perhaps, and certainly Perugino and Pinturicchio, in the room in which Raphael is supposed to have executed the *Fire in the Borgo*. In addition, as documents of October 1508 attest, there were Sodoma, protected by the Sienese banker Sigismondo Chigi, Giovanni Ruisch, Michele del Bocca da Imola, and Bramantino, who were joined in March 1509 by Lorenzo Lotto. Raphael, as we have seen, does not figure among them until January 1509; but even if we want to give the first " installment " the meaning of an actual payment in advance for beginning the work, it does not exclude the fact that the task had been entrusted to him earlier. The brush could not be applied to those walls without the prior elaboration and division of the great allegorical discourse that was to cover them, like the plan of a literary work with its divisions into chapters. Even supposing that the definitive versions of the drawings and cartoons were begun in January

92 Detail from the Disputa del Sacramento: Angels. Stanza della Segnatura.

85

93 Detail from the Disputa del Sacramento: Head of the Virgin. Stanza della Segnatura.

94-95 Detail from the Disputa del Sacramento: putti carrying the Bible. Stanza della Segnatura.

1509, there must have been general and detailed sketches submitted earlier so that the commission could be confirmed and legitimized. This is even more likely in this case, in which the subject matter to be treated was different from every figural precedent, did not derive from any familiar repertory, and required an entirely new vision of general composition in the rendering of detail that in itself makes the fact that it was finished in only two years nothing short of miraculous. To those two years, then, must be added the last half of 1508, in which Raphael must have been actually engaged in those " heavy and unceasing labors " required for putting his new creation, conceptually and figurally, into focus.

96 Detail from the Disputa del Sacramento: Saints, Patriarchs, Prophets (St. Peter, Adam, John the Evangelist, David, St. Stephen and Jeremiah). Stanza della Segnatura.

97 Detail from the Disputa del Sacramento: Heads of St. Peter and of Adam. Stanza della Segnatura.

JULIUS II

In his short *Life of Raphael*, Paolo Giovio asserts that he painted "cubicula duo *ad praescriptum* Juli pontificis" in the Vatican.[74] This passage has been interpreted to mean that the iconographic programs of the two Stanzas were proposed by the same pontiff, Julius II, in particular the more organic program, that of the Stanza della Segnatura. This is a plausible interpretation in the light of the grandiose character of the theme that gathers in all the loftiest activities of the

98 Detail from the Disputa del Sacramento:
Heads of John the Evangelist and of David.
Stanza della Segnatura.

human spirit and their final fulfillment in the Faith: it is almost a new *Summa*, a celebration of the Church, supreme mediatrix between the Divinity and the world of human action. This is why the decoration of the Stanza della Segnatura with its grandiose allusions—*Truth* sought through reason by Philosophy (the *School of Athens*); *Good*, in the two-fold aspect of the Virtues and of the Law; *Beauty*, signified by the Muses listening to the music of Apollo (the *Parnassus*); and the greatest spiritual "categories," all converging around the exaltation, in the Eucharist, of the fundamental mystery of the Christian Faith (the *Disputa*) has been considered the presentation of Renaissance Humanist and Christian thought in a new synthesis almost comparable to what the *Divine Comedy* achieved at the conclusion of medieval thought.[75]

A program of this kind suited the pontifical action of Julius II, to which consideration is generally given only to the political campaigns, often conducted with unscrupulous and violent means in order to assure the Church a territorial base from which she could not be overcome by the fierce competitions among the great monarchies contending for the mastery of Europe. But at the roots of the actions of a political leader sometimes lacking in scruples, lay the deep convictions of a spiritual leader whose overweening desire was the unification of Christianity beyond the crises that were undermining it, the truth of the Faith beyond the dramatic dialectic that was being traversed by Renaissance thought. These were the intentions, in addition to the necessity of defense against threats and schisms, that later inspired the Lateran Council which death prevented Julius from bringing to a conclusion. But they are certainly manifest in his action through art. Thus a single idea of Christian reaffirmation guides the reconstruction of St. Peter's. The commission to Michelangelo to decorate the vault of the Sistine Chapel with the re-evocation of Revelation, beginning with the biblical origins, was to be followed by the presence of Revelation in the actual world, the demonstration that also the newest conquests of thought could converge and find a point of reference in it. This was to be the significance of the illustrations of the Stanze, a continuation of the Sistine theme. This also constitutes the great difficulty in its interpretation, as is attested by an immense literature.

99 Detail from the Disputa del Sacramento: Saints, Patriarchs, and Prophets (Judas Maccabaeus, St. Lawrence, Moses, St. Matthew or St. James the Elder, Abraham and St. Paul). Stanza della Segnatura.

100 Detail from the Disputa del Sacramento: Heads of Abraham and of St. Paul. Stanza della Segnatura.

103 Detail from the Disputa del Sacramento. Stanza della Segnatura.

101 Detail from the Disputa del Sacramento. Stanza della Segnatura.

102 Detail from the Disputa del Sacramento. Stanza della Segnatura.

In fact, the will to achieve a higher reconciliation of the most diverse facts has allowed the exegetists to indulge in infinitely varying points of view, ranging from the rigidly scholastic exposition, almost a return to the Middle Ages, through a totally Platonic conception, an exclusively religious reaffirmation, to a manifesto of secular thought. Critics have perceived emblematic significations, abstractly allusive, or they have attempted to justify everything with reference to the contingent facts of Julius' polity. Whatever the critical point of view, it has been possible to justify it by the multiplicity of facts that converge in this synthesis—truly the synthesis of the entire thought of the epoch whose metaphors can express the facts of contemporary history, but whose point of reference lies in a transcendent sphere. Herein lies the true and higher conclusion of what had been begun on the walls of the Sistine Chapel in the late quattrocento. Thus Julius II was resuming the tradition of his predecessors, the Popes who had wanted to make Humanism Christian and Catholic, from Nicholas V to Sixtus IV, his uncle, who had promoted the pictorial decoration of the Sistine Chapel. Without the presence of this basic conception of reconciling all in the renewed exaltation in the Faith, every interpretation of the discourse developed from the Sistina to the Stanze is bound to be unilateral and incomplete. But this was a discourse through imagery, expressed not with conceptual means of theological or philosophical exposition, but with the figural means of art. In the Renaissance, art, since its theoretical expression by Alberti, had been the new instrument of an investigation of reality in all its complexity in order to assert its immanent value and its point of reference was " *storia, somma opera del pittore.*" It was this recognized, affirmed immanence that had to be conjoined once again with the transcendental truth of the Faith, without losing anything of the new thought that had been conquered. This required the very language of art to be sublimated and that not only iconography but the entire formal expression should be capable of symbolizing meanings beyond the historicity that had determined it and remained at its base. This intention, already circulated in thought from the Neo-platonic proposal of a rationally renewed theological system, now found the possibility of a total fulfillment in the theologico-historical synthesis proposed by the Church. This was the task that was presented to the artists Michelangelo and Raphael: to translate into imagery the new *Summa* of Christianity. It was a demand upon art to thrust beyond its own immense conquest, to bring its own historicity to the clarity, essentially simplified, of the " concept " and to adapt its potential for expression to that philosophical language. It enjoined the artists to immerse themselves totally in these new concepts in order to translate them integrally into the metaphor of a new image, to create a language in which art definitively was placed in the class of speculative disciplines, crowning the function that it had performed for more than a century in the renewal of thought through the rediscovered value of reality. The artists themselves were to go beyond the rational sublimation of the Neo-platonic " Idea " to the point of expressing in a realistic image the ineffable transcendence, and to translate into form that which surpassed every form without ever having recourse to the pure abstraction of the medieval symbol. The artists summoned to the construction of the spiritual center of this movement—the mother church of Christianity, St. Peter's, and the residence of the head of the Church, the Vatican—were tried in the crucible of this tremendous task. It is not surprising that many did not survive the test. The destruction in 1508 of all that had already been accomplished in the Stanze was not due

90

104 Detail from the Disputa del Sacramento: Head of Dante. Stanza della Segnatura.

to a whim of Pope Julius but to the obvious inadequacy of the representations to express his thought, which was the same as that of the Church. The obscure, confused allegories of Perugino, the only surviving parts of the earlier decorations of the Stanze, are proof of this. The task called for a loftier intellectualism and the youthful energy of artists like Michelangelo, slightly over thirty, and Raphael, still in his twenties.

Raphael, in the period that preceded the actual commission (i.e., the second half of 1508), was to pass every test, in particular the comparison with Michelangelo, so that he could work alongside him, and himself become the creator of a new classicism in competition with him.

THE STANZA DELLA SEGNATURA

Although the figural theme of the Stanza della Segnatura, in its general outline, could be enunciated by Julius II, it was the artist's task to articulate it within the frame of a discourse through an imagery that was no less logical than the conceptual discourse of philosophy. Raphael, who was not a learned man (as is attested to by the crudity of expression in the letter of April 1508 to his uncle), had to become familiar with the highest culture, the ecclesiastical culture of the theologians no less than the secular culture of the Humanistic men of letters and philosophers. He himself had to become a man of culture, capable of understanding the subtleties to which he had to give form. Without this capacity for personal interpretation, he would have been merely a translator of the programs of others. Available to him, however, was another, profound culture that in the novelty of ideological positions had surpassed that of written texts: the figural culture he had mastered from adolescence in Florence as Leonardo's perfect pupil. Even before coming to Rome, he had acted as an innovator in that new discovery of realism which overthrew every previous hypothesis; he had brought to the metaphysical inquiry of Florentine drawing the revelation of color, and going beyond the Florentine ambit had experimented with the proposals of the whole of Italian painting. Consequently, his potential for understanding the requirements of the new figural language was immense. He could endow with real historicity the abstract enunciations of intellectual speculation, and compare them with art's discovery of a new meaning of reality: the ceaseless play of relationships and transformations, the eternal dialectic of being identified with becoming. In this comparison the entire datum of scholastic and humanistic culture lost every assertive significance: it posed itself almost as terminus to an ulterior, definitive overcoming. The "system," the monolithic construction of thought, was being cracked by the same overthrow of every system, the dialectic immanent in the very means in which it had to be expressed in the image. The dramatic reconciliation of opposites that had determined the papal program identified itself with the very figural drama of its interpreter; it could not be overcome save in the impetus of a renewed act of faith. Michelangelo was capable of it, renouncing every contingent flattery of the material world in a sublime expressive asceticism, denying painting itself in an expression different from every other, in which nothing

105 Detail from the Disputa del Sacramento. Stanza della Segnatura.

106 Detail from the School of Athens: Plato and Aristotle. Stanza della Segnatura.

107 Detail from the School of Athens: Head of Aristotle. Stanza della Segnatura.

else existed save the bare evidence of the drama. Rightly the inquisitor of Paolo Veronese could later assert that in him " there was no thing that was not of the spirit."

But Raphael had contemplated the " natural beauty of the universe " with too much sensuousness to be capable of such an absolute renunciation. His youthful themes had been the lyrical revelation of the sweetness of the hour of day, of subtle reactions, in individual characters, to the infinite, evanescent nuances of the daily drama of life itself. This appreciation of every facet of reality, even the most marginal and fleeting, was convinced historicity; and it had to be reconciled to the essentiality of a transcendant affirmation in the theme that had been proposed to him. In the elaboration of this theme, Raphael could but arrive at a concordance of opposites, albeit at the loftiest level, at an equilibrium between dialectic terms that remained, however, basically irreconcilable.

It was precisely this equilibrium, in which nothing was rejected but everything was transported into a higher poetic assertion, that was the great achievement of his art, the result of the immense task imposed upon him by the decoration of the Stanza della Segnatura. A patient, tenacious attempt to construct a new language, by calling upon all his previous experiments and in testing new ideas, in using the entire vocabulary of art available to him. Michelangelo could rightly say, if we consider only this phase, that Raphael had learned art not from nature but in the studio; and also, not without reason, that " what he had of art, he had from me."[76] For while Raphael was exhausting himself in seeking his equilibrium of opposites, Michelangelo remained the living demonstration of how this equilibrium could be surpassed by going beyond the " language " of painting—even Alberti's—to the roots of things in order to renew expression itself and to attempt to arrive at the extreme limits of

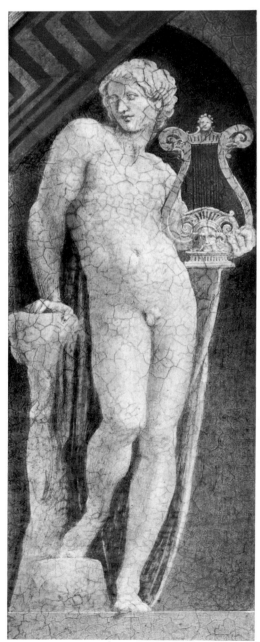

the possibilities of art. Raphael, however, remained a painter only, even if he clearly perceived in Michelangelo how painting itself was a limit. This journey into painting in order to broaden the ambit of its expression was Raphael's drama; it was not exasperated and rebellious, as was Michelangelo's, but a drama tenaciously played out in patient labor whose tireless progress is legible in the Stanze. He first worked to achieve a coherent language, in order later to be able to reach new goals of expression which, at one stroke, made those reached before him appear alien and remote His disinterest in that language was to come later, his leaving it to the endless analyses of pupils and followers, while Raphael, in all his most genuine creations, up to the last, the *Transfiguration*, continued to propose to himself, over and over again, the awesome problem of giving form to the dialectic of an historicity that anxiously tries to transcend itself—the problem of the whole Renaissance.

The first phase of the Stanza della Segnatura is that in which the problem is recognized, is posed, and finds a first solution in an equilibrium that will seem definitive for centuries, even if for Raphael it was to represent only a point of departure. It is the equilibrium determined by a unitary program that proposes to grasp the whole history of human thought in a total synthesis and to give it figural form.

Raphael's problem is first and foremost a compositional problem: the immense problem of understanding in its profound complexity the significance of the theme, and to articulate it in a clear expositional sequence without ever departing from its unitary character. But this unitary synthesis came to the mind of its very planner, Julius II, from the whole thinking of

110 Detail from the School of Athens. Stanza della Segnatura.

111 Detail from the School of Athens: Francesco Maria della Rovere (?). Stanza della Segnatura.

the Renaissance, from its lofty illusion that it could lead back to unity the discovery of the universe as an infinite dialectic tension. In art it was the search for the perfect form, the synthesis of every tension, the centralized structure in which Bramante, emblematically, was renewing St. Peter's. Bramante must have been Raphael's teacher from the moment of his arrival in Rome. They were of the same land, friends if not, indeed, kinsmen. And if Bramante was truly behind the call to Raphael to work on the papal project, it indicates a critical recognition of the great potentialities of the young man who was to measure himself against Michelangelo. It has rightly been thought that Bramante was Raphael's guide in understanding the lesson of Rome,[77] in orienting himself in that world in which historical continuity was imprinted in a millenium of uninterrupted construction and re-elaboration of figural thought, from classicism to Christianity. But the Renaissance idea of the centralized architectonic form in the full mastery of space permitted by the use of perspective had dominated the mind of Raphael, who had been educated in the discipline of perspective since his adoloscence in Florence, and is already evident in the temple in the *Marriage of the Virgin (Sposalizio,* 1504*)*. The continuation of the Albertian line, the search for perfect proportionality, *concinnitas,* and harmonic unity now found its fulfillment in the contact with the Albertian Bramante and in the continuous demonstration—and confirmation—of its origin, the architecture of Rome.

This was the way to the figural structuration of the Stanza della Segnatura. We do not know how the problem was elaborated before its grandiose solution was arrived at, since no architectural drawings by Raphael are extant; but what emerges from the solution with absolute clarity is how the foundation of that total figural unity was the foundation that had been practically and theoretically posed to the Renaissance: perspective. It made it possible for Raphael to utilize that which had been fixed by the artist who had preceded him in the decoration of the Stanza, the dividing of the vault. Someone, probably the Lombard Bramantino, had already opened the regular geometry of the intersected vaulting ribs to the infinity of the sky, in the extreme foreshortening of the central *putti* who hold up the coat-of-arms of the first builder of the apartment, Nicholas V. It was the Mantegnesque, and also Albertian idea, of the Mantovan *Camera degli Sposi.* For Raphael it was the point of departure

95

112 Detail from the School of Athens: Averroës, Empedocles or Boetius, Pythagoras, Telange (?), Francesco Maria della Rovere (?), Parmenides or Xenocrates or Aristoxenus. Stanza della Segnatura.

PLATE IX La Disputa del Sacramento (detail). Stanza della Segnatura, Vatican. ▷

96

for centralizing around this central "tuyere," like the interior of the Pantheon, the entire construction of an interior that was to combine, not a series of allegories, but the unitary unfolding of the phases of a history of the loftiest character, the history of the whole of humanity that began in time in order to end in eternity. In his profound by intuitive understanding of the theme, more than in its interpretation, in his reliving of it not only in its logicalness but in the winged impetus of fantasy, Raphael seized all the resources of perspective, all its equilibrating proportionality. But he immediately sensed that harmonious metric balancing would not be enough to enclose a figural drama that went beyond human measure. All that could be done, if one wanted really to signify this balance in all its "terribilità" (awesomeness), was to allude to a straining beyond it, while still accepting the harmonic coherence of that intellectual measure. The metric *concinnitas* of the architechtonic-perspective form executed around a median axis was the extreme outreach of this intellectual contemplation. From the outside it could be appreciated in its totality and enjoyed as such. But Raphael, and this has been clearly seen by Mellini in his recent reading of the Stanze,[78] makes the viewer not one who contemplates from the ground, but one who lives and moves and looks out from within the same ambience in which the protagonists of the paintings move and live. Consequently he becomes the focal point in which, whatever his position, ever renewed impressions of spatial coherence are always bound to converge. The perspective is unified only in the viewer: the coherence is no longer given by the equidistance from a fixed center, but from

◁ PLATE X-XI La Disputa del Sacramento. Stanza della Segnatura, Vatican.

PLATE XII La Disputa del Sacramento (detail). Stanza della Segnatura, Vatican.

◁ PLATE XIII-XIV   The School of Athens.   Stanza della Segnatura, Vatican.

PLATE XV   The School of Athens (detail).   Stanza della Segnatura, Vatican.

◁ PLATE XVI-XVII Parnassus. Stanza della Segnatura, Vatican.

PLATE XVIII Parnassus (detail). Stanza della Segnatura, Vatican.

PLATE XIX-XX The Cardinal Virtues. Stanza della Segnatura, Vatican.

a convergence toward a center that can shift. A guide to this shifting is given only in a longitudinal axis: that which links the beginning and point of arrival of this traversing in time and beyond time—the grand arcade in the background of the *School of Athens* and the infinite sky in which appears, suspended, the ultra-terrestrial vision of the *Disputa*. It is almost a grandiose basilica, like that in which idealized rationality is asserted by Bramante—St. Peter's, but it is stamped with an entirely new tension, the very tension of the drama that it must enclose. The character of the Stanza della Segnatura is that which Mellini has precisely defined as an "intense and dramatic cosmos, not simply olympic and apathetic," not only because of a connection through the window with the Bramantesque conception of the Court-yard of the Belvedere, but because of a total coherence in the emblematic significance of the composition, in which the past, signified in the thought of antiquity, is linked to the present of Christian thought. The complex multiplicity of the structures, not St. Peter's, but of a Roman bath with its alternations of centralized salons and great corridors covered by barrel vaults, is transfigured almost into an immense basilica, like the early Christian basilicas of Rome, terminated by an equally immense exedra from which the heavenly vision dominates. This is the exedra of the *Disputa*, which continues the transposition of the ancient theme already

113 Detail from the School of Athens: Heraclitus (Michelangelo). Stanza della Segnatura.

97

98 114 Detail from the School of Athens: Head of Pythagoras and Telange (?). Stanza della Segnatura.

realized in the full Renaissance by Melozzo in the apse of the Santi Apostoli (later destroyed, but then visible). The solemn progress of the two supreme philosophers, Plato and Aristotle, through the whole personified dialectic of ancient philosophy ideally had to finish at the foot of the altar on which the small Host is elevated in its bare essentiality. It is alone and simple amid the dramatic tumultuousness of the " disputa," from which the Church had risen. And in the background, behind the great figures of the western Fathers of the Church—Jerome, Gregory the Great, Ambrose, Augustine surrounded by the throng of Popes, the founders of the Orders, the exegetists, and also the poetic interpreter Dante—appear allusions to the emblem of the actual reaffirmation, the construction of the new St. Peter's. But from that small Host, surrounded by the delicate nimbus of the ostensorium, one is lifted in a series of rising chords, to the effulgence of the Holy Ghost, to the circular glory of Cherubins around the Epiphany of the Redeemer, who, His pierced hands uplifted, shows the sign of the Sacrifice until above all appears the Eternal One blessing, in the barely suggested dome of the infinite heavens, where every form seems to dissolve Dantesquely in an apparition of myriads of angels in a sublime light. This the vision of the Church Triumphant, mediated to human contemplation by the figures of the elect of the Old and the New Testaments, by the two major apostles, Peter and Paul, by the Patriarchs, the Prophets, the Evangelists, and the first martyrs flanked on an exedra of clouds at the center of which, on an advancing foreground, appears the Epiphany of the Trinity in a perfect axis with the altar of the Sacrifice.

Thus Raphael, recreating poetically the whole significance of Rome, ancient and Christian, as it appeared to him in its own structures, knew how to give a powerful organic character to his theme, an entire synthesis of the course of the centuries, including that in which he was living. If he repeated the already begun transposition of the Stanza from an organism arranged in the form of a cross with a centric coherence around the " tuyere " at the top of the vault, it was because he saw the possibility of inserting in it the alternations of forms constituting the nave of his ideal basilica, concluded not by a cupola but by the immense exedra that became the vault of heaven itself, open to infinity. And in that room the real person, the viewer, could linger, his gaze contemplating that immense history that was continuing in him.

115 Detail from the School of Athens. Stanza della Segnatura.

100   116 Detail from the School of Athens.   Stanza della Segnatura.

In the few months that preceded the actual beginning of the work, from the summer of 1508 to January 1509, the young artist had become capable of comprehending the world of classical and Christian Rome much more profoundly than when he was initiated into it by Bramante; he had relived it in the dialectic of all his architectonic themes, surpassing his teacher by far. From the construction of the first Stanza he must have more exactly defined the research that later made him master-builder of St. Peter's and the ideal reconstructor of ancient Rome: the creator of a new architecture that infused movement into the antique harmonies, inserted into them into a new feeling, and proposed the themes and the whole construction of the cinquecento.

The plan of the artists who had begun the decoration of the Stanza della Segnatura, starting from the vault, was entirely different, more confused and limited. Perhaps the original purpose of the Stanze, which was intended to have been used as the Pope's private library, limited them to a doctrinal program, to the formal classification of knowledge into its branches,

117 Detail from the School of Athens: Below Zoroaster with the celestial sphere. Stanza della Segnatura.

101

118 Detail from the School of Athens: Head of Zoroaster. Stanza della Segnatura.

theology, philosophy, poetry, jurisprudence, that had been adopted, for example, in the ducal library of Urbino.[79] Neo-platonic culture had associated these divisions with a cosmic and moral order alluded to in the four elements: fire, water, air and earth. They are referred to in the narratives inserted among the *tondos* where Raphael later was to place his allegories, each in two superimposed panels alongside a historical subject taken from Titus Livy and a mythological one from Hyginus. In them can be recognized a labored expression of the most exacerbated Neo-platonic intellectualism in an attempt to make a metaphorical allusion to the whole culture of antiquity, including its most minute details, and of Christianity and to clothe the concepts of the medieval Christian exegetists, already far-fetched in themselves, in the forms of an erudite rhetorical classicism. Along this path it would have been impossible to arrive at the proposition of a new synthesis that was the real program of the Stanze della Segnatura. It can be supposed that it was precisely because of his annoyance with this first elaboration, the work of tarrying Neo-platonists, that Julius II conceived his own plan, clearer and more basic, and commissioned a new artist, Raphael, to realize it. Raphael reacted to this contorted allegorism with his own substantial " Humanism " historically anchored in reality, by simplifying the minutely detailed and particularized decoration in a monumental construction of great figures. With hard work, and not without occasional discrepancies, he succeeded in harmonizing the prefixed theme of the four elements with his new division of the subject matter, resolving the abstruseness of the concepts with his clear sense of history. Precisely because of the difficulty, and also the tedium, of the task, he must not have begun his work with the vault, according

119 Detail from the School of Athens: Raphael and Sodoma (?). Stanza della Segnatura.

102

120 Detail from the School of Athens: Bramante appearing as Euclid, Zoroaster, Ptolemy, Raphael, Sodoma (?). Stanza della Segnatura.

to the usual procedure. His mature style strongly suggests that he must have gone back to it when the painting of the walls was already far advanced. Thus Raphael's development, which reached its crucial phase in this Stanza, cannot be followed in the usual sequence from the vault to the walls, and nor even from one to another of figural compositions. Rather it must be traced in the internal coherence of single episodes, as if the artist worked simultaneously on the articulation of the whole complex, unitarily dominated by his conception.

This hypothesis is not negated even in the physical procedure of the work. The scaffoldings necessary to paint those vast mural surfaces in fresco had to allow a control of the emerging composition from a distance. Like those used by Michelangelo for the Sistine vault, they must have been constructed of a single framework supported by vertical beams that allowed the artist to carry forward the entire decoration, while gradually executing the episodes in a sequence determined by the exigencies of the moment and by his intuitive choices. The only real limitation, and one that was valid for the individual walls but not for the vault, was the procedure of working from top to bottom in order to prevent color dropping from the parts already executed. But at different levels Raphael could freely pass from one part of the composition to another. Thus, in order to follow his posing and reposing of ever new problems in the two years of work in the Stanza we have no other means at our disposal save that of an attentive reading of his work, and to retrace in it the coherent procedure that was rooted in the premises of an integral dynamic of the image, which began in his Florentine apprenticeship and culminated in an Albertian fulfillment of " *storia, somma opera del pittore* "—a history that was now the history of the world.

In order to conceive this task, he had to avail himself of the whole culture of his time and to draw freely from ecclesiastical and secular thought alike, but only for his own artistic inspiration. He could choose his counsellors freely from among the greatest exponents in every field of that culture; this was possible thanks to the liberalism of Julius II, whose court was open to all currents and was a meeting place for the great thinkers of the day. Perhaps the portraits that appear many times among the imaginary heroes of the great frescoes often have no other reason for being than as an act of gratitude toward Raphael's cultural collaborators. For the grandiose allegory of the Eucharist, the *Disputa del Sacramento*, generally called simply the *Disputa*, Pastor [80] has rightly pointed out Raphael's sources in the scholastic-mystic sphere

103

121 Detail from the Parnassus: Corinna. Stanza
della Segnatura.

of the Dominicans, the theologians of the pontifical court, then as now. The doctrine proposed by them is that clearly expounded in the *Summa* of St. Thomas. But others who appear alongside the portrait of the great theologian were drawn from a Dominican circle that was well known to Raphael, that Florentine circle of San Marco of which his great friend Fra Bartolomeo was a member. They are dispersed among those that group around the Church Fathers. We do not know which of the many friars is Fra Giovanni Angelico, whom Vasari says is portrayed; but he is certainly not the lean old man on the left with whom he is commonly identified and who, instead, fits the current descriptions of the great prior of San Marco and later archbishop of Florence, Sant'Antonino, in his old age. This cannot be Fra Angelico, who died at fifty. Perhaps Julius II, in his openness of mind, consented that the figure of Savonarola, who supposedly is seen on the right almost hidden by a black cowl, be included in it. These are Dominican reminiscences of the Florentine convent so dear to Raphael and which seemingly also enjoyed the sympathy of the Pope who himself came from the Franciscans. But the poetic source is portrayed alongside the ecclesiastical source in Dante, who had given historical concreteness to the mystic vision. Fischel[81] has rightly and perceptively seen how Dante's Paradise, the kingdom of pure light, is related to the luminosity peopled with forms of the Paradise of the *Disputa*.

For the synthesis of the whole of ancient philosophy in the *School of Athens* Raphael had to draw from secular thought. The portrait of Pietro Bembo has been recognized in the panel; he was the learned spokesman of the Neo-platonism that Raphael had acquired at the court of Urbino and who now, in the frequent visits from Urbino to Rome, was a leading figure in the papal court. The artist could avail himself of Bembo's guidance through the cultural world of

122 Detail from the Parnassus: Alcaeus, Corinna, ▷
Petrarch, Anacreon, Ennius, Dante; below,
Sappho. Stanza della Segnatura.

104

105

antiquity and also be helped by him in retracing the features of his protagonists from the ancient documentations. He painted him in the group at the right of the fresco, where he placed his own portrait next to that generally supposed to be Perugino or Sodoma, or perhaps it is the portrait of a learned man, as is suggested by the doctoral cap. The same reasons must hold for the portraits of contemporary poets in the *Parnassus*, both those of uncertain identification, of Tebaldeo or of Sannazzaro, and also that of Ariosto, clearly identifiable. Cavalcaselle's study [82] contains the vague account of a letter, noted in the 18th century and later lost, in which Raphael is supposed to have turned to Ariosto for information relative to the *Disputa*. Only the recovery of this document could establish whether there is also a reference to the whole Stanza and therefore also to the *Parnassus*. But, hypothetical possibilities apart, the presence of Dominicans in the *Disputa*, of a man of letters in the *School of Athens*, and of contemporary poets in the *Parnassus* can be interpreted as a statement of appreciation on the part of Raphael for the lofty collaboration that had supported his work. It becomes an affectionate homage when the portrait is that of his teacher, Bramante, who is portrayed twice, in the *Disputa* and in the *School*, and never merely as a static portrait, but in action as teacher: he alone is on an equal footing with the philosophers of antiquity and Christianity. Only later, in the *School*, was he to be flanked by the portrait of another teacher: Michelangelo.

There has been discussion on the priority of execution of the *Parnassus* and the *Disputa*. Aside from the probability that he started from the principal wall, in front of the entrance to the Stanze from the inside of the apartments, and from the central composition of the whole cycle, the very style of painting of the *Disputa* leads to the belief that it was begun first, because of its strict concordance with the artist's previous work. In order to translate the ultra-terrestrial vision into imagery he had to have recourse to his own experiment in the *Paradiso*, painted in 1499 by Fra Bartolomeo, in which Raphael probably helped to translate into perspective accuracy the spatial scheme conceived by Fra Bartolomeo. Perhaps the great exedra of figures in the fresco of San Severo in Perugia, was also his. He recalls it here in an immense spatial dilation, making it the exact base of a hemispherical vault on whose radius the group of the trinitarian Epiphany is suspended. In the uppermost part the curvature is indicated by the symmetrical groups of angels and by the convergent movement of the golden rays, beyond which luminous clouds of cherubim fade into infinity. There are obvious reminiscences of the Signo-

123 Detail from the Parnassus: Vergil, Statius (Raphael?). Stanza della Segnatura.

106

relli of the Orvieto *Resurrection* in this pullulating web of real luminosities and of luminosities alluded to in a fine spray of gold and in the celestial scene itself, pressing down on the narrow terrestrial zone. There are also remembrances of the glory of Perugino, as in the aura of tiny heads around the Redeemer. Raphael rallies all his experience and that of others in order to overcome the difficulty of this highly emblematic figuration that he must portray in concrete terms; but the preparatory drawings of the *Disputa*, and especially those that seem to be the first (in Windsor and in Oxford),[83] indicate how the way to a solution was suggested to him by his fundamental Florentine experience. It is light, which Leonardo had identified with the incessant, mutable life of the universe itself, and which for Raphael became the means for transfiguring history into vision in subtle gradations, from the strong chiaroscuro of the figures in the lowermost part to the delicate, tenuous hints of shadow of those beyond the diaphragm of gold in the uppermost part. Dante's Paradise was suffused in light, as is this new Paradise unfolding above the terrestrial shadow. The influence of Leonardo is strong in Raphael's color, in the rich contrasts of intense chiaroscuro in the chromatic masses structuring the great figures of the Elect on each side of the Redeemer. The study of the cartoons of the *Battles* had given his figures this ample sweep and had resolved them, in the Dei Altarpierce, in a structural emphasis on color. In the *Disputa* the structures assume a stronger, and at the same time, a more refined dialectic of transitions. The gradation of chromatic intensities emulates Leonardo's chiaroscuro, not that of the later works, but that of the *Adoration of the Magi*, in which form is developed through the ceaseless play of light and shadow. Even though there was in Rome no example of Leonardo's works, there was their theoretical justification in the writings of the master. We do not know how Raphael had access to them, but such a powerful correspondence in operative technique posits a knowledge of them almost as necessary. It was not the derivation from a model, but from a theoretical proposition that impelled Raphael constantly to thrust forward in the creation of new painting.

The known drawings of the *Disputa*,[84] all relating to the upper part and the group below on the left, enable us to follow the conception as it evolved. In the Windsor drawing there is a reference, in the lower part, to an architectonic scene that can relate to the drawing (Oxford 107

125 Detail from the Parnassus: The Muses Thalia, Clio and Euterpe. Stanza della Segnatura.

76) for the Nativity scene supposedly sent to Francia in 1508. If such it be, it would confirm the assertion that the execution of the *Disputa* was preceded by a lengthy preparatory phase. Other drawings suffice to attest it, however—that in Chantilly, and especially the more evolved drawing in the British Museum. We can discern in them subtly critical facts indicating much pondering on the previous Florentine painting: for example, an obvious derivation from the Botticelli of the Sistine Chapel has been perceived in the group of kneeling youths near St. Gregory the Great. What to many modern critics has seemed like an artist's lingering over superseded, indeed medieval positions, instead appears as the work of an innovator of painting, a creator of the most boldly taut formal rhythms, a master of composition, an artist capable of raising the most dramatically historical representation to lyrical heights of significance. Consequently, he is in a sense his own forerunner in the problem of poetic transposition which the Stanze proposed to him. The conception of the *School of Athens*, with that tension between an impassive metric architecture and the animation of the figures acting in it, appears as a deliberate and meditated resumption of the figurative theme of the *Calumny*.

In the lengthy experiments that Raphael during his formative period had conducted on all the Renaissance enunciations of Florentine art there had been, besides "naturalism," the historicity of the image, "gentilezza," the law of harmony which, since Ghiberti, had had its model in classic art. Now the immensity of his task imposed this law of harmony upon him as an ultimate point of arrival. All the parts of the Stanza which, precisely because of the ever more urgent presence of this finality, appear as a new direction on Raphael's part—the vault and the *Parnassus*—mark a degree of evolution vis-à-vis the Paradise of the *Disputa*, leading to the conclusion that they must have followed it in execution.

If in the *Disputa* there was a whole figural tradition from Angelico to Signorelli to guide Raphael's inspiration, there was none for the earthly paradise which was to allude to the Neoplatonic idea of beauty as being itself a spiritual category, not unlike, perhaps, that mythological "conversazione" of Botticelli's *Primavera*. Raphael's *Parnassus* also is "a very shadowy forest of laurels in which, because of their verdancy, we almost discern the trembling of the leaves in the exceedingly sweet auras." [85] But it is a forest on the summit of a hill, along which climb not graces and nymphs but the men who for centuries were active in the search for beauty, the poets advancing toward the goal which is the music of Apollo surrounded by the Muses. Raphael's Apollo does not play the ancient lyre, but the modern viol, capable of new harmo-

108

126 Detail from the Parnassus: Apollo and the Muses. Stanza della Segnatura.

127 Detail from the Parnassus: Heads of Melpomene, Terpsichore, and Urania. Stanza della Segnatura.

nies, like that portrayed by Botticelli in the *tarsia* of Urbino. Dante is among these poets, and Dante too is of Urbino, faithfully recollected from the ducal library in order to suggest to the artist his " divine forest dense and verdant," the summit arrived at after the laborious ascent of the slopes of Purgatory. All these themes converged to excite the fantasy of the creator of the new allegory; but yet another poetic forest appeared to him in Bramante's Belvedere, the garden of oranges peopled with the sculptures that had emerged from the soil of Rome and that Julius II, with his Humanist taste, had collected: Apollo, the sleeping Ariadne, the Laocoön. Among the green trees, their whiteness gleamed, the harmonious play of their movements were transpositions in stone of the sublime harmony of human events, even the bitter and violent ones such as Laocoön's struggle with the serpents (Raphael was called by Bramante to judge the competition of the artists for the copy of this work).[86] This vantage point became the angle from which Raphael positioned himself in order to interpret and to make poetry of history. We do not know what questions he posed to his poet-collaborators, such as Ariosto, and to Bembo himself; but they must have been eagerly formulated in his desire to penetrate ever more deeply into the world of poetry. Perhaps they would explain his own attempts to write poetry, laboriously elaborating Petrarchian sonnets on the same sheets on which, a little later, he drew the last figures of the *Disputa*. The uncultured man wanted to test himself even with the artists of the word, perhaps to experiment himself with all their techniques of study. The value of these efforts for Raphael's biography lies not so much in the identification of the inspiration, who could be any one of the women he admired, if not loved, but in her becoming in this phase the Muse, the awakener of poetry, who assumed attitudes like the antique figures; the " pure white arms enwrapt around my neck " are the marble arms of a statue, like the raised arm of Ariadne.

It cannot be asserted whether the conception of the *Parnassus*, or even the beginning of the execution preceded the re-elaboration of the vault; but it is evident that both figurations belong to that phase in which Raphael tests himself by trying every mode of expression, figural as well as literary, in the desire to achieve a harmony that will give coherence to his language, make his figures part of the unitary rhythm already achieved by his architectural composition, so as to enclose and order, from the beginning, the whole multiform theme of the history proposed to him.

The episode of the Muses around Apollo on the summit of Mount Parnassus, totally achieves this goal. They are linked by harmonious rhythm of movements, as in a dance frozen in the rhythms of the divine music. It is a harmony that is participation, rapt abandonment, that effectively binds one figure to the other, guiding their glances toward the figure of the musician and enlivening with mysterious sentiments the classic model that can be recognized in the sarcophagus of Achilles in Scyros (now in the Louvre). It is not by chance that Raphael, always self-aware, portrays himself with this group, wearing a poet's crown. The Virgilian epigraph "numine afflatur" could be affixed to the whole of this profoundly poetical work. It is the epigraph that is placed in the vault, next to an allegoric image of Poetry.

128 Detail from the Parnassus: The Muses Polyhymnia, Melpomene, Terpsichore, Urania, Erato and the Poets Tebaldeo (or Michelangelo) and Boccaccio. Stanza della Segnatura.

It would require certain documentation, that is, however, missing in order to reconstruct the exact sequence of two similarly inspired creations. Certain pen drawings for the Muses and the poets Dante and Homer seem less freely drawn in the upper part of the *Parnassus*, and less replete with inspiration than those for the figures of the vault, but there is no way of knowing the period of time that lapsed between the conception and the execution. It was certainly a brief span of months, and perhaps on occasion of days, so feverish was Raphael's concern to conquer this phase. We can only think that it must have been at this time, and not earlier, that Raphael resolved the problem of the adaptation of the vault with its minutely detailed metaphors, to the profound emblematic representation of which he now felt himself to be capable. The architecture of the whole had included also the suggestion of the "tuyere" at the summit of the vault, which subsequently had been respected, as were allusions to the four elements; however Raphael does not proceed along the lines of this symbology, but rather along those required by his clear figural divisions. After overcoming the obstacle of a forced connection, he places a single figure in each of the pre-existing *tondos*, in order to allude emblematically to the composition on the wall below; and in order to declare its meaning more emphat-

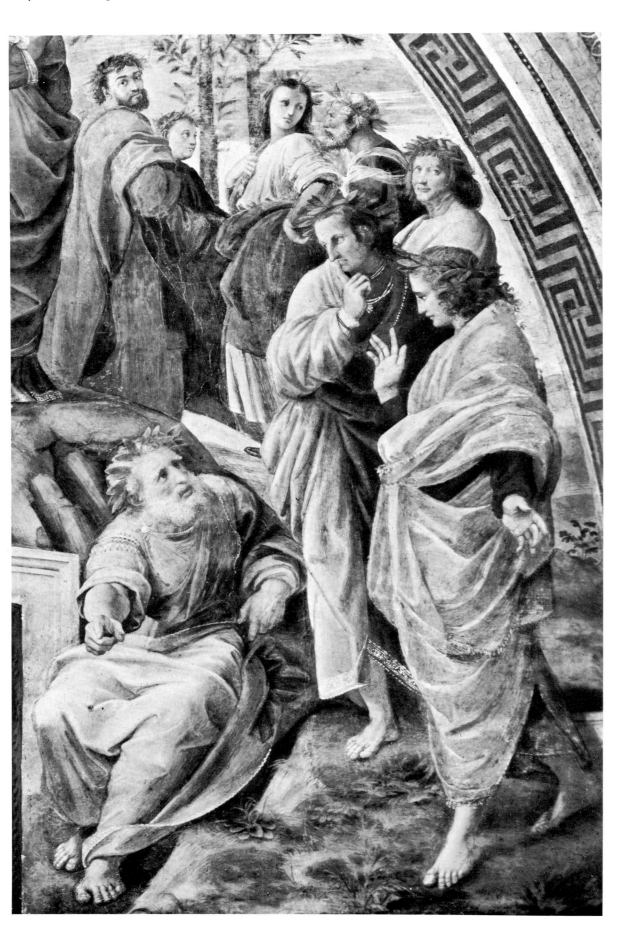

129 Detail from the Parnassus: Tebaldeo or Michelangelo, Boccaccio, Tibullus, Tebaldeo (?), Propertius (?), Ariosto (?), Sannazzaro (?), Horace (?). Stanza della Segnatura.

130 Detail from the Parnassus: Heads of Propertius (?, above), of Ariosto (?), and of Sannazzaro (?). Stanza della Segnatura.

131 The Cardinal Virtues Wall. Stanza della Segnatura.

ically, he inserts angular panels with biblical, mythological or philosophical scenes such as the *Original Sin*, the *Judgment of Solomon*, the *Victory of Apollo over Marsyas*, of the " First Motion " of the Universe.

To the contorted ideology of the previous Neo-platonic plan for the Stanza, he reacts with the force of his own Humanism. His figures do not have as background the reality of a landscape or of a sky, but the other-worldly light suggested by an imitation of a mosaic of gold, like those he saw in the early Christian basilicas of Rome. The structures fill out, they become emphatic, sonorous; and they are all animated with a spiritual intensity which seems about to be translated into action. This expression is far removed from the noble calm of the *Virtues* in the Cambio, even though there is still a sweetness in the color in the gentle faces of *Justice* and *Theology*, rich in memories of Perugino's archangels. But *Philosophy*, the " causarum cognitio," turns as though to move beyond the solid niche of the throne framed by the pillars where the impassive idol of Artemis of Ephesus stands. The whole figure leans over to follow the eye of *Poetry*, who looks upward far into the distance. It is beyond understanding how the idea of these representations or of those in the angular panels that clarify their meaning, could have been attributed to others than Raphael.[87] Even if the hand of Sodoma can be seen in the execution, or of the many other assistants of whom Raphael had to avail himself in so vast an undertaking, there can be attributed to them only a purely instrumental function, in works in which there is the unmistakeable sign of the imagination of the Master and, indeed, of its soaring to new heights of poetry. The preparatory drawings, from the first conceptions, suffice to attest his exclusive presence. The drawing of *Theology* in Oxford, surpasses in intensity of design the drawings executed for the *Parnassus*, and even the final version; this cannot be explained only by the lack of skill of the assistants, there was also the enormous difficulty of translating these freely drawn images into the exacting technique of fresco. Raphael was again faced with the problems posed in Florence, when the great drawings of the *Battles* were a challenge to his use of color. He had not fully resolved them, even in the Paradise of the *Disputa;* but the necessity of finding a solution presented itself again with greater urgency in these paintings. This can be seen most clearly in the most inspired of figures, the one positioned between *Poetry* and *Philosophy* (which has been interpreted as the " First Motion," the " divine principle of the causal series, the spirit that sets in motion the machine of the world "—Castelfranco).[88]   The conception is wonderfully lyrical in this figure with upraised hand, who seems to be driven by a superhuman impulse to set the sphere of the Universe in motion which will never again be stopped.   In the preparatory drawing, rapid and sure pen strokes delineate the figure; but in the pictorial translation too many things, including the color, intervene to arrest the *élan* of the figure and to weigh it down.   In the *Original Sin*, Leonardo's *Leda*, which had already inspired the *Graces*, returns in

132   Detail from the Virtues: Fortitude with *putto* symbolizing Charity.   Stanza della Segnatura.

133 Detail from the Virtues: Temperance with *putto* symbolizing Hope. Stanza della Segnatura.

the figure of Eve, linked by a marvelous rhythmic chain to Adam as he turns toward the face of the tempter. Such coherence becomes more difficult when the scene is crowded. In the *Victory of Apollo* the vigorous rhythm of the seated god is not successfully terminated in the verticalism of Marsyas flayed at a tree; but rhythmic balance is successfully achieved in a more complex scene—the *Judgment of Solomon*, in which multiple and diverse actions, the brutality of the executioner, the cold argumentation of the lying woman, the desperate parrying gesture of the true mother and, in the judge, the hesitation of the final decision all converge in harmony. Here the color also supports the improvisation of the design, breaking it down into contrasting, clear intensities. The echo of another teaching, that of Michelangelo resounds.

In the very construction of grandiose figures in the vault and in their very arrangement, there is evident the decisive impression made upon Raphael by the ceiling of the Sistine Chapel. Vasari posed the question of how Raphael could have known the ceiling, inasmuch as Michelangelo seemingly did not unveil the first part of his work to the public until September 1509, at which time the decoration of the Stanza della Segnatura must have proceeded quite beyond the vault.

Vasari resolves the problem offhandedly with an anecdote.[89] Raphael, during one of Michelangelo's absences from Rome, is supposed secretly to have climbed the Sistine scaffolding, with the complicity of Bramante, who had the keys to the chapel. But it seems that Michelangelo's absence occurred in 1510, after the partial unveiling of the ceiling, which would have made any such subterfuge unnecessary. The anecdote, moreover, loses every reason for being if it is acknowledged that Raphael's vault was finished only after the completion of more than half of the *Disputa*, which was enough to occupy a great part of 1509. It was only then, while

Raphael was intent upon drawing from classic art all the teaching of its ideal harmony, that Michelangelo must have appeared to him as the fulfillment of his own research and as having surpassed it in achieving a coherence of language in which classic harmony was reached and overtaken by the force of his inspiration. This was no longer the Michelangelo that Raphael had studied and followed in the Florentine drawings and sculptures; the Leonardesque game of shadow and light with its subtle transitions had given way to the contrast, harsh to the point of dissonance, of chromatic intensities in order to shape figures almost into gigantic high reliefs, breaking the classical continuity of rhythms. A new vista suddenly opened up before Raphael, making all the paths of research he had followed up to then seem narrow and without exit. Michelangelo taught him what could be taken from the classical model beyond the musical beauty of rhythm; how the most dramatic representation could be intensified to attain universality if it were strained to the point where it was almost surpassed. Raphael had already approached this understanding in the drawings of the *Battles*, but it is in the vault of the Segnatura that his comprehension of Michelangelo's style reaches fulfillment. The Sistine Chapel became the model for constructing the figures of the Segnatura almost like a huge high-relief and for modeling with color alone, particularly in the intensely dramatic figures such as the actors of the *Judgment of Solomon*. This play of contrasts, of clear tones without any murky shadows and the use of white as a luminous intensity had its first complete realization in the *Parnassus*.

The drawings for the figures of the vault are placed alongside—very often on the same sheet—the studies for another composition that Raphael was working on at the same time: the *Massacre of the Innocents*, which was not, however, destined to be translated into color; perhaps it was originally intended for an engraving.[90] Marcantonio Raimondi, a pupil of Francia, was an engraver who had already made a name for himself before he came to work in

134 Detail from the Virtues: *Putto* symbolizing Faith. Stanza della Segnatura.

Rome. He probably had known Raphael earlier, but after their meeting in Rome Marcantonio became his most faithful interpreter and popularizer. We know from Vasari that a real work association developed between Raphael and Marcantonio, and that Baviera, Raphael's boy-servant, whose talent Raphael had discerned and encouraged, also assisted in the work. It is thanks to Marcantonio that the first composition for the *Parnassus* is known, and also the *Massacre of the Innocents* to which innumerable detailed drawings refer and in which can be followed a whole chapter in Raphael's research along the guide lines marked out by Michelangelo. The composition of the *Massacre* as a whole joins together several single groups into a perfect rhythmic conclusion. In the drawings the groups are studied, one by one, from their single figures to their relationship within the unity of the composition. The influence of Michelangelo appears everywhere: the mother of the *Deluge*, holding her child so tightly that the figures interpenetrate, can be seen in the mother who flees before the executioner; the chase by the hired ruffians has as its base the assistants of the *Sacrifice of Noah*, and that of the son who covers him in the depiction of *Drunkenness*. Yet there is never any trace of copying; there is only abundant evidence of an imagination kindled by the enthusiasm of discovery. These revelations found new pictorial expression in the vault, and in particular in the *Parnassus*, in which color becomes limpid, clear, vivified directly by the light and the modeling shadows become translucid and reabsorbed by the color which itself molds the powerful figures. It can be seen how the first idea for the *Parnassus*, known through Marcantonio's engraving, which was an idyllic evocation of the sylvan glade of the poets, changed to become a plastic construction of figures alone in the fresco which fills the spaces at the sides of the window.

It is to this phase, in which Michelangelo's influence opened new horizons for Raphael's painting and poetic language, that the profound reflections for the synthesis which was to be

135 Tribonian Handing the Pandects to Justinian.
Stanza della Segnatura.

118

the *School of Athens*, must belong. In this composition it is no longer mystic contemplation or poetic escape, but history with its concrete reality that becomes the artist's theme—a history, however, not of violent actions, but of human thought, the pictorial expression of which, consequently, does not require emphatic gestures and movement, but the reflection of the inner life of each of its actors. Multiple meanings have been given to it: an exaltation of Platonic thought has been seen in the entire composition, and its antithesis to Christian thought celebrated in the *Disputa;* or the convergence of the whole of ancient philosophy in the dialectic between immanence and the material, personified in Aristotle, who points downward, to the earth, and Plato who points upward, to heaven. It has also been supposed that there is an allusion to the medieval division of knowledge in the arts of the Trivium and of the Quadrivium, personified by their antique initiators. Many attempts have been made to identify these figures, with more or less success.[91] In addition to Plato and Aristotle, identified by the titles of the books they carry (*Timaeus* and *Ethics*), the most probable other identifications are those of Socrates with his pupils, among whom is Xenophon and, perhaps, Alcibiades in the guise of a youthful warrior; the florid Epicurus, crowned Bacchus-like with vine-leaves, Pythagoras, near whom a young disciple shows the tablet of harmonious concordance to the savant Averroës, and finally Euclid, personified by Bramante, next to Ptolemy and Zoroaster, who has the quite recognizable features of Pietro Bembo and who turns toward Raphael himself. Alone, in disdainful negation, is Diogenes, "with a pensive air, lying on the steps, a figure admirable for its beauty and the disordered drapery" (Vasari) among the solemn cloaks of the philosophers.

More valuable for art than the various interpretations and indentifications is the way in which Raphael articulated the history of the whole of ancient thought in groups of teachers and pupils who fervently listen to them or engage in passionate discussion. Vasari saw the whole composition as portraits "of all the wise men of the world in disputation," suggesting 119

137 Madonna and Child, called the " della Torre " or " Mackintosh Madonna." London, National Gallery.

the modern interpretation implicitly critical, of the *School of Athens*. Raphael's history of the centuries of thought is not a series of dogmatic enunciations, but an eager, continued dialectic which proceeds from its most ancient beginning to the present signified by the *Disputa*. In the *School* Raphael expresses his dialectic sense of history in an animated articulation of groups that are themselves rhythmic components of the vivacious whole which fills with animation the great space of the vaults and *tondos*.

Raphael made this newly acquired wisdom the object of a deepened critical reflection. In the cartoon now in the Ambrosiana, which shows the last stage of the idea before its final pictorial translation, other more distant influences return—those of Leonardo; not the Leonardo of the *Gioconda* or of the *Battle of Anghiari*, but the Leonardo who in the youthful *Adoration of the Magi* first expressed language which became the prototype of all the conquests registered by Florentine art from the fourteenth to the fifteenth century: the announcement of a new " pittura." Indeed, so advanced was it that Leonardo himself had faltered before the difficulties of definitively translating this tension of chiaroscuro. Several of the figures that seem to have been self-engendered there return in Raphael's cartoon, emerging from the shadowy depths, as if the artist knowingly leads the language that he is creating back to that original premise and to the problem it proposed, the problem set by Alberti in his identification of painting with history, an expression not of a motionless " existing " but of a constant " becoming."

Raphael directs all the knowledge that he has experimented with, assimilated, and mastered to this single problem. Just as his infinite variation in form becomes in movement the dialectical point of his unitary spatial measure, so does color, in the violent contrast of relationships that Michelangelo taught him, bring dynamic tension to the homogeneity of the light diffused throughout that space and shaped by the perspective. These extreme contrasts, however, pushed as far as complementarism, must not fragment the composition in a multi-colored play that is an end in itself; they must flow together with that dramatic tension of Albertian and Leonardesque " Storia." Just as the movement of the single figures and groups was combined to form the rhythm of the whole composition, so must the heightening of the color in

138 Madonna and Child with the Infant St. John, called the " Aldobrandini Madonna." London, National Gallery.

139 Portrait of Cardinal Francesco Alidosi. Madrid, Prado.

bold relationships lead back to that sublime light. Now, for the young artist of Urbino who had seen without yet comprehending Piero della Francesca, it is the final revelation of " tone," the understanding of a luminous unity that dominates and pacifies the infinite world of color. The Greek word on the tablet of the pupil of Pythagoras, which indicates sonorous concordance, seems by analogy the epigraph of the whole composition.

" A certain friendship of colors is found to exist," Alberti had written,[92] " so that one joined with the other brings it dignity and grace. The color red next to green and pale blue confer honor and beauty upon each other. The color white, placed not only next to grey and next to saffron, but next to almost all colors, is conducive to gladness." In the *School of Athens* the white toga of Pythagoras and that enveloping the young man (supposedly a portrait of Francesco Maria Della Rovere, the new Duke of Urbino), stand out among the gilded green of the robe of Averroës and the dark red cloak, shaded with blue, of the unknown with the open book as if Raphael, in this new synthesis returned to his oldest theoretical manifesto and totally carries it out in a dynamic of color not arrived at by even the most coherent expressive research of the Renaissance, the Florentine.

The path traversed from the Leonardesque compromise of the " Paradise " of the *Disputa*, to the classic harmony of the *Parnassus*, to the Michelangelesque tension of the vault, is concluded in the grand equilibrium of the *School of Athens*, in which Raphael brought to bear his entire knowledge of the theories of Alberti, Piero and Leonardo and endows them with the most authoritative stamp of legitimacy. Truly the answer to the problems of the earlier

140 Madonna and Sleeping Child with the Infant St. John, called the " Diadem Madonna." Paris, Louvre.

142 Madonna and Child, called the " Madonna of the Veil " (detail). Paris, Louvre.

masters appears total; painting as it was later conceived for centuries here has its " birth certificate."

Yet Raphael's progressive development does not halt even on this vertex. New problems are posed by the perfect solution of problems already posed; and that fundamental phase of art that is the Stanza della Segnatura comes to a close in their announcement.

At the center of the *School of Athens*, inserted after the fresco was finished, there appears a figure that is missing in the cartoon: a solitary figure, closed in a private meditation alien to the general colloquy, believed to be the figure of Heraclitus. It is isolated itself among the free-flowing rhythms, precisely because of its plastic concentration, forming almost a single mass with the marblelike block on which it rests. It is a chromatic mass of mat tones, violet in the raiment, bronze-colored in the flesh-tones, hollowed out in deep densities of shadow in which form loses every contour. There is also a play of the brush, insistently searching as nowhere else, for the signs of the torments of intellect, even in the frowning of the face and in the shadows cast by the mass of air. It is a figure different from every other personage of the *School*, even in technique. It does, however, find coherence with almost the all of the group at the base of the *Disputa*, a compact group condensed like a great wall of rock in 123

which an impetuous sculptor's tool has rapidly and roughly sketched the salient essentials of a dramatic action. This group, in which we no longer perceive any continued rhythmic modulation in the tight interpenetration of the figures, occupies almost all the lower zone of the fresco, from the erect figure, seen from behind on the left, up to the figure on the right which leans over, further developing the theme of the " First Motion " in the vault. It is matched by the kindred group of Bramante and his two pupils which concludes the composition on the left. In the Louvre and in Montpellier[93] there are magnificent drawings for the figures in the outermost corners of the great lunette in which the line grows thicker and intersects in order to follow the flowing movement of the relief. New rhythms follow on each other's heels in the fresco, flashing suddenly from the breaking up of the classic harmonious cadences; dense color is the substance of this intensified plasticity, no longer limpid, but deep in value, such as the heavy red cloak of St. Bonaventure or the great cope of Sixtus IV, woven of gold and of a metallic stiffness.

The " tone," the pictorial unity achieved in the *School of Athens*, a synthesis of the " clear and more graceful " play of gradations, now has also to encompass the differentiated intensity of real values, those which had given the dimension of greatness to Raphael's youthful portraiture and which now are used together with the delicate, airy luminosities to create an expression of fantasy combined with history and achieving a plenitude of poetry.

This new direction opened up to Raphael at the end of the stylistic journey mapped out on the walls of the Stanza della Segnatura. Its evolutionary phases, furthermore, can be exactly defined further in concordance with external circumstances. In the lower part of the *Disputa*, which seems to show the highest degree of maturity in expression, Innocent III listening to St. Thomas wears the face of Julius II, frowning and almost hidden by a hirsute beard, as he must have looked upon his return to Rome on June 26, 1511 after the ill-starred undertaking against the French in which Bologna had been lost. There is a second papal portrait in the Stanza della Segnatura in which Julius II, in the beard he had assumed during the war,

144 The Triumph of Galatea. Rome, Farnesina.

146 The Prophet Isaiah. Rome, Sant'Agostino.

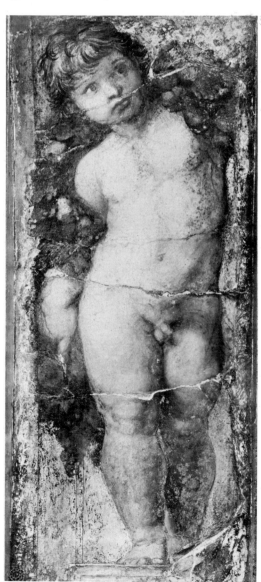

145 Putto. Rome, Accademia di S. Luca.

impersonates Gregory IX in the act of receiving the text of the Decretals from St. Raymond of Peñafort.

Both these frescoes, the second one of which is in a very poor state of presevation, have the aspect of the works conceived by Raphael in the tight compositional vigor of that part of the *Disputa* which, in our opinion was the last, albeit weakened by the partial intervention of assistants.[94]   The figure of the seated Pope, whose cloak is held by the Cardinals Giovanni dei Medici (the future Leo X) and, perhaps, Antonio Dal Monte and Alessandro Farnese, has a new and rich development of draperies, almost baroque, and a free, loose animation of color. But in the restorations the face has lost the energetic expression of the portrait in the *Disputa*. A strange hand, quite evident in the figures of the Pandects on the right, makes us think that Raphael may have left his drawing to be executed by an assistant so that he could dedicate himself to the completion of the larger figures.

The presence of two papal portraits in this same room complicates, rather than helps, to solve the chronological problem posed by the letter, dated August 16, 1511, with which Giovan Francesco Grossi informs Isabella d'Este that the Pope wants Raphael to paint a portrait of her son Federigo Gonzaga " in a room which he is having decorated in the palace in which His Holiness is painted from nature with a beard. " [95]

The child, then eleven years old, who was being held as a hostage in the papal court, is generally recognized in that florid and curly-haired figure that appears behind the shoulders of Averroës in the *School of Athens*. Since he also figures in the Ambrosian cartoon, it would induce us to accept an incredibly late dating for the whole lower part of the fresco. A date, however, that is still previous to the insertion of Heraclitus to the lower part of the *Disputa* containing the second papal image. Even admitting that Grossi's letter refers to the fresco of the *Decretals* already executed, or in course of execution, by Raphael and his assistants, the total stylistic difference, its greater development in comparison with the parts of the *School* which should follow it would always remain inexplicable. At any rate, there is the difficulty of admitting that such a large and important part of the Stanza della Segnatura as the half containing the *School of Athens* and the *Disputa*, could have been executed in the few months between August and the end of 1511, the date marked twice on the walls of the Stanze. Nor, on the other hand, does it seem probable that work was already proceeding on that date in the Stanza di Eliodoro.

In the face of such grave difficulties that crop up it may be asked whether Grossi's letter and the consequent identifications of the young Gonzaga may not have been given too much importance by Passavant, followed by Müntz and others. Grossi does not refer to an event that had already occurred but to an intention of the Pope, with no mention that it was to be included in the Stanza. Later, indeed, in letters to Isabella, dated 1512 and 1513, there is still talk of a portrait of her son as an easel painting in which he was to appear in armor.

147 Head of the Prophet Isaiah. Rome, Sant'Agostino.

127

128　148　The Vault of the Stanza di Eliodoro. Vatican.

149 Detail from the Stanza di Eliodoro: The Burning Bush.

150 Detail from the Stanza di Eliodoro: Jacob's Dream.

We can legitimately deduce therefrom that in August of 1511 at least one of the papal portraits was completed in the Stanza della Segnatura, and that that stylistic phase which we maintain is legible in the last part of the *Disputa* was already in progress, as also in the *Decretals*. The ill-starred military undertaking, which had lasted from August of 1510 to August of the following year, slowed down the work of the artists whom Julius II had called to the decoration of the Vatican. It was a feverish year for Michelangelo. We know of his furious cavalcades between Rome and the papal headquarters in Bologna in order to solicit payments so that the work in the Sistine Chapel, which now engaged his whole attention, could go forward.[96] Despite all obstacles, he did manage to complete it, so that the Pope, upon his return to Rome could celebrate Mass on the feast of the Assumption on August 15, 1511, under the almost finished vault of the Chapel, from which it seems only the lunettes with Christ's forbears were missing.[97]

Raphael, instead, had to react differently to the sudden difficulty that arose when he probably had finished the *Parnassus*, the *Virtues*, and to a large measure, the *School of Athens*. All that remained for him to do was to put the finishing touches to the *Disputa*, interrupted at the Paradise and at the beginning of the lower part on the left. In November 1510, there is news of his work for Agostino Chigi, the rich Sienese banker, financial adviser to the Pope himself, from whom he would have received handsomely remunerated commissions regardless of the outcome of the war. Chigi, whom Raphael could have known since the beginning of his Sienese activity, was also the patron of Baldassarre Peruzzi, for whom he gave security in November of the following year in the case of a contract of the lease at a ground rent in perpetuity, and who must have been one of his most active collaborators in this phase.

The Chigi document, dated November 10, 1510,[98] concerns a part payment made to the Perugian goldsmith Cesarino Rossetti for the execution of two bronze vases " cum pluribus floribus de mero relevo, secundum ordinem, et formam eidem dandam per Magistrum Raphaelem . . . pictorem." Two drawings, in Windsor and in Oxford, have been attributed to this commission. In them figurations of the most fanciful classicism appear on the edges of the plates, centaurs and nymphs in one, tritons and naids in the other, interlaced in richly

developed rhythms; this is Raphael at the peak of the classical enthusiasm which the *Parnassus* had inspired in him. The discovery on the back of the Windsor drawing of a sketch for the *Massacre of the Innocents* justifies the attribution of that composition with greater sureness to the summer of 1510. In the unrestrained vitality of these sketches, Raphael approaches the festive symphony of rhythms of the *Galatea*, painted in fresco on a wall of the Chigian Farnesina, so that it may be supposed that it also was at least conceived during the months of respite from the work of the Stanza della Segnatura. Away from those lofty themes, Raphael could pause in these fantasies, almost as a kind of relaxation from the hard work of his construction of a language. But it was a respite that itself was tantamount to the creation of poetry.

In August 1511, however, when the war was over and the vault of the Sistine Chapel was unveiled, Michelangelo's severe warning resounds anew and once more points out other goals to Raphael. In the Sistine narratives of Genesis, in the last Prophets, in the last Sibyls, the form went beyond itself, reabsorbed itself, undelineated and "unfinished," in those grand imprecise masses, a primordial material almost, laden with latent energies. Once more the equilibrium that Raphael had found again in the rhythmic and chromatic tensions towards which Michelangelo's example had impelled him, namely the lofty tonal equilibrium of the *School of Athens*, was to undergo a new, disturbing comparison. Michelangelo was once more far ahead of him in a painting that was no longer only form, but the revelation of energy emerging from the deep matrix of the material as if in an extreme effort of liberation. The expression of the biblical theme of Genesis immersed into a total identification with the artist's creative toil itself. Once again Raphael's creation, painting that was the sublime adaptation and contemplation of beauty, was contradicted by this negation of every pause in the serenity of contemplation, by this "desperate beauty" that overwhelms every harmony in a mad race to the infinite.

Just as at one time the Florentine cartoons of the *Battles* had flawed with problems the young Raphael's lyrical abandon to the "natural beauty of the universe," so now did the "awesome" Sistine paintings appear to the young master as the contradiction of all his conquest, and pushed him anew toward more difficult paths beyond the balanced harmony that had been his last point of arrival. The lower part of the *Disputa*, painted after the summer of 1511, must have been an attempt to surpass his own achievement, a total overthrow of all that he had sought in the peace of Paradise; it was its dialectical turning point, giving the entire composition its true and profound significance: that of sublime certainty opposing the drama that was stirring on earth among men eager to find truth, truly the *Disputa*. It was then that Raphael, at the end of his undertaking, inserted among the teachers of antiquity in the already completed fresco of the *School* his true teacher, the man who had directed his great experiment of the Stanza della Segnatura: Michelangelo, in the likeness of the solitary Heraclitus meditating on the eternal transiency of things.

At the end of 1511 when the two works, the vault of the Sistine Chapel and the Stanza della Segnatura were both completed, it truly must have appeared to the viewer who went from one to the other—in an incredible comparison—as the manifestation of a new world in all its fullness. It was a language that in one stroke nullified all that which had been stated in art up to then. Julius II had to find consolation for the failure of his whole political action in this affirmation of the greatness of the Church executed by two young artists whom

153 Detail from the Expulsion of Heliodorus from the Temple. Stanza di Eliodoro.

154 Detail from the Mass at Bolsena. Stanza di
Eliodoro.

he had summoned to Rome to interpret his thought. They, and not his " condottieri " had
crowned his program, celebrating the universality of the Church, a synthesis of all times, from
Genesis to the tormented present, itself also the dramatic genesis of a vaguely defined future.
Art had accomplished what theology and philosophy had not succeeded in doing: it had re-
united the eager dialectic of the Renaissance into the synthesis of a system which did not
conclude it but, on the contrary, left it open to an infinite discussion in the sole certainty
of a higher point of arrival. It had created the language of this history which was the synthesis
of every history, capable of extreme realisms but also of its total glorification. A language
that henceforward it would be impossible not to speak, even when the matter to be expressed
was much more modest than these extreme propositions, and that would become the difficult
path of Mannerism. But the " bella maniera " created in the Julian decoration of the Vatican

still seemed to Vasari " the last word " permitted to art. Only its creators could dare to step beyond it. In this effort the palm of victory was to be awarded to Raphael.

In fact Michelangelo, later, was to pursue further his figural theme of the liberation of form, making of its very tension an end in itself. It would be the " harsh chain " within which the sorrowful figures of the Medicean tombs of Florence, or the very Giants of the Judgment would struggle in order to arrive at the formal destructions of the late *Pietàs*. Raphael, on the other hand, did not set himself the task of surpassing that which in the Stanza della Segnatura appeared definitive to him. He had touched the outermost limit between reality and symbol, and he did not want to cross the frontier into pure abstraction. He saw, as Vasari was to say,

155 Detail from the Mass at Bolsena. Stanza di Eliodoro.

that painting " has a large field," as spacious, that is to say, as infinite reality. In it the artist could still trace, in inexhaustible Leonardesque discovery, those same events that he had enunciated, almost theoretically, on the walls of the first Stanza. His subsequent procedure as artist was to verify his own conquest in a renewed comparison with the realities of life, and therein for him lay the possibility to go beyond Michelangelo himself, to return to the origins of that profoundly lyrical terrestrial contemplation which he had learned to sublimate in the " poetry of knowledge," the insuperable achievement of the Stanza della Segnatura.

This was his way of humanizing the language of the loftiest contemplation and making it accessible to all, a means of universal expression, and of infusing into it by his own example the possibility of adapting it to every content. His " storia " was still the history of man in action and feeling. To him, more than to Michelangelo, was granted the privilege of being the teacher of generations of artists, not by crushing them under the weight of his superiority but by guiding them to grasp motives of poetry in an unlimited field of experience. For him the daily drama of life, an actual reflection of the eternal drama and its infinite dialectic, once more became the protagonist. Thus he was continuing his true research, in which he had been moving from the time when he had subjected the teaching of his first master, Perugino, to an incessant comparison with reality. In his subsequent work, therefore, the restatement of the symbolism of the Segnatura was almost a sign of fatigue, a concession to a taste which, to be sure, he had created but of which he himself had perceived the risks and the incipient misunderstandings. This can explain how, by leaving to his many and expert assistants the execution of the *Histories* of the Vatican palace, he reserved to himself that in which he was granted complete freedom of expression, namely the Madonnas and the portraits.

MADONNAS AND PORTRAITS

Raphael's deepest research as a poet was carried out in connection with the Madonnas and the portraits; but he achieved full and complete mastery of figural means in drawing. The Florentine and pre-Florentine Madonnas subtly pried into the most hidden accents of feeling. The portraits were the single moments, personalized, of history understood as drama. This research accompanies the great experiments of the Segnatura without interruption. We can follow it in the small paintings in which in the docile technique of oil the same grandiose formal propositions of the fresco are stated, although more tenuously and allusively. The so-called *Aldobrandini Madonna*, now in London, transposes a composition, actually by Lorenzo di Credi,[99] to a more ample formal consciousness, opening it in a Leonardesque manner beyond the arches to landscapes that now shade off into the light like the landscape in the left part of the *Disputa*. Thus the *Madonna of the Tower* (Mackintosh), also in London, despite the extreme toning down of the color and because of the theme itself, appears to be the spiritual sister of the last Florentine Madonnas, such as the *Tempi* or the *Niccolini Madonnas*. The rhythmic tension of the Muses of the *Parnassus* or of the mothers of the *Massacre of the Innocents* is effused into a spacious landscape, more of a dream than a description in its luminous peacefulness, in the *Alba Madonna* (Washington) and appears again in the Virtues of the *School of Athens*. This is a phase not far removed from that of the *Madonna of the Diadem* (Louvre), in which the landscape predominates over the inspired composition of the figures seemingly closed in an ideal ellipse underlined by the wavy motion of the veils. It is a landscape in which the light is differentiated in a subtle play of reflections, a novelty in Raphael and which could possibly have been suggested by a first influence of ancient painting in some landscape tenuously emerging from the Roman " grottoes." The color of the figures, less identified with the form than that of the *Alba Madonna*, has warranted the not improbable supposition of the collaboration of Penni, but it must be recognized as only a partial technical intervention in a work in which Raphael's unexhausted imagination is unmistakeable. It renews the theme of the Madonna who raises the veil to show the sleeping Child, already seen in the drawing of the Nativity scene sent to Francia in 1508 and in which what is enunciated in the landscape is the chromatic fantasy of the *Madonna of Foligno*. This induces the supposition of a date not far from that of the latter work, between 1511 and 1512. It is also the most probable date for the version of the same theme, formally more evolved, that was to appear in the Madonna for Santa Maria del Popolo, unfortunately lost, and which we know only from copies, among which is that in the Louvre, perhaps given to the church together with the portrait of Julius II.

157 Detail from the Mass at Bolsena: Julius II. Stanza di Eliodoro.

158 Detail from the Mass at Bolsena: Cardinal Raffaele Riario (?) and others. Stanza di Eliodoro.

Thus Raphael's portraiture continued along with his work on the frescoes. Now his subjects were no longer rich Florentines with their frank personalities solidly anchored in the realities of life, but the sophisticated personages of the papal court, intellectually refined, spiritually complex and at times ambiguous, like that young cardinal of the Prado whose inner personality Raphael cruelly revealed. He has been identified as Cardinal Francesco Alidosi, the refined and perverse youth who nevertheless enjoyed the trust of Julius II to the extent that he granted him the governorship of Bologna in the delicate period following its reconquest by the Church, in 1506.[100] Of Alidosi Bembo said: "cui nulla fides, nulla religio, nihil tutum, nihil pudicum, nihil unquam sanctum fuit." Nothing, except the art with which he liked to surround himself in his hedonistic way of life. There is a whole drama of refined and cynical depravity in that extenuated and cruel countenance, in that veiled look which nevertheless fixes the spectator with its pitiless and chilling penetration, in that spectral pallor, and in the deep red of the cardinal's raiment. It is the figure which Gamba already saw return in one of the bishops in the lower left part of the *Disputa*, which, in our opinion, was the first part to be executed. Indeed, the work seems to have come to a halt precisely with this figure, and since the cardinal died in May 1510, assassinated by Francesco Maria Della Rovere, the latest possible date we would assign to it would be the beginning of 1510, regardless of what has been asserted in this regard.

A medaillon of Alidosi, in his Bolognese period, bears on its reverse side the figure of Jove on his throne transported by two eagles. It would be wholly arbitrary to link this with the description given by Malvasia of a small picture for which Count Vincenzo Hercolani paid Raphael in 1510, "in which there is a Christ in the manner of Jove in heaven and around him the four evangelists."[101] This small painting, at that time in the Hercolani residence in Bologna, is described by Vasari in a way as to leave no doubts for its identification with that now in the Galleria Palatina in Florence, the famous *Vision of Ezekiel*. But Vasari states that it was executed after *St. Cecilia*, dated 1514, and critics are divided between Malvasia's and

136

Vasari's indications, leaning toward the latter, which would seem to be coherent with the mature grandiosity of the composition. Passavant had already tried to effect a reconciliation by supposing that Hercolani's payment was only an installment on the final one, supposedly was made many years later—a rather improbable hypothesis inasmuch as it involved not a great cycle but a small work of modest cost. Every doubt of authenticity is excluded for the reason that none of Raphael's pupils could have arrived at the mastery of light in the mobile texture of reflections in the landscape in which the minuscule Ezekiel is almost lost. Nevertheless there remains a subtle discrepancy between the masterful composition and a pictorial treatment which, despite its richness, does not attain the boldness that marks the last frescoes of the Segnatura. In the drapery of the angel there is not the heroic movement of the cloaks of the *School of Athens* or of the *Parnassus*. Indeed we note something that hints at embroidery, something that is lightly calligraphic, as in the locks of the *putti*, which in fact recall the last Florentine period. Hence it seems that we should not discard the possibility that the work is contemporaneous with the Paradise of the *Disputa*, when Raphael had already reached the maturity of the Canigiani *Holy Family* and of the Dei Altarpiece, but not yet the surpassing poetry of the first Stanza. The year 1510, furthermore, coincided with that phase of his contact with Bologna evidenced by the letter to Francia and the drawing for the Nativity scene, as well as by the collaboration with Marcantonio, by the portraits of Alidosi in the Prado and in the *Disputa*, up to the point of its conclusion in the *St. Cecilia*.

We still believe that one of Raphael's most powerful portraits, that of Tommaso Inghirami,
also was not executed beyond 1509-1510, in the course of his experience in the Stanze. Inghirami, called Fedra,[102] was the learned Ciceronian who had been prefect of the Vatican
Library since 1505, and a person of prominence in the entourage of Julius II; he delivered
the funeral oration to the cardinals on Julius' death.

Two versions of the portrait exist, one formerly in the possession of the Inghirami family
and now in Boston, the other in the Galleria Palatina in Florence. The authenticity of both
is incontestable, even though the one in Florence appears to be a copy, but still one by the
master's hand, of the other which has all the spontaneity of the first inspiration. It required
all of Raphael's formal mastery to move the rounding masses in the space in which the obese
and squat figure is simplified in that oblique direction that permits an attenuation of the squint
of the eyes. But these masses are moulded in the most solid chromatic material: the lucid
crimson of florid flesh-tones, the shrill red of the heavy fabrics of the cloak and the cap,
the black and white brightnesses of objects, all emerging clearly defined from the gloomy
background. Once more, as in the portrait of Alidosi, we discern the evolution of the last
Florentine enunciations, those of *La Gravida* with their intensely acute perception of values,

animated but not tonally unified by the subtle play and gradation of light. The portraits of the real people, luminously " abridged," that Raphael introduced among the imaginary heroes of the *School of Athens* and of the last part of the *Disputa*, appear markedly different. They, and not those equally admirable easel works, find consonance with those that appear in the next Stanza painted in fresco, the Stanza di Eliodoro.

THE STANZA OF HELIODORUS

The decoration of the second Stanza painted by Raphael, the Stanza di Eliodoro, bears an inscription with two dates: 1512 and 1514. There is no reason not to consider them as the dates between which the work was carried out. As has been seen, some critics would like to push back the date to the summer of 1511, after the return of Julius II to Rome from the unsuccessful undertaking in Romagna. They base themselves on a passage in a letter from the messenger of Isabella d'Este, July 12, 1511, that made reference to the work of two Stanze. But it is a vague indication, which could refer to the entire program of work, and not necessarily to its actual continuation in the second Stanza.[103] According to our hypothesis, that the conclusion of the *Disputa* and the insertion of the figure of Heraclitus-Michelangelo in the *School of Athens* post-dated the unveiling of the whole vault of the Sistine Chapel in August 1511, this undertaking sufficed to occupy the rest of the year, while Raphael's assistants executed the *Decretals* and the *Pandects*. It is difficult to say who they were. At that time Penni and Giovanni da Udine were already working alongside Raphael and documents attest to his friendly relations with Baldassarre Peruzzi, the artist in the employ of Agostino Chigi, who also com-

161 Detail from the Mass at Bolsena: Head of a bearer. Stanza di Eliodoro.

139

missioned Raphael himself. There is little, however, that supports a distinguishing of styles, because the presence of the master weighs so heavily also in those frescoes that it does not even leave the possibility of a convincing comparison with that which the assistants executed by themselves. We can infer their participation by comparison of the pictorial qualities which are heavier on the one hand and appear limpid in the neighboring figurations that bear the mark of his authentic signature. It is only on this basis that we can note the presence of assistants, but not their individual contributions in the Stanza di Eliodoro.

This Stanza follows a program quite different from that of the Segnatura. It also seems that this underwent changes in the course of the work itself. The vault, divided into four triangles that simulate a pavilion adorned with historical scenes, has biblical figurations that refer to the intervention of the Divinity in the crucial moments of the history of the Patriarchs: Noah entering the Ark that will save him from the *Flood;* Abraham about to sacrifice his son Isaac; Jacob's vision of God the Father in a dream, at the top of a ladder on which Angels are ascending and descending; and Moses in the Burning Bush, whose vision of God incites him to the liberation of Israel. Single concordances have been established with the figurations beneath them, but not without great difficulty: it is better to think of the generic allusion to divine aid that always crowns true Faith. It was the only hope of Julius II who in those terrible days of 1511 had seen the wreck of all his political initiatives and within the Church itself the defection of the cardinals favorable to the hegemonic ambitions of the King of France and their convocation of a Council in Pisa, tantamount to schism.

If the decoration of the Stanza was already under consideration at the end of 1511, it could be due only to the firm trust of the Pope who, undaunted even by the grave illness of August, feverishly took steps to repair and to dam the disaster. But events precipitated variants in the figural elaboration from the moment work was begun on the Stanza in 1512, and probably at the very beginning of the year. Variants, moreover, which did not digress from the initial significance: it was still the celebration of divine intervention in which Julius II had believed and for which he had fervently prayed, and which miraculously suddenly gave a different course to the event, transforming disaster into victory. The search for posterior concordances, for solely celebratory significations in the *Expulsion of Heliodorus*, the *Mass at Bolsena*, in the *Liberation of St. Peter*, and finally in the *Repulse of Attila*, mark a failure to reflect that these events were taking place while Raphael was working and that they could not have determined changes in the composition if we take account of the time to pre-arrange and execute them. We can justify the intervention of assistants, by this necessity to make swift changes; but the variants, and their executory consequences occurred within a comprehensive conception already ideally divided at least in regard to its three principal parts: the *Mass*, the *Expulsion of Heliodorus*, the *Liberation of St. Peter*. It could have been the events which, in their unpredictable succession, determined procedures and justified the coexistence of different evolutive moments

163 Detail from the Liberation of St. Peter. Stanza di Eliodoro.

142 164 Detail from the Liberation of St. Peter. Stanza di Eliodoro.

among the parts of the same history which has always constituted the difficulty in the reading of this Stanza; but they do not suffice to destroy its coherence, which is the conceptual coherence of the artist's general program, so concordant with the outcomes of reality, that they could refer to no one else save Julius II himself.

It was no longer, as in the Segnatura, the vision beyond historical time of the spiritual unity incarnated by the Church. Now that everything was in danger there remained only the supreme truth of the Faith. The theme that links everything together could be said to be that of the Pope's prayer, of his passionate colloquy with the Divinity, like that primordial

165 Detail from the Liberation of St. Peter. Stanza di Eliodoro.

143

colloquy of the Patriarchs. The spiritual Head who had lowered himself to use the secular sword, now, in the moment of failure that was almost a divine admonition, turned to the sword that was more proper to him, that of ecclesiastical authority against errors and schisms. The oration of the Dominican Tommaso da Gaeta on May 17, 1512, at the second session of the Lateran Council, which had opened on May 13, summed up the direction of papal policy in this metaphor.[104] And the Council, convoked one month before the battle of Ravenna which had seemed to be the last blow inflicted upon the Julian policy of expansionism, in reality was a victory that smashed the schism at its birth and greatly contributed to the reversal of the situation and caused the French, victorious at Ravenna in April, to march back over the Alps at the end of June, abandoning all the conquered territories.

What is narrated on the walls of the second Vatican Stanza is in reality the history of Julius II in the concluding and loftiest pages of his dramatic life, in which brightest light and the deepest shadows alternated. When everything that he had wished to establish had crumbled—his authority had been denied by a schismatic Council and in France his very person was the object of public and cruel mockery—he still believed in the Church of which he felt himself to be the head, and he placed himself at the feet of the Divinity with the unshakeable faith of the ancient Prophets. This was to be portrayed by his great interpreter, positioning him in prayer like the High Priest Onias in the Temple profaned by the usurpers with the complicity of the priests themselves, and positioning him once more in prayer, certain of his faith, in front of the unbelieving priest of the *Mass at Bolsena*, still trustful in the supernatural power that had destroyed Heliodorus and liberated St. Peter from prison. These suggestions were not made to him by the occasion of circumstances; Julius himself must have

◁ PLATE XXII-XXIII The Expulsion of Heliodorus from the Temple. Stanza di Eliodoro, Vatican.

PLATE XXIV The Mass at Bolsena (detail). Stanza di Eliodoro, Vatican. ▷

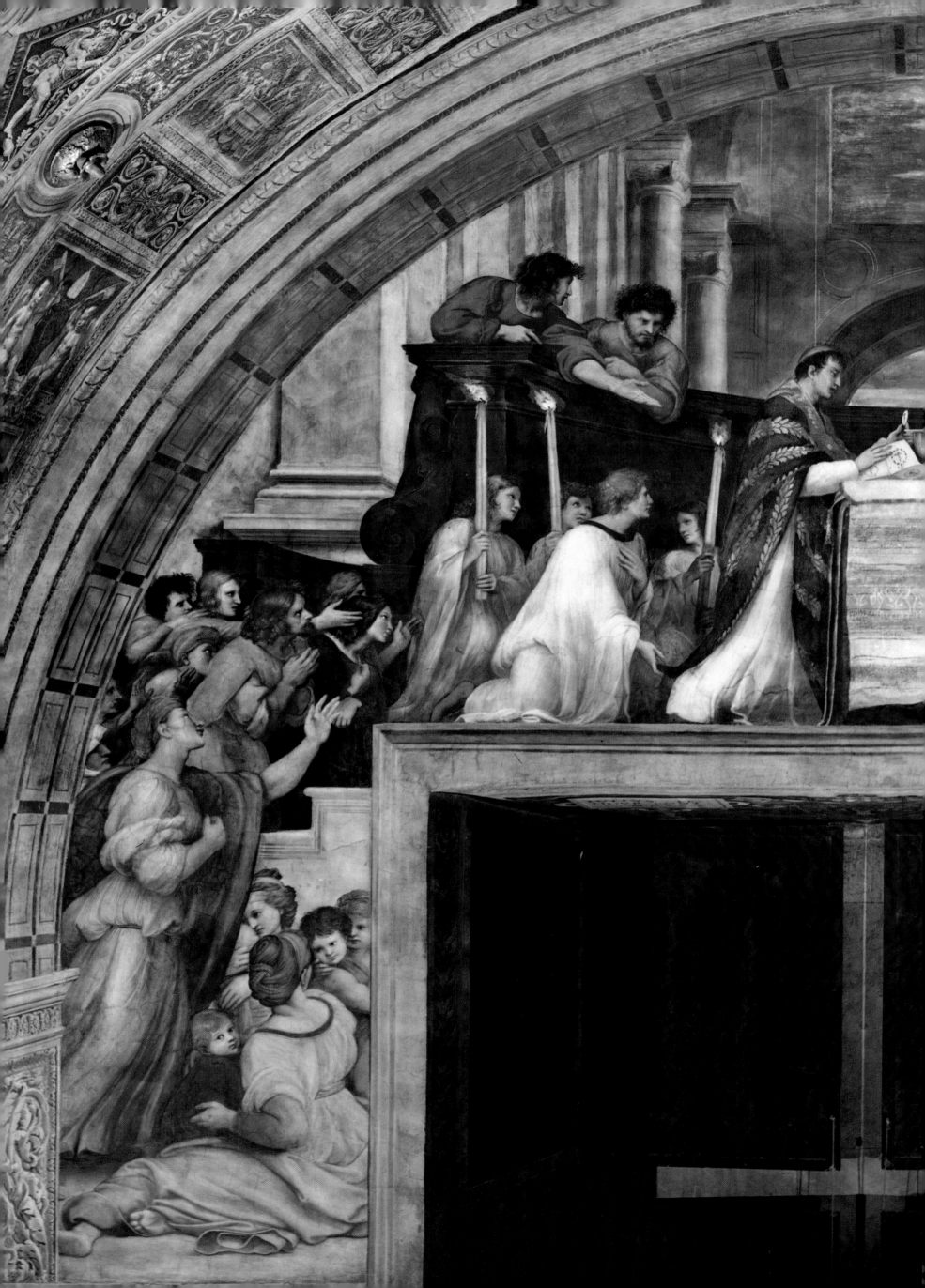

Plate XXV-XXVI   The Mass at Bolsena. Stanza di Eliodoro, Vatican.

Plate XXVII   The Liberation of St. Peter (detail). Stanza di Eliodoro, Vatican. ▷

◁ Plate XXVIII-XXIX   The Liberation of St. Peter.   Stanza di Eliodoro, Vatican.

Plate XXX   Encounter of Attila and Leo the Great (detail).   Stanza di Eliodoro, Vatican. ▷

selected them from among the infinite recollections of his sacerdotal life: of his pause to visit the Corporal of Bolsena on his way to the conquest of Bologna; of his titular church, San Pietro in Vincoli. They were the "exempla" which he, following the method of ecclesiastical preaching, adduced in order to clarify, to signify in images the high religious purposes of his practical, vigorous action against every form of scepticism, of the consciousness of his papal mission, expressed in his very motto: "Dominus mihi adiutor, non timebo quid faciat mihi homo." He had to propose his spiritual and active program, which at that time was only a great hope shared by few, to the only one capable of understanding it, Raphael—his great interpreter in the Stanza della Segnatura. Raphael had to set to work immediately, leaving to his assistants the last frescoes of the Stanza—the *Pandects* and the *Decretals*—in order once more to give the papal thought its most faithful figural translation. The confirmation of events followed Julius' proposals only much later, and it was then that Raphael inserted direct allusions to them in the figuration of the whole. But the dramatic moment in which only the strength of a great soul, of a lofty sacerdotal conscience which at that moment triumphed over all the miseries of human life like a dike against the universal storm, remained the theme of this second Stanza, more profound and more passionately human than the first, which was sublimely theoretical. From it a different accent came to Raphael's art, not of exaltation but of an intense realism. He was truly the hand with which Julius II, through the image, signed his general confession, that which the Christian rite prescribes at the point of death. And death was near. The only truly celebratory figure, in the *Repulse of Attila*, of the defeat of the French, bears the countenance of his successor, Leo X.

In the anxiety of this declaration, which was the reply of faith to the spreading discouragement, Julius II had to have everything that had been painted previously in the Stanza destroyed in order to leave a free field to Raphael. The artist, probably, proceeded immediately along the general lines of the program in his division of the episodes and in that architectonic structuration that is read, unitarily, from the vault with the biblical allusion to the divine aid which the Pope implored, to the three principal walls where the *Expulsion of Heliodorus* was the total proposition of the theme of which the *Mass at Bolsena* and the *Liberation of St. Peter* became the analogical illustration. The hypothesis of a first unitary design coherent with the iconographic unity finds confirmation in the organic figural structure. Apart from the *Repulse of Attila* which, as we shall see, was conceived and added at a later

167 Detail from the Encounter of Attila. Stanza di Eliodoro.

169 Portrait of Julius II (copy). Florence, Uffizi.

168 Raphael's Assistants: Portrait of a Cardinal (Cardinal Dal Monte). Naples, Museo di Capodimonte.

time, the other representations are staged in grandiose and rigourously symmetric architectural forms, whether they allude to basilical interiors, as in *Heliodorus* and the *Mass*, or in the *Liberation of St. Peter*, to a prison, which also has the grandeur of a nave among very solidly built walls. The analogous amplitude of the central embrasures, their perfect axial coordination once more unfold the architectonic theme rationally posed in the *School of Athens*. But the flight of the perspetive that is repeated on all three walls imprints multiple tensions on the space, as if the original embrasure had become only the point of departure of an opening of the vision towards the infinite. This straining towards the limit, beyond the rationality of the perspective, is accentuated by the mobile play of the light that fills these embrasures in a subtle texture of shadows broken by sudden flashes of waving, tiny flames, of a metallic glinting of jewelry and suits of armor, and, in the brief patches of sky, fleeting shadows of clouds. These solemn perspectives are no longer, as in the *School of Athens*, a dialectical apposition to the agitated tension of the figures; on the contrary, they participate vitally in their animation and become, so to speak, themselves actors in an intensely dramatic history that coinvolves every figural element. It is this history in its entirety that is marked out in expressive intensity on all the walls. Therefore, considering the episodes in their totality and not in an exactly determined sequence, we must read in the pauses and accents the continuity of a single discourse.

This discourse is not the lofty dialectic of the Stanza della Segnatura, in which every opposite tension was reconciled in the higher equilibrium of a painting that was itself theory, the ideal contemplation even of the most violent historicity. Here the theoretical propositions themselves seem to vacillate in the fearful confrontation with an actual dramatic reality. The pictorial violence does not pause; it grasps the most fleeting moments of an action that is

146

articulated feverishly in infinite " movements of mind." Form no longer becomes definition; it is solely suggestion, allusion only to that which is essentially expressive. The color is wholly one with the light and capable of qualifying, of defining and, simultaneously, of alluding beyond every definition. Here we can see a return to the first determining teaching, that which Leonardo—carrying out Donatello's theory—had proposed from the *Adoration of the Magi:* a painting that would be genesis in action, history caught in the actuality of its becoming, the image not of an immobile world, almost an abstract symbol of itself, but of a world in the incessant transformation of birth, death, and rebirth which is the perpetuity of history.

Only in the understanding of this problem, present throughout Raphael's life, will we be able to follow his evolution from the Stanza della Segnatura to that di Eliodoro and within it the succession of experiences which at times are placed side by side in the one figuration and have constituted the perennial difficulty of their critical reading. It is all the more difficult when an attempt is made to declare data valid from a single experience in order to establish the chronological sequence of various episodes. This has often led to partial interpretations, giving a categorical value to single episodes, forcing purely philological distinctions into critical premises, fractioning the expressive unity in a particularistic distinction of influences and hands. Thus the individual contribution by assistants has been seen where, instead, there was only the creativeness of the master badly translated, an eclectic oscillation between Michelangelesque suggestions and new Venetian influences, or also a continual deviation on Raphael's part from Renaissance positions towards Manneristic, pre-Baroque, even Baroque positions, almost as if these stylistic categories were already so exactly outlined in Raphael's time as to be able to represent a goal for him

Rather, the coherence of the Stanza di Eliodoro, its representation of a further stage and not of a negation of his precedent painting, appears only if we see the artist as acting in the fullness of his time, individually assuming and vivifying its problems which, in painting, were those of the total renewal of expression. In this intention, namely that of increasingly adapting the image to the ever deepening dynamic of history, those experiences that are feverishly renewing themselves and reciprocally integrating into each other, and are diverse only in appearance, will find their place. The homogeneity that has been seen in the inspiration can be noted in every aspect of the synthesis that is more properly pictorial if we know to perceive these events in an attentive reading, not according to an arbitrarily prearranged sequence but according to that suggested by circumstances of every kind, and first of all by the style, that converge in these figurations. The painting, in contrast to the preceding Stanza, must have been begun from the vault, as was the custom.

170-171 Portraits of Tommaso (Fedra) Inghirami. Boston, Isabella Stewart Gardner Museum, and Florence, Galleria Palatina.

According to Vasari, Piero della Francesca and Bramantino had painted the two walls occupied today by the *Expulsion of Heliodorus* and the *Mass*, and in the Bramantino part there were portraits which Raphael had his pupils copy and which then, through Giulio Romano, passed on to the collection of Paolo Giovio in Como.[105]   It seems that, as in the vault of the Segnatura, Raphael had respected also here a pre-existent division made by Baldassarre Peruzzi.   However, a certain time must have been required for the new preparation of the grooving of the walls and the destruction of the old frescoes; this was the time, between the end of 1511 and the beginning of 1512, when Raphael might have been occupied with projecting the whole and preparing drawings and cartoons for the representations of the Patriarchs in the vault.   Only one of these has come down to us, the Moses of the Burning Bush, now in Naples in the Museum of Capodimonte.

This is the most disputed part of the whole Stanza, both in regard to chronology and execution. The disputation is justified by the diversity of this section from the others; at its most manifest the influence of Michelangelo at times comes close to copying, as in Noah entering the Ark, whose layout recalls that of Judith in one of the spandrels of the Sistine, and the whirling flight of God the Father borne by the Angels, modelled on the Sistine *Genesis*.   But we cannot deduce from it a dating that is too late.   If it is true that the entire Sistine vault, including the lunettes, was unveiled on the eve of All Saints Day of 1512, it is also suggested that the first two triangular spandrels, precisely those with Judith and David were already unveiled as early as September 15, 1509.   Even if we wish to reject this hypothesis, advanced by Tolnay, there is the other, universally accepted, according to which the whole vault, including the spandrels, was unveiled in August 1511 except for the lunettes, which were executed from October 1511 to October 1512.[106]

172 Detail from the Foligno Madonna: Head of the Baptist. Pinacoteca Vaticana.

In the Stanza di Eliodoro visions appear like rapid lightning flashes to the men who believe and pray. The oblique ladder of Jacob's dream furrows the sky like a streak of lightning; whirling angels as in the Dei Altarpiece swoop down from the heights to arrest Abraham's already upraised arm; Moses covers his dazzled eyes, a man incapable of looking at the Beyond which suddenly reveals itself to him. The drawings for this figure, in its broad folds of light and shadow, has reminiscences of the Heraclitus. In these representations everything points toward to the Michelangelo influence of the later parts of the Segnatura. It makes us think that Raphael must have prepared this work immediately after the latter; but even if he started painting then, the presence of assistants appears undeniably in many parts where the vigorous movement is arrested in the contortion of the arabesque, for example in the clouds curled around God the Father of the Bush. Several attempts have been made to identify the assistants: Baldassarre Peruzzi, Penni, finally Guglielmo di Marcillat, the expert master who decorated the Vatican Stanze with legend-illustrated stained glass windows;[107] but until some new document is discovered every supposition is bound to remain unconfirmed, because every pupil became

149

too unlike himself when the Master was alongside him, imposing upon him innovations which the pupil could repeat but not relive, and at times, actually not understand. If those were the artists alongside Raphael then it is an arduous task to determine who among them collaborated in painting the vault. The damage, greater here than elsewhere, further increases the difficulties. Consequently, all that remains is the certainty of the collaboration and the strong probability of a comprehensive beginning of this part of the work, even if Raphael let it be finished by other hands because he was pressed by his commitments to the other great mural decorations.

The chronological succession of the *Mass at Bolsena* and the *Expulsion of Heliodorus* also is not wholly clear. The reason for this, perhaps, may lie in the persistent critical habit of comparing the figures in their totality, a comparison that does not succeed in explaining diverse elements that coexist in them and that poorly lend themselves to a retracing of the whole in a unitary evolution. Hence we must presuppose that the same operative procedure which we discovered in the Stanza della Segnatura must also have been followed in this Stanza. Raphael did not execute the single figures one by one, but worked simultaneously on the whole complex at the levels marked out by the landings of the single scaffolding, and at times he did not even let himself be totally bound by those. In this Stanza also concordances of stylistic phases are discernible without any apparent rule on the one and another of the frescoes. Consequently only the evolutive coherence of Raphael's style can be of help to us in attempting to establish a plausible chronological sequence.

It is probable that the *Expulsion of Heliodorus* was the first to be painted. It was the most important, the entire proposition of the argument, namely the profaned Church in the allusion to the Hebrew Temple in which the traitorous priests had allowed entry to the foreigner Heliodorus to plunder the monies of widows and orphans. The prayer of the High Priest Onias has obtained divine intervention in the form of the horseman and the celestial messenger who fiercely scourged and expelled the usurper. The prayer is the figurative center of the fresco. The perspective lines of the long empty nave converge in the priest who has the features of Julius II, kneeling before the altar in the gleam of candles while the faithful and the avengers who strike the culprit to the ground throng in tumultuous groups on the sides. The group of the pontiff is lacking in drawings showing the first plan, and the supposition that it was added later is confirmed by an examination of the plastered surfaces prepared for fresco painting.

Perhaps the crowded church is an allusion to the aula of the Lateran Council convoked by the Pope in 1511, but which was to open only in May of the following year. It was the spiritual arm from which he awaited the liberation of the Church and her reform, as in fact happened. But at that time it was only a great hope and the goal of a fervent imploration for divine aid: the theme of the entire allegory. The atmosphere seems filled with this spiritual tension; it is an obscure ambience, shot through with dazzling flashes that become pure light only in the background where it comes from above to illuminate the prayer of Onias. The crowd is a thick texture of figures, arranged in the manner of Michelangelo, marked by chromatic masses as in a febrile, rough-hewn sculpture. The light strikes them in violent strokes, but now it also infiltrates and consumes them until, in the rearmost planes, it reduces them to extremely rapid, sudden suggestions emerging from the dense shadow. Raphael the painter, surpassing the Michelangelesque teaching itself, arrives at that splendid episode of the two who climb on the column which is, in an admirable rhythmic concatenation, sheer impetuous movement, grasped beyond every formal definition by the color, by reddish, blue, and yellow dazzling gleams as in a fleeting tongue of fire. It is a new point of arrival of his art, even beyond the achievements of the last parts of the Segnatura.

Not even Michelangelo can provide a suggestion for the ideation of the group of the heavenly horseman who jumps on the prostrate enemy and the two scourgers. It is again Leonardo who provides that unsurpassable example of the furious combatants of the *Battle of Anghiari*. There the difficult compositional problem has been resolved forever, and there too the problem of making light the dramatic coefficient of action was also resolved. In its tight unity of composition the horseman group isolates itself in the interlacing of its own impetuous rhythms. It is so studied a work of elaboration that even the central episode of the priest's prayer passes to the second plane. This, which is the only criticism that can be made of this lofty creation, is justified, however, by the attenuation of the luminous fusion with the entirety of the scene due to the undeniable and recognizable presence of a strong collaborator. The surviving drawings of the heads of the scourgers[108] have the sudden chiaroscural impetus that is a prelude to the chromatic *élan* of the two figures on the column; but whoever translated them in fresco made the shadows heavy, arrested the suggestion and gave to them and to the entire group a sculptural quality which disturbs the lyricism of the whole figuration. To be sure the assistants were most expert, but in them we can recognize only Giulio Romano, at that time only thirteen; could they have included Penni, who had been with Raphael since adolescence, or Baldassarre Peruzzi? We confess that we cannot answer this question since their presence is evident only in this inability to follow Raphael's fancy, even if they translated its forms with great skill. Rather, we can ask ourselves how is it that Raphael, who had executed all the rest with his own hand, left precisely this essential episode, which must have been laboriously prepared, to the execution of others? It must have been necessary to go ahead with the histories of the lateral walls, and in particular the *Mass at Bolsena*, in which the figure of Julius II assumed the role of protagonist, the asserter of a faith in which everyone else was vacillating.

174 Detail from the Foligno Madonna: The House of the Donor struck by lightning (?). Pinacoteca Vaticana.

The *Mass of Bolsena* is the most unitary of the figurations bearing Raphael's authentic signature in every part, to demonstrate his commitment in this celebration of his spiritual hero. The light is diffused, without the sudden tensions of the precedent composition in this grand aula opened to an even grander sky, and it again permits the tonal ecstasy of the *School of Athens*. The Michelangelesque impetuosities of the color of *Heliodorus* are attenuated and fused in this luminous tone without losing anything of their structural vehemence. They further permit, in the dense formal texture of the women on the ground, the tender interplay of maternal affection and infantile vivacity, and in the adoring impulse of the woman who rises to her feet an ethereal luminosity that imbues her yellow garment. A more subtle perception of real values converges in this tonal fusion with a more imaginative chromaticism, as if the pictorial discovery has penetrated more deeply into the fastnesses of reality in order to find new inspiration. The white surplices of the assistants of the celebrant are of the whiteness of light linens, subtly pleated in multiple folds. The embroidered chasuble emits metallic reflections, reflecting the flame of the lighted candles, as does the gold of the chalice and of the sacred church ornaments. The force of the color is intensified in the lyrical description of the inanimate things themselves. But it achieves its loftiest accents in the figure of the Pope. Here it is not the violences of Heliodorus that form this powerful plastic nucleus; the power is effected solely by the contained and dominated spiritual vehemence of the motionless figure who interrupts his prayer only to fix the unbelieving priest with an awesome stare from which nothing is hidden. A few masses of gloomy reds, of whites, of the yellow backgrounds of old gold, permeated by light, construct this essential plasticity in which the most dramatic "movement of mind" is enclosed. Everything is interiorized in Raphael's painting, it has been humanistically led back to the image of man—the Renaissance man who could still bring back to the feet of the Divinity the bitter experience of a whole life, and for him, it was totally incarnated in Julius II.

If we place the *Mass of Bolsena* chronologically to the time when the assistants were bringing *Heliodorus* to completion, it shows us the fulfillment of what was being enunciated there: the extreme conformative and suggestive capacity acquired by color is brought back from the field of vision to the direct confrontation with reality almost as if by an investigation that was beginning once more. Portraits abound in this fresco, and figures obviously drawn from life, which have been variously explained and analyzed, but which are evidence of Raphael's need for the substance of reality to express the transfigurative power that he had achieved. This is conformed by all his subsequent creativity. That universal contemplation of the whole of life, which had been the Leonardesque initiation of his first youth, now returns to lead him back from the sublime creation of symbols of the Stanza della Segnatura, to the plenitude of Renaissance historicity. This was not a descending from achieved heights, a retreat, but rather a further 151 thrust forward in order to discover in the depths of reality the primordial germ of that exaltation and to actualize it, to reveal infinite, hidden " reasons " even if up to then " they were never in experience." This was also a great admonition of Leonardo.

Even if this new turn to reality was a necessity of style, Raphael seized its possibilities when they were offered to him by the very events of these decisive months of 1512. The Pope's diplomatic activity and the powerful aid that was being prepared by the Swiss, organized by Cardinal Schinner, was undermining the success which the French army had registered in April at the battle of Ravenna. The Lateran Council, which held its inaugural ceremony on

175 Detail from the Madonna of the Chair. Florence, Galleria Palatina.

152

176 Madonna and Child with the Infant St. John, called the "Madonna della Tenda." Munich, Alte Pinakothek.

177 Detail from the Sistine Madonna. Dresden, Gemäldegalerie.

May 2 and its first session on the following day, the feast of the Holy Cross, from the outset nullified the competency of the schismatic council which a few weeks earlier in Milan had declared the suspension of the Pope. Instead, Julius succeeded once more in rallying around his person the greatest European powers, isolating France, victorious up to then, and compelling her to abandon her Italian conquests. On June 3 Bologna was retaken, and three weeks later on June 22 news reached Julius of the total retreat of the French towards the Alps. The miracle that had been invoked was taking place, and as a token of thanksgiving the Pope betook himself, almost in pilgrimage, to his titular church of San Pietro in Vincoli on June 23, and remained there in prayer until June 27. This was followed by the triumphal return of Julius to the apostolic seat across the illuminated streets of an exultant Rome. His firm faith had been crowned with the most unforeseeable success. Sanuto and the faithful chronicler Paride de' Grassi report his words: " Now we have nothing more to ask of God, only we must thank the Most High for the splendid victory." [109]

All this had taken place with a lightning-like swiftness while Raphael rapidly, and with the indispensable help of his pupils, was working on the compositions that had been evolved when victory was but the hope of the man who was preparing it and who entrusted himself to the Most High as the sole help. But now the fulfilled hope imposed a different tone. New personages came into the foreground, and perhaps the Pope himself wanted their likenesses alongside his. Hence the lower part of the *Mass of Bolsena*, still unfinished, had to be filled with portraits. Raffaello Riario, cardinal of San Giorgio, who had celebrated the inaugural Mass of the Lateran Council, is rightly recognized as the old, very proud old man with arms folded across his breast. Next to him some have thought to identify Cardinal Schinner. Their bright red robes allowed Raphael a splendid pictorial episode opposite the mat tones of the two unknown prelates in the corner. But even more superb is the episode of the Swiss kneeling in the foreground. They had been the faithful assistants, the greatest architects of the victory and the Pope nominated them " protectors of the Church." From that moment on they became the papal guard alongside the gestatorial chair; here they are portrayed holding the gifts of sword and hat with which the Pope had honored then on July 5. The references to all these events are too evident to be denied and therefore we must deduce therefrom the dating of the summer of 1512 for the completion of the fresco.[110] In the powerfully characterized faces of these soldiers and in their rich, multicolored garments, luminous silks and velvets, the discovery of chromatic values, the ascending degrees of which are marked precisely in this fresco, reached its apex.

It has been suggested that this new direction in Raphael's painting was due to an influence of Venetian painting, which at that time, after the death of Giorgione in 1510, was continuing along the lines of supreme tonal unity in which the deepest chromatic substance converged. The hypothesis has been pushed to the point of seeing precisely in the episode of the Swiss the collaboration of Sebastiano del Piombo, who was in Rome from 1511, or of Lorenzo Lotto, who in 1509 appeared in the documents among the artists active in the Vatican.[111] But, aside from the unconvincing comparisons whith the known work of the two artists, it remains for us to consider the coherence of this painting an evolution of the Segnatura and *Heliodorus*, in the images of the Pope and of the cardinals in the upper part of the *Mass*. It is entirely probable that Raphael knew the new directions of the Giorgionesque painting. Works circulated no less than men, and to an exceptional sensibility and intelligence such as his the least reference

could disclose wide horizons, as Gamba has rightly noted.[112] Thus it must be pointed out that these possible influences could only join the flow of pictorial evolution that was the fruit of a continued, meditated experience from the first manifestations to maturity. Raphael, from his youth on, must have known of those premises of " Giorgionism " that were the " Marches " works of Giovanni Bellini, and Leonardo had given him at first hand those determining propositions on which Giorgione's own renewal is based. We could already speak of a Giorgione influence *ante litteram* in such works as the *Graces* and the *Connestabile Madonna*. In the fullness of his Roman painting he no longer needed any indications or examples, and all the less so from artists who, to be sure, were of notable talent but doubtlessly inferior to his own, as was Sebastiano and even Lotto, and inferior also to those whom he recognized as his only teachers: Leonardo and Michelangelo. Only in their teaching, which was to last through Raphael's life, was born the capacity of Raphael's painting constantly to renew itself, the capacity to adapt to every pictorial discovery of his time and also constantly to surpass them, including even the most sublime discoveries of Giorgione.

From now on he entirely dominated the field of art. In the Stanza di Eliodoro the most profound reality and the most winged vision stood miraculously side by side. Contemporaneously with the *Mass* he had to finish the *Liberation of St. Peter*, and quickly, incited by the great thanksgiving service in San Pietro in Vincoli. It had been conceived, probably, as a counterpoint to 155 the diffused light of the *Mass at Bolsena*, almost as if the luminous dialectic enunciated in the central figuration of the *Expulsion of Heliodorus*, should become the dialectic between two entire figurations, one clear and luminous, the other a fanciful nocturne. But even the intensified effulgence of the central episode, the ultra-real light of the halo of the angel bent over St. Peter, revealed profound realities of things and men. Under the scrutiny of that light the stones of the prison, in their gloomy roughness appear with a crudeness that would have moved Caravaggio. An opaque net, the black iron of bars and chains, separates us from that angel who is light alone, bent to the form, and to the most rhythmically harmonious form, by a few great brush strokes of yellow and dark red. Never did the most loudly proclaimed impressionism thus succeed in grasping a fugitive moment like a flash. The other angel who accompanies the liberated saint outside the prison seems to delay, if only for an instant, his beauty defined and revealed by the light. Because of the work of an assistant, no doubt able, the suddenness of the vision that Raphael had miraculously grasped is lost. It returns in the lower part on the dark stairs on which the guards abandon themselves to sleep. The master's hand is certainly seen in the radiance of the white lights on the metallic armature in which the human form is closed as in a shell, on the breast-plate of the other guard who hides his face and the intense chromaticism of his attire in the shadows. It had required a whole life in order to rethink this way and to filter, up to its extreme lyrical purification, the theme of the sleep that is a dream, already enunciated alongside Perugino in the youthful Vatican *Resurrection*. On the other side the stairs are clear, illuminated by the torch and the shining reflections of the metal are reduced to a skillful play. But in the upper part, a figure wholly in shadow, with only tenuous reflections on the helmet and on the arm guard, flees in front of a large crepuscular sky, still red with twilight as night rises and the fugitive clouds shine with the silver of lunar luminescences. Here no one else but Raphael is at work, and the artist whom some would have learning the lyricism of Giorgione from Sebastiano or from Lotto, in one stroke soars higher than the whole span of the Venetian conquest, beyond Giorgione and including Titian and Tintoretto.

There were no longer any frontiers for Raphael's great lyricism between reality and vision. Both flowed into to it together in a transposition on a universally poetic plane which had been possible only to a few in all times. The moment of the supreme test which had made of Julius II one of the loftiest figures of history had found in Raphael its great cantor, as great as Vergil, as Dante. Raphael was so conscious of it that he wanted, and this can be supported without arbitrariness, on his own iniative to insert the sovereign image of his hero in the figuration which had exalted his unbreakable faith when the Church was in danger. He must have been present at the annihilation of the adversary powers, in the glory of that triumph marked by the Pope's return after the thanksgiving in San Pietro in Vincoli. But now it was not the Swiss who carried the gestatorial chair, but the artists who had glorified him in the very moment of his humiliation. Vasari indicates the figure of Marcantonio Raimondi among the bearers, the erect figure with the emaciated face who seems to dominate over the tiny band. Had he been Raphael's major assistant in this undertaking? This supposition is validated by Raimondi's great experience in drawing, even if he is not known as colorist. The other, further in the rear, according to Fischel is Raphael himself but the resemblance is superficial and it is strange to see him thus in the background. Others instead have elected to recognize him in the figure on the left in curial raiment[113] which, for that matter would befit Raphael, inasmuch as since 1509 he had held the post of writer of apostolic briefs. The writing which has identified this figure as Giovanni de' Foliari, a most obscure functionary of the Curia, has turned out to be apocryphal and stems from a later time. But dominating over all the figures is Julian II, truly heroic in his tense immobility, poised as if ready to move so that his hands contract instead of resting on the arms of the chair, heroic above all in his countenance, truly " awesome," in that look which is but a black pupil and a gleam of white. Yet the look of the great Julius who, like the Patriarchs had not doubted, dominates, judges, execrates. Pictorial wisdom itself vanishes from this synthesis of an exceptional personality, still it draws radiant lights from the velvet of the *mozzetta*, the red tippet, and rapidly models, sculpturally, the fabric of the chemise. Painting is forgotten for the image that is its ultimate end. This is the art of Raphael, this surpassing of the media, from now on.

In this brief cycle, from the Stanza della Segnatura to that di Eliodorus, heights are reached which are not only those of a great artist at work, but are among the greatest of art in all times. For in Raphael there was a gathering of the thought of a decisive moment of human history, becoming itself an inspiration; and the person who dominates it in all its totality, the great Pope Julius II, had been the mediator of this thought to him.

The Pope was not a man of letters; he would not have been capable of separating thought from action and expounding it in conceptual form. But he was capable of living, exhausting in himself the experience, all the dramatic contradictions of his epoch and of intuiting their point of arrival. He did not call in the men of the pen, entangled in their laborious demonstrations and in their polemics, in order to signify this intuition, but the artists, and alongside the mature Bramante, young men not yet imprisoned in their conquests but open to following the advice of the teacher as he felt himself to be. Michelangelo and Raphael, only they, in the happy openness of youth could have unconditionally believed in him and become his interpreters. The old Pope who, in his long life, had approached the greatest masters must

179 Detail from the Sistine Madonna: The Virgin and the Child. Dresden, Gemäldegalerie.

have been quite aware of the fact that in his time art was in the vanguard of a new discovery: namely, that art and not philosophy, with its worn out and conceptual means, knew how to look deeply into reality and to reveal a new history different from the hypotheses of the ideological systems, indeed irreducible to any formulation in its infinite dialectic, in its perpetual transformation. He, the spiritual *condottiero* understood how a point of arrival was necessary for this eager searching and that this could take place only beyond the rational chain of causes and effects in the sublime *absurdum* of a renewed act of faith. For this he called the artists, the ingenuous " discoverers " of a new wisdom to give expressive form to the reaffirmation of the Faith, to the vision that was his vision, of a Church as the synthesis of all history from the remote times of Genesis to the future already germinating in the tumultuous present. But the dramatic difficulty of this renewed act of faith had been lived by the Pope himself in a total experience that by his own confession, in the supreme sincerity of the last hour, was the experience of martyrdom.[114] After the assertive proclamations of St. Peter's, of the vault of the Sistine Chapel, of the admonition of Julius II in the first Stanza, this Stanza was to be almost autobiographical but only to propose himself, in the moment in which " to believe " had a dramatic significance, as an *exemplum* of predication, the witness who in the etymological sense is the " martyr."

All this was represented by Raphael, not as an obedient executor but as a disciple, fascinated by the word and the example of him whom he felt to be his spiritual teacher. This is why the whole composition cannot be read in exclusively visual terms, so much does the form fuse with the ideological content, finding its justification exclusively in it and being generated by it. The image immediately passes over to the metaphor of the idea and from it flows clearness and efficacy of communication which was the primary meaning of the ancient " rhetoric." But for this reason also, it will be impossible to write a history of Renaissance thought without the reading of this, its fundamental text, written jointly by one of its great spiritual leaders and by one of its greatest artists. The reading of a figural test, however, is often barred to those who know very well how to read written texts. It is from such persons that the points of view emanate with which the figuration of the Stanzas has been considered, a posteriori. All of them have found confirmation, but without exhausting the significance that can be read only in its totality.

180 Sacra Conversazione (Madonna and Child with St. Catherine, St. Elizabeth, and the Infant St. John), called the " Madonna dell'Impannata." Florence, Galleria Palatina.

158

181 Sibyls and Angels. Rome, Santa Maria della Pace, Chigi Chapel.

Raphael had so deeply lived his lofty task that he personalized it finally in the very history of his hero. He followed him to the last, even when after the transient terrestrial victories there remained to the Pope only his greatest victory: that of seeing his thought fixed in art by Michelangelo and by Raphael: the triumph of faith over the whole effort of the intellect, a faith of which the depository was not only the corrupt Church of his time, but the Universal Church, Revelation in action for the whole span of time. When contingency again imposed its problems on the old Pope who stood on the threshold of death, Raphael portrayed him again in the last struggle between the spirit, eternally alive and the flesh which was yielding. It was the likeness intended for Santa Maria del Popolo, which has been lost and can only be ideally reconstructed from the copies, especially from that which has greater claims to authority inasmuch as it is presumed to be the original, now in London, of a portrait completed by Titian, now in the Galleria Palatina of Florence. It is still the great Pope whom the artists had borne in triumph before the defeat of his enemies in the *Expulsion of Heliodorus*. But he is no longer a dominator and judge, but pensive, beyond that momentary glory, of that which transcends and annuls it. The fading look no longer turns to the things of this world but beyond them, to the eternal void, to the obscure profundity of the soul. History is still in the painting, now the last history of the man, as it had been for Donatello. Every technical limit is surpassed for this history. The rapid technique of fresco is brought to the minute definition of oil and brings into the easel painting expressive impetuousness, the capacity to abbreviate, to suggest, to infuse the dramatic tension of the great frescoes also into the single image. Nothing anymore is an obstacle, but everything is a means toward realizing the entire significance of the man, physicality in which the " movement which is the cause of every life," the eternity of the spirit, tarries for a moment.

This portrait, sealing the events of Julian's life, can be supposed to have been executed in the first months of 1512, when the Pope still wore the beard of his moment of struggle (he removed it, as we know, in April 1512). Death was near and he departed this world on the night between February 20 and 21, 1513. In the span of these two years Raphael had been assigned the task of completing the Stanza di Eliodoro; a miracle had been seen in the sudden retreat of the victorious French, to which an allusion is seen in the *Repulse of Attila*, the invader of a thousand years before, in the presence of papal authority. But the theme itself was outside the great ideological synthesis which the Stanza had represented when the miracle was only imploration, prayer. Raphael had to work in a cold state, merely unfolding the bravura he had attained, not totally redeemed by the enthusiasm of inspiration. There was still a touch of this inspiration in the first ideation which has come down to us, not by his hand, in which the Pope, in the glory of his pontifical insignia, is being brought towards the battle; once more it was the waiting for the miracle, not its accomplishment. But at this point the great protagonist vanished from the scene, taken by death. His prophetic vehemence as supplanted by the cold calculation, the earthly ambition of his successor Leo X. He who had been portrayed at the side of Julius II in the papal cortege wanted to place himself on an equal footing with the great deceased, and himself became the pontiff of the miracle. Thus his likeness was repeated in that of St. Leo the Great, and his face, that of a shrewd hedonist, replaced that suffused with spiritually of the bearded old man who, it can be thought, would have summarized the whole dramatic character of this scene in himself. Thus also the face of his antagonist, the barbarian Attila remained dispersed amid the anonymity of the tumultuous combatants. History became narrative, and perhaps for this reason Raphael left its completion to assistants, of whom we shall make specific mention later, even though the dramatic contrast between the spasmodic interlacing of the battle, its impetuous chromaticism,

159

182 Detail from the fresco with Sibyls and Angels: The Persian Sibyl, two Angels and a *putto*. Rome, Santa Maria della Pace, Chigi Chapel.

and the monumental peace of the Pope who advances among his courtiers in a solemn scansion of great masses of colors is Raphael's alone. Even so there is no lack of very beautiful episodes in the horses, in the squires, above all in that fiery red sky against which the papal likeness stands out.

Raphael could not paint now that he had lost his great inspirer. On February 19, Grossino, an agent in Rome of the Marquis of Mantova, Francesco Gonzaga, informs his lord that Raphael will not paint his son, prince Federico, despite the commitment assumed years before: " he says that Your Lordship should forgive him for now: it would not be possible for him to have the mind to paint this portrait." [115] Even the practical, balanced Raphael for once had to feel himself depleted. If his interest in the decoration of the Vatican Stanze diminished, if its execution was increasingly entrusted to pupils, all of whom were now capable of availing themselves of the language that he had created as their own means of expression, it was because there were no longer the great motivations that had determined it, and it was the followers, and not the Master, who were to elaborate this language until it became that ductile instrument of which all could avail themselves, and until they emptied it in the inert mechanism of Mannerism. But it was Raphael himself who pointed out the way to its real utilization which was to be its evolution: as the perfect versification open to every content of poetry. This was still be the path trodden by Raphael in his last years.

AGOSTINO CHIGI " IL MAGNIFICO "

The evolutionary process that we have been able to follow in the first two Stanze receives almost an exact comment from the work that Raphael was carrying out at the same time in a different field, not under the highly theoretical inspiration of the thought of Julius II, but in response to the requests of a very rich patron, Agostino Chigi. The Sienese banker for whose family he, like Perugino, had worked in Siena, represented a financial power before which the political powers of Europe bowed. His life, in terms of sumptuousness and display was that of a sovereign, and his very relationship to culture, his patronage of men of letters and artists bore the stamp of a refined pastime: *otium*, escape from the practical world of business. The villa which his fellow-Countryman Baldassarre Peruzzi had built for him on the banks of the Tiber, the present-day Farnesina, in the midst of a vast garden, was a place of delight, the *Suburbanum*, the *Viridarium* which soon had its aulic singers: Egidio Gallo in 1511, Blosio Palladio in 1512. Both singled out for admiration the fresco of " the nascent Venus borne on the waves in a shell," which commonly is considered as an inexact allusion to Raphael's *Galatea*.[116]

The two citations tell us that at least the *Galatea* was a work in progress in 1511 and in the following year. This corresponds, as has been said before, with that phase of the artist's contact with Chigi already attested by the commission of the designs for precious trays in November 1510. By a coincidence of dates, it has been related to the period in which the work on the Vatican frescoes stagnated because lack of money during the war, so that Raphael,

183 Detail from the fresco with Sibyls and Angels: The Phrygian and Tibur (?) Sibyls. Rome. Santa Maria della Pace, Chigi Chapel.

184 The Vision of Ezechiel. Florence, Galleria Palatina.

in contrast to Michelangelo, looked for another patron in " il Magnifico " Agostino Chigi. At that time Chigi was negotiating a huge loan to the Venetians and, upon visiting their city in the spring of 1511, he received the honors accorded to the Doges.[117]

All this is confirmed by the stylistic phase reflected in the *Galatea*, a festive evocation of the classic fable of the nymph blown upon by the wind that makes her large red cloak shimmer like a flame while flying cupids, tritons, and nymphs, bound to each other in unbridled, joyous play, whirl in fanciful rhythms of forms in the brightness of the sky and sea. It is the moment, for the artist, of his most ardent enthusiasms for the beauty that was revealed in classic art, for the musical harmony of its rhythms, thematic impulses grasped and freely relived in the arcadian idyll of the *Parnassus*. But it is also the phase in which the bold chromaticism of Michelangelo, his capacity to suggest form in extreme animation is transposed by Raphael in a refinement of the relationship that seeks even in the Albertian " friendship " of colors the coefficient of a unitary harmony of the composition. Outside the great restraint of the theoretical content of the *School of Athens*, then a work in progress, the fantasy of the young Raphael erupts and

185 Detail from the St. Cecilia: Head of St. John the Evangelist. Bologna, Pinacoteca Nazionale.

186 Sacra Conversazione (St. Paul, John the Evangelist, St. Cecilia, St. Augustine and St. Mary Magdalene), called " St. Cecilia." Bologna, Pinacoteca Nazionale.

163

effuses itself, liberating all the richness of his color in this joyous exaltation of life, as the ancient fable exalted it in beauty.

In the ceiling of the loggia facing the Tiber, Baldassarre Peruzzi had alluded to the signs of the zodiac. On the walls the subjects are taken from Ovid's "Metamorphoses" and perhaps, for *Galatea*, from Politian's "Giostra." But what there was vivid description became interpretation in Raphael's ideation: not the circumstances of the joyous legend, but its evocation of a play of winds and waves from which the figures seem spontaneously to germinate. And next to it in the lunette, translating the Ovidian subjects with an equal enthusiasm, another great artist was at work, Sebastiano the Venetian, later called del Piombo. According to Vasari, Chigi in his Venetian contacts had induced Sebastiano to come to Rome after his master, Giorgione, died in 1510. Still according to Vasari,[118] Sebastiano supposedly began the work in the loggia from these lunettes where he did " some poetical fancies in a style that he had brought from Venice, very unlike that in use among the prominent painters then in Rome. " This can be a reference only to Michelangelo and Raphael, who at that time were alone in enunciating that which only later would be widespread as a common language. The comparison that is instituted and that is proposed to critical investigation, consequently, is not that between them and Sebastiano, but between the painting that they created and that which in Venice had been renewed by Giorgione and in which the student had already made great strides forward and made a name for himself. Hence the debated critical question on the relationship between the two artists whom Chigi had almost placed in competition, and on their reciprocal credits and debits: a question which, going beyond their persons, went to the definitive comparison between the two directives represented by them, and on their contribution to the future of painting.

According to Vasari the lunettes executed by Sebastiano were earlier than Raphael's *Galatea*, followed, in its turn by the *Polyphemus*, in which the Venetian did " his utmost, spurred by the competition of Baldassarre of Siena and of Raphael." But if we study the previous works of Sebastiano, such as the altarpiece of St. John Chrysostom in Venice, executed in the most profound Giorgionesque tonalism, in none of them can we discern that formal boldness, that capacity to decompose and recompose classic rhythm in a more impetuous, fanciful agitation which had no precedents in Venice but which, on the other hand, were precisely the road on which Raphael had embarked at the time of the *Massacre of the Innocents*, and especially of the *Galatea*. Nevertheless critics have wanted to insist on the alternative posed by Vasari and trace back these innovations of Sebastiano to the influence of Peruzzi. It seems that an artist of such a high degree of talent could not but have looked at Raphael's work when, after all, creations like the *School of Athens* were visible, albeit unfinished, or, if not, the drawings for the furnishings of the Chigi residence.[119]

Even if we wish to lend full credence to Vasari and accept that the lunettes preceded the execution of *Galatea*, Sebastiano as an artist, from the first moment of his arrival in Rome must have noticed the total diversity of the pictorial world, being disclosed to him, from that in which he had been formed, a diversity that posed the same problems that had also presided over Giorgione's revolution but in a broader and deeper way. In Rome, as in Venice, they were constructing a new painting which released the image from every traditional limit, suffused it with free movement and endowed it with animation wholly through the unarrestable play of color in light; but what in Venice was lyric contemplation, abandonment to dream, the deployment of form in the beauty of the universe vibrant with that diffused life, in Florentine painting became what was being carried out in Rome, an intellectual tension which did not permit abandonments, a search within form itself for an expressiveness: " history " with all its drama compared to Venetian " poetry." Before applying the brush to the Chigi walls Sebastiano, as soon as he arrived in Rome, had had time to perceive the new paths and to embark upon them himself and it was precisely their immediate impact, not recast in terms of his own thought, that permitted the freshness of his concepts and their very irregularity, which is the richness of a barely aroused fantasy and of a not yet acquired wisdom. Although the question cannot be exhausted in the brevity of an allusion, it seems possible to us that whatever the executory sequence may have been, Sebastiano worked in the Chigian *Suburbanum* in the throes of an enthusiasm over what Raphael had, if not painted, prepared in the drawing and in the cartoon for the *Galatea*. Further Sebastiano, who had never before tackled fresco painting, must have drawn lessons from the Stanza della Segnatura with its clear color effused in luminous tone. Thus the two directions of sixteenth century painting flowed together and were integrated. For if Raphael in his youth, at the suggestion of Giovanni Bellini and of Leonardo, had achieved Giorgionesque equivalents in works like the *Connestabile Madonna* or the *Graces*, now through Sebastiano he was getting to know the more mature achievements of the Giorgione school, of the tonal fusion it had achieved even when the chromatic values were the profound substance of real things. Perhaps precisely this newly aroused reflection was not without an echo in his pictorial evolution in the Stanza di Eliodoro. The precise dialectic of these years between 1511 and 1513, moreover, is a page of the history of art which still has only been barely outlined and which can be written only if we posit Giorgionesque painting not as an irreducible antithesis to the Florentine-Roman school, but only as a different solution to the same problem, the problem of expression besetting the whole Renaissance. It was Raphael who recognized it in its entirety, so much so that each one of his experiments was neither occasional nor determinant: it was necessary for the synthesis at which he was consciously aiming. The Giorgionesque suggestion of Sebastiano could also flow into it, and immediately dissolve. The latter, on the other hand,

187 Portrait of Baldassarre Castiglione. Paris, Louvre.

had his first initiation into the " bella maniera " from none other than Raphael, with whom at the time of their Chigian collaboration his relationship was an admiring one of pupil to teacher, even if later he separated himself from Raphael and sided with Michelangelo when a deep antagonism divided the two artists. Even after the break, the constant observation of Raphael's work, the attempt to insert himself in his undertakings, indeed to compete with him, indicates an aversion that was still admiration, as if the painting of Raphael, and not that of Michelangelo

188 Detail from the Fire in the Borgo: Head of Ascanius. Vatican, Stanza dell'Incendio.

166   189   Detail from the Fire in the Borgo: Anchises, Aeneas and Ascanius. Stanza dell'Incendio.

190 Detail from the Fire in the Borgo: Heads of Anchises and Aeneas. Stanza dell'Incendio.

who was close to him and a friend, were his true goal. This, on the part of a Venetian, was the first critical recognition of Raphael's art, the beginning of that synthesis of the two solutions which, later, were to be effected in Titian.

The collaboration between Raphael and Sebastiano did not continue, moreover, beyond the decoration of the loggia of the *Viridarium*, this has led Cavalcaselle to suppose that the preference shown to Raphael by Chigi over Sebastiano, whom after all he had induced to come to Rome, was the cause of a resentment that was never placated. At any rate, Raphael alone was entrusted with the decoration of the Chigi chapel in Santa Maria della Pace, which had probably already been the intention of " il Magnifico " since 1512, when the decoration of the loggia was in progress. The recent investigations of Hirst[120] have acutely and exactly defined all the circumstances of this undertaking. Above all, however, they have irrefutably demonstrated that it was ideated by Raphael according to a general project which from the beginning, beyond the decoration of the façade with figurations of the Prophets in the upper part and sybils in the lower zone, provided for the altarpiece with the Resurrection of Christ which, however, Raphael never executed.

167

191 Detail from the Fire in the Borgo. Stanza dell'Incendio.

It is not certain when the Chigi chapel decorations were actually painted. For Vasari the style, "considerably finer and more magnificent than his first" is a further development of the "sweetest manner" of the *Galatea*, owed to Michelangelo's influence "before the chapel of Michelagnolo was opened publicly, though he had seen it." But if this indication would lead precisely to the last phases of the Segnatura, there is also the not improbable interpretation that Vasari is referring to the completion of the Sistine vault, including the lunettes of the *Forebears of Christ*, and therefore to late 1513. This would open the possibility of the dating that the style suggests, precisely between the end of the Segnatura and the execution of the Stanza di Eliodoro, for all of 1512, even though the final finishing touches were protracted into the following year. It does not seem possible, moreover, to go beyond this date, because the rich, ringing Michelangelism of these forms is not discernible in the later parts of the Stanza della Segnatura, but only in the paintings of the vault.

In the paintings of the Chigi Chapel, as in the impetuous visions of the Patriarchs, the language of the Sistine vault is present almost to the point of copying. Indeed, in the drawing now in Stockholm (National Museum),[121] which is a faithful copy of Raphael's first ideation, a figure of the *Forebears of Christ* returns exactly, and further exactly fixes the dating between 1512 and 1513. But in the comparison with its declared source the individuality of Raphael's interpretation emerges all the more, his transposition of that world closed in its own tragedy to the open fantasy of the vision in a convincing lyricism which excels and does not terrify. The powerful plasticity, actuated now by the force of color, expands harmoniously in a musical concatenation of rhythms that moved Vasari to hail this as the "best of his works and the most beautiful among so many others" because it is represented with "great vivacity and perfect coloring." These are the achievements of the time of the Stanza di Eliodoro. Nevertheless the work is only partially Raphael's; in the sibyls and especially in the angels and in the *putto* with a torch which is the "key" of the arch of the figures, there are fragments that are among the

192 Detail from the Fire in the Borgo. Stanza dell'Incendio.

169

193 Detail from the Fire in the Borgo. Stanza dell'Incendio.

195 Detail from the Fire in the Borgo. Stanza dell'Incendio.

194 Detail from the Fire in the Borgo. Stanza dell'Incendio.

most beautiful of this pictorial movement of the great Raphaelesque form. The *putto* is wholly created by the light in the tight plastic knot; the harmonious articulations of the Virtues of the Segnatura are deepened and locked in everywhere. But moments of figural fatigue appear in the Prophets, and they can be referred to collaboration, usually indicated as that of Timoteo Viti. Raphael, having employed all the possible Roman collaborators in the execution of the Stanza di Eliodoro, spurred on by the haste of Julius II, must have had recourse to his old associate in the workshop of Urbino. According to the documents, Viti was absent from Urbino from March 1512 to September 1513 as well as throughout 1514 and up to May 1515.[122] In particular the period of more than one year between 1512 and 1513 seems to be the most probable time for his participation in the execution of Santa Maria della Pace. Nor should this be improbable considering, as has been done, the persistent quattrocento manner of Viti also in his later works. Raphael must have left very little to the initiative of his assistants, in particular when the task, as in this case, was of the most exacting character. Even the most backward had to act in his "bella maniera." Here, more than in the Prophets but also in certain

171

parts of the Sibyls, we note the work of a fastidious brush following the impetus of the drawing, the breadth of the modelled pictorial and the rapid incidence of the light: an arduous labor, moreover, sustained by Raphael's constant intervention.

The theme of the Resurrection developed in the whole of the composition, from the personages to the Greek and Latin inscriptions, selected by a refined culture that was more literary than theological, in addition to the documentary references relative to a projected completion by Sebastiano following Raphael's death, have led Hirst to suppose that the altarpiece, already provided for in the project as a whole, was to feature the Resurrection. Thus a precise reference was given to the whole group of drawings that elaborate this theme and that Hirst would date around 1514, but only on a stylistic basis, although there are powerful references to the *Expulsion of Heliodorus* so as not to make impossible a date closer to this fresco. In these drawings for the first time Raphael's grand style, the " bella maniera " is extended, as Hirst has perceptively noted, to the altarpiece and removes it from its iconic traditions and conventions in order to make of it the heavenly vision that suddenly appears to the faithful. In the beautiful sketch in Bayonne, Christ, as in the *Disputa*, opening his arms to show his pierced hands is borne toward the heavens by a company of exulting angels wheeling in a light which, by the same extremely subtle pen stroke, is intuited as sublime, while below the soldiers throw themselves to the ground in the shadow. Here the figural theme of the Stanza di Eliodoro becomes the point of arrival of a meditation that had had a beginning in the altarpiece painted for the church of Aracoeli at the instance of the papal secretary and great historian of his times, Sigismondo de' Conti: the *Foligno Madonna*.

196 The Battle of Ostia. Vatican, Stanza dell'Incendio.

The altarpiece had been commissioned, but probably also executed, before the death of Conti, February 18, 1512, and perhaps also in the preceding year if we want to find an index in the color which has not yet achieved the freedom of touch of the Stanza di Eliodoro. But here the technique is different; the rapid abbreviation, the broad synthesis of the fresco were to be slowly conquered in oil painting which, on the other hand, had permitted the solid definition of values of the Raphael's portraiture. Below the potent masses of figures form a solid plastic base; above, the intense luminosity of a solar aura, of cherubims barely emerging in the diffused splendor surrounds the appearance of the Virgin, as if the theme of the *Disputa* with its heavenly vision weighing upon the remote terrestrial world is present also within the limits of the altar painting. The connection is given by the *putto*, inspired by the Michelangelesque *putti* among the lunettes of the Sistine, and above all by that landscape lighted by a subtle play of dazzling flashes representing the phosphoric lightning of the meteorite, or projectile, that fell near the house of Conti in Foligno without hitting it and which occasioned this exceptional *ex voto*. This is a landscape so intimately created by light as to have no comparison in Raphael's painting and which indeed has led to the supposition of an intervention by Battista del Dosso in his years

172

197 The Coronation of Charlemagne. Vatican, Stanza dell'Incendio.

of Roman apprenticeship. But if we think of how now Raphael passes from real landscape to fantastic projection also in other works, as in the *Madonna of the Diadem*, and above all in the imaginative luminosities which soon thereafter were to fill the temple of the *Expulsion of Heliodorus*, it becomes less impossible to attribute to him alone even this admirable anticipation in which there is the germ of that which was to have unfolded in the Resurrection. This painting was not finished, however, nor was that commissioned from Sebastiano del Piombo as a substitute for it. From now on there will be only few works totally autographed by Raphael, because fundamental changes were taking place in his artistic and cultural interests. Further, Julius II was no longer present to impose a single direction on Raphael's work, and implicitly, on its development, but now there were the multiple commissions dictated by the cultural eclecticism of Leo X.

LEO X

In 1514 a new period in the life and work of Raphael began. The first two Stanze showed his greatness to all. Even the comparison with Michelangelo was resolved in his favor. Vasari tells us that two parties of critics were emerging: " . . . his friends said his paintings were superior to those of Michelagnolo for beauty of color, excellence in design and grace, and they judged Raphael superior or at least equal to him in painting, but absolutely superior in coloring. " This was why, according to Vasari,[123] Michelangelo took Sebastiano under his wing, thinking that the latter's beautiful Venetian color sustained by his own drawing could reach a higher synthesis than Raphael's. Nevertheless the antagonism between the two artists, which did

198 The Oath of Leo III. Vatican, Stanza dell'Incendio.

not exist when Raphael had placed the likeness of Michelangelo in the *School of Athens*, is amply documented from then on. The attitude of the new Pope, Leo X, contributed to it. The official recognition of Raphael came from him. Whereas Michelangelo, after the Sistine Chapell, was to be utilized by the Medicean Pope for his Florentine initiatives, for the glorification of his family, and was to be taken away once more from his most beloved undertaking, the tomb of Julius II, the highest commissions of the papal seat were to be conferred on Raphael. The decoration of the Stanze is confirmed and continued and, at Bramante's death, Raphael is honored definitively with the lofty post of architect of St. Peter's. After he had worked and collaborated with his friend and protector, since April 1514, the papal brief of August 1, [124] upon Bramante's recommendation as he lay dying, nominates him as his successor "*cum praeter picture artem, qua in arte te excellere omnes homines intelligunt, is a Bramante Architecto etiam in construendis aedibus es habitus.*" The handsome stipend that goes with the commission assures Raphael's well-being and will permit him that "life of a prince" which will place him in the forefront of the most distinguished Roman society. The two letters that he sent in this year to Count Baldassarre Castiglione and to his uncle Ciarla echo this promotion in every field, artistic and social, and of the satisfaction that ensued therefrom. We feel in them the pride of the citizen of Urbino declaring his success to his homeland.

He addresses, almost jokingly, Castiglione, ambassador of the Duke of Urbino to the Curia, as an equal, in a style so cultured and elegant that it makes us rightly suppose that the letter was written, or at least corrected, by Pietro Aretino.[125] It contains the famous declaration thanking the Count for the praises he had lavished on the *Galatea*, explaining that since he could not choose for that beauty among the many beautiful women available, " I follow a certain Idea that hovers before me, living in my mind. I do not know if this has in itself some excellence of art. I strain myself mightily to have it." This declaration has often been invoked in support of the claim that Rapheal had an idealistic esthetic, whereas it should be reduced, rather, to a witty remark reflecting no less than a mode of thought common to the two friends. But this elegant nonchalance is only the frame in which to enclose the real reason for the letter, to announce the commission to St. Peter's: " Our Lord, by honoring me, has placed a great weight on my shoulders. This is the charge of the construction of St. Peter's. " The model, already completed, " is praised by many beautiful minds. " But for Raphael this commission is not only a satisfaction, but solicitation... " I raise myself higher with thought. I would like to find the beautiful forms of the ancient edifices, nor do I know whether the flight will be of Icarus. Vitruvius gives me much light, but not enough. " The uncultured man now tries the vast fields of culture. Painting is already behind him, the consummated conquest that no longer suffices for the artist's commitment. The field of research shifts: if in order to paint a beautiful woman he depends on a " certain Idea " the reasons for that Idea are much more profound, namely the harmony which for the early Renaissance appears as the inner law of the universe. Following in the path of the first Renaissance enunciators, of Brunelleschi and Alberti, Raphael also resumes, patiently, the investigation of classical antiquity, which had raised harmony to a theoretical principle, in the edifices of ancient Rome. Here is still " l'ingegno scorgitore erudito, " which the artist had been for the Renaissance.

The letter to his uncle Ciarla, dated July 1, is marked by an entirely different tone.[126] Here in his crude language, Raphael considers the practical side of the honorific promotion. There is talk of money with the exact objectivity of figures, figures of stipends and of dowries that can come to him from the marriage that Cardinal Bibbiena is proposing to him with one of his nieces, and also figures relative to the undertaking of St. Peter's which is " the largest construction ever seen and which will come to more than a million in gold coin. " There is no talk here of rising higher in thought but of the practical rising in the world. Yet this was the only language that could be spoken to the kinsman back in the province who is requested " to go to the Duke and Duchess and to tell them this news, for they will find it pleasing to know that one of their servants is distinguishing himself. " Alongside the Raphael deified by universal esteem and consideration, here appears Raphael in his everyday humanity, with his apparently niggardly limitations. Yet it was precisely from these limitations, from this continual participation in everyday life, from which that vivifying reality came to the artist that was to drive him further still.

It is from the letter to his uncle that we learn that at that time, in July 1514, work on another Stanza had begun, that later called the *Incendio di Borgo*, " the Fire in the Borgo, " named after one of its principal themes—the intervention of Pope Leo IV who, with a blessing, extinguished the fury of the fire that raged among the small houses around St. Peter's. The lofty ideological program of Julius II was reduced, in his successor, to a self-celebration in which he preferred to impersonate especially the popes who had borne his name. The heights reached by the art of Michelangelo and Raphael thus were replaced by rhetorically celebratory narrations. Raphael's enthusiasm for the decoration of the Vatican rooms must have declined for this reason, as well as because of the commitments of his new commissions and plans. Now he had his expert pupils like Giulio Romano and Penni, who could fluently translate his ideations, and who were in full possession of the language which he had transmitted to them. Their work and that of other assistants, who increasingly worked alongside them, is prevalently discernible in the subsequent Vatican frescoes, be it in the Stanze or in the Loggias. We shall postpone an exhaustive exegesis of this activity to another part of this book. But in this work, and in the most recent particular studies of it, it is rightly recognized that this assiduous " group "

200 Portrait of Cardinal Bibbiena. Florence, Galleria Palatina.

199 St. Peter. Pinacoteca Vaticana.

activity is always carried out according to directives from Raphael. It is to him, and not to his able interpreters that we must refer the further evolution that is read in the very ideation of the frescoes, in their compositional and formal structure, more clearly than elsewhere in the *Fire in the Borgo* where Raphael's autography still exists in many parts.

In this work which for many reasons, specified in the discussion that follows, seems to have been the first to be executed we are very far from the unitary rhythm of the precedent figurations of the Stanze. Indeed the narration seems to fragment itself into innumerable episodes, architectonically no less than figurally. In the precise description of the ancient St. Peter's, of the classical ruins incorporated and scattered among the dense clusters of tiny houses of medieval Rome, there already appears the fruit of that erudite analysis that Raphael was conducting for his dream of an ideal reconstruction of the antique city with the guidance of Vitruvius and of his distinguished commentators such as Marco Fabio Calvo, the learned native of Ravenna with whom he was in correspondence until the end of August 1514 and whom, even later, he held as dear as a father.[127] Even in the scenographic intentions of architecture peopled by the agitated action of the figures, critics have seen a possible influence of Baldassarre Peruzzi, who in that year designed scenery in perspective for the comedy the *Calandria*, by Cardinal Bibbiena. Raphael, outside the frame of the grandiose proposition of the thought of Julius II, seems now to address himself once more to the reality of an immediate happening, even if from now on the words and the syntactic nexuses of his narratives are those that have had the heroic timbre of the classic example. But analogically the color has been intensified, all one with the light through modeling, and lyrical accentuation in its ringing gradations. It is this intense pictorial life that justifies the episodic swarming of the poetic discourse. The *Isaiah*, painted somewhat earlier for the Luxemburger Jan Goritz in Sant'Agostino, had given the example of how it could be enclosed even in a single episode: the Prophet between two festoon-bearing *putti*, the whole dramatic

175

201 The Miraculous Draught of Fishes, Cartoon for the Vatican tapestry. London, Victoria and Albert Museum.

impetus of a Michelangelism totally translated into color. In the *Fire* whole groups are held tightly in that chromatic force and it is those which, isolated in our attention, permit the greatest enjoyment of this work: against the background of the fire, the man who rescues his whole family, modeling himself on the Virgilian Aeneas; or in the center the taut group of *contrapposti*, no less of gestures than of intense yellows, blues, dark reds; or that, without formal ligatures, of the mother who beats her boys in order to spur them to run faster than the fire—a goddess of antiquity, who in her anxiety becomes a woman of the people, the harmonic cadences breaking up in a febrile piling up of rumpled fabrics and disarranged locks of hair. The intervention of artists such as Penni and the very young Giulio Romano, more evident on the right, is discernible everywhere and is eminently skillful and inventive; but in the autographic parts the inventiveness is pictorial power, innovation through which classicality once more descends into the character of everyday life. This is the miracle of the extremely cultured yet popular art of Raphael.

In it, in this phase, the theoretical enunciations of the first Stanza is identified with happening, becomes a mode of life, and permeates all of its circumstances from the most solemn to the most humble. The celebratory themes which Leo X wanted included in the same

202 The Giving of the Keys, or " Pasce oves meas," Cartoon for the Vatican tapestry. London, Victoria and Albert Museum.

176

PLATE XXXIII Madonna and Child with the Infant St. John, called "della Seggiola." Galleria Palatina, Florence.

PLATE XXXIV   Sistine Madonna. Gemäldegalerie, Dresden.

PLATE XXXV   The Fire in the Borgo (detail). Stanza dell'Incendio, Vatican. ▷

PLATE XXXVI-XXXVII   The Fire in the Borgo. Stanza dell'Incendio, Vatican. ▷ ▷

LEO·PP·IIII

PLATE XXXVIII Portrait of a Woman, called "The Veiled Woman" or "The Fornarina." Galleria Palatina, Florence.

203 The Blinding of Elymas, Cartoon for the Vatican tapestry. London, Victoria and Albert Museum.

Stanza, the execution of which was protracted by Raphael's workshop up to 1517, whether they be *Battle of Ostia* the ritual figurations of the *Coronation of Charlemagne*, or the *Justification of Leo III*, are constructed in open rhythms, in which the very architecture follows the articulation of the action, and the loftiest figural dignity comes into being through its coherence, which is painting.

The same ultra-terrestrial vision, the new meaning given by Raphael to the great altarpiece, becomes the immediate transposition in a rhythm of which the classicality from now on is alone the remote generatrix of an actual historicity. We have seen how in the St. Cecilia, commissioned for San Giovanni in Monte in Bologna in 1514 by Blessed Elena Duglioli, the very likeness of the saint, rapturously listening to the celestial music, is permeated with human feelings to the point where she forgets her instrument, the little hand organ, turned upside down, from which the pipes fall. Here Raphael's autograph is reduced to a few elements, perhaps only to the inspired countenances of the Saint, of St. John, of Mary Magdalen. But the very attribution to the executor, probably Giovanni da Udine, of the stupendous still-life of the instruments abandoned on the ground, indicates the intent to humanize the symbol, to give it as foundation the sensitive world where music is something created by man, a subdued echo of the divine harmony, the listening to which nullifies it.

204 The Sacrifice at Lystra, Cartoon for the Vatican tapestry. London, Victoria and Albert Museum.

Raphael's best loved theme, from his first activity in art, namely the Madonna locked in the most passionate knot of affection for her Child, returns once more in this phase as the metaphor of a loftier life. The *Madonna della Seggiola*, now in the Galleria Palatina, is the point of arrival of the theme that had had its poetic stages throughout Raphael's life, from the *Connestabile Madonna*, to that of the *Granduca* and to the *Tempi Madonna*, almost marking the vertex of his conquest. Now, in the full maturity of a language that has exhausted every experience, that woman of the people returns in the robust floridness and even in the multicolor dress of the women of Trastevere, set in a formal rhythm so that her embrace is locked in a vehemence of affection around the extremely vivacious Child. The color welds this interpenetration of forms in the spontaneity of a simple gesture, in which all intellectualizing disappears. If there has been a desire to consider the *Madonna of the Veil*, now in Munich, anterior to this work, almost as a stage to that full achievement, this is due exclusively to the discernment of its poetic incompleteness. The color of the *Madonna of the Veil* is more luminous, ringing, its fusion more technically advanced, not because it was a preparatory stage for a further advancement, but rather an exhaustion of the lyrical inspiration in the process of thinking it over.

On the other hand, lyrical inspiration is raised to an even higher pitch, miraculously, when the brief episode is exalted to the dimension of vision in the *Sistine Madonna*. In my opinion the lengthy controversy on its origins, its dating, and on the destination of this most famous painting has been definitively closed by Düssler: [128] it was probably commissioned by Julius II and intended by him for the Benedictines of San Sisto in Piacenza as a token of appreciation for the city's voluntary annexation to the Papal States.

The altarpiece must not have been finished until later, in 1513 or perhaps in the following year in which, moreover, it was already on the altar when the reconstructed church was consecrated. This must have been its destination from the beginning as proved by its significance as a grandiose "Epiphany," the apparition of the Virgin to the faithful assembled in the church. In this work, desired by his great inspirer Julius II, who himself was to figure in the company of Saints, Raphael worked with the creative enthusiasm of the first Stanze, in the purest declaration of his creativity. Every scenic accessory disappears: the text opens on an immense luminous sky from which the Virgin descends toward the world, placing a foot on the bank of the clouds on which the saints are kneeling. There is no forced modulation in the simple rhythm, only a limpid equilibrium of masses and spaces. There is no classical reminiscence in that generation of the figure from the grand curves of the mantle, from the raiments still waving in the flight. Everything is essential reality. Only the gesture of St. Sixtus and the lowered gaze of St. Barbara link the miraculous apparition to the human multitude that has implored her with prayer. This is still the grand theme of the Stanza di Eliodoro, the theme of the Faith that fulfills itself. This Madonna, maternal, of a universal maternity, in all the loftiness of her glory is still the humanly loving mother clinging closely to her Child, evoked throughout Raphael's life.

206 Detail from the Healing of the Cripple,
Cartoon for the Vatican tapestry.   London,
Victoria and Albert Museum.

By merely looking at this work from the point of view of its essential simplification, we can derive from it a critical conclusion with respect to Raphael's art. In order to convince ourselves of this, all we need is to make the most summary comparison with the *Foligno Madonna* that precedes it. Here even conversation has vanished: Paradise is solely a sublime light, the personages are taken directly from life: a mother with her child, an old priest, a comely young girl, two children as angels. The color does not effuse in subtleties, the modelling of it identifies completely with the form like a welding. A whole infinity of intellectualization is forgotten for this refound naturalism. It is as if the Renaissance, after a century of feverish experimentation, has returned to its first formulations: the "arte naturale," the natural art that Ghiberti said was "brought about" by Giotto.

THE TAPESTRIES

This is the conclusion, this return to "naturalism," to which criticism arrives also with respect to the great cycle that occupied Raphael's mind much more deeply than the decoration of the last Stanze and Loggias of the Vatican in the years between 1513-14 and 1516, that series of colored cartoons for the tapestries that Leo X had executed in Flanders for a display to be exhibited during the solemnities in the Sistine Chapel. The first payment to Raphael on June 15, 1515, attests to the work being already in progress; the last is dated December 2, 1516. Raphael executed them along with his larger commitments in connection with St. Peter's and his studies regarding the restoration of ancient Rome, to which was added, on August 27 of that same year,

207 Raphael and Pupils: Sacra Conversazione (Madonna and Child with the Archangel Raphael, Tobias and St. Jerome), called the "Madonna of the Fish." Madrid, Prado.

180

the job of acquiring for the Fabric of St. Peter's marbles from the ruins of ancient edifices, of supervising the operations and of preventing any further destruction of those edifices. Therefore collaboration was inevitable, as was the consequent question of attribution which will be discussed in another part of this book.

It suffices solely to point out how the ideation of this cycle, entirely by Raphael, is integrated into the framework of that more severe, immediate historicity that was his intent after the Julian Stanze. The subject matter, ten scenes from the lives of SS. Peter, Paul and Stephen taken from the Acts of the Apostles, was also a driving force. Consequently this was a history, and not an embroidery of fantasy in order to allude to contemporary events in antique dress, as in the figurations ordered by Leo X in the new Stanze. It was a history, moreover, in itself essential, concise, agitated in a continuous contact between the first Apostles and the life of men. Three of the cartoons have been lost. The others, acquired by Charles I of England, seemingly on the advice of Rubens, in Brussels where they had remained after the weaving, are today again preserved in the Victoria and Albert Museum, after various vicissitudes. Their execution, extended over at least a year and a half, has posed the problem of chronological sequence, which in terms of stylistic evolution does not seem to accord with the historical sequence of the cycle. Critics, in a general agreement, tend to group in the first period the *Delivery of the Keys*, the *Death of Ananias*, and *Paul on the Areopagus*, and in a second period the *Healing of the Lame Man*, *The Blinding of Elymas*, the *Sacrifice after the Healing of the Cripple at Lystra* and also the cartoons for the *Martyrdom of Stephen*, the *Conversion of Paul*, and the *Imprisonment*. The time at which the *Miraculous Draught of Fishes* was executed has occasioned greater controversies. The succession proposed is probable, but not incontestable. It seems

181

210 Detail from the dome of the Chigi Chapel: God the Father. Rome, Santa Maria del Popolo.

to be based on the greater dramatic tension that the narrative progressively assumes in the groups presumably effected later, from the agitated closing in of the figures as in massive high-reliefs in which the light sets into bold relief revealing "movements of mind" more than figures or faces. But we have seen these knots of drama in Raphael at other times: in the part to the right of the *Disputa*, in the Heraclitus of the *School of Athens*, when Michelangelo's example in the *Genesis* of the Sistine Chapel was immediately at hand. Here Raphael seems to return to the first formulation of the problem of the total resolution in movement of the whole image: the Leonardesque problem enunciated at the time of the now distant *Adoration of the Magi*. Painting as living history is once more the problem of the artist who had resolved infinite problems, forcing him to reconsider in full maturity the whole great research of which it had been the point of arrival. Critics have seen in the *Delivery of the Keys* a recollection of the Masaccio's *Tribute Money*; in the *Miraculous Draught of Fishes* accents of the time of the *Battle of Cascina* resound. Elsewhere, there are echoes of the taut Botticellian groups of the Sistine. No exact citations, but the reflowering of distant recollections in the renewed inspiration. Here, where the "history" has to be narrated and not alluded to or elevated to emblem, we see a return of the great Albertian identification of "storia" as the "somma opera del pittore," the synthesis of the "movement of the mind" which is the action of man on earth. Thus the great teacher, celebrated as an absolute dominant figure in the field of art, consciously presented himself as the ultimate fulfillment of an effort of generations. He added the apostolic history of his tapestries to the historical cycles created by Masaccio, Donatello, and those projected jointly by Leonardo and Michelangelo in the cartoons of the *Battles*.

SANTA MARIA DEL POPOLO

209 Detail from the dome of the Chigi Chapel. Rome, Santa Maria del Popolo.

The execution of the cartoons proceeded together with another undertaking that Raphael was engaged in at the behest of Agostino Chigi, and which brought into play his total experience in the whole field of art. Probably from the time of the *Galatea* and of his works in Santa Maria della Pace, Raphael had projected the architecture and decoration, in its entirety, of the funereal Chapel of the Chigi in the church of Santa Maria del Popolo. But only the cupola must have been completed in 1516, as the inscribed date attests, with its decoration in mosaic executed by the Venetian Luigi De Pace based on drawings by Raphael. It is not our task

182

particularly to discuss this chapel, which is dealt with in the part of this book dedicated to Raphael as architect. But we cannot refrain from making some remarks about it even in our discussion of Raphael as painter. For now that he was in his full maturity, painting was assuming a wholly different meaning which went beyond the limited field commonly assigned to it, as a product of colors and brushes. Now it was the Albertian " pictura " that was realizing itself for him, the theoretical tension inherent in every form, be it constructed, carved or painted. For this reason Raphael, like all the great men of the Renaissance, did not act only in a delimited field of art. In this moment his thought " rose higher." Beauty, raised to a theoretical principle by antiquity, was read not only in the superiorly human image given to it by the gods, but also in the pure abstraction of architectonic form, in the very city where that abstraction adhered to the life of man: classic Rome, which Raphael, at the suggestion of the Humanist Leo X, hoped to restore ideally in its integrity, to see entirely as a work of art.

The Chigi chapel gives us the total synthesis of Raphael's thought, since there the whole complex—the architecture, projected by Raphael, the sculptures executed on the basis of his drawings by Lorenzetto, the colored mosaic of the cupola and, perhaps, also the actual painting of the altarpiece—is resolved in a unity whose significance is that indicated at the and of a lengthy exegetical work by Shearman: [129] in the funerary chapel the passage from time to eternity is expressed, a theme later resumed by Michelangelo in the Medici Chapel of Florence.

It was the last theme that proposed itself alike to the Neo-platonic and Christian syntheses. Here, while the religious synthesis of the Stanza della Segnatura was coming to a close, Raphael " omo sanza lettere " became the most lofty interpreter of the reconciliation between the Platonic Idea and the Christian Revelation proposed by Neo-platonism. The cultural ambience in which Agostino Chigi moved was permeated with this philosophy; from it the " maggiore mercante della cristianità," the " greatest merchant of Christendom," acquired the conception of life as harmony which had inspired the creation of the *Viridarium* where Raphael had placed his *Galatea*. How could this terrestrial joy confront, in serenity of spirit, the last goal? The mausoleum of Santa Maria del Popolo signified the transposition from a terrestrial harmony to a higher harmony without the terror of a final judgment that weighed so awesomely on Michelangelo's entire history of the Sistine Chapel.

Shearman has seen, and rightly I think, in the whole Chigi Chapel the Christianization of the cosmic idea enunciated by Plato in his *Timaeus*, the book that Raphael places in his hands in the *School of Athens*. The soul, created from the same matter of the celestial spheres, returns to them after the temporary imprisonment in the body, the " earthly prison." These celestial spheres, moved by the angels in a fusion of the Beyond of the Dantesque Banquet with its Platonic counterpart, in the vault of the chapel are the last garland of the Godhead, who appears in the open sky in a gesture that Shearman rightly interprets as a gesture of welcome. The tension imprinted on the whole chapel is concluded in the impetus of those upraised arms, in its structure animated by the sculpture and the adornment and perhaps also by the altarpiece which, according to Shearman, was to represent the Assumption of the Virgin.

211-212 Details from the dome of the Chigi Chapel. Rome, Santa Maria del Popolo.

But also this time the work, never brought to completion, was to be substituted by Sebastiano del Piombo with his *Nativity of the Virgin*.

The cupola of the chapel of Santa Maria del Popolo resolved in movement the same perspective exactness of the structures. If its sources are in ancient edifices, as critics have discovered, as in the ideations of Melozzo in Loreto and in the apse of the church of Santi Apostoli, its very tension from which the radial division seems to wheel in the infinite like the spheres moved by the Angels, recalls Donatello in that turning wheel inside his pulpit in Prato, that constitutes its baldacchino.

It required the splendor of the mosaic to diffuse that tension in a resplendent, ultra-real light, the blue and gold of a celestial Paradise. But that light was now at the base of Raphael's vision. From the beautiful drawings that the mosaicist had to translate into his resplendent material, miraculously emerge the broad gestures of the winged figures, the only, essential allusions to their initiation of a movement that shall have no end: the " First Motion " already alluded to in the vault of the Segnatura.

This extreme structural tension that is resolved in a color that is tantamount light, in a sublime " pittura," a race of form towards the luminous, eternal dissolution, will certainly be able to anticipate the most visionary Baroque, but in itself it is but the winged conclusion of the great Renaissance dream: Alberti's "pictura," which is motion, an infinite tension of form which from the abyss of eternity engenders itself in order to return to eternity, the synthesis through image of the whole philosophy of the Renaissance.

THE LAST WORKS

In 1516, when Raphael saw the completion of his work in the Chigi Chapel, ideated several years earlier, he must not have felt it as alien, if even his painting, in the *Sistine Madonna* and the apostolic histories of the tapestries, had gone in a different direction. The " Beyond " of the chapel was the point of arrival of a historicity that was directing the whole effort of its drama thereto, and from which goal it received a higher dignity. But this history from now on could be only that of the Apostles, of the Martyrs, illuminated by the loftiest finality. All the rest receded in the distance, incapable of stirring the artist's inspiration, whether it was the rhetorical celebration of the Vatican chambers or the classical fable which Agostino Chigi once more called upon him to evoke in his suburban villa: the fable of Psyche as it had been narrated by the fanciful Apuleius. Raphael was to translate it into images, dividing it into episodes, enclosing all his rhythmic sapience within it. But only his pupils were to translate it in color. The informers of Michelangelo, then in Florence, could stigmatize it with ill-concealed satisfaction, on January 1518, as a " thing vituperous to a great master, much worse than the last room of the palace." [130]

But the censure was directed at the pupils. The " great master " was elsewhere, absorbed in his dream of restoring life to ancient Rome, the pure mirror of classical antiquity. " Romam in Roma querit reperitque Raphael / Querere magni hominis sed reperire Dei est," sang the poet and apostolic pronotary Celio Calcagnini. [131] In the letter of 1519 to Leo X he will expound the method, but he will also betray enthusiasm over his " querere " and " reperire." The assiduous research was often gladdened by discovery and this, not the fable of the literati,

214 Portrait of a Young Man. Formerly in Cracow, Czartoryski Museum.

could still nourish his fantasy. Fresh pictorial inventions, which at first he had known only from the colorless marble of the sculptors, emerged from the " Grotte " chambers submerged in the earth for centuries. This vivid fantasy of forms inspired in him delightful " grotesques," the cupids, dragons, snails, and butterflies in the frame of brief mythological fables with which in 1516 he decorated the small bathroom, or Stufetta, of Cardinal Bibbiena in the Vatican. [132] He brought this same droll escapist figuration as a fanciful contour to the narratives of the events of the Old and the New Testaments in the Loggias of the Vatican Palace, probably executed between 1516 and 1519, to which the Loggetta, with allegories of the Seasons, also executed in 1519, was contemporary. But that which was called the " Bible of Raphael " was only his for the general program, and the ideation of several scenes. The execution and, perhaps, also this time, the invention was the work of a band of pupils and followers who are discussed in the section dealing with Raphael's workshop. They demonstrate how the great language could become the " vulgar " tongue, accessible to all, capable of historical narration, but also of the most popular and entertaining poetic recreation. The Bible was narrated to the people, it became the sequence of animated episodes, a popularization without problems, a melodrama and not history. But this, too, was an aspect of Raphael's art, of his communicability, of the colloquy with the public that he accepted without disdain, the man whose nature was " so full of gentleness and love," as Vasari writes, and who throughout his life gave an example of how to be " courteous alike to the upper, the middle and the lower classes." His art was dedicated to the totality of men.

And men, the actors of his sublime " Storia " were his field of experiment, incessant also in the higher maturity which his art had achieved in those years which were to be his last. Those superb human images that were never to be surpassed extend over the time span be-

216 Holy Family with St. Elizabeth, the Infant St. John and two Angels, called the " Madonna of Francis I. " Paris, Louvre.

187

tween about 1516 and 1520. In them his epoch, as is his life, is reflected in its entirety. It is the woman tenderly loved, idealized in the late Madonnas, the famous Fornarina, who appears to us in her florid beauty veiled like a saint, ornamented like a queen in that sumptuous raiment of white silk and gold, which corrugates into a convulsive plasticity, incredibly taut like that which grasps entire multitudes in the cartoons for the tapestries. This plastic furor is attenuated in the other portrait of this woman, now in the Galleria Nazionale in Rome, in which the light penetrates directly, modelling her as in marble in the florid flesh-tones, anticipating Titian, but also in which the interventions of Giulio Romano must have frozen, especially in the face, the pictorial enthusiasm. The portrait remained unfinished at the time of Raphael's death. Next to the beloved woman were his friends: especially the learned gentleman, Baldassarre Castiglione, in the portrait in the Louvre, where a shadow of a smile, more enigmatic than that of Leonardo's *Gioconda*, suffices to allude to the open cordiality of the great Humanist, and all its subtle light is in the silvery grey velvet of the raiment. In April 1513 Raphael went on an excursion to Tivoli with Castiglione, Bembo, two Venetian literati and poets, Andrea Navagero and Agostino Beazzano, in order to see, writes Bembo,[133] " the old and the new, and what is beautiful in that countryside ": a gathering of learned men and poets in front of the relics of the classicism to which Raphael wanted to give new life. Critics have thought to recognize the images of the two Venetians in the *Double Portrait of Two Friends* in the Doria Gallery in Rome. But it seems to us to be two different portraits, executed by the pupils and not by the master, that are brought together in this format, copies of the separate versions of which are in the Prado: one, the bearded man, heroic in the emphasis of the pose and of the fabrics, is modelled in the color which in the original we can presume was as intensified as in the Fornarina; the other is more subdued and human, also in the powerfully sculptured tension in the broad sleeve. The color is that live mass in which Raphael was now digging out his forms with a brush that had the strength of a scalpel. We find a similar sculpture of color in the portrait of Cardinal Bibbiena, admirer of the " divine " Raphael to the point of wanting to bring him into the family, in the bust, in the Galleria Palatina in Florence, moulded with Berninian impetuousness in the bright red of the cardinal's vestment. In a style that intensified every reality of form and substance, the likenesses of men who now surrounded him, the heroes of culture were placed on an equal footing with the potentates. There has been tendency to recognize Francesco Maria della Rovere, up to 1516 the Duke of Urbino, in the Czartorisky portrait of a young man of a beauty that is almost feminine, but cruel. But even if the identification is rejected today it is still the typical image of a lord of the cinquecento, refined and ethically insensible, in this face that looks at us contemptuously from the chromatic glory of the rich vestments. These red velvets streaked with light shond have been the plastic-pictorial protagonists of the portrait of Joanna of Aragon (now in the Louvre), the terms of contrast, perhaps, with a pallid spectral face, if this idea had not lost its poetic vigour in the almost total translation of the assistant, perhaps Penni. Even in portrait of Bindo Altoviti, the young banker, although it is delicately poetic to the degree that it recalls the Urbino portraits and the early self-portrait of Raphael in the Uffizi, nevertheless has a descriptive insistence that bespeaks the intervention of a collaborator albeit expert. But wholly Raphael's at least in its essential part, is the most sublime of these portraits, the point of arrival not only of portraiture but of the painting of all time, that of Pope Leo X, now in the Uffizi, a universal image which gathers all history in that which dominated it through its high authority. The son of Lorenzo il Magnifico is caught in his entire personality as

217 Venus and Cupid, in a spandrel of the Loggia of Psyche. Rome, Villa Farnesina.

218 Cupid and the Graces, in a spandrel of the Loggia of Psyche. Rome, Villa Farnesina.

pope and man. Nothing is attenuated in the deformity of the countenance, yet the consciousness
of a higher dignity enobles it. The beautiful, sensitive Medici hands rest on things of a refined
beauty—the pages of a subtly illuminated book, a tiny bell of the most refined workmanship,
Values are assiduously sought for in order to signify the intimate history of inanimate things
themselves: the sphere of the back of the chair, which like a lucid mirror collects all the
light of the room in penumbra, a frayed silken tassle wore by time, the velvet of the mantle
that creases in rigid folds on the softness of the damask. Everything is an infinite play of light
revealing the vital movement that joins men and things: the majestically alive texture of which
history is woven. And of these values, which are the purest pictorial values, gradations of
reds, from the vermillion of the carpet to the carmine background of the mantle, to the reddish-
ness of the flesh-tones, which fill the whole space and follow its oblique perspective tension, a
bringing together of this perfect equilibrium in the process of becoming. Here Raphael, painter,
acts in the totality of art: he constructs, models, paints in order to grasp, without arresting it,
the image of the historical actuality of existence. The head of Christendom, who did not
have the great mind of Julius II, is his equal in the higher dignity of the history evoked by
Raphael.

The artist was then meditating in the creative fullness on that which he did not know was
destined to be his last work: the *Transfiguration*, the great altarpiece commissioned in 1517
by Cardinal Giulio de' Medici, who at the same time had ordered the *Raising of Lazarus* from
Sebastiano del Piombo. For the Venetian it was the coveted opportunity to compete with
Raphael. From a letter of Leonardo Borgherini to Michelangelo, then in Florence, dated
January 19, 1517[134] it seems that Raphael obstructed Sebastiano's commission; but surely not
for the reason, as Borgherini insinuates " per non venire a paraghoni " " to avoid comparison."
Rather, we can suppose he did so because of the consciousness of his uniqueness which made

220 School of Raphael: Raphael and His Fencing
Master (?). Paris, Louvre.

221 School of Raphael: Portraits of Andrea
Navagero and Agostino Beazzano. Rome,
Galleria Doria-Pamphili.

190

it almost humiliating for him to compare himself with anyone else. Anyhow Raphael worked slowly, because of his great task in connection with the restoration of ancient Rome, and by those tasks that were requested of him from all sides. From the documents we know of his continuous delay from 1517 onward regarding the request from Alfonso I d'Este, Duke of Ferrara for a *Triumph of Bacchus* to be placed alongside the mythological paintings of Gian Bellino and Titian in the "camerini d'alabastro" the "little rooms of alabaster," in the Ferrarese castle. Even the works destined for the King of France, the *St. Michael* and the *Holy Family*, now in the Louvre, dated from 1517 to 1518, in view of the urgency of the Pope's solicitations and those of the Duke of Urbino, Lorenzo de' Medici, were left totally to the execution of his pupils. The painter's thought was far from them, absorbed as he was in the research of ancient Rome, of which, in 1519, he gave a programmatic exposition in the famous letter to Leo X, and of the *Transfiguration* which he alone was executing, meditating on it slowly while Sebastiano worked feverishly in order "to arrive first" with his *Raising of Lazarus*.

It was in fact the theme in which he glimpsed the synthesis of his whole artistic thought: the most dramatic reality that "transfigured" itself in vision. The discontinuity that critics have chosen to see between the two parts of the painting, the lower part gloomily suffused with shadows, the upper part resplendent with light, is instead the sublime dialectic of the image which would have declared itself whole if it had not been slowed by the intervention which, as always was also incomprehension, of the assistant who finished it. If we suppress the lower part on the right, the episode of the boy possessed, totally painted by Giulio Romano, up to

222 Portrait of the Fornarina. Rome, Galleria Nazionale.

223 The Finding of Moses, in the eighth vault
of the Vatican Loggias.

the sutures badly completed in the center, the admirable poetic coherence of Raphael's ideation will appear to us in its totality. It is amazing that Vasari himself, who was such an acute
exegetist of Raphael's work, could have disapproved of the dark shadows of the lower group,
and suggest that the colors would not have become faded " if he had not employed printers
lampblack, through some caprice, which darkens with time . . . and spoils the other colors with
which it is mixed." But in Vasari's time no one had yet ventured to resolve the whole chromatic
relationship in that extreme solution of the densest shadow in the brightest light. No one,
save for Leonardo, in his *Adoration*. There still was no Caravaggio to assume precisely this
Raphaelesque consummation of that intuition as the foundation of a new painting. Instead,
it is possible for us to rejoin it ideally with the first Renaissance propositions, those of Donatello and of Leonardo who had seen light as the revealer of form from the primordial chaos of
shadow and had made of this effort at liberation the theme of their art. It had also been the
theme of Michelangelo and of Raphael in their mature phases, in which the intuition of art
became consciousness, the foundation of a whole interpretation of the existent, and in which

224 The Burning Bush, in the eighth vault of
the Vatican Loggias.

earthly life with its individualization and incessant trasformation appeared only as a brief moment of infinite eternity, caught in human time. Both had lived in their work of expression the life of their own epoch in its entirety, going back to the first, essential enunciations. And just as Michelangelo, in his later Pietàs, was to arrive at the total dissolution of form to its genetic energy alone, so did Raphael, at the apogee of his expressive conquest, reach this suggestion, this primordial emergence from formless darkness. The plastic tension of the mother in the *Massacre of the Innocents* which became the flashing gesture of a white hand of light in order to drag a whole khot of tenebrous, interlaced plasticity toward the effused brightness where the form itself dissolved, was only a light allusion: the fugitive touch of the brush in the countenance of Christ.

On Holy Saturday, 1520 "at the head of the dead man, in the room where he worked, they put the *Transfiguration*," unfinished, Raphael had died on the previous night between April 6 and 7, on Good Friday; as he had been born thirty-seven years before on Good Friday. Vasari tells us [135] " the sight of the dead and of this living work filled all who saw them with poignant sorrow."

The sudden departure from this world of him who seemed to be the very incarnation of art filled those around him with terror. It looked like a sign from Heaven that the Vatican Loggias during those days threatened to collapse; Marcantonio Michiel writes " it was a miraculous sign due to the decease of him who gave to the Loggias their decoration." He was laid to rest in

225 The Baptism of Constantine. Vatican, Sala di Costantino.

the Pantheon, and Bembo wrote the epitaph. But that learned Latin does not achieve the loftiness of Vasari's simple vernacular: " With the death of this admirable artist painting might well have died also, for when he closed his eyes she was left all but blind . . . It is indeed to him that the arts, coloring and invention have all been brought to such perfection that further progress can hardly be expected, *and it is unlikely that anyone will ever surpass him.*"

[1] For the extremely vast literature on Raphael and his time readers are referred to the article *Raphael* by O. Fischel in *Thieme-Becker, Künstler-Lexikon*, Leipzig, 1907-1950, vol. XXIX (1935), and to that by A. M. Brizio in *Enciclopedia Universale dell'Arte*, vol. XI, Venice-Rome (1963).

We shall give the complete titles of the fundamental works, the only ones cited in the brevity of the present " outline." In the following notes only the name of the author will be given, followed by the abbreviation indicated in square brackets next to the titles when more than one work refers to him: G. Vasari, *Le Vite* (1568), edited by G. Milanesi, Florence 1878-85, passim; Quatremère de Quincy, *Histoire de la vie et des ouvrages de Raphaël*, Paris 1824; L. Pungileoni, *Elogio storico di Raffaello Santi da Urbino*, Urbino 1829; J. D. Passavant, *Raphael von Urbino und sein Vater Giovanni Santi*, Leipzig 1839-1858; G. B. Cavalcaselle and J. A. Crowe, *Raffaello, la sua vita e le sue opere*, 3 vols., Florence 1884-1891; E. Müntz, *Raphaël, sa vie, son œuvre et son temps*, Paris 1900; L. von Pastor, *Storia dei Papi dalla fine del Medioevo* (Ital. ed.), vols. III and IV, Rome 1925-26; O. Fischel, *Raphaels Zeichnungen*, 4 vols., Berlin 1913-1923 [Fischel, Diss.]; A. Venturi, *Raffaello*, Rome 1920 [Venturi, Raff.]; id., *Storia dell'Arte Italiana*, vol. IX, *La pittura del Cinquecento*, P. 11, Milan 1926, pp. 1-336 [Venturi, St. A.]; C. Gamba, *Raphaël*, Paris 1932; O. Fischel, article *Santi, Raffaello* cited in *Thieme-Becker*, vol. XXIX, Leipzig 1935 [Fischel ThB.]; id., *Raphael*, 2 vols., London 1948 [Fischel, R.].

226 Detail from the Transfiguration: The mother of the boy possessed by the devil. Pinacoteca Vaticana.

For documentary citations, when there is no particular indication in the footnote, the reference is always to the complete collection that has been made of them by V. Golzio, *Raffaello nei documenti, nelle testimonianze dei contemporanei e nella letteratura del suo secolo*, Vatican City 1936. They are indicated in order of date.

For the literature and the questions relative to the single works, either of Raphael or Perugino, the reference, save in cases of divergent opinion, specified from time to time, is to the critical listings of the complete works in: E. Camesasca, *Tutta la pittura del Perugino*, Milan 1959 [Camesasca, *Perugino*]; id., *Tutta la pittura di Raffaello*, 2 vols., 2d ed., Milan 1952 [Camesasca, *Raff.*]; P. L. De Vecchi, in: *L'opera completa di Raffaello*, Milan 1966; L. Dussler, *Raffael*, Munich 1966.

Only the works of the most certain attribution are cited in the text. We have neglected those around which the greatest controversies rage, since we could not deal with the questions relative to them within the present limits.

[2] The *Cronica di G. Santi* is published in Passavant's work. For the relative passages, see vol. III, p. 310 ff.

[3] The hypothesis of an apprenticeship with Viti, formulated by Müntz and by Schmarsow, was already disproved by Cavalcaselle, I, p. 33 ff.

[4] R. Longhi, *Percorso di Raffaello giovine*, in "Paragone" 1955, no. 65, p. 11 ff.

[5] F. Canuti, *Il Perugino*, Siena 1931, pp. 23 and 146 ff.

[6] Fischel, Diss. I, 5-10 and Castelfranco, *Raffaello*, in: *I grandi maestri del disegno*, ed. Martello, Milan 1962, nos. 1-6.

[7] Ashmolean Mus. 515. Cf. Castelfranco, *op. cit.*, no. 7, who, however, would date it later.

[8] G. Dalli Regoli, *Lorenzo di Credi*, Cremona 1966, Plates 114..., 125..., 126..., 105.

[9] *Ibid.*, Plates 85 and 79. For the paintings cited successively cf. Plates 107..., 97..., 93.

[10] B. Degenhart, *Di alcuni problemi di sviluppo della pittura nella bottega del Verrocchio, di Leonardo e di Lorenzo di Credi*, in "Rivista d'Arte," XIV, 1932, pp. 263-300 and 403-444, and Dalli Regoli, *op. cit.*, pp. 147-148.

227 Detail from the Transfiguration: The Apostles.
Pinacoteca Vaticana.

[11] L. B. Alberti, *Della Pittura* (critical ed. by L. Mallè, Florence 1950).

[12] Dalli Regoli, *op. cit.*, p. 60.

[13] S. Ortolani, *Raffaello*, Bergamo 1942, p. 16; G. Castelfranco, *op. cit.*, p. 8.

[14] Fischel, *R.*, German ed., Berlin 1962, passim.

[15] For the entire question see Camesasca, *Perugino*, pp. 76-77.

[16] Cavalcaselle, I, p. 37 ff.

[17] E. Carli, *Il Pintoricchio*, Milan 1960, p. 12 "...I am not certain of Pint, nor of the minor collaborators... figures such as the mighty Angel with the unsheathed sword and the group of the Circumcision, especially the women, and in the Baptism... the stupendous seated youth who is undressing himself, etc."

[18] Longhi, *op. cit.*, p. 14.

[19] Longhi, *op. cit.*, p. 19 ff. The *Resurrection* in São Paulo, Brazil (formerly Kinnaird coll.) is not directly known to us, and consequently we share Dussler's doubts as regards attribution, p. 71, no. 124. As for the *Resurrection* in the Vatican Pinacoteca we agree with Cavalcaselle (I, pp. 90-92) who attributes the lower part with the sleeping guards and the sarcophagus to Raphael.

[20] Cavalcaselle (I, pp. 37-38) refers the greater stylistic robustness of the *Assumption* to the influence of the young Raphael on Perugino, though not excluding his hand for the portrait of the monk Blasio (Uffizi), referred to his predella, but not with total agreement. Fischel (*R.*, p. 21, and ThB.), on the other hand, admits collaboration in the altarpiece which, on the basis of an attentive direct reading, we consider even more extensive.

[21] For the question of the frescoes of the Cambio see Camesasca, *Perugino*, p. 80 ff. Here Raphael's participation is denied whereas, on the other hand, it had been maintained by A. Venturi (St. A., VII, 1913, p. 764 and p. 824 ff). But we believe

228 Detail from the Transfiguration: St. John.
Pinacoteca Vaticana.

that this question, which is a closed one for many critics, should be reopened because of the strong collaboration, and also the strong qualitative discrepancies that are noted in the decoration of the Cambio. Fischel (*R.*, p. 21) admits the collaboration, but limits the extension given to it by Venturi.

[22] R. Wittkover, *The young Raphael*, in "Allen Memorial Art Mus. Bull." vol. XX, 1963, no. 3, pp. 150-168.

[23] Camesasca, *Perugino*, pp. 71-76 . . .

[24] F. Canuti, *op. cit.*, vol. II, p. 258, doc. 430 "... prout tabula Mag.cae Alexandrae... de Oddis " in S. Francesco of Perugia.

[25] Fischel, Diss. I, 15, 32.

[26] Vasari, IV, p. 318.

[27] Golzio, pp. 7-8.

[28] Fischel, Diss. I, 6.

[29] Benedetto Dei. Cronaca ms. Florence, Bibl. Riccardiana, cod. 1853.

[30] Vasari, IV, pp. 117, 118, no. 1 (with doc. relative to the execution of the *Judgment* in 1499).

[31] The pulpit had been completed in 1476-77. V. W. Paatz, *Die Kirchen von Florenz*, Frankfurt a. M., 1940, I, p. 68.

[32] Golzio, pp. 11-14. The docs., that is the contract and the first payments, are dated December 12, 22 and 23, 1505. The list of the places is in the first (p. 13). *Ibid.*, on pp. 8-9 there is the passage from the " Liber reformationis " ms. of the monastery where it is said in 1503 the Abbess, Suor Chiara de' Mansueti, had found ." el Maestro el migliore " (" the best Master "), advised " by several citizens and also by our Venerable Fathers " " who is called Maestro Raffaello da Urbino. " The *Coronation* was completed only after Raphael's death, by his pupils.

[33] Carli, *op. cit.*, p. 61.

[34] Vasari, IV, p. 319, and III, p. 494.

[35] Fischel, Diss. II, 60-65 and relative text. Note how the very beautiful, luminous landscape of the Contini-Bonacossi drawing has been translated without comprehension in the fresco, interpolating a group of houses in it. It may be that the Leonardesque horses suggested to Vasari the indication, although chronologically erroneous, that Raphael had heard in Siena about " a fine group of horses " in the *Battle of Anghiari*, which work, moreover, was not yet in progress.

[36] Fischel, *R.*, pp. 22-23.

[37] Vasari, III, p. 576; Camesasca, *Perugino*, p. 147, furnishes information about Perugino's activity in Siena, the results of which, unfortunately, are almost totally lost.

[38] Golzio, pp. 19-20 (text and summary of the question); F. Filippini, *Raffaello a Bologna*, in: *Cronache d'Arte*, II, fasc. 5, September-October 1925, pp. 201-234. Filippini, moreover, would have Raphael arriving in Bologna on the occasion of the triumphal entry of Julius II on November 11, 1506, which is neither proved nor probable. Malvasia, *Felsina Pittrice*, 1678 (edited by G. P. Zanotti, Bologna 1841), I, p. 47, recalled a Nativity Scene by Raphael in Bologna in the house of Giovanni Bentivoglio, hence before the latter's expulsion in 1506. The drawing of which the artist speaks in the letter to Francia is called " very different " from one that he had previously praised. Was it Bentivoglio's?

[39] Vasari, III, pp. 545-547. Raphael assertedly entered into an epistolary relationship with Francia through several Bolognese gentlemen who had spoken about him in Rome, and he is supposed to have turned to him for the placing of the *St. Cecilia* in 1514. The old artist is supposed to have been so shaken in the face of the breathtaking novelty of Raphael's art that he died as the result of his upset. But the account seems to be a fictional amplification, on the part of Vasari, of the actual data on Raphael's relationships with Bologna. For other works which he sent to Bologna, about which nothing else is known, cf. Malvasia and Filippini, *locc. cit.* Malvasia also published a laudatory sonnet of Francia to Raphael, which others reject. It contains the well-known verses: " Tu sol cui fece il Ciel dono fatale / Che ogn'altro eccede..." (" Thou alone to whom Heaven made the fatal gift, that surpasses all others ") and " Fortunato Garxon, che nei primi anni / Tant'oltre passi..." (" Fortunate youth who in your first years, pass so far beyond..."); these are indices of the early fame of the artist (published in: Golzio, p. 333).

[40] For the Oratory see D. Scaglietti, *La Cappella di Santa Cecilia*, in: " Il Tempio di San Giacomo Magg. in Bologna ," Bologna 1967, pp. 133-142. It seems that San Giacomo also contained, from around 1496, Perugino's *Madonna in Glory*, now in the Pinacoteca Nazionale of Bologna. Cf. Camesasca, *Perugino*, p. 66, no. 78.

[41] Camesasca, *Raffaello, Quadri*, pp. 40-41, no. 37.

[42] Venturi, St. A., VII, p. 871, fig. 639.

[43] C. Volpe, " Due questioni raffaellesche," in *Paragone* 75, March 1956, pp. 3-18.

[44] For the altarpiece of Pesaro, and its probable dating around 1474, cf. G. Robinson, *Giovanni Bellini*, Oxford 1968, p. 66 ff. For Raphael's drawings that recall it cf. Fischel, Diss. 384 (very late).

[45] For the text and relative questions cf. Golzio, pp. 9-10.

[46] Vasari, *La Vita di Michelangelo*, edited by Paola Barocchi, Milan-Naples 1962, 5 vols., II, p. 248, nos. 193 and 194.

[47] Fischel, Diss. II, 80. Fischel also notes the rapid impression made by this Leonardesque design and not Raphael's study of it.

[48] *Ibid.*, text, pp. 87-126 and relative plates.

[49] Fischel, *Die Zeichnungen der Umbrer*, in "Jahrbuch d. Königl. Preusz. Kunstsamml.", XXXVIII, 1917, Teil II, *Das Venet. Skizzenbuch*, p. 85 ff,. with reproductions of all the drawings and previous bibliographies.

[50] Cavalcaselle, I, pp. 15 and 18: Elisabetta supposedly invited G. Santi to Mantova to do a portrait of Lodovico Gonzaga. *Id.*, pp. 204-205. After December 1504, while Guidobaldo, having become a captain general of the Church, resided in Rome,

the duchess remained in Urbino and, in the Carnival season, she had an allegorical play staged depicting the invasion and the expulsion of Cesare Borgia from the duchy. According to Cavalcaselle Raphael's *St. Michael* also alluded to it.

[51] Vasari, III, p. 544.: " A pair of caparisons painted by him for the Duke of Urbino increased his reputation marvellously. In these he represented a great forest which has caught fire, and out of it come all manner of birds and beasts, with some remarkable figures agitated by fear. "

[52] Cavalcaselle, I, p. 285 ff.: Guidobaldo in 1506 received in Rome from the ambassadors of Henry VII of England the insignia of the Order of the Garter. The investiture took place in Urbino on April 23. In the following July, Baldassarre Castiglione went to London in order to present to the King Raphael's *St. George*, now in Washington.

[53] For the relative questions see Camesasca, *Perugino*, pp. 106-109. Gamba, *op. cit.*, p. 37.

[54] Cavalcaselle, I, 244.

[55] A. De Rinaldis, *Storia dell'opera pittorica di L. da Vinci*, Bologna 1926, pp. 231-232.

[56] E. Panofsky, *Herkules am Scheidewege*, in " Studien Bibl. Warburg," XVIII, Leipzig 1930.

[57] For the events and questions relative to these portraits, see Dussler, pp. 33-34, nos. 44 and 45.

[58] The identification proposed here will be more amply demonstrated in a particular study. The medallion of Bembo, young and still beardless, is that by Valerio Belli, reproduced in C. von Fabriczy, *Medaillen der Ital. Renaiss.*, Leipzig n.d., p. 97. The passage from Michiel (*Der Anonimo Morelliano*, edited by T. Frimmel, Vienna 1888, p. 20) recalls in Bembo's house in Padova " The portrait of this Messer Pietro Bembo when as a youth he was in the court of the Duke of Urbino was by the hand of Raphael of Urbino in m...ata." Frimmel interprets the abbreviation to mean " in miniature " which would correspond to the " ritratto piccolo, " the small portrait. It could have been the copy of a larger one, namely the one in question, whose identification moreover is based on its iconographic and stylistic correspondence with the portrait of Guidobaldo in the Uffizi, which is also referable to the years 1505-1506, when Bembo was repeatedly in Urbino where he finally remained for six years. Cf. article (Dionisotti) in: *Dizionario Biograf. degli Italiani*, vol. VIII, Rome 1966.

[59] Dussler, pp. 31-32, no. 40. For the period of Elisabetta's regency in 1504-1505, in Guidobaldo's absence, cf. footnote 50.

[60] Volpe, *op. cit.*, in *Paragon*, 1956.

[61] Vasari, V, p. 350.

[62] Vasari-Barocchi, *Vita di M. A.* cit., II, p. 248 ff., no. 194.

[63] Gamba, *op. cit.*, p. 44 and ff.

[64] Golzio, pp. 15-16.

[65] *Ibid.*, pp. 18-19.

[66] For every circumstance relative to this work see A. Riedl, *Raffaels " Madonna del Baldacchino,"* in *Mitteil. des Kunsthist. Institutes in Florenz*, vol. VIII (May 1959), pp. 223-245.

[67] Golzio, pp. 370 and 22.

[68] Cf. notes 38 and 65.

[69] Cf. Golzio, p. 14 " *1507, Stanze del Vaticano* ": Julius II had gone to live in the chambers above in order to avoid those formerly inhabited by his execrated predecessor Alexander Borgia.

[70] Cavalcaselle, II, pp. 5-6; Fischel, *R.*, p. 70.

[71] A. Condivi, *Vita di Michelangelo* (Florence 1927), p. 45.

[72] Filippini, *op. cit.* for all the Bolognese information. For the drawing of the Nativity Scene, Fischel, Diss. 361.

[73] Vasari, II, 492; Golzio, p. 21, Signorelli's activity is attested only by Vasari (IV, 329-330).

[74] Golzio, p. 192.

[75] For every question relating to the Stanzas, but especially to their iconological interpretation, see besides Vasari L. von Pastor, III, pp. 783-832 (with a broad review of the preceding bibliography); F. Hartt, " The Stanze d'Eliodoro and the Sixtine ceiling " in: *Art Bulletin* XXXIII, 1950, pp. 115-145; E. Wind, " Typology in the Sixtine ceiling," Ibid., XXXIII, 1951, pp. 41-47; Fischel, *R.*, pp. 70-109; S. J. Freedberg, *Painting of the High Renaiss. in Rome and Florence*, Cambridge, Mass. 1961, pp. 112-133, 151-166 and 293-312; A. M. Brizio, article in *Encicl. Univers. d. Arte*; D. Redig De Campos, *Le Stanze di Raffaello*, Rome 1966; Dussler, pp. 78-98.

[76] Condivi, *op. cit.*, p. 101; Vasari-Barocchi, cit., II, p. 432 (from a letter of Michelangelo of 1542).

[77] Cavalcaselle, II, pp. 67-68.

[78] G. L. Mellini, *Raffaello: Le Stanze Vaticane (Forma e Colore)*, Florence 1965.

[79] A. Chastel, *Art et Humanisme à Florence*, Paris 1961, pp. 470-474.

[80] Pastor, III, p. 811.

[81] Fischel, *R.*, p. 81 ff.

[82] Cavalcaselle (II, p. 25, no. 1) cites from Richardson (1754) the information that a letter of Raphael to Ariosto, requesting advice for defining the personages of the *Disputa*, was supposed to have been seen in Rome at that time.

[83] Fischel, Diss. 258 (Windsor), 259-60 (Oxford).

[84] See the part relative to Raphael's drawings in the present vol. (A. Forlani Tempesti, Chap. III).

[85] Vasari, IV, p. 334; Fischel, *R.*, p. 88 ff.

[86] Vasari, VII, p. 489.

[87] For the questions of attribution cf. Dussler, p. 81.

[88] Castelfranco, *Raffaello*, cit., no. 38, pp. 18-19.

[89] Vasari, IV, pp. 339 340. It is not clear, however, to what precise moment the anecdote refers. For the relations between Raphael and Michelangelo, cf. Vasari-Barocchi, cit., II, pp. 262-266, 429-437 and 437-441.

[90] Vasari, V, p. 433 ff.

[91] Dussler, p. 83.

[92] L. B. Alberti, *Della Pittura*, ed. cit., pp. 101-102.

[93] Fischel, Diss. 282 (Louvre), 287 (Montpellier).

[94] Pastor, *op. cit.*, III, p. 646, for the return of the Pope to Rome. The cardinal on the right is identical to that portrait with the extensive intervention of assistants in the painting on wood now in Naples, Capodimonte (Fig. 168).

[95] Golzio, pp. 24, 26-28.

[96] Pastor, *op. cit.*, III, p. 766. The journeys took place in September 1510 and in January 1511.

[97] Vasari-Barocchi, II, no. 426, pp. 426-428.

[98] Golzio, pp. 22-23; Fischel, *R.*, pp. 176-177.

[99] It is the Madonna in the Galleria Borghese (Dalli Regoli, *op. cit.*, figs. 85 and 79).

[100] The identification was sustained with valid arguments by Müntz " Il ritratto del Card. Alidosi di Raff." in *Arch. Stor. d. Arte*, IV, 1891, pp. 328-332) and resumed by Filippini, *op. cit.*, pp. 221-222. We see no reason to doubt it, all the

more so because it also agrees with an ancient indication in a catalogue of the Prado. The arguments presented by Fischel (*R.*, p. 112) to identify him with Ippolito d'Este are much more vague; he is followed by Dussler (pp. 45-46, no. 76) who, moreover, points out, as Gamba had already done (*op. cit.*, p. 68) the identification of the personage with the bishop on the left, in the lower part of the *Disputa*. For the personality and tragic death of Alidosi, see Pastor, *op. cit.*, passim and especially III, pp. 637-638.

[101] For the relative questions cf. Camesasca, p. 65 (plate 125) and Dussler, p. 29, no. 35. There is no iconographic correspondence with the medallion of Cardinal Alidosi: only an echo of the emblem of Jove, assumed by him, which could have had repercussions in the Bolognese ambience.

[102] Pastor, III, p. 723.

[103] This is also Dussler's opinion, p. 87, relative to the document of which cf. D. Redig De Campos, in: *Miscell. Bibl. Hertz.*, Vienna 1961, p. 194.

[104] Pastor, III, p. 681.

[105] Cf. note 73.

[106] Vasari-Barocchi, II, pp. 426-428, no. 335, and p. 443, no. 344. The vault of the Sistine was totally unveiled on the eve of All Saints Day of 1512.

[107] Dussler, p. 88, for the entire question.

[108] Louvre 3853. Cf. Castelfranco, cit., p. 21, no. 59.

[109] Pastor, III, p. 685.

[110] The cap and the sword, symbol of the independence of the federated canton, had been brought to the Swiss by Cardinal Schinner in May 1512 (Pastor, III, p. 682). On July 5 the Pope nominated them the " protectors of the liberty of the Church " in perpetuity (ibid., p. 686).

[111] P. Zampetti in: *Catalogo della Mostra di L. Lotto*, Venice, 1953, p. XX, Pallucchini, *Sebastian Viniziano*, Verona 1944, pp. 43-44, which, however, challenges the opinion of Wackernagel (" S. Del Piombo in den vatik. Stanzen," in *Monatsh. f. Kunstw*, 1909, p. 319 ff.) according to whom Sebastiano participated in the decoration of the Stanza di Eliodoro. See also p. 123, no. 45 for a cautious suggestion regarding the *Delivery of the Pandects* in the Segnatura.

[112] Gamba, *op. cit.*, pp. 73-74.

[113] Fischel, *R.*, pp. 103 and 320; Dussler, p. 89.

[114] Pastor, III, p. 708.

[115] Golzio, p. 28.

[116] Fischel, *R.*, p. 177, denies that the verse written by Blosio Palladio " Hic Venus orta maris et concha sub sydera fertur " refers to the *Galatea*, completed in his opinion only in 1512, and that the poet is thinking of a Venus painted by Raphael to which a drawing of the Capitoline Venus assertedly would refer (id., Diss. VI, 264). But, apart from our different dating, Palladio could have seen the fresco in its planning state.

[117] Pastor, IV, p. 360.

[118] Vasari, V, p. 567.

[119] Pallucchini, *op. cit.*, p. 33.

[120] M. Hirst, " The Chigi Chapel in Santa Maria della Pace," in *Journ. of the Warburg and Courtauld Inst.* XXIV, 1961, pp. 161-185.

[121] *Ibid.*, Plate 28 c.

[122] Cavalcaselle, II, p. 244 in note.

[123] Vasari, V, pp. 5, 6, 8.

[124] Golzio, pp. 33-34.

[125] *Ibid.*, p. 30 and *R., Tutti gli scritti* edited by E. Camesasca, Milan 1956, pp. 28-30.

[126] Golzio, pp. 31-33.

[127] *Ibid.*, pp. 34-35.

[128] Dussler, pp. 24-25, no. 24.

[129] J. Shearman, " The Chigi Chapel in Santa Maria del Popolo," in *Journ. of the Warburg and Courtauld Inst.* XXIV, 1961, pp. 129-160.

[130] Golzio, p. 65.

[131] Fischel, *R.*, p. 207. The letter to Leo X is published by Golzio pp. 78-92 and in *Tutti gli scritti*, cit., pp. 44-72.

[132] For this and the other Vatican works of these last years of Raphael we refer the reader to the treatment of the school of Raphael in this same book by A. Marabottini (Chap. II).
Here we make only a brief reference, for expositional completeness, but without confronting the questions that involve those of the collaboration of his pupils. Consequently, in the treatment that follows there will be references also to several of the illustrations from the present article, as for example the *Madonna with the Fish* and others not alluded to in the text.

[133] Golzio, p. 42. A double portrait of the two literati was seen by Michiel (cf. note 58) in the house of Bembo in Padova. Since it was painted on wood, the present one on canvas, it could be a copy of it. But the obvious discontinuity between the two figures conduces to the suggestion that, originally separate, they were brought together long before by pupils of Raphael, and perhaps also to give to Bembo the combined likeness of both his friends. But see Dussler, p. 64, no. 115.

[134] Golzio, pp. 52-53.

[135] Vasari, IV, p. 383; Michiel, *Lettera ad Antonio Marsilio*, in Golzio, pp. 113-114. A likeness of Raphael in these last years of his life is given to us by that portrait, in the Louvre, that sometimes is designated " Raphael and his fencing Master," but today (Ortolani, *Raffaello*, p. 62; Dussler, p. 61, no. 107) it is called " Raphael and a Pupil." Indeed, a great part of the execution was the work of a pupil.

II

RAPHAEL'S COLLABORATORS

by Alessandro Marabottini

Premise

The study of Raphael's workshop is a difficult task because the relationship between Raphael and his pupils does not appear to be completely analogous to that in other known workshops.

For example, Giovanni Bellini had without doubt several collaborators and many works attributed to him and even some with his signature were in reality the works of students; Rubens in his studio-house in Antwerp directed a squadron of helpers who under his guidance transferred on vast canvases his ideas and sketches. On the other hand Giorgione's assistants were not necessarily his collaborators, they were his spiritual creations and took from him impetus for that Giorgionesque diaspora that colored Venetian and Lombard artistic life for two decades.

The connection between Bellini, Rubens and their assistants does not give rise to any particular commentary on the part of historians; it seems to have remained on a practical level, not unlike the traditional usage in artisans' workshops. On the other hand the Giorgionesque artists evidently gained inspiration from the master each according to his own character and then went on their way toward a search for personal expression.

Bellini's and Rubens' collaborators worked from the inside of the artistic *corpus* of their masters who, in turn, hid and absorbed them as much as possible. Their presence had no importance for the history of art—rather they incised their mark more or less negatively on the quality of this or that particular work. The case for the Giorgione shop was different. The assistants began from the poetry of Giorgione in order to interpret, modify, and elaborate it, each in a different direction. Thus they continued on a course which had not been started by Giorgione but by Bellini, and which Savoldo, Dosso and Titian developed in different ways without provoking an irreparable break with the art of Giorgione. Notwithstanding the

1 G. F. *Penni* (?). Alexander Places in Safety the Poems by Homer. Vatican, Stanza della Segnatura.

199

difference between their works and those of the master, the assistants almost always belonged to the same "culture" and not merely from the formal point of view.

To the degree that they were absolutely faifthful and were dominated by the master, the pupils of Raphael were so absorbed with his language that even the most perceptive art criticism has produced a conflicting series of attributions whenever it has wished to single out the hand of one or another assistant within a work by the master. However, as soon as the fidelity was broken and the autonomous personalities began to emerge, especially after Raphael had died, each one had to fend for himself. The relationship between the style of the assistants and that of their former master has always been seen as one of contrast; it seemed not a question of an inevitable break but of programmatic opposition. The reason for this condition should now be explained, if possible.

Raphael's workshop makes its massive appearance between 1514 and 1515. Up to that time Raphael occasionally had some collaborators who may also have felt the influence of his style but on the last wall of the Stanza di Eliodoro there appears the personality of an assistant that is identifiable.

In 1514 Raphael was made head of the works of St. Peter's; by 1515 he was named conservator of antique marbles and inscriptions. In 1517 this assignment was enlarged to include all the antiquities, a position analogous to that of a superintendent of archaeological antiquities, by modern standards.

These weighty responsibilities encouraged him to meditate upon the grandiose scale of ancient architecture and to examine the forms of Ancient Rome, as well as to rediscover her among the imposing ruins, in the vast, hidden *Domus Aurea* and in the porticoes decorated with stucco. From these meditations and passionate yet solemn visions, Raphael was elaborating his magnificent ideas for the Vatican tapestries.

The grace of Raphael's language continued to acquire energy and his idealization was enriched by a full vitality from the time he began to work in the Stanze and reached the apex in the Stanza di Eliodoro. But it was only in the cartoons for the tapestries that the idealized beauty and harmoniously vigorous elements that constitute his Renaissance Classicism become colored with a severe and magnificent dignity. Raphael is a great artist; not even at this point does he copy his forms from antique art. Depicting the Acts of the Apostles, he immerses them in a new poetic climate. The groups are no longer articulated in elegant and musical *contrapposto;* they follow instead the new non-centralized compositions, inaugurated in the scene of *Attila Stopped at the Gates of Rome*, or they are disposed in simple and monumental symmetry. The figures have a solemnity and accentuated plastic weight and the personages tend to become exemplary types in the Aristotelian sense: the Apostles, heroes and kings; the

2 *G. F. Penni* (?). Alexander Places in Safety the Poems by Homer, Drawing. Oxford, Ashmolean Museum.

200

3 *Raphael and Assistants.* Attila and Leo I (detail). Vatican, Stanza di Eliodoro.

figures in the crowd, on the other hand, capable of assuming violent, realistic physiognomies. But the heroes, both positive and negative, are eloquently enlarged: Paul and Peter, Elymas and Ananias. The architectural elements also have a new quality. There are no longer the wide Bramantesque vaults that collect the protagonists; rather, they are simpler structures, less related to contemporary architecture.

Without being true and exact reconstructions of classical monuments, they are nevertheless very similar to an antique ideal city which for the Rome of the early sixteenth century held solemn historical evocations: the twisted columns on the old Constantinian ciborium, the sacrificial altars of pagan temples. An equivalence between the grandeur of the classical world and holiness of the Christian one is decisively affirmed. The two histories, that of the city of Rome and that of the Holy Bible, are fused in a noble rhetorical language. The culture of the Leonine court was both reflected and sublimated in Raphael's inventions.

This ideal reality, so violent because of the power of its protagonists and so calm for the perfect layout of the composition, is not a contemporary reality. Contrary to the Stanze, here the chronicle is not sought; history dominated, and it is an ancient and Christian history that is the only one accepted as true by Renaissance Classicism.

Whatever the critical evaluation of Raphael's language might be, which is in continuous change, it will be recognized that at the moment of the cartoons, the highest point of Classicism was reached by the master. Artists and writers on art up to the Romantic Age, however, saw and loved something more: not the high point of Raphael's Classicism, but Classicism in painting, the discovery of the Grand Manner, of the *bella maniera*, as the only means capable of expressing the ethical and political virtues of history. Thus an absolute value was recognized for this language; it was one of the poles between Classicism and Anti-classicism: the ideal Classical pole.

Following the interlude of Mannerism, Annibale Carracci, Domenichino, and Poussin saw Raphael in this way. Similarly David and Ingres saw him after the Baroque. Vasari already admitted as much, even though he sided with the opposing faction, that of Michel-

5 *Giulio Romano* (?). Attila and Leo I, Drawing. Paris, Louvre Museum.

6 *G. F. Penni* (?). Attila and Leo I, Drawing. Oxford, Ashmolean Museum.

4 *Raphael and Assistants (Giulio Romano).* The Madonna dell'Impannata (detail). Florence, Pitti.

angelo: "Now for us, who are after him, it remains to imitate the fine, indeed, excellent manner he left us as an example. . . . We have from him the art, the colors, the inventions combined in the finest fashion that could be wished for; one could not imagine that anyone could surpass him."

Raphaelism and Classicism become identified with each other. In the nineteenth century the Romantic artists in search of a congenial art assumed the name of Pre-Raphaelites. This explains why the position of Raphael's students is so different from the pupils of Bellini and the followers of Giorgione. There was never truly a pre-Bellinian or pre-Giorgionesque movement because these two masters, although very great, never had been identified with an eternal aesthetic movement where the personalities are annulled, as was the case with Raphael.

The classical aesthetics since Alberti place a special accent on the mental and ideal value of invention; it can easily corroborate the conviction that the ideas of the master, even if realized by pupils, gave a completely convincing life to the works. The material language for concretizing them was classical, discovered once and for all by Raphael, and it is understandable to the degree that it is codified. Thus with their activity those pupils of Raphael play a dual role: in the first place, they were substitutes for him, they were the voice of his thoughts, they worked in his stead when he was occupied with responsibilities other than painting, especially during the late years. In the second place, they used that patrimony of form to which the various Raphaelesque revivals had recourse. Their art was, therefore, fundamental for the history of European art.

7 *Raphael* (?). Christ's Descent to Limbo, probably a drawing for a medallion in Santa Maria della Pace, Rome. Florence, Uffizi, Gabinetto dei Disegni e Stampe.

These same pupils could not avoid creating polemics with their master in their search for an autonomous personality despite the fact that Raphael's language was absolute and perfect, as even Vasari had admitted. Here is the key, even today, for understanding all the best of Raphael's collaborators from Giulio Romano to Perino and Polidoro, and it was already implicit in the thinking of artists and writers on art in the sixteenth century.

From what has been said up to this point, a number of critical errors and prejudices may have been created by identifying with his most rigorously classical phase. Thus, for example, it seems quite evident that from the Carracci to Poussin up to the first Neoclassicists, the real Raphael was considered to be Raphael of 1511 to 1520, that is, from the *School of Athens* to the *Transfiguration*, or more specifically from the Stanza di Eliodoro to the Vatican tapestries. With the new romantic taste, it is this estimate of Raphael that was rejected. The Purists in their manifesto of 1843, which was signed by Bianchini, rejected "all the works of Raphael from the *Disputa* and following." On the other hand, during the first half of the nineteenth century, modern Raphaelesque philology contemporary with Pre-Raphaelitism, Purism and the Nazarene Movement, restricted the *corpus* of authentic works, that is autographs up to the second Stanza (for Dollmayr) [1] and by the end of the century even the cartoons for the tapestries were considered totally executed by Penni.

Recent art historical criticism is theoretically freed from the exclusive romantic predilection for the lyric and spontaneous world of the very early Raphael. But since these ideas are not completely dormant and since the results often are exaggerated by the philological research which had definitively assigned the works from 1515 onward to the workshop, and due to the old but still valid identification of Raphael and Classicism, modern critics have only half-heartedly accepted a late Raphael whose production does not seem to agree with certain fixed analyses that have been made about him. And so Raphael ends up by being embalmed by about 1515.

We ourselves, maintaining in these very pages that his style in the cartoons for the tapestries seemed to coincide with an eternal moment of taste, have in part supported a similar position. However, it obviously is an absurdity to uphold that the style of a single artist coincides with an abstract aesthetic idea. The contemporaries of Raphael indeed believe it, as the painters and the theoreticians from the seventeenth to the nineteenth centuries believed it, and historically this fact had great importance for the artistic life in Europe and also, of course, for the history of art. An error passionately followed often produces greater fruits than a truth without fascination. But the fact is that Raphael did not cease to elaborate his own language in 1515 and regardless of many demanding tasks other than painting that were thrust upon him, he never

8 *Raphael.* The Prophets. Rome, Santa Maria della Pace, Engraving, by Salvatore Cardelli.

9 *Raphael.* The Sibyls. Santa Maria della Pace, Engraving, by Volpato.

203

10 *Raphael and Assistants (Giulio Romano and Giovanni da Udine). St. Cecilia (detail).* Bologna, Pinacoteca.

11 *Raphael and Assistants (Giulio Romano).* Caryatids and architectural compartments of the socle in the Stanza di Eliodoro, Vatican.

ceased to be the head of the workshop, the responsible and real inventor of what was made public with his name, up to the time of his death (and even somewhat beyond it).

In spite of some recent art criticism which upholds, for the reasons already mentioned, that from the time of the frescoes of the Stanza dell'Incendio del Borgo, Raphael did not even plan the compositions, limiting himself to slight corrections of the projects of others (that is, his best pupils and in particular, Giulio Romano), I am not able to accept absolutely this analysis

of the relationship between master and students because I see it as an extreme consequence of the tendency of raising to a rule the language of Raphael as it appeared when he began the third Stanza.

If it is true that Raphael's language in 1515 reaches the apex of Classicism, there is nothing that would prove that the same master was not able to renew himself and move beyond those limits. Rather, his incredible ability for enrichment and transformation exhibited in the first two decades of activity, leads one to think the contrary.

For this reason I am in full agreement with Shearman,[2] Freedberg[3] and Pouncey[4] in rejecting the opinion of Hartt[5] who concludes by making Giulio Romano responsible, or nearly so, for about five years of Raphael's creativity.

A draftsman of Raphael's ability, as Pouncey correctly observed, would hardly have found it difficult to make a sketch or a project for one of his works, even with many pressing duties. And in the works after 1515, it is possible to see the results of a genius in continual self-perfection, as Brizio among other Italian scholars, has very astutely shown.[6] An interpretation of the master's inventions over a long span that goes from the first projects to the development of the designs actually used for execution, makes it clear that the pupils altered them, sometimes even significantly, but the invention was always Raphael's. This point will be discussed at greater length at the proper time.

I wish to add, finally, that the image of an *équipe* of young artists collaborating in the creation of a work of art, discussing and perhaps elaborating the idea of the master, or even the image

12 *Raphael*. Christ for the tapestry with the scene of the "Pasce oves meas," Drawing. Louvre, Paris.

13 *Raphael*. Christ and the Apostles, for the tapestry with the scene of "Pasce oves meas," Drawing. Windsor, Royal Library.

14 *G. F. Penni* (?). Model for the cartoon for the tapestry with the scene of "Pasce oves meas," Drawing. Paris, Louvre.

205

16 *Giulio Romano.* Miraculous Draught of Fishes, Drawing. Vienna, Albertina.

15 *Raphael.* Soldiers and horsemen, for the tapestry with the Conversion of St. Paul, Drawing. Chatsworth, Devonshire Collection.

of a master taking ideas from the pupils—in short the notion of a unified team that gives life to the late work of Raphael, may appear today especially fascinating to group acting workshops, to team scientists and to the creative aspects of industrial production. Interpreting in this way the dynamics of Raphael's studio, however, seems to me highly unhistorical. On the contrary I think that the shop was subject to and devoted to the creative authority of the master, and totally dependent on him. So dependent that even after, when the material ties were released by death, the spiritual bonds remained. And I think that if one would abstain from interpreting the autonomous steps of the students polemically with the master's art, if one would recede from the critical and historical viscosity sketched above, it would improve not only our understanding of Giulio and others, but also the art of Raphael, and in general the whole panorama of sixteenth century painting.

[1] H. Dollmayr, " Raffaels Werkstätte," *Jahrbuch der Kunst Sammlungen in Wien*, Vienna, 1895, pp. 232-363.

[2] J. Shearman, " Giulio Romano " (review of the volume of Hartt, 1958), *Burlington Magazine*, 1959, pp. 456-460.

[3] S. J. Freedberg, *Painting of the High Renaissance in Rome and Florence*, Cambridge, Mass., 1961.

[4] F. Pouncey and J. A. Gere, *Italian Drawings of the Department of Prints and Drawings in the British Museum. Raphael and his Circle.*, London, 1952.

[5] F. Hartt, " Raphael and Giulio Romano with Notes on the Raphael School," *Art Bulletin*, 1944, pp. 67-94.

[6] A. M. Brizio, *s.v.* Raphael, *Enciclopedia Universale dell'Arte*, vol. XI, Rome-Venice, 1963.
    Idem, *Arte Lombarda*, 1965.

17 *Raphael and Assistants.* Cartoon for the tapestry with the " Pasce oves meas." London, Victoria and Albert Museum.

18 *Raphael and Assistants*. Cartoon for tapestry with the Healing of the Cripple. London, Victoria and Albert Museum.

19 *Raphael and Assistants*. Cartoon for tapestry with the Death of Ananias. London, Victoria and Albert Museum.

20 *Raphael and Assistants*. Cartoon for tapestry with the Sacrifice at Lystra. London, Victoria and Albert Museum.

Raphael and his workshop

In his letter of April 19, 1516 to Cardinal Bibbiena, Bembo points out the existence of Raphael's pupils for the first time, as far as I know. Here is the passage: "The portrait of M. Baldassar Castiglione or the portrait of the fine and always honored memory of our Duke, blessed by God, seems to be by the hand of one of Raphael's pupils, in that by comparison they resemble the one of Thebaldeo, ..."[1] Not only is the existence of a well-staffed workshop documented here, but it is also implicitly admitted that the helpers of Raphael often executed works in his name, attaining aesthetical results inferior to those of the teacher. The first time the independent activity of these young assistants is recognized by an administrative act, that is, the payment made directly to them, is to be found in volume 2241 of the Archivio Camerale, Part I, *spese minute di Palazzo*, located in the Archivio di Stato of Rome, where on folio 24 verso, under the date of July 1, 1517, is written: "and more, on the first day of July to Raphael of Urbino's young men who painted the room in front of the guardaroba ... 20 ducats."[2]

Naturally these citations are somewhat after the effective formation of Raphael's shop. It must have occurred more or less as a consequence of the important and extensive effort required by the frescoes of the Segnatura. From mere helpers, as they were, the pupils of Raphael must have developed into efficient assistants in the course of that work and when between 1511 and 1512 Raphael's great success was acknowledged, the new commission for the Stanza di Eliodoro and an additional series of urgent charges were entrusted to him, these pupils must have begun to assume the role of faithful executors of some minor and decorative parts of the frescoes not found in the first Stanza.

The first universally recognized example of a massive participation by the workshop in the execution of a large Raphael fresco, is found in the Stanza di Eliodoro, in the *Encounter of Attila and Leo the Great*, where the repeated presence of Leo X, first as a Cardinal surrounded by papal Court, and then as Pope, reveals that the fresco was begun when Julius II was still alive, but finished after his death, that is, after January 1, 1513. As matters stand, the figure of Leo I, planned at the beginning as a portrait of Della Rovere, assumed in the final version the likeness of the Medici pope, his successor. Between the period from the end of 1512 and the first half of 1513 the problem of Raphael's workshop took shape. This does not signify that all that we find before this date in the Stanza is entirely Raphael's. Moreover the sections that are not his are attributed to independent masters who were occasionally brought in to work on the same decorations, executing them of their own responsibility. They were not part of Raphael's workshop and subsequently his pupils substituted for them.[3]

The pupils of Raphael, as I have mentioned, appear in a recognizable manner in the secondary parts of the Stanza della Segnatura (grotesques, ornamental motifs, plus the two much discussed *grisailles* under the *Parnassus*) and in the *Encounter of Attila and Leo the Great* in the Stanza di Eliodoro; other than that, their style may be seen in less important areas of the other frescoes and the entire decoration of the socle of the same room.

It is impossible to date with certainty the completion of the Stanza della Segnatura, but it was probably executed within the year 1512. At that date among the known pupils only the Florentine, Giovanni Francesco Penni, called "Il Fattore," was old enough to have worked there, given that Giovanni da Udine, the oldest of the group, seems to have joined the shop later. Vasari says that Penni died in about 1528 at the age of forty, born therefore in 1488, but Milanesi,[4] on the basis of documents, advances his date of birth to 1512, a proper age to begin to paint in Raphael's workshop when one considers that the master was not yet thirty. Giulio Romano, *l'enfant prodige* of the shop, was not quite fifteen when he started to work in the Stanza di Eliodoro. Penni was, consequently, the first pupil of Raphael in order of time, and always remained the favorite along with Giulio. It is by no means easy to form a judgment about Penni because so little of his work as an independent artist is known. Studies on Penni outside of the traditional repertory are for all practical purposes non-existent. Only one signed painting, a portrait of a youth in Dublin's National Gallery, exists. After Raphael's death, we know that Penni and Giulio Romano executed the frescoes in the Sala di Costantino, the *Coronation of the Virgin* in the Pinacoteca Vaticana and a copy of Raphael's *Transfiguration*, today in the Prado; traditionally a *tondo* with the *Holy Family and St. John* in the Museum of Cava dei Tirreni, is attributed to him.[5]

Against the scantiness of autograph paintings by Penni, there exists a rather remarkable list of accomplishments, either in fresco or on wood, under Raphael's direction, and above all, an abundance of drawings connected with Raphaelesque frescoes, paintings and drawings that are now attributed to Il Fattore and they seem to indicate that Giovanni Francesco was the workshop specialist in this field. Vasari was explicit on this point: "He imitated the manner of Raphael in his drawings and studied it continuously and it is not surprising that one sees many of them, since they were finished with diligence; he applied himself much more to drawing than to painting." This information from Vasari is important because it tells us that Giovanni Francesco's drawings were in general finished designs. We shall see that, for the most part, the folios that are attributed to him have this characteristic. The question will be better discussed in its proper place, that is, when we shall analyze the Loggias, the scenes to which the "finished designs" attributed to Penni, are related. At this point, however, it should be said that, although they show a finished quality and notable ability, these drawings all lack

fascination. There is an absence of emotional elements and there is also a commendable yet deluding artisan's correctness in the effort to adhere to Raphael's language. One has the sensation that Penni identified himself, although ineffectively, with the master. The drawings we attribute to him are not copies, they are originals, but they lack creativity " and cannot be described as studies in the real sense of the word." [6] We are probably dealing with executive projects from which the cartoons will derive. Behind these projects lies the first creative idea that one must suppose is by Raphael.

Penni's function tends to clarify itself especially in the preparatory stage of the cartoons which presumes the inventive participation by the master. Unfortunately we are unable to indicate the actual sequence even in single cases that would clarify the whole program: sketch by Raphael, executive drawing by Penni, cartoon, and finished work. Freedberg believed he was able to indicate something of this sort with respect to the scene of *Pasce Oves Meas* in the Vatican tapestries but the traces of the first idea, that of Raphael, in general is completely lacking.[7] I hardly know how to explain this situation, even if one could suppose that the sketches, inherited jointly by Penni and Giulio or left to one or the other, were destroyed.

The idea that we do not possess the first original sketches by Raphael today simply because they never existed is not very convincing.

But to return to the initial activity of Penni, it probably had its start with the *grisaille* frescoes beneath the scene of the *Parnassus* in the Stanza della Segnatura (Fig. 1). They were engraved by Marcantonio Raimondi [8] and there is a drawing in the Ashmolean Museum of Oxford for one of the two (Fig. 2).[9] The subject matter of the two scenes has been discussed and variously interpreted in accordance with the iconographic significance of the paintings in the entire room.[10] The style reveals that absence of vitality but correct Raphaelesque orthodoxy which we have already indicated for the drawings attributed to Penni. It is almost certain that Il Fattore also participated in the other secondary decorations of the Stanza della Segnatura (excluding the socle painted by Perino under Paul III) all painted from the master's idea; typical, I think, is his part of the *Story of Attila*, a fresco begun around the end of 1512 and finished perhaps in 1513. Naturally there is no documentary proof of his participation, but the noticeable lowering in quality that marks the whole right side of the fresco, alludes without doubt, to the execution by pupils. The stamp of this work " correct " and opaque, as if it were a miniature Raphael, coincides remarkably with the idea we have already sketched for Penni. I do not believe, therefore, that the proposal to assign to Giulio Romano a considerable part of the work has any validity.[11] First of all, Giulio was still too young for perhaps any assignment, much less such a demanding one.[12] Secondly, the characteristics of his style are not apparent here. There is nothing of his compact plasticity, his accentuation of naturalistic detail and psychological vivacity, nor his preference for contrasts of light. The energy in a group of horsemen (Fig. 3) is attributable to the idea, to the drawing and here and there to last minute touches by Raphael, while a certain dullness, the absence of secure concentration, and the coloristic aridity in many sections are remote from Giulio's temperament.[13] It is my opinion, therefore, that Penni is the principal assistant of Raphael throughout 1513 and somewhat later. As a matter of fact, he had already held the position for two years and was aiming at the role of organizer of the shop. But around 1514, the star of Giulio Romano, the most energetic of the pupils is rising. He is an interesting painter and a significant architect. The position he will play in the development of Italian art after Raphael's death is of primary importance and involves a vast cultural area.

It is indicative that he was developing at the moment when Raphael was passing from the dynamic and illuministic researches in the Stanza di Eliodoro to classical-archaeological ones in the tapestries. Giulio was always to demonstrate an interest in light, a passion for movement, care for an imitative reality of physical features, and an antiquarian erudition, all aspects of Raphael's first crucial years. Two large altarpieces executed between 1513 and 1514 mark the beginning of the collaboration by the workshop in easel painting also. We are dealing here with the *Madonna of the Fish* and the *Madonna dell'Impannata*. The first, which is also the earlier, must have been entirely by Penni who translated a monumental idea by Raphael with his usual haziness, uncertainty in the ponderous figures and psychological vacuity. The relationship between the construction of large parallelepipeds for the base of the throne and the geometric taste of the architectural elements on the socle of the Stanza di Eliodoro could not be more convincing for dating the *Madonna of the Fish* to that creative phase of Raphael which corresponds to the last year of work in the second Stanza. Penni, even in the execution of these purely architectural parts of the altarpiece, was limited to the Raphaelesque idea which he had to follow as is demonstrated by a comparison with that socle of the Stanza di Eliodoro, a result of an analogous invention, but treated somewhat more splendidly in the painting. The execution of that socle was by Giulio Romano, as we shall see and must have been more or less contemporary with his work on the *Madonna dell'Impannata*.

As with the *Madonna of the Fish*, undoubtedly it was entirely the invention of Raphael but its execution allows, unlike the case with the work of Penni, the recognition of a gifted personality with a certain autonomy.[14] A confrontation with the detailed drawing in Windsor is sufficient to make one realize that the figures in the painting are massively blocked out, the plastic contours are tighter, without movement and the shadows are deeper, thus the images have a more statuesque and less natural appearance. At the same time a lively satisfaction in underscoring and almost forcing the expression and the tendency to chisel some of the realistic

23 Predella of the tapestry with the Miraculous Draught of Fishes, Scene from the Life of Leo X (detail).

details, forced the idealized measure of Raphael to an opposite direction. It should be underlined that by using the unique idea of the window with the shutters open, the personages become housed as if in a bourgeois interior: an exceptional case for Raphael's Madonnas but found instead in Giulio Romano, who with this kind of environment was able to insert, within heroic Raphaelesque compositions, fascinating elements from daily life. An example for this is the stupendous detail of the work-basket in the *Madonna della Gatta* in the Capodimonte Museum. For all these reasons it seems to me that here we should recognize the first appearance of Giulio and not, as Adolfo Venturi thought, a work by Penni. It can hardly be otherwise because it is not possible to find in the *Madonna dell'Impannata* that softened, precise fidelity to Raphael which is typical of Il Fattore. The errors here, on the contrary, are notable and show the inexperience of a debutant; nor are infidelities absent and they indicate the predilections of a person with strong autonomous tendencies. Among others, the young St. John with his muscular and statuesque nudity is a clear prototype of the plastic autonomy of Giulio Romano (Fig. 4).

The year was especially difficult for Raphael. Besides completing the Stanza di Eliodoro, executing the memorable *Sistine Madonna*,[15] the *Madonna della Seggiola*, the *Madonna della Tenda* and the *Madonna dell'Impannata* (which if actually executed by Giulio, as has been said, was nevertheless projected by the master and partially retouched by him), Raphael was occupied that year with two other very noteworthy commissions: the frescoes of the Chigi Chapel in Santa Maria della Pace and the altarpiece of *St. Cecilia*, begun even if not finished before 1515. These last mentioned works are quite different from each other; the first one seems to sum up and conclude the whole Roman phase of the master which is characterized by the elegant and contrapuntal compositions of the Stanza della Segnatura, the inspiration from Michelangelo, the dynamics for the Stanza di Eliodoro, and finally certain rethinking of Leonardo (see the angel that bears the tablet for the so-called *Persian Sibyl*. It is related to, and similarly Leonardesque in taste, to the seated figure on the tomb in the preparatory drawings for the *Resurrection* conserved respectively in the Bayonne Museum and in the Ashmolean in Oxford, and to another of the *Annunciation to Joachim* in a drawing also in the Ashmolean). The *St. Cecilia*, instead, opens the next period of classicizing meditations between 1515 and 1516. In both, the workshop participated however.

Today it is difficult to recognize the hand of the collaborator who worked in Santa Maria della Pace, and it is not even sure that we are dealing with only one. The frescoes are quite damaged. The alterations and restorations have practically obliterated the architectural framing that connected the two scenes—the *Sibyls* over the entrance and the *Prophets* at the sides of the window in the lunette above—and, to form an idea of the overall scheme of decoration, recourse must be made to the engravings, for example, those of Volpato and Cardelli (Figs. 8, 9). The *Prophets* are greatly ruined.

24 Predella of the tapestry with the Sacrifice at Lystra, Scene from the Life of St. Paul.

The set of paintings was completed by two bronze relief medallions (*Christ in Limbo* and *The Doubting of Thomas*) which were to be placed at the sides of the apsidal niche, on the chapel front under the *Sibyls*. Hirst, I think rightly, presumed a drawing in the Uffizi (Fig. 7) attributed to Giulio Romano, to be a study in Raphael's hand for one of these two bronze medallions which, executed perhaps by Lorenzetto, are now in the Abbey of Chiaravalle, and in their place are two seventeenth century reliefs.

It is well known that Vasari suggested the name of Timoteo Viti for the frescoes. He was "called to Rome with much insistence by Raphael; he made the *Sibyl* by his own hand and invention in Santa Maria della Pace with the master. This is affirmed by some who remember him working, and is proved by the cartoons which are still to be found with his heirs." [16] The statement by Vasari has always been rejected and whoever has in mind the archaizing style of Viti cannot fail to agree with Adolfo Venturi: "Certainly Raphael used assistants in the execution of the fresco, but Timoteo, quattrocentesque even in his last works, was not among them." [17]

One cannot deny, however, that Vasari's reference is quite explicit. He cited people who had seen Timoteo working in Santa Maria della Pace (as if Vasari, doubting himself, sought witnesses) and gives the important information about the cartoons in the possession of the heirs. He also speaks of some letters written by Raphael as testifyng to Raphael's desire to make Viti return to Rome from Urbino. Vasari shows that he had seen these letters and we understand just how, since he was acquainted with Giovanni Maria, son of the painter, who had given him some drawings by his father to insert in his famous book. It was certainly at Giovanni Maria Viti's that Vasari saw the cartoons. They are the proof that makes one reflect and which indicates a firsthand documentation. Possibly in Viti's home the merits of Timoteo were exaggerated with respect to the frescoes but it is difficult to imagine that they were wholly invented. Surely the style of Timoteo Viti is very removed from Raphael's and when, as often happens in the drawings, he tends to approach it with an archaizing manner (not without attraction) is almost purist like Minardi or Pre-Raphaelite.[18] But who can say what would have been the result of this timid and "correct" hand if he had to execute in fresco a part of Raphael's cartoons, working side by side with the great master, guided and controlled by him? Once the invention was given and the manner of execution determined, perhaps Timoteo would have been able to proceed. I believe, in fact, that one must always keep in mind, before considering the participation of assistants, the absolute value of the idea, the universal significance of the language that was already known around 1514 for the works of Raphael.

It is another matter to specify the parts eventually done by Timoteo Viti in the frescoes of Santa Maria della Pace. The *Sibyls* have always been considered totally autographic. Despite a certain exaggeration, in substance, these frescoes form one of the most authentic contexts (leaving aside the damage and the restorations) Raphael has left us. On the other hand, the *Prophets* above have always been considered of the school by an unidentified assistant.

It is known that there are also splendid drawings by Raphael for the *Sibyls* (in the British Museum, in the Ashmolean in Oxford and in the Albertina Museum in Vienna), but also for the upper zone there is the sheet in the Uffizi with two angels and two studies for the prophet seated at the extreme right. Yet, if the invention of the *Prophets* and the drawings were by Raphael and if it is admitted that the master could have intervened with corrections on the fresco, it is evident that had some part of the decoration been left to the assistants, it was logically this. The two figures are very high up and the window in the center of the lunette locates them against the light; therefore they can never be seen well. Today the extensive damage has aggravated the situation. Thus, one gets the sensation that the quality here is inferior to the series of the *Sibyls*. How much this derives from the work and inexperience of an assistant or from the damage and poor visibility is difficult to say. If it is up there among the *Prophets* that we find Timoteo Viti (Vasari speaks of his collaboration on the *Sibyls*, but it seems to me clear that he mentioned the most famous and best visible part) or others, is even more difficult to say. If he really was there, this modest painter from Urbino was able to stand briefly on this single occasion beside the great master. He offered devoutly his own ability which is a masterpiece of scrupulosity and artisan achievement within the shadow of Raphael's poetry.

Viti cannot be found, nor was he named in the other activities of the workshop. He was too old to belong to the very youthful group who was at that time affirming itself. Precisely during the course of the year 1514, Giulio Romano was developing, and together with Penni he constituted the effective nucleus of the *équipe*. At the beginning of 1514 when the works in Santa Maria della Pace should have been completed, probably while one of them was too occupied with finishing the Stanza di Eliodoro, the other was too close to beginning to take part in the Chigi Chapel. This would explain the employment of Timoteo Viti, or some other unknown helper. By the end of the year Timoteo was no longer needed. Not only were Raphael's Dioscuri at the master's disposal for any new commission but probably from then on they carried out, first under orders and then always more independently, all the ornamental decoration (Giovanni da Udine master of the stuccoes, of the grotesques, of the flowers, prints, animals and of still lifes). Penni, Giulio Romano and Giovanni da Udine were to constitute such an exceptional team between 1514 and 1520 that it is certainly difficult to find the equivalent in any other workshop.

"Raphael when making the altarpiece of *St. Cecilia*, made Giovanni depict an organ which

27 *Giulio Romano.* Study for two female figures in the Fire in the Borgo, Drawing. Vienna, Albertina.

26 *Giulio Romano.* Study for female figure in the Fire in the Borgo, Drawing. Paris, Louvre.

the Saint holds in her hands ... also all the other musical instruments that are at her feet; and what is more important, he made his picture so similar to Raphael that it seemed by the same hand " (Fig. 10).[19] This is the first in a series of information by Vasari concerning the activity of Giovanni da Udine in Raphael's shop. It would appear certain that this is correct considering the close friendship between the Aretine and the Friulian; it also is easy to assume that Vasari obtained this information directly from him. Less certain is the year to which this activity should be assigned. In fact, since the publication by Filippini of the document for the commission of the work, the *terminus post quem* of 1514 cannot be doubted; the completion of the altar is variously presumed within the years 1514-1516, and even by some as late as 1518.[20] Personally it seems to me that the painting must have been finished not too long after the commission, by the end of 1514 or at the latest by the beginning of 1515, because it accords very well stylistically with the phase of Raphael's high classicism.

In the figures, Giulio Romano must have been the principal collaborator to whom the physical type of the *Magdalen* remained fixed for a long time. This is an example of another of those enrichments by Raphael that little by little went into consituting the patrimony of forms for the young artist. Anyway, Raphael keeps solid control over the picture in which he painted large sections and which he had conceived in its entirety.

More or less at the same time Giulio Romano must have carried out the solid caryatids on the base of the Stanza di Eliodoro (Fig. 11) based upon Raphael's design. Raphael's new dedication to the ancient world in this socle decoration reveals itself more than in the mono-chromatic figures of the architectural decoration on the front wall whose surface is marvelously divided into three framed rectangular areas one on top of the other with subtle proportions

28 *Giulio Romano* (?). Study for a group with Aeneas and Anchises in the *Fire in the Borgo*, Drawing. Vienna, Albertina.

that match the most distilled proportions of Piet Mondrian. The whole feigned architecture, including the dados upon which the caryatids rest, contributes to the extraordinary effect of equilibrated harmony in a more composed manner than is seen in the base of the throne of the *Madonna of the Fish*, which, nevertheless, as we have already noted, anticipates the same vision. There is no doubt that Giulio Romano was not the inventor but only the executor. Perhaps in the little stories in relief within the framing below, between caryatid and caryatid it would be possible to recognize some autonomous work by the pupils. It would have been natural for Raphael to have left areas for them. But today after Maratta's reworkings, an examination is no longer possible.

In 1515 Raphael had to divide his energies between two important activities: the preparation of the Vatican tapestries, and the decoration for the third Stanza in the papal apartments, which takes its name from the scene of the *Fire in the Borgo*.

These were not his sole preoccupations: there were architectural activities quite increased at that time by the new assignment to take charge of the Fabric of St. Peter's, the works to finish in Chigi Chapel in Santa Maria del Popolo and the always present minor commissions. Although there must have been insistent requests in 1515 no easel picture seems to have been released by Sanzio except for the altarpiece of *St. Cecilia*, as we have said.

Naturally in such a situation, it was inevitable that the help of the workshop was relied upon to a large extent. Probably of the two commissions, the tapestries and the Stanza dell'Incendio, Raphael first received the latter, since in a letter of July, 1514 we are already informed

29 *Giulio Romano*. Study for figures for the Battle of Ostia (?), Drawing. Vienna, Albertina.

213

30 *G. F. Penni.* Study for the Bishops in the Coronation of Charlemagne, Drawing. Düsseldorf Museum.

that he has " begun to paint another Stanza for the Pope " [21] from which it can be assumed that at that date he must have at least begun to prepare the projects for the decoration.[22]

But first I shall discuss the cartoons for the tapestries.[23] We are certain that they were not begun within the year 1514, and they must have been done rapidly in the course of 1515, if already by June of that year Raphael received a first payment equal, it seems, to the total for three scenes.[24]

31 *G. F. Penni.* Study for the left side of the Oath of Leo III, Drawing. Florence, Horne Foundation.

214

32 *Raphael.* Study for female figure with *putto* (Fire in the Borgo?), Drawing. Zurich, Artistic Society.

Speaking of the tapestries, Vasari writes in the life of Raphael that "he made the colored cartoons in natural size with his own hand." [25] However, in the life of Penni he says that "he was a great help to Raphael in painting a large share of the tapestry cartoons of the papal Chapel and the Consistory, and especially the friezes." [26] As I said, Dollmayr, on the basis of this notice ends up by attributing to Penni the total execution of the cartoons. But more recently Hartt, in his book on Giulio Romano, has attributed the projects for the cartoons to Giulio and claims that the young assistant had executed them with no graphic assistance from the master, basing himself instead on simple verbal suggestions. [27]

This is quite evidently an absurd hypothesis. How could one imagine that an artist like Raphael, finally called upon to produce a work destined (through the mediation of tapestry-maker) to represent him in the Sistine Chapel, entrust the projection of the designs to a fifteen-year-old youngster with only oral instructions? It is true that in the sixteenth century the invention of a story was held in the highest regard, and literary men and poets were sought for it. They made their suggestions to the painters in writing or orally; however this invention is what today we would call the iconographic theme, the literary content, and is not the same as invention in the modern sense which is conceived as the formal idea of an art work.

Besides, in the sixteenth century a written guide or verbal instruction for the execution of a painting was a procedure that could have taken place in a rapport between a poet and a painter, but not between two artists. The painter, the "silent poet," as might have been said then, citing Simonides, would not have made suggestions with words but with drawings. Although Raphael was by universal consent considered a pleasant companion and therefore was an able talker, there is no doubt that he was much better as a draftsman and for those who drew as he did, making a rapid sketch certainly was not a dismaying matter. It is hardly worth pursuing this point further. There could be a problem if we had projects and designs for the cartoons by Giulio Romano. If the cartoons had been executed by him, without the least shadow of doubt good sense would lead us to presume the existence of lost studies by Raphael. But this is not the case.

Hartt's hypothesis is not based upon a shred of proof (not even on a utilization of the sources, as Vasari did, though proposing Penni's name). The hypothesis of Hartt is based simply upon an unjustifiable stratagem in dealing with the *corpus* of Raphael's drawings. He transfers to Giulio Romano with only self-determined authority the two autographed studies by Raphael (in the Louvre and at Windsor) for the cartoon with the scene of the *Delivery of the Keys* (Figs. 12   215

34 *Raphael and Giulio Romano.* The Battle of Ostia. Vatican, Stanza dell'Incendio.

35 *Raphael.* Study for God Father in the dome of the Chigi Chapel in Santa Maria del Popolo, Drawing. Oxford, Ashmolean Museum.

and 13), as well as the finished drawing in the Louvre, and also for the cartoon which is generally attributed to Penni (Fig. 14). He is silent over the existence at Chatsworth of the splendid drawing of St. Paul in the *Sacrifice at Lystra* and the drawing with soldiers and horsemen for the *Conversion of St. Paul* (Fig. 15), and he considers as projects for a first version of the *Miraculous Draught of Fishes*, assigning them to Giulio, the finished drawing and its verso sketched with pen from the Albertina in Vienna (Fig. 16), which instead is probably a derivation and variation on the theme of the cartoon, that is, *from* and not *for* the tapestry cartoon.[28]

All these distortions of the facts have already been indicated with extreme clarity by Shearman in his review of Hartt's book and if here we are insistent, it is only because it is necessary to demonstrate with these examples how easy it would be to deform the problem of Raphael's workshop and create a paradoxical connection between the activity of the master and that of the pupils.

The situation for the tapestry cartoons was actually quite simple and traditional. Raphael had three excellent assistants with him in Penni, Giulio Romano and Giovanni da Udine and undoubtedly he used them. But he used them in subordinate roles. It is possible, as Vasari says, that Giovanni da Udine, specialist in painting animals, did the wading birds in the foreground and the beautiful still life of fish on the boat in the *Miraculous Draught of Fishes*. Penni with his preference for finished designs would have helped in preparing small models for the cartoons; he would have made the copies for keeping them in the workshop as documentation, or to be engraved, or to preserve the autographed model. As for Giulio Romano, he would have, together with his two companions, helped to color the cartoons. In fact when the originals are carefully studied three different hands are perceived, of which Raphael's is without doubt the finest; another one more delicate but weak should be Penni's and finally the solid but rough one is Giulio's. If Giovanni da Udine was employed according to his inclinations to execute the decorative architectonic elements and the architecture itself, who would dare say that he could not recognize them? When Raphael is present, the pupils are always rather dominated or assimilated. In this case one should also bear in mind that the reading of the cartoons can be deceptive. One is dealing here with surfaces that have been extremely altered; recomposed after they had been subdivided into numerous fragments for the tapestry-makers, then restored many times (was not Christ's mantle in the *Miraculous Draught of Fishes* repainted in white? The mantle was originally red which is its color in the tapestry as well as the color of its reflection in the water in the cartoon). It would certainly be amusing if one would end up with arguing for either Penni or Giulio in a particular section made by an English restorer at the end of the seventeenth century.

The truth of the matter is that the attribution of one or another part to one or another of the pupils has little importance when the work appears powerfully unified. But since it is difficult to avoid these often fruitless pursuits, we shall make some fleeting observations in looking quickly at the cartoons. It has already been suggested what could have been the section made by Giovanni da Udine in the *Miraculous Draught of Fishes*. We should add that in this scene the weakest figure, the only one that would suggest an assistant seems to be the main one, that of Christ. But the observation already made about the repainted mantle reminds us that this is a damaged figure whose lesser qualities should not be imputed to Penni or Giulio, but to injuries and restorations: a good lesson for those who have too much faith in simple stylistic readings. In *Pasce oves meas* (Fig. 17) the quality is very high, and except for the modest execution of the sheep, one hardly knows where he can point out eventual collaborators.

In the *Healing of the Cripple* (Fig. 18), the youth seen from the back and so plastically defined in an anatomy of a gigantic infant, seems to show the hand of Giulio, while the twisted columns with their agile friezes of *putti* and vines could belong to Giovanni da Udine. Here and there the intervention by one or more of the pupils is seen in some of the weaker heads. But more important than noticing some sections by Giulio Romano is observing how the figurations in

36 *Anonymous (Raphael?).* Study for the Prophet Jonah, Drawing. Windsor, Royal Library.

38 *Lorenzo Lotti called Il Lorenzetto.* The Prophet Jonah. Rome, Santa Maria del Popolo, Chigi Chapel.

37 *Lorenzo Lotti called Il Lorenzetto and Raffaello da Montelupo.* The Prophet Elias. Rome, Santa Maria del Popolo, Chigi Chapel.

39 *Raphael and Assistants*. The Coronation of
Charlemagne. Vatican, Stanza dell'Incendio.

this cartoon, above all, the potent images of the crippled so violently characterized within the
limits of brutal realism and yet so exceptionally universal, concentrate within themselves the
symbolic aspect of misery and physical suffering. They are the basic foundation for Giulio Romano's language who takes lasting direction from the violent representative art of Raphael.

This is, in my opinion, the correct view of the relation between Raphael and his workshop
at least up to this point. The shop gives able assistance, although on an entirely subordinate
level. Raphael creates and imprints profound impressions on his pupils, building in them little
by little a personality.

Continuing the examination of the cartoons, the whole central portion of the *Death of Ananias*
(Fig. 19), that is, the two splendid figures in the foreground and the group of Apostles in front
of the drape on the second plane are absolutely autographs. Giulio probably worked on the
group at the left; another assistant who does not seem to be Penni, worked on the figure in
the second plane at the right.

Predominantly by Raphael, I believe, is the *Blinding of Elymas*. The truly extraordinary
invention of the *Sacrifice at Lystra* (Fig. 20) is only partially Raphael's but that part is among
the most impressive and new that he ever painted. We are dealing with the eight figures (six
men and two women) in the crowd at the extreme left. Probably the image of the Apostle is
by the master. Giulio Romano is, it seems to me, easily recognized in the somewhat awkward
colossus who in the foreground on the extreme left leads the ram to sacrifice. Penni must have
worked in the central zone, in that group of figures with their heads covered. Also the somewhat
finicky grace of the boy and his companion near the altar does not seem worthy of Raphael.

There is an even greater intervention of the workshop in the last cartoon, the *Preaching of
St. Paul;* Penni and Giulio had a large share in its execution.

Naturally it is impossible to form an hypothesis on the role of the pupils in preparing the three,
unfortunately lost, cartoons. All three of the respective tapestries: the *Stoning of St. Stephen,*
the *Conversion of St. Paul, St. Paul in Prison* (Fig. 25) have, for various reasons, the flavor of
Giulio Romano's taste.[29] This is an inappropriate, if not reverse way of explaining the situation. In fact it was Giulio who was to find models of certain brutal figures of his *Stoning,* the
fleeing horsemen in the *Battle of the Milvian Bridge,* the typology of his Mantuan giants in various
Raphaelesque creations of those tapestries. The root of Giulio Romano's language is to be sought
in these works by Raphael between 1514 and 1515 and seems to me to coincide with the beginning of his rapid growth in the master's workshop in precisely these years. Thus, as the diverse
artistic personalities of Raphael and Romano correspond very well, so all these Raphaelesque
inventions are to reappear, interpreted by Giulio in a very different and also relentlessly
diminished context.

Besides the cartoons for the main scenes, those for the borders and the predellas must have been prepared. None of them survives, but it is not difficult to recognize, even through the distortions of the Flemish tapestry-makers, that in all these parts Raphael must have contributed little. Naturally this must have been clear even in the sixteenth century and it explains the lack of attention given to them. According to Vasari the *fregiature* were the main contribution of Penni's collaboration.

Based upon what can be judged from studying the fabrics, the tasks must have been subdivided: the lateral borders (today of the nine only five remain, those with the representation of the *Fates* (Fig. 21); of the *Theological Virtues;* of *Hercules* with the celestial and terrestrial globes; of the *Seasons and Hours* (Fig. 22). Lost are those of the *Four Elements*, the *Arts of the Trivium*, the *Arts of the Quadrivium*, the *Cardinal Virtues*) conceived according to the system of the grotesque, are attributable to Giovanni da Udine, the specialist in this field. Certainly they would not have been made without suggestions by Raphael nor without his final approval, but in this case I am disposed to admit that to Giovanni da Udine was left the honor of actually making the projects.

The predellas, instead, are reminiscent of Penni's art. The stories contained in them, as is known, are of two different types. The five tapestries, that is, the *Stoning of St. Stephen* and all the *Stories of St. Peter* contained in the predellas depict the salient events in the life of Leo X from 1492 when he returned to Florence as a Cardinal to the *Adoration* after he was made Pope in 1513 (Fig. 23). The predellas of the remaining tapestries, all dedicated to St. Paul, recount events from the life of the Saint according to the Acts of the Apostles (Figs. 24 and 25). The single scenes in monochrome, since they imitate antique relief, follow a manner

already inaugurated on the base of the Stanza di Eliodoro, where the use of caryatids and the reduction of the scenes into small compartments framed within vast and open fields remove from the imitative reliefs the typical aspect of a continuous narrative, characteristic of Roman historical reliefs of the Imperial age. In the tapestries, however, the distention of the scenes along the whole length of the predella and the adding together of two or more different narratives in the same compartment recall vividly prototypes from the Imperial columns and constitute the most direct precedent for the painted socles done after Raphael's death in the Stanza di Costantino. Once again we find in a section of the tapestries, a motif that will be taken up by Giulio Romano.[30] Giulio's love for Trajan's Column which dominated his house nearby at Macel de' Corvi must have predisposed him very favorably toward similar decorative solutions. It does not appear, however, that the cartoons for the predellas of the tapestries could have been his own. The subject matter was surely suggested by a literary figure in the Medici circle and Raphael must have supervised the translation into stories suggesting, with his usual exceptional ability, the iconographic solutions so rich in ancient references and as such, constituting a sort of erudite and passionate re-evocation of historic Imperial sculpture. It is possible nonetheless that the share of the master was limited to suggesting some sample solution and the overall supervision, leaving a free hand to the assistant charged with the work. Since the style, as it can be deduced from the tapestries, does not contradict Vasari's information that the author of these parts was Penni, it seems to me convenient in the absence of more certain data to retain the attribution of the Aretine historian.

Thus we have seen the role of the workshop for the tapestries; contemporaneously the young assistants of Raphael were called upon to help him in the third Vatican Stanza.

None of the preparatory drawings or the supposed ones for the frescoes of the third Stanza can be convincingly attributed to Raphael.

From the point of view of composition, that is, the distribution of the figures in space, from their relationship with the architecture and the landscape, from the choice of the vanishing point of the perspective, and finally from the rapport between the main scene and the minor ones, the four histories of this room differ from each other, and excluding the *Oath of Leo III before Charlemagne*, they fail to show connections with the scenes of the Stanza di Eliodoro.

From the point of view of the workmanship that is the pictorial execution, not only is the general quality inferior to the other frescoes by Raphael but what is more important, the hand of pupils is apparent.

The evaluation incidentally expressed by Leonardo Sellaio, while announcing to Michelangelo the unveiling of the frescoes depicting Cupid and Psyche as "not worthy of a fine master; much worse than the last Stanza of the Palace" has inevitably found an echo in the writings by scholars.[31] The sparse autography was already proclaimed by Vasari: "There was nothing else to do but follow the order that he started in the papal rooms and halls in which he kept constantly helpers who were carrying out the designs under his continuous supervision. It was not long before he uncovered the chamber of the Borgia Tower in which he painted a scene on every wall."[32]

Hartt has reduced to a minimum Raphael's responsibility in this room by utilizing his

43 *Raphael and Giulio Romano.* Egyptian telamon, Detail from Stanza dell'Incendio, Vatican.

44 *Giulio Romano.* Study for a herm-caryatid in the socle of the Stanza dell'Incendio, Drawing. Haarlem, Teylers Museum.

attitude taken with regard to the cartoons and tapestries. For the American scholar, Giulio Romano had the real responsibility for the frescoes: Giulio devised the scenes, he executed the preparatory drawings, he painted the two most famous histories, namely the *Fire in the Borgo* and the *Battle of Ostia*. This is Hartt's most radical position which was taken before his monography,[33] in a long article devoted to the relationship between the master and the pupils where Hartt concentrated on an examination of the two scenes.[34] The essence of this text by Hartt is to be found in the observation that their plan and its realization went beyond the language of Raphael. They revealed a new and different personality, precisely that of Giulio Romano.

More recent criticism is less extremist. De Campos who has frequently studied the problem since the recent restorations, examines with great objectivity Raphael's share in the project and in the direction of works and without abandoning traditional opinions he did not fail to notice that here the master was physically exhausted.[35]

Others, like Pouncey and Shearman limit themselves to rejecting Hartt's extreme position without offering detailed judgments.[36] Still others, like Freedberg and Brizio, attempt although aware of the works of the pupils, to find traces of Raphael's personal vision and his continual renewal in the Stanza dell'Incendio.[37]

45 *Anonymous (Raphaelesque).* Venus and Cupid, (after original drawing of Raphael for decoration of the Stufetta for Cardinal Bibbiena?), Drawing. Windsor, Royal Library.

47 *Raphael and Assistants.* Detail for decoration of the Stufetta for Cardinal Bibbiena, Vatican.

46 *Raphael and Assistants.* Venus and Cupid, detail from the Stufetta for Cardinal Bibbiena.

The point is crucial for a study dealing with Raphael's workshop. The real question here is to what degree one can admit the autonomy of the pupils and how one goes about establishing their identities.

The phrase of Vasari already cited seems to answer the question better than any of our suppositions. He presents us with a completely normal situation: a master who prepares the designs upon which the assistants "carry on the work" and finally the master himself "continuously checking everything." The procedure corresponds to artistic practice. It is understandable that finding himself almost contemporaneously occupied with cartoons for the tapestries and frescoes for the third Stanza, Raphael busied himself more with the cartoons. The tapestries were to be executed by Van Aelst in Brussels, far from his control; the ideas were to be transferred from the quite different technique and material of painting into weaving. Therefore, the greatest concentration on the cartoons was necessary. After all, the tapestries with the Acts of the Apostles, were intended for the Sistine Chapel, an even nobler place than the private papal apartments and there they would form a dialogue with Michelangelo's ceiling: the challenge was great. This does not mean that Raphael would have lost interest in the scenes for the third Stanza. Though less important than the Sistine Chapel, the papal apartments were always a worthy location. "The chambers of N. S. that Raphael painted, because of the singular and excellent painting, and also because they are full of Cardinals, are very beautiful . . .," Bembo writes to Bibbiena on July 19, 1517.[38] This supplies the information that the just completed frescoes in the Borgia Tower were destined for an important public.

The correspondence of Costabili to the Duke of Ferrara proves that Raphael, and not others, was the author of the cartoons and that the master considered the frescoes entirely his responsibility. In a letter of November, 1517 there is mention of the cartoons "that Raphael of Urbino donated to Your Excellency of a scene of Pope Leo IV which he painted in the Pope's room."[39] This cartoon is lost, but it must refer to the *Fire in the Borgo* or to the *Battle of Ostia*, and 221

48 *Raphael and Assistants.* Grotesque in lunette of the Stufetta for Cardinal Bibbiena (detail). Vatican.

49 *Raphael* (?). Detail from preceding grotesque. Vatican.

it is improbable that Raphael would advertise a pupil's work as his own. In fact, as Shearman pointed out on another occasion, after having sent the Duke the cartoon of the portrait of Giovanna d'Aragona done by a pupil, Raphael through Costabili stated that "he had not sent the portrait . . . as his own; he sent His Excellency the portrait made by his pupil who was sent to Naples to make it, since it was desired for Santa Maria in Portico." [40]

In another letter from the same correspondence we read: "Raphael of Urbino told me he still has two days work in the Pope's apartment, after which he promised to begin without fail Your Excellency's work." [41] Bearing in mind the desperate efforts by Raphael to justify the continuous delays in delivering the works of important patrons (often paid in advance), the responsibility for the papal chamber may seem to be only an excuse. But it could not have been a good one had everyone not known that Raphael was really looking after the work there. Do not tell me that in the Vatican, at that time, as it is now, they would not know the smallest detail about such an important and envied favorite as Raphael. An indirect confirmation that Raphael really had supplied the drawings for the frescoes is found in the behavior of Giulio Romano and Penni, when after Raphael's death, they had to face the insidiousness of Sebastiano del Piombo who wanted to take over from them the inherited commission for the last Stanza, that of Constantine.

On that occasion they asserted that they had Raphael's design and projects for the decoration. The appeal to the famous name of the deceased master was a *deus ex machina* without recourse for Sebastiano's claims. But would the expedient have been effective had Raphael not failed to personally provide drawings for his decorative commission? Certainly not! It is quite probable that Giulio and Penni did not have even a single sketch by Raphael for the *Stories of Constantine* but their claims must have been credible enough to have weight in the Pope's decision. This decision was based on Raphael's work on the other Vatican frescoes.

Now it will be asked, where are Raphael's drawings for the Tower of Borgia frescoes, and why are they so different and irreconcilable to his art? Is not this the proof that they were all done by the workshop? Are not the studies for the *Fire* by Giulio (Figs. 26, 27 and 28); [42] the single but very famous study for the *Battle of Ostia* also by Giulio (Fig. 29); [43] the preparatory folios for the *Coronation and Oath* (Fig. 30 and 31), are they not Penni's? [44] The sketches and drawings by Raphael are lost. But there is nothing strange about this when one remembers the quantity of graphic works irremediably lost over the centuries. Besides Shearman's suggestion that the study for *Aeneas and Anchises* may be an autograph should be refuted (see note 42). The same writer has called our attention to a drawing of the Artistic Society in Zurich (Fig. 32). [45]

50 *Raphael* (?). Amorino, detail from decoration of the Stufetta of Cardinal Bibbiena. Vatican.

51 *Anonymous.* Decoration of the Stufetta for Clement VII. Vatican.

Published by Fischel as a study for one of the female figures in the *Expulsion of Heliodorus*, he maintains that it is one of the early Raphaelesque ideas for the group of women with children in the foreground of the *Fire in the Borgo*.[46] The female figure and the *putto* from Zurich clearly derive from an antique Niobe, were then doubled, so to speak, during the process of the theme's elaboration, in the four figures drawn by Giulio (Vienna, Albertina S.R. 274; Fig. 27) and then translated into fresco. Also this hypothesis by Shearman can be accepted with the result that the graphic preparation of the fresco by Raphael would be illuminated and partially proved. The basic point is something else, however. What value is there in showing that Raphael executed the drawings for the frescoes, if they are so foreign to his language and the context of his work? Furthermore is this a correct affirmation?

Generally, the *Fire in the Borgo* (Fig. 33) is considered to have been the first in the series. Only Freedberg, as far as I know, dates it after the *Battle of Ostia* (Fig. 34) but his reasons are highly disputable.[47] If the *Fire* was the earliest in the series, it is quite probable that it was already planned in 1514 almost contemporaneously with the conclusion of the work in the Stanza di Eliodoro. In fact the horizon line upon which the whole perspective is hinged falls here as it does in the scenes of the Stanza di Eliodoro in about the middle of the composition. In the other three frescoes (Figs. 34, 39 and 41), the horizon is raised as it is in the tapestry cartoons and in all the late works (for example, the *Transfiguration*). It is undoubtedly interesting that he was becoming involved with new architectural problems connected with Saint Peter's. Raphael represented the façade of the Basilica in the fresco but more interesting and quite persuading both as absolute evidences of the paternity of the fresco and for a dating of 1514, at least for the design, are precisely these traces of a new archaeological taste characteristic of Raphael's concerns in the summer of 1514. At that time he received from Fabio Calvo the translation of Vitruvius which he intended to illustrate and he discussed it with Fra Giocondo, specialist in archaeological and Vitruvian matters whom the Pope had placed beside him for the work on Saint Peter's.[48] Probably under the influence of the Veronese friar, Raphael proposed to find in antique architecture the guidelines for carrying out the large structure which Leo X had commissioned him to do. For this great task Raphael exclaimed "Vitruvius offered me clarification for it." [49]

52 *Giulio Romano and Assistants* (?). Diana and Cupid, detail, from Decoration of the Stufetta for Clement VII. Rome, Castel Sant'Angelo.

53 *Giulio Romano and Assistants* (?). Stufetta for Clement VII. Rome, Castel Sant'Angelo.

At the same time he followed the advice of the archaeologist Andrea Fulvio "with whom he went in search for fine antiquities that can be found around these vineyards and I drew them by order of our Lord." [50] Clearly such an accentuated classical and erudite climate (note the cultivated allusion to the *Burning of Troy* at the left of the fresco) pervades this work and fits very well with Raphael's mental attitude during the summer of 1514 when the already cited letter to his uncle Simone Ciarla assures us that Raphael had begun to work on the third Stanza. Thus, the fresco of the *Fire* is not only compatible to Raphael but it expresses exactly his thoughts of the moment. It is entirely his and not Giulio's, still too young to be able to impose anything on his master. Begun when the work on the tapestries had not yet absorbed the painter, the *Fire* is the most Raphaelesque of the frescoes in the room. But in the course of its planning, the second assignment brought Raphael's attention away from the Tower of Borgia. At this point Giulio Romano intervened. It is not surprising that he never again succeeded in executing anything of such a high level; it is, simply, the product of the invention, preparation and continuous participation of Raphael.

Brizio has suggested that one should perceive in this fresco some typical scenographic qualities in connection with theatrical preparations.[51] It is possible, and if it is true that Raphael only later began working in the field of scenography, one cannot remain silent about the fact that there were highly important theatrical preparations for the Carnival in 1514. Peruzzi staged the *Calandria* by Bibbiena, repeating in this way the production and perhaps the scenery used in Urbino the year before, which had been conceived by Genga. Therefore, even this scenographic element tends to date the project for the *Fire in the Borgo* in 1514. Nor is the connection with the scenes by Peruzzi entirely improbable, if one recalls Baldassarre's theatrical drawings. They are rich in archaeological elements and the one in the Uffizi with modern buildings and famous Roman monuments may be identified with the scene from *Calandria*.

It is probable that while Raphael was preparing the execution in fresco of the *Fire in the Borgo* the commission for the Vatican tapestries came up. At this moment Giulio Romano entered into the execution of the fresco and, supported by the master's guidance, he carried on in excellent fashion. Nevertheless, he was not able to avoid a greater plastic hardness, a certain rigidity that separates the groups from each other and the single figures within the groups, rendering them more like statues than living people. At this point I do not know if one should bring in Penni. It is usually done by assigning to him the very small figures at the back, but I ask myself if the lightness of the touch which is normal in the treatment of backgrounds is not being confused with the greater softness that usually distinguishes the sweet but weak brush stroke of Penni from the constructive one of Giulio.

In 1515 Penni and Giovanni da Udine were probably recruited for the work on the cartoons while Giulio continued to look after the frescoes which could not be interrupted. Thus the *Battle of Ostia* is Giulio's work, the idea is Raphael's but he did little on it and the quality of the fresco consequently suffers. Nevertheless only Raphael could have decided to raise the horizon line to enlarge the vista as he did also in the tapestry cartoons. In this way he was able to arrange the scene in two different planes. The composition on the first plane with victors and vanquished, all inspired by classical reliefs, is from a still archaeological climate, like the *Fire in the Borgo*. The motive is not new in Raphael. There is a folio at Oxford, a pen drawing, that has an analogous scene on the retro and verso.[52] Datable some five years earlier, this drawing proves that Giulio Romano cannot be credited with an idea already formulated when the young assistant of Raphael was still a child, completely outside of the thoughts of art. The idea of the boatman who, placing his left foot on the frame of the fresco to shove off on his boat, appears to come out of the illusionary space of the painting to enter the real space of the spectator, is also Raphaelesque. The vision of the *triregnum* in the *Sistine Madonna* placed on a kind of parapet over the infinite which constitutes the base of the picture, offers a similar sensation. With a strange sense of reversed situation almost as if one watches the secret interior of a room from the bright outdoors, the two little angels show themselves from the sky.

The sixteen-year-old Giulio Romano was left to his own devices, giving in the execution of the *Battle of Ostia* a formidable example of his precocity. Thickening the plastic contrast of the groups and obscuring the composite clarity of Raphael, in a continuous laced mass of bodies in battle, the personality of the young assistant begins to develop and we perceive here the future author of the enormous *Battle of the Milvian Bridge*.

The frescoes in the Stanza dell'Incendio proceeded slowly. In 1515 and certainly still at the beginning of 1516, Raphael was very busy with the tapestry cartoons. Penni and Giovanni da Udine assisted him with precise assignments; they executed the borders and the predellas. But they also helped in the main scenes as did Giulio himself in more than one instance as we have seen. In 1516 Raphael finished other commissions: the dome of the Chigi Chapel in Santa Maria del Popolo, dated during this year, was decorated with mosaics. Raphael prepared splendid drawings (Fig. 35) which the Venetian mosaicist Alvise de Pace executed.[53] It is possible that one of the pupils prepared the cartoons. Also in 1516, indeed before June 20, of that same year, the apartments of Cardinal Bibbiena were terminated.[54] In the meantime there was a change among the collaborators in the Stanza dell'Incendio. Giulio finished his task by executing the *Battle of Ostia*. On the third stanza it was Penni who substituted for him. He probably had finished the predellas for the tapestries and was available. Raphael

54 *Raphael and Assistants*. Loggetta of Cardinal Bibbiena. Vatican.

55 *Raphael and Assistants*. Loggetta of Cardinal Bibbiena. Vatican.

56 *G. F. Penni* (?). Lunette with Vulcan's Forge, detail from Decoration of the Loggetta of Cardinal Bibbiena. Vatican.

57 *Giovanni da Udine and Collaborators.* Detail from decoration of the Loggetta of Cardinal Bibbiena. Vatican.

58 *Taddeo Zuccari and Collaborators.* Decoration of the Sala dei Palafrenieri. Vatican.

gave him the *Coronation of Charlemagne*, using Giulio Romano and Giovanni da Udine for the more subtle and refined works for Cardinal Bibbiena. Nor is to be excluded the possibility that Giulio executed the cartoons for the mosaics of the Chigi Chapel.

In 1516 work was being done in the Stufetta and in the Tower of Borgia.

The construction of the fresco with the *Coronation of Charlemagne* (**Fig. 39**) is one of the most original of Raphael's thoughts showing us to what point this great painter might have arrived, had not death stopped him. The horizon is very high, allowing for the creation of a vast space and here the groups of figures are disposed obliquely in space, multiplying the directional axes and suggesting crossed diagonals in space. The light was to have underscored this vitality of human masses with its dynamics and this would have produced a completely new whole in comparison to the symmetries of a central vision adopted in the other Stanze.

Also new are the no-centralized compositions used by Raphael in the *Repulse of Attila* and in the *Battle of Ostia* and in some tapestries like the *Conversion of St. Paul*, the *Miraculous Draught of Fishes*, the *Giving of the Keys*, the *Sacrifice at Lystra*, and the *St. Paul Preaching*. In them the movement which runs across the space parallel to the picture's surface has a mono-directional intensity that ends at the culminating element of the scene, namely the protagonist, who since he becomes the antagonist of the choral movement, is isolated and enlarged. But in the *Coronation*, the protagonist is the interweaving of masses and spatial thrusts. With this dynamic vitality, Raphael conceived the representation of a scene as a contemporary chronicle. There is no doubt that this is the first time that Raphael leaves a symbolic representation controlled by norms of a classical ideal (and this is the case in the *Mass at Bolsena*), to venture into a lively contemporary account. Compared with the scenes of the Stanza di Eliodoro, the *Coronation of Charlemagne* is completely new and in a certain sense foreign to the fundamentals of a classical language. The Mannerist painters of the sixteenth century were to recognize it and take it as a point of departure. How frequently do we see that stupendous passage of obliquely seated bishops with solemn white miters!

229

59 *G. F. Penni.* Drawing, the Evangelist Matthew in the Sala dei Palafrenieri. Paris, Louvre.

61 *G. F. Penni.* Drawing, the Evangelist John in the Sala dei Palafrenieri. Paris, Louvre.

60 *G. F. Penni.* Drawing, the Evangelist Luke in the Sala dei Palafrenieri. London, British Museum.

Unfortunately the executor took the color out of Raphael's invention but I agree with Cavalcaselle and Venturi that the group of bishops is worthy of the master who probably intervened personally. Besides Penni there were other minor assistants but it is impossible to name them. The more modest assistants in Raphael's shop are too difficult to identify when working under him since we know practically nothing of their work as independent artists. In such a situation, each name suggested is only a guess. Only in the Vatican Loggias will it be possible to identify other hands besides Penni, Giulio and Giovanni da Udine. They are beginners but with pronounced personalities well known by their autonomous works—painters like Perino del Vaga and Polidoro da Caravaggio.

Penni's responsibility for the execution of the *Coronation of Charlemagne* has always been upheld by modern criticism beginning with Cavalcaselle and Dollmayr even if it must be admitted that the sources (that is, Vasari) in no way mention Il Fattore in relation to the Stanza dell'Incendio. Hartt opposes the current opinion for stylistic reasons, and advances the name of Raffaellino del Colle in place of Penni.[55] This new attribution has an uncertain foundation in the sources, to say the least. (Vasari records Raffaellino del Colle in Rome among the assistants of Giulio Romano, not of Raphael) and Hartt does not cite a document published by Degli Azzi from which it is learned that on November 11, 1517, a painting commissioned from Raffaellino by the friars of Santa Maria della Neve was paid for in Borgo San Sepolcro.[56] Nevertheless we cannot exaggerate the authority of Vasari, whose errors are known to all and there is nothing to exclude the possibility that the painting for Borgo San Sepolcro was made in Rome and sent home by the painter, or less probably, it was painted some years before and paid for only in 1517. In addition, although Raffaellino's date of birth is not known, the fact that he made his first will in 1554 and died on November 17, 1566, does not conflict with the possibility that he was born at the end of the fifteenth century and therefore around 1516 he was old enough to collaborate with Raphael.[57]

The more serious problem is that of stylistic concordance. Raffaellino is not in the same situation as many of the minor assistants of Raphael and Giulio, who are known only by name. Vasari tells us that they were employed in this or that decoration but we do not possess any certain and independent works by them. There are a certain number of Raffaellino's pictures. This does not mean we are able to say that we know his style for this period; indeed everything that remains of his work is certainly later. His works are all found outside Rome, the majority in his native area between Città di Castello and Borgo San Sepolcro, where he returned after the Roman years. They all betray, with the possible exception of the *Resurrection* in the Cathedral of Borgo, influences not only from Rosso but also from a Mannerist Tuscan culture of the mid-century. Most contradictory to Hartt's proposal is the fact that late paintings by Raffaellino are so mediocre and with such a typical provincial stamp. Serious doubts arise over the possibility that such a fabricator of altarpieces for the country churches between Umbria and Tuscany could have obtained in his youth decisively superior results as the executor of the *Coronation of Charlemagne* had. And to go as far as Hartt's supposition that he was the author of the project for the composition whose great novelty we have indicated, is hardly worth discussing. Even less so is the same scholar's contention made in the appendix to his article that the question may be raised to attribute to him, together with other famous pictures from Raphael's workshop, the fascinating masterpiece, the so-called *Fornarina* in the Galleria Nazionale Romana di Pittura in Rome.

62 *Raphael and Assistants.* Decoration of the Loggia of Psyche, general view. Rome, Farnesina.

65 *Raphael* (?). Study for the Three Graces in the Wedding of Cupid and Psyche, Drawing. Windsor, Royal Library.

63 *G. F. Penni* (?). Study for the figure of Omphale in the Wedding of Cupid and Psyche, Drawing. Haarlem, Teylers Museum.

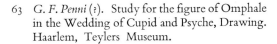

64 *G. F. Penni* (?). Study, for the figure of Ganymede in the Wedding of Cupid and Psyche, Drawing. Paris, Louvre.

It is common, I admit, the case of artists who returning to the provinces from a center of high culture, undergo a powerful involution. But this analysis of Raffaellino is not acceptable; rather it may be supposed that in Rome he was just a modest assistant of a greater master.

Observing then with attention the only work that still permits the recognition of the painter as a member of the Roman fraternity, that is, the already mentioned *Resurrection of Christ* in the Cathedral of Borgo San Sepolcro, there is nothing here but a rather awkward re-use of Raphael's ideas for his never-realized *Resurrection* (ideas that Raffaellino could have known well through the drawing inherited by Giulio). It is in a heavily emphatic plastic style with gloomy and violent shadows revealing an author who was more the follower of Giulio than of Raphael. Here for once Vasari was correct. Nor does the landscape background with Roman ruins in Raffaellino's altarpieces recall Raphael but Giulio. They are certainly not comparable, as Hartt claims, to the sublime view of Rome in *Attila and Leo* where the measure between reality and idealization marks this passage in Raphael, a prelude to seventeenth century classical landscapes. In fact they derive from those passionate and capricious syllogisms of antique architecture and monuments that populate the horizon in the *Oration of Constantine* and the *Stoning of Stephen* and they open a direction for fantastic and archaeological landscapes that recall the extreme effects of Niccolò dell'Abate and Antoine Caron. Giulio is also in this case the source for our painter, but in Raffaellino, I am afraid, all that remains is the inert echo in a country-style performance.

Finally the Morellian comparisons brought in by Hartt between certain profiles in the *Coronation of Charlemagne* and certain others in the *Resurrection* from Borgo San Sepolcro or in the *Presentation of the Virgin* from the Pinacoteca in Città di Castello, are not unfounded but it seems to me, they cannot prove anything more than a generic taste in drawing, applicable rather generally among painters in central Italy during those years.

Conclusion: However much there is to appreciate in Hartt's efforts to bring from anonymity and individualize more precisely the collaborators of Raphael, it seems very dubious that his attribution of the *Coronation* fresco can be easily accepted. Hartt has, nonetheless, shown something: there is in the fresco a zone, namely that above at the left with the groups of bishops and captains near the altar that shows greater graphic insistence. It is probable that here we should discern someone other than Penni who is generally inclined to more unified painting with soft masses of colors. We are perhaps witnessing at this moment the appearance of assistants of the assistants. In fact Penni must have prepared the cartoons on Raphael's design and executed most of the fresco, assisted by an anonymous collaborator, and perhaps several, to which the name might be applied although other names might also be taken from the regiment cited by Vasari and of the other fifty or more who also, according to Vasari, encircled Raphael and who accompanied him like a retinue on the street when he was on his way to the Vatican.[58]

In any case the participation of this collaborator whether he was Raffaellino or not, can never be included in the project for the whole, as Hartt wants, nor for a major portion of the execution of painting which in my judgment belongs to Penni. Rather it is confined to

66 G. F. Penni (?). Study for the figure of Venus showing Psyche to Cupid, Drawing. Paris, Louvre.

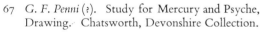

67 G. F. Penni (?). Study for Mercury and Psyche, Drawing. Chatsworth, Devonshire Collection.

some sectors where, as has been said, the taste for graphic outlines of the figures shows itself with greater insistence.

The last fresco in the room, the *Oath* or the *Justification of Leo III* (Fig. 41), remains to be discussed. Reading it is not easy because it is badly preserved and placed in a fastidious position against the light, from the window cut into the wall. Despite his good intentions Freedberg wanted to see in the composition of the scene a conscious return to the measured monumentality of the tapestry cartoons after the dynamic attempt in the *Coronation*, rather than an inert repetition of the scene in the *Mass at Bolsena:* it is difficult to avoid a feeling of delusion in front of this work, as when one encounters familiar things already known, but in finer garb. The execution must fall during the first half of 1517 (the project could not have been undertaken before December 19, 1516, cf. note 22). The year 1517 was also a busy one for Raphael; besides minor works, there was the large altarpiece of the *Spasimo di Sicilia;* the frescoes in the Loggia of Psyche in the Farnesina (finished by the year's end); probably the organization and supervision of the lost frescoes in the Sala dei Palafrenieri; the direction of the restoration of the Loggetta of Cardinal Bibbiena and the completion of the architecture for the Loggias in the courtyard of San Damaso.

In addition, Raphael had important responsibility derived from his position as director of the works of St. Peter's; he was engaged in the study and conservation of Roman antiquities; and he received three important French commissions for paintings. At the beginning of the year Cardinal de' Medici ordered the altarpiece of the *Transfiguration* for the Cathedral of Narbonne; [59] at the end of the year there was added the request for the *St. Michael* and the *Holy Family with St. Elizabeth* for the King and Queen of France.

There is enough here to explain Raphael's relative disinterest for the lost fresco in the Stanza dell'Incendio, the twelfth large painted wall in the rooms of the papal apartment.

If, as I believe, Raphael gave to Penni little more than a general suggestion, the latter conducted himself predictably. He conformed to Raphael's most obvious style consecrated in the preceding rooms. He was, as always happens with those of minor ingenuity, more realistic than the " King." He retained for the sake of uniformity with the other two scenes executed in the preceding room only the horizon which is somewhat higher than in the *Mass at Bolsena.* He approached thus the more modern solutions of the tapestries like the *Death of Ananias.* The finished drawing in the Horne Foundation (Fig. 31) blocked out for transfer into a cartoon which seems to me without doubt by Penni, proves that he was certainly responsible for all the final preparation of the fresco. As for the execution, the possibility that he availed himself of the help of assistants as with the *Coronation* cannot be overlooked. It hardly seems possible to impute the low quality in many sections to the correct mediocrity of Il Fattore.

The collaborator evidently cannot be identified here as the one individualized in the *Coronation* (Raffaellino for Hartt) and I agree in this case with the opinion of the American scholar. It must have been another assistant (or perhaps several), but it is impossible to advance any names.

The base of the Stanza with caryatids in the form of herms in imitation marble and the interspersed figures of protector kings of the Church painted in *terretta gialla* (Fig. 42) belong to Giulio.[60] We can even suppose that he was, under the generic control of Raphael, the one in charge of the complete composition, the date of the execution of which must fall in 1517. Giulio was already eighteen years old and this trial was commensurate to his ability. Unfortunately Maratta's repainting obscured almost all, the vigorous figures but where it has been removed especially in a herm with a youthful and vital aspect, the hand of Raphael's best assistant is easily recognized. He is here already a formed artist yet the solid plasticity of these images, their richness and formal articulation are below the level attained in the figures of the *Fire in the Borgo*, done almost two years earlier when the painter was still a boy; Raphael's presence before and during the execution was indeed valuable.

Perhaps the idea and surely the execution of the Egyptian telamons that flank the frescoes were Giulio's (Fig. 43). The antique originals from which they were copied was discovered at Tivoli a few years before and today are part of the Vatican collections (Museo Pio-Clementino). This typically archaeological element is added to the many antique motifs present in the Stanza, in the *Fire in the Borgo* and in the *Battle of Ostia.* The climate of the Rome of Leo X was no longer the Rome of Julius II. We have seen how Raphael was involved in the study of Antiquity by the wish of the Pope. In this, which is the first of the Stanze made for the Medici Pope, the archaeological erudite passion on the one hand and a descriptive interest in contemporary narrative on the other, dominate. Thus, as the archaeological elements bear testimony of the humanist Pope's passion for antiquities (the Loggias will be shortly arranged to house the collection of Leo X's statues), the mitered bishops in the *Coronation* evoke the solemn assembly of the Lateran Council and the likeness of Francis I dressed as Charlemagne reflect the proposals, views and anguish of Leo's diplomacy. Raphael is the sensitive interpreter of this more profane and less heroic reality where refinement of the culture and the anxiety of nepotist ambition take the place of the noble thoughts of Julius II. Raphael's pupils obediently respond following as well as they can the extraordinary ability of the master to transfer the situation and the ideas into images. While the works in the Stanza dell'Incendio were half finished Raphael did the Stufetta for Cardinal Bibbiena (Figs. 46-50) with his pupils. It is perhaps the finest result of the archaeological culture of the master. The date of the Stufetta is certain: on June 20, 1516 it was already finished.[61] However, a couple of months

68 *G. F. Penni* (?). Study for Venus and Mercury in the Wedding of Cupid and Psyche, Drawing. Chatsworth, Devonshire Collection.

before at least the small mythological stories were still to be finished; he executed them following a book given to him by the patron.[62]   The program for the Stufetta is unified: the architecture and pictorial decoration are so interdependent that we must conclude that they were conceived together.   For about a century Italian Renaissance artists engaged in an ideal competition with the ancient world.   But if exception is made for the special world of small bronzes and carvings, no one achieved such an identification, either spiritual and formal, with Hellenistic-Roman art.   This actually could also be considered a limitation in this art if the decisively imitative intention were not redeemed by the truly palpable enthusiasm with which

234

69-70 *Raphael and Giulio Romano.* Cupid and the Three Graces – Venus, Ceres and Juno. Rome, Farnesina, Loggia of Psyche.

71-72 *Raphael and Giulio Romano.* Venus on a Golden Chariot – Psyche give Venus the Vial with Water from the Styx. Rome, Farnesina, Loggia of Psyche.

Raphael offers proof of his own culture to one of his learned patrons. The stories from Ovid and Servius suggested by the Cardinal of Santa Maria in Portico are returned, as it were, to the environment and mode of dress they would have assumed had the authors ordered them painted by an artist of the first century. The dialogue between humanistic and philological culture of Bibbiena and the archaeological one of Raphael, under the excited eyes of Bembo, was so intense that any other consideration becomes secondary and futile. What importance is there in weighing the roles of the collaborators for this delightful undertaking? Raphael had first guided them in exploring the Roman sites and gave them the taste for archaeology.

73 *Raphael and Giulio Romano. Cupid and Jove.* Rome, Farnesina, Loggia of Psyche.

74 *Raphael and G. F. Penni. Mercury and Psyche.* Rome, Farnesina, Loggia of Psyche.

75 *Raphael and G. F. Penni. Mercury.* Rome, Farnesina, Loggia of Psyche.

76 *Raphael and G. F. Penni. Venus and Jove.* Rome, Farnesina, Loggia of Psyche.

77 *Raphael and G. F. Penni. Venus carried by cupids.* Rome, Farnesina, Loggia of Psyche.

78 *Raphael and G. F. Penni (?). Venus showing Psyche to Cupid.* Rome, Farnesina, Loggia of Psyche.

Through Raphael they not only became acquainted with the antique, but had contact with men like Bembo, Fulvio, Navagero, Beazzano, and Calvo who taught them the history of Antiquity.

Giulio Romano and Giovanni da Udine, the two most lively and sensitive temperaments in the workshop had adopted this patrimony of ideas, this passionate predilection and it is therefore natural that Raphael employed them for this very special assignment.[63]

I think that the decorative sections and the grotesque motifs are to be assigned to Giovanni da Udine;[64] nearly all of the figurative scenes are usually given to Giulio.[65] The poor state of conservation and the nature of the paintings that willingly imitate the technique and the economical and rapid style of Hellenistic art make single attributions rather risky. The important thing is the general stamp which is qualitatively very high. A comparison with analogous works produced by the workshop alone, like the Loggetta in the same apartment (Figs. 54-57) and soon after Raphael's death, the Stufetta of Clement VII in the Vatican (Fig. 51) or the other in Castel Sant'Angelo (Figs. 52 and 53) is sufficient to indicate here in the Stufetta of Bibbiena the dominating presence of the master.

Thus the conclusion of De Campos seems to me very judicious: "the restoration made in 1942 would counsel, in my opinion, a revision of the critical judgment, perhaps too drastic, that assigns to Raphael's school, guided by his drawings, the painting of the entire Stufetta excluding any direct intervention by the master. That which remains of the little Venus born from the waves and the one who suffers with Cupid from the wounds of love are not unworthy of his brush. I also believe that some of the figures in the lunette imitated subsequently by his disciples in the second Loggia and in that of Bibbiena though never equaled, are by his hand."[66]

I also believe that in this case Raphael did not limit himself to the project but from the

81 *Raphael and Giovanni da Udine. Amorino* with Lion and Sea Horse. Rome, Farnesina, Loggia of Psyche.

79 *Raphael, Giovanni da Udine and Assistants. Amorino* with Shield and Helmet. Rome, Farnesina, Loggia of Psyche.

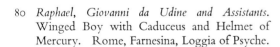

80 *Raphael, Giovanni da Udine and Assistants.* Winged Boy with Caduceus and Helmet of Mercury. Rome, Farnesina, Loggia of Psyche.

same pleasure of experiencing in the work the aesthetic emotions confirmed by contemplating antique decorations, he executed not only some of the mythological scenes but also certain passages of the splendid grotesques, for example those with the *amorini* at the sides of the niche (Fig. 49) and certain delicious small inventions, like the section with the *amorino* who drives a bizarre chariot (Fig. 50), a large vat pulled by a pair of serpents around which, a masterpiece of fantasy and realism, runs a decoration emitting *lattarini*, those tiny fish so well known to Roman cookery.

Only a little time was required to carry on those decorative passages where not only the fresco technique but the style, for example, imposed rapid execution. Even if he was overburdened with commissions I am certain that Raphael would not have divorced himself from the satisfaction of personally working for his friend and protector demonstrating in this way to his assistants the direction to follow in this new type of decoration which was destined to have an important following but never with such brilliant results. For Giulio and above all for Giovanni da Udine the lesson was of decisive importance.

The effects can be seen a few steps from the Stufetta, in the decoration of the Loggia constructed for the Cardinal's apartment (Figs. 54-57). The date of this decoration is generally placed in 1519 because it is related to the contents of Michiel's letter already mentioned.[67] We should, therefore, discuss the Loggetta later. Certain reasonable doubts remain suggesting that it may have been painted earlier, perhaps in 1517, the year in which it was restored (cf. note 54) if not in 1516 as Hartt believes and Freedberg supports, although without discussing the documentary arguments.[68] For this hypothesis one must believe that the rebuilding in 1517 was also partial and that the paintings were restored. The type of decoration is so close to the Stufetta that it is intimately tied to and even in a certain sense derived from it. Only here Raphael's hand is absent, and he probably did not produce a detailed project. Bearing in mind the general type of decoration in which narrow motifs of the grotesque prevail and the scenes on the figurative panels have a distinctly accessory role it seems to me that the minuscule-like project of the whole can be assigned beyond doubt to Giovanni da Udine whose brilliant coloring and truly Neo-Hellenistic spirit is found everywhere. Naturally some collaborators assisted him whether the work was made around 1517 or in 1519; the pupils of Raphael already had their *équipe* of assistants and there are traces of these collaborators in the heaviness of the quality in some passages of the decoration. De Campos who wrote about the Loggetta after the restorations that have permitted its re-evaluation, believes that besides Giovanni and his helpers, Penni, Giulio Romano and Perin del Vaga worked there.[69] He attributed to Penni at least the design of the four *grisaille* figures in the niches, which he identified as the *Seasons* (only three are original, the fourth being a restoration) and that of the lunette with the *Forge of Vulcan*. To Giulio he gave the very fragmentary scene of the lunette over the entrance door and the three little scenes on a black ground with mythological subjects (only two are left today) which appear at the center of the zone of the wall compressed between the painted niches. Finally Penni would appear as an assistant of Giovanni da Udine (the same role he plays in the Vatican Loggias) and would be the recognizable author of at least the two spinners who flank the third painted niche and the two small mythological scenes in a similar position at the sides of the fourth niche.

I confess that this *équipe*, in my opinion, is a bit too numerous and perhaps also a bit heterogeneous but De Campos was able to study the frescoes with complete leisure, a possibility not granted to one like myself who can enter these quarters connected with the Segreteria of the Vatican State only rarely and for a short time. Perino seems to me recognizable in the

237

parts indicated by De Campos, quite close to the Perino we shall meet on the Biblical stories of the Loggias (which would suggest that the two were executed nearer together in time).

A very interesting circumstance for stabilizing the rapport between Raphael's pupils and the ancient world that inspired them is furnished by the study of the two surviving panels attributed by De Campos to Giulio Romano: *Olympus Beseeching Apollo* and *Apollo and Marsyas*. Both derive from analogous scenes that decorated, it seems, a Roman columbarium. Those paintings are today lost but we know them from the copies in a drawing collection put together around the middle of the sixteenth century by the German Stefan Vinand or Wynants Pighius and conserved in the Library in Berlin with the name "Codex Pighianus." Basing himself on them, De Campos has been able to suppose that the third scene, now lost, represented the *Punishment of Marsyas*. It was proved that when there was no help from the suggestions by a man of letters, as in the case of the Stufetta, the painters went ahead on their own to select their material, sacking the wealthy mines of Antiquity. Nor should we be surprised if it were made by Giulio whose familiarity with Roman archaeology we have already underscored.

In 1517 we have the last large decorative commission in which Raphael directly guided his young assistants and the first one, as far as we know, when the assistants are paid directly without his mediation; to a certain extent this is an official recognition of their autonomy.

I have already mentioned the payment of twenty ducats to the "young assistants of Raphael" for painting "the room in front of the Guardaroba." This room is to be identified with the so-called Sala dei Palafrenieri or dei Chiaroscuri and Vasari gives us further details about its lost decoration. He writes in the life of Raphael, "Continuing his series, he (Raphael) did a room with some figures on the ground-level of Apostles and Saints in tabernacles and employed Giovanni da Udine, his pupil, unique in drawing animals, to do the animals of Leo X: a chameleon, the civet, cats, apes, parrots, lions, elephants and other curious creatures." [70] And in the life of Giovanni da Udine: "In a hall next to this (the Sala dei Lanzi or degli Svizzeri, mentioned immediately before) where the chamberlains are, Raphael depicted in certain tabernacles life-size Apostles in chiaroscuro. Over the cornices, Giovanni drew parrots of various colors then in the Pope's possession, with baboons, apes, civets and other curious animals. But Paul IV destroyed everything to make some retiring rooms, depriving the palace of this remarkable work." [71]

Taking both the above together, we have not only a rather exact description of this decoration but also we come to learn when it was irremediably destroyed. [72]

The Zuccaresque remakings (cf. note 72; Fig. 58) in part took into account its illustrious predecessor but to form an idea of what Raphael projected for the room we have more precise evidence. Two drawings in the Louvre (4261 and 28954) [73] and the one in the British Museum (Pouncey and Gere, no. 63) show us the finished studies, sectioned and ready for transfer to the cartoons, of the Evangelists *Matthew*, *John* and *Luke* (cf. note 65; Figs. 59-61).

Notable similarities between the corresponding figures frescoed by Zuccari and the designs for *St. Luke* and *St. John* mentioned above indicate beyond any doubt that the drawings are related to the decoration of the Sala dei Palafrenieri and that Zuccari based himself, at least in part, on Raphael's prototypes when renewing the frescoes. The style of the three drawings suggests Penni with his soft lighting and his short delicate strokes devoid of energy. The weakened interpretation of Raphael's monumental ideas, on the type of those expressed in the tapestry cartoons almost two years earlier, is here recognizable.

In a series of engravings by Marcantonio Raimondi, two Apostles from the Louvre by Penni (the *St. Luke* is absent) appear in reverse and with variations but it is doubtful that we are dealing here with the same decoration. [74]

What was Raphael's role here? In the life of Taddeo Zuccari, Vasari says that: "Taddeo was commissioned to remake those Apostles in the Sala dei Palafrenieri, that Raphael had made on the ground-level and that they were torn down by Paul IV." [75] That word "remake" and the similarity already indicated between some of the Apostles now existing and drawings by Penni as well as the presence also of new tabernacle frescoes that contain the figures, all lead to the thought that Zuccari, as was natural given the importance to the prototype, would remain as faithful as possible to what Raphael and his collaborators had made. Naturally the animals painted by Giovanni da Udine, dear to Leo X, were not recovered because they were not suitable to decorate the papal rooms of the new Tridentine climate of Pius IV, the Pope who had called Cardinal Borromeo to direct the politics of the church. But the motif of the tabernacles between the columns that support the feigned trabeation, that is the general system of decoration, was surely, I believe, borrowed from the Raphaelesque example, with modification, it is understood, in the details that the new taste demanded. This general system I think may also be attributed to Raphael who for the first time made wide use of illuministic architecture. Nor is it an accident that it happened in 1517 when Raphael returned to plan a decoration on the ground floor of the Farnesina. Around 1516, in fact, Peruzzi had executed on the *piano nobile* of that building the celebrated Sala delle Prospettive, which is the highest achievement in the field of painted architecture of the Roman circle in those years. Raphael understood immediately the high decorative possibilities of it and used it in the Sala dei Palafrenieri.

The following year he was to push architectural illusionism to the limits in painting in the *sotto in su* of the Loggias.

238

82 *Raphael, G. F. Penni and Assistants.* The Council of the Gods. Rome, Farnesina, Loggia of Psyche.

From what we can reconstruct of the lost frescoes, this is what only Raphael would have received, the fruit of his vigilant and innovating invention. As for the rest, the individual figures, the material execution of the plan, the animals of the frieze—without doubt his pupils were already able to do it on their own. There is no doubt that Giovanni da Udine had no guide for his share; rather it suits so well his specialization to make one think that it was introduced for the Pope's pleasure, and also because of the good fortune of having at hand an artist with the ability to paint animals that Giovanni had.

To have an idea of how this most attractive parade of animals must have been, this last trace of the adventurous delights of the late Gothic within the Medician Renaissance climate, it is sufficient enough to think of the beautiful birds, the lions, griffons, wolves, sea horses, that Giovanni painted that year for the Loggia of Psyche and the variously colored multitude of animals that climb among the grotesques of the Vatican Loggias.

As for the Apostles, the trace that Penni leaves in his two drawings does not allow us analogous fantasies. Perhaps Penni himself executed them with correctness but without genius. Perhaps, too, as in part of the *Coronation of Charlemagne* or the *Oath of Leo III*, for which frescoes Penni, as has been seen, supplied the preparatory drawings, the execution was perhaps given to some assistant even less able than Il Fattore.

The payment of twenty scudi speaks clearly for Raphael's pupils and indicated that the execution was certainly not by the master. It must have referred to a partial payment because twenty scudi would have been too modest a sum, even if intended for simple apprentices (and Penni and Giovanni da Udine could not have been considered as such) for a decoration like the one we have described.

Raphael's effort was without doubt much greater for the painting in the Loggia of the Farnesina, the last work for Agostino Chigi (Figs. 62 and 69-83).

As proof, the famous drawing in the Louvre is sufficient.[76] Raphael's presence is doubtlessly felt and his spirit is expressed in the decoration, where he, in harmony with the profane climate

83 *Raphael and G. F. Penni and Assistants.* The Wedding of Cupid and Psyche. Rome, Farnesina, Loggia of Psyche.

84 *Raphael and Assistants.* The Spasimo di Sicilia. Madrid, Prado.

of the Farnesina seems to resume in a more luxurious and picturesque tone the discourse left interrupted with the *Galatea* in the adjoining Sala dell'Oroscopo. Hence in front of this joyous exaltation of physical and natural beauty it is not important if some passage or even large segments of the Loggia show a decline in quality. The sharp comment of Leonardo Sellaio, "the vault of Agostino Ghizi (sic) was unveiled, a shameful thing for a great master; a good deal worse than the last Sala of the palace," [77] sounds fundamentally unjust. Besides, the weakest parts are found precisely in the two large scenes of the *Council of Gods* and the *Marriage of Cupid and Psyche*, which, because they are at the center of the vault, are less visible than the figures on the pendentives and in the triangles above the lunette. In fact, only by looking at them from an unnaturally twisted position is it possible to perceive these scenes, while all the others can be seen almost frontally.

The plan for the decoration of the Loggia, conceived as a trellis stretched under the open sky with a provisional covering obtained from two suspended trapestries (Fig. 62), is certainly Raphael's and is in harmony with the ambient's functions, as it was destined to mark the passage from the closed spaces of the house to the open air of the garden. Besides, this taste for the commingling of the internal and the external space by means of the painting seems typical of the Farnesina, where Peruzzi had provided a much more illusionistic example in the Sala delle Prospettive. Another element of harmony between the project for the Loggia of Psyche and the preceding decorations on the villa is visible in the selection and distribution of subjects. Raphael has in fact represented on the vault, which in a certain sense is the sky of the room

85 *Giulio Romano.* Studies for the Holy Women in the Spasimo di Sicilia, Drawing. Florence, Uffizi, Gabinetto dei Disegni e delle Stampe.

(and it is truly represented as a sky), only the "celestial" sequence in the *Fable of Psyche*, precisely as in the adjacent Sala di Galatea (or dell'Oroscopo) the lunettes and the vault contain only the images of the gods of the air, while those of the earth and of the water were to have occupied the walls, to be in this way, closer also materially to the ground (as it is known, only the *Polyphemus* by Sebastiano del Piombo and the *Galatea* by Raphael were executed). This has produced the supposition that the decoration in the Loggia should have proceeded on the walls with the narration of the earthly events of Psyche, and that it was interrupted by unexpected new commissions to Raphael in 1518. An hypothesis that is difficult either to accept or deny today.[78]

The execution of the frescoes belongs to Raphael's three principal disciples: Francesco Penni, Giulio Romano and Giovanni da Udine, and for once, there is reasonable agreement among the scholars in assigning respective parts to each of these painters. Of the ten pendentives, five were surely done by Giulio (*Cupid and the Three Graces; Venus, Ceres and Juno; Venus in the Chariot;*

86 *Giulio Romano.* Study for a Mary and back-view of a ruffian in the Spasimo di Sicilia. Drawing. Florence, Uffizi, Gabinetto dei Disegni e Stampe.

241

88 *Raphael and Giulio Romano.* The Holy Family of Francis I (detail). Paris, Louvre.

87 *Giulio Romano.* Study for the Holy Family of Francis I, Drawing. Florence, Uffizi, Gabinetto dei Disegni e Stampe.

Psyche with the Vial from the Styx; Cupid and Jove: Figs. 69-73). The other five more or less decisively reveal the presence of Penni. Of these, three of them are commonly agreed upon (*Mercury and Psyche; Mercury; Venus and Jove:* Figs. 74-76); another, *Venus Carried by Cupids* (Fig. 77), not universally ascribed to him is, in my opinion, his). Finally, the tenth pendentive with *Venus Showing Psyche to Cupid* (Fig. 78), was attributed by Hartt to Raffaellino del Colle and has been accepted.[79] Personally I remain doubtful over the name of the artist whose style, as we have said, cannot be easily identified, nor has it been sufficiently described as such by Hartt, at least from 1516 to 1517. The attribution is based on information by Titi, who cites Gaudenzio Ferrari and Raffaellino del Colle among the masters active in the paintings of the Farnesina (without specifying in which parts).[80] How little Titi can be counted on in this is shown by the fact that Gaudenzio Ferrari was in Novara from 1515 to 1518, an irrefutable documentation attests. Personally, in conclusion, I would attribute the scene of *Venus Showing Psyche to Cupid* more generally to an artist in Penni's orbit, since the fresco has a fundamental affinity to the art of Il Fattore, but perhaps a little inferior in quality.

At this point, however, we must recall the prudent observation by Shearman.[81] He recalls how the damaged frescoes of the Farnesina were in large part greatly restored by Maratta who besides refixing and repainting the background and reworking the contours of the figures, apparently was obliged to do also actual remakings, using as models in some cases antique copies, in others projects by Raphael (or those he thought to be his).[82] Such a reworked text even after the restoration conducted by Sartorio in 1930, does not seem to offer great confidence for subtle distinctions based upon inferior quality. It must also be added that Penni reveals in the Farnesina that he is beginning to feel the influence of a personality not only more talented but also more decisive than Giulio Romano's in such a way that we perceive here the antecedence of the collaboration between the two artists with the clear supremacy of Giulio, a collaboration that will bear fruit in the Loggias and above all in the Sala di Costantino.

Precisely this influence of Giulio on Penni makes any attribution of the figures of *amorini* (in the fourteen triangular squinches, with their sides slightly curvilineal, over the lunettes: Figs. 79-81) very difficult if not undesirable. They are *eroti* who fly in the sky carrying the attributes of various goods and are accompanied by their symbolic animals. As for these figures of boys, the names of Penni, Giulio, the assistants of each of them and the artists that lie halfway between the two, could be infinite. Only with great difficulty could we arrive at a precise definition. On the other hand it is certain that the animals, birds, and admirable festoons of fruits and flowers that surround these and the other scenes are the work of Giovanni da

Udine, as Vasari also assures us; and even more, it is possible to read in Vasari that Giovanni also made the *amorini*.[83] Now, whoever wishes to consider this hypothesis should also reflect on the fact that, at least in most cases, as in the one of the boy with the lion and the sea horse (explicitly mentioned by Vasari in the life of Giovanni da Udine), if the two animals are by Giovanni, it is extremely probable that so is the *amorino* (Fig. 81). It is a painted fresco and in fresco painting, a fact that even astute connoisseurs tend to forget; it is not easy nor advisable to fragment the work in too many sections, so that its distribution among many different people is unlikely. It would have caused notable practical difficulties in delimiting the various zones of the intonaco, that would end up making the procedure of painting almost impossible and evidently quite slow. It could in effect annul all the practical advantage of collaboration.

More clear and generally agreed upon, or nearly so, is the situation for the two scenes, the *Marriage of Cupid and Psyche* and the *Council of the Gods*, on the ceiling. They are by Penni with the help here and there of less skilled assistants (Figs. 82 and 83).[84]

Giovanni da Udine, who already must have achieved splendid results in the Sala dei Palafrenieri, reveals himself to us in this decoration for the first time in the total integrity of his felicitous art. The festoons of fruits and flowers are handled with an extraordinary self-possession without ever becoming precious; they have a luminous naturalness and perform admirably structural and decorative functions. The secret of casting within an appropriate balance the detail and the whole, and the ability of not going beyond the boundaries of a subordinate function to the realism of the still life, so that from a distance, that which counts, is the festoon understood as an architectural structure, the real frame and support of the scene— it is not by chance that at the top of each pendentive there is a large floral element like the

89 *Raphael and Giulio Romano*, small Gonzaga Madonna. Paris, Louvre.

243

keystone of an arch—all this reveals in the Udinese artist a profound assimilation of Raphaelesque measure, the comprehension of the Master's Classicism and the ability to transfer
it to a new genre of which Giovanni was an uncontested specialist. Once again we should give
credit to the critical capacities of Vasari's reading, if observing the festoons of the Farnesina,
we recall the following passage from the *Lives:* "A Fleming whom Raphael named John, an
excellent master of fruits, foliage and flowers, though with a somewhat dry and labored style,
taught Giovanni da Udine to do them like a master, soft and mellow, and he introduced them
successfully into some things as I shall relate." [85] Here not only is the style of Giovanni
admirably described, but here all the difference between the analytic spirit of the Flemings,
inherited from the late Gothic and the ability of synthesis of Italian Renaissance painting, is
outlined for the observation of nature. Giovanni da Udine's brush work is indeed rich and
mellow, his chiaroscuro is luminous and transparent; there is in his painting a serene and gentle
vitality that fully reveals itself in the images of animals: the candid grace of Venus' doves, the
fierceness of Jupiter's eagle, the gliding speed of the jackdaws, the planar distension of the
falcon, the feathers of the swallows, the play of the birds are rendered with an acute spirit of
observation, but what is more important, they become pretexts for splendid formal structures
and vivacious color notations. If there is any meaning in speaking of a Neo-Hellenistic art, it is
in relation to the art of Giovanni da Udine who certainly, more than from the perfect micro-
cosm of Giovanni Fiammingo, would have learned from Roman paintings of the first century
which are close to the beautiful gardens of the House of Livia at Prima Porta. Compared
with the passages by Giovanni da Udine, certainly the most fascinating parts of the decoration,
those by Giulio Romano leave us less impressed. Yet their quality is quite high. The youthful
assistant of Raphael had by then achieved a considerable maturity and it is clear that he presents

us with his own interpretation of the Master's art. The comparison between the drawing in the Louvre of *Psyche Offering Venus the Vial of Water from the Styx*, a Raphael autograph as we have said, and the Giulio realization in fresco (Fig. 72), is illuminating. In Raphael the figures are large and imposing, but a subtle vibrant chiaroscuro, a coherent transferal of movement to all parts of Venus' body, the vigorous gesture and expression of Psyche, the abstract but not aloof beauty of the faces, all this holds the images suspended in an unique equilibrium between the real and the ideal, moderating the fullness of the form with the graciousness of execution. Thus, Venus and Psyche at once are natural and remote, human and divine. In Giulio's fresco the plasticity of the two figures has become much more dense, almost tangible. The nudes are transformed into powerful anatomies, the draperies, by means of high shadows and clear lights have assumed a bronze-like consistency. From living figures these images have become statues. Their abstraction is now like that of marble sculpture. The interior life diminishes but the physical beauty of the figures is exalted.

Penni has neither the luminous naturalism of Giovanni da Udine, nor the marble grace of Giulio. Compared with Giulio his contours are less clear, in seeking perhaps vibration he achieved often only uncertainty. Thus his chiaroscuro is less decisive, but it produces softer bodies though not more delicate ones. And yet, as has been observed, Penni tries to adjust himself to the style of his younger companion, but he cannot overstep the limits of his own nature. In the scenes of the ceiling he appears even more unsteady and inaccurate than in the pendentives,

91 *Giulio Romano*. The Stoning of St. Stephen. Genoa, Santo Stefano.

245

and this is certainly due to the intervention of the helpers. Nevertheless he is quite unable to show real energy and to make harmonically measured structures. The drawing at Chatsworth (no. 55) with *Mercury and Psyche* for the *Council of the Gods* (Fig. 68) is more successful than its realization in fresco (Fig. 82). Nevertheless also in the drawing Mercury is an uncertain figure with a neck too long, a poorly proportioned head which is swollen as if by a lymphatic ailment, illogically connected with the body, while the tiny head coincides poorly with the long and flat abdomen, and the legs are short in relation to the rest of the figure. Everything in the fresco, perhaps due to the damage, restoration, or the intervention of an assistant, assumes even more incorrect aspects to the point of being comic. It almost seems that the *Council of the Gods* was made by a Neoclassic, second-class brush, rather than a classical sixteenth century one. Actually some time ago, finding myself in the village of Giove on the border between Lazio and Umbria, when visiting a modest little palace near the imposing Mattei palace, I saw a provincial copy of the *Council* in a room that has pretentions of being a salon. It was as if an evil-minded critic had put into bold relief all the inaccuracies, the wide deviations from the poetic line of Raphael which are present in the fresco of the Farnesina, and had ferociously put them in evidence with the harshness of a caricature; but there was no doubt that nearly all the defects of the miserable copy were deeply rooted in the original. Apparently Leonardo Sellaio alluded to these poor anatomies when he so ferociously reviewed the frescoes of the Loggia of Psyche. Ill-disposed and perhaps not very understanding, the spirit that pervades the entire decoration and makes unimportant the weakness of some parts, escaped him. Vasari started with these works in beginning his peroration on the inferiority of Raphael compared to Michelangelo when he ventured to treat the nude. But with less

92 *Giulio Romano.* Altarpiece. Rome, Santa Maria dell'Anima.

malevolence than Sellaio, even though Michelangelesque deep in his heart, and clearly more shrewd and less implicit, now that Raphael was dead, in a lively polemic Vasari recognized the other virtues of Raphael's art and in addition conceded that many of the anatomical errors were due to pupils: "the nudes that were similarly made by him in the vault of the palace of Agostino Chigi were not satisfying because of that lack of grace and sweetness that was Raphael's. It was largely because he had them painted by others from his design." [86] We surely have seen that not only the modest parts by Penni but not even the more successfully executed figures, those by Giulio Romano, could ever boast to have among their qualities "grace and sweetness." The personality of the various assistants of Raphael is therefore more clear in the Farnesina. It is miraculous once again, despite everything, that the fundamental intuition of Raphael is preserved.

We know that the *Spasimo di Sicilia* (Fig. 84) was executed in 1517 from the engraving reproducing it by Agostino Veneziano which bears that date. It is quite a famous picture though truthfully not worthy of its fame. Destined for the church of Santa Maria dello Spasimo in Palermo, which must have seemed very distant indeed to Raphael, it is doubtful that it interested him greatly. Nonetheless he must have dedicated some studies to it in the preliminary phase when he was preparing the composition. The general distribution of the groups, the invention of the grotto in a space enclosed by the arms of the cross in the empty center that gives relief to the fallen Christ, the suggestion of a large, convex, arc-like movement that progresses from the entrance gate of the city deeply into the space of the countryside: are among the better parts of the work and perhaps are by Raphael in addition to a few strokes on the rather intense face of Christ. The rest is by Penni and Giulio who conducted the work to its conclusion almost, I believe, unaided. Naturally the single figures reveal traces 247

94 *Giulio Romano*. The Holy Family. Naples, Galleria Nazionale di Capodimonte.

of Raphaelesque motifs. For example, the Holy Woman kneeling in the foreground, the movement of the drapery with that falls from the shoulder to the knee forming a kind of oval shape with the curve of the thigh and the nude foot that appears under counter movement of folds, those are motifs that return the following year in the *Virgin* painted for Francis I. In this case Raphael applied himself much more deeply and Giulio plays the role of simple assistant.

But finding Raphaelesque motifs in Giulio and Penni or even apparent precursors of forms adopted later in work by Raphael should not be so surprising. But they were very heavily nourished by ideas of the master. As for the precursory motif, how many drawings as well as autographed studies are lost? How many exercises and variations on the theme of Raphael's ideas had Giulio Romano and all the young artists of the workshop drawn? It can be said that their formation was nothing other than that. And in 1517 Giulio was still studying. Raphael's death in 1520, the resulting autonomy of Giulio Romano and Penni, their rapid growth of importance and fame, falsify our a posteriori judgments. But in 1517 no one dreamed that the radiant season of Raphael would turn out to be a late autumn and his pupils were far from considering themselves as mature artists but what else could they have felt alongside such a master? Therefore their attention was certainly turned to studying and imitating the thoughts, that is to say, the drawings, of Raphael. And when these drawings hardly existed there were rapid sketches, allusive ideas as surely was the case for the *Spasimo;* in developing them, in giving a detailed form to a note of movements and masses, the pupils sought the most Raphaelesque solutions possible by dipping into the very rich graphic materials existing in the workshop. Yet the scanty presence of Raphael in the realization of a painting is clear at once. For the *Spasimo*, doubtless Giulio prepared the final drawings, studying the figures carefully. Drawings like those in the Uffizi for the group of *Holy Women* (E 543 r; Fig. 85) or the ruffian with his back to us and the Mary standing (E 543 r; Fig. 86) that are of very high quality and show what a high graphic force Giulio had attained, were insufficient to sustain

248

the weak execution, which was probably mainly by Penni. I would attribute to Giulio the best parts of the "Marys," for example, the *Magdalen* and the *Virgin*, and perhaps the *Christ* and the figure in the foreground. Certainly by Penni are those sorry wooden horses that have no counterpart in Raphael's work nor in Giulio's; all those figures in the black and the darkish background in addition to the large parts of the groups in the foreground, are also by Penni. Seen as a whole the *Spasimo di Sicilia* is an exemplary work, for it demonstrates what is truly workshop painting, in comparison with pictures in which Raphael obviously used some assistants only as helpers.[87]

This is the case of the two commissions for the king of France, the *Holy Family of Francis I* (Fig. 88) and *St. Michael* today in the Louvre. Ordered in 1517 by Lorenzo de Medici, they were delivered to the king at Fontainebleau in June, 1518. The date of that year and Raphael's signature appear in both.

On July 2, of that same year, 1518, Sebastiano del Piombo wrote to Michelangelo "It pains me that you were not in Rome to see two pictures that were sent to France by the Prince of the Synagogue of which I think you could not imagine anything more contrary to your opinion of what you would have seen in similar work. I shall not tell you more than that; they seem figures made of smoke or figures of iron that shine, all bright and black and drawn in the manner of Leonardo, it will be said." [88]

The observation of Sebastiano del Piombo is pertinent. It is affirmed in these pictures in which the chiaroscuro in the dark tends toward black and the light is reflective. Vasari realizes it when speaking of the *Transfiguration*; but his judgment is neither partisan nor hostile (rather the picture is highly regarded by the Aretine), and he seeks to explain the overly dark shadows

96 *Raphael, Giulio Romano and Collaborator.* The Madonna of the Oak. Madrid, Prado.

95 *Giulio Romano and Collaborator.* The Madonna of the Rose. Madrid, Prado.

98 *Raphael, G. F. Penni and Collaborator.* The Visitation. Madrid, Prado.

99 *G. F. Penni.* The Madonna of the Divine Love. Naples, Galleria Nazionale di Capodimonte.

97 *Giulio Romano.* St. Margaret. Paris, Louvre.

as a technical device, by means of which Raphael " in this work almost capriciously used the smoky black of printers, which, as has been said on several occasions, becomes even more dark with time and offends the other colors with which it is mixed." [89]

These dark, deep blacks are also a characteristic of the work of Giulio Romano, and since Giulio undoubtedly assisted Raphael in the two pictures in question (and also in the *Transfiguration*), the problem is posed as to whether this aspect, so basic to the late works of the master and being such a contrast with the transparent "Venetian" phase from the time of the Stanza di Eliodoro should not be imputed to be by the student rather than the master.

It would be, in this case, an important trace regarding the influence of Giulio on Raphael, or slightly less as regards his independent development in the commissions after 1517.

Personally, once again I am convinced that the movement of the influences had only one direction: from Raphael to his pupils and not vice versa. During the preparation of the tapestry cartoons, Raphael had moved away from the chromatic richness of the Stanza di Eliodoro because he was aware that the weavers would never have been able to transfer on cloth a range of such various and vibrating colors. Thus the coloration was simplified and the play of lights and the darks were contrasted in schemes of violent opposition. We witness, it can be said, a sort of radicalization of chiaroscuro; the darks became strong and neat, the lights vivid; the blendings, the intermediate tones, disappear. In so doing Raphael discovers that this new language of color has its advantages; the figures acquire a statuesque monumentality and everything becomes more vivid and definite. Through this process of simplification of the bright and chromatic aspects, it is possible to achieve a chosen intellectual atmosphere but at the same time, for the plastic concentration and the clarity of narrative, it was possible also to impress an heroic dramatic effect to the story.

In this way, while on the one hand the study of Classical painting which was, to be sure, primarily ornamental, induced Raphael to invent a sparkling, impressionistic and rapid decorative style; on the other, the contact with the grand ideas of the ancient world (pagan and Biblical) and the influence of Roman statuary, which was primarily historical, are the origins of the solemn language of the frescoes and the altarpieces of the late Raphael. Here the violently contrasted chiaroscuro, the deep almost black shadows " like figures that shine," correspond to a precise narrative intention, elevating the chronicle on an abstract ideal plane. In Raphael's activity the different genres of painting are defined according to a criterion that will always be dear to Classicists. Nor is it an accident that in the workshop various pupils specialize not only in subjects but even in styles: carried along with the genres are the exclusivity of contents and of functions as well as resultant formal characteristics. Giovanni da Udine on one side, and Giulio Romano on the other become symbols of this dichotomy not only in practice but also in style.

The violent chiaroscuro and the statuesque appearance of the forms characteristic of Raphael's late work, are the starting point for Giulio Romano's style of these years and not vice versa.

And it is in this development of Raphaelesque chiaroscuro that we should place the double portrait in the Doria Gallery as a splendid autograph by the master while the so-called *Bindo Altoviti* of the Washington National Gallery is ascribed instead to Giulio. [90]

But returning to the pictures of *Francis I*, we may conclude that, without any doubt, the new taste for shadow belongs to Raphael and not Giulio.

The collaboration of Giulio may be quite well ascertained in the *Holy Family;* it is less so in the *St. Michael*, due in part to its condition. Raphael surely made the drawing for the *Holy Family* though Giulio painted some parts, among them the Virgin's clothes, in which the perfection of the detail is carried to the limits of metallic neatness, characteristics of Giulio Romano (Fig. 88). He prepared himself, besides, for this difficult task with the beautiful drawing in the Uffizi (535E; Fig. 87) which is a study not of the Virgin but indeed of the drapery of the figure. Also it seems to me that Giulio abandoned himself enthusiastically to imitating the veins of marble in the pavement: his sculptural predilections have found a challenge here. In other places, in secondary figures, the intervention of the pupil was that of simple execution, revised and corrected by the master. To be convinced of the dominating control of Raphael, it is sufficient to observe the detail of the cradle and compare it with those in the small *Gonzaga Madonna* (Fig. 89), the Madonna called *La Perla*, the *Madonna of the Oak* (Fig. 96) and still better in the *Madonna della Gatta* (Fig. 94): all works that still bear Raphael's name in that they came from his workshop, but from his young assistant, sometimes aided by a secondary collaborator. Well, the cradle in the *Holy Family of Francis I* is a secondary element in the painting, hierarchically removed in comparison to the true protagonists of the composition; in other cases, however, the always more lively taste for naturalistic details for the " tranche de vie " lights Giulio Romano's passion and he employs it in a stupefying realism foreign to Raphael's mentality. It is not, in fact, in these insertions of passages from daily life within a highly idealized and abstract context that Raphael anticipates the tendencies of Mannerists' taste; this is a characteristic of Giulio. The anticipations in Raphael are of another type and we have seen them very clearly in the *St. Michael*.

The pure gratification for abstract forms seems to prevail in this painting, pushing Raphael into a search for the perfect combination of the two diverse spiral movements described by the body of the Saint and that of the Demon. The seductive exactness of the meeting of forces derives neither from its ability to excite passions nor from the ability of justifying the action described, but simply from a kind of refined pleasure for formal perfection in itself. And this is a main feature of Mannerism that (and not accidentally), will evoke similar painting up to the very end, that is, up to Cavalier d'Arpino.

Giulio Romano had nothing to do with the planning of the picture. We know from Raphael's own mouth that he himself was the author of the cartoon that is today unfortunately lost (cf. note 40); on this rare occasion Hartt is disposed to accept this affirmation. It is probable instead that Giulio intervened in the execution (for example, in the accessories of the Saint and the figure of the Demon), but the picture has by now undergone so many restorations and re-workings besides its transference from wood into canvas, that one cannot place too much trust on an analytic examination of the surface. The two pictures for the King of France cannot be considered from the workshop; on the contrary, because of their fundamental autographic nature, they were of great importance in influencing Giulio Romano's style because he collaborated on them as an assistant under the guidance of the master.

It is quite probable that the group of the Holy Families, in which Raphael must have been responsible only for the general project but in no case, or very rarely, for detailed drawings, are all after the commission for Francis I. They all carried out the same theme of the *Holy Family* for the King of France and in those done by Giulio Romano the subject of the cradle recurs. We deal here with the small *Gonzaga Madonna* in the Louvre, *The Pearl*, and the *Holy Family under the Oak*, both in the Prado (Figs. 89, 90 and 96). In all three the ambient is different from that of Francis I's *Madonna*, because the scene occurs out of doors. In all of them there is, so to speak, less narrative, less action, and in their place a pleasing search in the study of elegant static poses of figures grouped together. The small *Gonzaga Madonna* (Fig. 89) seems to have been wholly executed by Giulio. To establish its date is not easy. The absence in the landscape of those archaeological elements that are dear to Penni in these

100 *Giulio Romano.* St. Margaret. Vienna, Kunsthistorisches Museum.

101 *Giulio Romano.* The Infant St. John. Florence, Accademia.

102 *Anonymous (Raphaelesque).* The Infant St. John. Paris, Louvre.

251

years may also induce one to think that the execution came after Raphael's death.[91] Completely fantastic is the idea held by some that the hand of Polidoro da Caravaggio may be perceived here.

More interesting is the so-called *Pearl*, that is the painting of the *Madonna and Child with Saint Anne and the Infant St. John* in the Prado, Madrid (Fig. 90). The relationship between the St. Anne of the *Pearl* and the St. Joseph of the *Holy Family of Francis I* is evident but the similarities more or less stop here: in the Madrid painting the landscape has an enormous value. It is not an ordinary landscape, but is closed on the left by a splendid background of Roman ruins and opens on the right in a valley populated with small figures and crossed by a river in which modern and ancient buildings (recognizable among the others is the Tempietto of the Sibyl at Tivoli) face each other while a sky striated by lights and clouds, " a much praised sunrise " (Vasari), throws back their reflections on the countryside. A not dissimilar sky where the branches of the trees are seen in profile against the light can be observed in the Vatican

103 *Giulio Romano* (?). The Madonna of the Candelabra. Baltimore, The Walters Art Gallery.

Transfiguration and there is little doubt that the two paintings were being made contemporaneously in Raphael's workshop; the problem still remains as to whether the landscape motifs in the so-called *Pearl* are inventions of Giulio or of Raphael. Little help in resolving the problem can be gained from a comparison with the *Transfiguration* which, as far as the landscape is concerned, was probably completed only after Raphael's death.

The question is important because this type of background is to be absolutely typical of Giulio's works in particularly architectural motifs lighted by a radiant sun that fascinatingly place in profile the details and projects mysterious shafts of shadows and dazzling impressions of light. The backgrounds of the *Stoning of St. Stephen* (Fig. 91) and the *Santa Maria dell'Anima* (Fig. 92) altarpiece will be so. All the fascination of the small *Madonna and Child* in the Barberini Palace (Fig. 93) and the *Madonna della Gatta* (Fig. 94) is based upon similar effects. In substance the question is to decide once again if Giulio depends totally for his vocabulary on Raphael or not. Well now, these evasions of the picturesque seem imputable to Giulio; so also to Giulio, as we have already said, seem ascribable, on an opposite pole of inspiration, the passion for certain splendid naturalistic passages: here in the *Pearl*, the wicker cradle with its little frame fixed by nails, the trimming, the simple knots of wood, the confused pile of thin covers. Here is an introduction to what we will see in the *Madonna della Gatta*.

All of this appears to me extraneous to Raphael's spirit which he liberally accepted in a painting that came out of his studio but which had been assigned for execution totally to his most gifted pupils.[92]

Analogous observations may be repeated for the other *Holy Family* of the Prado, the so-called *Madonna of the Oak* (Fig. 96) where Giulio, besides the motifs of the cradles, introduces *bravura* passages of antique marbles in the foreground—the ruins of the so-called temple of Minerva Medica. Nevertheless the hand of a weaker collaborator is rather easily recognizable and to him we may assign certain errors like the poorly proportioned *Infant Saint John*, the thin left hand of the Virgin, as well as a certain pedantic graphic insistence. This man recalls Penni somewhat and also other masters. That Raffaellino could have collaborated with Giulio in this *Holy Family* is possible even if not easily demonstrable.[93] A copy of the *Holy Family of Francis I* executed by Raffaellino in the Church of the Corpus Domini at Urbania, would indicate that around 1518 he had already started to work in Raphael's workshop.

To Giulio with the collaboration of Raffaellino around 1518, Freedberg also assigns the *Madonna of the Rose* (Fig. 95), variously thought to be by Giulio or Penni and considered by Gamba as simply of the school and painted after Raphael's death on his design.[94] Personally, though some passages recall Penni, I, too, think that the attribution to Giulio with an assistant who could be Raffaellino, is more useful. The same assistant must have collaborated with Penni rather that with Giulio in the *Visitation* (Fig. 98), conserved, as is the *Madonna of the Rose*, in the Prado, and painted (and signed) by Raphael for Marino Branconio.[95]

Finally the hand of Penni alone is recognizable, it seems to me, in the very famous *Madonna of Divine Love* in the National Gallery of Capodimonte of Naples (Fig. 99). This picture, so famous and often reproduced is in reality a modest work precisely because of Penni's execution which academically interprets Raphaelesque motifs of the moment.[96] The five *Holy Families* and the *Visitation* seem the only works, with the exception of some portraits that, executed by the workshop in those years, can boast to have been, at least in a literal sense, projected by Raphael. Among them the only one that really rises to a very high level is the so-called *Pearl* in the Prado. It is a picture where the youthful genius of Giulio Romano shines although through a composition of the master; he is nevertheless able to express his own personal vision.[97]

A completely different case is that of the celebrated portrait of the so-called *Fornarina* from the Galleria Nazionale Romana di Pittura at the Barberini Palace. On the blue armband is written in gold " Raphael Urbinas " and there is no reason to doubt the autographic quality of the picture. The tendency to consider as typical modes of Giulio Romano, the dark shadows, the marked and powerful passages, that sense of reality evident in the light that characterizes the painting, has misled scholars. As we have repeated several times, these are instead motifs that were passed on to the pupil from a late Raphael. The dating of around 1518 for this picture seems correct, which shows, besides, in the vibrant forms on the hands, in the transparent ripplings of the veils, in the very precious appointments of the turban and in the search for geometric perfection in the face, qualities superior or at least different from those of Giulio's art; qualities that did instead greatly interest Parmigianino when around 1524, he was studying the works of Raphael. Absolutely untenable, hence it seems to me, the attribution to Raffaellino del Colle, advanced with great assurance by Hartt overlooking the fundamental value of the work's quality.[98] The only limitation that I believe can be made for the total autography of Raphael is to concede a minor role for Giulio Romano as a simple and completely submissive helper.

The problem presents itself almost analogously for the *Portrait of a Woman* in the Musée des Beaux-Arts of Strasbourg, which, after the excellent cleaning, was exhibited and in a certain sense unveiled, at the Paris Exhibition of 1965-66. On that occasion Michel Laclotte produced a careful entry for the catalogue, proposing three attributional solutions: Giulio Romano; Raphael and Giulio Romano in collaboration; Raphael himself alone.[99] With great honesty and prudence Laclotte left the final judgment to the specialists but declared on his own to have rejected the first possibility, that is, to Giulio Romano alone, because the qualities of the picture " témoignent des mérits dont aucune autre œuvre contemporaine de l'artiste ne fait preuve."

I agree with him and I believe that without doubt the picture belongs to Raphael. The damage which restoration was unable to eliminate, impedes, however, a definite judgment for a possible subordinate assistance on the part of Giulio Romano. Nor does it seem to me that the agreement in the measurements is sufficient to justify the hypothesis proposed in the entry by Laclotte, that the Strasbourg painting can be paired with the so-called *Bindo Altoviti* in Washington. The American portrait is of a different quality and in my opinion belongs, as I have already said, at least for the execution, completely to Giulio; such a partial distribution of personal participation on Raphael's part would seem to me strange, if the two pictures had really been executed for a husband and wife.

In concluding our discussion on the vicissitudes of Raphael's workshop and the activity of its members while the master still lived, we must deal with only two undertakings, but surely fundamental ones, in order to complete the picture of what we had proposed to do. They are the large altarpieces of the *Transfiguration* and the decoration of the Vatican Loggias.

The *Transfiguration* is not merely the last work by Raphael on which the premature end of the master and the fact that it was used as a background for the catafalque bearing the dead painters's body, cast a Romantic light; the *Transfiguration* is a powerful message that Raphael

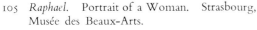

253

106 *Raphael and G. F. Penni*. Christ, detail from the Transfiguration. Vatican, Pinacoteca.

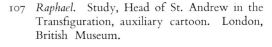

107 *Raphael*. Study, Head of St. Andrew in the Transfiguration, auxiliary cartoon. London, British Museum.

left us and from which artists in the past had learned much and from which we today can understand a great deal about the possible changes in Raphael's own personality. It was commissioned in 1517 together with and directly in competition with the *Resurrection of Lazarus* by Sebastiano del Piombo, and it was out of this rivalry that the chronological data which we possess concerning the progress of these two works, spring.[100] We shall ignore if, or up to what point at the death of Raphael, the picture was finished; it is quite possible that it was not. Certainly it was finished in 1522, if Giulio Romano, probably more in the guise of Raphael's heir than as an assistant on the work, asked for its payment.[101] And even if the completion of the *Transfiguration* came after Raphael's death, and at the middle of 1518 no part had been painted, it is quite likely that the master had begun to study the composition around 1517. Vasari gives testimony that up to the end, Raphael personally and passionately devoted himself to it. There is no doubt that the painting was projected, even down to the details, by the Master as the remaining " auxiliary cartoons " by the hand of Raphael confirmed in an absolute manner (Figs. 107 and 109).[102] As to the final execution, that is, the painting, there is naturally not complete agreement among scholars in assigning to one or another hand this or that part. But there is more agreement in this case than for any other work by Raphael. Usually the St. Andrew in the foreground is believed to be by Raphael. With greater reserve scholars have assigned to him one or the other of the other six figures of Apostles, for whose heads there are final studies in London, Oxford, Chatsworth and Vienna (cf. note 102). The female figure on her knees in the foreground and the whole group at the right (Fig. 108) are commonly assigned to Giulio Romano; the upper part with the scene of the *Transfiguration* (Fig. 106) to Penni. Naturally all on precise projects are by Raphael. Strangely the only name of a collaborator put in rapport even if vaguely, with the *Transfiguration* by contemporary sources is that of Battista Dosso, whose hand is not recognizable in any way in his work.[103] This does not substantially alter what was said earlier: if the Emilian artist had worked there, he must have played an extremely subordinate role in the *Transfiguration*.

Actually in this picture, if it is possible to recognize the attentive but slightly soft brush stroke of Penni in the upper part (quite typical in the head of Christ with the almost indecisive and scarcely expressive lines) and if in the lower part on the right, the decisive, bold, powerfully plastic and detailed manner is very evident, still it is the personality of Raphael that reigns supreme. Penni's interpretation is nothing other than a weakened transcription of the lightening of the forms with which Sanzio wanted to express the bright transcendence of the upper zone of the picture; the strong contrasting formal precisions of the figures on the ground executed by Giulio in the lower section with all that emphasis in the search for the expression and for the states of mind by means of almost theatrical gestures, also derive totally from Raphael and are nothing other than the continuation of what Raphael himself made with his own hand in the groups of the Apostles in the same zone. Thus, once again, Giulio develops Raphaelesque ideas and radicalizes them, so to speak, carrying them to perhaps excessive programmatic positions because of the absence of that relative liberty from the same principles that come precisely from a creative genius. From the time of the tapestry cartoons we have seen Raphael occupied in describing his personages with theatrical and nobly historical attitudes, and able to underline the characters and expressions with great vivacity and even with violence. Now, while in the dynamic and unitary groups of the Apostles executed primarily by Sanzio, these same aspects reappear in solemn grandeur, in the group that faces them with the obsessed boy and his companion, the execution by Giulio breaks up the harmony of the whole. Excessive local finish and his insistence on expressions become superfluous. If in Raphael's work we find admirably reflected and interpreted the Renaissance artistic theory of classical inspiration, which insisted on the necessity that the figures be effectively equipped to express the states of mind, but recommended as well the dignity and beauty of the images— ideal brake for every excess—in Giulio, it seems that these two essential elements of creativity, instead of interpenetrating, are completely separated. All the physical beauty is centered within the splendid statuesque female figure in the foreground and all the psychological and expressive violence in the obsessed boy supported by his father. In their extreme exasperation both motifs tend to be academicized and Giulio Romano appears more Classicistic than Classic.

Not to Giulio's and even less to Penni's, but only to Raphael's genius is the profound invention of the whole imputed, unified in its apparent contrast: that opposition between the upper zone of the picture where all is movement, but a movement balanced and harmonic in the orbital gravitation of all the figures around the luminous and solemn center of Christ, and the lower zone where instead, the groups of the Apostles and the supplicants agitate each other as they are confronted in two parallel diagonals, with a grandiose contrast of lights and shadows that give plastic and earthly substance to the passions and movements. The scheme of this grandiose altarpiece will be taken as an example for all Classic painting of the late sixteenth and seventeenth and eighteenth centuries. The Carracci, Poussin, Reni and Maratta will find treasures in it. But on the other hand, those violent black shadows from which emerge dramatic and statuesque, the illuminated passages of the figures, could, I believe, have pleased Michelangelo da Caravaggio and certainly Ludovico Carracci and his followers.

Whether or not this blackness of the shadows was a result that went beyond the desire of the author as a consequence of alterations in the color employed, the effect that it produced

254

108 *Raphael and Assistants*. The Transfiguration (detail). Vatican, Pinacoteca.

impressed Italian and other painting profoundly. But that this effect was largely due to Raphael is proved by the fact that it is the final point in the line of development of Raphaelesque chiaroscuro from the time of the tapestry cartoons onward, as we have already sufficiently indicated.

The altarpiece of the *Transfiguration* is truly Raphael's last work; the last in the main line of his art, the grand religious-historical genre. With his emphasis, with his impressive embroidery of lights and shadows, with his complex construction articulated in physical masses and extremely alive in its psychological research, the *Transfiguration* documents how much there was new in the master's art at the end of his life. Notwithstanding that the work was probably completed after Raphael's death, the presence of pupils, which must have been extensive in the execution, weighs less heavily than in the Holy Families and in the other late works already examined, and this is because Sanzio, urged on by the rivalry with Sebastiano del Piombo and then certainly taken with the novelty of his own invention, conducted the *Transfiguration* in an infinitely better manner with the drawings, studies and cartoons. It is a fine document that shows how, till the end, the assistants, including Giulio Romano, had little to say and nothing new to propose to the master, when Raphael made his presence felt.

Completely different is the case of the decoration of the Vatican Loggias (Fig. 111), a great undertaking, in fact the greatest in a minor genre: decoration. From now on, speaking of the Loggias, we shall mean the large Loggia on the second floor (by American standards, the third), that faces east to the Cortile di San Damaso and is adjacent to the Stanze, that is, to the papal apartments. This environment with its prestigious decoration commonly is called the "Raphael's Loggias." The Loggia underneath, decorated more or less at the same time by Giovanni da Udine is called Loggia of the first floor. On the third floor there is also a Loggia decorated by Giovanni da Udine and today in very bad condition but since it was painted some decades later, it is beyond the scope of our study and we shall not mention it again. The three floors of the Loggias on the north and west sides of the Cortile of San Damaso were constructed much later and decorated during the course of three centuries from the sixteenth to the nineteenth.

The Loggias are the triumph of Raphael's workshop and also, indirectly, a triumph for the master who was able to see the work carried out by the assistants that he had taught without intervening in person. There is no graphic proof that Raphael made drawings for the Loggias and, on the other hand, the documents speak of payments "to the assistants that had painted the Loggia." [104]

However, that a Raphaelesque paternity of the whole cannot be refuted, is provided by the sources and the older literature. The diary of Michiel informs us that in the Loggias "there were paintings of great value and of much grace, the designs of which came from Raphael of

109 *Raphael.* Study for heads and hands of two Apostles in the Transfiguration, auxiliary cartoon. Oxford, Ashmolean Museum.

110 *G. F. Penni (?) (from Raphael ?).* Study of Three Apostles for the Transfiguration, Drawing. Vienna, Albertina.

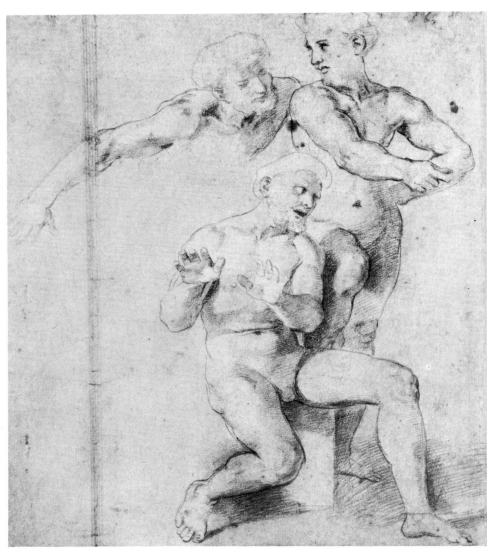

256

Urbino." [105] And Vasari: "Raphael made the designs of the ornamental stuccoes and the stories that were painted and also of the compartments." [106]

No one, on the contrary, attests that Raphael had painted in the Loggias, and the attempts on the part of modern criticism to attribute to him some passages have not been successful and sometimes even a bit comic.[107] In substance, Raphael must have made a general project, planned the divisions, studied in large measure the Biblical scenes and here and there some details of the grotesques and the stuccoes. After having examined and discussed this preparatory material " as for the stuccoes and the grotesques, he placed in charge Giovanni da Udine and over the figures, Giulio Romano, who had worked with him for a brief time." [108] The Loggias remain Raphael's creation in that they were born from his ideas, fruit of the passionate investigations of Hellenistic-Roman decorative art that he conducted for years and in which he had encouraged his best pupils, giving as precedents the Bibbiena apartments, the Loggia of Agostino Chigi and the Sala dei Palafrenieri and finally absorbing the stamp of that bright and serene culture and of harmonic beauty that is the quintessence of Raphael's poetry: the Loggias are therefore his because without him they could not have existed precisely as the colors cannot exist without the light; although for me, it is not possible to find in the long series of scenes, *grisailles*, and grotesques, a single brush stroke by Raphael himself.

The complex of decoration remains without doubt the most grandiose result that the Classicism of the Renaissance attained in ornamental genre, and is able to weld with incredible felicity the stucco to the painting in the grotesques, to harmonize the real and the illusionistic architecture of the small vaults and finally to insert the grand motif of Biblical history, the noble subject, within a dominatingly decorative context without diminishing or violating the one or the other; it is a miracle of equilibrium between the antique and the modern, between the sacred 257

112 *G. F. Penni* (?). God Separating Light from Darkness, Drawing for the First Vault of the Loggias. London, British Museum.

and the profane, between ornamentation and representation. Never after did even the best of Raphael's pupils succeed in emulating a similar achievement working when the light of the irreplaceable master no longer burned.

And yet, it is precisely in the Loggias or better in the Biblical stories of the Loggias that, either because of the absence of precise preparatory drawings or rather of close control by Raphael, the individual personalities have the opportunity to express themselves in a more independent fashion. Besides, the subordinate function of the particular scenes, each rather

113 *G. F. Penni* (?). Jacob's Dream, Drawing for the Sixth Vault of the Loggias. London, British Museum.

258

small, and decidedly conceived as a series, allows for this independence, a freedom that is attractive for us, even if unimportant in the large unified context.

There exists, consequently, two ways of seeing the Loggias: one, which all things considered is the best, consists in viewing the whole, and then the extraordinary beauty of this work will be enjoyed, and we shall see Raphael; the other is the one we must examine here, which consists of the dissection of this harmonious unity. Only then, the individual pupils of the Master will be found; the enjoyment will be lessened but some interesting information for scholars will be discovered, which is also useful for explaining the manner in which the decoration was executed.

Besides Giovanni da Udine and Giulio Romano, who according to Vasari were put in charge of the work (and the former also executed much of the work, as far as the stuccoes and the grotesques are concerned), it is the same Vasari who gives us the names of another group of assistants: " Giovan Francesco, Il Bologna, Perino del Vaga, Pellegrino da Modena, Vincenzo da San Gimignano and Polidoro da Caravaggio with many other painters that did the stories and figures and other things that were necessary for the entire work." [109]

Consequently and for the first time, we have the description of a rather vast workshop, a confirmation that as the years passed, the pupils of Raphael were multiplied, and one suspects than even in earlier works where everyone, including ourselves, had always mentioned the usual names of Penni, Giulio, Giovanni and perhaps Raffaellino del Colle, or some anonymous artist, one may believe in the presence of some of these new people described by Vasari in the work on the Loggias.

114 *G. F. Penni* (?). David and Bathsheba, Drawing for the Eleventh Vault of the Loggias. London, British Museum.

115 *G. F. Penni* (?). Baptism of Christ, Drawing for the Thirteenth Vault of the Loggias. London, British Museum.

116 *G. F. Penni* (?). Expulsion of Adam and Eve, Drawing for the Second Vault of the Loggias. Windsor, Royal Library.

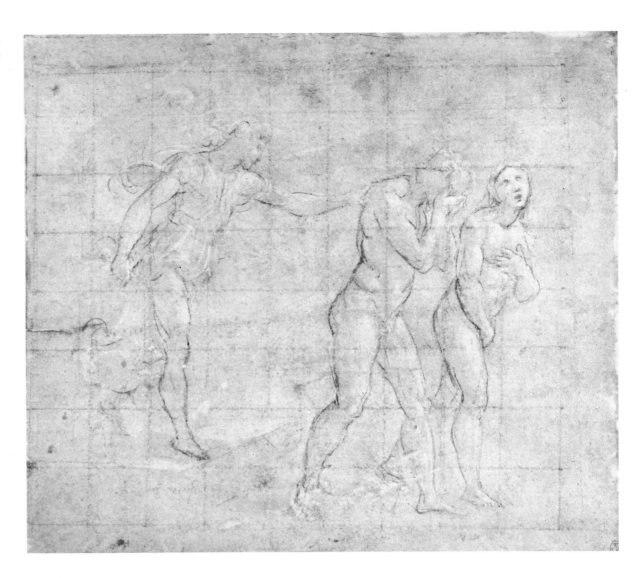

From Vasari's remarks, however, the impression remains that, more than a real Raphael workshop, here there was a kind of pupils' workshop. That is to say, it looks like Giulio and Giovanni are operating now as masters and they feel responsible for the new young artists (some like Polidoro were beginners in this work); there could have existed, therefore, a sort of delegation of power to the real and loyal pupils in order to organize and direct the "troupe" of the Loggias.

When, at the beginning of this study, we spoke for the first time of Penni and his characteristic drawings, it was said that we would return and go more deeply into the discussion when dealing with the Loggias. Actually since then we have already encountered some other typical graphic examples by Il Fattore, like the drawing in the Ashmolean in Oxford corresponding to the *grisaille* in the Stanza della Segnatura (Fig. 2), the study in the Horne Foundation for the *Oath of Leo III* in the Sala dell'Incendio (Fig. 31), or the three folios (Louvre and British Museum)

117 *G. F. Penni* (?). Dividing of the Promised Land, Drawing for the Tenth Vault of the Loggias. Windsor, Royal Library.

with the Apostles in the Sala dei Palafrenieri (Figs. 59-61); but the most rich series of drawings that usually are ascribed to Penni remain those connected with the Biblical scenes of the Loggias: four are in the British Museum (Pouncey and Gere, nos. 64-67; Figs. 112-115), one in the Victoria and Albert (Dyce, no. 185), two at Windsor (Popham, nos. 806-807; Figs. 116, 117), one in the Ashmolean (Parker, no. 574), one in Muncie (Indiana, U.S.A.) in the collection of the Ball State University, and three others in Florence in the Gabinetto dei Disegni degli Uffizi (E 509, 510, 1222). From the technical point of view, not all of these twelve drawings are homogeneous and some doubts remain in certain cases also on a stylistic level, but in general there emerges a personality whose identity with Penni has been, if not absolutely proved, at least supported with good reasons.[110]

Consequently, we come to know that Giovanni Francesco played an important role in the preparation of the Biblical stories (the drawings are concerned with scenes from the first and last vault), probably carrying along the graphic project up to the point of the cartoon. And precisely for the transference on the cartoon, it seems plausible that they would use his finished studies. It is not possible to think that we are dealing with copies from the frescoes or from original drawings because there are instances in which important elements that do not correspond with the features of the finished works, indicate that we find ourselves confronted with preparatory work.[111]

Giulio directs the operation and Penni prepares the finished drawings; but he is not necessarily the inventor of the stories; rather, looking at the scarcely engrossing aspect of his drawing, it is easy to deduce, and we have already said it, that it is not the product of invention but rather a definitive organization of the ideas of others. These ideas in some cases may have been

118 *G. F. Penni* (?). Joseph recounting Dreams to his Brothers, Drawing for the Seventh Vault of the Loggias. Vienna, Albertina.

Raphael's as in the stories of Genesis (first and second vault) or in *Jacob's Dream* (sixth vault) and in others of Giulio and finally also of Perin del Vaga who worked for the occasion in the workshop as collaborator both for the decorative as well as the figurative parts and seem to acquire an ever-increasing authority in the course of the work.

Before proceeding further with the distinctions, it is necessary to make quite clear that the attribution to one or another of the assistants of individual scenes of the so-called "Bible of Raphael," is an extremely difficult endeavor whose results will be, at least in part, always more or less fanciful and hypothetical for the following reasons: above all the frescoes are very damaged, spoiled and repainted and offer therefore an untrustworthy text; and secondly we do not know how Tommaso Vincidor called "Il Bologna," Pellegrino da Modena, Vincenzo da San Gimignano, Polidoro da Caravaggio and even to a certain extent Perino, painted in the years from 1518-1519.[112] As for Giulio and Penni, even they at this date are known to us only by hypothesis, and as collaborators within the paintings by Raphael. Some of these artists like Il Bologna and Vincenzo will always remain unknown to us or virtually so. As for Pellegrino da Modena, the frescoes in San Giovanni degli Spagnoli display an unique character, between Ferrarese and Roman in manner (quite exacting and tight) that is not easily recognizable in the scene of the Loggias.[113] We have already spoken of Penni, especially as a draftsman. We know Giulio, Perino and Polidoro much better. The independent works of Giulio are numerous and quite individualized—true they were all made after 1519 but near enough in time to be utilized. Giulio, however, worked little in the Loggias even though he directed a

119 *Giovanni da Udine and Giulio Romano and G. F. Penni*, General View of the First Vault. Vatican, Loggias of Raphael.

good deal: a fact attested by Vasari and it is quite possible that he was correct. All things considered, the artist we know best, among the actual executors, is Perino: Vasari's exact attributions are confirmed by a comparison with other works by the Florentine in the Vatican which were quite close in time (for example, with the planets in the Sala dei Pontefici executed during 1521) and even with some details of his Genovese pictures. Polidoro, on the contrary, was a beginner in 1519. We know little of his personal style until around 1523-24. From that moment onward, Polidoro becomes a more easily identifiable personality, above all through the beautiful series of drawings; but to discover him in the Loggias, it is necessary to rely on the dangerous criterion of seeking characteristics of an already mature and strongly personal master in the exercises of a beginner who certainly works from the drawings and under the direction of others.

That having been stated, here is what we can conclude: [114] of the thirteen small vaults with four Biblical scenes each, the first nine display the dominant presence of Giulio and Penni with assistants under their charge; the tenth is completely by Perino as is the eleventh except for the scene with the *Consecration of David;* the twelfth reveals two distinct collaborators, each author of two scenes, the more gifted seems to be Polidoro da Caravaggio; the thirteenth is once again dominated by Perino. Now we shall seek to be more precise and if possible justify these opinions. Of the four scenes from the first vault (Fig. 119) I think that the design belongs unquestionably to Sanzio giving answer here "a passo ridotto" to the great Michelangelesque invention on the Sistine Ceiling. The *Separation of Light from Darkness* (Fig. 120) differs somewhat from the other scenes; although damaged, it is in a certain sense more energetic and less decorative and therefore, I think it was done by Giulio Romano. Penni appears to dominate in the other three, probably assisted by Giovanni da Udine in the fourth, where he painted the animals (Fig. 121). Giulio must have directed the second vault (Fig. 122) on the basis of designs of Raphael by utilizing and adjusting old ideas of the master (the group of the *Expulsion from Paradise,* Fig. 125, besides recalling the *Progenitors* by Masaccio, recalls the *Aeneas and Anchises* from the *Fire in the Borgo*). In the *Creation of Eve* (Fig. 124) and in the *Expulsion of Adam and Eve* (Fig. 125), Giulio had by his side a more delicate assistant than Penni, who could have been Perino; while in the *Original Sin* (Fig. 123) the participation of Il Fattore is recognizable. *Adam and Eve Laboring* is in such a ruinous state that it cannot be judged. The third vault (Fig. 126) is also dominated by Giulio Romano. It is difficult to say who was his assistant for the two scenes of the *Building of the Ark* and the *Flood* (Fig. 127); particularly in the second, the frenzy of the draperies twisted by the wind and the tension within the poses might make one think of Pellegrino da Modena. Giovanni da Udine must have been the author of the animals for the *Coming out of the Ark;* Penni, instead, is recognizable in the *Sacrifice of Noah* (Fig. 128) where the design of the first figure on the right derives from the analogous figure in the cartoon for the *Sacrifice at Lystra.* The scenes of *Abraham* for the fourth vault (Fig. 129) includes two rather fine stories whose design might be traced back to Raphael and whose execution belongs to Giulio and Penni. They are the *Abraham and the Angels* and the *Flight of Lot* (Fig. 131). *God's Covenant with Abraham* is quite ruined and cannot be judged. An assistant that cannot be identified as either Penni or Perino must have aided Giulio in painting the story of *Abraham and Melchizedek* (Fig. 130). This assistant, especially in the figure of the armed Abraham and in the kneeling figure in the foreground, shows a notable affinity to the painter of the *Crowning* and the *Judgment of Solomon* from the twelfth vault.

120 *Giulio Romano.* God Separating Light from Darkness. Vatican, Loggias of Raphael, First Vault.

The Isaac stories in the fifth vault (Fig. 132) contains two damaged scenes and are of more modest quality (*Isaac Blessing Jacob*, Fig. 135, and *Isaac and Esau*), perhaps assignable to Penni. The other two are much more interesting; *God appearing to Isaac* (Fig. 133) and *Abimelech spying on Isaac and Rebecca* (Fig. 134) are in fact, it seems to me, by Giulio. The latter is absolutely one of the most successful achievements of the whole Biblical series and perhaps the idea could be traced back to Raphael.

The quality is maintained at a high level in the sixth vault (Fig. 136): *Jacob's Dream* (Fig. 137), with its simple yet intense composition could have been utilized again for a similar scene in the ceiling of the Stanza di Eliodoro, according to the hypothesis of Cavalcaselle. The execution appears worthy of Giulio.

Giulio, perhaps assisted by Polidoro, is recognized in the *Jacob, Rachael and Leah at the Well* (Fig. 139) while in the two other scenes of the vault, *Jacob Begs for the Hand of Rachael* and *Jacob on his Way to Canaan* (Fig. 138), it seems to me that Perino was at Giulio's side in a prevailing way, especially in the latter scene. The seventh vault (Fig. 140), that is the central one, contains four scenes of Joseph. The first, *Joseph telling his Dreams to his Brothers* (Fig. 141), is distinguished for its well-balanced handsome landscape that almost anticipates classical seventeenth century landscape painting. It could very well have derived from a drawing by Raphael but the execution remains in Giulio's orbit, assisted perhaps by Penni or another disciple.

Giulio and Penni are responsible for the *Joseph sold by his Brothers* (Fig. 142), a picture destined to exert a powerful influence on Roman seventeenth century painting. Again Giulio, perhaps based upon an idea by Raphael, is to be recognized in the scene of *Joseph Tempted by Potiphar's Wife*, while that of *Joseph interpreting Pharaoh's Dreams*, quite beautiful and worthy of Raphael for the composition, shows together with Giulio an assistant who could have been either Penni or perhaps Polidoro.

On the basis of an explicit assertion by Vasari and confirmed by stylistic examination, Giulio Romano alone painted the *Finding of Moses* in the eighth vault (Fig. 143) and perhaps also *Moses and the Burning Bush*. Perino is responsible for the entire translation in paint of the *Crossing of the Red Sea* (Fig. 145); Giulio and Polidoro, the *Moses striking the Rock* (Fig. 144).

121 *Giulio Romano, G. F. Penni and Giovanni da Udine.* God Creating the Animals. Vatican, Loggias of Raphael, First Vault.

Giulio with Penni's help, is responsible for the four scenes of Moses in the ninth vault (Figs. 146 and 147). On the other hand there is no trace of these two masters in the four stories of Joseph in the tenth (Figs. 148-152). These seem frankly the work of Perin del Vaga. Similarly, as has been said, are those of the eleventh (Figs. 153-155), except the *Consecration of David* which is by an unidentifiable assistant of Giulio Romano; as I have already stated, in the twelfth vault (Fig. 156) the *Meeting of Solomon and the Queen Sheba* (Fig. 159) and the *Construction of the Temple* (Fig. 160) should be assigned to Polidoro. If Pellegrino da Modena may really be recognized in the *Anointing of Solomon* (Fig. 157) and in the *Solomon in Judgment* (Fig. 158), it may never be proved, but it is definite that the author of these two scenes is quite a characteristic artist, with his dryness, his torsions, his twisted draperies; he is less correct, indeed incorrect at times, than the other collaborators in the Loggias, but never unpleasing. A certain inability to absorb fully the harmony of the classic vocabulary (see how an idea derived from the tapestry cartoons becomes deformed in the *Judgment*) would seem to indicate that he was a Northener.

The last of the small vaults (Fig. 161) contains four New Testament scenes. Vasari decidedly ascribes them to Perino and two of them, the *Nativity* and the *Adoration of the Magi* (Fig. 162), are his without any doubt. The *Baptism of Christ* (Fig. 163) may be his. *The Last Supper* is probably much altered by repainting and therefore cannot be judged. As it appears, it has passages similar to Perino's style, while in others Penni is recalled and finally, I would not know to whom to attribute certain parts.

With this doubt, I finish my attempt (which I did not know how to avoid undertaking, after all) to distribute among the known personalities the fifty-two scenes making up the "Bible of Raphael." I am conscious of having honestly expressed my deep-rooted convictions but I am equally convinced that many if not all will be inevitably challenged by the next scholar to confront the problem.

I must add that diverse scholars ascribe the various landscape elements in the scenes to Giovanni da Udine. I am not of the same opinion.[115] Giovanni was too busy with the stuccoes and the grotesques to allow himself something more engaging than the modest share in the animals that we have mentioned. Besides, the landscapes are not all by the same master; furthermore they represent one of the most interesting but least solvable aspects, at least for now, of the whole attribution problem of the Loggias. It seems to me that it should always be kept in mind that excessive subdividing of the execution of the individual scenes among the collaborators is an erroneous criterion. The reduced dimensions of all the scenes allows the supposition that each one was executed by one or at the most by two painters, with some very rare exceptions. A greater participation of hands would have produced only delays and confusion. The collaboration is explained instead by work on many scenes at the same time and hence, many vaults, operating in such a way that all the tasks and the sections be divided and standardized as much as possible.

Giulio Romano and Penni, admitting that the identifications proposed are exact, do not offer us much by way of innovation in the Loggias. More than his share as executor of the frescoes, we appreciate in Penni the quality in certain of his final drawings which, even if derived from Raphael, have still great refinement for light touches, and delicate lights and shadows. So it is, for example, in the two drawings of *God the Father separating the Light from the Darkness* and for the scene of *Jacob's Dream*, conserved in the British Museum.[116]

124 *Giulio Romano and Collaborators.* Creation of Eve. Vatican, Loggias of Raphael, Second Vault.

Giulio is rarely the actual author of the frescoes. In general he must have had (as Vasari says) a managerial role, of itself very important. But the *Finding of Moses*, assigned to him by the Aretine with an admiring comment, demonstrates the abilities that induced Raphael to entrust Giulio with full authority "over the figures." In *Pharaoh's Daughter* with the elegant group of maidservants we recognize the final fruit of those splendid groupings of female figures that Giulio Romano had first been able to study in the works of the Master (recall the women that take part in the *Mass at Bolsena* or in the *Expulsion of Heliodorus*) and, later more

123 *Giulio Romano and G. F. Penni.* The Original Sin. Vatican, Loggias of Raphael, Second Vault.

125 *Giulio Romano and Collaborator.* The Expulsion from Paradise. Vatican, Loggias of Raphael, Second Vault.

265

126 *Giovanni da Udine, Giulio Romano and G. F. Penni.* View of the Third Vault. Vatican, Loggias of Raphael.

profoundly, in endeavouring to carry out the ideas of the master, as in the *Fire of the Borgo*. The landscape of the scene, with the expanse of water, the high horizon, the clear transparency of the color had its prototypes in Raphael, for example, in the cartoon of the *Miraculous Draught of Fishes*. Yet, even if it is not altogether possible to exclude a Raphaelesque project for this work of Giulio, the contrast between the handsome fleshy reality of the female figure and the unreal suspended lightness of the background generates a strange almost dream-like sensation that removes itself from the balanced harmonies of the Master or from the dramatic accents of his greatest phase. In other figurations Giulio is generally more typical and flowing. However it is necessary at least to recall the mysterious, fascinating dark-against-the-light in the scene of *Abimelech spying on Isaac and Rebecca* with those luminous effects dear to the painter, in a more bizarre and emotional key. The idea of the romantic embrace with an arc of light projected by the sun while around, the cast shadows lengthen and the profiles are caught flashing in the rays, or are chopped neatly in the shadows like nocturnal "silhouttes," is certainly of a strange order halfway between the enchanting naturalism of the illuminator of "Cœur d'amour épris" and the most successful luministic adventures of the new Mannerist style.

Despite everything, the passages by Giulio Romano, Penni, and their assistants remain generally within the limits of Raphaelesque poetry.

The same cannot be said for the scenes done by Perino del Vaga. The fundamental element in Perino's compositions is the search for a determinate rhythm. The scenes do not actually have any dramatic charge even when treating battles. What is more important is that the legion of figures confronting another legion and the motifs of one and the other are matched in an elegant *contrapposto*. Thus the gestures and poses tend to repeat themselves and one has the impression of watching an action performed in a dance as if the war were transferred into a Moorish ritual. Quite typical in this sense are the two scenes with the *Fall of Jericho* and *Joshua arresting the Course of the Sun*.

That elegant butterfly, Perino, who will be exemplary for the whole of Italian Mannerism within a few years and whose style will be the basis of Northern refinement had not yet left his chrysalis, and sometimes appears like a caricature. It is the first reaction of Perino in passing from the very light field of grotesques where he worked under Giovanni da Udine and from where he came, to the solemnity of historical painting by Raphael's demiurge, the powerful Giulio Romano. Yet the expansive forms, the almost excessively muscular bodies, large curly heads of hair, the swelled massive heads, do not succeed in removing from Perino's figures their essential lightness. It is in fact quite characteristic of the painter at this moment that, after having discovered an effective pose, elegantly assumed, he repeats it, he alters it, making use of it in all possible ways. A typical example is the soldier, seen backview, hurling a lance from above. There he is dominating the scene of *Joshua arresting the Course of the Sun* using the gesture as in a "fugue" with the shields of the enemy; there he is again in the story of *David and Goliath*; and finally we see him reappear in the high relief on Bathsheba's terrace in the last of the David scenes. The significance of these repetitions is illuminating: a canon of formal beauty survives from one scene to another, from one story to another. A certain neatness and elegance become the true protagonists of the action indifferent to the change in contents. Schema of movements, invariably pleasant, are transmitted from one

127 *Giulio Romano and Collaborators (Pellegrino da Modena ?)*. The Flood. Vatican, Loggias of Raphael, Third Vault.

composition to another and end by substantiating them. The elegance of these movements does not permit any dramatic sentiment to crack; its harmony is rhythmic and fluent as that danced by an intermediary, never aware of the stasis of a solemn action or restrained idealization of a contained passion. All of which if not yet Mannerist, is at least quite mannered.[117]

128 *Giulio Romano and G. F. Penni*. Noah's Sacrifice. Vatican, Loggias of Raphael, Third Vault.

129 *Giovanni da Udine, Giulio Romano and G. F. Penni.* View of Fourth Vault. Vatican, Loggias of Raphael.

The profound drama and conviction in the action which are absent because they do not interest Perino are, however, characteristic of Polidoro, a painter who up to the end, in spite of his fame as a Classicist, was to cut deeply into the most tense passions and conclude his own career on the razor's edge of a violent expressionism.[118] It is this interior charge that induces us to suppose as his the *Meeting of Solomon and Sheba* and the *Building of the Temple*, basing himself also on certain types and specific poses.[119] In other scenes where we have indicated his presence, as the *Moses Striking the Rock*, particular features besides these dramatic aspects speak of him to us: the rock, for example, and the plants that grow beneath it are all passages that we shall recognize in later works by Polidoro, like the scene of the *Finding of the Sibylline Books* frescoed on the ceiling of the saloon of Villa Lante and now retouched and transferred after many vicissitudes to the Palazzetto Zuccari. Even the excessive passion in Polidoro, even his naturalist acuteness are, like the elegance of Perino but on the opposite pole, within the boundaries of Raphaelesque language. Still Polidoro is too close to his beginnings in the Loggias for his voice to be truly audible and it will be difficult for many to hear him without being confused.[120]

Of the supposed Pellegrino da Modena I have already spoken. Tommaso Vincidor, called "Il Bologna," to whom Filippini proposes to attribute the New Testament scenes of the last vault, did not take part in this decoration, I believe.[121] He is one of many whom we cannot recognize, or if you wish, we do not know how to recognize: as similarly to pause at those named by Vasari, Vincenzo da San Gimignano, or to list other possible people present not recorded by the Aretine but presumed by some scholars, for example, Raffaellino del Colle.

The real physical nature of the Loggias is not the one found in the study from the Biblical scenes. They are actually absorbed in the decorative totality which is the protagonist of the entire invention.

The interest that art historians have in finding within the Biblical scenes the beginning of many masters destined to have a determinant weight in artistic development of the sixteenth century and the influence of many scenes (taken largely from copies and engravings) on the culture of painters from the sixteenth to the eighteenth centuries, should not induce us to misinterpret the real pictorial motif of the decoration which is an organic whole where stuccoes, illuministic motifs in the frames of the frescoes and in the partitions of the vaults, play not only a structurally supporting role, but are actually the real protagonists. For all this, Giovanni da Udine was director and in a large measure executor as well (Figs. 164-168). That does not mean that Raphael did not have a project in the beginning for this fundamental aspect of the enterprise; but, in my opinion, it is certain that Giovanni da Udine concretized the Master's ideas with considerably more freedom that the other executors. As far as I know, there are no drawings of grotesques attributable to Raphael and although this does not mean that he never made any, it proves only that they did not constitute a group as fertile, rich and varied as the incomparable patrimony of his figure studies in the workshop.

And speaking of Giovanni da Udine's activity in the Loggias, Vasari gives us the most vivid picture of the evolution that occurred in Raphael's workshop; its formation, especially in the decorative sector where a nearly independent group was headed by Giovanni: "and so Raphael made chief of that work for the stuccoes and the grotesques Giovanni da Udine who was rare and unique in those things but especially in animals, fruit and other small objects;

130 *Giulio Romano and Collaborator.* Abraham and Melchizedek. Vatican, Loggias of Raphael, Fourth Vault.

since he had come to Rome and had brought many masters from abroad, he had a company of able persons for working in stuccoes, grotesques, foliage, festoons, stories and other things. Thus according to who was better, they were given assignments and were paid best; competing in this work there were many young artists who were to become excellent in their own careers. Of this company Raphael assigned Perino to Giovanni da Udine to work with two others on the grotesques and scenes. . . ." [122]

Perino was among the collaborators of Giovanni da Udine and his hand is recognized among the grotesques, for example in the lunette of the second vault in the Loggias.[123] Probably Tommaso Vincidor was also occupied in this part of the decoration (cf. note 121). Nonetheless the personality that dominated indisputably is that of Giovanni da Udine who repeats here with an incredibly enlarged richness the successful types of the Loggia of Psyche.[124] Two half pilasters brought to light in 1952 during the restorations on the arch at the end of the Loggias, miraculously retained intact the colors of the grotesques and the gilding of the stuccoes and gives us some measure of the decoration's splendor (Fig. 168).[125]

Underneath the area that we have been examining up to this point there is another identical one: the Loggia of the first floor (Fig. 169). On May 2, 1519, Michiel announces, when the Loggia of the second floor was finished, Raphael "went on painting two other

131 *Giulio Romano and G. F. Penni.* The Flight of Lot. Vatican, Loggias of Raphael, Fourth Vault.

132 *Giovanni da Udine, Giulio Romano and Assistants.*
View of Fifth Vault. Vatican, Loggias of
Raphael.

Loggias that will be very beautiful." [126] It has been said that one of these Loggias is probably
that in the Bibbiena apartment (cf. note 54 and 67); the other is certainly the one on the
first floor.   When it was finished Marc'Antonio did not like it very much, as he notes in his
diary: "in these days the Loggia below the Palace with the three stories . . . was painted
rather vulgarly with foliage, grotesques and other similar fantasies and with little expense. This
was the case because it was a communal work where all went on the scaffolding even though
only at the first stage." [127] Once again Vasari certifies that the paternity of this decoration
belongs to Giovanni da Udine whose frescoes were "lovely for their fine invention of the false
trellises in many sections and all full of vines laden with bunches of grapes, of clematis, of
jessamines, rose bushes and various kinds of animals and birds." [128] The paintings are still

133 *Giulio Romano.* God appears to Isaac. Vatican,
Loggias of Raphael, Fifth Vault.

270

134 *Giulio Romano.* Abimelech spying on Isaac and Rebecca. Vatican, Loggias of Raphael, Fifth Vault.

preserved but " the compartments of stuccoes and the paintings for the façade " are either completely lost or repainted.[129]

The fine idea of the trellises that transform in a highly plausible and naturalistic manner the illusionism of the painted architecture made in the Loggia in the floor above, allows Giovanni da Udine to furnish a final proof of his pleasing ability as decorator. Notwithstanding the alteration, the first floor Loggia, unfortunately difficult to enter, stands as one of the most noticeable additions to the decorative style of the Renaissance born in Raphael's shop. It is difficult to say whether Raphael had suggested the theme of the trellis, but it is quite probable that he did. Besides his position as head of the workshop and architect of the Loggias,

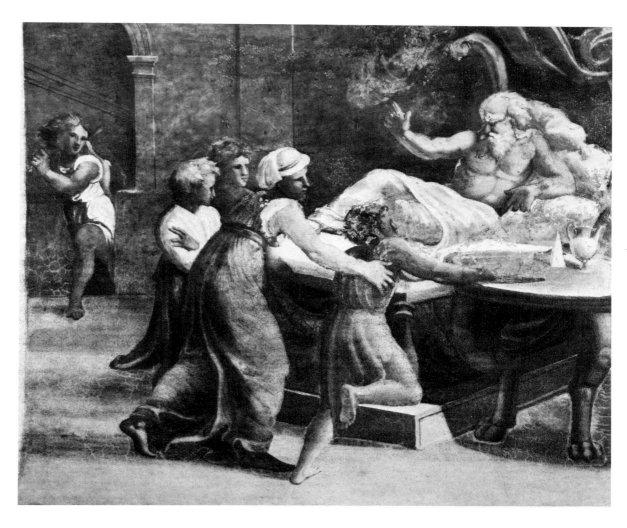

135 *Giulio Romano and Collaborator.* Isaac Blessing Jacob. Vatican, Loggias of Raphael, Fifth Vault.

271

136 *Giovanni da Udine, Giulio Romano and Collaborators.* View of the Sixth Vault. Vatican, Loggias of Raphael.

he officially played the role of superintendent of artistic affairs for the *Sacri Palazzi*. Surely Giovanni da Udine had no more than a hint from the master and permission to proceed. He worked with a good number of assistants but there is not a single authentic piece of painting among those ascribable to the assistants that can be attributed to Polidoro da Caravaggio, as Pacchiotti maintains.[130]

This Loggia must have been the last large work finished by the workshop while Raphael was still alive.

On April 6, 1520, Raphael of Urbino died unexpectedly from a continual and acute fever.[131] Even his enemies could hardly have done less than weep over him. Sebastiano del Piombo, the antagonist for the commission of Narbonne, writes to Michelangelo, the great rival: "I believe you have learned that poor Raphael of Urbino is dead. I believe you are greatly saddened by this news, and may God pardon him." [132]

137 *Giulio Romano.* Jacob's Dream. Vatican, Loggias of Raphael, Sixth Vault.

272

138 *Giulio Romano and Collaborator (Perino del Vaga ?).* Jacob on the road to Canaan. Vatican, Loggias of Raphael, Sixth Vault.

[1] *Lettere di M. Pietro Bembo*, Rome, vol. I. pp. 88-89.

[2] Golzio, p. 56.

[3] As has already been said, much of the problem of Raphael's workshop constitutes an art historical problem, since it coincides with a very specific period in Raphael's art around 1514 and includes the formation of a unified language within the limits of what had been interpreted as a universal moment of taste. In this phase Raphael operated primarily through his pupils, at least in the field of painting.

A simple problem of collaboration or of assistance would not have been of such interest as to justify a separate treatment.

Consequently it does not seem necessary to speak of the youthful collaboration with Evangelista di Pian di Meleto and of the relationship with Timoteo Viti or to cite the anonymous and truly quite awkard assistant who completed the *Madonna del Baldacchino*, in the Pitti.

Nor relevant to our summary is the study of the connection between Raphael and the masters who worked earlier, or beside him, in the vault of the Segnatura; they included Bramantino and Sodoma. Finally, even the hypothesis advanced by others that Guglielmo di Marcillat was the author of *Justinian Consigning the Civil Laws* does not enter into our scope. It is a discourse on a different level than a study of Raphael's workshop when it is held that the vault of the Stanza di Eliodoro or part of it was the work of Marcillat or of Peruzzi. Neither of them is a Raphaelesque artist; rather they are independent figures who found themselves, admitting that the above-mentioned hypothesis is correct, working in competition or alongside Raphael, feeling his great attraction but acquiring afterwards their total independence.

Venturi, *Storia*, 9, 11, p. 236; Donati, "Dell'attività di Guglielmo di Marcillat nel Palazzo Vaticano," in *Atti della Pontificia Accademia Romana di Archeologia, Rendiconti*, 25-26, 1950-51 pp. 267-276 and also for Marcillat see Vasari, IV, pp. 417-430; M. Salmi, Una pittura ignorata di Guglielmo di Marcillat," in *Arte*, 1911, XIV, VI, pp. 438-441.

139 *Giulio Romano and Collaborators (Polidoro da Caravaggio ?).* Jacob, Rachael and Leah at the Well. Vatican, Loggias of Raphael, Sixth Vault.

140 *Giovanni da Udine, Giulio Romano and Collaborators.* View of the Seventh Vault. Vatican, Loggias of Raphael.

For the collaboration of Sodoma and Peruzzi, see: G. Gombosi, " Sodomas und Peruzzi Anteil an den Deckenmalereien der Stanza della Segnatura," in *Jahrbuck für Kunstwissenschaft*, 23, 1930, pp. 14-24.

For the collaboration in the ceiling of the Stanza di Eliodoro particularly, see: Dollmayr, " Die Zeichnungen zur Decke der Stanza di Eliodoro," in *Zeitschrift für Bildende Kunst*, 1890, pp. 292-299; *Idem*, " Raffaels Werkstätte," in *Jahrbuch der Kunstsammlungen in Wien*, 1895, pp. 224-245; F. Baumgart, " Beiträge zu Raffael and seiner Werkstatt," in *Münchner Jahrbuch der bildenden Künste*, 1951, pp. 49-52; O. Fischel, *Raphael*, London, 1948, p. 362; F. Hartt, " Lignum Vitae in Medio Paradisi: The Stanza d'Eliodoro and the Sistine Ceiling," in *Art Bulletin*, 1950, pp. 124-129; Freedberg, 1961, pp. 147-150.

For the relationship between Raphael and Lotto for the Stanza di Eliodoro see: E. Zucca, " La decorazione della Stanza di Eliodoro e l'opera di Lorenzo Lotto a Roma," in *Rivista dell'Istituto Nazionale dell'Archeologia e Storia dell'Arte*, 1953, pp. 329 ff.

4 Vasari, IV, p. 643.

5 For the essential bibliography on Penni see the appendix of biography and bibliography. A drawing for the *tondo* of Cava dei Tirreni which is considered today an autograph (see Pouncey and Gere, 1962, p. 51) is preserved in the Ashmolean Museum in Oxford (Parker, 1956, no. 571).

6 Pouncey and Gere, p. 50.

7 Freedberg, 1961, p. 274. We are dealing with studies by Raphael: one, reduced to a fragment, with the single figure of *Christ* (Paris, Louvre; Fig. 12); the other with the scene of the *Giving of the Keys* (Windsor, Royal Library; Fig. 13). Freedberg correctly notes that it is among the early versions not only because the figures show many variations from those in the final solution, but also because they are clothed in contemporary dress, that is, costumes of the models. One is the counterpart of the other because Raphael controls the double effect of the cartoon and the tapestry which are themselves reversed. There is also a finished drawing similar to the cartoon (Fig. 14) in the Louvre and it is attributed to Penni by Freedberg and to Giulio Romano by Hartt. It would appear that here the sequence was more or less complete (the cartoon is in the Victoria and Albert and the tapestry in the Vatican Pinacoteca). Nevertheless Freedberg in this case doubts that the drawing which he assigns to Penni is the final and executive one for the cartoon and presumes a final drawing by Raphael himself like the one in Windsor with the *Blinding of Elymas*. The drawing by Penni would be the copy of such a lost original made with two purposes: " to protect Raphael's original for deterioration resulting from use and to simplify the transfer to the cartoon." Others, however, like Shearman (review of F. Hartt, " Giulio Romano," *Burlington Magazine*, 1959, pp. 546-460), attribute the Louvre drawing to Raphael himself and consider instead the Oxford drawing with *Punishment of Elymas* by Giulio Romano but not preparatory of the cartoon from which it differs in some figures, especially on the right side, but made from the cartoon for the engraving by Agostino Veneziano.

8 H. Delaborde, *Marc-Antoine*, n. d. pp. 218, no. 190.

9 K. T. Parker, *Drawing in the Ashmolean*, 1956, no. 570, pp. 312-313. Parker does not believe that the drawing was made as a preparation for the fresco but rather for the engraving by Marcantonio Raimondi because there is a head in the engraving which is not present in the fresco. It should be noted that, as with all the frescoes in the Stanza especially in the lower registers, this one alsoh as been damaged and was largely repainted by Maratta, and precisely in the zone where the missing head is located there are visible traces of damage and reworking. In my opinion, however, it is impossible to discard the hypothesis that this is the final drawing for the cartoon. The attribution to Penni is entirely convincing.

10 In his iconographic study, E. Wind (" Platonic Justice Designed by Raphael: the Four Elements in Raphael's Stanza della Segnatura," in *Warburg Journal*, I, 1937-38; II, 1938-39) on the Stanza della Segnatura tends to interpret the subject of the two *grisailles* as Augustus impeding Virgil's friends from burning the Aeneid and Alexander placing in safety the Poems of Homer. This interpretation is convincing and is confirmed by the gestures and the types of figures, prevailing over the opinion of F. Wickhoff (" Die Bibliothek Julius II," in *Jahrbuch der preuszischen Kunstsammlungen*, 14, 1893), based upon a passage of Valerio Massimo in which it is told how the Consuls P. Cornelius and Bebius Panphilus had ordered the conservation of some Latin books discovered in a sarcophagus and the destruction of other works in Greek. The older interpretation of the two scenes, which seeks to identify them with the discovery of the Sibylline books in the tomb of Numa Pompilius and their eventual destruction, fails.

11 A. Bertini in *Critica d'arte*, 1959.

12 Giulio Romano's date of birth was for a time fixed in 1492 but today it has been demonstrated that Giulio was born in 1499. It is true that a dating of 1512 for the *Meeting of Attila and Leo I* is not universally accepted and some scholars, basing themselves on the fact that here Raphael had abandoned the symmetric compositional system of the other frescoes in the room, tend to date this scene, the last of the series, in 1514. But this opinion, already rejected by Cavalcaselle, is poorly supported since the historico-iconographical reasons already mentioned lead one to believe that the work was started when Julius II was still living; nor is there any reason to believe that it was left interrupted for a considerable time before its completion at the end of 1514.

13 It is Penni rather than Giulio who was involved in the graphic versions of the two notable variants of the *Attila* fresco (Fig. 5 and 6).

In the first, in the Louvre (H. de Chennevières, *Dessins du Louvre, École Italienne*, n. d. Raphael, 15) the hand of Giulio Romano can be recognized; in the second, in the Ashmolean in Oxford (Pouncey and Gere, 1962 p. 58, with an entry

141 *Giulio Romano and Collaborator (G. F. Penni ?).* Joseph telling his Dreams to His Brothers. Vatican, Loggias of Raphael, Seventh Vault.

devoted to early ideas for the fresco) the bearded figure of the Pope is probably Julius II who returned to Rome with a beard after his Bolognese sojourn. They are copies and elaborations of lost drawings or sketches by Raphael which served perhaps to document the discarded ideas of the Master or executed for practice by the pupils.

[14] Autograph drawings are found in the Uffizi *(Madonna of the Fish)* and a Windsor *(Madonna dell'Impannata).* As is known the *Virgin and Child and St. Elizabeth* in the sheet at the Royal Library (Popham, 1949, no. 800, pp. 312-313) corresponds to those figures as they appear in the first blocking of the picture revealed by a radiography (P. Sampaolesi, " Due esami radiografici di dipinti," *Bollettino d'arte,* 1938, pp. 495-505) but then altered (the most serious change was the substitution of a St. Joseph, not in the Windsor drawing, with the figure of the Infant St. John) by Raphael himself, if the drawing for the second and definitive version conserved in Berlin and published by Grote (VI, no. 158) is really the autograph it appears to be. A knowledge of this last-mentioned drawing is important for confirming what had been intuited, namely that the changes of the composition are never applicable to the very young assistant. It is impossible, however, to establish from the radiography whether Giulio also executed the first edition of the picture.

[15] The opinions concerning the date of the *Sistine Madonna* are more disparate. I agree with Freedberg and Brizio that this work must fall within 1514 and was done before the *St. Cecilia.* In the latter, the monumental composition already seems to be a prelude to the solemn Classicism of the tapestry cartoons, detaching itself from the luminous and dynamic climate of the Stanza di Eliodoro which had animated the *Dresden Madonna.*

142 *Giulio Romano and Collaborator (Perino del Vaga ?).* Joseph Sold by his Brothers. Vatican, Loggias of Raphael, Seventh Vault.

275

143 *Giovanni da Udine, Giulio Romano and Collaborators.* View of Eighth Vault. Vatican, Loggias of Raphael.

[16] Vasari, IV, p. 495.

[17] Venturi, 9, II, p. 259. Cf. *idem, Grandi artisti italiani*, 1925, p. 181 ff.

[18] There is no complete study of Viti's drawings which are no more than generally dated. I think that their archaizing appearance tends generally to trick the scholar into dating them too early. I wonder if certain drawings, like numbers 254 and 255 from the British Museum (cf. Pouncey and Gere, 1962, pp. 151-152) and plates 236-237 should not be placed in relationship with Raphael's graphic style between 1514 and 1515, that is, the studies for the *Resurrection* in Windsor and Oxford, or with the famous sheet in the Albertina referred to as by Raphael or Giulio and given to Raphael by Dürer as the inscription attests.

[19] Vasari, VI, p. 550.

[20] Filippini in *Cronache d'arte*, 1925.

[21] *Lettera allo zio Simone di Battista di Ciarla*, with the date July 1, 1514.

[22] It is said that Castiglione furnished Raphael the theme of the decoration, since in an undated letter (though certainly of 1514) addressed to Castiglione himself, Raphael speaks of having made " drawings in various manners upon your invention." I do not believe that this invention was for the stories of the Stanza dell'Incendio because the context not only does not offer any connection with that commission but rather suggests that we are dealing with various studies on a single theme, probably a subject for an easel picture. In any case at least two of the subjects for the decoration, that is, the *Coronation of Charlemagne* and the *Justification of Leo III*, are connected with events that took place after 1514 and unpredictable at the time. The *Coronation*, where the Emperor has a resemblance to Francis I, alluded to, as Pastor (*Storia dei Papi*, IV, part I, pp. 469-470) has shown the alliance between Leo X and the French king; result of a meeting in Bologna in October 9, 1515; the *Justification* is connected with the Confirmation of the Bull of Boniface VIII, *Unam Sanctam*, discussed by the Lateran Council in its XI session on December 19, 1516 (*Ibid.*, p. 471).

[23] Concerning the weaving and the original disposition of the Vatican tapestries in the Sistine Chapel, their iconographic significance, the predellas and the side borders, and finally their stylistic interpretation within Raphael's œuvre, the article by J. White and J. Shearman, " Raphael's Tapestries and their Cartoons," in *Art Bulletin*, 1958, pp. 193-221 and 299-323, is fundamental.

[24] The payment was 300 ducats and Marcantonio Michiel in his diary of 1519 writes that Raphael was paid 100 ducats for each scene.

[25] Vasari, IV, p. 370.

[26] Vasari, IV, p. 644.

[27] F. Hartt, *Giulio Romano*, New Haven, 1958.

[28] This group of drawings was mentioned in note 7. The Louvre drawing (O. Fischel, *Raphaels Zeichnungen*, Berlin, 1913-1941, part I, p. 20 and fig. p. 20) is a fragment of the first autograph study (Fig. 12); the Windsor drawing (Fig. 13; Popham, 1949, no. 802, plate 62) is the complete study traced in reverse from the original in the Louvre before it was mutilated. As to the finished drawing of the same scene on the verso, also in the Louvre (Fig. 14; Freedberg, 1961, Fig. 353), it is not in my opinion an original by Raphael, as Shearman supposes but more likely, notwithstanding the high quality, one of Penni's best achievements. There is no possible doubt that the *St. Paul* at Chatsworth is a very beautiful original by Raphael (A. S. Strong, *Chatsworth Drawings*, no. 7).

As for the drawing in the Albertina of the *Miraculous Draught of Fishes*, the argumentation of Shearman seems to me convincing. Given the severe spiritual climate of the cartoons, it would be absurd to consider it as an early idea by Raphael for the cycle, a drawing with an anonymous crowd that dominates the foreground and the second scene in small portions relegated to the background. Hartt's idea should be rejected and Shearman's, that we are dealing here with a *capriccio* on the theme of the Draught of Fishes, done a posteriori by Giulio, accepted. The attribution to Giulio is more convincing than the one to Penni sustained by Freedberg.

[29] A silver-point drawing that seems to be a study for the figure of the subterranean giant, symbolizing the earthquake in this tapestry, is in the Janos Scholz collection in New York (J. Bean and F. Stample, *Drawings from New York Collections*, I. *The Italian Renaissance*, 1965, no 50, pp. 41-42 and fig. 50). I only know the drawing in reproduction. In the cited book it does not appear of sufficiently high quality to be considered a Raphael autograph and I am tempted to think of it as a copy after a lost original; naturally a judgment based upon a reproduction is not of great value, however. A curious pen drawing with the story of Conte Ugolino attributed to Penni in the Sotheby's sales catalogue dated March 12, 1963 (Old Master Drawings, no. 18) shows the same figure with limited variations. It is testimony to the effect of Raphael's invention which derives more from the tapestry or from the engravings of it than from the knowledge of the cartoon or the original drawing.

[30] The monochromatic friezes on the socle in the Stanza di Costantino are, in my view, by Polidoro da Caravaggio; but the detailed project of the room and therefore the decision of how to paint the bases is due to Raphael.

[31] Letter from Leonardo Sellaio to Michelangelo, dated January 1, 1518 (Golzio, p. 65).

[32] Vasari, IV, pp. 358-359.

144 *Giulio Romano and Collaborator (Polidoro da Caravaggio ?).* Moses Striking the Rock. Vatican, Loggias of Raphael, Eighth Vault.

33 F. Hartt, *Giulio Romano*, New Haven, 1958.

34 F. Hartt, " Raphael and Giulio Romano, with notes on the Raphael School," in *Art Bulletin*, 1944, pp. 67-94.

35 D. Redig De Campos, *Raffaello e Michelangelo*, Rome, 1966. *Idem, Le Stanze di Raffaello*, Rome, 1952. *Idem, Itinerario Pittorico dei Musei Vaticani*, III ed., Rome, 1964. *Idem, I Palazzi Vaticani*, Rome, 1967.

36 Pouncey and Gere, 1962. J. Shearman, 1959. The types of these two studies, one a catalogue of drawings and the other a review, do not lend themselves to lengthy observations about Raphael's style.

37 Freedberg, 1961. A. M. Brizio, *s.v.* " Raffaello " in *Enciclopedia universale dell'arte*, XI, Rome-Venice, 1963.

38 Golzio, p. 57.

39 Golzio, p. 63.

40 Letter by Costabili to the Duke of Ferrara dated March 2, 1519 (Golzio, p. 77).

41 Letter by Costabili to the Duke of Ferrara dated June 16, 1517 (Golzio, p. 54).

42 There are three drawings usually attributed to Giulio as preparatory studies for the *Fire in the Borgo*: two figures of women with two children for the central group of the fresco (Vienna, Albertina, S. R. 274; Fig. 27); the woman seen from the back with arms raised for the same part of the fresco (Paris, Louvre, 4008; Fig. 26); the so-called *Aeneas and Anchises* (Vienna, Albertina, S. R. 283; Fig. 28); cf. Hartt, *Giulio Romano*, 1958. Shearman, in his review of Hartt's book, doubts Giulio's authorship for the drawing of *Aeneas and Anchises* which he finds so high in quality that he attributed it to Raphael.

43 There is a drawing in the Albertina (S. E. 282) with two male nudes, one of which is a study or at least has the same pose as the captain standing at the extreme right side of the *Battle of Ostia* fresco (Fig. 29). At the side of the figure is an inscription held by some to be Dürer's and by others of a late period (cf. J. Passavant, Raffael von Urbino, II, p. 443) which says " 1515 Raphahill di Urbin der so hoch peim Papst geacht ist gewest hat der hat dyse nakete

145 *Giulio Romano and Collaborator (Perino del Vaga ?).* Crossing of the Red Sea. Vatican, Loggias of Raphael, Eighth Vault.

146 *Giovanni da Udine, Giulio Romano and G. F. Penni.* View of the Ninth Vault. Vatican, Loggias of Raphael.

Bild gemacht und hat sy dim Albrecht Dürer gen Nornberg geschickt Im seim Hand zu weisen " (1515 Raphael of Urbino so highly esteemed by the Pope made these nude figures and sent them to Albrecht Dürer in Nuremberg to show him a work by his hands). Vasari, in the life of Raphael writes, " Albert Dürer paid him the tribute of his homage and sent him his own portrait painted in water colors on cambric so fine that it was transparent, without the use of white paint, the white materials forming the lights of the picture. This appeared marvelous to Raphael who sent back many drawings of his own which were greatly valued by Albert. This head was among the things of Giulio Romano, Raphael's heir in Mantua " (Vasari, IV, pp. 353-354). The Vienna drawing that could be the only remains of the " many drawings " sent by Raphael to Dürer does not seem to be an autograph by Raphael. It is usually considered to be by Giulio. Hartt thinks it is by Giulio but retouched by Raphael. From here the hypothesis arises that Giulio made the drawing and project for the frescoes and Raphael limited himself to the supervision and correction. Shearman (*loc. cit.*) is not convinced of the attribution to Giulio and thinks that the drawings can be assigned to Raphael. He considers absurd Panofsky's idea that Dürer would consider or would write that the drawing was by Raphael because of the different conception of art people had in the North. Shearman holds with Vasari to the contrary. Besides, Vasari must have been informed of the whole matter by Giulio Romano. We know from the cited passage that the Dürer portrait was in Mantua among other things inherited by Giulio; Vasari in the life of Giulio Romano repeats that he had seen it in Mantua. It seems impossible for Shearman that Giulio would not have told Vasari, had the Vienna design really been a youthful work, since Dürer would have been cheated by Raphael in the exchange. I do not agree with Shearman's reasoning on this point. Above all, Giulio might not have known which drawings Raphael had sent to Dürer: there must have been hundreds in the studio and it is possible that everything that was done under the master's direction was his property; hence Raphael could have taken whatever he wished. If among the various things selected to send to Dürer he happened to come upon a good copy by his best pupil, he could have easily added it to the group after correcting it a little and would thus have kept the original. With all the esteem that he could have had for Dürer, I doubt that Raphael considered him as highly as the Marquis of Mantua, or the Duke of Ferrara. A small trick of this type would not be repugnant to him in this case. It is therefore quite possible that Raphael, after having retouched it, sent a drawing by Giulio to Dürer as if it were his own and that Giulio knew nothing of it and further that Dürer accepted it in good faith. The case is different for a small drawing sent to a German artist and for cartoons of a famous work such as the scene of *Leo IV* and the *St. Michael* for the Duke of Ferrara. As for the date of 1515 given by Dürer it does not mean much. It only indicates when the German artist received the two works and who had sent them. For the dating of the fresco, the year 1515 written on the design is not useful, in my opinion. In fact it only assures us that there already existed in the workshop in that year a drawing from which derived the first figure on the left side of the *Battle of Ostia.* A very vague *terminus* actually acquires strength only because the fresco can be dated by other elements as we shall see.

Finally in conclusion, I must say that the drawing has very little fascination. I cannot agree with Shearman, therefore, in attributing it even doubtfully to Raphael. Raphael's drawings of 1514 are among the most beautiful that we know. It is sufficient to think of the stupendous series for the *Resurrection.* This one instead seems academic. The figure at the left leaning on the staff is especially academic. That staff which returns in drawings of many other artists from the sixteenth to the nineteenth centuries (for example, in those of Viti) is a typical ingredient of the nude drawing-class pose. It is possible that this figure was originally thought of as a papal guard. But the feeling is that it is a study for its own sake and that the two images were united arbitrarily, copied or studied from different sources: an exercise by Giulio Romano.

[44] A study for the seated bishops on the foreground at the right side in the *Coronation* is located in the Düsseldorf Museum (Fig. 30). At first sight it is fascinating, then we realize that the fascination lies in the idea, the invention of the group. The drawing has various weak passages including bungled drapery folds and broken structures under the mantels. The usual attribution is to Penni. It is quite possibly a derivation from what must have been the splendid Raphael original.

The finished model for the left section of the *Oath* is now typical of Giulio. (Florence, Horne Foundation; Fig. 31). The drawing has been squared as if it had served for transfer to the cartoon.

[45] Shearman, 1959.

[46] O. Fischel, " An Unknown Drawing by Raphael in Zurich," *Burlington Magazine,* 1925, p. 134.

[47] Freedberg, 1961. Freedberg's arguments are not very convincing for his proposed dating. The connection with the first cartoon for the tapestries makes one think that the *Battle of Ostia* chronologically is the second in the series. Raphael had begun to work in this room during the summer of 1514 while the work on the cartoons could not have been undertaken before the beginning of 1515. The comparison of the plan of the *Battle of Ostia* with that of the drawing of the *Miraculous Draught of Fishes* conserved in the Albertina is rather superficial, deriving perhaps from the suggestion of a similar placement near a water course. The Albertina drawing seems to us by Giulio, derived from a Raphael study of the cartoon and not a first idea for it (cf. note 28). The observation of the disposition of the frieze on the base of the painting of all the principal figures of the *Battle of Ostia* which corresponds to the analogous solution of the *Giving of the Keys* and certainly inspired by ancient reliefs, is still valid.

[48] Letter by Raphael to Fabio Calvo, dated August 15, 1514.

[49] Letter to Baldassarre Castiglione, without date, but certainly of 1514 and probably at the beginning of the summer.

[50] Letter to Fabio Calvo, cited.

[51] A. M. Brizio in E. V. A., cited.

[52] Parker, 1956, no. 538, fig. CXXVII. Parker, following Gronau, dates the drawing *ca.* 1506-08 and places it in connection with the famous battle scenes planned by Leonardo and Michelangelo for the Palazzo della Signoria in Florence. I believe it should be dated later (1510) as does Shearman. The drawing appears to be very close to the nudes on the ceiling of the Segnatura.

[53] Oxford, Ashmolean Museum (Parker, 1956, nos. 566 r. and v., 567; Fig. 35); Lille, Musée Wicar. The figurative decoration of the Chigi Chapel was completed with a projected series of sculptures. Of the four prophets, only two were executed: the *Jonah* and the *Elias* (Figs. 37 and 38). They were done by the Florentine, Lorenzo Lotti, called " Il Lorenzetto " who under the will of Agostino Chigi (1519) had the commission to sculpt the statues in the niches, the altar, and the obelisks, after drawings by Raphael. The commission was renewed by Sigismondo Chigi in 1521. We also know that while the *Jonah* was done by Il Lorenzetto himself, the *Elias* was executed at least with the collaboration of Raffaello da Montelupo who came to Rome in 1523. As is well known, the series was completed more than a century later by Bernini.
To what degree do Lorenzetto's sculptures depend upon Raphael? Or putting it another way, in what sense does this sculptor, like the mosaicist Alvise del Pace, become a member of the workshop? Judging from the rather awkward forms Lorenzetto displays in his Tuscan works before working in the Chigi Chapel, that is, the Forteguerri monument divided between the Cathedral and the Museo Civico of Pistoia, it must be said that he was enormously influenced by Raphael. And if in the *Elias*, perhaps because it was done later and with the help of Raffaello da Montelupo, the elegant harmony of the *Laocoön*, its prototype, was marred by the academic exercises of imitating its grand expression, in the *Jonah* instead we are witnessing the ardent interpretation of the forms of Raphael. This to such a degree that many have been led to suspect that Raphael had a hand in it; a suspicion validated by the fact that we know Raphael had modeled figures in terra cotta to be translated into marble. This was in 1516, precisely the year in which he was planning the decoration of the Chigi Chapel (cf. Golzio, p. 51). Excluding the possibility that a plastic model might have existed (but no one ever names it) I think that Raphael limited himself to studying the two figures with precise drawings and that only the *Jonah* fully respected those drawings.
There is a drawing at Windsor (Popham, no. 811) which represents the figure of Jonah with many variants (Fig. 36). I believe that it is a copy of one of Raphael's preparatory drawings for the statue. A copy, to be sure, of a rejected idea but one quite close to the definitive one. The drawing is one of the many by anonymous Raphael followers, almost certainly a painter rather than a sculptor, as Popham suggests (which excludes Lorenzetto).

[54] " The Loggia, the Stufetta, the rooms, the hangings of leather of Your Honor are furnished, everything awaits you;" letter by Bembo to Cardinal Bibbiena of June 20, 1516 (Golzio, p. 48). An earlier letter of April 19, 1516 has requested Bibbiena to send new subjects to be painted in the Stufetta because the ones which were sent had already been executed. There is no doubt therefore that on the finished Stufetta there was a painted decoration. The problem is different for the Loggia. In a letter dated July 19, 1517, Bembo informs Bibbiena, " once again the Loggia of Your Honor is being built and is coming along beautifully. . . . "
What had happened? That " once again " seems to allude to damage that occurred after all was done. It is probable that the decoration that we know was remade after the reconstruction. Based on a letter of Marcantonio Michiel of May 2, 1519 (Golzio, p. 98) in which he says that Raphael had painted " a very long Loggia (evidently the large Loggia of the second floor) and is working on the other two Loggias that will be very beautiful . . . ," it can be supposed that these two Loggias were the one on the first floor (actually by Giovanni da Udine) and the Bibbiena Loggia. There are no other Loggias in the Vatican Palaces decorated at this time; the Loggia of the third floor was completed by Giovanni da Udine for Pius IV many years later. Among recent studies that do not follow this dating, Freedberg (1961) considers all the decoration of the Bibbiena apartment as executed in 1516. De Campos is of the other opinion. (*I Palazzi Vaticani*, p. 110).

[55] F. Hartt, " Raphael and Giulio Romano, with Notes on the Raphael School," in *Art Bulletin*, 1944.

[56] *Inventario degli archivi di San Sepolcro* (extract from Volume IV of the *Archivi della storia d'Italia*). Rocca San Casciano, 1914.

[57] For biographical information and a list of Raffaellino del Colle's work see: A. Venturi, *Storia dell'arte italiana*, IX, 5, pp. 607-620.

[58] The position of scholars with regard to Hartt's attribution has been unusual. De Campos, although rejecting Hartt's fundamental position and revindicating Raphael's authorship for at least the design of the *Coronation of Charlemagne* does not discuss the reference to Raffaellino either on stylistic or documentary grounds.

147 *Giulio Romano and G. F. Penni.* The Worship of the Golden Calf. Vatican, Loggias of Raphael, Ninth Vault.

279

Freedberg (1961, pp. 307-310) does not mention Raffaellino at all (he does later, in relation to the Loggia of the Farnesina) but limits himself to speaking of Penni with minor assistance. He also thinks the project was Raphael's. Camesasca (*Tutta la pittura di Raffaello*, II, *Gli affreschi*, Milan, 1956, p. 53) cites for the fresco in question " drawings by Sanzio " which unfortunately we cannot recognize and for the execution he believes it " belongs to Penni (rather than Giovanni da Udine according to the opinion of older authors, including Gamba) perhaps assisted by Giulio Romano to whom could be assigned some figures at the left: especially the bishops on the other side . . . tend to reveal the participation of Raffaellino del Colle." Even in this case the acceptance of Hartt's idea (which was not cited) is limited to the group of bishops and was not discussed.

Finally Pier Luigi de Vecchi in a generally careful critical catalogue of a recent popular study on Raphael (*L'opera completa di Raffaello con presentazione di Michele Prisco*, Milan, 1966) speaks, as does Camesasca, of Penni, Raffaellino and perhaps Giulio Romano, but maintains that Hartt also assigns to Raffaellino the other fresco with the *Oath of Leo III*, which is not exact because Hartt assumes the presence of another anonymous collaborator for this work. These examples taken from works of various levels are sufficient, I think, to give an idea how fluctuating and often gratuitous are the opinions of modern historians on the problem of Raphael's workshop. The fluctuation is excusable where the facts are lacking but errors are not. It is for this reason that I shall never attempt to make easy stylistic attributions, convinced on the other hand that in a similar context the results achievable are always, or nearly always, illusory.

[59] Letter of Leonardo Sellaio to Michelangelo dated January 19, 1517.

[60] Drawings by Giulio in Haarlem, Teylers Museum (cat. A. 64 and A. 65; Figs. 40 and 44).

[61] Letter by Bembo to Cardinal Bibbiena (Golzio, p. 48).

[62] On April 19, 1516 Bembo wrote to Bibbiena begging him on behalf of Raphael to send " the other histories that are to be painted on your Stufetta, that is, the text of the histories, since the ones you sent will be prepared for painting this week." (Golzio, p. 44).

[63] Giulio Romano's famous passion for Trajan's Column and his drawings and studies of archaeology prove how his beginnings under Raphael from 1514 to 1516, that is, during his period of greatest enthusiasm for the antique, was crucial for the young artist. Giulio knew very well how " to draw perspectives, measure the buildings and make plans " (Vasari, V, p. 525) and he was so employed by Raphael not only as an assistant in his architectural works but also for the methodic recognition of antique monuments that he was preparing for a projected map of Rome. It is probable that for this enterprise Raphael elaborated upon the modern techniques of relief upon which Brizio had cleverly insisted, and he taught it to Giulio Romano.

Regarding the relationship between Raphael, Giovanni da Udine and archaeology, this passage from Vasari is illuminating: " Not long after, in digging near San Pietro in Vincoli among the ruins of the Palace of Titus, they found some rooms roofed in, covered with grotesques, small figures and scenes in stucco. Giovanni and Raphael, who were taken to see them, were amazed at their beauty, freshness and excellence, which had been preserved so long; but it is not remarkable, because they had been protected from the destructive influence of the air " (Vasari, VI, p. 551). Vasari's account vividly immerses us in the discovery and in the emotion it caused among the artists of Leonine Rome. There follows the discovery by Giovanni da Udine, after a long search of the technique, to make real antique stuccoes in all the parts he wished to employ them (Vasari, VI, p. 552).

[64] Giovanni da Udine's name for the part of the decoration was first advanced by De Vito Battaglia (" La Stufetta del Cardinal Bibbiena," in *L'arte*, 1926, pp. 30 ff.).

[65] Dollmayr was the first to attribute to Giulio Romano, in addition to the ornamental motives, the execution of the compartment with the exception of the *Birth of Erichthonius* which he holds to be Penni's (" Lo stanzino da bagno del Cardinal Bibbiena " in *Archivio storico dell'arte*, 1890, pp. 272-280). Earlier scholarship, from Passavant to Cavalcaselle, believed that Raphael himself was dominant in the execution. The attribution to Giulio Romano was upheld by De Vito Battaglia but he attributed the decorative parts to Giovanni da Udine (cf. note 64). Hartt (*Giulio Romano*, 1958) considers the stories with *Venus and Cupid*, *Pan and Syrinx* to be Giulio's but correctly insisted upon the importance of the Raphaelesque

149 *Perino del Vaga.* Crossing of the Jordan.
Vatican, Loggias of Raphael, Tenth Vault.

conception. In the Royal Library at Windsor there is a drawing for the scene of *Venus and Cupid* painted for the Stufetta (Popham, 1949, no. 810, fig. 159)· The same subject is repeated in a drawing attributed to Giulio Romano in the Albertina (cat. III, no. 82), which Popham, following Cavalcaselle's opinion, correctly considers a copy of the Windsor drawing. The latter seems to be a delicate study by a Raphael pupil very close to the Master, from the original drawing for the fresco. The characteristics of the Windsor drawing have induced Popham to relate it to a series of Raphaelesque drawings conserved in Chatsworth that represent the Apostles painted by the workshop in the Sala dei Palafrenieri. Of that last decoration we know three executive drawings ready to be transferred to the cartoon and certainly by Penni: two in the Louvre (4261 and 28954) show *St. John the Evangelist* and *St. Matthew* and one in the British Museum shows *St. Luke* (Pouncey and Gere, 1962, no. 63). The Chatsworth drawings seem instead, like the Windsor drawing, copies *from* rather than studies *for* those figures. Their handsome delicacy nonetheless does not permit an attribution to Penni. I often ask myself if we are not dealing with personal studies by Giovanni da Udine. The Raphael pupil, whoever he was, was occupied in the Stufetta and in the Sala dei Palafrenieri, but he must be excluded as the author in the parts of the drawing which reproduce figures because he worked in grotesques, still lifes and animals.

The Windsor drawing has notable formal connections with the figures in the *Vision of Ezechiel* (Florence, Pitti), a Raphaelesque painting attributed to Giulio Romano as the executor but which has nothing to do with his imposing style and little with that of Penni, for that matter. This little masterpiece, instead, where the figures of animals and the landscape dominate (two specialities of Giovanni da Udine), could be assigned to Giovanni around 1517, if the high quality, not only

150 *Perino del Vaga.* Fall of Jericho.   Vatican,
Loggias of Raphael, Tenth Vault.

151 *Perino del Vaga.* Joshua Arresting the Course of the Sun. Vatican, Loggias of Raphael, Tenth Vault.

in the invention (no one would wish to deny Raphael here) but also in the execution (especially the landscape) were not to indicate with greater reason Raphael's personal role here.

The scene with *Venus and Cupid* in the Stufetta from which the Windsor drawing derives was engraved by Agostino Veneziano (Bartsch, XIV, pp. 218, 286) with the date 1516.

[66] D. Redig De Campos, *I Palazzi Vaticani*, Bologna, 1967, p. 112.

[67] See note 54. It is worthwhile to note that the remarks of Michiel are not very clear, at least on this point. He speaks of " four papal rooms " painted by Raphael but in 1519 he had painted only three Stanze; the fourth, that of Constantine, was probably commissioned to him but he did not execute it.

Hence Michiel is not exact unless he meant to allude to the Sala dei Palafrenieri to be identified with the " Stanza avanti la Guardaroba " as the fourth room, which decoration was paid for in 1519, " to those young assistants of Raphael." If not, Michiel was poorly informed and then the notice about the two Loggias being executed in 1519 could also be wrong and put in doubt the dating of the Loggetta of Bibbiena for that year.

[68] Freedberg, 1961.

[69] D. Redig De Campos, *Raffaello e Michelangelo*, 1946, pp. 48-49.

[70] Vasari, IV, pp. 361-362.

[71] Vasari, VI, p. 555.

[72] For the details surrounding the Sala which was demolished under Paul IV, was redecorated in the pontificate of Pius IV by Zuccari but completed under Gregory XIII only in 1582, see D. Redig De Campos, *I Palazzi Vaticani*, Bologna, 1967, p. 145 and p. 164.

[73] See Freedberg, 1961, p. 321 and figs. 395 and 396; also Pouncey and Gere, 1962, no. 63. In the Devonshire Collection at Chatsworth there is a series of Raphaelesque copies of drawings for or from the figures of Apostles (see note 65).

152 *Perino del Vaga.* The Dividing of the Promised Land. Vatican, Loggias of Raphael, Tenth Vault.

[74] Bartsch, XIV, nos. 64-76.

[75] Vasari, VII, p. 90.

[76] There is no doubt possible about Raphael's paternity of the Louvre sheet (3875) preparatory for the fresco of *Venus and Psyche*. The attribution to Giulio (Hartt, 1958), although attenuated by the inclusion of corrections by Raphael is not supportable. The quality of the drawing and its relationship to the fresco indicates quite well the boundary of the two personalities. More doubtful as an autograph is the study for the *Three Graces* at Windsor (Popham, no. 804, Fig. 61; Fig. 65). A certain open sensuality, the weakness of drawing, the absence of preparatory marks made with a stylus typical of Raphael's autographs, leave open the possibility (but nothing more than a possibility) that we are dealing with a pupil. Still less possible for consideration as an autograph are the supposed preparatory studies in Haarlem and Dresden. The study for Omphale in the *Wedding of Cupid and Psyche* (Haarlem, Teylers Museum; Fig. 63) seems ascribable (with reservations) to Penni as well as the Ganymedes (Paris, Louvre; Fig. 64) for the same scene. Weaker but within the same correct taste is another folio from the Louvre with *Venus showing Psyche to Cupid* (Fig. 66). With reservation, the study for Mercury and Psyche in the *Council of the Gods* (Chatsworth, Devonshire Collection, no. 55; Fig. 68) and from the same collection, the penned study with *Mercury and Psyche* (Fig. 67), is given to Penni. The drawings here assigned to Penni have connections with Giulio Romano, but an influence of Giulio on Penni is also noticeable in the paintings by Il Fattore. All of these drawings probably derive from original ideas by Raphael.

[77] Letter by Leonardo Sellaio to Michelangelo of January 1, 1518. From the date of this letter, the dating of the frescoes may be set without doubt within the year 1517.

[78] Certain gestures toward a lower level, as that of *Venus showing Psyche to Cupid* or of *Cupid and the Graces*, may be interpreted as support to the projected existence of an earthly cycle of Psyche for the walls of the Loggia (and perhaps for tapestries destined for a place there). These gestures may also be explained naturally as a looking down from the sky without presuming another series.

It has also been said that the well-known series of engravings (Bartsch, 39-70 and 235-38) by Agostino Veneziano and " B nel Dado " with early stories of Psyche may give us some trace of the Raphaelesque projects of this unexecuted part of the decoration. Yet in no way can these drawings for the engravings be made to revert back to autographs by Raphael or of the workshop at the time of the decoration of the Loggia. Instead they seem to have been produced in the post-Raphaelesque Roman orbit, perhaps by the school of Giulio.

[79] F. Hartt, " Raphael and Giulio Romano, with notes on Raphael's School," in *Art Bulletin*, 1944, pp. 67-94.

[80] F. Titi, *Studio di pittura, scultura e architettura nelle chiese di Roma*, Rome 1675, p. 22.

[81] J. Shearman, " Giulio Romano " (review of Hartt, 1958) in *Burlington Magazine*, 101, 1955, pp. 456-460.

[82] See P. Bellori, *Descrizione delle immagini dipinte da Raffaello d'Urbino nel Vaticano e di quelle alla Farnesina*, Rome, pp. 160 ff.

[83] " There one sees similarly many animals made in the lunettes that are surrounded by festoons and some *putti* that hold the signs of the gods. A lion and a sea horse are held to be divine things. " (Vasari, VI, p. 558).

[84] Once again Hartt (in *Burlington Magazine*, 1944, *op. cit.*) proposes the name of Raffaellino del Colle as Penni's assistant and his suggestion has generally been accepted. The distinction made by Hartt of the parts belonging to Penni and Raffaellino are minute and it seems to us useful to repeat them here: In the *Wedding of Cupid and Psyche*, the American scholar gives to Penni: the Apollo, Flora, the two Muses between them, Hercules, Hebe, Thetis, Neptune, the first two winged figures, Ganymedes, Cupid, Psyche, Bacchus and the three Graces; all the other personages are given to Raffellino. In the *Council of Gods*, to Penni: Psyche, Mercury, Janus, Venus, Pluto, Cupid, Neptune, Jove, Juno, Diana and Minerva; the rest to Raffaellino. This distinction is based naturally, nor could it have been otherwise, on a praiseworthy stylistic reading but it is spoiled, as we have often said, by the poor (not to say, non-existent) knowledge of Raffaellino's style in these years. This difficulty causes contradictions even for Hartt. If the head of Neptune in the *Council of the Gods* is compared with the bearded warrior with a chain around his neck (above, at the left) in the *Coronation of Charlemagne* (Stanza di Costantino), it becomes clear that they were executed by the same hand, or by two artists so close that distinctions cannot be made. Nonetheless Hartt attributes, as we have seen, the first to Penni and the second to Raffaellino del Colle.

[85] Vasari, VI, pp. 550-551.

[86] Vasari, VI, pp. 377-378.

[87] It can be admitted that the *Spasimo di Sicilia* appears today in a considerably ruined state because it had suffered from numerous vicissitudes beginning with a shipreck before the picture had even arrived at its destination, followed by its transfer to Spain in 1662: in 1813 it was taken from Spain to France with other Napoleonic booty. The picture was transferred to canvas and underwent a probably excessive cleaning, at least from what can be judged today in its present state. The painting is also defaced by old retouches that were made rather indiscriminately on the surface. It was brought back to Spain in 1822 and is now in the Prado Museum.

[88] Golzio, pp. 70-71.

[89] Vasari, IV, p. 378.

[90] If the Doria picture is really the double portrait of Andrea Novagero and Agostino Beazzano, it must have been executed before the end of April, 1516 (see the famous letter by Bibbiena with the notice of the Tivoli trips made with Raphael and the two men depicted " for the pleasure of M. Andrea " on his way to Venice, in Golzio, p. 42). A similar dating which coincides with the last phase of work for the tapestry cartoons agrees perfectly with the stylistic characteristics of the former. As for *Bindo Altoviti*, it seems to me that it is a kind of academicizing of the figure of Novagero, insistent in the details and exasperatingly plastic, just as we have seen done by Giulio during 1516 and 1517.

[91] It was painted for Cardinal Gouffier de Boissy who seems to have ordered it from Raphael on the occasion of the meeting in Bologna of the Pope and Francis I. It certainly cannot belong to those years. Its dating is based upon a stylistic hypothesis only. Personally, I do not think that Raphael had any part in it. The landscape, in form, can be compared rather than with the landscapes in the Madonnas from 1517 and 1520, to those considerably later by Giulio, like the *Jove suckled by Amaltea* (Hampton Court).

Equally difficult is the dating and attribution of another Raphaelesque painting, also in the Louvre, that belonged to Cardinal Gouffier de Boissy, namely the *San Giovannino* (Fig. 102). For the pose of the gesture it is related to Raphel's drawings around 1514 (angels for the *Resurrection*, etc.) and it has no stylistic connection with works of that period. Badly ruined by cleanings, its condition does not permit a clear reading. The idea of painting two coats of arms on the surface at the sides of the Saint's head cannot be Raphaelesque and only with difficulty can it be given to a pupil of Sanzio. It would rather make one think of a Northern artist; or the arms might have been a later addition. The landscape of this type and the acutely realistic passages like the trunk on the first plane, are hardly Raphaelesque. The attribution to Raphael is thus rejected without, however, suggesting the name of a collaborator or a date that is at all convincing.

[92] The identification of the picture with the most beautiful *Nativity of Our Lord* which Vasari records was sent by Raphael to the Counts of Canossa in Verona, is almost certain. It is possible to follow the subsequent transfers up to its present location, through the Este, Sforza, Gonzaga collections, and the collection of Charles I where it was purchased by Philip IV of Spain who called it " the Pearl " (its present name). In 1813 it was brought to Paris but was returned to the Prado in 1815. The dating is not supported by any documents. It is usually placed in 1518 and was almost certainly executed in that year or in the following one.

[93] F. Hartt, " Raphael and Giulio Romano," in *Art Bulletin*, 1944.

[94] Freedberg, 1961.

[95] It was done for the Church of San Silvestro in Aquila where it was already in place on April 2, 1520.

F. Hartt (" Raphael and Giulio Romano," in *Art Bulletin*, 1944) assigns it completely to Raffaellino.

[96] Despite Vasari's enthusiasm for this picture, explainable perhaps as an act of devotion to the son of the orderer, " the Most Reverend Cardinal of Carpi . . . great amateur of our arts " (Vasari, IV, pp. 348-349), no one today assigns the picture to Raphael. Dollmayr already attributed it to Penni, basing himself on a drawing for the *St. Joseph* in the Albertina (Catalogue III no. 117) that he recognized to be by Il Fattore. Fischel includes the Albertina drawing in his *Corpus* (VIII, 378c) considering that if Penni was almost certainly the executor of the drawing, the idea must have gone back to Raphael, to whom implicitly he assigns the projection of the picture. In the catalogue of his volume on Raphael which appeared in 1948, Fischel still ascribes the execution as well as the projection of the painting to Penni, contradicting what he had asserted in the *Corpus*.

283

153 *Giovanni da Udine, Perino del Vaga and Collaborator.* View of the Eleventh Vault. Vatican, Loggias of Raphael.

The preparatory drawing by Penni which was acquired along with the picture by Cardinal Alessandro Farnese is conserved along with the painting at Capodimonte and was sent to Naples with the Farnese Collection.

Another cartoon which reproduces to scale a part of the *Madonna of the Divine Love* is found in the British Museum (Pouncey and Gere, 1952, no. 51, pp. 40-41) and must have served for the execution of a copy.

[97] To what degree the rapport with Raphael was still important to sustain Giulio Romano's quality is attested by two paintings, the *St. Margaret* in the Louvre (Fig. 97) and the *Infant St. John* in the Accademia, Florence (Fig. 101) which are believed to have been done between 1518 and 1519 but which, I think, were only by the pupil. The *St. Margaret* takes up the theme of the juxtaposition of two different forms in torsion, which inspired Raphael's *St. Michael.* The *Infant St. John* reminds us in the movement of the legs of the pose of Jonah (executed by Lorenzetto on Raphael's design) and in the gesture of the arm the never-forgotten Leonardesque motif from the drawings of angels in the *Resurrection.* Both paintings came out of the workshop as works of Raphael or at least controlled by him but his actual share must have been minimal. In connection with the *St. Margaret,* Adolfo Venturi's opinion that the hand of Garofalo is here perceived, is worthy of mention. The softness, especially in the face, could make one think of the sweet Raphaelism of the Emilian painter, but I think the effect is the result of numerous restorations.

Freedberg (1961) attributed the *St. Margaret* in the Kunsthistorisches Museum of Vienna (Fig. 100) to Giulio Romano with Raffaellino del Colle. It is a type of repetition of the Louvre picture but more coherent from a point of formal structure, so that some, including Venturi, consider it a copy of a lost Raphael original. The attribution to Giulio and Raffaellino is convincing.

To complete the list of pictures executed by Giulio in Raphael's workshop we must mention at least two other pictures: the copy of *Tommaso Inghirami's Portrait* now in the Pitti which was executed, I think, around 1516 after an original Raphael of about two years earlier that can be identified with the picture in the Boston Museum. The lower quality in the accessories and the greater realism in the face speak decisively in favor of Giulio for the picture in the Pitti. The *Giovanna di Aragona* in the Louvre, the cartoon of which Raphael sent to the Duke of Ferrara saying that it was not " his work " (see note 40 and also p. 223), should also be assigned to Giulio. The letter speaks of the cartoon on March 2, 1519 but the picture had already been sent by Alfonso d'Este at Fontainebleau in November of 1518 and perhaps was executed around 1517. Even though the plan of the composition can be given to Raphael, there is no doubt that Giulio found himself quite comfortable in handling the architectural theme in the background, in treating this female figure whose beauty was purely physical and worldly which he evidently was requested to represent in all her splendor, decorated with handsome clothes and refined jewelry.

And finally it is possible that the *Madonna* called " dei Candelabri " in Baltimore's Walters Art Gallery (Fig. 103) which came from the Borghese collection in Rome, was also by Giulio. It is a strange picture with a singularly nineteenth century flavor that almost could be attributed to Ingres rather than Giulio Romano. It may be dated around 1514 and must mark the beginnings of the very young Raphael assistant even before his collaboration on the *Madonna dell'Impannata.* There is a replica of it in which the Madonna wears a veil which was exhibited for some time at the London National Gallery. Fischel (" Raphael," London, 1948) speaks of the London picture referring to it as Cavalcaselle had for the Boston picture.

I do not think that the portrait of *Giuliano dei Medici* from the Metropolitan Museum of New York (Fig. 104) can be assigned to Giulio. It can be better considered as an anonymous copy of a lost original by Raphael. An analogous judgment can be applied to the portrait of *Julius II* in the Uffizi which came into the Medici collection with the inheritance of Vittoria della Rovere, bearing Giulio Romano's name (changed in Florence in the inventory of 1631 to Raphael's). Possibly the other copy of the lost Raphael today in the Pitti which entered the Medici collection together with and with the same attribution as the previous one, is really by Titian. In the inventory of 1691 it was already attributed to him and today, after some discussion, this attribution prevails. Cavalcaselle attributed to Giulio Romano the fresco with the elephant Annone basing himself on the copy by Francisco de Hollanda in a notebook now in the Escorial. Leo X commissioned it from Raphael who executed it on the Torre della Cinta Vaticana (destroyed during the time of Paul V). More likely it was carried out by Giovanni da Udine, the specialist in representing animals (L. Pastor, *Storia dei Papi,* IV, I, p. 49).

[98] F. Hartt, " Raphael and Giulio Romano," in *Art Bulletin,* 1944.

[99] Catalogue of the exhibition, *Le Seizième Siècle Européen, Peintures et Dessins dans les Collections Publiques Françaises,* October, 1965-January, 1966, no. 245, p. 198.

[100] From Sebastiano del Piombo's letters we learn that Raphael was behind in the completion of the work. In July of 1518 Raphael had not yet started painting (Golzio, p. 70).

[101] The request was made by Baldassarre Castiglione in Giulio Romano's name to Cardinal de' Medici (Golzio, p. 146).

[102] Two studies are relevant: one for the head of St. Andrew (Fig. 107) and one for another Apostle both in the British Museum (Pouncey and Gere, 1962, no. 37 and 38); of the study of the two Apostles' heads and hands (Fig. 109) in a single sheet in the Ashmolean Museum of Oxford (Parker, 1956, no. 568); of two Apostles' heads in two drawings in Devonshire Collection at Chatsworth (file 59, nos. 66 and 67) and finally that of the Albertina in Vienna (Catalogue

154 *Perino del Vaga.* David and Goliath. Vatican, Loggias of Raphael, Eleventh Vault.

III, no. 79). These seven heads on six folios represent most of those that we can see in the group of Apostles at the center and on the lower left of the picture (there are really nine Apostles but one turns inward and only his hair is seen and of the other one we have no study). This series of drawings was mentioned for the first time by Fischel in November, 1898 (*Raphaels Zeichnungen Versuch einer Kritik,* Strasbourg, 1898) and since then attentively examined by the same scholar almost forty years later (" Raphael's Auxiliary Cartoons," in *Burlington Magazine,* 71, 1937, pp. 166-168).

The attribution of the six drawings is not fully agreed upon. Fischel assigns, to Raphael only the *St. Andrew* in the British Museum (no. 37) and the double study in Oxford (Parker, 1956, no. 568). In the Albertina catalogue (1932) where Raphael is assigned the drawing in that collection, mention is made of a positive oral opinion by Fischel; nonetheless the attribution is dropped in his cited article in the *Burlington Magazine* of 1937 where the Vienna drawing and the British Museum one are assigned to Penni.

Hartt, " Raphael and Giulio Romano " in *Art Bulletin,* 1944, p. 87, assigns the two Chatsworth drawings to Raphael, to which proposition U. Middeldorf (Raphael's Drawings, New York, 1945, no. 87) agrees. P. Pouncey and J. Gere (pp. 33-34, nos. 37, 38), mentioning the retouches in the head of St. Andrew, consider both drawings as originals by Raphael, pointing out the substantial affinity of hand and quality between the Oxford drawing, those of Chatsworth and of Vienna, seeming to hold the entire group of " auxiliary cartoons " as autographs. It is not possible to accept as autographs the other studies

155 *Perino del Vaga.* Triumph of David. Vatican, Loggias of Raphael, Eleventh Vault.

285

156 *Giovanni da Udine, Giulio Romano and Collaborators.* View of Twelfth Vault. Vatican, Loggias of Raphael.

for the whole figures of the *Transfiguration* like the group of Apostles on the highest range at the center of the lower zone of the picture which is in the Albertina (Fig. 110). It shows nude figures taken directly from models but the quality does not permit an attribution to Raphael; it seems, rather, to be a copy by Penni from an original by the master done for some reason during the long study for the large altarpiece.

The sheet in the Louvre with the Apostle who points upward and the figure of John kneeling in front with his hands at his breast is of higher quality. In this study, too, the models are nude and belong therefore to an early phase of the projection. The psychological intensity and the vibrant quality in many passages induce me to think that we find ourselves, perhaps, in front of a Raphael drawing completed and hardened by Giulio Romano.

As for the term " auxiliary cartoons " coined by Fischel for the six head studies mentioned above, it illuminates an interesting phase in the preparatory work on the *Transfiguration*. After the execution of the final cartoon from which, using the *spolvero* method, these details were obtained (the heads have, as do all the details of the cartoons or the *spolveri* from the cartoons have, the same proportions as their corresponding parts in the painting) in carrying the study a step further than was attained in the cartoon itself, not only carefully executing the composition of lights and darks but also modifying (as is easily seen, for example, in the hands of the Oxford sheet) the traces of the *spolvero* with a new drawing.

[103] The name of " the brother of Dosso " was given by the Ferrarese Ambassador Paolucci, writing to Alfonso I (Golzio, p. 106). As has been said already, Giulio Romano's request, advanced through Baldassarre Castiglione to Cardinal

157 *Anonymous (Pellegrino da Modena?).* Anointing of Solomon. Vatican, Loggias of Raphael, Twelfth Vault.

286

158 *Anonymous (Pellegrino da Modena?). Solomon in Judgment. Vatican, Loggias of Raphael, Twelfth Vault.*

de' Medici for payment of the *Transfiguration* in May, 1522 does not prove the collaboration of Giulio on the painting because it was to be advanced to him in his role as Raphael's heir (see J. Vogel, " Zu Raffaels Transfiguration," in *Monatsheft für Kunstwissenschaft*, 13, 1920, pp. 298-305.

[104] Payment of 25 ducats on June 11, 1519 (Golzio, p. 99).

[105] Diary of Marcantonio Michiel (Golzio, p. 104).

[106] Vasari, IV, p. 362.

[107] It is surprising, for example, that an important scholar like Fischel (" Le gerarchie degli angeli di Raffaello nelle Logge del Vaticano," in *Illustrazione Vaticana*, VIII, 1937, pp. 161-164) could seek the hand of Raphael in those little angels painted like diamonds between the interwoven motifs that surround the scenes of Genesis in the first vault (Fig. 119). How could we believe that a master like Raphael wishing to leave traces of his work, would do so in those tiny figures absolutely invisible from the ground!

[108] Vasari, IV, p. 362.

[109] Vasari, IV, p. 362.

[110] The greatest obstacle for assigning to this or that pupil of Raphael the group of drawings in question consists in the fact that still today, notwithstanding the hypotheses and adventurous attributions, we do not know with any degree of certainty how Perino, Polidoro, Giulio or Penni to whom from time to time these drawings have been attributed, drew

159 *Giulio Romano and Collaborator (Polidoro da Caravaggio?). Solomon and the Queen of Sheba. Vatican, Loggias of Raphael, Twelfth Vault.*

160 *Giulio Romano and Collaborator (Polidoro da Caravaggio).* Building of the Temple. Vatican, Loggias of Raphael, Twelfth Vault.

around 1518 and 1519. The reasoning in favor of an attribution to Penni given by P. Pouncey and J. Gere in the *Catalogue of Drawings by Raphael and by His School in the British Museum* (pp. 50-52) is based upon a comparison and full stylistic concordance between the group of drawings cited and the three sheets in the Albertina with scenes of classical subjects (S.R. 278, 279, 290). The three drawings in Vienna cannot be dated before 1530 for stylistic reasons and at that date we know well enough the graphic styles of Giulio Romano, Perino, and Polidoro to exclude the possibility that these are their works. The only name left is Penni's. Besides, Vasari's insistence on his ability as a draftsman and his " finished drawings " serve to confirm what the two English scholars acutely observed. More doubtful is the attribution to Penni of other drawings connected with the Loggias, such as that in the Albertina with *Joseph recounting his Dreams* (Fig. 118).

¹¹¹ A typical example is the drawing of the episode with *David and Bathsheba* (British Museum, no. 66; Fig. 114) where the form of the frame terminates in a semicircle above as in many scenes from the Loggias but not in this one; the finished frescoes are purely rectangular in form as are the other three in the same vault (Fig. 153). It is important that the variation is neither original nor capricious as in so many a posteriori exercises on Raphaelesque themes common in the drawings of the shop which invest them with a detail both fundamentally practical and aesthetically negligible which would only represent a phase of the projection.

¹¹² The start of the painting in the Loggias is variously dated but it seems to me reasonable to suppose that it must have fallen around the end of 1517, as Dollmayr has already proposed, or better at the beginning of 1518. All work was finished during the summer of 1519 (cf. Golzio, pp. 98, 99, 104).

¹¹³ Shortly after Raphael's death, Pellegrino da Modena returned home where he was killed in 1523. Before that date, therefore, and actually around 1520-1521 are to be dated his only remaining Roman frescoes and even these are in mediocre condition. They include the *Conquest of Granada* and the *Stories of San Jacopo* in the church dedicated to that Saint (see A. Venturi, IX, 2, pp. 448-452 and G. Fiocco, " Pellegrino da Modena," in *L'arte*, 1917, pp. 195-210).

¹¹⁴ For the reasons presented, a notable difference is found between the attributions advanced for the individual scenes

161 *Giovanni da Udine, Perino del Vaga.* View of Thirteenth Vault. Vatican, Loggias of Raphael.

by various art historians from Cavalcaselle, to Dollmayr, Venturi and all the others who have studied the problem. To discuss and rebut all these opinions is almost always extremely tedious and not very useful. To note them is a duty, but to avoid weighing down the text and the notes, see the excellent summary in the volume by E. Camesasca (*Tutta la pittura di Raffaello*, 1956, vol. I, pp. 58-65).

[115] It is true what Vasari says that "He also learned to make landscape with ruins and fragments of antiquities, coloring them in a style since adopted by Italians as well as Flemings;" still, when speaking of the Loggias, Vasari goes on to say that Giovanni made "all the vaults with very beautiful ornamentation of stucco enclosed with grotesques like the antique" and "embellished the ornamentation with little stories, landscapes, foliages and various friezes" (Vasari, VI, pp. 550 and 553). Hence the landscapes by Giovanni da Udine, at least according to Vasari, in the Loggias are only those that are part of the grotesque decoration and not within the scenes: they are the tiny landscapes inspired by Roman painting and not the backgrounds of the Biblical stories.

[116] Pouncey and Gere, 1962, nos. 64, 65. The drawing in the British Museum (*ibid.* no. 66) for the scene of *David and Bathsheba*, although it reveals the same technique and the same hand, is so connected to the style of the scenes by Perino (certainly executor of the fresco) that I would be inclined to consider it done by Penni but completing a project by Perino. On the other hand, the *Baptism* (*ibid.*, no. 67) in the same collection, despite the different technique, seems to me more exclusively by Penni. If Penni executed the fresco, as I believe he did, he did so by developing and then transforming an idea that was not his (see the significant attenuation of the angels' arms).

[117] On Vasari's authority, the *grisailles* which are found on the socle of every bay are generally assigned to Perino. The precarious state of preservation of these elements does not permit any certain affirmation on the discussion.

[118] Vasari says that Polidoro "came to Rome in the time when the Loggias for the palace of the Pope were being built under the orders of Raphael of Urbino" and worked until he was eighteen years old as assistant *(garzone)* of the masons employed in that task. But when Giovanni da Udine had begun to paint them, Polidoro became friendly with the painters and had acquired practice in their art; he was brought into the *équipe* and did not leave that work until he had achieved the true glory of greater beauty and greater ingenuity than most of the others" (Vasari, V, p. 142). From this passage we learn when Polidoro began painting and that he must have been born around the year 1500 if he was eighteen years old when he began the decoration of the Loggias.

[119] The picture of Rachael's face in the scene of the *Meeting with Jacob* is quite typical of Polidoro. It derives from Giulio's female types but he exaggerates and deforms the features. A comparison, among others, may be made between the head of the Virgin in a youthful drawing in the Berlin Museum (Cabinet of Drawings and Prints, no. 22473) representing the *Adoration of the Shepherds* or the female figure in the two stories of *Clelia* frescoed in the salon of the Villa Lante and now transferred with all that decoration to the Palazzo Zuccari. Analogously, the figures frescoed in the works for the *Construction of the Temple of Solomon* recall those for the *Finding of the Sibylline Books* in the aforementioned frescoes of Villa Lante, or the painting in imitation bronze on the socle of the Sala di Costantino in the scene of the *Foundation of the Vatican Basilica*.

[120] A recent example of this confusion, which is quite excusable considering the fluidity of the problem, is the attempt to attribute to Polidoro the scene of the *Dividing of the Lands* (see E. Borea, "Vicenda di Polidoro da Caravaggio," in *Arte antica e moderna*, 13-16, 1961, pp. 211 ff.) in my opinion surely executed by Perino. There is a drawing at Windsor for this scene (Popham, no. 807, Fig. 156) which seems to me assignable to Penni, as it does to Pouncey and Gere (1952, p. 51).

[121] Filippini, in *Bollettino d'arte*, January, 1929. The little that we know about Il Bologna is actually connected with the drawings for the tapestries called *Giuochi dei Putti*. He seems to have been a sort of assistant to Giovanni da Udine (and therefore worked on the decorative parts in the Loggias) invited to Flanders to supervise the weaving and perhaps for complet-

162 *Perino del Vaga*. Adoration of the Magi. Vatican, Loggias of Raphael, Thirteenth Vault.

163 *Perino del Vaga* (?). Baptism of Christ. Vatican, Loggias of Raphael, Thirteenth Vault.

164 *Giovanni da Udine and Assistants.* Stuccoes and grotesques in the Second Compartment of the Loggias. Vatican, Loggias of Raphael.

ing the cartoons for this and other series of tapestries (see *s.v.* H. Voss in *Thieme Becker*, 1940, and the long, documented entry in Pouncey and Gere, 1962, no. 155, pp. 87-90 with a re-examination of the criticism related to the tapestries of the *Giuochi dei Putti* and drawings and engravings connected with them).

122 Vasari, V, pp. 593-594.

123 A. Venturi, *Storia*, 9, II, pp. 408-410.

124 D. Redig De Campos, *I Palazzi Vaticani*, 1967, p. 117. To obtain an idea of the whole cycle of the Loggias before much damage had rendered many parts of the decoration unintelligible, it is useful to consult the excellent engraved reproductions of the whole by Volpato, for example, or others, as those in water color made in 1745 by the Spaniard, Francisco La Vega (Codex Vat. Lat. 13751).

125 We know of no autograph drawings by Giovanni for his work in the Loggias. A splendid study for a perched pheasant conserved in the British Museum (Pouncey and Gere, 1962, no. 153) has on the recto in a nineteenth century hand " for the decoration of the Vatican." There is no corresponding element in the painted decoration but if another barely traced outline of a bird in the same pose as the pheasant but in a reversed direction is taken into account, it can be observed, as the authors of the catalogue have done, that pairs of birds in such a way recur in the ornamentation of the twelfth vault. A drawing in the Uffizi (S. 461) with two studies of a little bird is by the same hand that executed the pheasant in London and corresponds in taste and spirit, but once again not in letter, to the zoomorphic motifs in the Loggias. Another pen drawing in the British Museum (Pouncey and Here, 1962, no. 154) is very close, except for minor variations, to the representation of a cormorant on the second pilaster at the left of the Loggias. The quality leads the authors of the catalogue to consider this drawing as a copy and with good reason. For a full discussion of the few drawings of grotesques attributed to Giovanni da Udine and for the correct conclusion that none of them can be considered his, see once again Pouncey and Gere, 1962, no. 184 and pp. 109-110.

We have no studies for the stuccoes. The presence in them of reproductions of famous Antique and Renaissance sculpture should not be surprising when one bears in mind that the Loggia was destined to house the collection of sculpture gathered together by Julius II and Leo X; it was potentially, and in fact, the Vatican's first Gallery of Art.

126 Golzio, p. 98.

127 Golzio, p. 104.

128 Vasari, VI, p. 554.

129 Vasari, *loc. cit.*

130 C. Pacchiotti, " Nuove attribuzioni a Polidoro da Caravaggio," in *L'Arte*, 1927, pp. 189-221. The small classical scenes reproduced in a series of engravings by Cherubino Alberti as works by Polidoro and which Pacchiotti sees as taken from passages in the Loggia on the first floor, are absolutely not traceable to that cycle. Besides, Polidoro entered, I think, immediately in the orbit of Giulio Romano and worked in the circle of Pippi at least until 1524 and he never worked in the circle of Giovanni da Udine.

131 Letter from the Ambassador Paolucci to Alfonso I d'Este of April 7, 1520 (Golzio, pp. 115-116).

132 Letter of April 12, 1520 (Golzio, p. 125).

Epilogue

With Raphael's death, the history of his workshop is not automatically closed. Many works and some of great importance remained unfinished and his pupils hoped to be able to complete them. We have already discussed the *Transfiguration*. In the Vatican palaces the series of paintings for the papal apartment remained unfinished: between the three finished Stanze and the Sala dei Palafrenieri and the Loggias is a large room, the Sala di Costantino (Fig. 174), whose decoration the Pope had already discussed with Raphael and the Master had decided to paint this in oil, that is, with the new technique successfully employed by his rival Sebastiano del Piombo in the Borgherini Chapel in San Pietro in Montorio. After a heated battle for settling the commission, Giulio Romano and Penni won in competition with Sebastiano del Piombo and executed the frescoes from the summer of 1520 till September, 1524. Also for the

Vatican palaces while Leo X was still alive, that is, before the end of 1521, Giovanni da Udine and Perino del Vaga decorated the vault in the last room of the Borgia apartment, the Sala dei Pontefici (Figs. 170 and 171). This was not *de rigueur* based on a commission inherited from Raphael, nor dependent on his interrupted projects although it is closely tied to inventions in the Loggias. Finally the construction of the Villa of Cardinal de' Medici at Montemario was left half-finished.[1] Naturally the problem here is principally architectural, that is, the relationship between completing and the project of Raphael and the role that his successors played in the enterprise. As for the decoration, Giulio Romano and Giovanni da Udine continued the language of the Vatican Loggias. The same holds true for the Stufetta of Clement VII in Castel Sant'Angelo (Figs. 52 and 53) which is a re-edition, but without the ideal splendid dimensions of the prototype of the Stufetta in the apartment of Cardinal Bibbiena.

Also, in these years an old commission that had been given to Raphael in the early years of the sixteenth century, was finally completed by Penni and Giulio: we are dealing here with the *Coronation of the Virgin* for the Nuns of Monteluce (Fig. 172) delivered in 1525 and today located in the Vatican Pinacoteca.[2] The cartoons for the tapestries with *putti* playing games around the Medici emblems, projected almost certainly by Giovanni da Udine, perhaps assisted by Tommaso Vincidor and woven in Flanders, probably depend upon an idea by Raphael.

In addition, the second set of Vatican tapestries was also directly inspired by the master.

Besides, in these Raphaelesque works (in the strict sense) the art of Raphael continued to live on through the work of his direct collaborators who were all bound to him in the decade after Raphael's death in one way or another. This is a matter that transcends the boundaries of the history of Raphael's workshop and is instead the beginning of the powerful effect the Master's art was to have for the next four centuries on the development of European painting.

Giulio's and Penni's battle for the award of the commission of the Sala di Costantino is the most important episode in the juridical vitality of the shop after the Master's death. They claimed to have in hand, as Raphael's heirs, his drawings and his projects for the decoration. The workshop was therefore still alive and could extend the life of the departed Master beyond the grave.

The whole undertaking of the Sala di Costantino is confusing in the narrative given by Vasari, but by utilizing the other sources it can be reconstructed reasonably well.

The chronology proposed by Hartt, based upon an incomplete utilization of the documents, has not served to clarify the problem.[3] But Hess, re-using his earlier study,[4] has re-established the real chronology of the work quite well;[5] and Freedberg has used these results to his advantage.[6] Without retracing the whole discussion for which the cited studies may be consulted, we can conclude today that while he was still alive, Raphael planned a division of the walls (Vasari) that is as a general idea, and he prepared part of the room with a mixture appropriate for receiving oil paint. The idea of placing on each wall a large historical scene between two commemorative groups in which is represented a Pope enthroned with two Virtues at the sides, is Raphael's idea. It is unlikely that he could have gone beyond that point in the general projection. Giulio Romano and Penni, in order to receive the commission, executed in oil on the prepared two walls, two Virtues (Justice, Fig. 173, and Meekness). After overcoming the resistance of Sebastiano who, at one point, had been assigned half of the decoration and being the masters of their own, they removed the preparation from the walls for oil paint (maintaining however, the two Virtues already executed) and returned to the familiar technique of fresco painting and actively dedicated themselves to the enterprise. The first phase of the work took place from the summer of 1520 until the death of Leo X in December, 1521. In this period of about a year and a half the *Dream of Constantine* and the *Battle of the Milvian Bridge* (Fig. 175) and at least four of the papal groups were completed and perhaps one of the large scenes was begun. They must have, at least, studied the composition. It is difficult to say whether the socles with imitation bronze had been started at this time. From a letter to Leo X of July, 1521, it would seem that the twenty tapestries with the *Giuochi di Putti* and papal emblems (now in the Louvre) were then being woven in Flanders and it is difficult to understand where they were to be placed if not to form the base for the painted walls.

The death of Leo X interrupted the work which was suspended for the entire duration of Hadrian VI's pontificate and was only taken up again at the beginning of 1524 under Clement VII and finished in September of the same year.

Giulio Romano was the dominant personality in the Stanza di Costantino. He collected the heredity of Raphael and in a certain sense gathered together under him the group of pupils who had been the earliest young assistants of Raphael. Even though the composition of Giulio's workshop as listed by Vasari is made up of nearly all new names, "Bartolomeo da Castiglioni, Tommaso Paparello Cortonese (that is Papacello), Benedetto Pagni da Pescia, Giovanni da Lione, Raffaellino del Colle,"[7] Penni was always present with him and Polidoro too, who we find employed on the socle in imitation bronze (Fig. 174) in the Sala di Costantino and in the frescoes for the main salon of Villa Lante (constructed by Giulio and decorated under his direction).

The Sala di Costantino, although nourished by Raphael's art, is nonetheless irremediably removed from his spirit. Giulio took over the High Classicism of late Raphael and changed it into archaeology; he took the plastic force and solidity of chiaroscuro and transformed it in an exasperating formal definition and in a nearly statuesque taste; he took the dramatic sense of the action and resolved it in violent gestures; he took the examination of character and of

165 *Giovanni da Udine and Assistants.* Stuccoes and grotesques on a pilaster of the Loggias. Vatican, Loggias of Raphael.

167 *Giovanni da Udine and Assistants.* Grotesques on a pilaster. Vatican, Loggias of Raphael.

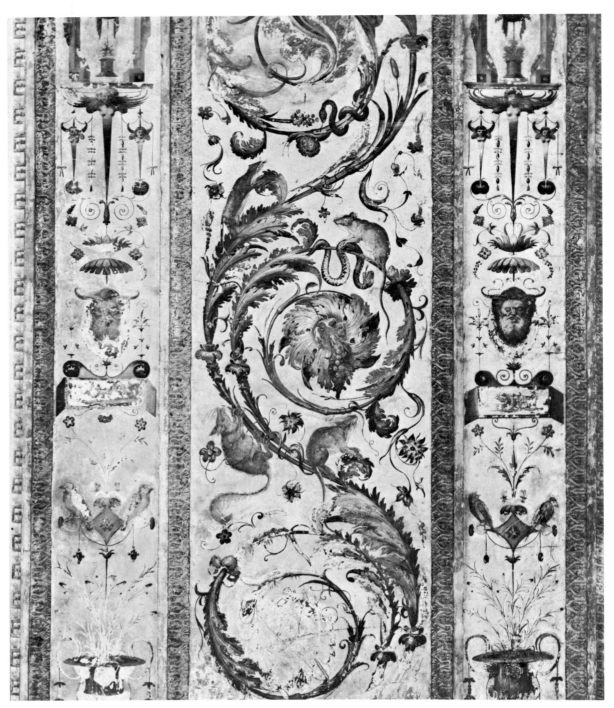

167 *Giovanni da Udine and Assistants.* Grotesques on a pilaster. Vatican, Loggias of Raphael.

166 *Giovanni da Udine and Assistants.* Grotesques on a pilaster of the Loggias, Vatican, Loggias of Raphael.

292

expressions and thus transformed them into mimical masks. All these single elements, however, cannot be fused. The marble-like precision of the forms isolates the images and freezes the gestures; the violence becomes a superficial cuirass and fails to move internally while the faces are frozen into mimical masks. The large tangles of bodies in the *Battle of the Milvian Bridge* (Fig. 175) become encased in bronze, brownish torsos of warriors, shining horses and armors. We recognize the *Dioscuri of Monte Cavallo* and the *Belvedere Torso* but the heroic and elevating humanity of Raphael has vanished. The Classicism is still present but the classical language is a mere presupposition and not a reality in these pictures. The tie with the ancient world and the formal tie with Raphael, still recognizable starting points, are sufficient for the grandiose invention of the *Battle of the Milvian Bridge*, to become, for example, the foundation of the "heroic battle scene." And perhaps it is that frozen perfection of bas-relief, that detachment from the passion of sentiments but not, to be sure, from the passion of the forms that provided this picture with so much fascination for the eyes of a Cortona or a Poussin.

The assistants count for little in Giulio's art. As opposed to Raphael, he had neither a Giulio nor a Giovanni da Udine. His Raffaellino del Colle or his Giovanni da Lione were much more modest than was Penni in comparison with Raphael: as for Penni, quite well-imitated in the *Oration* (where, perhaps, he had not taken part and Raffaellino rather was the only important assistant) and in the *Battle*, he reappears more actively and independently in the *Donation* (Fig. 176) and in the *Baptism of Constantine* (Fig. 177), with the result that these two later scenes have decidedly less new flavor that the paintings done in 1521 and, leaving aside passages by Giulio, they evoke Raphael in a minor tone with a certain deferred melancholy air. Still, notwithstanding the differences in quality, the Sala in its decoration is impressive and unified (Fig. 174). What is striking is not so much the division of the walls (which could also be Raphael's idea) but the way it had been achieved, which is certainly by Giulio. The groups with the Popes and the Virtues (Fig. 179) have a cast, three-dimensional monumentality derived from sculpture and with their vanishing point lowered, they contrast with the large narrative scenes; these, on the other hand, have a rather high horizon according to the system

169 *Raphael and Giovanni da Udine.* View from the First Floor Loggia on the Courtyard of San Damaso. Decoration by Giovanni da Udine. Vatican.

168 *Giovanni da Udine and Assistants.* Detail from decoration of a pilaster, rediscovered in 1952. Vatican, Loggias of Raphael.

of the late Raphael; thus they generate an illusion of deep space. The fiction that they are tapestries, two-dimensional hung materials, contradicts their spatial appearance, however. A whole series of exciting and contradictory sensations are born of this fiction. The luxurious richness of the forms and the sonority of the ornamental elements are exalting and we are taken with the fascination of all the plastic politic perfections, but we cannot do less than remain disillusioned by the absence of any human warmth or of any authentic interior vitality.

The Popes in their niches, even when, as with Clement I, they show the recognizable physiognomy of Leo X (Figs. 178 and 179) have no connection with the vivid papal portraits in the Stanza by Raphael. Constantine on his large horse in the *Battle of the Milvian Bridge*, taken from the relief on his triumphal arch, is equally remote from the crucial battle that surrounds him.

Thus, those elements which we have seen flashing in the *St. Michael* by Raphael and which Giulio had already emphasized in executing some of the Master's late works, now are liberated here in the Sala di Costantino and especially in the main scenes of the cycle which Giulio seems to have conducted with the enthusiasm of a programmatic affirmation.

Giulio Romano's other motive is his extraordinary ability to insert violently in this " machine " of his, the unexpected contradictory emotion of a sweet note from daily life, this fragmentary realism, which we so often find in the Mannerists, is met in the altarpiece for Santa Maria dell'Anima (Fig. 92), where the ray of light which ignites the background isolates the very delicate motif of the woman who faces the door to watch the hen with its chicks; or in the small *Madonna and Child* in the Galleria Nazionale Romana di Palazzo Barberini (Fig. 93), almost anti-Mannerist in its polished elegance, we discover beyond the partially opened door, a pair of humble domesticated pigeons caught in a shaft of light. Thus we turn to recognize the romantic motifs of the ruins, so dear to Giulio from the time of the *The Pearl*, forming the background of the *Stoning of St. Stephen* (Fig. 91) where, as Venturi noted with acuteness, there is " a compromise between the lights of the *Transfiguration* of Raphael and the lighten-

293

170 *Giovanni da Udine and Perino del Vaga.* Decoration of the Sala dei Pontefici. Vatican.

171 *Perino del Vaga.* Jove, detail from the decoration of the Sala dei Pontefici. Vatican.

172 *G. F. Penni and Giulio Romano*. The Coronation of Monteluce. Vatican, Pinacoteca.

ing in the *Resurrection of Lazarus* painted by Sebastiano del Piombo in competition with the artist from Urbino." [8]

In comparison with the new elements by Giulio in the Sala di Costantino, the splendid stuccos and grotesques by Giovanni da Udine for the Villa Madama, begun perhaps in 1520 but dated and signed in 1525 are not different from the achievements in the Loggias, continuing, as in the Sala dei Pontefici, that long decorative direction.

The Roman works of Perino between 1520 and 1527 (they are not very well studied) are decidedly more interesting for their flavor of independence from the old dialect of Raphael's workshop. Perino is one of the richest personalities belonging to the generation in full development at the dawn of Mannerism. It was precisely for this reason that he rapidly liberated himself from ties with Raphael and his vicissitudes go beyond our study. The same may be said for Polidoro. Of his youthful decorations on the façades of Roman houses, practically nothing remains and the indirect documentation furnished by engravings and drawings serves little to reconstruct his style. Around 1524, we encounter him in the series of "gouaches" formerly belonging to Charles I of England and presently at Hampton Court, except for the story of Psyche that went to France when the royal collection was dispersed and is today in the Louvre. We observe his work at the same time on the frescoed ceiling, perhaps executed under Giulio's direction in the salon of the Villa Lante. Polidoro, if on one hand, he maintains contact with the Neo-Hellenistic spirit that characterized the products of Raphael's workshop between 1516 and 1520 in the small scenes of grotesques, on the other, he shows already the germ of his visionary stylization, of his propensity for a dramatic and anti-Classical language in a range of peculiar expressions.

Parmigianino arrived in Rome in 1524 and his refined elegance was contagious for the young Romans while the presence of Rosso suggested Michelangelesque evasions. Giulio Romano departed for Mantua in the autumn of 1524 and Penni also left Rome shortly thereafter. Four years had passed since Raphael had been laid to rest. The fervor of his inventions were extinguished. The secret of his human warmth was lost, as was lost the intellectual attraction. "Heaven endowed him with the power of showing a disposition quite contrary to that of most painters. For the artists who worked with Raphael, not only the poor ones, but those who aspired to be great, and there are many such in our profession, lived united and in harmony, all their evil humors disappearing when they saw him, and every vile and base thought deserting their minds. Such a thing was never seen at any other time, and it arose because they were conquered by his courtesy and tact, and still more by his good nature, so full of gentleness and love that even animals loved him, not to speak of men." [9]

[1] For the Villa Madama and on Giovanni da Udine's and Giulio Romano's pictorial activity in the Villa see: W. E. Greenwood, *The Villa Madama in Rome*, London, 1828, p. 62; F. Hartt, 1958; J. Shearman, "Giulio Romano," in *Burlington Magazine*, 1959, pp. 456-460 which effectively combat Hartt's tendency to attribute too much to Giulio and too little to Giovanni.

[2] Hartt (1958) gives to Penni alone the *Coronation* of Monteluce, but it is contradicted by the documents (see J. Shearman, "Giulio Romano," in *Burlington Magazine*, 1959, pp. 456-460).

[3] F. Hartt, "The Chronology of the Sala di Costantino," in *Gazette des Beaux-Arts*, 1949, pp. 301-308.

[4] J. Hess, "On Raphael and Giulio Romano," in *Gazette des Beaux-Arts*, 1947, pp. 73-106.

[5] J. Hess, "The Chronology of the Sala di Costantino (reply to Mr. F. Hartt)," in *Gazette des Beaux-Arts*, 1950, pp. 130-132.

[6] Freedberg, 1961.

[7] Vasari, V, p. 533.

[8] A. Venturi, *Storia*, 9, 11, p. 369.

[9] Vasari, IV, p. 384.

173 *Giulio Romano*. Justice. Vatican, Sala di Costantino.

Appendix

From time to time in the notes to the text, the individual references have been indicated.

Here below are listed the fundamental studies for orientation on the problem of Raphael's workshop (the bibliographic citations used most frequently show, in parenthesis, the short form titles as they have been presented in this study).

The principal sources for any examination of Raphael's workshop remain:

G. Vasari, *Vite de' piu eccellenti pittori, scultori e architettori*, Florence, 1568, edition edited by G. Milanesi (9 vols.), Florence, 1878-1885.

For all the other sources and documentary material, reference is made to the exhaustive compilation by Golzio:

V. Golzio, *Raffaello nei documenti, nelle testimonianze dei contemporanei e nella letteratura del suo secolo*, Vatican City, 1936.

Almost all the bibliography on Raphael is involved in subjects which concern the study of the workshop. It has been gathered up to the year 1883 in:

E. Müntz, *Les historiens et les critiques de Raphaël*, Paris, 1883.

From 1883 to 1961 in the excellent bibliographic repertory, extended also to the principal pupils of the Master in:

S. J. Freedberg, *Painting of the High Renaissance in Rome and Florence*, Cambridge (Mass.) 1961, vol. I, pp. 600-606.

Particular studies directly and indirectly devoted to the question or to the aspects of the problem of the workshop:

H. Dollmayr, "Raffaels Werkstätte" in *Jahrbuch der Kunstsammlungen in Wien*, 16, 1895, pp. 232-263 (Dollmayr, 1895).

F. Baumgart, "Beiträge zu Raffael und seiner Werkstatt," in *Münchner Jahrbuch der Bildenden Künste*, 8, 1931, pp. 49-68.

174 *Giulio Romano and Assistants.* Sala di Costantino. Vatican.

In addition, in chronological order:

E. Müntz, *Raphaël: Sa vie, son œuvre, et son temps*, Paris, 1881.

G. B. Cavalcaselle and J. A. Crowe, *Raphael: his life and works*, London, 1882-1885, ed. Florence, 1884-1891.

E. Müntz, *Les Tapisseries de Raphaël au Vatican*, Paris, 1897.

A. Venturi, *Storia dell'Arte Italiana*, vol. IX, part II, Milan 1926 (Venturi, 9, II).

C. Gamba, *Raphaël*, Paris, 1932.

S. Ortolani, *Raffaello*, Bergamo, 1942, 1946, 1948.

F. Hartt, " Raphael and Giulio Romano, with Notes on the Raphael School," in *Art Bulletin*, 26, 1944, pp. 67-94.

D. Redig De Campos, *Raffaello e Michelangelo*, Rome, 1946.

J. Hess, " On Raphael and Giulio Romano," in *Gazzette des Beaux-Arts*, 32, 1947, pp. 73-106.

O. Fischel, *Raphael*, London, 1948.

F. Hartt, " The Chronology of the Sala di Costantino," in *Gazette des Beaux-Arts*, 36, 1949, pp. 301-308.

J. Hess, " The Chronology of the Sala di Costantino," in *Gazette des Beaux-Arts*, 37, 1950, pp. 130-132.

J. Pope Hennessy, *The Raphael Cartoons*, London, 1950.

E. Camesasca, *Tutta la pittura di Raffaello*, Milan, 1956.

175 *Giulio Romano and Assistants.* Battle of the Milvian Bridge. Vatican, Sala di Costantino.

176 *Giulio Romano and G. F. Penni.* The Gift of
Constantine. Vatican, Sala di Costantino.

177 *Giulio Romano and G. F. Penni.* Baptism of
Constantine. Vatican, Sala di Costantino.

J. White and J. Shearman, " Raphael's Tapestries and their Cartoons," in *Art Bulletin*, 40, 1958,
pp. 193-221 and 299-323.
S. Freedberg, *Painting of the Renaissance in Rome and Florence*, Cambridge (Mass.), 1961, (Freedberg, 1961).
D. Redig De Campos, *I Palazzi Vaticani*, Bologna, 1967, (De Campos, 1967).

Besides these works, indispensable instruments of study for any examination of Raphael's workshop, are critical collections and catalogues of Raphael's drawings and those of his school, particularly:

O. Fischel, *Raphaels Zeichnungen*, parts 1-8, Berlin, 1913-1941.
Beschreibender Katalog der Handzeichnungen in der Graphischen Sammlung Albertina, 1926-1941, vols. I-VI
(in particular vol. III, 1932, ed. by A. Stix and L. Frohlich-Bum, dedicated to the schools of
Tuscany, Umbria and Rome), Vienna (Albertina, III).
A. E. Popham and J. White, *The Italian Drawings of the XV and XVI centuries in the Collection of His
Majesty the King at Windsor Castle*, London, 1949. (Popham, 1949).
K. T. Parker, *Catalogue of the collection of Drawings in the Ashmolean Museum*, vol. II, *Italian Schools*,
Oxford, 1956. (Parker, 1956).
P. Pouncey and J. A. Gere, *Italian Drawings in the Department of Prints and Drawings in the British Museum,
Raphael and his Circle*, London, 1962. (Pouncey and Gere, 1962).

179 *Giulio Romano and Assistants.* Leo X as Clement I between Temperance and Meekness. Vatican, Sala di Costantino.

178 *Giulio Romano.* Study for the head of Leo X as Clement I in the Sala di Costantino, Drawing. Chatsworth, Devonshire Collection.

BIOGRAPHIES WITH ESSENTIAL BIBLIOGRAPHY OF THE PRINCIPAL PUPILS OF RAPHAEL

Giulio Romano

Giulio Pippi, called Giulio Romano, born in Rome about 1499, died in Mantua the first of November, 1546. He entered Raphael's workshop around 1514 and assisted the Master on the fresco of the Stanza di Eliodoro (socle, *ca.* 1514), the Stanza dell'Incendio (*Fire in the Borgo, ca.* 1514-1516; *Battle of Ostia, ca.* 1515 and socle, *ca.* 1517), the Stufetta of Cardinal Bibbiena (1516), the Loggia della Farnesina (1517), the Loggetta del Bibbiena (1519?) and the Loggias (1518-19). And besides, he was the executor, at least in part, of some of the most important easel works by Raphael, sometimes in collaboration with Penni or with other assistants (*Madonna dell'Impannata,* 1514; *St. Cecilia* 1515 [?]; *Spasimo di Sicilia,* 1517; *Madonna of Francis I* and the *St. Michael,* 1517-18; *St. Catherine* in the Louvre and Vienna; *The Infant St. John* in the Academy in Florence; the *Holy Family,* called the "Pearl," all *ca.* 1518-20; The *Holy Family under the Oak,* 1518-20; the small *Gonzaga Madonna,* 1518-20; the *Coronation* of Monteluce, after 1520; the *Transfiguration,* 1518-after 1520). Between 1515 and 1516 he assisted Raphael in the execution of the tapestry cartoons. After the death of the Master from the summer of 1520 to the fall of 1524 (with an interlude during the reign of Hadrian VI from the winter of 1522 till the end of 1523) he directed and executed the decoration of the Sala di Costantino. In 1524 he also worked in the Loggia of Villa Madama (the lunette with Polyphemus) and executed the *Stoning of St. Stephen* (Genoa, Santo Stefano) and the large altarpiece for the church of Santa Maria dell'Anima in Rome besides some minor works like the *Madonna della Gatta* (Naples, Capodimonte), the *Portrait of a Woman* in the Hermitage, the small *Madonna and Child* in the Galleria Nazionale Romana di Pittura (Palazzo Barberini). It seems that in the year 1524 together with Giovanni da Udine he could have directed the works on the Stufetta of Clement VII in the Castel Sant'Angelo while he surely programmed the pictorial decoration of the Villa Lante on the Janiculum but had it executed by others.

From October of 1524 until his death he was in Mantua. He was, besides his activity as a painter, engaged as an architect (already started as a Raphael assistant and then independently in the Villa Lante on the Janiculum and later the Palazzo Maccarani; perhaps also at the Villa Madama).

298

His principal undertakings during the Mantuan period were the contruction and decoration of the Palazzo del Tè (*ca.* 1520-35), the reconstruction and decoration of part of the Ducal Palace (1536-39), the reconstruction of the Cathedral begun in 1545, besides a series of easel paintings.

BIBLIOGRAPHY:

G. Vasari, *Vite*, 1568, ed. Milanesi, 1880, V. pp. 417-430.
F. Hartt, " Raphael and Giulio Romano," in *Art Bulletin*, 1944, pp. 67-94.
J. Hess, " On Raphael and Giulio Romano," in *Gazette des Beaux-Arts*, 1947, pp. 73-106.
F. Hartt, " The Chronology of the Sala di Costantino," in *Gazette des Beaux-Arts*, 1949, pp. 301-308.
J. Hess, " The Chronology of the Sala di Costantino," in *Gazette des Beaux-Arts*, 1950, pp. 130-132.
F. Hartt, *Giulio Romano*, New Haven, 1858.
J. Shearman, " Giulio Romano " (review of F. Hartt, 1958), in *Burlington Magazine*, 1959, pp. 456-460. (Shearman, 1959).
P. Pouncey and J. Gere, *Italian Drawings in the British Museum*, 1962, vol. I, pp. 58-85.

Giovan Francesco Penni

Called Il Fattore, born in Florence in 1496, died in Naples about 1528 (Vasari) or during the course of the fourth decade of the sixteenth century, according to the most recent opinion which is based upon the style of his last drawings. An assistant of Raphael, perhaps as early as 1512, he collaborated with the Master completing decorative *grisailles* and secondary parts of the Stanza della Segnatura, the fresco of *Attila* in the Stanza di Eliodoro (1513?), the *Coronation of Charlemagne* (1516) and the *Oath of Leo III* (1517) in the Sala dell'Incendio. He is the principal assistant (Vasari) in painting of the tapestry cartoons and is perhaps also responsible for the cartoons of the predellas for them (1515-16). He executed a large share of the Loggia of Psyche in the Farnesina (1517), some Biblical scenes and many drawings for the Loggias (1518-19), collaborated on the Loggia of Cardinal Bibbiena (1519?). He was executor, at least in part, of various easel works by Raphael (*Madonna del Pesce*, 1514; *Spasimo di Sicilia*, 1517; *Madonna of the Divine Love*, 1518-20; *Visitation*, 1518-20; *Madonna of the Rose* [?], 1518-20), and the upper part of the *Transfiguration* (1518-after 1520), and a copy of it (after 1520) begun with Giulio Romano. Together with Giulio Romano he did the *Coronation* of Monteluce (after 1520 but before 1525) and the frescoes in the Sala di Costantino (1520-24), where his presence is best seen in the last two stories of the cycle (*Donation* and *Baptism*). Having left Rome, he first went to northern Italy, then to Naples where he died. Only a single work by him is known (*Portrait of a Youth* in the Dublin National Gallery) and to him is traditionally attributed the *tondo* in the Museo di Cava dei Tirreni.

BIBLIOGRAPHY:

G. Vasari, *Vite*, 1568, ed. Milanesi, 1880, IV, pp. 639-643.
F. Baumgart, in *Thieme Becker*, 1932, *s.v.* (with earlier bibliography).
P. Pouncey and Gere, *Italian Drawings in the British Museum*, 1962, vol. I, pp. 50-58.

Giovanni da Udine

Giovanni Recamador, called da Udine (Udine 1487-Rome 1561, or according to Vasari, 1564). Pupil of Giovanni Martino da Udine and of Giorgione, he was painter, maker of stuccoes and architect. He entered the workshop of Raphael around 1514 where he functioned primarily as a painter of still lifes, animals and grotesques, besides producing stuccoes. Vasari mentions him as author of the musical instruments in the *St. Cecilia* by Raphael (1515?); he is responsible for the cartoons with grotesques for the lateral borders of the Sistine tapestries (1515-1516), for the decorative parts in the Stufetta of Cardinal Bibbiena (1516), in the Loggia of Psyche (1518) and those in Bibbiena's Loggia (1519?) as well as in the Loggias of Raphael (1517-19). Probably alone but assisted by his own personal helpers, he did the decoration of the Loggia on the first floor.

Between 1520 and 1525 (signed and dated in that year) he made the stuccoes and the grotesques in the Loggia of the Villa Madama; meanwhile in 1521, with Perino del Vaga, he frescoed the vault of the Sala dei Pontefici and he prepared and arranged the execution of the tapestries with the *Giuochi di Putti* with Tommaso Vincidor. He transferred himself to Florence from 1523 and 1534 where he did the lost decoration for the Cupola of the New Sacristy in San Lorenzo. He was active in his native area in Udine and in the Friuli as an architect after 1534. Between 1539 and 1540 he was in Venice where he worked in the Grimani Palace of Santa Maria Formosa. He died in Rome, where in 1560 head painted, according to Vasari, the Loggia on the third floor and retouched his own paintings in the Loggias on the first and second floors. His fame is tied to his inventive inspiration as stucco and fresco decorator. Vasari claims that he rediscovered ancient stucco technique after a series of long experiments.

BIBLIOGRAPHY:

Vasari, *Vite*, 1568, ed. Milanesi, 1881, VI, pp. 549-567.
S. Battaglia, " La stufetta del Cardinal Bibbiena," in *L'Arte*, 1926, pp. 30 ff.
A. Ghidiglia, " Di alcune opere di Giovanni da Udine," in *L'Arte*, 1927, pp. 150-170.
G. A. Dall'Acqua, in *Thieme Becker*, 1939, *S.V.* (with precedent bibliography).
P. Pouncey and J. Gere, *Italian Drawings in the British Museum*, 1962, vol. I, pp. 86-90.

Tommaso Vincidor

Tommaso di Andrea Vincidor, called Il Bologna, born probably in Bologna (we do not know when), died perhaps in Breda during the fourth decade of the fifteenth century; Vasari recalls him among the painters who worked on the decoration of Raphael's Loggias (1518-19). He was sent to Leo X in Flanders with a letter of recommendation of May 12, 1520, probably in order to prepare the cartoons for tapestries or to supervise their transferance onto canvas. His activity seems to have been connected with a series of the *Giuochi di Putti* and of the materials made for the drapes for the bed of Leo X. From ca. 1527 he worked as an architect in Breda.

BIBLIOGRAPHY:

H. Voss, in *Thieme Becker*, 1940 *s.v.* (with precedent bibliography).
P. Pouncey and J. Gere, *Italian Drawings in the British Museum*, 1962, vol. I, pp. 87-90.

Raffaellino del Colle

Born at Colle near Borgo San Sepolcro, probably in the last decade of the fifteenth century; he died in 1566 in his native land.

On November 11, 1517 he was paid for a picture commissioned by the Friars of Santa Maria della Neve in Borgo San Sepolcro.

Vasari calls him an assistant of Giulio Romano and his principal collaborator together with Giovanni da Lione in the Sala di Costantino but does not record him ever among Raphael's assistants. Hartt, instead, attributes to him the planning and execution of the *Coronation of Charlemagne* in the Sala dell'Incendio (ca. 1516) and basing himself on a note by Titi (*Studio di pittura e architettura nelle chiese di Roma*, Rome, 1675, p. 22) he identifies him among Raphael's collaborators in the Loggia of the Farnesina. This opinion is shared by Freedberg and by many other modern scholars without convincing documentary or stylistic proof, in my opinion. He is considered by Hartt as the author, or at least a collaborator, in some late works of the Raphael studio (*Madonna of the Rose, Visitation, Madonna of the Oak*, all between 1518 and 1520 and even the *Fornarina* in the Palazzo Barberini). These opinions by Hartt have had a certain following, at least in part. His Roman works listed by Vasari are all lost. In 1524 Raffaellino left Rome. He then went into the service of the Duke of Urbino (worked, on several occasions, in the Villa Imperiale in Pesaro) and also perhaps in Mantua as an assistant to Giulio Romano. He came in contact successively with Genga (at Pesaro), Rosso (at San Sepolcro and Arezzo), Bronzino (collaboration for the Medici tapestries) and Vasari (decorations for the arrival of Charles V in Florence, works in Naples, decoration of the Cancelleria in Rome). With the destruction of the fort, Raffaellino's works executed in Perugia in the Rocca Paolina were lost. There remains however, a considerable group of paintings executed in his own land of origin between Borgo San Sepolcro and Citta di Castello. These show him a follower of Rosso and of mature Tuscan Mannerism, from Bronzino to Vasari. Recollections of Raffaellino, perhaps mediated by Giulio, are still recognizable in the *Resurrection of Christ* in the Cathedral of Borgo San Sepolcro.

BIBLIOGRAPHY:

B. Patzak, *Die Villa Imperiale in Pesaro*, 1908.
W. Bombe, in *Thieme Becker*, 191 *s.v.* (with precedent bibliography).
Degli Azzi, " Inventario degli Archivi di San Sepolcro," from vol. IV of the *Archivi della Storia d'Italia*, Rocca San Casciano, 1914.
A. Venturi, *Storic*, 1926, 9, V, pp. 607-620.
F. Hartt, " Raphael and Giulio Romano, with Notes on the Raphael School," in *Art Bulletin*, 1944, pp. 67-94.

Pellegrino da Modena

Pellegrino Aretusi, called il Munari or Da Modena, was born about the middle of the seventh decade of the fifteenth century, and died in Modena around the end of 1523. From his activity at home, dominated by the taste of the great Ferrarese fifteenth century school, there are traces in an altarpiece today in the Pinacoteca of Ferrara (perhaps from the Modenese Church of Santa Maria della Neve) and in a drawing showing *St. Francis Receiving the Rules from the Virgin* in the Academy of Venice.

Vasari mentions him among the assistants of Raphael in the Loggias where he can perhaps be identified in the two scenes of the *Consecration* and the *Judgment of Solomon*. All the other Roman works mentioned by Vasari are lost with the exception of the frescoes in San Giacomo degli Spagnoli with scenes of *St. James* and the *Conquest of Granada*. He seems bound to Raphael but still rich in Emilian stylizations. He returned home after Raphael's death and shortly thereafter was murdered in *vendetta*.

BIBLIOGRAPHY:

G. Vasari, *Vite*, 1568; ed. Milanesi, 1880, IV, pp. 649-651.
G. Fiocco, " Pellegrino da Modena," in *L'Arte*, 1917, pp. 199-210.
A. Venturi, *Storia*, 1926, 9, II, pp. 448-452.

Perino del Vaga

Piero Buonaccorsi, born in Florence in 1501, died in Rome in 1547. Pupil of Ridolfo del Ghirlandaio in Florence, he moved to Rome after having worked in Tuscany as an assistant of the painter, Il Vaga (from whom derived his name). After entering Raphael's orbit, he worked in the Loggias (1518-19) assisting Giovanni da Udine in the grotesques and Giulio Romano in the Biblical stories (the stories of Joshua, of David and the New Testament scenes). During his first Roman period which was protracted until 1527 (except for a trip to Florence in 1522), he executed with Giovanni da Udine, the vault of the Sala dei Pontefici in the Vatican (1521), the frescoes in the Palazzo Barberini; the Pucci Chapel in the Trinità dei Monti (1522-23); two chapels in San Marcello al Corso (one probably before 1523 and lost today; the other, of the Crucifix, begun around 1525 but interrupted and only taken up again after his return to Rome in 1539); the Deposition of the Cross in Santa Maria Sopra Mineva (partially destroyed, fragments in Hampton Court). In 1525 he married Penni's sister.

In Genoa where he went having left Rome following the Sack, his principal work is the decoration of the Palazzo Doria (probably finished in 1533). Between 1534 and 1537-38 he worked in Pisa and Genoa. Around 1538 he must have returned to Rome where he completed the Chapel of the Crucifix and decorated the Massimi Chapel in the Trinità dei Monti, subsequently destroyed (fragments in the Victoria and Albert Museum). His final activity was entirely in the service of Paul III Farnese (socle of the Stanza della Segnatura, stuccoes in the Sala Regia; project for the socle under the Last Judgment of the Sistine Chapel; decoration in Castel Sant'Angelo).

BIBLIOGRAPHY:

Vasari, *Vite*, 1568, ed. Milanesi, 1880, V, pp. 587-632.
M. Labò, *Vita di Perin del Vaga* (comment to Vasari), 1912.
M. Labò, in *Thieme Becker*, 1940, *S.V.* (with precedent bibliography).
A. E. Popham, " On some works by Perino del Vaga," in *Burlington Magazine*, 1945, pp. 56-66 and p. 85.
P. Askew, " Perino del Vaga's Decorations for the Palazzo Doria, Genoa," in *Burlington Magazine*, 1956, pp. 46 ff.
B. F. Davidson, " Drawings by Perino del Vaga for the Palazzo Doria, Genoa," in *Art Bulletin*, 1959, pp. 315 ff.
J. A. Gere, " Two late Frescoes by Perino del Vaga; The Massimi Chapel and the Sala Paolina," in *Burlington Magazine*, 1960, pp. 9 ff.
M. V. Brugnoli, " Gli affreschi di Perin del Vaga nella Cappella Pucci," in *Bollettino d'Arte*, 1962, pp. 327-350.
P. Pouncey and J. Gere, *Italian Drawings in the British Museum*, 1962, vol. I pp. 90-116.
B. F. Davidson, *Catalogo della Mostra di Disegni di Perino del Vaga e la sua Cerchia*, Florence 1966, Gabinetto dei Disegni e Stampe degli Uffizi (with complete bibliography).

Polidoro da Caravaggio

Polidoro Caldara, born in Caravaggio around 1500, died in Messina in 1543 (?). He began his activity as a painter, according to Vasari, in Raphael's Loggias as an assistant to Giulio Romano, and his hand is perhaps recognized in some scenes (the *Meeting of Jacob and Rachel, Moses Striking the Rock; Solomon and the Queen Sheba*, the *Building of the Temple in Jerusalem*). Joining in partnership with the Florentine painter, Maturino (who died in 1528), they executed in Rome between 1520 and 1527 many façades with subjects from history or ancient mythology (traces of the decoration of Palazzo Milesi *in situ;* frescoes of the now-destroyed Casino del Buffalo in the Museo di Roma; four scenes of the friezes from a house on Piazza Madama now in the Palazzo Barberini; frescoes in the Palazzo Ricci repainted *in situ*). Before 1524 he must have done the dispersed scenes of the *Passion* in the Church of Santa Maria della Pietà in Camposanto, today reduced to a few fragments (this attribution is still anything but proved). In the spring of 1524 he was in Naples where he decorated palace façades. Having returned to Rome, he probably executed in the same year the socle in the Sala di Costantino and the frescoes in the Salone of Villa Lante (now in the Zuccari Palace). Of the same time, perhaps done in Naples, are the two stories of *Psyche* (Hampton Court and the Louvre storerooms) and the scenes of satyrs, nymphs and *amorini* (Hampton Court), painted with tempera and all belonging to Charles I of England.

The frescoes of the Chapel of Fra Mariano in San Silvestro al Quirinale are from his late Roman period. After the Sack he went to Naples where, however, nothing remains of his work; from Naples he went to Messina. He was intensely active in Messina (from 1528 until his death) where he assumed a preeminent position in the local art scene. Few of the works survive: *The Doubting of Thomas*, London, Seilern Collection (*ca.* 1530); the *Adoration of the Shepherds*, Messina, Museo Nazionale (1533); *The Way to Calvary* (1534), Naples, Capodimonte Museum (studies in Rome, Palazzo della Cancelleria; Naples, Capodimonte; London, Pouncey Collection); *St. Albert the Carmelite*, Turin, Galleria Sabauda (*ca.* 1535); *Crossing the Red Sea* (Scotland, Ellesmen Collection). A series of strongly expressionistic sketches in Naples (Capodimonte) and in Palermo (Museo Nazionale) are from the late period. His very rich and exceptionally interesting graphic production is to be found in the major collections of such works. In 1535 he executed arches of triumph for the entrance of Charles V into Messina (drawings in Berlin, Cabinet of Drawings of the State Museum).

BIBLIOGRAPHY:

G. Vasari, *Vite*, 1568, ed. Milanesi, 1880, V, pp. 141-154.
F. Susinno, *Le vite de' Pittori Messinesi*, 1724, edited by V. Martinelli, Florence, 1960, pp. 53-60.
G. S. in *Thieme Becker*, 1911 *S.V.* Caldara (with precedent bibliography).
K. Cassires, " Zeichnungen Polidoro da Caravaggio in den Berliner Museen," in *Prussian Jahrbuch*, 1920, pp. 344 ff.
H. Voss, *Die Malerei des Spätrenaissance*, 1920, I, pp. 78-85.
C. Pacchiotti, " *Nuove attribuzioni a Polidoro da Caravaggio in Roma*," in *L'Arte*, 1927, pp. 179 ff.
R. Kultzen, " Die Malereien Polidoros da Caravaggio in Giardino del Bufalo in Rom," in *Mitteilungen des Kunsthistorischen Institutes in Florenz*, 1960, pp. 97-120.
C. Pericoli Ridolfini, *Le case romane con facciate graffite e dipinte*, Catalogue of the exhibition, Rome 1960, Palazzo Braschi.
R. Kultzen, " Der Freskenzyklus in der ehemaligen Kapelle der Schweizergarde in Rom," in *Zeitschrift für Schweizerische Archäologie und Kunstgeschichte*, 1961, pp. 19 ff.
R. Kultzen, " Bemerkungen zu einer Fassadenmalerei Polidoros da Caravaggio an der Piazza Madama in Rom," in *Miscellanea Bibliothecae Hertzianae*, Munich, 1961.
E. Borea, " Vicenda di Polidoro da Caravaggio," in *Arte Antica e Moderna*, 13-16, 1961, pp. 211-227 (with bibliography).
P. Pouncey and J. Gere, *Italian Drawings in the British Museum*, 1962, vol. I, pp. 116-134.
A. Marabottini, " Intorno a Polidoro da Caravaggio," in *Commentari*, I-III, 1966, pp. 129-145.
A. Marabottini, " Genesi di un dipinto (L'Andata al Calvario di Polidoro da Caravaggio a Capodimonte)," in *Commentari*, II-III, 1967, pp. 170-185.

THE DRAWINGS

by Anna Forlani Tempesti

The " divine " harmony in Raphael also is manifested in the organic interdependence and reciprocity between his drawings and his paintings. His work as a draftsman does not interfere at all with his work as a painter, rather it clarifies the painting, and at the same time it does not allow the viewer to forget the various stages of drawing that precede the painting. Indeed the limpidity in the paintings never becomes facility precisely because of that preliminary ground-work, never overdone, which was concerned with selecting the best in the minor passages and the most subtle variants, the most appropriate allusions to tone and sentiment which the sketches and drawings could suggest.

From the very beginning Raphael knew that "it is art to hide art," that harmonious and simple art, as was his, could not be achieved without long study and without careful selection among that which fantasy dictated. The means to achieve this was the drawings, as the quattrocento practice of the Umbrians and Perugino had taught him, and as he had gradually verified in his Florentine and Roman contacts, especially when he looked to Leonardo.

"...When the Painter tries out in the first sketches those fantasies which history generate in his mind, he must not content himself with only one, but should execute many inventions and then choose the one that comes out best, taking everything into account as a whole and separately as well; Raphael himself, so rich in inventiveness, worked this way, always making a work in four or six ways, each one different from the other and all of them were pleasing and looked well." This is how Dolce, through the mouth of Aretino, in 1557,[1] described the secret of that inventive fertility which was admired in Raphael by his contemporaries and thereafter, and which has its most tangible demonstration in the quantity and exceptional variety of his drawings.

Among the autographs and attributions under his name, some hundreds have come down to us (almost four hundred are catalogued in Fischel's work, which comes to an end at the point of the first years of his Roman period), and these are certainly nothing more than a part of all the drawings that Raphael made or had made, sometimes retouching them and in all cases supervising them personally in his workshop. What with sketches, studies, models and cartoons, there must have been many more, and this is attested by the various copies of originals that are no longer known,[2] and by the occasional lacunae regarding some works and certain periods, unexplainable unless by the loss of entire groups. For example, compared to the more than forty studies for the *Disputa* still extant, there are only eight or ten left for the contemporaneous *School of Athens*, while there are none at all for the *Mass at Bolsena*.

Raphael's drawings are mentioned in contemporary documents and books while he was still alive and there are notices of them throughout the sixteenth century. If it is an autograph, Raphael himself in the letter addressed to Francia in 1508 furnished a very early mention with a reference to a drawing of a Nativity he had sent to the old artist. Nevertheless it is certain that in 1514 Raphael spoke of his " drawings in several manners " on themes supplied by Castiglione,[3] and the folio with two nudes for the *Battle of Ostia*, which Raphael had sent to Dürer as an example of his work, is dated 1515 (see note 160). The mention of *beletissimi* (most beautiful?) sketches for a *Chase of Meleager* and for a *Triumph of Bacchus*, found in the correspondence regarding the unsuccessful commission of the Duke of Ferrara, is from 1519.[4]

In 1587, Armenini says of Raphael that " dispiegava molti disegni di sua mano, de quelli che li pareva che fossero più prossimani a quella materia, della quale egli già gran parte n'havea concetta nella Idea, et hor nell'uno, hor nell'altro guardando et tutta via velocemente dissegnando, così veniva a formar tutta la sua inventione, il che pareva che nascesse per essere la mente per tal maniera aiutata, et fatta ricca per la moltitudine di quelli." [5] Here, besides evidence of the quantity of Sanzio's drawings, we also find an academic interpretation of Raphael's draftsmanship (the adherence to an Idea already conceived and the selection of the best in order to come close to that Idea) which was partially evident in the passage of Dolce and which was to meet with great favor. It is certainly a schematic interpretation and one linked to the Neo-Platonism of late-sixteenth century theory, but one which is true in part, above all as regards the mature period of Raphael, as he himself seems to affirm in the letter to Castiglione: " ... to paint a beautiful woman, I need to see many beautiful ones ... in order to select the best. But ... I make use of a certain Idea, which comes to my mind. If this has in itself any great value in art, I do not know; I work hard to achieve it." (See note 3).

It is chiefly the numerous engravings based upon Raphael's inventions, which became so popular after the first decade of the sixteenth century, that amply demonstrate the widespread interest in drawings that were done by him or were inspired by his work. Once again we refer to Dolce in 1557, " ... many of his very beautiful sheets were engraved in copper ... were passed around, and also those by his hand were in the possession of so many people that their number is vast; they are a most effective proof of the fertility of his divine genius, for in each one admirable inventiveness may be seen." [6]

Case by case and often for complete groups it is possible and interesting, especially for the history of taste, to see how many of these drawings have been conserved down to our times. Besides the singular example of the sheet sent by Raphael himself to Dürer in 1515, which passed from the heirs of the artist to the Royal Collections and is now in the Albertina, we know of other drawings that were in the hands of friends and patrons of the artist. Still known are the sheets, almost all from his youth, that perhaps through gift or heredity, came into the hands of his friend Timoteo Viti. Recognizable by the initials "R. V.," they were passed on to his son Giovan Maria (who apparently gave some to Vasari together with others by his father) and gradually came down to the successors of the Vitis, the Antaldi di Urbino. [7]

In the seventeenth century that family owned at least forty-eight folios, according to an old inventory; but even at that time Raphael's originals were mixed with copies (if not actual forgeries) probably made or commissioned by Timoteo himself and, by his successors (in the Viti family there were a number of painters), for the purpose of documenting sheets not in the possession of the family. Directly from the Antaldis, the French collector Pierre Crozat acquired a part, perhaps twenty-six sheets, in 1714, while another fifteen pieces were purchased by the English merchant Woodburn in 1828, from the last descendent of the Antaldis. [8]

The group of Raphael's drawings left in his workshop upon the Master's death must have been considerably richer and more varied than those owned by Viti. They were probably quickly divided up among the various pupils and heirs. At the middle of the sixteenth century, the antiquarian Giacomo Strada spoke of having purchased in Rome from the widow of Perino del Vaga, "two boxes of drawings ... all drawn by hand," by Perino himself and by Raphael, "who had been his teacher," and he speaks also of a large number of drawings he purchased in Mantua from the son of Giulio Romano, "where there were gathered together the most beautiful things of Raphael of Urbino." [9] There is further information about these sheets that had been the property of Giulio Romano. From the ownership of the Duke of Mantua some of them passed at the beginning of the seventeenth century to the collections of Lord Arundel and of Charles I of England, and they were dispersed half a century later; some of them are still identifiable in various collections.

As for Vasari, who liked so much to enrich his *libro di disegni*, he says that he has nothing by Raphael other than "some sketches," made to help Pinturicchio in the Library of the Cathedral of Siena. However, there are no autograph drawings by Raphael among the known sheets of the reconstructed *libro*.[10] There must have been many other owners and seekers of Sanzio's drawings since the middle of the sixteenth century, if Dolce, who incidentally claimed to possess the *carta* with the *Coronation of Rossane*, asserted that " all his sheets and drawings are prized, as gems and gold are prized." [11]

In the seventeenth century this admiration continued. It is symptomatic that Raphael's drawings were in classicist Bologna, in the possession, for example, of Malvasia, who was not particularly fond of Raphael, and in the possession of the Bonfiglioli family from which some passed during the eighteenth century, through the Venetian Zaccaria Sagredo and the Englishman Smith, into the collection of George III at Windsor (see figures 88, 89, 145). The classicist Maratta, restorer of Raphael and his standard-bearer, had some others.[12] But, as was natural in a period of infatuation for Raphael's art, there was already a great deal of chaff in the wheat, and drawings by other artists falsely bore Raphael's name. One example is sufficient: in the collection of Father Resta, one of the most notable at the time, notwithstanding the large number of sheets attributed to Raphael perhaps only one was an autograph.[13]

At the end of the seventeenth century and even more in the eighteenth century, the great interest in collecting drawings, and therefore also those by Raphael, no longer existed in Italy, although Italy was to remain the principal center for the acquisition of sheets which had not yet entered the international art market. The French and the English were the most able collectors, the former turned almost naturally to Sanzio because of the classical predilections of their culture, the latter because of that passion for collecting; it is not by accident that even today the largest number of drawings by the artist are found in England.

Most formidable of them all was the Jabach collection in Paris, which according to the inventory of 1671 included six hundred and forty sheets attributed to Raphael and his school. Equally impressive was the already-cited Crozat collection, also in Paris, with acquisitions from the most illustrious sources; in the sales catalogue of the collection, edited in 1741 by Pierre Jean Mariette, it appears that there were 155 drawings by Raphael (still known today),

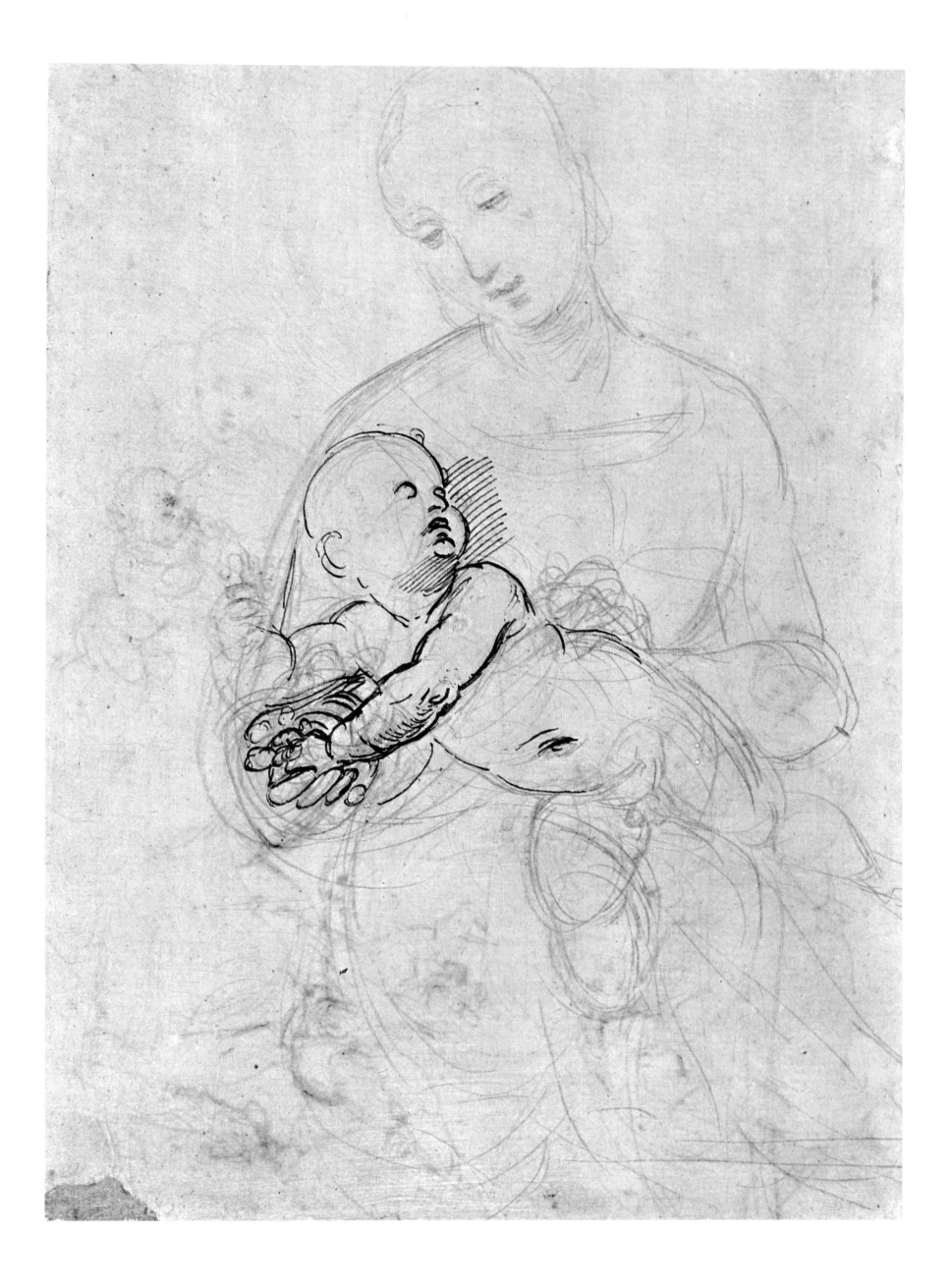

PLATE XLII   Study for the Statue of Minerva and other Statues, for the School of Athens.   Ashmolean Museum, Oxford.

PLATE XLIII   Study for the Alba Madonna.   Wicar Museum, Lille.

Madonna embracing the Child. Ashmolean Museum, Oxford.

PLATE XLV Study of Landscapes with Ruins, for the Morbetto. Royal Library, Windsor.

the best of which passed on to Mariette, highly selective collector and scholar.[14] In England at the beginning of the seventeenth century the grand collections of Lord Arundel and of King Charles I contained a large number of important Raphaelesque drawings, some of which were dispersed by the middle of the century and others of which came into the possession of the painter-collector Peter Lely. In the eighteenth century there were some in the collections of Richardson and of the painter Reynolds, and some remained in the Royal Collections. Others appeared in Russia at the Court of Catherine II and in Sweden.

For the most part these were the same works, which went singly or in groups from one owner to another until the principal public collections were stabilized in the period between the eighteenth and nineteenth centuries.

However, in the period between the two centuries the market held some pleasant surprises for the connoisseurs of Raphael; it was still another Frenchman, Jean Batiste Wicar, commissioner for works of art in Italy since 1797, who succeeded in putting together over a period of time three different collections with Raphael's drawings, the last of which he left to his native city of Lille, and it contained some sixty drawings. Symptomatic of the fervor for collecting of the time and especially of the persistent favor in which Raphael was held is the story of the sheets gathered first by Wicar, then received unscrupulously by the Florentine painter Antonio Fedi, and then passed on, through Ottley, to the large collection of Thomas Lawrence; others were secretly repurchased by Wicar himself.[15]

The English merchant and connoisseur Samuel Woodburn played a notable part in that occasion, as throughout the first half of the eighteenth century now and then he bought and sold many drawings by Raphael, among which were the finest examples then in circulation. It was Woodburn who, after having furnished the best examples to the most important collection of the time, that of the painter Lawrence, who possessed 180 of Raphael's sheets, actively concerned himself with the passage of the whole collection the Ashmolean Museum in Oxford, by means of funds raised by public subscription; he succeeded in 1846 only as regards Raphael's and Michelangelo's drawings, and not without some lacunae, since some sheets had been previously acquired by William of Orange and were dispersed shortly thereafter in a sale of that Prince's collection held in 1850. The Oxford collection which came from Lawrence is still the most complete and most beautiful collection of Sanzio's drawings, comprehensive of the various stages, styles and techniques with its sixty autographs and hundred copies and workshop pieces. Following in importance is the collection left by Wicar to the Lille Museum in 1834, which also has about sixty drawings attributed to the master and his close circle. Comparable to the approximately forty autographs in the British Museum are those in the Albertina of Vienna which came from a collection of more than 140 (according to the attributions found in the old inventories) belonging to Prince Albert of Saxe-Teschen, also a renowned collector of drawings. Somewhat farther behind follow the collections in the Louvre and the Uffizi (in which the quantity of old attributions does not at all correspond to the actual autographs), and those of Windsor, Chatsworth and other private and public European museums. There are very few drawings by Raphael in America.

From this summary review of the history of collecting, we can implicitly deduce an outline for the history of criticism of Raphael's graphic works; the major collectors were also the greatest critical connoisseurs of Raphael's drawings. It has been seen that he was always among the favorites on the market, even at times or among persons that were less enthusiastic about his art, as was the case with Malvasia. It is obvious that the collectors sought to ennoble their possessions to the maximum, even beyond truth, but in the case of Raphael, his drawings had the good fortune of being collected frequently by authentic connoisseurs, such as Crozat and Mariette, and the old attributions almost always, therefore, had some elements of truth; Fischel quite wisely advised to keep in mind both the provenance of the work and the opinions of the older and more qualified collectors before rejecting a reference.

But every rule has its exception, and many traditional attributions are to be regarded with skepticism, even those of drawings of high quality, especially if they are works from the late period of Raphael's activity, when the workshop was intensely productive. As for the paintings, so also for the drawings: the question of the authenticity of the collaborative works and the sense of that authenticity is a weak point and perhaps an unresolvable one in the study of Raphael. For this reason the eye of the connoisseur will always be the most valid instrument of judgment, especially for the drawings, which lack precise documentation.

From the passages by Dolce and Armenini quoted above we can form an idea of how Raphael's drawings were evaluated during the sixteenth century; however, their observations although not generic, were certainly general and were based on the idea of the existence of many drawings rather than on a direct knowledge of single drawings.

Instead, the connoisseur-collector Mariette had a personal, penetrating and affectionate knowledge of them, and he left some of the earliest perceptive critical observations on the question in his catalogue of the Crozat collection and his *Abecedario;* he wrote, " Quand on n'auroit pas une idée de Raphaël aussi avantageuse qu'on la doit avoir, il ne faudrait que ces Desseins pour montrer quelle étoit la sublimité de son génie: les autres jettent sur le papier leurs premières pensées et l'on s'aperçoit qu'ils cherchent, Raphaël, au contraire, en mettant au jour les siennes, lors même qu'il paroit entraîné par la véhémence de son imagination, produit du premier coup des ouvrages qui sont déjà tellement arrêtés, qu'il n'y a presques rien à y ajouter, pour y mettre la dernière main." [16]

Collecting, therefore, had a certain critical function, direct and indirect, and in order to follow it and to serve it, after the eighteenth century there began to be formed numerous collections of facsimiles and engraved reproductions of Raphael's drawings, the originals of which were in various collections; these collections were formed for the enjoyment of amateurs but also as an instrument of study (and for the market), according to a tradition originated by Jabach in 1660, which continued throughout the nineteenth century with the first photographic reproductions. The initiative of the Prince Consort of England was to foster this activity. He selected Raphael for his experiment of collecting photographs of the complete pictorial and graphic œuvre of the major artists;[17] this is the first example of exploitation, for the purpose of study, of an instrument of work today considered indispensable (and the choice of Sanzio was indicative of the cultural climate in England around 1870).

With the nineteenth century there began the full critical and historical consideration of his drawings, besides that of his paintings; there was Passavant (who began in 1839 his praiseworthy effort of compiling a complete critical list of the drawings then known, a list that was gradually amplified in successive French and Italian editions); there was Robinson's catalogue of the sheets conserved in the Ashmolean Museum, and the exemplary monograph by Crowe and Cavalcaselle. The authors of this monograph, without repeating Passavant's systematic list, carefully took into account Raphael's graphic works, availing themselves of a romantic enthusiasm in making refined judgments and chronological and critical selections.

The drawings of Raphael appear at the end of the nineteenth century in some specialized studies and in catalogues of various collections but it was not until this century that a specific and exhaustive work on the subject was produced, namely that of Fischel.[18] After his first study, Fischel began in 1913 the preparation of the complete illustrated œuvre of all the drawings he considered to be autographs; with this he presented not only the sole collection of Raphael's graphic works to this day, but also an incomparable source of information and of study and a model of wisdom in attributions, after the excessive generosity of the Romantic period and the hypercritical attitude of Morelli. Unfortunately Fischel was unable to complete his work, to which his later monograph, issued posthumously, added little. In Italy Venturi, who initiated a new epoch of studies of Raphael, treated the drawings in an unsystematic manner, sometimes using a priori reasoning, in short particularized studies or marginally in relation to the paintings. Nonetheless, his works are still today the most comprehensive treatments in Italian, if we except the equally marginal but extremely perceptive suggestions of Ortolani and the short monograph by Castelfranco.[19]

The book by Middeldorf, which inaugurated the notable revival of interest in Raphael's graphic works after World War II, especially in England and America, has a specific interest, with its exhaustive selection of examples and acute observations regarding methods and styles. Parallel studies of some artists in Raphael's circle and particularly of the workshop during the later period (with the recent tendency to restore to the Master many old attributions that modern criticism had gradually put aside or at least left in doubt) have fostered this revival; the catalogues of the two major English collections (Parker's for the Ashmolean Museum and Pouncy-Gere's for the British Museum), as well as such recent articles as those by Shearman and Oberhuber,[20] may be considered true monographic studies.

Contrary to Leonardo and Michelangelo, Raphael left no direct testimony of what drawing meant to him, either in his own writings or in the writings of his contemporaries. What we know about his ideas and his method of work is, therefore, only what we can deduce from an examination of his drawings.

Probably from the time of his Marchigian and Umbrian apprenticeship drawing was for Raphael a systematic method of working, as it was for his teachers and as was the workshop practice during the fifteenth century; it took the form of sketches and studies, almost always from life, executed in a careful and refined manner so as to provide practice for the hand and in order to evaluate a gesture, a pose, a perspective view, a shade of expression in the over-all context of the painted composition, and this is the scope of the drawing. Raphael was always faithful to this final conditioning of the drawing by the painting, and this is what distinguishes him from the Florentines, even in the many moments when he seems to abandon himself to the dictates of vivid fantasy in sketches which seemed to be ends in themselves. Instead, Raphael always kept the picture in mind, and his choices are evidence of this.

His drawings were always made as preparatory studies for paintings (except a few, which are in fact from the Florentine period) and if sometimes we are not able to determine the final destination of a sheet, it is because the connecting links are missing or because the painted work has been lost or perhaps was never completed, although it existed in the artist's mind from the start. Because of this and also because he adhered to the ancient Umbrian workshop practice, Raphael often used in later paintings motifs that he had long before elaborated in drawings that were for him the arena of invention but not the point at which the invention would cease. It was thanks to his exceptional richness that the motifs were echoed but never repeated and that he always chose for his paintings the most harmonious and unique note from among the many sketched.

He also has a wide range of tools and techniques: black pencil, sanguine, black pencil and sanguine mixed, pen, lead point, silver point, stylus, brush, watercolor, white lead, tracings; applied with sharp or shaded lines, roughly sketched or carefully finished; on white paper, or greyish pink, or cream tinted paper, according to fifteenth century practice.

All these elements were used with extreme freedom in different years and at various stages of the same composition, with a sensitive adaptation to the different themes.

As for his actual method of work, it is difficult to systematically establish the successive phases followed by Raphael in the preparation of a work,[21] if it is true that he did follow the same process in every work, rather than allowing the problems presented by each painting to determine the type of preparation necessary.

In any case, we may deduce from the various types of drawings conserved that after a first general sketch of the composition, usually done in pen, Raphael elaborated the parts in more finished drawings, either of the whole or of single figures or groups of figures, in different techniques, to better define the spatial and expressive relationships as well as the individual poses. A peculiarity typical of Raphael, but rather unusual with other artists of the time, is the frequent use of the stylus in one or another phase of the drawing to make the first outline of the figures which were then delineated with pen or pencil, following or deviating from the groove left on the paper by the stylus. In further studies the artist made more precise elaborations especially of heads, hands, and draperies, of which he then made detailed drawings, always keeping naturalness in mind; at this point the whole composition may already have been established in a squared sheet that served for enlarging (almost always done in pen or brush).

The true cartoon, in the same dimensions as the painting (the early ones were usually in pen, those of the later period were in charcoal), must have been executed at the last stage, when all the various parts of the composition had been decided upon, together with the details of the figures; this is not to say that there may not have been some changes and consequent further detailed studies. It seems certain that besides the general cartoon, and principally for frescoes, Raphael used auxiliary cartoons, that is, highly finished drawings on a natural scale in black pencil or charcoal, which bear the marks of the tracing, for some details (especially the heads, so important in Raphael's paintings); these were more effective in guiding the pictorial execution and took the place of the corresponding parts in the large cartoons.[22]

As has been said, Raphael always keeps naturalness in mind both when he drew from a live model, as was often the case (the model might have been a workshop companion or a pupil who posed in his everyday clothing), and when he copied a model dressed in real clothes, or when he worked from memory. The theme is, with rare exceptions, the human figure (usually assuming a pose, rarely in action), not, however, in the exclusive and almost exhibitionistic manner of Michelangelo or in the highly scholastic fashion of Fra Bartolomeo and the other Florentines; and not with the all-encompassing sensibility of Leonardo, who softens the figure in its ambient and in its movement. In the drawings as in the paintings, the human figure is for Raphael the supreme norm of representation, but in a harmonious dimension of gestures and emotions, which accepts and concentrates an infinite variety of tones and environments, and thus also includes landscapes or architectural backgrounds.

There is no contrast between this adherence to nature and Raphael's aversion to true anatomical studies, so basic to the Florentines, because the study for its own sake of musculature, nerves and bones is something which forces and falsifies nature, isolating parts which are otherwise harmoniously connected.[23]

We may read Vasari in this regard, who despite his disposition to place Raphael after Michelangelo, does not fail to appreciate Raphael's variety according to nature: " When Raphael began to change and improve his style [that is, in Florence], he had never studied the nude as it should be studied, but had only drawn nudes from nature, as he had seen his master Pietro do, assisted by his own natural grace. Accordingly, he studied the nude comparing the muscles of dead men with those of the living... But seeing that he could never achieve the perfection of Michelangelo in this respect, and being a man of good judgment, he reflected that painting does not consist of representing nude figures alone, but that it has a large field," in which he could " express well and with ease the inventions and caprices of history...," enriching them with backgrounds, with " living and beautiful " heads, with clothing, with various elements, " and an infinity of other things," and thus he became an excellent universal artist." (Vasari-Milanesi, IV, p. 375).

If not anatomy, the nude became the natural object of study for Raphael in Florence, once he had overcome the impediment of his Umbrian heritage and realized the classicality and expressive truth of the nude human body; because of his awareness of this truth he habitually will draw whole figures (usually in the nude) even when in the final composition they will be half-hidden by others and will, therefore, be only partially painted.

We have spoken of the close connection of the drawings with the paintings, where it is relatively easy to follow the chronological development, once the correct dating of the painting is determined, bearing in mind, however, that the drawings may precede by some time the execution, if not the commission of the respective paintings. The point can be taken conversely, also; for the works for which we have no precise dates, the study of Raphael's graphic development can offer some valuable suggestions, more so because the constant search for a better solution produced a crescendo of variations, often in clearly marked phases.

In order to follow them carefully to develop a well-defined history, it will be necessary to keep in mind certain factors: the loss of many sheets which would have filled the lacunae or would have added subtle dimensions to the various phases which we are able to recognize today (for which there are precious documentations in copies, derivations, engravings, and documents of various kinds related to the drawings); the often disconcerting flexibility of Raphael's imagi-

1 Study for the altarpiece with the Coronation of S. Niccolò da Tolentino, formerly in Sant'Agostino in Città di Castello. Lille, Wicar Museum, recto (28).

nation, which resulted in reworking and rethinking of techniques and styles; during his second Roman phase, his practice of working in a team with his pupils, which, if typical for the paintings, is also present in his drawings. In this regard, one should note that often Raphael's sheets have come down to us rather altered, not only by later owners, but also by the hands of Raphael's pupils: especially the finished drawings that immediately preceded the execution of the cartoon or painting have large zones that are worked over, and the later drawings sometimes were integrated or finished by pupils.

From what has been said, there will appear clearly, if not the possibility of an interpretation based solely on the drawings themselves, certainly a special poetry that can be enjoyed even independently of the paintings. This is the case, as Passavant says so well, because: "... to the beauty of the composition, Raphael's drawings unite vivacity and the attraction of the expression: nor are they less admirable for the frankness, purity and correctness of treatment... His studies from life are simple in their imitation and are scrupulously true ... His manner is always simple and there is no effort evident in his drawing, notwithstanding the various corrections." [24]

The Umbrian Period

THE FIRST DRAWINGS: THE S. NICCOLÒ DA TOLENTINO AND THE LIBRARY IN SIENA

It is by now traditional to begin any more or less detail study of Raphael's drawings with the famous sheet in Lille of the *Coronation of S. Niccolò da Tolentino*, the first certain drawing by Raphael for his first independent work, surely datable to 1500-1501, when the artist was just seventeen years old. It would certainly be fascinating to avoid following the tradition, but if one wishes to see further back into Raphael's drawing activity, one must move into the untrustworthy field, not yet been re-explored by the most recent critics, of Umbro-Marchigian art of the end of the fifteenth century, studying the drawings sheet by sheet, and this is not the appropriate place for such a study.

Clearly, however, if the first modern Raphael scholars, from Passavant to Crowe-Cavalcaselle, thought they could recognize his hand in too many sheets of a typical Umbrian stamp,

2 Various studies for the altarpiece of S. Niccolò da Tolentino and other sketches. Lille, Wicar Museum, verso (28).

later criticism, led by Morelli, who was followed by Venturi, has erred by excessive severity. This was the result, as Fischel has noted, of an attitude that tended to idealize the possibilities of the young Sanzio, to whom even a minimal deviation was denied, while his first graphic experiments could well have been, sometimes, uncertain in the result or awkward in appearance, as were his early exploits in painting. Even in the well-known but discredited notebook in Venice (variously considered entirely Raphael's or entirely Pinturicchio's, or generically of the Umbrian school, or even an eighteenth-century forgery),[25] it is undeniable that among the many sheets of poor quality there are some that are worthy of greater attention, at least as a reflection of the interests and the types of exercises of Raphael as a beginner. Indeed, the drawings of Raphael's masters and fellow-students were certainly of this type and were known to him both during his early apprenticeship with his father, Santi, and during his apprenticeship in the workshop of Vannucci in Perugia around 1494-95.

At the end of the fifteenth century, the Umbrian and Marchigian schools were linked by a single drawing tradition, one that was rich mainly in Florentine echoes, in elements derived from Signorelli and in more vaguely Emilian accents. As we have mentioned, drawings served this school almost exclusively as phases of elaboration for the execution of painted works, or at most, as a working basis of iconographic and compositional motifs, as were the repertories of drawings of the workshops of the later period of the International Gothic style. The technique, varied in means (pen, black pencil, metal point, tinted papers of various colors), is sharp and precise; the models are often draped models or workshop helpers in contemporary clothing and in repeated poses; the types are usually standard and anonymous. The only personality easily identifiable and very much above these schemes was that of Perugino, while that of Pinturicchio was yet to be delineated, along with those of the others, who are, at least from the point of view of graphic expression, little more than names: Eusebio da San Giorgio, Spagna, Evangelista da Piandimeleto. Fellow-disciple and imitator of Raphael, rather than possible teacher, was Viti, who was quite well known as a draftsman. [26]

Naturally, young Raphael was instinctively attracted to the best that the school could offer him, and, studying his master's drawings, he drew from them not only their purest qualities but also their sources, which he was shortly to seek out directly. Although it is possible to trace in painting a number of Raphael's personal efforts during the period of his " pre-history," when he worked alongside Perugino, it is a much more difficult task regarding the drawings, because even the drawings of his " historic " period give rise to uncertainties, as we shall see.[27] Leaving aside the uncertain material, we must put our trust in the famous drawings for the altarpiece with the *Coronation of S. Niccolò da Tolentino*, formerly in Sant'Agostino in Città di Castello, which was commissioned from Raphael and Evangelista da Piandimeleto December 10, 1500 and was finished September 13, 1501; ruined during the earthquake of 1789 and recovered in fragments, the altarpiece can be reconstructed on the basis of the preparatory drawings and the partial copy of the eighteenth century in the Pinacoteca of Città di Castello. Although at least some portions of the finished work were painted by Evangelista di Piandimeleto, it is to be believed that the conception was wholly that of the young Raphael, who, in a drawing now in Lille made a study of the composition with the unity of a work to be executed personally. It is indeed unusual and fortunate to have a design for an altarpiece, especially one which is so complete and which regards the first sure work by Raphael.

The artist must have made studies of the theme of his altarpiece on many sheets, and that in Lille (Fig. 1) [28] must be one of the last of the series because it shows clearly the curved form of the picture and the architectural frame of the scene; also evident is the squaring of the surface that served for the transfer on a larger scale. That the figures are the definitive ones is demonstrated by a comparison with the surviving fragments of the painting and with the copy. The only notable variations are the inversion of the figure of the demon, the addition of the two angels on the right (for which space is left in the drawing but which are not traced there) and the costumes and the types of the personages; the figures of God the Father, the Virgin and S. Niccolò are drawn from models in contemporary dress, a male model was used even for the Virgin and a youthful model even for God the Father, who in the painting was to have a long white beard. These variations and the disparities of technical and iconographic treatment of the figures, as well as the stylus tracing under the study of St. Augustine lead to the supposition of the existence of other drawings for the single figures that could have preceded or followed the drawing in Lille.

The existence of this type of detailed studies, which must originally have been numerous, is attested by the verso of the sheet in Lille and by the analogous one in Oxford. In the first, Raphael the artist had drawn the head of God the Father, or of S. Niccolò, two folds of the

4 Study of an angel and other studies for the altarpiece of S. Niccolò da Tolentino. Oxford, Ashmolean Museum, verso (29).

311

drapery of the angel on the left and, with pen, a group of swans with a bird as well as an architectural element with a loggia which has been identified as a detail of the Ducal Palace in Urbino (Fig. 2). On the Oxford sheet,[29] on the recto Raphael drew a study of the hands of S. Niccolò and St. Augustine, along with other sketches, and on the verso he drew the same angel on the left, St. Augustine and the hand of God the Father (Figs. 3, 4). We should note that these lastmentioned studies are on different planes and on a different scale; there is no reciprocal spatial relationship, and St. Augustine is drawn in full figure, indicating that Raphael considered this purely a study that served to define his ideas, and he did not give it the organic quality of the recto of the Lille sheet. Thus, Raphael's method of working in various phases of drawing had already evolved, and it endured up to the end of his career, manifested in sketches of the whole, preceded and followed by detailed studies, especially of hands and heads, as preparatory to the small or natural-scale cartoon.

And the style? Such clarity of choice is surprising in such a youthful artist, whose timid stroke does not clearly render the form and who has an ingenuous faith in manneristic articulations. Ortolani saw in it signs of the "substratum of the figurative background of Raphael before his training (with Perugino), which is as easy as it is plausible, although it has not been proved, to relate in its basic plastic solidity to the corporeal modeling of Melozzo da Forlì ... and for the tapering of the form, developing in easy helicoidal rhythms and in a full symmetry of cadences, to the manner of Timoteo Viti." We should, perhaps, insist more on the influence of Signorelli which appears also in other drawings of the very young Raphael,[30] and which is particularly evident in the chiaroscuro firmness of St. Augustine's mantle in the Oxford drawing and in the slightly harsh acuteness in the renderings of the structure of the head on the verso of the Lille sheet and the palm of the hand and the solid legs on the verso of the Oxford sheet. Also notable is the evident knowledge of Florentine art, through Verrocchio, Pollaiuolo and, above all, Leonardo (the group of animals on the verso of the Lille drawing is directly derived from him). Although this knowledge could have been gained from his experiences with Perugino, it would, however, authorize the hypothesis of other trips by Raphael to Florence before 1500, that is, before the documented one of 1504.[31]

The close connection with Perugino in this work is beyond discussion, not only in the Umbro-Peruginesque conception of the altarpiece but also in the manner of bending the fingers and shading them with sparse crosshatchings with a fine pencil (the central hand of the Oxford drawing), of turning the figures, of rendering the folds (see the mantle of St. Augustine in the Lille work). Fully indicative of Perugino's manner are the long, somewhat dry strokes, which are very suitable for rendering light and using it to soften the structure of Florentine form, with which Raphael sketches the angel and S. Niccolò on the Lille sheet and the smaller

5 Study for a group of soldiers for the Piccolomini Library in the Duomo of Siena. Oxford, Ashmolean Museum (33).

312

6 Small cartoon for the Departure of Aeneas Sylvius Piccolomini for the Council of Basel, in the Piccolomini Library of the Duomo of Siena. Florence, Uffizi (34).

figures on the Oxford drawing; they are the same strokes Vannucci used in such general studies as the *Adoration of the Magi* in the British Museum. Above all, however, Raphael already shows himself to be " the most congenial heir of Leonardo, for the pictorial quality of the drawing . . . The point in which the chiaroscuro sense of Peruginesque form . . . loses the drowsy inertia dear to the Umbrian master and begins to expand, to come alive " (Ortolani).

Those long and luminous strokes, which delineate the Florentine forms more softly and with some uncertainty and repetition, are seen again in another drawing in Oxford, one related to Raphael's much-discussed contribution to the work in the Library of the Sienese Duomo, soon after 1502. [32] Although his participation in the pictorial execution of the cycle is now com-

313

7 Study for the guards of a Resurrection. Oxford, Ashmolean Museum (38).

monly excluded, there remains the explicit testimony of Vasari concerning his graphic collaboration with Pinturicchio: who "being a friend of Raphael and knowing him to be an excellent draftsman [even at that time], he brought him to Siena, where Raphael made some of the drawings and cartoons for that work"; and, further, "... it is true that the sketches and cartoons of all the stories which he [Pinturicchio] made there, were by the hand of Raphael from Urbino, then a young lad ... and of these cartoons there is still one in Siena, as well as some sketches by the hand of Raphael in our book" (Vasari-Milanesi, III, p. 494; IV, p. 319). In fact, some preparatory drawings for the frescoes survive (F. 60-65), and their attribution to Raphael has repeatedly been proposed, with good reason.

An example of a first sketch for the frescoes would be the cited drawing in Oxford (Fig. 5),[33] with a group of soldiers quite similar to those on the second plane at the center of the scene showing Aeneas Sylvius Piccolomoni crowned poet by Frederick III; the figures in the drawing are in fact exactly the same as those in the fresco, though dressed and grouped differently. Betraying Raphael's hand here are the beautiful, luminous head of the third figure, turned in a three-quarter view typical of Raphael, and that very gentle face in the half-shadow of the central figure, not to mention the fluidity of the gestures and the fresh boldness of the over-all presentation, notwithstanding the weakness of certain parts (feet, hands, joints). Pinturicchio could never have achieved these, nor had he ever arrived at the agility of composition which is found in the frescoes in Siena, especially, and this is indicative, in those for which there exist preparatory drawings attributable to Raphael; this is a sign that there was a collaboration, consisting at least in certain suggestions by the young but already well-known Sanzio to his more sluggish countryman.

The small cartoon in the Uffizi for the scene of the *Departure of Aeneas Sylvius Piccolomini for the*

314 8 Madonna and Child with SS. Sebastian and Rocco. Paris, Louvre (39).

Council of Basel is examplary (Fig. 6). Together with the one formerly in the Baldeschi Collection in Perugia for the scene depicting Aeneas Sylvius leading Eleonora of Portugal to marry Frederick III (F. 65), it could be one of the cartoons cited by Vasari and categorically attributed by him to Sanzio.[34] Placing Vasari's assertion in the proper dimensions, it may be that the biographer was inclined by his enthusiasm as a collector to attribute the execution of the cartoons and drawings, some of which belonged to him, to the more famous artist; but it seems strange that such an inclination would lead Vasari to the point of inventing the collaboration of Raphael and Pinturicchio, for which there were no valid indications, not even from tradition.

A careful study of the drawing, made as early as the nineteenth century by Crowe and Cavalcaselle,[35] leads to a confirmation in this sense and justifies the persistence of the attribution of the entire group to Raphael. The sheet in the Uffizi which had already " suffered greatly " at the time of Passavant and had underdone retouching, perhaps during the actual working phases, at the time it was transferred onto a larger cartoon for the fresco. But the very poor state of conservation does not, however, impede the discovery of some quite beautiful passages: the languid lines of the clouds on the left, the subtle entanglement of the sails and the rigging, the spatial precision of the small boats in the background with their small, neat shadows. The tiny figures of sailors and bearers, and of the infantry and cavalry on the bank are barely traced with the straight, sparse lines already seen in the drawing for the altarpiece of S. Niccolò da Tolentino; the background of the city and the port has a luminous intensity of atmosphere that displays Peruginesque and Leonardesque characters derived from their very nature, not with the discursive obstinacy of Pinturicchio. The foreground, notwithstanding the frequent reworkings in ink and white lead, displays the ingenious inventiveness and freshness of Raphael's hand, above all in the youthful heads in which the vaporous line gives new life to Perugino's dreamy types, and in the handsome, trembling horses, which once again postulate an early knowledge of Leonardo on Raphael's part. The variations carried out by Pinturicchio in the fresco give a maudlin aspect to the figures that are almost mawkish in the drawing and diminish the airy compositional idea, by an excess of crowding and ornament. The almost Neo-Gothic alteration of the perspective which Pinturicchio had used in the background of sky and sea, which is still almost in the manner of Piero della Francesca in the Uffizi drawing, contributes to it.

There is another drawing, also in the Uffizi,[36] of a detail of that mentioned above. It is rapidly sketched with pen and shows cavalrymen and a foot soldier (F. 60-61). Besides confirming the reference of the whole group to Raphael, it gives evidence, in the evident reflections of the drawings, if not yet the cartoon, of the *Battle of Anghiari*, of a previous trip to Florence by Raphael. Besides, on the verso, this same drawing has a copy of a figure from the frescoes by Signorelli in Orvieto which gives evidence not only of a visit to that city by Raphael (which is attested by other later drawings) but also of his repeated interest in certain compositional ideas and certain types of the artist from Cortona.[37]

At this point it should be also noted that, although Raphael derived some elements of the drawings from Signorelli (as in some hardness of outlines, above all in the nudes, and some dense shadows, especially in the woolly garments that do not have so many looped folds as those in the Umbrian drawings, cf. note 30), still he never shared in the harsh world of Signorelli and was, instead, fully imbued with the sweet, classic spirit of Perugino.

This is evident in two analogous drawings at Oxford, quite Peruginesque in style, connected with the much-discussed *Resurrection* now in São Paulo and datable to around 1502.[38] If these drawings can be used to confirm Raphael's authorship of the painting (but this does not preclude the possibility in the drawings of common prototypes from the Umbrian tradition for the types of the various figures, among which there are only two that coincide perfectly in the painting and the drawings), they appear surely to be by Raphael at the time when he was closest to the master. Compared with Perugino's work, here there is a more nervous spring of articulations in the rhythmic poses, still with echoes of Signorelli and Florentine style, together with an ingenuousness in the standing figures and the details of line—a Peruginesque manner that was transposed in the " brilliant and decorative manner " of Pinturicchio, as Roberto Longhi noted with regard to the painting in São Paulo (Fig. 7).

Pinturicchio could have suggested the curving of the headdresses and a certain contraction of the limbs apparent in the two drawings, and there is a connection with Pinturicchio in another sheet with a much-discussed attribution to Raphael, showing the Madonna with Ss. Sebastian and Rocco[39] in the same scheme as the Ansidei Altarpiece although it is much earlier (Fig. 8). Here the mannered modules of the looped folds, of the hooked fingers, the latticework shadows, the exuberant poses of the two saints are not sufficient to mitigate the spatial clarity of the whole and the luminosity of the parts, especially in the tender group of the Madonna and Child, so close in composition and chronology to the *Solly Madonna*.

THE CORONATION OF THE VIRGIN AND OTHER DRAWINGS

Another sure point of reference in the evolution of Raphael's drawing consists of the group of drawings for the *Coronation of the Virgin* in the Vatican Pinacoteca commissioned by Maddalena degli Oddi for San Francesco in Perugia, apparently around 1502-03.

There are about a dozen drawings for this work (F. 15-30) of various kinds and in various techniques that survive.[40] Their unusually large number leads us to suppose that Raphael

had prepared an exceptional quantity of sketches, studies and cartoons for this altarpiece, which must have been one of the most important commissioned from him up to that time, and which was destined for a church in the Umbrian capital, a gift of one of the most powerful families of the region. That the very young artist, despite so much care, failed in part in the painted execution, with the exception of the very beautiful predella, does not diminish the value of the work and of its creation, which the drawings help us to understand. There is no sketch of the whole to document the early compositional ideas of the artist, who from the beginning must have chosen the general scheme of the altarpiece from examples by Perugino, with juxtaposed terrestrial and celestial zones; once the general scheme was selected, he must have been more preoccupied with the various particulars than with the over-all effect. And it is precisely in the details that the painting has its greatest fascination, for that direct search of *affetti* which shows that the young Raphael was already seeking to escape from the vague sentimentalism of the Umbrian school, to define not only the physical differences between the figures but also, and primarily, their various psychological aspects.

The drawings attest this study step by step; they are in large measure intended as studies of the heads of the various protagonists, the subtle variations of their expressions, the gradations of light on the surfaces of their faces, underscored by the variety of graphic techniques employed.

The sheet at Lille [41] with studies of the head and hands of St. Thomas is executed with a delicate silver point, with a sparse stroke that " hardens and vitrifies the surfaces " of the grey paper (Ortolani). It has a compact quality almost like that of the preparation of a painting; and as the latter is ready to receive its colors, so the former is full of luministic-painterly effects that render the drawing more airy and almost more mature than the corresponding passages in the painting, where the ecstatic expression of the saint results more puppet-like than ingenuous, more frozen than spontaneous (Fig. 9).

The expression of another youthful saint for the same altarpiece, the St. James, is only slightly different; the study of the head in the British Museum (Fig. 11) [42] was destined for this figure; this time it was executed with black pencil and traces of pin-pricking and pounce that lead us to believe it to be a direct preparatory drawing for the cartoon, or an " auxiliary " cartoon itself (that is, as has been said, one of those studies made after the actual cartoon for the purpose

11 Auxiliary cartoon for the head of St. James in the Vatican Coronation. London, British Museum (42).

10 Study of an angel playing the cymbals, for the Vatican Coronation. Oxford, Ashmolean Museum (44 a).

of improving certain parts, immediately before proceeding to the execution of the painting). In fact, the deviations from the painting are few and the scale is identical. But here too, the fuzzy quality of the hair and the hatched parts that lightly indicate the play of light and shadow on the facial planes, make the drawing preferable to the corresponding painted section. To a lesser degree this is also true of the surviving sketches of the old Apostles,[43] where Raphael seems to follow Perugino's schemes and perhaps also the optical effects of the Flemings, with which he had been familiar since his Urbino phase; but those "tremors of emotion" and those "vibrations" that were even then Leonardesque in spirit (Venturi) and which are the fascinating aspect of the two studies for the young saints, are missing.

There also remain drawings for an angel[44] for the *Coronation* in the Vatican, and they bear already familiar motifs. From a model in contemporary clothes the artist made studies of the most appropriate gestures to give his figures and then elaborated on the young figures, sheathed in their tight hose, the flourishes of the garments and light outlines of wings which contrast curiously with the berets and the sixteenth-century tights. The painting thus gradually was composed as a sacred representation and the boundary between human reality and divine representation almost disappeared; the young artist seemed to enjoy portraying his workshop companions, dressing them up as angels, and offers us passages of a freshness that in the painting he had to sacrifice because of the iconographic necessities and the iconic nature of the altarpiece (Figs. 10, 12).

Another study of an angel[45] recalls the type of drawing for the head of St. Thomas. The study of the angel is quite similar to the corresponding element in the painting; here too the advantage is completely in favor of the drawing, with its less stereotyped expression, with its large luminous areas of the facial planes, as pure as those in a Luca della Robbia, with its subtle atmospheric vibrations of shadows and the flowing curls which, as always, reveal a preceding acquaintance with Leonardo's work. How unsure and completely Peruginesque does the painting appear in comparison with this "classic" head, which had absorbed and transformed the acquired cultural motifs into its own language and fused them in a manner that perhaps had never before been so perfectly achieved (Fig. 13).

317

12 Two studies of angels for the Vatican Coronation. Lille, Wicar Museum (44 b).

It is the same perfection that we find in the predella and above all in the very beautiful *Annunciation*, for which there is a small preparatory cartoon in the Louvre, [46] almost without variations with respect to the painting, except for a closer point of visualization (Fig. 15).

It is well known that for the composition of this scene Raphael had made reference to the analogous predella of Perugino's altarpiece of Fano, on which he may have collaborated as a youth. But compared with the sister composition of Fano, notable in this *Annunciation* is a more balanced neo-quattrocento disposition of the figures and the architecture, which recalls Luca della Robbia and confirms once again a Florentine experience on Raphael's part before the known trip of 1504. The columned interior with the floor marked off in squares is of a Brunelleschian purity which could not have come about without a direct experience of Florentine architecture, while the landscape in the background (the only part not fully delineated in the small cartoon) recalls, in its clean rendering and its spatial juxtaposition of trees, hills and houses, the beautiful landscape drawings of Fra Bartolommeo. While the gesture of the Madonna, the ridges of the folds and the wing-spread of the angel keep alive the formulas of the Umbrian manner, the unified discourse of the rhythms and the light purifies every part to which the painted execution will in this instance add the splendor of atmospheric sense and the union of colors.

The scene of the *Adoration of the Magi* in the same predella is a bit more trite; there exists a preparatory drawing for it in Stockholm, a drawing that is somewhere between a sketch of the whole and a true small cartoon (F. 29).

Still more directly inspired by the corresponding scene in the Fano predella is the *Presentation in the Temple* in the predella in the Vatican, for which there is a little sketch depicting the central group conserved at Oxford (Fig. 14).[47] Here Raphael transposes "in a cursive and painterly mark the applied calligraphy of his models" from Umbria (Ortolani) and shows a knowledge not only of the major Florentine works but also of the drawings by Florentine artists: Leonardo; Ghirlandaio, in the lines of the shadows; the brilliant turning of the

13 Study of a head and hand for the angel-musician in the Vatican Coronation. London, British Museum (45).

14 Sketch for the Circumcision in the predella of the Vatican Coronation. Oxford, Ashmolean Museum (47).

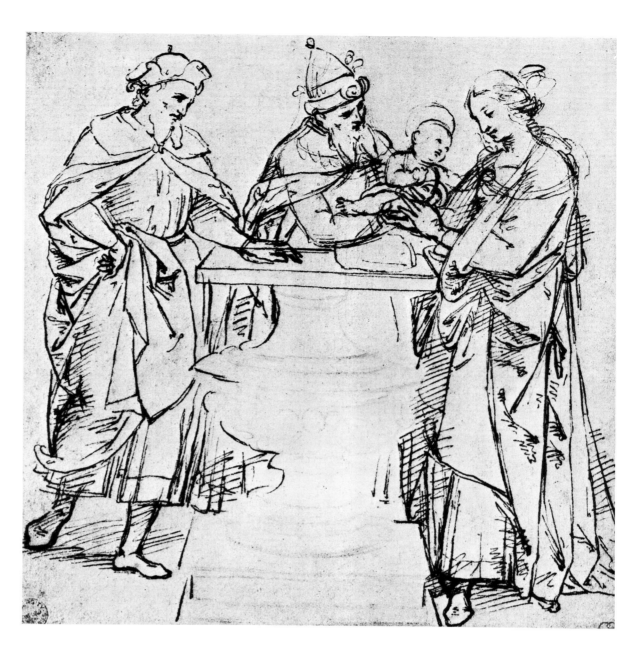

line of Filippino; in a pictorial variety of pen work which is also found in Fra Bartolommeo and which returns gradually in an ever more diffused manner in Raphael's sketches up to his maturity.

The beautiful profile of a girl in the Uffizi[48] has been linked to the *Presentation in the Temple* of the same predella; nevertheless, more than a study of the woman with the doves in that scene, it seems to be a portraitlike digression on this type of woman—a type that is once again Leonardesque, as the complex mass of the hair testifies. But the somewhat rigid fullness of the

15 Cartoon for the Annunciation in the predella of the Vatican Coronation. Paris, Louvre (46).

319

16 Female bust, in profile. Florence, Uffizi (48).

bust and the full face modeled in light go back still further to Raphael's fifteenth-century sources, to Luca della Robbia and even to Piero della Francesca, with results that correspond in part with those of a Florentine, Piero di Cosimo (Fig. 16).

As in the preceding case, the head of the lad in Lille is also a portraitlike digression on a motif of the Vatican altarpiece; in the drawing the model of the aforementioned drawing in Oxford for the angel on the left of the *Coronation* is studied from a closer viewpoint, with the same hairstyle and turn of the head and the same play of light (Fig. 17).[49] It is as if Raphael, while studying his workshop companion in order to create his angel, at a certain point became aware of the expressive qualities of the model and moved closer to him, studying him again for his own sake, beyond the scope of altarpiece (where, in fact, the corresponding angel re-enters the anonymity of Umbrian typology). This is one of the first portrait-drawings by Raphael and one of his most delicate ones. In painting, Raphael rarely succeeded again in capturing such vivid and easy naturalness, which has placed this drawing in relation to certain Emilian products of Francia's circle (and it is probable that the path led through Viti, who had by then returned from Bologna), but which above all shows all Raphael's knowledge of the beautiful portrait drawings of Lorenzo di Credi.

A lovely drawing in Oxford [50] recalls the sweet, balanced rhythms of Francia, though in a full Peruginesque climate; it is executed in a transparent silver-point technique similar to that in some studies for the *Vatican Coronation*, and it may have belonged to the same notebook, the only relatively plausible one among the various notebooks reconstructed thus far.[51]   The various links established between this drawing and the altarpiece of the *Mond Crucifixion*, formerly in Città di Castello, are not entirely convincing; however, whether or not it was destined for the painting, and whether or not it belonged to the same notebook of sheets mentioned above, this study is datable to around 1502-03, still within the Umbrian years (Fig. 18).

The situation is similar for the sketch in Frankfurt [52] for an unidentified altarpiece, one that perhaps was never executed, representing the Virgin enthroned with Saints (Fig. 19). On the left there is a S. Niccolò da Tolentino, on the right there was to have been another saint, in a final composition of the type of the drawing in the Louvre (cf. Fig. 8) or the Ansidei Altarpiece: the motifs of the throne and of the architectural background open onto a distant landscape

320   17 Head of boy. Lille, Wicar Museum (49).

19 Study for an altarpiece with the Madonna and S. Niccolò da Tolentino. Frankfurt, Städelsches Institut (52).

18 Kneeling youth. Oxford, Ashmolean Museum (50).

recall the Ansidei Altarpiece, as do the gestures of the Madonna and of the saint, whose three-quarter pose is analogous to that of the Baptist in the London altarpiece, while the Child recalls the small picture of the *Madonna and SS. Jerome and Francis* now in Berlin. Chronologically it seems to fall between these two works, because this drawing does not have the compositional breadth of the Ansidei Altarpiece, which already had elements of Fra Bartolommeo, but, on the other hand, it is more advanced with regard to the drawing in the Louvre, because of its greater spatial confidence and the composed but decisive pose of the saint, which is the result of the experiments in pose of the saints in the Vatican altarpiece.

A group of three sheets that were certainly intended for the same, lost pictorial composition recall these drawings but have a slightly more mature character. The group consists of a drawing at Lille for a full-length Madonna, the gesture of whose hand recurs in a sketch of a half-length Madonna and Child in Oxford, and whose face recurs in a drawing in the British Museum for a veiled female head.[53] The relationship between the three drawings is precious evidence of the variety of technical, stylistic and emotional refinements that Raphael was able to derive at the same time from a single iconographic motif.

The sheet in Lille, perhaps also a piece from the already cited notebook in silver point on prepared grey paper (cf. note 51), is a study from the usual male model in contemporary dress of a figure of the Madonna, which is taking on the appropriate attributes: the sweet face with a hint of a veil, the necklace with a pendant. This is new evidence of the point at which the reality of the model meets the invention of the divine figuration. According to a scheme typical

321

20 Study for a seated Madonna and for a hand. Lille, Wicar Museum (53 a).

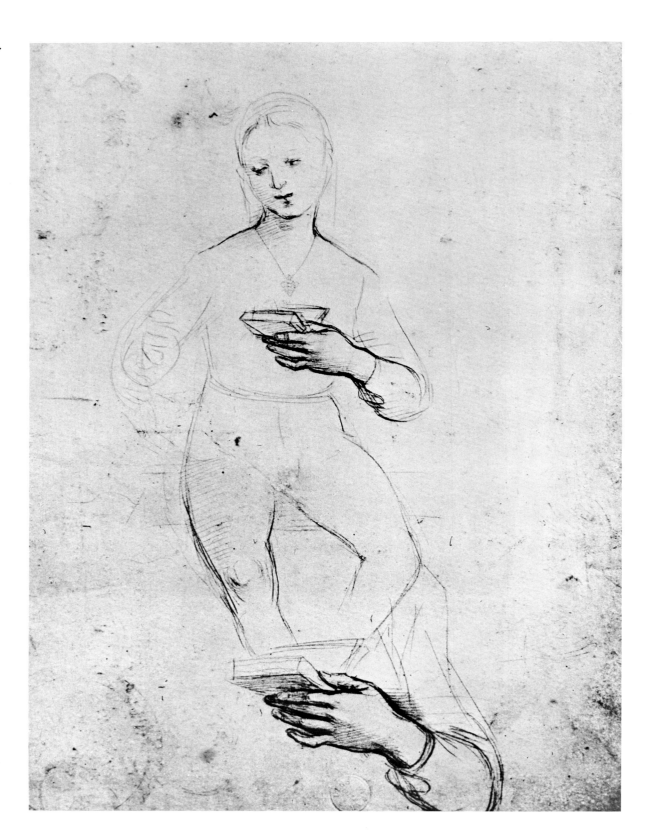

of Perugino, the hand of the Madonna is restudied on the same sheet in a large scale while her left arm, which will be covered by the figure of the Child in the painted version, is here hardly delineated (Fig. 20).

The study in the British Museum with only the head is almost without variations. The eyelids are only slightly more lowered and the arrangement of the hair is different; the necklace has given way to a brooch, which according to the traditional iconography holds the veil at the neckline. The luminous intensity and the purity of the face recall once more the shining surfaces of Della Robbia terra cottas, and this effect is heightened by the lightly tinted, almost glossy ground of the paper (Fig. 21).

The small Oxford sketch (Fig. 22), which seems the final compositional result of the two previously mentioned drawings, appears to recall the Madonnas of Luca or Andrea della Robbia, both for its clear outlines, for the pose and for the affectionate relationship of Mother and Child. It makes little difference whether this drawing was done before or after the other two. What seems certain is that a composition of this type was what Raphael had in mind when he executed the drawings of the details of the head and of the hands. He is gradually and more clearly breaking away from the traditional Umbrian manner, once more showing his direct knowledge of the Florentine artistic culture. His pen has lost its Peruginesque character and has assumed the pictorial breadth of Leonardo; note the tender figure of the Child, which, although retaining the forms dear to Perugino, has broadened the planes, bending them to receive the light more fully and delineating the outlines in a manner that recalls Verrocchio. The landscape in the background, studied again at the right and on the verso (Fig. 23), fuses the scratched lines of Piero di Cosimo with the slow juxtaposition of planes in

21 Head of a veiled Madonna. London, British Museum (53 b).

22 Sketch of a Madonna and Child. Oxford, Ashmolean Museum (53 c).

23 Sketch of a landscape. Oxford, Ashmolean Museum (53 c).

24 Study of a female head for the Marriage of the Virgin in the Brera. Oxford, Ashmolean Museum (55).

landscape drawings by Fra Bartolommeo, as it had also in the small cartoon for the *Annunciation*, in a union unknown to Perugino.

This is perhaps the first pure landscape in Raphael's graphic production.[54] We will not find in his œuvre a large number of drawings of such explicit landscapes, but we shall sense that the perception of nature is always present, according to Leonardo's teachings, in his drawings. Even where nature does not appear directly, and this is true in the greatest number of instances, there circulates around Raphael's figures a sense of space, of light, and of air which are the very elements of nature and which suggest the landscape in which the figures move and which is necessary to their existence. "They are not landscapes in the Venetian sense; Raphael had no eye for the romantic charm of the unexpected... Nature, for him, was the friend of man, not his puzzling and awe-inspiring antagonist... Raphael's landscapes are perfectly built. They present nature at its best, in full harmony with itself and with the man... Such a sublimation of nature presupposes the most assiduous study, not always with the pencil but forever with the eye and mind " (Middeldorf).

25 Bust of a woman. London, British Museum (56).

324

The Florentine Period

THE DRAWINGS ABOUT 1504

We have now reached the period about the year 1504, the date of the highly celebrated painting which eloquently demonstrated these experiences and which concluded Raphael's Umbrian activity: the altarpiece with the *Marriage of the Virgin*, now in the Brera, painted for the church of San Francesco in Città di Castello.

The only sheet known for the picture is the one in Oxford,[55] which has on the recto a study for the fourth woman on the left and on the verso studies for the woman in profile in the foreground and for the one on the extreme left, all studies for the heads only. Here Raphael's hand is delicate in drawing the broad facial planes and in the intensity of their gazes, but his art remains slightly below that manifested in the picture and in other sheets, also datable to this time (Fig. 24). It may be held that Raphael executed many other drawings for this important painting and perhaps also some sketches of the whole, of the type of those for the S. Niccolò altarpiece of 1500. However the typical Peruginesque juxtaposition of two planes, the figurative and architectural, leads to the supposition that the artist had no great need to study the composition as a whole and that he chose primarily to study in separate sheets and cartoons the single heads and details of the poses, intending directly in the painted execution to link the various figures and to unify them with the background, principally by means of the magical purity of the light on the enamel-like color.

28 Cartoon for the Agony in the Garden in the predella of the Colonna Altarpiece. New York, Pierpont Morgan Library (60).

27 Cartoon for the Magdalene in the Contini-Bonacossi Collection. Berlin, Kupferstichkabinett (61).

The more detailed drawings for the painting must have been on the type of the one of a woman at the British Museum,[56] perhaps intended to be a female portrait in the guise of a saint, as it would appear from the trace of a halo above the head (Fig. 25). This head, which is similar to that of the first assistant on the left in the *Marriage* in the Brera, was certainly taken from life, notwithstanding its Umbrian typology. The connection with Umbrian models is still clear in the handling of the drapery and in the doll-like expression of the eyes and mouth, which perhaps was the reason for its attribution to Timoteo Viti by Morelli. But the free treatment of the hair and the veil, as well as the light and the Leonardesque sense of

30 Madonna of the Pomegranate, perhaps a cartoon for the Connestabile Madonna. Vienna, Albertina (63).

atmosphere that surrounds the figures suffice to distinguish it from Mannerist formulas. And some physical details masterfully accentuate the defects of the model, whose face is a bit sheeplike, almost a subtle caricature of the Umbrian types.

There are no longer traces of these types in another portrait-drawing in the British Museum,[57] also usually placed in relation with the Brera painting although it is not a study for any of the figures in it (Fig. 26). The reality of this masculine head is such as to lead one to see here more than in other, earlier drawings the portraitist's digression on a model which Raphael contemporaneously had occasion to study for a painting. Whether or not it was for the Brera painting is of little importance, once the date of 1504 is accepted for the drawing, as it commonly is, correctly rejecting the too-late dating of 1508 suggested by Robinson. Still, a certain similarity of this head with that of the S. Niccolò in the Ansidei Altarpiece could better date our drawing to the period around 1506. According to what Robinson observes, this head has links with certain Leonardesque types, rather than with those less fierce and truer ones by Fra Bartolommeo. The " sweet . . . airs of the heads " which Vasari admired in Raphael and which were to be his glory in the Roman works up to the *Transfiguration* had their beginnings here, in this determined and at the same time detached observation of the live model. The severity of this adherence to nature recalls the portraits of ancient Roman sculpture and what had come down from them to Tuscan sculpture of the fifteenth century; this was now being restated by Fra Bartolommeo. Besides if, as we shall see, Raphael looked

◁ 29 Cartoon for the Dream of the Knight in the National Gallery of London. London, National Gallery (62).

31 Study for a Holy Family with an angel. Lille, Wicar Museum (64).

32 Study for the St. George in the Louvre. Florence, Uffizi (67).

to the Donatello of the St. George, why could he have not looked to Donatello's Joshua or his Jeremiah with equal interpretative ability?

The so-called self-portrait in Oxford,[58] once again sweetly Peruginesque in appearance, is rich in suggestions from Florentine sculpture of the fifteenth century, which now seemed to be based, not only on the purity of Della Robbia but also on the dry delicacy of Desiderio da Settignano, in the extraordinary capacity for capturing the youthful charm of the model and in the rendering of the surface quality of light on the face. But, above all, there is an evident influence of the drawings of heads by Lorenzo di Credi, and their importance for Raphael is emphasized by Luisa Becherucci in this volume.

These influences from fifteenth-century Florentine sculpture and from painting, from Credi to the early Fra Bartolommeo, together with the many echoes from Leonardo, are so mature and have been so assimilated by around 1504, that they seem to confirm the precocity of Raphael's Florentine experience; however that may be, he seems to have established himself in Florence precisely in that year.[59]

A series of small cartoons for painted works, datable between the late Umbrian period and the early Florentine phase, seem to appear at this point as if by design, and since they are cartoons, that is to say drawings immediately previous to the painting, they have a particular importance as documentation.

The one in the Pierpont Morgan Library[60] for the *Agony in the Garden* in the predella of the Colonna Altarpiece (Fig. 28) shows some variations with respect to the painted panel, with the advantage of a greater simplicity that did away with all remnants of Umbrian preciousness to arrive at a fully " Attic " quality of rhythms and to a complete truthfulness of observation; thus, if the idea of Crowe-Cavalcaselle that the altarpiece was begun before but finished after the trip to Florence is true, the predella and its cartoon could have coincided with the end of the work. In addition, the part of the predella which is at the National Gallery in London contains such evident citations from Leonardo's cartoon of the *Battle of Anghiari* as to justify such a conjecture.

The small cartoon in Berlin for the Magdalene in the Contini-Bonacossi Collection (Fig. 27) pendant to the Rothschild cartoon for the St. Catherine,[61] its companion piece, differs from the

33 Study for a horseman fighting with foot-soldiers. Venice, Accademia (68).

329

35 Half-length portrait of a woman. Paris, Louvre (72).

34 Leda with the swan, from Leonardo. Windsor, Royal Library (71).

painting only in the absence of geometric motifs in the background, which while giving the effect of painted glass, diminished the purity of the space and of the soft, almost neo-Botticellian contours of the figure.

The small cartoon in the National Gallery in London for the *Dream of the Knight*, in the same collection, is exceptional (Fig. 29).[62] And even if it lacks that "softness and velvet weave of colors" (Crowe and Cavalcaselle) which gives the picture fascination, there is a limpidity of rhythms, a diffuse luminosity intelligently mixed with areas of shadow in minute strokes on the foreground of the figures which give the masterpiece its tone. One can deduce from it that Raphael had achieved in the drawing the precious, balanced scale of the whole composition. The drawing, therefore, is to be regarded not as the uncolored version of the painting and therefore as a factor of limited importance in comparison to it, but as the necessary breaking down of the planes because the harmony of the colors has its base in the harmony of the poses, of the proportions, of the clear relationships between figures, objects and landscapes.

It was by means of the graphic elaboration that Raphael composed his paintings and it is unfortunate that in this case no other drawings survive to exemplify such an elaboration to us from the beginning. Unfortunately also, no drawings survive for the companion picture to this one, the *Three Graces* in Chantilly. From the examples already seen, it is certain, in fact, that Raphael made a long series of studies before arriving at the selection of each minor detail of a picture, even those works of small dimensions, and therefore it is quite possible that this small cartoon was preceded by sketches and studies for the figures and the very beautiful landscape, sketches of the type of those for the Vatican predella or of the *Little Madonna* in Oxford (cf. Figs. 14-15, 22-23). To repeat here once again what has been said of the Florentine

influence would seem superfluous regarding a work connected to a painting which many concur in dating to the fringes, if not actually within the limits of, the Florentine period of Raphael. But what is perhaps more evident in the drawing than in the painting, is the rapport with the lingering fifteenth-century phases of that culture, that is, with the linear modulations of Botticelli (the girl at the right), with the glassy clarity of the pen strokes of Fra Bartolommeo and of Albertinelli, with the sharp furrow of the contours in Donatello's low reliefs.

The very beautiful drawing in Vienna for the *Madonna of the Pomegranate* (Fig. 30),[63] a sheet not pin-pricked but of such precision, technique, balance, and scale to make one suspect that it, too, was conceived as a cartoon for a unidentified picture, presents aspects similar to those of the aforementioned drawings. The connections established between it and the *Connestabile Madonna*, are supported only in part and, precisely, in the head and shoulders of the Madonna, in the head of the Child, in the lightly drawn landscape which on the right seems to indicate water reflections and in the fact that the first version of the picture, as was seen in a nineteenth-century cleaning, represented the Child playing with an apple, as in our drawing. But the position of the Child and of the Madonna's arms, the rectangular form which seems to have been intended to remain as such, the presence of the pillow on which the Child is placed and of a window sill upon which the book and the left hand of the Virgin rest indicate a precise destination, but one different from the *Connestabile Madonna*, although the dating of around 1504 seems valid, and was proposed by Ortolani for the painting in Leningrad and by Fischel for the drawing.

In it the echoes of Della Robbia, frequently mentioned here as appearing in Raphael, seem determining factors in the clear arrangement on the background together with a sweet thoughtfulness of "affetti" which seems to hint at an early version by Raphael of Michelangelo's solutions. This is not yet on a formal level (although the foreshortened right arm of the Virgin has a distinctive plastic vigor) but it is at least on an interpretative level, as a softer variation of the melancholy that Buonarroti instilled in the *Pietà* or, speaking of a work which Raphael could have then seen at first hand, in the *Madonna of Bruges*. Perhaps, though, it was his friendship with Fra Bartolommeo that induced the tender pupil of the Umbrian school to such severity of vision.

There remain traces of their formulas in another sketch of the Madonna and Child (Fig. 31),[64] which can also vaguely be linked to one of Raphael's first Florentine works, the *Terranuova Madonna*; the sketch is an interesting indication, precisely in a certain unevenness, of the crucial problems that Raphael was attacking at that moment. The neo-quattrocento rhythms of the composition reflect Perugino, Della Robbia, and the linear qualities of Filippino Lippi; the free, broad juxtapositions of light (the foreground in shadow, the light background with deep hollows of the pen which outline the saint's face and the chin of the angel) are derived from Piero di Cosimo and, of course, Leonardo da Vinci. Pen strokes in the manner of Ghirlandaio and planes open to the light in the style of Fra Bartolommeo rest on the polished surfaces like fifteenth-century low reliefs, with the nervousness and the furrowed contours of the type of Verrocchio (see, for example, the legs and arms of the child). Raphael was experimenting here with the whole range of contemporary Florentine culture.

THE FLORENTINE PERIOD

What Raphael found in Florence and how he was received there, sometimes as a brilliant assimilator of old and new ideas, sometimes as a member of the vanguard, and sometimes as a raw and enthusiastic neophyte, is well known. What is said with regard to Raphael as a painter is easily demonstrable through his graphic works as well; there is no dichotomy between his painting works and his drawings, they are, rather, complementary.

For a youth who arrived in Florence with the specific intention of studying (if we are to believe Vasari and the much-discussed letter of introduction written to Soderini by Giovanna

37 Studies of heads and hands for the fresco of San Severo in Perugia and sketch from the Battle of Anghiari by Leonardo. Oxford, Ashmolean Museum (74).

Feltria, cf. note 59), he quickly became familiar with the artists working there and with their patrons, and it is quite natural to suppose an early knowledge not only of the most famous and impressive works of art in the city but also of the graphic works that were especially admired there: the first engravings of the northern artists (we should remember that even Michelangelo copied them) and those of the circle of Pollaiolo and Finiguerra, together with the sheets by Botticelli and Verrocchio, which were in Lorenzo di Credi's workshop, and above all those of Leonardo.[65] If Raphael had quickly become a friend of Ridolfo del Ghirlandaio and Aristotile da Sangallo, as Vasari said, it would have been simple for him to enter for a time in the respective workshops of the two families, both rich in active draftsmen and to leaf through the drawings of the masters of the shops and their pupils and those of the other more or less contemporary artists whom they admired and studied.

His knowledge of Florentine drawing must have proceeded for Raphael at an equal pace with his discovery of the great works of painting and sculpture in the city, both the older ones as well as the contemporary works, as, for example, the two cartoons by Leonardo and Michelangelo for the frescoes of the Salone dei Cinquecento.

In this regard, we should bear in mind the precise evidence in Vasari: " For he heard great things from some painters of Siena of a cartoon done by Leonardo da Vinci in the Pope's Hall at Florence of a fine group of horses, to be put in the hall of the palace, and also of some nudes of even greater excellence done by Michelangelo in competition with Leonardo. This excited so strong a desire in Raphael that he put aside his work and all thought of his personal advantage, for excellence in art always attracted him." Raphael, there-fore, came to Florence around 1504, if not for the first time (cf. note 31), at least to see for the first time the two cartoons that had just been published and which were so full of new ideas that they became " the school of the world " (Cellini).

It should also be noted that these new ideas which became emblematic for the whole figur-ative development of the sixteenth century, were established in precise graphic terms.[66] The two cartoons were basically two large drawings that translated the formal ideas of their two authors in a technique, which, because it was monochrome and graphic, was exclusively of the nature of drawing, even though it immediate preceded a painted execution and was of necessity subordinate to it in part. And Raphael, along with the others admired and copied them, seeing in them the formal innovations and their qualities as design, even though his particular sensi-tivity went beyond the purely technical aspects, and he was able to understand how much the cartoons had to offer from a purely pictorial and painterly point of view. And he did so before all the others, for echoes of the cartoons did not begin to appear in paintings and drawings by Florentines and others until after the first decade of the century, except in Raphael where it seemed to occur simultaneously.

As with his painting, so with his drawings, the romantically Leonardesque theme of *St. George* can be taken to exemplify the acute and precocious perception by Raphael's of the new features of the two cartoons. There is an extremely evident desire to rival the " very beautiful group of horses " of the *Battle of Anghiari* in the quivering horse of the *St. George* in the Louvre and its preparatory drawing in the Uffizi (Fig. 32),[67] which is datable, for precisely this Leo-nardesque element, to about 1504. Everything in it seems assimilated from Leonardo: the twisting of the dragon and its type, which is something between a fantastic and a scientifically rendered version based on studies from real animals; the face of the warrior cut in shadow and the way he turns violently in the saddle; the swift lines of the cape, the clouds, the horse's tail and mane. The " dynamic movement " of the spatial rhythms and the compositional cross patterns, pictorially interpreted, of the Pollaiolo brothers . . . " (Ortolani) are direct intuitions of Leonardo's art, derived not only from the *Anghiari* cartoon, but from the earlier *Adoration of the Magi*, a point of inspiration for so many of Raphael's works in various periods.

The interpretation of the *St. George* is pertinent also to the sheet in the Accademia of Venice (Fig. 33),[68] also evidently derived from the types of the *Battle of Anghiari*, in which for the first time we find Raphael concerned with problems of the nude in action first time. As long as he had remained tied to the Umbrian school, he studied anatomical forms only from models clothed in clinging garments, but he had never approached the basic theme, which had obsessed the Florentines throughout the fifteenth century and which had now been given its most inte-gral and dynamic statement in Michelangelo's cartoon of the *Cascina*. The extent to which Raphael remained fascinated by this theme was mentioned by Vasari, who in his excess of admiration for Michelangelo may have overemphasized Raphael's inexperience with anatomy; however, basically, he did not give a false picture of the situation.

It is a fact that up to the Florentine phase drawings of nudes by Raphael are very rare,[69] and, instead, this theme was frequently taken up and articulated in problems of groups and movement in a series of pen studies, such as this one in Venice, which are datable to the early part of his Florentine sojourn.

A large part of these studies were collected by Fischel in what he called the *Grosses Florentiner Skizzenbuch* and although the reconstruction of this notebook is not without uncertainties,[70] the thematic and chronological connections among the various sheets is unquestionable although there were some time lapses. In it there is confirmation of Raphael's special interest for anatomical problems, as a result of his contact with the Florentine environment and especially with Michelangelo, which proves the correctness of Vasari's assertion.

Nor should such an interest be understood in an exclusive sense, but rather in a teleological sense, as a means for a more complete understanding of nature, which remains the central point of development of all of Raphael's art, as we have attempted to demonstrate.

The drawing in Venice, together with the analogous one in the Uffizi representing a battle of centaurs (F. 58, 59), with its graft of nervous Pollaiolesque outlines on forms which are more fleshy and are rhythmical in the surrounding space, filled with pools of shadow, in Leonardo's manner is one of the most beautiful examples of how Raphael conceived the study of the nude.

He did not immediately achieve a great fluency, and those which seem to be among his first experiments on the theme are sometimes awkward, as in the studies from Michelangelo's *David* (F. 82, 85, 87), which are, however, very important indications of Sanzio's early interest in the dominating nude-athlete of Michelangelo. Raphael assumes the Humanistic imposition of the figure in the foreground, but he compromises it with the surrounding space, either through luminous and Leonardesque proportions, with a greater or lesser thickness of the pen stroke, or through neo-quattrocentesque rhythmic cadences. In all, while Michelangelo is present as a thematic and formal example, the true point of reference for Raphael was still Leonardo, and this is evident in the subjects of his drawings, with their definite citations.

This is true of the drawing in Windsor (Fig. 34),[71] directly inspired by the composition by Leonardo for a standing Leda, which we know through paintings of his school or of Leonardesque derivation, and through sketches by Leonardo himself; Raphael perhaps came to know this composition more from the drawing than from the original painting. It is also true of the drawing in the Louvre (Fig. 35)[72] with a portrait of the bust of a girl, which is stylistically quite similar to the Windsor drawing and clearly derived from the *Gioconda*. While the *Leda*, as Castelfranco correctly has noted, must have greatly impressed Raphael for its classical, sculptural pose, which more skilfully rendered the balanced Peruginesque rhythms, the *Gioconda* proposed

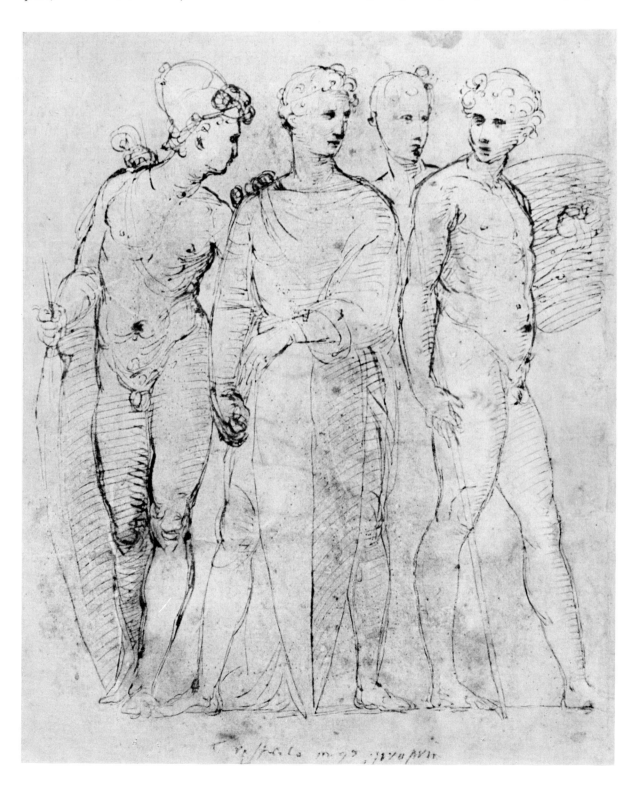

38 Study of four standing soldiers, one of them from the St. George by Donatello. Oxford, Ashmolean Museum (75).

334

to him, with infinite richness of psychological insight, both chromatic and spatial, models for portraits which he had already seen in Perugino and in the Flemings. Raphael's interest, however, did not consist so much in the study of the pose of the figure as in the atmospheric space in which the light plays, and the pools of shadow which the pen traces on the eyes, mouth and bust of the young girl show a sure ability to obtain pictorial effects solely with graphic means. Because of this the dating of about 1505 suggested for this drawing seems justified, as also for the paintings to which it is connected from time to time, the *Young Girl* in the Galleria Borghese and *Maddalena Doni* in the Pitti. It has in common with the latter the pose of the hands and the arrangement of the hair, while the expressive intensity of the face (although physically quite different), the motif of the two columns and the window sill which separate the various planes of the composition and which frame the soft landscape all serve to connect it with the former.

Less effective luminous contrasts and a more rigid, fifteenth-century pose, together with a greater perception in portraiture, in the still-Umbrian type of the model, characterize the drawing in the British Museum (Fig. 36),[73] which Fischel supposes to be from Raphael's Perugian period, but which was correctly believed by Passavant and now by Pouncey and Gere as from his Florentine period. The link is once more with the *Maddalena Doni*, with its somewhat doll-like and vaguely Leonardesque tone, and it cannot yet be connected with the truer portraits of a later date, such as *La Gravida*.

The discussion of the citations from Leonardo is pertinent to a very fine and famous drawing which, although linked with a dated painting, still presents uncertainties as to its chronological position. We place it here in order to follow in its various aspects the exchange between Raphael and Leonardo, but it also could be placed somewhat later in time because it has links with drawings that date from around 1507 and even with the first Roman works. This drawing is the one in Oxford (Fig. 37)[74] with studies for the fresco of S. Severo in Perugia,

335

40 Study for the Madonna del Granduca. Florence, Uffizi (77).

done in silver point on prepared paper in a clear neo-quattrocentesque style which was also dear to Leonardo and which we have already seen in Raphael.

The fresco of San Severo, we know, bears the date of 1505, about which critics have had some doubts, proposing a date of about 1505 for the beginning of the work but one toward 1507 for its completion. This makes the placement of the drawing somewhat more complicated, since its technical features seems to indicate a time immediately before the painted execution; however, it could also be a study made at the outset of the work and then put aside for a time, which would explain both the presence of sketches not relative to the fresco's theme and the difficulty of establishing exact parallels between figures in the drawing and those in the fresco. Indeed, if the studies of hands in the drawing are certainly for the figure of S. Giovanni Gualberto and the head in profile is similar to that of S. Mauro in the painting, the youthful head is quite problematic; it cannot be for the figure of S. Placido because the position of the body is reversed and indicates that the figure must have been at the right side of the fresco, although it is different from that of S. Benedetto, and it is impossible to establish whether it corresponded to the figure of S. Giovanni Gualberto, since the head in the painting has been totally erased.

Especially interesting the explicit link with Leonardo in the citation from the *Battle of Anghiari* which Raphael may have sketched from memory on the upper right of the sheet, and in the type of the head in profile, which seems an outright copy from Leonardo's drawings (e.g., those in Windsor, nos. 12276v, 12556). The special interpretation in a more classical and natural sense which Raphael offers of Leonardo goes beyond what the latter, in slightly caricaturesque tones, gives to his figures. Raphael, "has imparted to his imitation a delicacy and refinement of expression and an air of truthfulness beyond Leonardo's reach. He is here, in fact, seen surpassing Leonardo in his own particular field, just as he had already gone beyond his master Perugino" (Robinson).

An interpretation in this sense may be connected not only to Raphael's own nature but also to his friendship in these years with Fra Bartolommeo, according to Vasari and as we have often repeated here, precisely with regard to the S. Severo fresco, classically composed with figures of a solemn naturalness, as in the friar's art.

Certainly the friendship with Fra Bartolommeo meant more to Raphael on a spiritual ground than on a stylistic one: basically his affinity with the authoritative and somewhat older artist, who was less daring but not less curious, must have supported the young Umbrian artist's tendency for equilibrium and for a high " eclecticism " (the much discredited word can still be used in its etymological sense for Raphael). It is precisely the Perugia fresco, which clearly anticipates the division of the *Disputa*, that announces his relationship with the friar, both for its over-all aspect, which repeats features of Bartolommeo's *Judgment* of 1499, and for the severe arrangement of the single figures. Obviously the drawing, being a study of details, reveals less directly this relationship, except in the use of the silver-point technique, which is more sharp than in earlier examples. Still, Raphael's drawings that have evident citations from Fra Bartolommeo's types and manner are rare, and this is proof of what was said about the more spiritual importance rather than stylistic weight, of the friendship with Raphael.

In the most positive sense of the word, the eclecticism of Raphael reaches a high point in these years, as we can see in the drawings that reflect the whole vast range of the artist's Florentine interests. We have seen the breadth of the Leonardesque echo and the first shock of Michelangelo, the tendencies toward Pollaiuolo and Verrocchio and also Botticelli; we know from Vasari that Raphael admired and studied Masaccio in Florence (as Michelangelo had also done, but in the case of Raphael there is no graphic evidence of this admiration), and it is clear from the drawings that he studied the works of Donatello with profound interest.

It is symptomatic that Raphael would study the more youthful works of Donatello, those less insistent and more open to different solutions, such as the *St. George*. This statue which Perugino had already studied and which Michelangelo was now also studying, must have seemed to Raphael to be a paradigm, and he copied it several times, as in the Oxford drawing (Fig. 38) [75]

41 Studies for the Madonna del Belvedere. Chatsworth, Duke of Devonshire collection (79 b).

42 Study for the Madonna del Cardellino. Oxford, Ashmolean Museum (78).

·R·V·   337

43 Four sketches for the Madonna del Belvedere.
Vienna, Albertina (79 a).

44 Study for the Madonna del Belvedere. New
York, Metropolitan Museum, recto (80).

45 Study of a nude. New York, Metropolitan
Museum, verso (80).

in which it appears in a group with other soldiers taken from other sculptured motifs, according
to a system which was familiar to Raphael and which must have served merely the purpose of
compositional study (cf. the drawing in the British Museum, Fig. 90).

According to the intuition of Crowe-Cavalcaselle, the *St. George* now in Washington and the
relative cartoon in the Uffizi (Fig. 39) [76] are also related to Donatello's *St. George* and especially
to the low relief on the base. Raphael here reverses the compositional structure of his first
St. George, with the idea of making the horse and the knight run toward the background of the
picture, turning away from the spectator. That he had Donatello's relief in mind for this
motif seems to be further demonstrated in the figure of the princess, who keeps her arms folded

46 Studies for a Holy Woman and a Christ Crucified. Vienna, Albertina (81 b).

47 Six sketches of a Madonna and Child. Vienna,
Albertina, verso (84 a).

48 Study of a nude with hands joined, and of
an arm. Vienna, Albertina (81 a).

as in Donatello's version and functions in the composition as an element that provides an
opening onto the landscape background. A comparison with the drawing for the first *St. George*
(Fig. 32) shows that the time which had passed between the two (one or two years, if the second
is to be dated about 1506) had matured Raphael's enthusiasm for Leonardo, which was measured along with all the other influences: the detachment of the planes reflects the clean juxtaposition in fifteenth-century Tuscan sculpture; the broad landscape recalls Fra Bartolommeo,
while the linear intention which is so agitated in the first St. George is calmed, and the rhythms
return to an Umbrian purity, much less ingenuous in its now consummate " Attic quality ".

Raphael had achieved such mastery primarily through drawing exercises (besides, he did not
have many public commissions during the Florentine phase) and above all through the successive graphic elaborations of a theme which also in painting was especially dear to him: the
group of the Madonna and Child, with or without other figures. It was a theme which in its
long iconographic tradition and in its apparent simplicity presented compositional and psychological problems of a rather stimulating kind, especially after the very new solutions projected
by Leonardo and Michelangelo, from the *Adoration of the Magi* and the cartoon of St. Anne in
the first mentioned, to the *Bruges Madonna* and the *Doni Tondo* in the second.

Using such solutions as a starting point, Raphael worked hard in these Florentine years on this
theme, as his paintings also demonstrate, and he succeeded in giving it innumerable variations, with
an intellectual fertility which was nourished both by a loving adherence to nature and by all the
figurative stimulations that his Florentine experience provided. The drawings and the sketches
of the Madonna datable to this period number about fifty, some of which are connected with
compositions actually realized or realized in paintings, but the majority are so far from known
compositions as to appear ends in themselves, a free field of study and inventive elaborations, unlike
anything Raphael had done in drawing up to that time, and unlike anything he was to do later.

The small drawing in the Uffizi for the *Madonna del Granduca* (Fig. 40)[77] has signs of a circular
frame and of a landscape of which there are no traces in the painting, at least in its present
state; these elements better justify the curvilinear effects of the group, which maintains a still
fifteenth-century hieratical quality that is contradicted by the luminous effects, which are quite
close to those of Piero di Cosimo. The dating toward the early part of his Florentine period
usually proposed for the picture is confirmed by the drawing and by its evident stylistic separation from others for works usually datable years later.

In the drawing at Oxford for the *Madonna del Cardellino* (Fig. 42),[78] done around 1506, there
is an evident attempt to interconnect the three figures: the directional axes of the three heads; 339

50 Study for the Esterházy Madonna. Florence, Uffizi (82).

49 Study of a Madonna and Child and the head of St. Joseph, for the Madonna della Palma. Paris, Louvre (83).

the foot of the Child placed over that of the Virgin, according to the tender idea of the *Bruges Madonna;* the Infant St. John still separated from the group but placed in order to complete the base of the pyramid, with that " boyish and wholly lovable simplicity," which Vasari noted in the picture. The Madonna studied from the nude model as in the drawing also at Oxford (F. 122), with barely delineated draperies, shows a relationship with certain drawings by Fra Bartolommeo, while the Child is certainly derived from the one in the *Pitti Tondo* by Michelangelo, just as the Infant St. John is related to the same figure in the *Taddei Tondo.* But all is fused in a sweet simplicity which could only have been done by Raphael.

The motifs in the Madonna and Child compositions interconnected between themselves to an almost inextricable degree at times; for example, the drawing just mentioned, even though it is best related to the *Madonna del Cardellino,* is not too far from the ideas for the *Madonna del Prato,* also datable around 1506, in the pose of the head and the left arm of the Virgin and in the figure of the Infant St. John. For this picture there are a series of sketches which present, as in a cinematic sequence, the successive variations which the three figures were given before assuming the final pose of the painting—from the sheet in the Albertina (Fig. 43), which bears on its recto and verso studies relating to the *Madonna del Cardellino,* to the sketch in Chatsworth

52 Madonna and Child with an Angel. London, British Museum (85).

51 Various sketches for a Madonna and Child. London, British Museum (84 b).

(Fig. 41) where the two children embrace with a childlike and quite naturalistic turn, which Raphael renounces in the painting in favor of a more controlled presentation of the figures and their theological meanings. The sketch of the child on the upper right foreshadows the warm effects of the *Madonna della Tenda* or *della Seggiola*.[79]

A remarkable drawing in the Ashmolean Museum (F. 118) done in metal point, brush and wash and sanguine (one of the first examples of such a complex technique), shows the poses as they appear in the picture and in the definitive drawing in sanguine, recently rediscovered and now in the Metropolitan Museum.[80] It is an important sheet not only for its recto (Fig. 44), where Raphael in order to define the composition used, perhaps for the first time, the decisive and painterly technique of sanguine, but also for its verso (fig. 45), which shows a sketch of a nude that demonstrates how, together with all the Madonnas, Raphael also studied anatomy from nature during his Florentine stay. The problem of the destination of this sketch, which is believed with certainty to be the thief at the left side of a *Crucifixion* or *Deposition*, is quite interesting; these themes are not known in his paintings, but Raphael sketched them in other drawings during these years, such as those in the Albertina (Figs. 46, 48) for a Sorrowful Mary and for its nude male model, in which there is a clear echo of Michelangelo, because on the verso there are some soldiers inspired by the *Cascina* cartoon.[81]

Also connected with a painted work is the drawing in the Uffizi for the *Esterházy Madonna* (Fig. 50),[82] which unites high graphic quality to a new complexity of compositional problems, even within the extremely simple theme. The drawing with its measurements, the squaring, the pin-pricking and with its almost exact correspondence to the painting, is perhaps the first small cartoon. The most notable variations are in the gesture of the child's hand, in the curly head and the cross of the Infant St. John and above all in the landscape which in the painting appears with classical ruins that are not present in the drawing.

In order for Raphael to have achieved such balance, it must have been preceded by various other drawings on the type of those for the *Madonna del Prato* (Figs. 41, 43). The example of Michelangelo's figures is apparent, especially in the Infant St. John, which repeats the pose of the Child in the *Doni Tondo*, but Raphael brings to it the sweet and fleeting poetry that Leonardo inspired in him. Indeed, Leonardo's drawings for the cartoon with St. Anne return to mind because the cartoon created so much interest when it was shown in Florence in 1501: Raphael must have heard people talk about it and he could have known the preparatory drawings for it, since Michelangelo himself apparently copied from them (cf. Ashmolean Museum, Parker, no. 291). Perhaps no other drawing is more suited to Vasari's words: that Raphael

341

53 Study for the Child in La Belle Jardinière.
Oxford, Ashmolean Museum (87).

54 Study for La Belle Jardinière. Paris, Louvre
(86).

"surpassed [Leonardo] in sweetness and in a certain natural facility . . . [and] he was closer to him than any other painter, and especially in the grace of the colors."

The drawing in the Louvre for the *Madonna della Palma*, done in metal point and white lead on tinted rose paper, is of a less fluid manner and of a still fifteenth-century Leonardesque interpretation in the style of Lorenzo di Credi (Fig. 49).[83] Although the drawing is squared and below bears traces of the curved frame of the painting, it differs considerably from it in the pose of the Child, in the head of St. Joseph (who in the painting is in profile and in the drawing is foreshortened, in the manner of the spectators in Leonardo's *Adoration of the Magi*), and in the perspective of the figure of the Madonna, here with her legs shortened as if seen from above or in a convex mirror.

The technique and the motif of the turning Child are analogous to the recto side of another interesting sheet in the Albertina (plate XLI), which is one of a closely connected series of studies for a half-length Madonna with Child (F. 108-111, 136, 140). In this series there appears a type of Child which repeats to a greater or lesser degree the pose of the Child in Michelangelo's *Taddei Tondo*, a work which Raphael must have seen in the house of his patron and friend and which apparently he had copied in a drawing now in the Louvre (F. 108). The pose, which has a Leonardesque origin even in Michelangelo, was used by Raphael in his *Bridgewater Madonna*, of uncertain date; to this painting are related both the recto of the cited

56 Study of young girl in profile. Florence, Uffizi
(88).

55 Studies of figures which could be connected
with the St. Catherine in the National Gallery
of London. Oxford, Ashmolean Museum,
verso (90).

drawing in the Albertina and the handsome drawing in the British Museum which, as in the
verso of the other, also contains studies for the *Colonna Madonna* (Figs. 47, 51).[84]

The motifs of all these drawings are so interwoven among themselves and with those used
by Raphael in his paintings over the years that it remains quite difficult and basically of little
importance to connect these sketches to known works or to establish a relative chronology.
What is more interesting is the inventive richness which Raphael shows, and the fresh, very
personal manner with which he traces the figures on the page, now preoccupied more with the
compositional relationships between the figures than with the details of the hands or the head.

We now know which are the more likely exemplars of Raphael, although for example, if the
bald heads of the Madonnas and some of the tender but slightly rigid figures of children recall
Fra Bartolommeo, it may be asked which of the two was the real innovator, at a time when the
friar had not yet made known his best works and when Raphael, instead, showed himself to be
so sensitive and inventive. And with regard to Michelangelo, it seems to me that there is an
extraordinary ability on Raphael's part to distinguish in his work its most varied and secret
aspects, leaving aside what was too personal and incommunicable in Michelangelo's art.

The rare drawing in the British Museum for a *Madonna and Child with an Angel* (Fig. 52)[85] makes
us think precisely of certain summary outline drawings by Michelangelo (who often made them
for the purpose of reducing the image or for indicating the measurements to a stonecutter).
This is an early example of a composition which alters the usual grouping of the Virgin and

343

57 Standing woman in profile. Oxford, Ashmolean Museum (89 a).

58 Standing woman (St. Catherine?). Oxford, Ashmolean Museum (89 b).

Child with the addition of another figure, enlarging the pyramid and preparing the problems of the *Madonna with the Lamb* and the *Canigiani Madonna*.

The various drawings for *La Belle Jardinière* are re-elaborations of the pyramidal structure of the *Madonna del Prato* and the *Madonna del Cardellino*, although with greater freedom, given the diagonal placement of the figures. For this picture no elaborative sketches survive, though there are two highly finished studies in the Louvre and at Chantilly (F. 119), whose mutual connection is not very clear, since they are analogous and have similar variations with respect

59 Head for the St. Catherine in the National Gallery of London and studies of *putti*. Oxford, Ashmolean Museum, recto (90).

345

60 Cartoon for the St. Catherine in the National Gallery in London. Paris, Louvre (91).

61 Study for the Borghese Deposition. Oxford, Ashmolean Museum (93 a).

to the painting. In both, the pose and the dress of the Virgin and the figure of the Child are different while the Infant St. John of the painting is in the same pose as in the Chantilly drawing, but in the viewpoint of the Louvre drawing; notwithstanding the squaring, there is a more immediate rendering and the lower part of the Madonna has been studied from the nude model (Fig. 54).[86] The cartoon of the painting at Holkham Hall (F. 123-125) shows two variations for the left arm of the Infant St. John, as in these two drawings; the pose of the Child, instead, is the final one, which must have been studied from life in the sheet in Oxford where Raphael studied even the details of the feet, unusual for the Florentine years (Fig. 53).[87]

The broad stroke of the pen, concentrated in sparse pools of shadow on forms loosened by the light, and the sweet, thoughtful tone of these various studies of Madonnas are found again in drawings of a different type, not necessarily related to known paintings. For example, the sheet in the Uffizi (Fig. 56),[88] with an intense profile of a girl, recalls the already mentioned drawing in the Louvre (Fig. 35), but with a less obvious Leonardesque tone and a dryness in capturing the psychological and physical features of the model, which places it with such late portraits of the Florentine period as *La Gravida*.

Two summary sketches of a standing girl are quite similar in type (Figs. 57, 58),[89] and they are not directly connected with known compositions. Indeed, we cannot be sure of what the first drawing represents, whether a Virgin for a Visitation theme or a figure with a bundle, for some unspecified scene. The second drawing appears, instead, to represent a St. Catherine of Alexandria and is in a certain sense connected with the early ideas for the painting of this saint in the National Gallery in London. Such ideas are documented by a sheet in Oxford (Figs. 55,59),[90] which has on the recto a study for the head, similar in every way to the painting, together with various sketches of putti, and on the verso some studies from life for the full figure. The stupendous cartoon at the Louvre (Fig. 60)[91] is for the same saint; the somewhat frozen

ecstasy of the picture, as was also the case in the recto of the Oxford drawing, has a more
dramatic tone in the cartoon, since the point of view is slightly altered and forces the face
into a somewhat painful expression that is well-suited to the pathetic twisting of the torso,
clearly a Michelangelesque echo. The variations on the verso of the Oxford folio give evidence
that this twisting of the apparently classical pose, with subtle contrasts, had been carefully
studied by Raphael, perhaps in other drawings with which we are not familiar (cf. the copy in
Chatsworth, F. 206), and was originally less rigidly arranged.

No other work more than this cartoon shows how much the experience of Leonardo had
influenced the art of Raphael, who was then about to begin his Roman sojourn, contemporaneously with the Michelangelesque *tour de force* of the *Borghese Deposition*. The weight of the
sculptural forms derived from ancient statuary, the compact unity of the parts and of the facial
planes in foreshortening and in movement, the articulation of the anatomical structure beneath
the garments, do not relate to Michelangelo's intensity, but partake instead of the atmospheric
value of Leonardo, through shadings with the black pencil, softening of the contours, and an
" Attic " rhythm of linear surroundings.

63 Study for the Borghese Deposition. London,
British Museum, recto (94 b).

DRAWINGS FOR THE DEPOSITION AND FINAL FLORENTINE PERIOD

The key work of this moment is the *Deposition* now in the Borghese Gallery, painted by Raphael for San Francesco in Perugia and dated of 1507, but evidently commissioned from him some years earlier, as is shown by the slow development of the work, which can be followed through a series of preparatory drawings.

It is the first time we find so many general compositional studies for a single painting and this in itself gives evidence of Raphael's special dedication to this commission, not so much for the "social" importance of the commission itself (it was the first altarpiece commissioned from him since he had come to Florence that was destined for a public place), as for the commemorative-dramatic theme which he treated for the first time; it was a more difficult theme for him to resolve now, after his long, direct experience with Florentine art and its programmatic examples.

The studies for the large altarpieces that we have seen up to now were above all studies of details, of heads, hands, and draperies, along with a few quick sketches of the composition and the final small cartoon. But his Florentine apprenticeship had proposed to Raphael compositional problems and more complex thematic implications which he had studied in drawings, especially those of the Madonna and Child. Nothing was more natural, since he happened to obtain the commission from Atalanta Baglioni at the height of his Florentine experience, than that Raphael should hold the work in special regard and be anxious to find a suitable compositional context for its sorrowful theme, rather than concern himself with the minute details, in which he could by now consider himself quite skilled. He understood that for a theme of this kind what counted was the unified effect of the single parts and the expressive details of the single figures, and for this reason the drawings for the *Deposition* almost always contain several figures in group each one examined in his specific relation to the over-all theme. This had occured up to then only in the sketches for the Madonna and Child, to which the various drawings for the *Deposition* do indeed have an affinity of time and style, datable as they are between 1505 and 1507, which is the final date of the painting.

There are today a dozen autograph drawings for the work, to which there may be added one for God the Father in the *cimasa*, executed by Domenico Alfani (F. 180), and one for the Charity of the predella (F. 181). The precise chronological relation of the remaining drawings is

64 Standing man, from Michelangelo's St. Matthew. London, British Museum, verso (94 b).

impossible, because there are many missing links in the chain, as the copies from lost drawings attest (cf. Fig. 161): once these links are known, they could lead to notable variations in any reconstruction possible today, and assumptions in this sense are inevitably arbitrary, although it certainly would be fascinating to be able to follow step by step the development and evolution of this very famous work.[92]

What is possible today is the definition of two fundamental steps taken by Raphael in his conception of the works, that is, the passage from an ordinary interpretation of the subject as a Pietà or a Lamentation for the Dead Christ to a successive dramatization of it as the Carrying of the Body of Christ, at which the grieving Marys are present, an obligatory theme to commemorate the sorrow of the donor for the death of her son. A drawing in Oxford and one in the Louvre, with their relative detailed studies, are examples of the first interpretation.[93]

The Oxford drawing (Fig. 61) is certainly the more beautiful and the first of the series, closely connected to the best sketches of Raphael's early Florentine period, from that of the first *St. George* to those for the *Madonna del Prato* (see Figs. 32, 41, 43): the balanced relationship of the two groups of mourners united in the foreground by the dead Christ and in the background by the landscape have a neo-quattrocentesque scheme, along with luminous effects derived from Leonardo, which we have already seen in the sketches. The composition was inspired by the *Pietà* of Perugino, formerly in Santa Chiara in Florence, executed some ten years earlier, as Robinson noted, and it was a compositional type also taken over by Fra Bartolommeo and by Marcantonio Raimondi in his engraving (B. XIV, 37) inspired precisely by this drawing of Raphael and its analogous detail (Fig. 62) now in the British Museum. The two drawings in the British Museum[94] are in perfect concordance with it and they show the passage to a second, more dramatic interpretation (Fig. 65), the Carrying of the Body of Christ to the tomb, which was to be retained in the painting; apart from numerous variations in the details, the principal group of the picture was already established, especially in the later drawing of the two. The only noteworthy diversity concerns the right side with the sorrowful Marys, for which, in the painting, Raphael returned again to a static composition as in the already mentioned detail drawing in Oxford; the composition is one of pose and not of movement, as it is in the second drawing, in the British Museum. (Fig. 63).

It is commonly believed and it is possible that the idea of transforming the Pietà into the Carrying of the Body to the tomb had come to Raphael from the well-known engraving by Mantegna (B. XIII, 3). Nevertheless, Raphael was almost naturally carried to an evolution in a sense that was both narrative and epic by his matured experience with the programmatic, contemporary Florentine examples of monumental themes, first among them the two cartoons by Michelangelo and Leonardo, in which the movements of the figures were the basis of both, although they were highly diverse interpretations of the heroic subject matter.

Raphael's work substituted the pathetic for the heroic, but that he made use of the two great examples is demonstrated by the Leonardesque style of these two drawings and also by the evident Michelangelesque solutions of certain poses. In fact, Raphael's Christ recalls the Christ of the *Pietà* in St. Peter's, which Raphael could have known at least from drawings (Fischel supposes for this period a trip to Orvieto where Raphael would have once again studied Signorelli; could he not also have found a speedy way to Rome, before and perhaps precisely for the purpose of preparing the definitive drawing of 1508?), while the bearers are variations on Michelangelesque themes, as is demonstrated by the verso of one of the sheets in the British

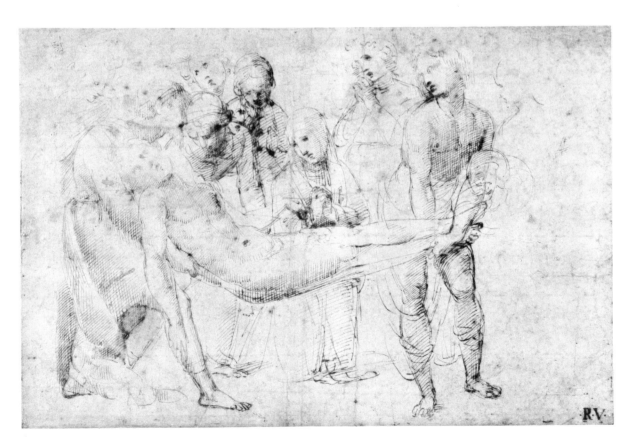

65 Study for the Borghese Deposition. London, British Museum (94 a).

349

67 Christ carried to the tomb. Oxford, Ashmolean
Museum, verso (95 a).

66 Sketch for the Magdalene of the Deposition.
Paris, Lugt collection (95 b).

350

Museum (Fig. 64), which is a copy of the *St. Matthew* by Michelangelo in the Florentine Duomo.
The reversed gesture of the *St. Matthew* must have inspired in Raphael possible solutions for
communicating the effort of the carriers, just as the spiral of the *Doni Madonna* must have
suggested to him the consoling gesture of the kneeling Holy Woman. For this right-hand portion
of the composition, we have no certain detailed studies, although it is logical to assume that
Raphael made some. For the central group, however, which is the most complex section of the
composition, there is the rather pathetic head of Christ (Fig. 67) in Oxford, a study of the bearers
(F. 173) also in Oxford, and a very lively sketch for the Magdalene, now in the Lugt Collection
(Fig. 66).[95]

These various studies are united and re-elaborated in a drawing in the Uffizi (Fig. 68),[96]
squared and partially pin-pricked, which seems to be the last of the series known to us, made
only a short time before the painted version, with which it shows variations only in secondary
elements. There must have been another one that does not appear here for only the right-hand
portion, which, together with this one, must have presented the total composition of the
painting, which apparently was conceived on two axes, subsequently united.

The Uffizi drawing is of a somewhat uneven quality (as is frequently true of this kind of
final study by Raphael), with highly finished zones that are almost dull in their even treatment,
as is true also of the copy of the St. Matthew, and with other, rapidly sketched zones, vividly
fresh and with fine lighting effects, as in the heads of the two women and in the leg of
St. John. One cannot exclude the possibility of another hand, perhaps that of a pupil, who
dulled Raphael's flowing strokes; however, perhaps for technical reasons even Raphael tended
to such cross-hatched chiaroscuro.

Of an analogous type to this drawing both because it underwent some reworking and because
it stands at a similar point of evolution with regard to the respective final solutions, are two
studies, the one in Windsor and one in Lille for *Madonna and Child*,[97] also to be dated at the
end of Raphael's Florentine period.

The Windsor study (Fig. 71) is for the *Canigiani Madonna*, for which there are various autograph drawings and copies of drawings (F. 130-133) that mark off the stages of the composition. Despite the high finish of certain parts, among the known studies it is the one furthest removed from the painting, both in the poses of the children, of the Virgin and St. Elizabeth and in the absence and the very impossibility of inserting the figure of St. Joseph in the composition. Still, it is the most beautiful of the series for the fluid movement of the bodies, especially vivid in the Child, and for the play of contrasts and of shadowy zones in the landscaped background.

To the spiral of the Virgin in the Leonardesque cartoon for the St. Anne the pose of the Madonna in the Lille drawing adds a broad abandon of the limbs derived from ancient statuary; according to the autograph inscription on the verso, the Lille drawing was sent by Raphael to his friend and collaborator Domenico Alfani. The allusion that the same inscription makes to a unpaid sum owed by Atalanta Baglioni has permitted the dating of the drawing to 1507-8 and at the same time is testimony of the links which Raphael still maintained with Perugia (Fig. 69).

He must still have had various interests there and a workshop, perhaps entrusted to various assistants and to Alfani, who a few years later executed the altarpiece for San Simone ai Carmini in Perugia, now in the Pinacoteca, copied faithfully from this drawing by Raphael. Since it is squared only up to the height of the figures, as Crowe-Cavalcaselle had noted, that is, up to the point in which Alfani's picture shows no variation with regard to Raphael's

68 Study for the Borghese Deposition. Florence, Uffizi (96).

351

352

69 Study for an altarpiece with the Holy Family, St. Anne and St. Joachim. Lille, Wicar Museum (97 b).

71 Study for the Canigiani Madonna. Windsor, Royal Library (97 a).

70 Study for the S. Bruno in the Madonna del Baldacchino. Florence, Uffizi (98).

drawing, it may be held that the squaring and the evident reworkings done by another hand over the original strokes were done by Alfani, who stiffened the soft effects of the pen, just as he later gave a sterile aspect to the painted execution.

" Among the large number of Raphael's drawings one does not find another up to this time which has more perfect lines, a more correct symmetry, more true attitudes and each appropriate to the specific figure, than this one " (Crowe-Cavalcaselle, I, p. 404). And, in fact, no composition by Raphael was so sage and novel in its fanlike development, where contrapuntal Leonardesque lighting effects (consider the *Canigiani Madonna* and the *Madonna of the Lamb*) and Michelangelo's contrasts are reduced to something else, in Raphael's own manner, and are mastered in a fully classical relationship. To this, the example of Fra Bartolommeo was probably not extraneous, if, according to Fischel, it was precisely from the *Assumption* which the friar delivered in 1508 to the Compagnia dei Contemplanti in 1508, now in Berlin, that Raphael took up once again the motifs of the three musical angels above.

It is also from this time that we have the picture which has stirred the most conjecture about the connections between Raphael and Fra Bartolommeo; this was the *Madonna del Baldacchino*, left unfinished by Sanzio when he set out for Rome. Among the series of drawings related to the picture (F. 142-148), only the one in Chatsworth (F. 143) serves to document the original idea of the painting, which was not excessively altered by the later finishing and by the restorations of Cassana; but the state of conservation of the drawing is such as to render any judgment difficult, and its value remains above all documentary, just as the variant in the Louvre for the Madonna (F. 144) gives evidence, instead, that Raphael still extracted from his studies for altarpieces certain thematic digressions for their own sake.

The best proof of Raphael's graphic quality during the elaboration of the painting is given by the little drawing in the Uffizi for the S. Bruno (Fig. 70),[98] which for its new technique of ink and watercolor over large areas is a prelude to the studies for the *Disputa*. The drawing is squared and, because of its variations from the Chatsworth drawing and its strong parallel with the relevant figure in the painting, it appears to preceed the execution of the painting 353

73 Group of three musicians. Oxford, Ashmolean
Museum, recto (95 a).

72 Sketch of two standing nude figures. Bayonne,
Bonnat Museum (99 a).

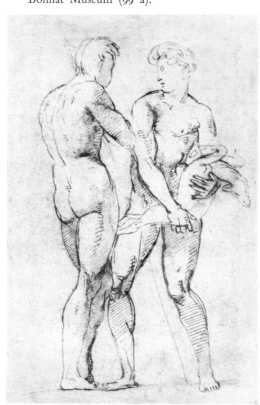

by very little. Its connection with Ghiberti's St. Sebastian, proposed by Fischel, gives further confirmation of the interest Raphael had for various aspects of Florentine art; however, the very new style of this sheet, pictorial, lively but extremely measured, in all, classical, shows the absolute autonomy of Raphael's choices. The Leonardesque expression, evoked again for example by the technique of other drawings for the same picture (F. 145, 147), takes on the solemnity of Fra Bartolommeo, but within a kind of abstraction of the figure in a revived manner of Piero della Francesca.

The Roman Period

THE BEGINNING OF THE ROMAN SOJOURN

Raphael was ripe for the Roman experience with its possibilities for total immersion in classical art; but from the time of his last Florentine works, he had showed an insistent desire for observing antique works, of which there were certainly many examples in Florence. The recto of the Oxford drawing of the Christ for the *Deposition* (cf. note 95), which represents three musicians and appears to have been directly inspired by an ancient relief or cameo, attests this interest; it is especially evident in the firm head of the woman, so close to his Madonna types of the period, and the figure of the young musician at the right, worthy of a Greek vase (Fig. 73). There are other examples of the same type (cf. F. 88, 101, 102, 197, 199). The musician of the Oxford drawing is connected in type and style with some studies of nudes in motion (Figs. 72, 75, 76),[99] often in groups or about to do battle, which are considered among the last drawings by Sanzio in Florence at the culmination of his experience of the graphic and sculptural art of Pollaiuolo, of Michelangelo and Leonardo, and with elements from Signorelli as well. They are themes and manners we already know but they are developed with greater formal knowledge and a dramatic connection between the figures, which shows that the laborious elaboration of the *Borghese Deposition* and the resolution of the problems raised by it had been effected. It is not accidental that this group of sheets includes motifs from works of the final Florentine phase and of the first phase of the Roman period, in such a way as to make it difficult to determine whether a given drawing was made in Florence and then developed for Roman works, or whether it was made in Rome from the memory of the most admired works in the Tuscan capital.

A study of nudes in the British Museum (Fig. 74) is a symptomatic case, which, as Pouncey and Gere note, unites echoes of the *Cascina* cartoon with motifs that are to return in the engraving of the *Massacre of the Innocents* (cf. Figs. 85, 87, 88). In this sense the drawing at Oxford (Fig. 77)[100] is especially interesting, since on the recto there is a study which can be interpreted either as the Carrying of the Body of Christ (according to an indication of an old inventory of the Antaldi Collection from which it came, and, as such, to be connected with the *Borghese Deposition*) or as the Carrying of the Body of Adonis (according to the interpretation of Mariette, who was then in possession of the drawing); on the verso of the same sheet there is a study for a Temptation of Adam (Fig. 78), which was to reappear in an engraving by Marcantonio (B. XIV, 1). Apparently Raphael either had drawn the recto while still in

74 Sketch of five male nudes. London, British Museum (99 b).

355

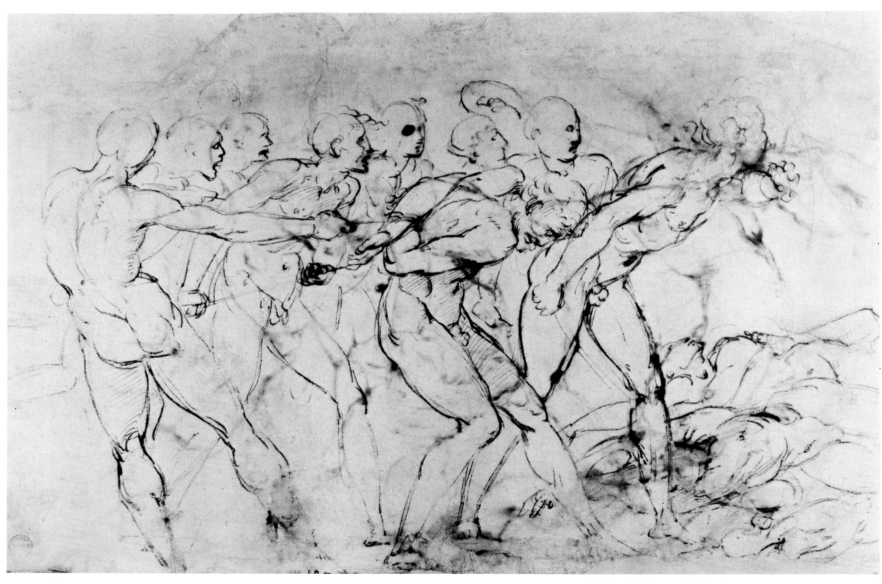

77 Christ (?) carried to the tomb, or the death of Adonis (?). Oxford, Ashmolean Museum, recto (100).

◁ 75 Battle scene with prisoners. Oxford, Ashmolean Museum, recto (99 c).

◁ 76 Battle scene with prisoners. Oxford, Ashmolean Museum, verso (99 c).

Florence when he was elaborating the ideas for the *Deposition* and brought the sheet to Rome, where he executed the drawing on the verso, or he derived the idea from it for further drawings to give to Marcantonio. It seems certain that Raphael brought to Rome many of the studies made during the Florentine years and gradually made use of them for certain motifs, as is attested by so many sketches of Madonnas which, connected in part with earlier works, are related also to paintings executed during the Roman years.

At this point it is necessary to specify that, especially in the first period of the Roman phase, Raphael did not have many occasions to vary his graphic experience. The truly great discovery that he was able to make in Rome at the end of 1508 was that of ancient art and of the new architecture of Bramante. As a friend of Bramante, Raphael must have already been acquainted with his work (according to Vasari it was Bramante who actually brought Raphael to Rome), just as he must have had some knowledge of the study of ancient art, by which he had already been stimulated for some time, especially during the later part of his Florentine sojourn, along with Fra Bartolommeo. But neither the enormously amplified spectacle of ancient art nor the vision of the new architecture could have presented him with exceptional stimuli from the point of view of drawing, as the works of Leonardo and Michelangelo had during his early Florentine years.

On the other hand the major part of the artists whom Raphael found active in Rome were already well known to him, especially those who had a specific graphic experience, such as Perugino, Pinturicchio and Michelangelo. Perhaps Sodoma was unknown to him and he must have found him interesting right from the start, but it is difficult to say to what degree Sodoma was then a draftsman and what his relationship was in terms of giving and receiving with regard to the more gifted Umbrian. The painted works which Raphael saw then in Rome were linked to a culture which he already knew and which he had already experimented, in its newest elements, at the Florentine source. The fervor of artistic activity, the patronage, the literary and philosophical interests of Julius II's court and the vision of ancient art in its

357

natural setting were certainly fundamental for the evolution of Raphael's personality; still, his experience as a draftsman was not greatly altered by this, except for the reflections that a radical change of social and cultural environment would naturally leave.

THE CEILING OF THE STANZA DELLA SEGNATURA

The first sure drawings for Roman works demonstrate this continuity, and they are those for the ceiling of the Stanza della Segnatura (F. 224-232, 237) executed presumably at the end of 1508, if the pictorial decoration of the ceiling is to be dated to the end of that year or the beginning of the following one.[101] This notable group of drawings, in fact, does not reveal strong continuity of solutions with regard to the style and problems of the last Florentine drawings: only the variety of techniques used and the range of ideas, sometimes dramatic, solemn, or concerned with plastic effects or with the luminous qualities of the surfaces, separate this group of drawings in their richness of problems from the earlier ones, and make one feel, as Fischel has so well emphasized, how much effort Raphael had to apply to this first and very important Roman commission. And, notwithstanding his affable character, Raphael must have felt quite alone in this enterprise, with all eyes on him and his audacious competition with the greatest artists of the period; he was certainly surrounded by envy and without skillful helpers, since the well-staffed Roman workshop was still in the future.

The first drawing of the series is the one in the Louvre relative to the section with the *Temptation of Adam and Eve* (Fig. 79).[102] The stylistic relation with the above-mentioned drawings of nudes is such as to make us think that this one also could have been one of the sheets Raphael brought with him from Florence. The fact that this drawing, at first sight, seems to have studies for a St. John the Baptist, rather than for an Adam, could show its original

78 The Temptation of Adam. Oxford. Ashmolean Museum, verso (100).

358

79 Five sketches of a male nude, some for the Temptation of Adam, from the ceiling of the Stanza della Segnatura. Paris, Louvre (102).

destination as different from the Vatican ceiling; of the whole drawing, only the idea for the seated figure in spiral form was used for the Adam on the ceiling, and none of the variations proposed corresponds perfectly to the fresco.

Also the sketch for *Theology* (Fig. 81)[103] in Oxford is connected without stylistic interruption to the Florentine drawings, from the one for the *Esterházy Madonna*, for example, to those for the *St. Catherine* or the *Deposition* (cf. Figs. 50, 59, 61-67). The softer sweep of the broad, quick strokes of the pen makes us think also of Filippino (of whose frescoes at the Minerva there are drawings which Fischel attributed to the workshop of Raphael, cf. F., V, Figs. 194-196), as also of the summary quality of the Sienese artists then active in Rome, such as Sodoma and Peruzzi. The extreme vivacity of the sketch, which is expressed also in the rapid gesture of the figure, is restrained in the fresco in favor of a more classical arrangement and a more harmonious rapport with the circular form of the moldings of the ceiling, according to the variation of the left arm hinted at in the drawing. Certainly for the purposes of the general painted version, Raphael made a wise selection in that variation, which left more space for the two lateral *putti*; but the charm of the vivid naturalness in this sketch leads to the regretful observation that the solemnity of the decoration had forced Raphael to control the fresh impulses of his first idea.

The phases leading up to the figure in the fresco are not known to us but it is probable that Raphael had made after this drawing various other studies for the figure, perhaps with different techniques or methods of drawing. The existence in Lille of a black-pencil drawing for the right-hand *putto* (Fig. 80)[104] demonstrates this; the drawing was also surely made from life, but it is in a stage closer to the corresponding painted figure and therefore closer than that for the *Theology* at the moment of its execution in fresco. This drawing, with its soft play of lights in the manner of Fra Bartolommeo, was perhaps preceded in turn by a more summary ink sketch and then followed by a true cartoon, such as that in the British Museum for one of the lateral *putti* of *Poetry* (F. 229).

For the latter there is at Windsor a preparatory study (Fig. 82),[105] which, together with those cited, gives us an interesting sequence of Raphael's method of working. The Windsor drawing in fact bears an evident mark of the stylus, presumably carried over from a preceding and more summary sketch, that traces the nude figure; on this, then, Raphael placed the form of the new figure, now draped and more carefully delineated, and now quite similar to the painted version, except for the more romantically inspired position of the head (" with the air and beauty of an immortal face," as Vasari was to say) and the absence of garments on the bust. The squaring of the whole sheet and the accent of curved lines at the corners

359

81 Sketch for the figure of Theology on the ceiling
    of the Stanza della Segnatura. Oxford, Ashmo-
    lean Museum (103).

80 *Putto* with scroll for the figure of Theology
    on the ceiling of the Segnatura. Lille, Wicar
    Museum (104).

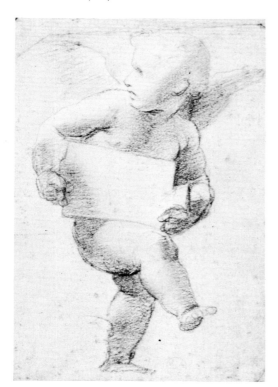

360

that allude to the *tondo* of the frame, indicate that this is the drawing immediately preparatory
to the cartoon, whose existence is attested by the already cited fragment of the *putto* in the
British Museum (F. 229).

Leaving aside these strictly technical considerations, there would remain much more to say
on the very high quality of this figure, as solemn as one by Fra Bartolommeo and as sweet
as a Perugino, or as sensual as a Sodoma and as frank as an ancient statue, but with that
sublime " grace " that only Raphael could give and which had begun to amaze the whole
of Rome.

For the rectangular scenes in the corners of the ceiling, besides the already mentioned Louvre
drawing of Adam (Fig. 79), there are other sketches (but not cartoons or definitive studies,
which Raphael must surely have made) for the *Judgment of Solomon* and for *Astronomy* which
demonstrate the particular technical accomplishment of Raphael in these fertile moments.
Unknown up to that time was the use of metal point on prepared paper for a summary sketch
of the whole, as in the case of the Oxford drawing for the *Judgment of Solomon* (Fig. 83);[106]
while the appearance on the same sheet of a rapid sketch in black pencil (little used during
the Florentine period) with a detailed pen drawing is unusual, as is the conjunction of a pen
sketch with a large study in sanguine (also little used by Raphael before this time), as occurs
in two sheets in the Albertina for the *Judgment of Solomon* (Figs. 85, 86) and for the *Massacre of
the Innocents* and for *Astronomy* (Figs. 84, 87).[107]

The style of these sheets is in perfect concordance with the relative frescoed scenes " all full of *senso* and sentiment, worked with pen with a very good design and vaguely gracious color " (Vasari).

But the most interesting fact is that those sheets, connected as they are with the frescoes on the ceiling of the Stanza della Segnatura, also contain ideas for a work of an entirely different character and purpose, that is, for the *Massacre of the Innocents*, which Raphael passed on to Marcantonio Raimondi for engraving; on the basis of these sheets, its conception could be dated at the beginning of the work for the Stanze, independently of the fact that Raimondi actually may have engraved it a few years later.

It is almost natural that, studying the violent and pathetic theme of the *Judgment of Solomon*, the idea came to Raphael of the *Massacre of the Innocents*, so that the ideas which he had elaborated in the " very beautiful nudes, women and *putti* " in dramatic movement should not be lost. That this idea was conceived for some other purpose perhaps for a painting, and then

82 Study for the figure of Poetry on the ceiling of the Segnatura. Windsor, Royal Library (105).

361

83 Sketch for the Judgment of Solomon on the ceiling of the Segnatura. Oxford, Ashmolean Museum (106).

was given to Raimondi for engraving, is not important, at least until there is some documentary proof of it. For the engraving there are two drawings, executed in the same sense as the engraving, one with pen in the British Museum with all nude figures (F. 233) and the other with sanguine at Windsor (Fig. 88)[108] with the figures of the mothers clothed. A rather interesting technical aspect of Raphael's method of working is that this last drawing was evidently taken from the one in the British Museum, which is pin-pricked and of the same dimensions, and then of having been delineated in summary fashion with a stylus, and then passed over again more accurately with sanguine, but only in certain parts, perhaps those that Raphael had not yet set clearly in his mind. It is notable that the great lacuna in the sanguine drawing in Windsor is filled by the above-mentioned drawing in the Albertina (Fig. 87), which seems, therefore, to be a very free complementary drawing executed shortly thereafter.

84 Sketch for the figure of Astronomy on the ceiling of the Segnatura. Vienna, Albertina, verso (107 a).

85 Study for the false mother in the Judgment of Solomon on the ceiling of the Segnatura and for an executioner in the Massacre of the Innocents. Vienna, Albertina, verso (107 b).

86 Study of an executioner for the Judgment of Solomon on the ceiling of the Segnatura. Vienna, Albertina, recto (107 b).

87 Studies for an executioner and for a mother in the Massacre of the Innocents. Vienna, Albertina, recto (107 a).

88 Study for the Massacre of the Innocents. Windsor, Royal Library, recto (108).

Compared with the pen drawing in the British Museum, Raphael has added in this one in Windsor the clothed figures of the women on the left and on the right in an immediate style with lines that are softly drawn down, as Polidoro da Caravaggio was to use later. On the verso there is a study of a plate (Fig. 89), which is a fantastic transposition into mythological terms of the same dramatic theme in a rather new manner of drawing with lines that are

89 Study of a plate with sea gods. Windsor,
Royal Library, verso (108).

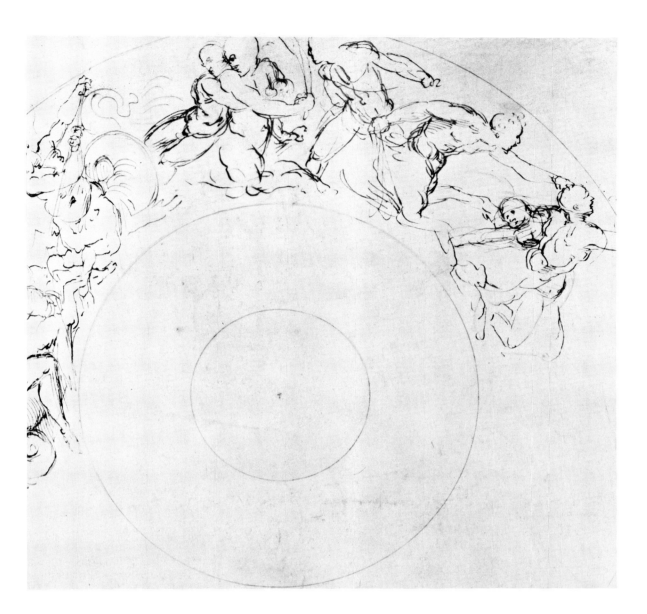

90 Sketches of various figures and a standing
Venus. Florence, Uffizi, verso (109 a).

91 Sketches of an old man and of a nude youth. Lille, Wicar Museum, recto (109 b).

92 Sketches of nude figures and of heads and a young man (Francesco Maria della Rovere? for the Disputa?). Lille, Wicar Museum, verso (109 b).

almost only contours, like those on an ancient vase, a manner which was later admired by Perino and by Giulio Romano. Worth nothing at this point, is the existence of autograph drawings by Raphael for decorative works of art which were to have a large following in the workshop and were to lead to the great popularity of objects of applied art inspired by Raphael's works.

The large quantity of definitive studies for the soldier on the left, the protagonist of the *Massacre of the Innocents*, on whom the eye of the observer falls first, may be pure coincidence. But it is also possible that Raphael gave special attention to the study of this key figure of the composition which he conceived in a dual aspect of classical derivation (it seems inspired by the Dioscuri of the Quirinale) and of defiance of Michelangelo, in the dynamic presentation of the large nude in the foreground.

It is relevant to mention here some other examples of engravings by Marcantonio based upon Raphael's ideas, but we shall leave to others in the present volume a more complete discussion of the importance and the manner of this collaboration between the neophyte engraver and the young master whose star was in the ascendance.

From Vasari we know many of the subjects that Marcantonio Raimondi engraved for Raphael, first among them the *Lucrezia* in Rome, but there are very few drawings by Raphael which would specifically document the collaboration. We have seen the *Temptation of Adam* (Fig. 78) and the group of sheets for the *Massacre of the Innocents*; more uncertain is the relation between the drawing of the *Last Supper* in the Albertina (F. 220) and the relative theme engraved by Raimondi (B. XIV, 26). Better documented, instead, is the idea for the print with the standing Venus (B. XIV, 311) which reveals few variations compared to a Raphael drawing in the British Museum, where the subtlety of the metal point on paper, with its minute interweavings in the shadows, seems to rival the effects of the engraver's tool.

As Pouncey and Gere note, this engraving by Marcantonio is the pendant to one representing Apollo (B. XIV, 335), also derived from a lost drawing by Raphael which was a study of the statue of the god in a niche for the *School of Athens*, and therefore the drawing of Venus could also be considered contemporary with the fresco. Still its closeness also to the fresco of the *Disputa*, or at least to the first ideas for it, seems documented by the verso of a sheet in the Uffizi (Fig. 90) which represents a Venus in a rather analogous pose to the one in the engraving, and a figure of a youth similar to the presumed figure of Francesco Maria della Rovere, in the *Disputa*. On the other hand, a sheet in Lille (Figs. 91, 92) in a style analogous to that in the Uffizi[109] has on the recto the figure of an Apollo (the theme of the engraving by Marcantonio pendant to the Venus) and of an old man, often identified as the Aristotle of the *School of Athens* but in reality of a traditional type that could also be related to the wise men of the *Disputa;* on the verso of the Lille sheet there are various sketches, among them a standing figure which unites motifs of the Apollo from the recto with motifs from the figure of Francesco Maria della Rovere for the *Disputa.*

As the many sketches of the Madonna and Child interwove ideas for various and different paintings on analogous schemes, building on each other, so in these Roman sketches we see an interconnection of motifs for the two major frescoes of the first Stanza, without however more than a vague indication that they were destined to one or the other, implying a precise chronological connection.

A rather logical consequence could be deduced from this: that from the beginning of his work on the frescoes Raphael had in mind the general scheme of the entire decoration and above all some key figures of the two principal scenes (as for example, the gesturing youth in the *Disputa* and the central philosopher of the *School of Athens*), and that therefore there are interwoven on probably contemporary sheets motifs of figures executed at different times, with that difference of style which distinguishes the two frescoes from each other. There are no other sketches that confirm this hypothesis and there are no early general sketches for the *School of Athens* which, by means of comparison with those for the *Disputa*, could clarify how and if the general outlines of the two frescoes were worked out contemporaneously.[110]

93 Model for the left half of the Disputa. Windsor, Royal Library (111).

94 Model for the upper section of the Disputa. Oxford, Ashmolean Museum (112).

95 Study for the lower left side of the Disputa. London, British Museum (114 a).

THE DISPUTA DEL SACRAMENTO

For the *Disputa*, an exceptional series of sketches documents the variations in the composition before Raphael arrived at the final solution as we see it in the fresco.

The series is exceptional both from the quantitative point of view, since until this work such a large number of drawings of the whole are known only for the *Deposition*, and from the technical point of view because it is the first time we find sketches in Raphael, in the pictorial sense of the term, that is, sheets with direct application of watercolor and white lead over the penciled outlines. An anticipation of the new technique was seen in the group of drawings for the *Madonna del Baldacchino* (cf. note 98) but now Sanzio displayed a chromatic richness until then unused, keeping a fundamental monochromatic effect; this chromatism elicited doubts

368

96 Study for the lower part of the Disputa. Windsor, Royal Library (113).

97 Study of nude figures for the lower left side of the Disputa. Frankfurt, Städelsches Institut (114 b).

from many, beginning with Morelli, regarding Raphael's autograph of these sketches. Today, however, there is a general tendency to accept them, above all for their genuine quality and for the variations which show themselves as studies " for " and not studies " from " the fresco.

The most interesting one is the Windsor sheet (Fig. 93),[111] which studies the entire left half of the *Disputa*, documenting the difference between the executed fresco and that which must have been the first or at least one of the first ideas for it. The choice of an architectural framework with side wings (the right part of the sketch had to be envisioned from the left side) is striking, and in it there are motifs from Pinturicchio and Ghirlandaio that are fully quattrocentesque. It is not surprising for the young Raphael just arrived in Rome, who had

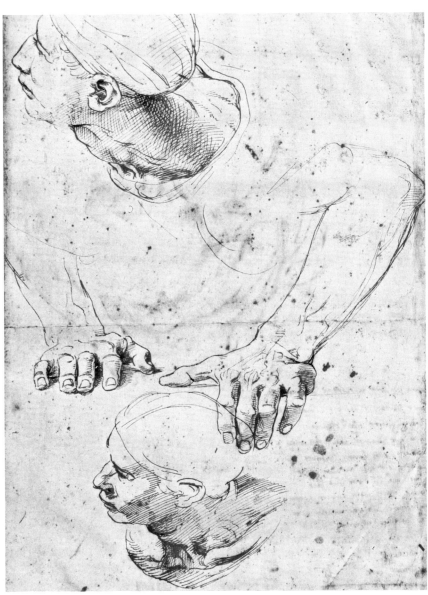

◁ 98 Study of a leaning man for the Disputa, and sonnet. Montpellier, Fabre Museum, recto (115 b).

◁ 99 Study of a leaning man and a head, for the Disputa. Montpellier, Fabre Museum, verso (115 b).

101 Studies of heads and hands for the so-called Bramante of the Disputa. Paris, Louvre (117).

◁ 100 Sketches of figures for the Disputa, and sonnet. London, British Museum (115 a).

found there as immediate examples for large wall frescoes precisely the examples in the Sistine Chapel, in the Ara Coeli and in the Borgia apartments and, a suggestion of airy heavenly vaults, the apse of SS. Apostoli, painted by Melozzo.

From the thematic point of view, the Windsor sheet is striking for the absence of the altar with the Host and the alignment of Christ and the Virgin (on the other side perhaps John the Baptist) in the same upper zone with other saints, two on each side; meanwhile, the Saints (Evangelists?) and the Prophets of the middle zone are paired instead in a series that continues as in the fresco, according to the system of S. Severo and the well-known example of Fra Bartolommeo in Santa Maria Nuova. The lower zone, with the learned men in discussion, already has the movement in planes which was to characterize the fresco, although with a more centralized arrangement. On the other hand, the line of the landscape and the balustrade which, given the absence of the altar, clearly marks the horizon at the center, confers on the whole a simplicity of planes which in the fresco was to be somewhat more complex, both in the various groups and in the interaction between the various groups.

The clearly Leonardesque inspiration is striking from the stylistic point of view: the monochrome technique, which utilizes to the best advantage the play of light and shade, is the same as in Leonardo's unfinished pictures; the groupings of the figures are those of the *Adoration of*

371

102 Studies for the flying angels in the Disputa. London, British Museum (116).

103 Study of seated man, for the figure of Adam in the Disputa. Florence, Uffizi (118 a).

104 Study for the figure of St. Stephen in the Disputa. Florence, Uffizi (118 b).

the Magi by Leonardo, from which the characteristic old men and ephebic youths are taken. On the left, the gesturing allegorical figure (the supposed Beatrice) is typical and is derived from a well-known drawing by Leonardo in Windsor (no. 12581); this is a figure had been sketched previously (Figs. 90, 92) and was a favorite of Raphael. He retained it in the fresco in the guise of the so-called Francesco Maria della Rovere. Besides, other types from this first sketch were to be retained in the fresco, from the figures of the divine group to St. Peter, from the seated scholar with the book on his knee to the youth with the long hair bending forward.

Executed with the same technique, but still more painterly in the soft dilution of the shadows and with the same compositional scheme, is another sketch at Oxford for the upper part of the *Disputa* (Fig. 94), which is often linked to an analogous sheet in Chantilly representing the lower part.[112] The latter seems to have been the most laboriously executed part of the entire composition because there are still other studies of the whole, with variations always more similar to the final solution. This does not mean to exclude the possibility that Raphael had made other studies for the upper part as well, at least for elaborating the alignment in a continuous row of the Saints and Prophets and the emergence of the divine group: but this was, in essence, the easiest zone of the scene, once the arrangement for it was selected, and it is probable that it required a lesser number of compositional sketches. The difficult elaboration of the lower zone, instead, is documented by autographs and by copies (F. 260-263, 267-269, 273) and by many detailed studies for single figures (F. 270-272, 274-281).

In the first group, a drawing at Windsor is unique (Fig. 96),[113] since we find Raphael there dealing with types already sketched in earlier sheets in Windsor and Chantilly, but in a more simple technique, black pencil, which until now he used only for detailed studies of heads or hands, or draperies and which, here for the first time since he went to Florence, is used in a compositional sketch. The manner of the Windsor sheet is quite an abbreviated one, which would almost make us doubt it as an autograph if there were not some completely Raphael-esque characteristics to confirm his authorship (the head of the youth behind the seated scholar who is reading, the leg and the foot of the latter, the group of figures standing at the extreme right), and if it were not for the certainty that we are dealing here with an immediate sketch, surely not a copy, that takes up motifs of the two preceding sketches in order to better specify the spatial planes and to work out the variations in the gestures.

The bilateral symmetry of these early ideas for the lower part of the *Disputa* could not have overly satisfied Raphael, who was to further alter the planes and gradually differentiate the poses and the types to the point of achieving solutions close to those in the fresco; there are traces of these solutions in a sketch in Frankfurt for only the left-hand part (Figs. 95, 97).[114]

The techniques of these two sheets in pen are more familiar to us, but notable in the first sheet is the use of a light watercolor which perhaps served Raphael to test the effects of the shadows in the fresco, and in the second the return to the nude model even after having made studies of the entire composition with clothed figures, according to the Florentine custom typical

105 Study for the figure of Diogenes in the School of Athens. Frankfurt, Städelsches Institut (120 a).

106 Studies of figures and of a head of Medusa
       for the School of Athens. Oxford, Ashmolean
       Museum (120 b).

of Fra Bartolommeo. The pin-pricking, the traces of squaring and the extreme refinement of
the stroke demonstrate that the drawing in Frankfurt was for a long time considered by Raphael as the definitive one, so much so that he carried it over onto other sheets of studies and
retained the gestures from it in many figures of the fresco. It may be held that the rhythmic
articulation of these groups of highly individualized nudes seemed to him to be too clear a
challenge to Michelangelo, who was working in the nearby Sistine Chapel, and that therefore
Raphael sought in the fresco not only to cancel the anatomical elements with soft, colored
draperies, studied in detailed sheets (F. 274, 275, 281) but also to loosen the gestures of the
figures and to fuse them in a Leonardesque manner in reciprocal communication (cf. the two
figures near the altar in the Frankfurt sheet).

That Leonardo and Michelangelo are the two constant poles of references for Raphael here
in Rome as in Florence is also demonstrated by the few studies that have come down to us for
the right side of the lower zone of the *Disputa*. An early, very vivid sketch in the British
Museum (Fig. 100) for the two figures conversing at the side, traced with a painterly line,
is developed in two later and nearly definitive studies for the figure leaning on the balustrade,
at Montpellier (Figs. 98, 99),[115] in which the Leonardesque stroke of the broad pen is united to
a structural interest and a plastic play of chiaroscuro networks derived from the graphic style
of Michelangelo. We are dealing here, too, with first ideas and not with final studies, as is demonstrated by the use Raphael himself makes of these two sheets as pages for poetry notes and for
figures to be carried onto other drawings more directly preparatory to the fresco.

Precisely of which type these drawings were, or in what technique, is not easy to say, both
because of the lacunae in the corpus of Raphael's drawings, and because it is probable that accord-

ing to the various problems, Sanzio used different ways and different techniques to move from the sketches to the studies and from these to the " modello " and then to the cartoon. After the pen sketches of the type of those in Montpellier or that in Oxford for the flying angels (F. 299-300), and after others in black pencil with further details, as that non-definitive one in the British Museum, also for the flying angels (Fig. 102),[116] it is possible that Raphael began to study his figures, nude or draped, from the living model, in a more detailed manner, either with black pencil or with the old technique of metal point on prepared paper. With this technique he studied, shortly before the painted execution, the details of the heads, hands and draperies, as he had done for the altarpieces of his Umbrian-Marchigian period, and as he was to do for the *School of Athens*.

We see in such a context the Louvre drawing for the so-called Bramante on the left in the *Disputa* (Fig. 101),[117] a figure which does not appear in any of the surviving plans for the lower part and which, with its absolutely Leonardesque type, substitutes the figures in the manner of Fra Bartolommeo of the British Museum sketch and the Michelangelesque nudes of the Frankfurt study (cf. Figs. 95, 97).

With a soft black pencil often heightened with white lead, Sanzio drew studies of the details of the draperies or of entire figures very close to the final version, thus approaching the technique of the true cartoon (a fragment of which is at the Louvre, F. 303) and the effect of the fresco. Examples of this type survive for figures in both zones of the *Disputa*, and especially for those in the upper one (F. 274, 281, 291, 296). Among them are the two drawings in the Uffizi for the figures of Adam and St. Stephen (Figs. 103, 104).[118] The first, with clearly Michelangelesque

107 Group of nudes fighting, for a low relief in the School of Athens. Oxford, Ashmolean Museum (121).

108 Cartoon of the School of Athens. Milan, Ambrosiana (122).

plastic intentions, achieves that " bringing to life of ancient statues " (Ortolani) which was to be from this point on the basis of all of Raphael's new experiences; the second, more fluid in the play of shadows and of light, achieves the fusion that Fra Bartolommeo had attempted to create between Leonardo's sfumato, the contrasts of Michelangelo and the solemn pathos of the ancients in a new uplifting poetry of *affetti*. The two sheets seem to be the mirror of the qualities which Vasari praised most in the fresco: " The saints in a group in the air seem alive, and are remarkable for the foreshortening and relief. Their draperies also are varied and very beautiful, and the heads rather more celestial than human...indeed, Raphael had the gift of rendering his heads sweet and gracious " (Vasari-Milanesi, IV, p. 336).

109 Cartoon of the School of Athens (detail) Milan, Ambrosiana (122).

376

111 Cartoon of the School of Athens (detail).
Milan, Ambrosiana (121).

110 Cartoon of the School of Athens (detail).
Milan, Ambrosiana (122).

THE SCHOOL OF ATHENS

As we have said, no sketches or drawings of the entire composition of the *School of Athens* survive, but there is only the famous cartoon in the Ambrosiana and some detailed figure studies, for a total of six original sheets (F. 305-312; nos. 309a and 310 are copies, while 310a is not for the *School of Athens*). Such an extremely sparse graphic documentation, as compared to that of the *Disputa* can have only one explanation, and that is the loss *in toto* of a whole series of preparatory drawings which, perhaps fallen into the hands of the same collector, was destroyed before they could become dispersed.

It is indeed inadmissible that Raphael had not prepared over-all sketches and many studies of details in pen and black pencil, analyzing single gestures and the grouping of figures, for the *School of Athens* as he had done for the *Disputa*. It is only on the basis of such sketches and studies that Raphael could have made the selection for the final solutions in the fresco, which, given its complexity also for the new relationship between figure and architecture that it presented, could not possibly have been conceived solely on the basis of the few drawings now known to us, together with the cartoon. There is proof of this in some sixteenth-century sheets that appear to have been inspired by lost sketches by Raphael for the entire composition.[119]

Unusual, with regard to the known variety of drawings for the *Disputa*, is the technical uniformity of the surviving drawings of the *School of Athens*, which are almost all in silver point on prepared paper. This technique was especially favored by fresco painters, as Fischel mentions, for its affinity with the process of preparation for the fresco and for its special luminosity, and we have seen that Raphael had preferred it ever since his early Umbrian period for those studies immediately precedent to the painted execution. Still, it should be borne in mind that among the many drawings for the *Disputa*, there is only one known to us in this technique (fig. 101). For the *School of Athens*, instead, these are in the majority, and they all must have been made only shortly before the execution of the cartoon and then of the fresco, because they show very few variations in both stages.

Thus it is with the three examples that we present here; it was perhaps precisely their close adherence to the cartoons that raised doubts among the followers of Morelli. One is a drawing in Frankfurt for Diogenes (Fig. 105) with very minimal variations with respect to the fresco (except that in the drawing the model is beardless); one is at Oxford (Fig. 106), for the two figures climbing the steps (below there is a head of Medusa which was to be used for the shield of the goddess in the following sketch); and another is also at Oxford, for the statue of Minerva and for the architecture at the right (Plate XLII).[120] Raphael shows an easiness in placing the figures in space and a confidence in modeling them, gaining inspiration from Antiquity (note the pose of Diogenes and the statue of Minerva, "worked in a manner to imitate the work of the carver," as Crowe and Cavalcaselle say), and observing the live model, as a clear consequence of the experiences in the ceiling and in the *Disputa*. Nonetheless, in these sheets the various echoes are not as isolated as in the *Disputa*.

377

Here Raphael has an absolutely unitary language which concurs with, but is not determined by, technical uniformity. Yet, however much of the new Roman culture and the classical culture is in the fresco, still the drawings and the cartoon are indebted to Florentine graphic tradition, perhaps here for the last time in such an evident manner.

Nothing shows this better than the sanguine drawing in Oxford, the only one in the series using that technique, which is a study for the simulated low relief beneath the statue of Apollo (Fig. 107).[121] The Pollaiolesque nudes of the last Florentine studies have become more solid as a result of the influence of the ancient statues and the hatching treatment and the Michelangelesque plastic contours seem to have assumed greater capacity of luminous effects, subsequent to the knowledge of engraving acquired from Marcantonio, while the knowing use of contrasts and of the interwining of bodies in space had gone beyond the Leonardesque expedient of the sfumato or the summary repeated strokes of the outlines. Still Leonardo remained Raphael's main source, as is seen in the head in the background, the same which was to serve for the Medusa on the shield of the statue of Minerva (see Plate XLII) and which is derived directly from the well-known soldier in the *Battle of Anghiari*.

The cartoon in the Ambrosiana (Figs. 108-111)[122] is a real ode to Leonardo, not only in the play of the various groups which although they have some elements from the *Last Supper* in Santa Maria delle Grazie, perhaps known to Raphael from drawings (Fischel), also draw on the

112 Studies of draperies and hands for the so-called Horace and of a hand for the figure of Tibullus in the Parnassus. London, British Museum (125 a).

378

solemn compositions of Fra Bartolommeo and the Florentine fifteenth-century tradition, but above all in the Leonardesque types, some taken in their entirety from the *Adoration of the Magi*, as for example the group of philosophers crouching in the left foreground (Fig. 109) and the presumed Xenophon, or Bramante, while Plato is the image of Leonardo himself. The manner of drawing with active lines and dense shadows on which the vivid white plays, the intensity of the faces, the dialectic of the gestures, are also used by Raphael to reinterpret Leonardo.

Nevertheless, the presentation of the whole is antithetical to the magical world of Leonardo. The solemnity of the ancient statuary and the robust Michelangelesque types (the old man to the left of Plato or Ptolemy), not to mention the continuous control of the natural aspects of the poses, of the fall of the draperies, of the faces, which are really portraits, all move away from Leonardo, and a final step further away from him will be made in the fresco, with the presence of the large architectural elements in the background which give new and definite clarity to the whole scene.

The architectural background is absent in the cartoon, and this creates an enormous difference of tone between it and the fresco which otherwise faithfully follows it. Not that the figures themselves, deprived of their architectural setting appear actually "common and of a second order," as Berenson said, but certainly the background had for Raphael a precise choral function with the figures, even at this phase of the work, so much so that the directional elements of the architecture are marked with a stylus on the cartoon.

Also absent in the cartoon are the Heraclitus at the center and the portraits of Raphael and Sodoma at the right, and on the second plane there is absent also the low relief with the battle scene at the left, and the two figures behind the two academicians on the stairs toward the

379

115 Study for the figure of the Muse Calliope (?) in the Parnassus. Vienna, Albertina (126 b).

114 Study for the figure of the Muse Melpomene in the Parnassus. Oxford, Ashmolean Museum (126 a).

right. Still Sanzio must have intended to fill at least the first two lacunae. In fact, in the cartoon Ptolemy and Zoroaster turn to the right, indicating that for that side at least one other figure was planned; on the other hand the free space on the stairs besides Diogenes is so large that Raphael from the beginning must have intended to place another figure there. But perhaps he had not yet been inspired, as he was to be later, while doing the fresco.

The hypothesis that the Michelangelesque Heraclitus was added later, after Raphael had seen part of the Sistine ceiling, is quite acceptable; this figure is a clear homage to Michelangelo, stylistically and physically.[123]

DRAWINGS FOR THE PARNASSUS

The *Parnassus* is, instead, documented by a rich series of drawings which for their uniform technique in pen and for their correspondence to the figures in the fresco seem all to belong to the same phase of work and may have been preceded, perhaps, by more summary sketches and followed, if not by studies in metal point as with those of the *School of Athens*, at least by cartoons.

We might think in this case as well of the loss of a whole group of drawings which would have documented the first and the last steps toward the final solution. But it should also be borne in mind that Raphael was then at an advanced stage in the decoration of the walls and that he had much experience in this type of work, and therefore the preparation of the single figures must have come to him more easily, and the passage between the first ideas and the cartoons could have proceeded in shorter stages, without a need for studies in complicated techniques. Besides, from this time on we see that his graphic preparations for the various works will be even more reduced, and this cannot be merely an accident to be imputed to circumstances of their preservation.

It should also be borne in mind that the *Parnassus*, from the technical point of view, required a different means from that used for the two large walls, because of the location of this fresco, which is set around the window, against the light.

116 Study for the figure of the Muse Erato (?) in the Parnassus. Vienna, Albertina (126 c).

Nevertheless the loss of part of the studies relative to it is documented by the existence of some old copies from lost originals by Raphael (F. 237a, 238, 239) and by the engraving by Marcantonio (B. XIV, 247), which certainly derives from an early project by Raphael, later abandoned.[124] The study appearing in the engraving and in a copy at Oxford from a drawing for the whole composition with nude figures (F. 237a, fig. 221) shows that Raphael must have found the greatest difficulties in the group of the Muses at the right and in the portions at the sides of the window, which in an early version he had conceived more harmoniously, with a less agitated general rhythm and with less naturalness in single poses.

This naturalness was mastered by Raphael precisely in the detailed studies (F. 240-252 for a total of seven sheets), which, as is well known, are all in pen and all have the common feature of being drawn on both recto and verso and of having only the drawings for the *Parnassus*. This shows that its conception must have been rather rapid, without the digressions and second thoughts which had occurred in drawings for other, more or less important works.

This fact, besides the sureness of style of the drawings and, naturally, of the fresco, confirms that this part of the decoration followed the execution of the two large walls, contrary to what Fischel thought, basing his judgment on the drawings; it is, in fact, the style of the drawings that show an achieved assimilation of earlier experiences with ancient statues which here seems to have remained the only direct source of inspiration for Raphael, so much do the earlier problems of light and movement and the dialectical play between the figures give way in favor of an exclusive interest for the sculptural rhythms of draperies *alla romana* and for exemplars of hands, feet, and heads in a kind of academic hand-book of gestures. Examples of these are the sheet in the British Museum which has on its verso studies of draperies and of hands for the so-called Horace (or Sannazzaro?; Fig. 112), and the famous drawing in Lille for the highly classical Apollo and for the drapery of Homer (F. 244-245), and that of Windsor (Fig. 113) for the heads "of the Dante type," of the so-called Anacreon and of Homer, the latter obviously taken from the pathetic face of the Laocoön.[125]

The suspicion arises that Raphael here, taken with ancient examples, adhered less to nature in his figures, which are so apropos even in the fresco, notwithstanding the many portraits among them; even the copious draperies have cadences more eloquent than real and the pen

381

strokes, with continuous tracings along the outlines and with hatched webs in the deep shadows of the folds, seem to be based upon sculptural examples, either in relief or in the round, and follow the method of the drawings of sculptors.

More varied are the three surviving studies for the Muses,[126] despite the fact that Raphael continued to use the pen with parallel or hatched strokes and to keep in mind the examples of ancient statuary. But although the study for Melpomene (Fig. 114), with its sharp form, seems to take up motifs of the Victories from Roman triumphal arches and sarcophagi and although the profile of the Muse is that of the figures on Attic vases, the stroke which is tangled in the draperies and in the hair with vivid movements returns to the beloved Leonardesque experiences, with a neo-Botticellian-Filippinesque note in the insistent waving of linear rhythms. Thus, although the study for Calliope (Fig. 115) evidently re-elaborates the complicated drapery of the Arianne in the Vatican and although her gesture has the flavor of an ancient orator, it is still to be noted that the pose of the Muse as it appears in the drawing, with her head in a pathetic *sottinsù* and not in profile as in the fresco, is the reverse of the pose of Michelangelo's Adam in the Creation in the Sistine Chapel (it should be noted that in August, 1511 the first part of the Sistine ceiling was uncovered for the admiration of all Rome). Thus, despite the similarity noted by Fischel to an ancient sarcophagus representing Achilles, a strongly Michelangelesque flavor is to be found in the study for Erato; the foreshortening of the head is of the type found in the Libyan Sibyl from the Sistine ceiling and the position of the bust is still that of the Florentine *Doni Madonna*.

A more exemplary classicism dominates the superb head of a Muse (Clio?) in the " auxiliary

382

118 Study of a detail of Gregory IX approving the Decretals. Frankfurt, Städelsches Institut (128).

cartoon " from the Norman Colville Collection (Fig. 117).[127] This very beautiful sheet, and the analogous one from the Horne Foundation for the *Polyhymnia* (F. 254), almost neoclassic in its more minute grace, puts forth once more an aspect already seen elsewhere in Raphael's method of work and interrupts the series of pen drawings for the *Parnassus* with its charcoal technique. The soft play of the light on large facial planes and the velvety strokes of the shadows, which were to be enjoyed later by Sebastiano del Piombo, preannounce the qualities of the relative fresco and of the accompanying one with the Judicial Virtues, for which there are no surviving drawings.

For the fresco below with Gregory IX who approves the Decretals, there is a partial pen study at Frankfurt with several variations from the painting; it goes back to early designs even though it has a somewhat dry quality which might make us think of the workshop, generally also held responsible for the execution of the fresco (Fig. 118).[128]

Interesting and little known is a drawing at Windsor (Fig. 119),[129] which Popham recognized as preparatory to one of the *grisailles* around the windows in the Stanza della Segnatura and which for its immediateness has all the elements to be considered an autograph. The rare theme of the Oath of Zaleucus, and the technique, akin to low relief, lead again to a fully classical climate, to the tone of the ancient world which was to become the rule and which had already appealed very much to Peruzzi. Indeed Sanzio seems to approach here certain illustrative and sculptural drawings by Peruzzi, and he was also in the future to show points of similarity with the Sienese artist, such as to raise discussions concerning not only the attributions of his paintings, as is known for example with regard to the ceiling of the Stanza di Eliodoro, but also of certain drawings (cf. note 143).

119 Study for the Oath of Zaleucus in a grisaille of the Segnatura. Windsor, Royal Library (129).

120 Sketch for the St. Ambrose in the Disputa, and sonnet (detail). Vienna, Albertina, verso (130).

121 Study for a reading Madonna and Child. Vienna, Albertina, recto (130).

384

123 Sketches of the Madonna and Child and *putti*. Florence, Uffizi, recto (109 a).

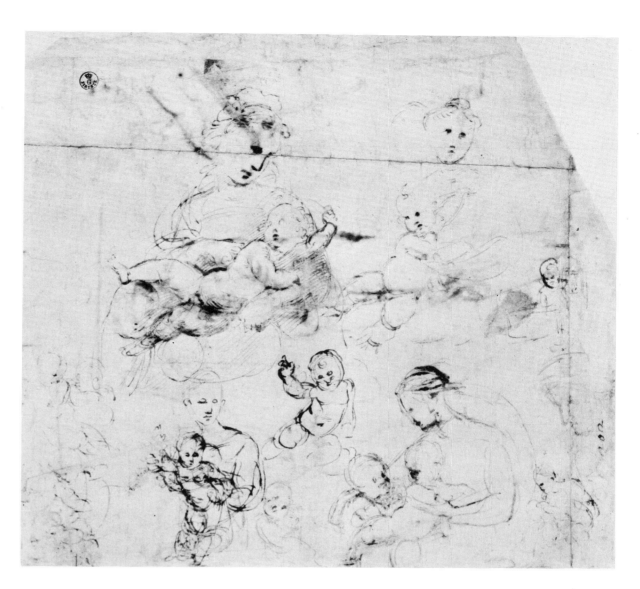

122 Various sketches for a Christ Child. London, British Museum (131).

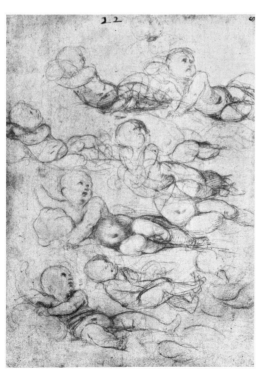

VARIOUS DRAWINGS OF THE FIRST ROMAN PERIOD

During the execution of the first Stanza, which certainly absorbed him above all else, Raphael also worked on minor projects; he was still able to retain control over his various projects and was almost always himself on the scene. We deal here with certain easel pictures datable between 1508-09 and 1511 and some drawings which unite sketches for the Stanza to others of a different destination.

A sheet from the Albertina which, having on the verso a rapid sketch for the St. Ambrose of the *Disputa* and therefore datable to the first period of the work at the Segnatura, has on the recto a sketch of the Madonna reading in a landscape with the Child (Figs. 120, 121).[130] It is still imbued with Florentine culture, from the pose in *contrapposto* of the Madonna that again repeats the *Doni Tondo*, to the type of the Virgin and Child, which are still within Leonardo's vision, as is the manner of the strokes of the pen, which are scattered in order to let in the light and are as brilliant as in the fine drawing for *Theology* on the ceiling (cf. Fig. 81).

The same type and style of Madonna is to be found on the recto (Fig. 123) of the above mentioned sheet in the Uffizi, which had on its recto the first references to a standing Venus and a figure for the *Disputa* (cf. note 109a), and therefore is also datable to the first Roman years. Of the many sketches of the Madonna and Child theme drawn on this sheet, only the largest one on the upper left could be carried over (in reverse, however) in a known painting, the *Bridgewater Madonna* in London, which precisely by virtue of this and by other drawings can be dated after Raphael's arrival in Rome and not, as it has been said, still in the Florentine years. The other sketches on the folio are variations on the theme, with only generic links to executed works: for example the Child isolated at the center is similar to the one we are to see in the *Alba Madonna* while the group below on the right anticipates, in reverse, the *Madonna della Tenda* and that on the left foreshadows the arrangement of the *Mackintosh Madonna*.

To the *Bridgewater Madonna*, more than to the *Madonna di Loreto*, with which it has sometimes been connected, is related the series of sketches for the Child on a sheet in the British Museum (Fig. 122). For its medium of metal point on prepared paper, for its dimensions and style, it is connected to a group of analogous sheets singled out by Fischel as forming part of an original notebook more or less contemporary with the preparation for the *School of Athens* and, in particular, to a page in Lille (F. 351), which effectively interweaves motifs of the Child from the *Bridgewater Madonna* and the *Madonna di Loreto*.[131]

From the same notebook would have come the extraordinary drawing in the British Museum with the very sweet head of Madonna (Plate XLIVa) of an almost Pre-Raphaelite flavor and the little head of the Child with the ambiguous Leonardesque smile which has occasionally been connected to the *Aldobrandini* and *Mackintosh Madonnas* but more likely does not refer to

124 Cartoon for the Mackintosh Madonna. London, British Museum (133).

125 Sketch for the Madonna della Seggiola (?), detail from Plate XLIII in color. Lille, Wicar Museum, recto (135).

126 Study of a figure for the Alba Madonna. Lille, Wicar Museum, verso (135).

any known paintings (but cf. also the drawings in Lille, F. 348, perhaps for the same composition).[132] For the *Mackintosh Madonna*, although, as we have seen, the identification of the preparatory drawings is vague, there is on the other hand the definitive cartoon in the British Museum (Fig. 124),[133] on an analogous scale with the painting and of a quality such as to dispel any doubts about Raphael's authorship of the very much deteriorated painting. The smile of Christ, quite similar to the one in the previous drawing, has the tender ambiguity of Leonardo, but the frontal placement of the group and the compactness of the forms from the smoky darkness are a return to Fra Bartolommeo and his special way of interpreting Roman statuary, as also occurred in portion of the *School of Athens*.

This recourse to Fra Bartolommeo should not be surprising, since we have seen him first as suggesting to Raphael the research of densely pictorial matter, in a work that must fall at the time of the strongest Venetian infiltrations into Raphael's Roman culture through Lotto and above all through Sebastiano del Piombo, who had arrived in Rome in 1511.

It is, therefore, the case to illustrate here the highest point from the point of view of graphics of these infiltrations: that is, the drawing in the British Museum for the *Foligno Madonna* (Fig. 127),[134] which for its technique of charcoal on cerulean blue paper shows evident relationships with Venetian habits of draftsmanship. The doubts of the autography of the sheet, in large

127 Study for the Foligno Madonna. London, British Museum (134).

128 Studies for a kneeling woman for the Expulsion of Heliodorus. Oxford, Ashmolean Museum, recto (138).

129 Study of a woman and two children for the Expulsion of Heliodorus. Oxford, Ashmolean Museum, verso (138).

measure due perhaps more to its technical peculiarities than to considerations of style, can all be dispelled by the reasons put forward in its favor by Pouncey and Gere, even though it remains an exceptional graphic experiment in Raphael's career. Compared to the picture it shows some variations (which could confirm its autography), among which the most apparent concerns the legs of the Child which are presented as in some of the earlier drawings, but which in the painting are disposed according to the scheme of the Child in the *Doni Madonna*, a scheme which Raphael used also for the angels for the key vault of the lunettes in the Stanza della Segnatura and in Santa Maria della Pace.

The Michelangelesque echo is still more evident in the beautiful sheet in Lille with studies for the *Alba Madonna* (Figs. 125, 126 and Plate XLIII),[135] which I think was executed around 1511, at the end of the work for the first Stanza and in any case after the vision of the first part of Michelangelo's Sistine ceiling. It is for good reason that the pose of the Madonna, as can better be seen in the study on the verso taken from a live male model in contemporary clothes, is the same as the one in the drawing for Calliope in the *Parnassus* (see Fig. 115) and, as it does also, it seems to be a version of the Adam from the Sistine ceiling. The vigorous technique with sanguine, the evident sculptural intention in the hatched shadows, on the verso the refined articulation of the forms in a compact group and, on the recto the juxtaposition, exceptional in Raphael, between the summary treatment of the figure of the Virgin and the more strongly plastic conception, instead, of the Christ (almost a transposition to drawing of the effects of the *non finito*, which Michelangelo also used in his drawings), are all elements in favor of a renewed contact with the works of Buonarroti.

The Leonardesque influence, transfigured, is also found here, above all on the recto, where a circular atmospheric sense between figures and landscape and an evocative play of light dominate. But one sees how the intense luminosity of the right-hand portion of the group, on the recto, gives way, in the verso and in the picture, to a concentration of shadows precisely on the right, for the sake of greater plastic quality—a proof of Raphael's continuing contact with nature and the way in which he gradually went beyond the lessons of Leonardo. About the pen sketches on the recto, the two above are to be connected with the later *Madonna della*

389

130 Head of an angel, fragment for the cartoon for the Expulsion of Heliodorus. Paris, Louvre (140).

Seggiola and the *Madonna della Tenda;* that of the Child below, which takes up a previously used motif (cf. Fig. 123), will be used again by Raphael in the *putto* guiding the shell of Galatea in the Farnesina.

For that fresco we have no drawings, but the occasional recourse in the sketches of those years to themes related to marine symbolism leads one to suppose that the dating of the fresco to around 1511, between the dates of the two Stanze, is correct.[136]

131 Model for the Liberation of St. Peter. Florence, Uffizi (141).

132 Studies of a sleeping woman, angels and architecture, for the ceiling of the Stanza di Eliodoro. Florence, Uffizi, recto (143).

DRAWINGS FOR THE STANZA DI ELIODORO

The body of graphic preparations for the Stanza di Eliodoro is notably smaller than that of the preceding Stanza, but the few surviving studies are autographs or at least copies from lost autographs, and consequently confirm Raphael's complete responsibility for the conception and for the major part of the execution of the decoration of the entire room, at least until about

133 Cartoon for Moses and the burning bush for the ceiling of the Stanza di Eliodoro. Naples, Capodimonte Museum (145).

391

134 Assumption of the Virgin. Stockholm, National Museum (146).

1513, when, with the *Repulse of Attila*, the intervention of others artists began. We have no initial sketches nor autograph general projects for the stories of the walls, as we had for the *Disputa*, nor are there complete cartoons, as for the *School of Athens*, and therefore any attempt to reconstruct the course of the general conception of the Stanza on the basis of the surviving copies must remain a hypothesis.[137]

There are only three fragments of the cartoon for the *Expulsion of Heliodorus* and one for the ceiling, besides a " model " for the *Liberation of St. Peter* and five or six studies of details.

Among them the most beautiful is certainly the sheet in Oxford of the two women kneeling on the left of the *Expulsion of Heliodorus*.[138] On the recto is drawn a woman with her back turned, similar to that in the fresco except for the higher position of the left forearm, with further studies of the feet and the head, according to the system habitual with Raphael since his Umbrian days. The figure shows a full " Roman " aspect in its rather rhetorical attitudes and in the sculptural placement of the forms, not to mention the archaeologically perfect headdress, a " Romanism " which does not signify only classicism but also a vital interest in Michelangelo (Fig. 128).

Sweeter in the play of light on her neck and on her profile, still more dramatic in her sudden gesture of clutching her children to her side, like a Niobe, as has been said, is the study of the woman on the verso for which there is another drawing in Zurich.[139] Here the summary interweaving of the lines in the lower part of the figure imposes a greater sense of movement on the image, which anticipates in the drawing, through movement, that rich and extremely vital sense which Raphael was to achieve in the fresco by means of color (Fig. 129).

More deeply regretted is the absence of any drawings for the *Miracle at Bolsena*, the most " tonal " of all the frescoes, for which Raphael must have prepared sheets of extraordinary pictorial quality. It is true that at this time more than any other Raphael expressed himself in color, to arrive at that quality of living flesh found in the fresco, which only color can render; therefore, the drawings must have served him more as an outline than as a real aid in his work. But it is also true that some drawings must also have been done for the *Miracle at Bolsena*, as for other parts of the Stanza that are not documented in their graphic elaboration.

Also for the *Expulsion of Heliodorus* there remain three fragments of the original cartoon, at Oxford and at the Louvre,[140] which, despite their poor state of conservation, are highly interesting, not so much as documents of the preliminary ideas for the final solution, given their exact correspondence to the fresco, but as an exceptional evidence of a precise point of passage from the graphic to the pictorial technique in a moment when the modes of this very same painting technique were undergoing radical changes in Raphael. And that this development was also felt in the graphic medium is demonstrated by a rapid comparison of the cartoon of the *School of Athens* with these fragments: here the charcoal is used in a painterly fashion, the area of Leonardesque shadow on the face or on the eye sockets is " colored " shadow, notwithstanding the monochrome, and the chiaroscuro is no longer the means of plastic emphasis, but rather it is the lively play of tones on the skin of the face together with the vivid dramatic crescendo of the narrative interpretation (Fig. 130).

Vasari's words seem more suitable for these heads than for the almost too noble St. Cecilia, of which they were written: " while we may call other works paintings, those of Raphael are living things; the flesh palpitates, the breath comes and goes, life pulsates everywhere ... " (which, for a partisan of Michelangelo, was to say a great deal).

That his contemporaries had already taken notice of the value of this particular stylistic approach of Raphael, and that it was fully embodied in his drawings as well, seems clear from testimony which Vasari supplies regarding these cartoons: " It was this work so stupendous in all its parts that even the cartoons are held in the highest esteem; thus Messer Francesco Masini ... has, among his many drawings, ... some pieces of the cartoon which Raphael made for this Story of Heliodorus and he holds them in the esteem which they merit " (Vasari-Milanesi, IV, p. 346).

It has been mentioned that there still exists, though extremely unclear, a " model " for the *Liberation of St. Peter*. Compared with the first sketches conserved for the *Disputa*, this drawing (Fig. 131) in the Uffizi[141] seems to indicate a different phase in the process of the work, as an actual model for the composition of the whole after early sketches and even detailed studies were probably made (some motifs from them are to return in figures in other works).

The model, besides giving an idea of the work to the patron, served the artist for ascertaining whether the placing together of the various figures previously studied could offer a convincing arrangement to be definitively used, or whether modifications were necessary in the context of the narrative and, therefore, whether further studies had to be made before arriving at the cartoon. It is natural, therefore, given their essentially utilitarian character, that many of the " models " which have come down to us are by the hands of pupils, at least in their finishing, and especially after 1513-14 when Raphael's workshop assumes a truly integral part of the master's work.

Even for the Uffizi model there is no absence of doubts, to which the disastrous state of conservation has also contributed; but the few passages intact and the inventive and original quality of the solutions, formal, luministic, and those pertaining to the gestures and poses, exclude here the collaboration of the workshop, even though, as time went by, this sheet must have undergone changes and inept restorations. The model reveals notable variations with regard to the fresco, above all in the two lateral groups and in the architectural framework, but the basic idea of the final composition is already clear and the principal problem of the fresco, which is essentially the problem of light, has been established. In the final version Raphael was to substitute the imprecise source of light in the drawing with the triple source of light in the fresco, a supernatural, natural and atmospheric light, according to the " realistic " bent (in the sense that this word could have for Sanzio) that Raphael's interests in these years tended to show. But this does not obscure the fact that, from the beginning, the scene of the *Liberation of St. Peter* was conceived by Raphael as a nocturnal scene, in which he might achieve a culmination of his Leonardesque experiences and even of those from Piero della Francesca and the northern followers. Such a drawing, if, as is probable, it was quickly known and subsequently admired by many, must have been astounding for the novelty of technique and narrative and must have had a powerful influence on the history of sixteenth-century graphic art, also through the popularization which Polidoro and Perino gave to this manner shortly thereafter.

For the other wall frescoes of the Stanza di Eliodoro, unfortunately, we do not know of any autograph drawings. We do have three for the ceiling and they confirm Raphael's paternity of it, at least for the conception, if not for the final executions as well, which recent studies have proposed as occurring at the end of the work in the Stanza, around 1513-14, rather than at the beginning.[142]

The most interesting among them is a drawing in the Uffizi, only recently reclaimed by Oberhuber as by the hand of Sanzio, with ample arguments which seem to dispel any instinctive perplexity before the unusual aspect of the drawings (Fig. 132).[143] It unites compositional studies which all pertain to the period 1513-14, especially the brilliant sketches of architecture on both the recto and verso, which appear to be ideas for the elevation and the vaulting of St. Peter's, of which Raphael was named architect in April, 1514. The fascinating sketch of a sleeping woman re-elaborates a classical pose which, by means of an engraving by Marcantonio (the conception of which is attributed by some to Parmigianino, by others to Raphael), was to have a vast diffusion during that century, to the extent that it inspired the St. Helen

135 Sketches for the plan of the wall of the Chigi Chapel in Santa Maria della Pace. Oxford, Ashmolean Museum (147).

393

by Veronese, now in London, for example, and influenced the lesser but skilled artists of late Mannerism.[144] The woman's romantic pose is enhanced by the play of light and shadow, the light of dusk if not that of the moon, and recalls figures and problems of the *Liberation of St. Peter*. And finally, the group of angels is clearly connected with the ceiling of the Stanza di Eliodoro; it studies, with minimal variations, the circle of clouds and the angels around God the Father in the panel with the appearance of God to Moses. This particular zone of the drawing, with its somewhat solemn stroke in the shadows with parallel lines and in the swirls of the clouds, leads one to think of Peruzzi, whose name has been mentioned in connection with the execution of the ceiling frescoes and in connection with a preparatory drawing in Oxford (see note 143), quite close to this one. But testifying in favor of Raphael are the airy luminosity of the conception and the presence of such characteristic Raphaelesque elements as the face of the woman, the beautiful angel on the left, and the hair and the gesture of the one on the right, which recalls the angels of Santa Maria della Pace with its rampant pose.

The motif of the figure turned in upon itself in order to hide its face, as if in an excess of emotion (also in Santa Maria della Pace Raphael was to tend to place in shadow the intense faces of the old Sibyl and of the very beautiful angel on the left on the arch), returns in the figure of Moses in the same scene on the ceiling, for which there is a cartoon in Naples exactly parallel to the fresco (Fig. 133).[145] For them the words of a nineteenth-century admirer, despite their romantic tone, are still valid: "a masculine thing, large and vigorous . . . which . . . perhaps in those days only Michelangelo could have equaled, but never surpassed . . . A fleeting concept more than a sculptural one . . . the conscious appearance of the interior motion as in a living person . . . no other reticence was ever more stupendous and loquacious "

136 Study for the figure of a young Sibyl in Santa Maria della Pace. Oxford, Ashmolean Museum (148 a).

137 Study for the figure of the old Sibyl in Santa Maria della Pace. Vienna, Albertina (148 b).

394

138 Descent of Christ to Limbo, for a medallion in Santa Maria della Pace. Florence, Uffizi (149).

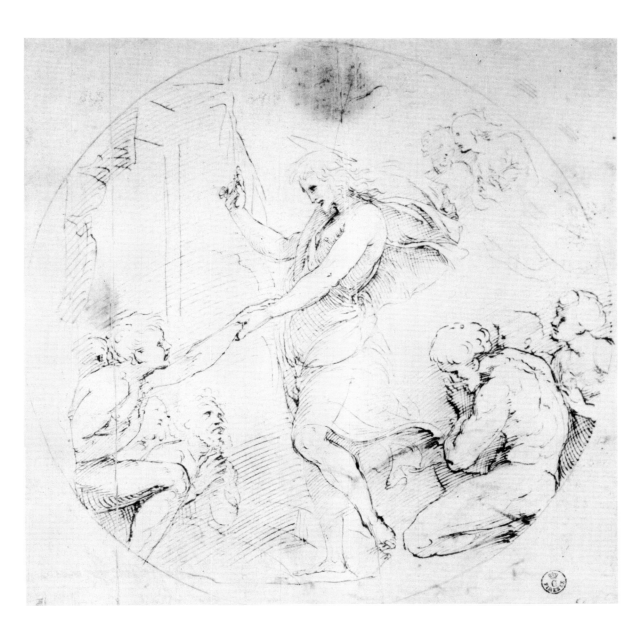

(F. Niccolini, *Di un cartone di Raffaello Sanzio, custodito nel museo Reale Borbonico*, Naples, 1859). More sober . . . no less authentic are the praises of Passavant: " It is impossible to be able to unite at the same time such a broad and sublime manner, such freshness, greater sentiment and expression and deeper intelligence in drawing " (vol. III, p. 118), which anticipates what could be said with regards to the cartoons for the Vatican tapestries.

139 Sketch for the lower part of a Resurrection. Oxford, Ashmolean Museum (151 c).

395

140 Sketch of a Resurrection (for Santa Maria della Pace ?). Bayonne, Bonnat Museum (151 a).

A beautiful sketch for the *Assumption* in Stockholm, which has raised many problems about its destination and, therefore, its chronology, shows a marked affinity with the group of angels in the above-mentioned drawing in the Uffizi (Fig. 134).[146]

We do not know how and if Raphael had had occasion to treat in painting the theme of the *Assumption of the Virgin*, which could be proved by the Stockholm drawing, a more summary drawing on the verso of the Oxford drawing with the figure of Theology (cf. note 103) and an engraving by the "Maestro del Dado" (B. XV, 7), of clearly Raphaelesque inspiration. Fischel thought that the altarpiece with the *Coronation of the Virgin* at Monteluce, commissioned from Raphael in 1505 but finished only after his death by Giulio Romano and by Penni, had the Assumption as its original theme and that the two drawings were, therefore, related to it; but Shearman recently has argued convincingly that an altarpiece of the Assumption was part of the original plan for the decoration of the Chigi Chapel in Santa Maria del Popolo and that the two drawings relate to this commission, partially finished in 1516 but begun perhaps as early as 1513. However that may be, the style, the poses of the flying angels, the tone of the composition which relies on new monumental and dramatically dynamic schemes closely link the drawing in Stockholm with the above-mentioned one for the ceiling of the Stanza di Eliodoro and with those mentioned below for Santa Maria della Pace (cf. Figs. 138, 140) and indicate therefore as quite certain the date of about 1513-14.

It should also be borne in mind the fact that in 1513 Leonardo was in Rome and that in 1514 Fra Bartolommeo also was there and renewed his contacts with Raphael. Now, while the penetrating strokes of the pen in this drawing and those related to it repropose Leonardesque experiences on Raphael's part, the summary handling of certain lines and the theme itself, so dear to the friar, could perhaps reflect the stimulus of these renewed contacts, even though it is believed that Leonardo's influence on Raphael was now only as a memory of a world thoroughly assimilated but now surpassed, and that the friar was now under the influence of the younger, highly admired Master, and would thus have not done more than offer him some advice.

DRAWINGS FOR SANTA MARIA DELLA PACE

The other very important cycle of these years, that in the Chigi Chapel in Santa Maria della Pace is no longer believed to have been executed around 1511 as Vasari indicates, but rather a few years later, around 1514.

It is the last fresco by Raphael for which there is a rich group of preparatory drawings and it is the last in which the participation of assistants, which there was in part of the

141 Various sketches for a Resurrection. Oxford, Ashmolean Museum (151 b).

397

pictorial execution, is not evident in the conception of the whole and of the details, and therefore not in the drawings either.

In this regard, a sketch in the Ashmolean Museum of Oxford (Fig. 135),[147] recently discovered, is indicative and gives in a quite general but definite and illuminating manner the idea of the general arrangement of the decoration, which must have come to Raphael's mind directly after the commission from Chigi. In the sketch is indicated the arch of the chapel with the torch-bearing angel and the figures on the right side: two Sibyls below, in movement and not at rest as they were to be in the fresco, and two Prophets above, with the gestures which they were to have in the final version and which were referred to earlier in a sketch from the above-mentioned Oxford sheet for the *Expulsion of Heliodorus* (cf. Fig. 129). A further step toward the general conception is documented by a drawing in Stockholm, a copy from a lost original by Raphael, which is also precious because on the sides of the chapel are indicated the architectonic arrangements envisioned by Sanzio and later destroyed, with two *tondi* which also were to be historied with bronze reliefs as we shall see.

This is not the place to further emphasize the exceptional value of the new and solemn decorative division of Santa Maria della Pace and the new way in which Raphael treated his figures, after all that has been said, beginning with Vasari. But it is relevant to remember that Vasari speaks of it as a " new manner," " more magnificent and grand," full of " mastery," for which they are considered the best and among the most beautiful works Raphael ever did; " because in the women and in the boys that are there, there is very great vivacity and perfect coloring." It is true that the biographer says also " before Michelangelo's chapel was open to the public, he must had seen it "; this was an indication that he considered Raphael's new style a consequence of Michelangelo's lessons and not, as it actually was, a natural development of Raphael's experience in the Stanza di Eliodoro; but certainly never as here is there so clearly evident the importance to this development of Michelangelo's Sistine ceiling.

142 Study of a nude figure holding an axe, for the Resurrection. Windsor, Royal Library (152 a).

398

143 Two nude figures defending themselves with a shield, for the Resurrection. Windsor, Royal Library (152 b).

144 Study of a seated nude. London, British Museum (153).

The drawings are the best testimony of this in their technique, which is more essential and, because it is monochrome, is in itself more Michelangelesque.

Not so much the first known drawing for the so-called Phrygian Sibyl in Oxford, as its further elaboration in the British Museum and the almost definitive study for the old Sibyl (Tiburtine?) in the Albertina (Figs. 136, 137),[148] in their powerful chiaroscuro, show the attention given by Raphael to the figures and the drawings of Michelangelo for the Sistine ceiling. Judging from the evidence that has come down to us, those Sibyls more than any other part of the decoration must have put to the test the inventive faculties of Raphael, and naturally so, since they were better visibile in the context of the frescoes and since they functioned as frames for the chapel. In fact the summary drawing in Oxford, the copy in Stockholm and these drawings show variations among themselves and with regard to the fresco, precisely in the poses of the Sibyls; it may be deduced that there was a whole series of now-lost drawings which had developed these variations, in a sequence analogous to those that it is possible to establish for the other cycles and, in this cycle, for the figure of the so-called Phrygian Sibyl.

From the stylistic point of view the drawings for the Sibyls show an advance in his classical-Michelangelesque studies, which had also characterized the drawings for the Muses of the *Parnassus* and for the *Alba Madonna*, but with a softer sense of the forms and a richer sense of subject matter, thanks to the softened shadows of the sanguine and to the sumptuous curves of the outlines.

To one of the *tondi* on the side walls of the chapel, according to Fischel's intuition, now demonstrated by Hirst, is destined the Uffizi sheet with *Christ in Limbo* (Fig. 138),[149] which brings us again to the type of drawing for the ceiling of the Stanza di Eliodoro and that for the *Assumption* (cf. Figs. 132, 134), with a pen technique alternating undulating with almost rigid lines, with the extreme luminous rarefaction that derives from it, and with it the new, almost theatrical sense of the narration. The theatricality, implicit in the solemn presentation of the figures, is underscored by the pathetic gestures and the " action " of the personages, and also by their placement in a space full of dimensional implications and completely habitable, though strictly within the small dimensions of the sheet; this is a completely Raphaelesque effect which was to be suffocated in the version in bronze by Lorenzetto.

Also for Santa Maria della Pace, Raphael was to execute the famous and numerous group of drawings of a *Resurrection* (F. 387-395 a) which were not easily placed in chronological context until Hirst convincingly proposed that they and the relative painting, perhaps never finished, were planned for the Chigi Chapel as a central altarpiece and as an iconographic conclusion of the complex decorative cycle.[150]

This group of drawings, for some time considered as belonging together, is centered on the drawing in Bayonne for the complete scene of the Resurrection (Fig. 140), to which the two Oxford sketches, one partial and one complete, for the lower part of the altar, are commentaries.[151] The chronological order of the three sheets is not clear, partly because the intermediate phases are missing and especially because we do not know the final resolution in the painting. Certainly the partial sketch in Oxford (Fig. 141) seems an early phase of notations and unites to figures clearly used for the Resurrection theme others that appear destined for a different theme, perhaps a battle; within the intricate vital interplay, there are still Leonardesque references: soldiers in battle who recall the drawings " in transition " between Florence and Rome (cf. Figs. 74-76), flying angels and some sketches of fallen soldiers which seem reworkings of the formal synthesis of certain drawings by Michelangelo. The Bayonne sheet, instead, which is clear in its various sections, may be next in succession and is linked once again to the drawing for the *Assumption* and to the one of *Christ in Limbo*, showing the new pathetic and dynamic interests of Raphael, who tended now toward the spectacular type of picture which was to culminate in the idea for the *Transfiguration*.

In this direction, which gave every possible opening to action and to space as the stage on which it takes place, together with the architectural and scenographic studies with which Raphael was now occupied because of his new commissions, and in anticipation of the solutions for the Vatican cartoons, the final version of the *Resurrection* must have been conceived.

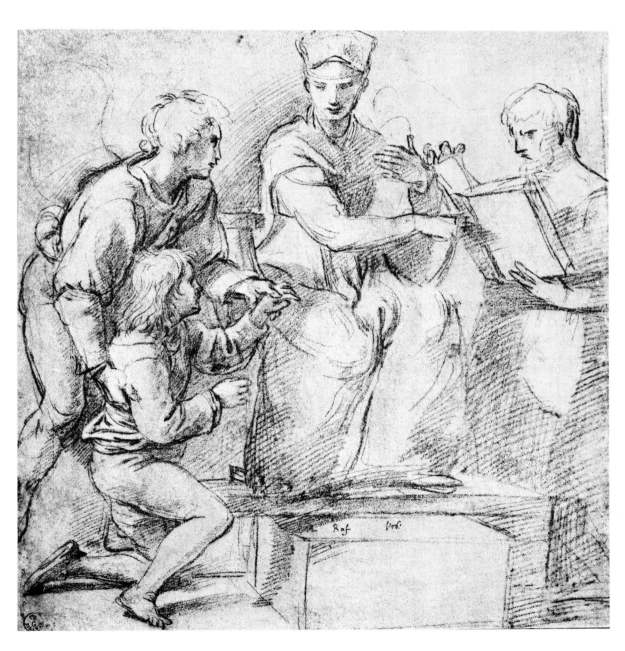

146 Study of the Madonna of the Fish. Florence, Uffizi (157).

147 Study of the Child for the Madonna of
Francis I. Florence, Uffizi (158).

To it seems best to relate the other Oxford drawing for the lower part of the composition,
given that the figures sketched there return in single studies evidently preparatory to the one
which must be the model for the projected altarpiece (Fig. 139).

So it is for the seated man on the left seen from behind, studied in detail on the recto
of the above-mentioned partial sketch (cf. note 151 b); so also for the reclining figure on the
right, studied in another drawing at Oxford (F. 391) and already sketched in several variations
in the general sketches; and so too for the standing soldier with the axe who appears both
in the partial sketch at Oxford and in the complete one in Bayonne, which takes up again
a motif already used in the *Liberation of St. Peter*.[152] The figure with the axe (Fig. 142) is one
of the most beautiful of the series because of the very natural gesture of the arm which covers
the face in fright; this, too, is an idea which Raphael had already studied in the Stanza di
Eliodoro and which here achieves its dramatic culmination in the vibrating movement of all
the parts. More calm in the pathetic attitude of the head between the arms is the gesture of
another figure in the British Museum, certainly destined for the same series although it does not
appear in any of the known over-all sketches (Fig. 144);[153] to this more than to any other study
in the series does the comparison with Michelangelo appear pertinent (Morelli attributed this
drawing to Michelangelo's school) because of its evident inspiration from motifs of the Sistine
ceiling (the Eve of the *Original Sin*, one of the figures in the *Flood*, the nudes at the sides of the
Creation of Light and Darkness and the *Sacrifice*) and in the tortured twisting of the sculptural limbs.
But the sensitivity of the shadows on the faces, the grace which the gestures of these nudes,
strong but not athletic, human beings seen within an ideal beauty, all held in action and in
reciprocal, natural spatial-luministic relationships, are all of the mature Raphael of these years.

It is known that around 1514 Raphael's activity underwent a radical change because of the important new architectural and archaeological commissions which forced the master to avail himself even more of the help of assistants in painting and to modify the working methods of the shop. From then on he was to intervene personally mainly in the conception and the supervision of the works, especially the less important ones, leaving a large part of the work to pupils, some of whom were by now well trained at least in the execution, as was the case with Penni and Giulio Romano.

But before we consider the intricate body of problems that this collaboration entails, especially in works of larger dimensions, it is necessary to examine a more or less autograph group of easel pictures datable after 1514, in order to determine which drawings can be linked to it and which others can shed light on the variations undergone by Raphael in these years. It is understood that those works for which there are no autograph drawings survive will not be mentioned here.

Among the first easel pictures for which a collaboration by assistants is mentioned is the *Madonna dell'Impannata* in the Pitti, generally dated around 1514, which an X-ray has shown to have been originally conceived in a different manner from what is seen today, a manner more in line with the drawing of it at Windsor.[154] In it the sweet figures of the Madonna and

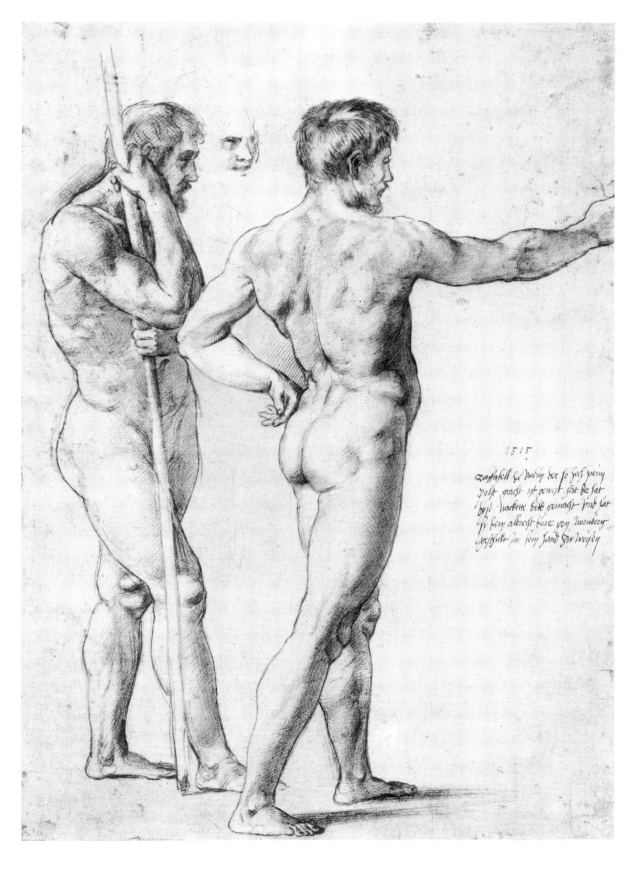

148 Raphael (?). Study of two standing nudes, for the Battle of Ostia. Vienna, Albertina (160).

149 The planet Mars and an angel, for the dome of the Chigi Chapel in Santa Maria del Popolo. Lille, Wicar Museum (161 a).

St. Elizabeth stand out; they are of the opulent and soft type of the Sibyls of Santa Maria della Pace and they are executed in the same drawing style, although in a different technique, here in metal point on prepared paper, rendered in a style that is plastic but insistently sprinkled with lights and therefore basically pictorial (Fig. 145).

A complementary sheet in Berlin (F. 374) studies the figure, here only hinted at, of the Child and that of the Infant St. John in the same neo-fifteenth-century technique of metal point, which Raphael now enriched with every possible chromatic and even painterly allusion. In the Windsor sheet the garment of St. Elizabeth, between " antique " and *ciociara*, and the striped peasant costume of the Madonna, which in the painting lost so much of its warm and vivid beauty, are notable.

This new descriptive taste, even within a traditional and long-tested theme, surely came to Raphael from the narrative experience of the Stanze, as it was perhaps his new activity as architect and archaeologist, which brought him to wander throughout old Rome, which was populated, however, by lively beauties, that elicited in him a rediscovery of the simple things which he had seen when he was younger. The fresh life of the angel-companions of the shop in the youthful drawings for the *Vatican Coronation* (cf. Figs. 10, 12) returns now in the images of the Fornarina-Madonna of the Windsor drawing or of the Madonna-woman of the people of the similar drawing in Oxford's Ashmolean Museum (Plate XLIV b).[155] The drawing, which has the same metal point technique and perhaps was from the same notebook, represents with an almost nineteenth-century impulse and ingenuousness the embrace of a young mother, just as a parallel sheet in Chatsworth (F. 375) represents the Madonna reading a book to the Child.

Belonging to this same climate is another drawing at Windsor with a landscape and ancient ruins, perhaps a view of Trajan's Forum (Plate XLV).[156] It is correctly placed in relation to the background of the engraving by Marcantonio known as *Il Morbetto* (B. XIV, 417), and the luministic interest of the drawing confirms the relation to the engraving technique, but what counts most is the true and solemn poetry of the great truncated columns in the foreground and the large shadows on the walls, in contrast with the serene stretch of trees in the background. A landscape seen with new eyes, almost pre-Romantic, beyond any archaeological or descriptive convention, and foreshadowing of some successful views by Polidoro da Caravaggio.

The drawing in the Uffizi for the *Madonna of the Fish* (Fig. 146)[157] is studied from the live model in contemporary dress. Passavant considered this drawing doubtful, but Crowe and Cavalcaselle recognized it as Raphael's for its "frank and resolute passages" which give form to the composition. The relationship proposed by Fischel with the Stanza di Eliodoro and the date of about 1513-14 seems apt, considering the strongly chromatic sense which characterized that moment and which comes through here in the soft fabric of the sanguine. But precisely the sparse, tight strokes of sanguine, in an over-all effect similar to a pictorial low relief (consider especially the Madonna), anticipate the later drawing methods for the Vatican tapestries and especially for the mosaics of the Chigi Chapel in Santa Maria del Popolo, where, as here, the dramatic fullness of the Stanza di Eliodoro is appeased.

Of such a type must have been the drawings which Raphael certainly made for the *Madonna della Seggiola* (cf. note 135) or for the *Sistine Madonna*, but as we have said, the graphic documentation for these mature Roman works is ever more rare.

Comparatively numerous, therefore, in contrast, is the group of drawings for the *Madonna of Francis I*, dated in 1518 and commissioned in 1517, and therefore chronologically more advanced with regard to the drawings discussed up to now. For this group, as for the execution of the picture, Giulio Romano is insistently proposed, on the basis of Vasari, who calls him the collaborator of the Master in this work and, indeed, mentions the work only in the *Life* of Giulio and not in that of Raphael; in fact, Hartt attributed to the pupil the three preparatory drawings which have survived. Still, given the important royal commissioner of the painting and Raphael's signature on it, it is obvious that the Master must have conceived the composition himself, making at least some sketches or preparatory drawings. Many of these, as usual, must have been lost, but for the three we have, it seems to me that the solution proposed here by Marabottini is quite probable, also for the parts of the pictures. Thus, while I continue to believe that Giulio Romano is author of the Uffizi drawing of the Madonna and Child (F. 377), I think that the more summary one in the Louvre for only the Madonna (F. 378a) demonstrates a more directly Raphaelesque sweetness and the one in the Uffizi for the Child alone clearly indicates the hand of the Master (Fig. 147).[158] The last-named has a soft stroke over

150 Angel with raised arms, for the dome of the Chigi Chapel in Santa Maria del Popolo. Oxford, Ashmolean Museum (161 b).

405

the original stylus tracings, a direct vivacity in the gesture and the expression of the face, and a warm tone of sanguine which lightly traces the hair, and shades with grace the smiling cheeks; how much more compact is Giulio's drawing, both in the psychology of the personalities and in the bronzelike substance of the sanguine and the chiseled chiaroscuro of the folds.

The question of the drawings for the Madonnas is no more than a small element of the complex question of the collaboration of pupils in the major painted works after 1514-15, and especially in such large-scale decorations as the Stanza dell'Incendio or the Loggia of Psyche in the Farnesina.

It is quite unthinkable that Raphael would not personally intervene in the general conception, even of single groups of figures, and in the supervision of the whole, and it is unthinkable that to do so, he did not avail himself of drawings. It would therefore seem that the drawings must represent the only truly autographic portion of Raphael's work. Instead, never as for the sheets of this period have there been more uncertainties and critical discussions, among the most difficult to resolve.

In fact the method of work had changed, and the more able pupils were engaged not so much on the final pictorial execution as on the various preparatory stages and therefore also on the drawings; they were the principal authors of the execution of the general " models " and of the definitive studies of individual figures, in which from time to time Raphael himself may have intervened either to finish certain parts or to outline a first scheme, or simply to select the solution best-suited to the idea which he wished to realize.

It is not my task here to analyze the methods of collaboration between master and pupils, since others in this volume have dedicated special attention to the drawings as well as to the paintings connected with this collaboration. I shall stop to examine some of the few sure or probably sure autograph drawings, seeking to determine in what direction Raphael turned in the last years of his life when other more intriguing and interesting assignments were taking him away from his drawing activity, and from painting as well.

It is true, however, that many of his drawings of these last years must have been lost, and in a greater number than usual, given the wider circulation and increased handling to which they were continually subjected in the shop, which used them not only in the execution of the painting but also for exercises in copying or for the reduction in other works, as, for example, engravings. But it may also be maintained that Raphael drew much less at that moment than he did earlier. His graphic activity had never been a carefree activity to him, but was above all else a practical necessity for the elaboration of his paintings; once these could be prepared by the pupils under his direction, and once he himself had less need for experiment his compositional ideas on paper, because of the practice he had already acquired in the field, it was almost natural that his drawings should diminish in quantity. The quality remains steady, however.

Therefore, in the highly intricate question of the late production of drawings by Raphael, notwithstanding the often generous efforts which more recent critics have made in order to enlarge the range of the Master's autographs (cf. note 20), I have here sought instinctively to reduce this field by illustrating only the cases of the highest quality and those on which there is the greatest critical agreement, leaving open many problems, in the basic conviction that presently at least, most of these are not resolvable on a demonstrated documentary basis.

151 Study of the figure of Christ for the tapestry " Pasce oves meas." Paris, Louvre (165 a).

152 Study for the tapestry " Pasce oves meas " (tracing). Windsor, Royal Library (165 b).

153 Study for the figure of St. Paul for the tapestry with the Sacrifice at Lystra. Chatsworth, Duke of Devonshire collection (166).

For the entire Sala dell'Incendio, for example, the drawings known are only fifteen or so, between models and studies that are surely from the workshop, copies, and sheets attributed to Raphael; and such a very well-informed scholar as Oberhuber, who nevertheless tends to add to the œuvre of the Master, does not attribute with certainty more than two or three sheets to him.[159] Yet Vasari says, with regard to the Stanze, that Raphael " continuously kept people who, working with his drawings, carried on the work," and it is known that Vasari had first-hand information of this subject. Thus, we see that Raphael still continued to make at least some of the drawings; the problem is to ascertain what kind of drawings they were.

From the little we know, it seems to me that we can deduce that the drawings Raphael made were, with few exceptions, simple tracings, if not actually rapid pen sketches of the type of the Oxford drawing for Santa Maria della Pace (cf. Fig. 135), on the basis of which the pupils were to develop more finished studies to be submitted to the master for selection and perhaps for corrections; the master finally may quite possibly have made some more complete studies to be used as examples.

Of this " exemplar " type just mentioned is the only drawing which has come down to us for the *Battle of Ostia;* it is also the only one for the entire Stanza dell'Incendio that has a " pedigree " that would justify an attribution to Raphael. We are speaking of the often-cited Albertina drawing (Fig. 148),[160] which bears the date of 1515 and an inscription by Dürer attesting that the sheet was sent to him by Raphael as a gift. Doubts have been raised concerning the authenticity of Dürer's handwriting as well as the attribution of the drawing to Raphael; but it would seem strange that Raphael should have sent Dürer, as his own drawing, one made by a pupil, and on the other hand we know that the writing, if not autographic, has a good base in a solid tradition, since the drawing comes from Dürer's heirs. In addition, exchanges of gifts between the two artists are attested by Vasari: " Albert Dürer the German . . . paid him the tribute of his homage and sent him his own portrait painted in watercolors on cambric . . . which appeared marvelous to Raphael, who sent back many drawings of his own which were greatly valued by Albert " (Vasari-Milanesi, IV, p. 354). That this exchange did not go beyond this point and that Raphael had limited himself to admiring the technique of the northern artist and to taking from him ideas for engravings which he then had made by his pupils, without necessarily being influenced stylistically by the northern artist, is another matter, and testifies that the so-called eclecticism of Raphael was limited to a very precise selection in the cultural ambient which was most congenial to him. But to return to the drawing in question, it is also important to consider that it presents many variations with regard to the fresco, not only in the poses but especially in the spatial rapport between the two figures that in the painting are placed in different zones; this seems to suggest that the drawing had been conceived for a general plan of the scene quite different from the one actually executed.

These are all external elements that speak strongly in favor of the hand of the master, rather than of a pupil. But it is certainly not so much the quality of the drawing, which is organic and has passages of intelligent chiaroscuro and linear flair, as it is the selection of the types of the personages, so serious and almost awkward, that creates a doubt; but it is also true that Raphael was inclined in these years to follow a direction sometimes especially naturalistic, which was to prevail in the tapestry cartoons and flourish in the " grotesques " of Giulio Romano.

154 Model for the tapestry with the Blinding of Elymas. Windsor, Royal Library (167).

DRAWINGS FOR THE MOSAICS OF SANTA MARIA DEL POPOLO AND FOR THE VATICAN TAPESTRIES

The quality is heightened, in the sense of freshness and of grace that we usually find in Raphael, in the drawings for the mosaics of the dome of the Chigi Chapel in Santa Maria del Popolo.

In all, there are four studies which seem to propose a system of work unknown up to now; in fact, two of the studies are drawn in the same sense as the mosaics and two are drawn in reverse (Figs. 149, 150).[161] The graphic manner also is varied respectively; the stroke of the two drawings oriented in the same sense as the mosaics is more open and flat, while the other two are more rapid and brilliant. It may be deduced that Raphael made some studies from life for this particular decoration, to which he dedicated a long ideological elaboration;[162] the studies from life were drawn with figures in the same direction as the cartoons (and therefore opposite to the mosaics), and then others were drawn with the opposite orientation, which thus came to correspond exactly with the poses of the figures in the mosaics, in order better to control the final effects of the mosaics.

The style of these drawings, with the movement in the oblique homogeneous lines of the shadows (perhaps determined also by the desire to facilitate the chiaroscuro effects for the mosaicist), and with the delicate but insistent manner of shading the faces, coincides with the style of drawings preceding the date of the execution of the dome, that is, 1516; consider, for example, the drawing for the *Madonna of the Fish* (cf. Fig. 146) and even those for Santa Maria della Pace. Thus, the hypothesis of Shearman that the commission for the decoration of the chapel can be

155 Study of Psyche offering a vessel to Venus, for the Loggia of the Farnesina. Paris, Louvre (169).

408

156 Study of a kneeling female nude, for the Farnesina. Chatsworth, Duke of Devonshire collection (170 b).

dated about 1513 would be confirmed by the fact that the studies for the mosaics give evidence of having been made more toward 1514-15 than toward the final date of the work on the cupola.

The affinity of these with the drawings for the cartoons of the Vatican tapestries, commissioned around 1515, confirms this.

The problem of the cartoons now in the Victoria and Albert Museum is quite different from that of the Stanza dell'Incendio, because we know that Raphael worked on them himself for the most part, both in the conception and in the basic execution, at least for the scenes if not also for the outlines: " Raphael made in their final form and size all the colored cartoons for all [the tapestries] in his own hand" (Vasari). But here, too, the documentation provided by the drawings is very scarce, and consists of little more than two autograph studies for single figures, a *calco* and a dubious general study, and two models also of dubious authorship.

Many designs, therefore, must have been lost, since the work was certainly one of those that, among various other commissions, Raphael studied more carefully, both because of its destination for the Sistine Chapel, and because of the complexity of the themes, historical, hagiographic and theological, and also because of the unusual character of the final medium, a medium which at that time was given more importance than a painted execution, because of the preciousness of the material and the difficulties of working in it.[163]

From the little that remains, though we are not able to follow the creative phases of the various tapestries, we can, however, gain a rather precise idea of the method of preparation of the cartoons, and it is interesting to see how also at this time, though he was very busy with other commissions, Raphael worked with extreme scrupulousness and without diminishing the quality.

157 Study of Venus in the clouds, for the Farnesina (tracing). Chatsworth, Duke of Devonshire collection (170 a).

409

158 Raphael (?). Study for the figures of two
Apostles in the Transfiguration. Paris, Louvre
(172).

After a first pen sketch of the scene, of the type for which there are traces connected with
other works and in the production of the school,[164] Raphael must have proceeded to his studies
from life for the individual figures (cf. Fig. 151) and to their composition in the scene (as in the
Uffizi drawing for *St. Paul Preaching*, no. 540 E, which, because of a certain flatness, is not clearly
an autograph). Sometimes Raphael would make a tracing from these more complete drawings
in order to control the effect that the scene would have in the tapestry. The tracing, in fact, done
in reverse with respect to the drawing and therefore to the cartoon, would be in the same sense
as in the final tapestry (cf. Fig. 152). At that point Raphael himself must have restudied all
the single figures, at least the more important ones, in the typical technique of metal point on
prepared paper, which ever since his youth he had used for final studies (cf. Fig. 153), and finally
he made or had made the "model" in the same sense as the cartoon (cf. Fig. 154 and note 165).
The tapestry is best documented is the *Pasce oves meas*, for which we have an autograph study
in sanguine, in the Louvre, and a retouched tracing also in sanguine by the Master himself for
the whole scene, at Windsor, and a model, perhaps by the school, also in the Louvre.[165]

The sanguine study for the single figure of the Christ (Fig. 151) in the Louvre could have been
either a single one or a fragment of a larger drawing with the whole scene, the one from which
the tracing at Windsor was taken, which exactly repeats this figure in reverse and which is the
basis for recognizing its destination, otherwise unrecognizable, considering the notable variations of the figure with respect to the corresponding figure in the cartoon. The freshness of a
first study from life is evident here, not so much because Raphael pictured the model in

contemporary dress (which he did not only for the Christ but for the Apostles, as is shown in the tracing), but because the drawing has the most genuine qualities of the Master, the same ones we find a bit flattened out in the tracing at Windsor (Fig. 152): a sweet peculiarity of shadows which veil the heads according to a mode dear to Raphael since the time of the Stanza di Eliodoro; a knowing selection of poses and of figure types, ideal and true in their grave beauty; a grace of linear concatenations and of the relationships of the personages, whose gestures are so immediate but are exactly calculated in space and in reciprocity of the action. Notwithstanding the different technical means, the same delicacy of luminous passages, tripled by touches of white, and the same naturalness and simplicity of action is seen in the study at Chatsworth for the St. Paul of the cartoon with the *Sacrifice at Lystra* (Fig. 153).[166] Because of its complete correspondence to the figure in the cartoon and because of the metal point technique on prepared paper, it must have been made as has been said, at the final stage of the work, in order to specify in every minimal nuance of pose and chiaroscuro the protagonist of the scene; Raphael had done precisely the same thing for the figures of the *School of Athens*, which this drawing recalls, although with a greater intelligence in the dramatic bearing of the personages.

The whole cartoon, then, declared the new steps completed by Raphael toward monumentality and the movement in the histories, on the background of ancient, scenographic architecture which was to remain exemplary for at least two centuries to come. But he must have studied such steps in other types of drawings, taken from the actual models, which have been lost and whose existence seems documented by the only final plan which has survived.

159 Auxiliary cartoon for the heads and hands of the two Apostles in the Transfiguration. Oxford, Ashmolean Museum (173).

411

We are dealing with the one, in the usual metal point technique on prepared paper with touches of white, for the cartoon with the *Blinding of Elymas* at Windsor (Fig. 154),[167] which shows the passage from the early, more descriptive cartoons to the later, more classical and historical monumental ones, such as the *Healing of the Lame Man* or the *Death of Ananias*. The drama was in progress on a stagelike perspective whose axes are traced exactly, with actors already in costume, with the same gestures that were to appear in the cartoon, except for some variations in the secondary types.

The model is in a very poor state of preservation and must have undergone many retouchings by pupils, even under the eyes of the Master, during the work on the cartoon, but many original strokes seem autographs, and there is a delicacy of *sfumato* especially in the figures in the background, and an immediacy of touch that make us think directly of the Master himself. The model remains, therefore, an interesting testimony of how Raphael worked and had others work at the final stage of one of his most important works, in about 1516.

DRAWINGS FOR THE FARNESINA AND FOR THE TRANSFIGURATION

The ceiling of the Loggia of the Farnesina and the *Transfiguration*, the last works in which Raphael surely executed himself, raise a type of problem of collaboration on the part of pupils also for the execution of the drawings, besides the paintings, which we have referred to with regard to the Stanza dell'Incendio, with analogous complexity and analogous resistence to satisfactory solutions. Here, too, we shall limit ourselves to illustrating only the drawings more commonly held as autographs, in the not ample number of surviving sheets, while we are conscious of the fact that many of those excluded may, for some reason, be referred to as the Master's, and they have, therefore, an enormous documentary importance for reconstructing the working stages and to give evidence of the graphic manner toward which Raphael tended at that time. In fact it has correctly been noted (Shearman) that the pupils tended to follow most closely the manner of the Master and that, therefore, the sheets which are surely by the workshop are rough but faithful copies of Raphael's style and, as such, are precisely indicative of his personal intentions.

The matter of collaboration is more difficult with regard to the drawings for the Loggia of the Farnesina,[168] to whose study Shearman has given an ample contribution, restricting to six or seven the sure studies by the Master and leaving either in a state of uncertainty or definitely to the pupils the others relative to this decoration, in which he detects a change in the system of division of the work. While in the Stanza dell'Incendio Raphael reserved to a particular pupil a particular zone of the fresco and the studies relative to it, here he tried to give homogeneity to the whole putting various students to work indiscriminantly here and there (except for Giovanni da Udine, to whom the trophies and the festoons were reserved) and continually supervising the whole, to which he himself furnished precise general ideas and some detailed drawings.

Among these the most surely identifiable with Raphael is the study in the Louvre for the Psyche offering a vessel to Venus, whether it is one with perfumes or with the water from the Styx (Fig. 155).[169] It does not show retouching by another hand, as some have supposed, but only a diversity in the methods according to the requirements of the work: more precise in the parts in which Raphael had already established the final disposition of the figure, as in the Venus, more summary in those for which he was still seeking a satisfactory solution, as in the Psyche. The "very beautiful grace" which Vasari praises in the fresco is already expressed in the drawing, in the sculptural elegance of the solemnly described figures ideally classical but of a lively and natural beauty in the free movement of the planes and of the light, which warmly invests the group. The magnificent intuition of Renoir comes to mind according to which "Raphaël qui ne travaillait pas dehors avait cependant étudié le soleil, car ses fresques en sont pleines."

The woman-child of the two highly delicate sheets in Chatsworth[170] has a still more subtle grace; very probably both drawings are relative to the frescoes of the Farnesina, even though they do not directly refer to any of the painted figures. Perhaps they were for scenes projected but never executed (Venus on the clouds, Fig. 157, for the scene of the *Departure of Psyche*; and the girl kneeling, Fig. 156, for the *Toilet of Psyche*) since the two fit perfectly with the above-mentioned one and with the other more probable autographs for the Loggia, to begin with the famous *Three Graces* at Windsor (cf. Marabottini, Fig. 65). Here is a Raphael especially inclined to delicacy and to an almost ingenuous contact with reality, as we have seen him in some drawings of the Madonna and Child (cf. note 155), held to beautiful forms but on the line of the *statuino*, which were to pass on into the seventeeth century and even into nineteenth-century pre-Raphaelitism. But on such a line Raphael is always highly controlled through a superb knowledge of the antique and a *humanitas* which excludes sentimentalism and pure idolatry of form.

That this *humanitas* has its most solemn culmination and conclusion in the *Transfiguration*, is recognized today as are the high intrinsic values and the vast cultural breakthrough of this most famous picture. We shall not repeat here what so many have wisely said of the newness of the theme's interpretation and of the theatrical placement of this great scene, as well as of the problems of the collaboration of Giulio Romano and Penni.

As is easy to understand, however, such problems of collaboration also involve the rather notable group of preparatory drawings which have come down to us, about fifteen in all, many of which are alternately referred sometimes to the Master and sometimes to the pupils, without ever any agreement among the critics, either the modern ones or those of the past. Yet it is certain that Raphael thought about the complex composition for a long time and made many studies for it before arriving at the actual cartoon, which is not preserved, however, not even in fragments.

A glimpse of his early compositional ideas come down to us in two models in the Albertina and in the Louvre, by pupils (there are also highly interesting copies of these by Rubens), in the general drawing for the upper part at Chatsworth, which is held rather convincingly to be by the hand of Raphael himself, and in the drawing in pen for the whole scene with nude figures in the Albertina, which seems to be by Giulio Romano on a tracing by Raphael.[171] But their examination, given the non-autography of the various pieces, regards the genesis of the pictorial work more than the real graphic problem, which arises instead with regard to some nude drawings from life, done with sanguine, for the Apostles below.

None of them has escaped the alternating attribution to Sanzio or to the pupils but none seems to have such a quality as to affirm itself as an autograph by the Master. The more delicate one in the passages of shadow on the faces, more immediate in the contours of the heads and attentive to the spatial aspects of the two figures is the Louvre study (Fig. 158)[172] for the mature Apostle gesturing on the left and the young Apostle next to him, bent forward; but certain stiff details in the legs and in the torsos do not exclude the hand of a pupil, who perhaps followed an original tracing of the master and attempted to interpret in it the ideas for the purposes of a final selection for execution.

Qualitatively more imposing and more homogeneous among them are the six sheets with definitive studies for the heads of the Apostles below, which Fischel already had recognized as auxiliary cartoons and which would confirm, once the Raphaelesque paternity for all of them was ascertained, the direct participation of the Master in this part of the work which is also recognized in its painted parts as the one most characteristic of him. But here too the opinions differ and the only drawing which has been recognized with little discussion as by Raphael is the magnificent study in Oxford for the heads of the so-called John and Peter, that is, the same young Apostle bent forward and the older one standing besides him (Fig. 159).[173]

The study is truly superb in the lively beauty of the young head and in the expressive intensity of the old Apostle, as also in the sensitivity of the hands and the active contours of the hair and in the immediacy of the shadows. These, which are decisively but delicately laid out, bring to completion the experiences of the Stanza di Eliodoro and of Santa Maria della Pace, of those " beautiful and lovely " heads which Raphael was master in creating so that " some heads are lost in the dark and others come forward with the light " (Vasari). Yet we are dealing with an auxiliary cartoon, the last part of the work before the painted execution and therefore one evidently preceded by many other studies for the same figures and heads, according to the usual method. But Raphael, when he works by himself, remains vital in every stage of the work.

It has been correctly observed that some of these heads, and, in this drawing, the one of the old man, have echoes of Dürer in their acute naturalistic perception of certain details: the eye sockets, the cords in the neck. On the other hand the study, here so evident, of the psychology of the personages, in the *incitamento devozionale* that their attitudes produce, were be exemplary for the art of *affetti* of the late Mannerist movement and the whole seventeenth to century, as Vasari says, " And in truth, here he made figure and heads being of such extraordinary beauty, so new, various and graceful that the common judgment of the artist on this work among the many that he made is that it is the most celebrated, the most beautiful and the most divine " (Vasari-Milanesi, IV, p. 372).

¹ L. Dolce, *Dialogo della pittura italiana, intitolato l'Aretino*, Venice, 1557, ed. by P. Barocchi, " Trattati d'arte del cinquecento », Vol. I, p. 170 (Bari, 1960).

² See, besides the various copies inserted in the catalogues of various collections, which we shall cite, those studied in order to understand the inventive process in many Raphaelesque works, both by Fischel in his œuvre, cf. O. Fischel, *Raphaels Zeichnungen*, 8 Vols., Berlin, 1913-41; and by K. T. Parker, " Some observations on Oxford Raphaels," *Old Master Drawings*, Sept.-March, 1939-40, p. 34; by J. White-J. Shearman, " Raphael's Tapestries and their Cartoons," *Art Bulletin*, 40, pp. 193 ff.; by K. Oberhuber, " Vorzeichnungen zu Raffaels Transfiguration," *Jahrbuch der Berliner Museum*, IV, 1962, pp. 116 ff.; and by J. Shearman, " Raphael's Unexecuted Projects for the Stanze," *Walter Friedländer zum 90. Geburtstag*, Berlin, 1965, pp. 158 ff.

³ Raphael writes about his drawings in a letter to Castiglione in 1514 (cf. V. Golzio, *Raffaello nei documenti . . . del suo secolo*, Vatican City, 1936, p. 30) and many suppositions have arisen about them—that these are drawings for a medal (cf. D. Passavant, *Raffaello d'Urbino e il padre suo Giovanni Santi*, Italian edition, notes and translation by G. Guasti, Florence, 1891, III, p. 65) or with those for the Stanza dell'Incendio (cf. Golzio, *op. cit.*, p. 30, note 2, and E. Camesasca, *Raffaello Sanzio, tutti gli scritti*, Milan, 1956, p. 30, note 2); Shearman, instead, more reasonably supposes that these drawings were made for the Loggias of the Farnesina (cf. J. Shearman, " Die Loggia der Psyche in der Villa Farnesina und die Probleme der letzen Phase von Raphael graphischem Stil, " *Jahrbuch der Kunsthistorischen Sammlungen in Wien*, 60, 1964, pp. 58 ff.).

⁴ See the letter by Gerolamo Bagnacavallo to the Duke of Ferrara, written from Rome the last day of February, 1519 (cf. Golzio, *op. cit.*, pp. 92-93).

⁵ G. B. Armenini, *De' veri precetti della pittura*, Ravenna, 1587, p. 75. For the letter by Raphael to Castiglione, cf. Golzio, *op. cit.*, p. 30.

[6] L. Dolce, *op. cit.*, p. 192. See Vasari on this point (cf. Vasari-Milanesi, *Le vite de' più eccellenti pittori, scultori e architettori*, Florence, 1878-85, IV, pp. 354 ff.; V, pp. 411 ff.), and, for Raphael's engravings, see what has been said in the chapter by L. Bianchi in this book.

[7] Vasari-Milanesi, IV, p. 499: " By this hand [of Timoteo Viti] are some of the drawings in our book, which I received from the very gracious Messer Giovanni Maria, his son "; that among those drawings there are some made by Raphael has been supposed by Milanesi (note 4) and that some of these drawings, bought by Vasari, may have been given to the Uffizi (cf. Fischel, *op. cit.* p. 7; and F. Lugt, *Les marques des collections de dessins e d'estampes*, Amsterdam, 1921, suppl., The Hague, 1956, no. 2463) has not been proven; in fact, none of Raphael's drawings in the Uffizi bears traces of its provenance from Vasari's book or from Viti's collection; the matter of the provenance of Raphael's drawings conserved in the Uffizi, is being researched by K. Oberhuber, who has already found many important elements regarding this argument, and one hopes that he will soon publish these and other results of his long studies of the Master's drawings.

[8] The seventeenth-century inventory of the Viti-Antaldi Collection is preserved today in the Ashmolean Museum in Oxford. On 26 of the 48 sheets listed in it, there is written " sold," and it was supposed that these 26 drawings were the ones bought by Crozat in 1714 which were dispersed after the sale of his collection in 1741; those which were bought by Woodburn then passed into the collection of the painter Lawrence and later almost all passed to the Ashmolean Museum in Oxford (cf. F. Lugt, *op. cit.*, nos. 2463, 2245, 2246; and K. T. Parker, *Catalogue of the Collection of Drawings in the Ashmolean Museum*, Oxford, 1965, pp. XII ff.).

[9] The Mantuan Giacomo Strada, who around 1558 was in Vienna as an *antiquario Cesareo*, must have bought them between 1550 and 1560 because Perin del Vaga died in 1547 and Raphael, son of Giulio Romano, died in 1562; cf. the notes to his edition of the *VII Libro di Architettura* by Sebastiano Serlio, Frankfurt a. M., 1575 (Golzio, *op. cit.*, p. 176).

[10] Of Raphael's sketches for the Library of the Sienese Duomo, which later became his property, Vasari speaks in the *Life* of Pinturicchio (Vasari-Milanesi, III, p. 494), but the few known sheets by Raphael for the Library (cf. notes 33, 34) do not bear signs of having belonged to Vasari, as it can also be deduced from the reconstruction of his " book " made by O. Kurz, " Giorgio Vasari's *libro de' disegni*," *Old Master Drawings*, 1937, no. 45, pp. 1 ff.; no. 47, pp. 32 ff.; for the collection of Vasari, see also the exhibition catalogue, *Giorgio Vasari dessinateur and collectioneur*, Cabinet des Dessins du Louvre, Paris, 1965.

[11] L. Dolce, *op. cit.*, p. 191; L. Dolce, *Lettere di diversi eccellentissimi huomini*, Venice, 1599 (cf. Golzio, *op. cit.*, p. 306). For the drawing representing the *Marriage of Rossane*, see the scholarly note by K. Oberhuber in *Le Cabinet d'un grand amateur*, *P. J. Mariette* (1694-1774) exhibition cat., Louvre, Paris, 1967, no. 123; and A. M. Hayum, " A New Dating for Sodoma's Frescoes in the Villa Farnesina, " *Art Bulletin*, 48, 1966. None of the drawings gradually identified with the one cited, seems, however, to have the high qualities of an original by Raphael, notwithstanding the good quality, for example, of the ones in the Albertina (no. 17634) and the one in Haarlem (Tayler Museum, A. 63).

[12] That Maratta possessed at least one drawing by Raphael, among the many of his collection reported by Bellori, has been demonstrated by no. 4370 of Windsor (Popham-Wilde, 788) with the two heads of the Apostles for the Vatican *Coronation*, which came from the Maratta Fund (cf. A. E. Popham, " An Unnoticed Drawing by Raphael, " *Old Master Drawings*, 1937-38, XII, p. 45. That Maratta was even the former owner of the so-called *Taccuino di Venezia*, not to mention the one of the Duke of Leicester, was assumed by Passavant, III, pp. 98, 217, according to an erroneous reading of the passage by Bellori in the *Life of Maratta*, in which he recalls a notebook of his observations on Raphael, and not a notebook of drawings by Raphael himself.

[13] For the collection of Father Resta, see L. Grassi, " Ricerche intorno al Padre Resta e al suo codice di disegni dell'Ambrosiana, " *Rivista del R. Istituto di archeologia e storia dell'arte*, 1941, and the volume in facsimile published by the Credito Italiano, *Cento Tavole del codice Resta*, Milan, 1955. Among those drawings, only the beautiful study for the Virgin of the *Disputa* (F. 291) has Raphael's quality. On the contrary, the drawing in the National Gallery of Ottawa (which also belonged to Father Resta and was attributed by him to Vincenzo Romano, while Popham attributed it to Sanzio) does not seem to have the qualities to be an autograph of the Master (cf. Popham-Fenwick, *Catalogue of European Drawings. The National Gallery of Canada*, Toronto, 1965, no. 12).

[14] An attempt to reconstruct the collections of Jabach and Crozat, in regard to Raphael's drawings, was made by Passavant (III, pp. 247, 227, respectively), who attempted the same for the collection of King William of Holland (III, p. 235). For Mariette's collection, see the already cited catalogue of the Louvre exhibition of 1967.

[15] See Beaucamp, *Le peintre Lillois J. B. Wicar, son œuvre et son temps*, Lille, 1939, Chap. X; F. Lugt, *op. cit.*, *s. v.*; (P. Mourois), *Raphaël, Dessins*, exhibition cat., Lille, 1961; Robert Scheller, *Dessins Italiens du Musée de Lille*, exhibition cats., Amsterdam, Bruxelles, Lille, 1968, pp. 8 ff.

[16] (P. J. Mariette), *Description sommaire des statues . . . du cabinet de feu M. Crozat*, 1750, p. 14.

[17] C. Ruland, *The Works of Raffaello Sanzio da Urbino as Represented in the R. Collection in the R. Library of Windsor Castle*, private ed., 1876.

[18] For the bibliography up to the last century, see O. Fischel, *Raphael Zeichnungen. Versuch einer Kritik der bisher veröffentlichten Blätter*, Strasbourg, 1898 (henceforth will be cited as Fischel, 1898, with the catalogue number). While he was writing various detailed articles, Fischel also published a vast corpus of Raphael's drawings, which unfortunately he could not finish, and three or five issues of reproductions in facsimile and at least another volume of text relative to the late Roman period of Sanzio are missing: O. Fischel, *Raphael Zeichnungen*, Berlin, 1913-41, 8 vols. of facsimiles and text (which henceforth will be commonly cited as F.). His opinions regarding the drawings of his late period can be deduced from the cited essay of 1898 and from the posthumous monograph: O. Fischel, *Raphael*, London, 1948 (trans.), Berlin, 1962.

[19] See especially Venturi: A. Venturi, " Disegno di Raffaello, avanti la venuta in Roma, " *L'Arte*, 1916, p. 315; " Raffaello disegnatore, " *La Nuova Antologia*, 1920, CCVI, pp. 19 ff.; *Raffaello*, Rome, 1920; *Storia dell'arte italiana*, IX, II, Milan, 1926; *Choix de cinquante dessins de Raphaël Santi*, Paris, 1927.
For other Italian contributions regarding the drawings, besides detailed articles cited below, see S. Ortolani, *Raffaello*, Bergamo, 1942; G. Castelfranco, *Raffaello* (drawings), Milan, 1962.

[20] K. T. Parker, *op. cit.*, 1956; Ph. Pouncey-J. Gere, *Italian Drawings in the Department of Prints and Drawings in the British Museum, Raphael and his circle*, London, 1962. Among the most ample recent articles on the drawings, see especially: K. Oberhuber, " Die Fresken der Stanza dell'Incendio im Werk Raphaels, " in *Jahrbuch der Kunsthistorischen Sammlungen in Wien*, 1962, 58; *Ibid.*, 1962; J. Shearman, *op. cit.*, 1964, 1965 (these two scholars tend to increase the number of Raphaelesque autographs with new attributions, not always convincing, as we will see below); R. Wittkower, " The Young Raphael, " in *Allen Memorial Art Museum Bulletin*, Oberlin College, Summer, 1963. After the great work by Fischel, the major anthological essay on Raphael's drawings remains that by U. Middeldorf, *Raphael's Drawings*, New York, 1945. For a vast bibliography, more or less recent, on Raphael's circle, see the chapter by Marabottini in this book and the notes on the drawings illustrated here.

[21] Raphael's working procedure, which became more and more complex as his assistants took part in his work, has been studied in a more or less systematic manner by Passavant (*op. cit.*, III, pp. 92-93), Fischel (*op. cit.*, 1913-41, pp. 20-22),

Middeldorf (*op. cit.*, 1945, pp. 11-12), Hartt ("Raphael and Giulio Romano," *Art Bulletin*, 1944, 26), S. J. Freedberg (*Painting of the High Renaissance in Rome and Florence*, Harvard University, 1961, pp. 261 ff.), Oberhuber and Shearman (*op. cit.*).

[22] Raphael's use of so-called "auxiliary cartoons" has been demonstrated by Fischel ("Raphael's auxiliary Cartoons," *The Burlington Magazine*, 1937, 71, pp. 167-168) and it has been accepted by the succeeding criticism.

[23] The only drawing of a skeleton among those more commonly considered as Raphael's autographs is the one on the verso of a drawing in the Ashmolean (cf. note 87); another example, although partial, is the one in the drawing in the British Museum (F. 178; Pouncey-Gere, II) for the Marys of the *Borghese Deposition*, in which one of the figures is studied on the skeleton. Besides, as L. Becherucci pointed out to me, the drawing in the British Museum (F. 4; Pouncey-Gere, I) for a standing nude seems a precise anatomical study of a *scorticato*.

[24] Passavant, *op. cit.*, III, p. 92. In Passavant one can find the first general information on the preservation of Raphael's sheets up to our time, on the reconstruction of the oldest collections of his drawings, and on the engravings and lithographic reproductions of them, for a total of 613 sheets, described and arranged by countries and by collections.

[25] The notebook preserved in the Galleria dell'Accademia in Venice, was acquired in Parma by Giuseppe Bossi in 1810 as an autograph by Sanzio and passed to the Academy in 1812 as a gift from Emperor Francis I. Passavant and Cavalcaselle accepted it as an autograph, but at the end of the nineteenth century Morelli advanced the first doubts (Morelli, *Die Werke Italienische Meisters*, etc., 1880, p. 318). Some thought of Pinturicchio and of an anonymous artist of the Umbrian workshop, until Kahl (*Das Venetianische Skizzenbuch und seine Bezeihungen zur Umbrischen Malerschule*, Leipzig, 1882) proposed the name of Genga, and Loeser ("Note intorno ai disegni conservati nella R. Galleria di Venezia," *Rassegna d'arte*, 1913, 12, pp. 177 ff.) raised the doubt that it might be a forgery of the eighteenth century. That opinion had quite a following, even though it was corrected according to Venturi's opinion, in the sense that they were copies and eighteenth century forgeries from Raphael's originals (cf. G. Fogolari, *I disegni della R. Galleria dell'Accademia di Venezia*, Milan, 1913). Fischel seems more cautious in considering them works of the Umbrian workshop, with traces of a Pinturicchiesque-Raphaelesque culture. Grassi also considers them eighteenth-century forgeries (*I disegni italiani, il Quattrocento*, Venice, n. d., p. XXXVII).

[26] After the still basic work by Fischel, "Die Zeichnungen der Umbrer," *Jahrbuch der Preussischen Kunst Sammlungen*, 1917, 38, parts I and II, not many other additions have been made to our knowledge of the Umbrian drawings of the fifteenth century, if one excludes the sporadic contributions to the argument of the catalogues of the various collections, especially those of A. E. Popham-J. Wilde, *The Italian Drawings of the XVth and XVIth Centuries at Windsor Castle*, London, 1949; A. E. Popham-Ph. Pouncey, *The Italian Drawings in the ... British Museum*, London, 1950; Pouncey-Gere, *op. cit.*, 1962; K. T. Parker, *op. cit.*, 1956. For a brief panorama of the argument, cf. L. Grassi, *op. cit.*

[27] An attempt in such a direction was made, for example, by Venturi in the article cited (*L'Arte*, 1916), in which, referring to Raphael parts of the execution of the frescoes of the Cambio, he also attributed to him such drawings as the Sibyl, no. 399 E, in the Gabinetto Disegni e Stampe degli Uffizi, which remains, instead, a typical graphic example of Perugino (cf. *Cento disegni italiani*, exhibition cat., U.S.A., 1960-Florence 1961, no. 21).

[28] Lille, Wicar Museum, 474-475: (r.), *Coronation of S. Niccolò da Tolentino;* (v.), head of a man, two studies of draperies, sketches of birds, elevation of a building with two stories. Black pencil and white lead (r.), black pencil and pen (v.), 395 × 250. Passavant, 396; F. 5-6; *Le XVIᵉ siècle européen. Peintures et Dessins dans les Collections Publiques françaises*, exhibition cat., Paris, 1965-66, no. 233; exhibition cat., Lille, 1968, no. 79.
Bear in mind that on the recto the figure of St. Augustine is already dressed with a mantle and a bishop's hat, in contrast with the other figures which are studied on the model in contemporary dress, and that the same figure of the saint is reworked on a preliminary tracing with the stylus, probably derived from a preceding drawing. We should also notice, besides, that the head on the verso, which had been studied from the usual model with a contemporary beret, unites the type of God the Father already studied on the recto (the large cheekbones, the pointed nose, the short hair) with the pose of the head of S. Niccolò, also indicated on the recto, bent toward the left and looking down.

[29] Oxford, Ashmolean Museum, 564: (r.), hand with a crown and various sketches; (v.), angel with "cartiglio" and other studies. Black pencil, 379 × 245. F. 7-8; Middeldorf 5 (v.); Parker, 1956, n. 504.
On the recto, the two hands at the left are, respectively, studies for that with the book and for that with the cross of S. Niccolò (of the latter we have, right beside, a weaker sketch), while the hand at the center which holds the crown seems to be that of St. Augustine, even though some have seen in it a variation for that of God the Father; in fact, there are too many differences from the divine hand on the surviving fragment of the picture, and there are, instead, many analogies with the hand of St. Augustine, as it appears in the Lille study (cf. note 28). Always on the recto, there are below at the center two quick sketches of complete figures which appear destined, one for the S. Niccolò and the other, perhaps, for the angel at the right of the altarpiece, but not without some analogy in the pose to the God the Father in the *Creation of Eve* in the standard for Città di Castello. On the verso there are studies of a full-length figure for St. Augustine, for the left angel and for the hand of God the Father, while the sketch can not be clearly identified.

[30] The influence of Signorelli is especially evident in the sheet in the Ashmolean Museum, no. 501 (F. 23), which bears on its recto a study for the God the Father for the standard of Città di Castello and a study for a nude copied from the archer of the *Martyrdom of St. Sebastian* by Signorelli, also in Città di Castello. The drawing in the British Museum (cf. Pouncey-Gere, 2, F. 11), which has been considered a sketch for the same standard, has on its recto a figure which seems inspired by the *St. Peter* in the altarpiece by Signorelli in Volterra. Raphael later shows influences from Signorelli, as, for example, in the S. Niccolò in the Ansidei Altarpiece which is inspired by the figure of the saint in the Signorelli altarpiece in Perugia, of 1484.

[31] Such a notion, proposed recently by Longhi, "Percorso di Raffaello giovine," *Paragone*, 65, 1955, seems also to be confirmed on the graphic level, according to arguments by Fischel, by a drawing in the Louvre, Inv. 1609 (F. 10), whose verso represents a saint clearly inspired in his pose by Donatello's *St. John the Evangelist* in the Florentine Duomo, while the type of the head is the same as that of the God the Father in the *Coronation of S. Niccolò da Tolentino;* the connection with that altarpiece is also confirmed by the recto of the same drawing (F. 9), which studies the head of the demon in the same *Coronation:* this is an indication that as early as the time of the execution of the altarpiece for Città di Castello, in 1500, Raphael knew the works of Florentine artists located in Florence.

[32] Although Vasari affirms explicitly, as we have said, the collaboration of Raphael with Pinturicchio in Siena, Milanesi, his commentator (Vasari-Milanesi, III, p. 256), excluded the possibility that Raphael could have invented the stories for Pinturicchio, and he has been followed by the greater part of contemporary criticism (E. Carli, *Il Pintoricchio*, Milan, 1960), which leaves the problem of the drawings unresolved, as Fischel had done already; he could not decide whether to attribute to Sanzio the group of known sheets for the Library (cf. notes 33-36), even though he includes them as documents in Raphael's œuvre. The first doubts that the drawings accepted as Raphael's by earlier criticism had been executed instead by the hand of Pinturicchio came from A. Von Beckerat, "Über einige Zeichnungen alter Meister in Oxford," *Repertorium für Kunstwissenschaft*, XXX, 1907, p. 293; but now the connoisseurs of drawings generally continue to follow Vasari, from Popham to Parker to Pouncey-Gere, even though no exact study has directly confronted the problem. Reasonable confirmation of Raphael's sojourn in Siena was recently provided by R. Longhi ("Un intervento raffaellesco nella serie 'eroica' di Casa Piccolomini," *Paragone*, 175, 1964, pp. 5 ff.), with the attribution to Sanzio of a Cleopatra (?) which might have been part of the Sienese cycle and which indirectly provides another element in favor of a collaboration between Raphael and Pinturicchio.

[33] Oxford, Ashmolean Museum, 510: (r.), group of soldiers; (v.), two cupids with a shield, silver point, grey-blue tinted paper, 213 × 223. Passavant, 530; F. 63; exhibition cat., London, 1930, no. 120; Parker, 510.

Among the figures which appear on the recto, the first at the left can be seen in the fresco at the extreme right of the group; the central one is similar to the central frescoed figure, with the arm outstretched, according to the variation alluded to in the drawing; the third figure does not appear in the fresco, while the fourth corresponds to the first figure of the painted group, although the head is turned. On the verso there are two putti supporting the coat of arms, quite similar to those by Pinturicchio at the sides of the various frescoes in the cycle.

[34] Florence, Gabinetto Disegni e Stampe degli Uffizi, 520 E: *Departure of Aeneas Sylvius Piccolomini for the Council of Basel.* Pen, bistre and white lead, with traces of black pencil, squared in pen. 705 × 415 (maximum measures). At the top it bears a pen inscription of the sixteenth century: " La historia è questa che M. S. Enea era in la comitiva de Ms. Domenicho da Capranica el quale era fatto Cardinale e non publicato quando il detto andava in Basilea al Concilio, e intrato in mare al porto di Talamone e essendo per intrare nel porto di Genova fu assalito da la tempesta e battuto fino in Libia"; it also bears the indication of a person and the places: " Sardinia/Talamone/MS Domenicho da Capranica." Passavant, 135; F. 62.

Also the drawing formerly in the Baldeschi Collection in Perugia, and now in the Contini-Bonacossi Collection in Florence, bears an inscription in a similar hand which confirms the original unity of the two small cartoons; this, also, has passages of high quality worthy of an autograph drawing by Sanzio, with few variations in regard to the fresco. The two drawings were considered copies from the frescoes and were decisively denied by Venturi as being by Raphael (*op. cit.*, 1916. p. 352), but Scalvanti accurately and passionately defended this attribution, which, among other things demonstrates that the drawing formerly belonging to Baldeschi, at the beginning of the seventeenth century was assigned to Raphael by earlier tradition and that it came from the Piccolomini heredity; he maintains, besides, that the inscriptions on the cartoons are by Raphael himself (cf. O. Scalvanti, *Il disegno raffaellesco dei Conti Baldeschi di Perugia per la Libreria Piccolomini del Duomo Senese*, Perugia, 1908).

[35] Crowe-Cavalcaselle (*Raffaello*, ed. Florence, 1884-91, I, p. 180) conclude the description of the sheet by saying: " admirable execution of this drawing, with its beautiful contrasts of light and shadow," with " the characteristic signs of Raphael's hand." The conclusion of the two great scholars regarding the problem that arose from the finding of the contract commissioned to Pinturicchio, in which it was specified that he was obliged to furnish all the drawings and the cartoons for the frescoes of the Library, is convincingly simple (p. 179): " we must believe that the assertions of Vasari and the contract of Pinturicchio are not irreconcilable, and admit instead that Pinturicchio was obliged only to furnish the first sketch, and that this was reworked by Raphael so as to make a more complete drawing, more inspired from nature." See also C, Gamba (*Raphaël*, Paris, 1932, p. 33), who accepts the attribution to Raphael.

[36] We are dealing here with a drawing in the Uffizi, 537 E. (F. 60-61), in pen, which bears on the recto a group of horsemen for the second plane of the *Voyage of Aeneas Sylvius to Basel*, and on the verso a sketch of a lion, some heads and a foreshortened reclining figure taken from one in the foreground of the *Last Judgment* by Signorelli in the S. Brizio Chapel in Orvieto.

[37] Also the Oxford drawing, 539 (F. 200-201), see note 100, takes up motifs from the frescoes in Orvieto. For further Signorellian citations on Sanzio's sheets, see note 30.

[38] Oxford, Ashmolean Museum, 505: Sketch for guards for a Resurrection. Silver point, white lead, grey-tinted paper, 320 × 220. It bears the mark " R. V.," in imitation of that of Viti-Antaldi. Passavant, 479; F., 1898, 394 a; exhibition cat., London, 1930, no. 118; Parker, 505.

For the *Resurrection*, formerly in the Kinnaird Collection and presently in the São Paulo Museum (Brazil), see the recent attribution to Sanzio made by R. Longhi (*op. cit.*, 1955), which also avails itself of the two drawings in Oxford (the cited 505 and the analogous 506); for contrast, see the negative opinion maintained in this book by L. Becherucci. After the first doubts of Morelli regarding Raphael's autograph of the two drawings in Oxford, Fischel also considers them of Perugino's school, and for this reason he did not list them in his corpus of Raphael's works, but only in his *Zeichnungen der Umbrer*, loc. cit., pp. 135, 140, nos. 74-75. Instead they are accepted as Raphael's by Parker, *q.v.* for the bibliography of the sheets.

[39] Paris, Cabinet des Dessins, Louvre, 1935: (r.), *Madonna Enthroned with SS. Sebastian and Rocco*; (v.), sketch of a *Nursing Madonna*. Ink (r.), black pencil (v.), 285 × 225. From the Vallardi Collection. F. 45. A. Riedl, " Raphaels ' Madonna del Baldacchino'," in *Mitteilungen der Kunsthistorisches Institutes in Florenz*, VIII, IV, 1959, p. 234. It should be compared with another drawing in the Louvre (F. 43), representing the half-length Madonna and Child, which as a composition has many analogies with this and with the *Solly Madonna* of Berlin, so much so that it could be considered as a preparatory sketch for that painting, if it had not been made in a more mature style subsequent either to the present drawing or to the picture in Berlin.

[40] These are the drawings F. 15-32, thirteen in all existing to which we might add the sheet in Windsor, Popham-Wilde, 788 (see notes 12 and 43). One must notice that the sheets listed by Fischel as no. 17 and no. 31 are lost, while nos. 20 and 32 cannot be connected with the Vatican altarpiece. With regard to the latter, its earlier date of 1499 *ca.*, should be pointed out, that is to say when Raphael still worked in Perugino's workshop, as Wittkower has proposed (*op. cit.*); but the drawings and their style, by now quite accomplished, confirm the chronology generally accepted for the altarpiece, that is, around 1502-03, since Wittkower himself admits that at least the auxiliary cartoons seem to contradict his hypothesis.

[41] Lille, Wicar Museum, 440: (r.), study of a head and two hands; (v.), sketch of Christ crowning the Virgin. Silver point, grey-tinted paper, 226 × 200. Passavant, 384; F. 15-16; exhibition cat., Paris, 1965-66, no. 234.

Notable is the verso of the folio, which was considered a copy by Morelli, while it is probably an autograph drawing, badly retraced in ink: the figures here are (as usual) sketched from the model in contemporary dress (the Virgin also is drawn from a male model), with few compositional variations with regard to the painting. The folio according to Fischel should have been part of the same notebook of his nos. 18, 19, 21, 22, 41, 50, 51 (cf. notes 44, 45, 50, 51).

[42] London, British Museum, 1895.9.15.610: Head of St. James in ecstasy. Black pencil, with traces of pin-pricking, 247 × 216. F. 23; Middeldorf, 13; Pouncey-Gere, 5.

The small folio in Oxford, no. 512 (F. 24), which shows a head in an analogous pose, is apparently a preparatory sketch for this drawing. The pose in the Oxford drawing is in its turn similar and upside down, in relation to the one of a Penitent St. Jerome in the Uffizi, no. 277 E. (F. fig. 31), which could very well be an earlier autograph. According to Fischel the Lille drawing, Wicar Museum, no. 482 (F. 26), should be connected with the figure of St. Jerome; on its recto is a head of saint which nevertheless seem similar to the one of St. Thomas of the same Vatican altarpiece, for its cut and physiognomy.

[43] We have here the Lille drawings, no. 470 (F. 25), for the third Apostle at the left, and the Windsor, Popham-Wilde, no. 788 (cf. note 12), for the two Apostles at the right of St. Thomas.

[44] a) Oxford, Ashmolean Museum, 511 a-b; two studies of a boy musician, a) with harpsichord, b) with violin. These drawings, now separated, were originally on the same folio, which was subsequently cut vertically. Silver point, body color, grey-tinted paper, 191 × 127 (a), 189 × 126 (b). Passavant, 493; F. 18-19; Parker, 511.

b) Lille, Wicar Museum, 444: Sketches for a musical angel. Silver point, grey-tinted paper. 202 × 221. Passavant, 383; F. 21; exhibition cat., Lille, 1961, no. 14.

The two drawings of Oxford and Lille perhaps belonged originally to the same notebook, which was reconstructed by Fischel (F. 15, 16, 21, 22, 41, 50, 51; cf. note 51).

[45] London, British Museum, Pp. l. 67; Head and hand of angel. Metal point, ivory-tinted paper, 276 × 196. Passavant, 440; F. 22; Middeldorf, 12; Pouncey-Gere, 4.

It is a sketch for the angel at the right of Christ with a minimal variation in the bending of the head. It probably belonged to the same notebook as the sheets mentioned above.

[46] Paris, Cabinet des Dessins, Louvre, 3860: *Annunciation*, small cartoon. Ink, bistre, traces of black pencil with light passages of watercolor: pricked for the trancing. 283 × 420. Passavant, 320; F. 28; Venturi (*op. cit.*, 1916) does not consider it as Raphael's autograph.

[47] Oxford, Ashmolean Museum, 513; *Presentation of the Child in the Temple*, Ink on stylus marks. 200 × 200. Passavant, 456 (as in the Chambers Hall Collection); F. 30; Parker, 513.

[48] Florence, Gabinetto Disegni, Uffizi, 57 E.: Female bust in profile. Black pencil on stylus marks, with light passages in pen on the nose and eyes and with a trace of white lead on the shoulders. 256 × 160 (maximum measures). F. 32; exhibition cat., London, 1930, no. 114; exhibition cat., Uffizi, 1960, no. 56.

The drawing was attributed by Meder to Viti, while Fischel compares it with a lost drawing (F. 31) representing the drapery of one of the saints in the Vatican altarpiece and a profile of a woman which would be a study for a young girl with doves in the predella but which is rather generically related to this Uffizi drawing.

[49] Lille, Wicar Museum, 641; Head of boy with hat, turned to the right. Black pencil and white lead, prepared paper, 211 × 186. Passavant, 407; F. 20; exhibition cat., Paris, 1965-66, no. 235; exhibition cat., Lille, 1968, n. 80. It was attributed to Viti by Morelli.

[50] Oxford, Ashmolean Museum, 509; Kneeling youth. Silver point, tinted paper. Passavant, 497; F. 41; exhibition cat., London, 1930, no. 117; Middeldorf, 11; Parker, 509.

The relationship with the *Mond Crucifixion* and its predella are vague; in fact this figure is similar to that of the Magdalene in the Crucifixion, but not in the pose of the arms; with regard to the predella, it is similar to the two spectators at the right of the *Miracle of S. Cirillo*, now in Lisbon, but its head is turned differently and it is similar to the youth at the right of the *Miracle of St. Jerome*, now in Richmond, which instead has the arms placed in a different fashion. This folio may have been part of the same notebook (cf. note 44).

[51] Of all the various notebooks assembled by Fischel (cf. O. Fischel, " Raphael's pink sketch book," *The Burlington Magazine*, April, 1939, pp. 182 ff.), the most plausible one appears to be the earliest, with drawings made with metal point on grey-ivory-tinted paper which includes nos. F. 16, 18, 19, 21, 22, 41, 50, 51, most of which are intended for the figures in the *Vatican Coronation* and are homogeneous among themselves because of their technical and stylistic criteria and because of their scale (cf. notes 41, 44, 45, 50, 53). The other reconstructions are less convincing, even those of the *grande taccuino fiorentino* (cf. note 70) and of the " Pink sketch book " (cf. note 154); the homogeneity which Fischel saw in the different sheets is, in fact, quite dubious, as Parker already noted (*op. cit.*, 1939-40), and as Pouncey-Gere had proposed in their catalogue of the British Museum (nos. 3, 4, 14). Besides, such reconstructions, which necessitate accurate and technical studies of the types of the tinted papers, have only a relative importance from a critical point of view because the folios of a notebook could have been drawn at different times and with different interests or stimuli, sometimes even made by different hands, without the possibility of deducing other elements than those merely external to an originally material unity of the sheets.

[52] Frankfurt, Städelsches Institut: *Madonna and S. Niccolò da Tolentino*. Ink and traces of black pencil and metal point, 233 × 156. Passavant 276; F. 52; Middeldorf, 15; Riedl, *op. cit.*, 1959, p. 235.

[53] a) Lille, Wicar Museum, 442; (r.), Study of a seated woman holding a book and a study of a hand with a book; (v.), two archers. Silver point, grey-tinted paper, 248 × 178. Passavant 375 (as a study for the *Madonna del Cardellino*); F. 50; exhibition cat., Paris, 1965-66, no. 236; exhibition cat., Lille, 1968, no. 81.

b) London, British Museum, 1895.9.15.611: Head of a veiled Madonna. Metal point, tinted paper, 258 × 191. F. 51; Pouncey-Gere, 3. This and the preceding folio in Lille belonged probably to the grey notebook (cf. note 51).

c) Oxford, Ashmolean Museum, 508 a-b: (r.), a) Study of Madonna and Child, b) Study of landscape; (v.), a) Study of Child, b) Study of landscape. This sheet, originally double, was divided afterward. Ink and traces of stylus, 116 × 132. Passavant, 486; F. 46-49; Middeldorf 7-8; Parker, 508.

There is no relation between these studies and the *Solly Madonna*, to which they had been connected by Koopmann.

[54] An example of a drawing for landscape earlier than the Oxford one, this should be considered a portion of landscape in a drawing also in Oxford, no. 501 v (F. 3), intended for the standard of Città di Castello, and therefore quite early. But there, as in other examples which we will see later, the spatial background is linked to a greater figurative composition.

[55] Oxford, Ashmolean Museum, 514: (r.), Head of a woman; (v.), Two heads of a woman, one in profile and the other in a three-quarters profile, black pencil. 161 × 111. F. 35-36; exhibition cat., London, 1930, no. 115; Parker, 514.

[56] London, British Museum, 1895.9.15.612: Bust of a woman, black pencil, stylus traces. 411 × 260. Passavant, 583; F. 34; Pouncey-Gere, 9. Morelli and Van Marle attributed it to Viti and it was erroneously believed to be a portrait of Raphael himself.

[57] London, British Museum, 1895.9.15.619: Male head and marks of stylus, brown paper. 255 × 190. F. 57; Middeldorf, 10; Pouncey-Gere, 8.

[58] This is the very famous " self-portrait " in the Ashmolean Museum (F. 1; Parker, 515), reproduced in this book in the chapter on Raphael's life, Fig. 4. The drawing, which represents a long-haired youth, more handsome than Raphael appears in his more certain and later self-portraits), bears an eighteenth-century inscription " self-portrait when young," which caused it to be considered a self-portrait of Raphael, an idea which we do not accept because of reasons validly demonstrated by Parker. Also the chronology of the drawing is uncertain, between about 1500 (a date which would forcibly bring our attention to the rather young age of the artist, if he is considered to be Raphael himself), and 1502, a date arrived at by means of a comparison with drawings for the Vatican altarpiece and the similar portrait of Lille (cf. note 49), and 1504. This drawing has also been attributed to Viti.

[59] That in 1504 Raphael was in Florence is documented in the letter of recommendation of Giovanna Feltria to Soderini, of October 1, 1504 (cf. Golzio, *op. cit.*, p. 9); and although the authenticity of that letter and its reference to Raphael have been questioned, nevertheless it appears quite plausible that precisely in about 1504 one should date the arrival of Raphael in Florence, according to Vasari, who places that arrival after the collaboration between Raphael and Pinturicchio in Siena, at the time when Leonardo and Michelangelo were working on their cartoons for the hall of Palazzo Vecchio.

[60] New York, Pierpont Morgan Library, U. 1. 15: The Agony in the Garden, cartoon. Ink, water color; pin-pricked for pouncing, 226 × 265. From the Antaldi Collection. F. 66; Middeldorf, 20; J. Bean-F. Stampfle, *Drawings from New York Collections, I, The Italian Renaissance*, New York, 1965, no. 58. On the verso it bears an attribution to Viti.

[61] Berlin, Kupferstichkabinett: The Magdalene, cartoon. Ink and watercolor, and pin-pricked for pouncing, 302 × 95. F. 56 a (without text); Middeldorf, 16.

The cartoon was published by Fischel (" Raffael's Heilige Magdalena im Berliner Kgl. Kupferstichkabinett," *Jahrbuch der Preussischen Kunstsammlungen*, 36, 1915, pp. 92 ff.) as a pendant of the one with St. Catherine in the Rothschild Collection (F. 56), both preparatory works for the small panels with the two saints, now in the Contini-Bonacossi Collection, which Longhi (*op. cit.*, 1955, p. 22) dates to the artist's first Florentine period.

[62] London, National Gallery, 213 A: *The Dream of the Knight*, cartoon. Ink and traces of metal point. Pin-pricked for pouncing, 168 × 202. F. 40; Middeldorf, 6; C. Gould, *Sixteenth-Century. Italian School*, cat., National Gallery, London, 1962, p. 147.
Venturi (*op. cit.*, 1916) denies its attribution to Raphael and considers it a forgery.

[63] Vienna, Albertina, 4879. Half-length Madonna and Child with a pomegranate in her hand. Black pencil, 418 × 298. Passavant, 183; F. 53; cat. Albertina (Stix-Froelich Bum, *Die Zeichnungen der Toskanischen, Umbrischen und Roemischen Schulen . . . in . . . Albertina*, Vienna, 1932, no. 49).
There is a drawing in Berlin (cf. note 64), that has been mistaken for the original cartoon since it was in the Madrazo Collection in Madrid (Passavant, 584); the same error is found in contemporary compilations which always cite the " cartoon " in Berlin with regard to the *Connestabile* painting even though Fischel had already recognized that it was a copy (p. 71). Perhaps it is a copy from the painting before the variation of the book in place of the fruit was made, or perhaps it is from another lost drawing, because the pose of the Child is similar to the one in the picture and not to the drawing in the Albertina (I thank Dr. U. Schlegel for having sent me the photograph).

[64] Lille, Wicar Museum, 431; *Holy Family with an Angel*. Ink, 168 × 158 (folded sheet). Passavant, 482; F. 54; exhibition cat., Lille, 1961, no. 16; exhibition cat., Lille, 1968, no. 84.
There is a more complete copy on the recto of a drawing in Berlin, Kupferstichkabinett (F. fig. 62), which bears on the verso a copy of the Umbrian school from the painting or from the drawing for the *Connestabile Madonna* (cf. note 63). Comparing it with the *Terranuova Madonna*, here we have variations in the gesture of the Madonna; in the picture the angel at the left and St. Joseph are absent, there is, instead, an unidentifiable *putto*, perhaps an angel.

[65] See what L. Becherucci writes with regard to the influence that Lorenzo di Credi, with the material in his rich workshop, might have had on young Sanzio.

[66] On the essentially draftsmanlike character of the two cartoons of *Anghiari* and *Cascina*, and on the influence which they had on contemporary and on future graphic developments, I have written elsewhere (A. Forlani, *Disegni italiani, il 500 nell'Italia centro-meridionale*, Venice, 1962, pp. XVIII-XIX, XXV-XXVI).

[67] Florence, Gabinetto Disegni, Uffizi, 530 E: St. George, semi-frontal, on horseback, killing the dragon. Ink, light traces of black pencil, some pin-prickings, 265 × 268. F. 57; exhibition cat., London, 1930, no. 119; Middeldorf, 9; exhibition cat., Uffizi, 1960, no. 57.

[68] Venice, Galleria dell'Accademia, 10; (r.), Battle of horsemen and foot-soldiers; (v.), Male nude with standard. Ink, 258 × 209. F. 97-98; exhibition cat., London, 1930, no. 122; Middeldorf, 29; exhibition cat., U.S.A.-Uffizi, 1960-61, no. 32.
This is the only sheet attributed to Raphael existing in the Accademia which is not part of the famous notebook (cf. note 25). According to Fischel it must have been part of the " large Florentine notebook " (cf. note 70).

[69] Among the drawings prior to 1504, in fact, one can consider as pseudo-anatomical studies, or at least as nude studies, the study by Signorelli in Oxford, no. 501 (F. 2), (cf. note 30), and the drawings in the British Museum, Pouncey-Gere, 1 (F. 4), and in the Uffizi, no. 277 E (F. fig. 31, formerly attributed to Pollaiolo, cf. note 50).

[70] The " large Florentine notebook " assembled by Fischel, nos. 81-82, contains drawings differing among themselves in time, technique and style: for example, the Vatican folio (F. 81), appears to be of the early Roman period, together with the drawing in the Louvre for the Stanza della Segnatura (cf. note 102); the drawing in the British Museum (F. 91, cf. note 99) seems more mature than the others, as likewise are the drawings in the Ashmolean Museum, 524-525, 528 verso (F. 88, 89, 101), and in the Christ Church Library (F. 102), cf. note 89. See also Pouncey-Gere, *op. cit.*, no. 14 and note 51.

[71] Windsor, Royal Library, 12759: Leda and the swan. Ink and traces of stylus and black pencil, 308 × 192. Passavant, 438; F. 79; Popham-Wilde, 789.
According to G. J. Hoogewerf (" Leonardo e Raffaello," *Commentari*, 1952, pp. 173 ff.), the drawing seems less early than is commonly thought, derived from the *Leda* which Leonardo must have brought to Rome and then to France and identified with the one in the Spiridon Collection, executed by the pupils. Among the drawings by Leonardo for the *Leda*, one in Windsor, 12516, for only the head, and those with complete figures, but in kneeling position, in Chatsworth, in the Devonshire Collection, and in Rotterdam, Boymans Museum, are famous.

[72] Paris, Cabinet des Dessins, Louvre, 3882; Bust of a young girl. Ink, 223 × 159. From the Jabach Collection. Passavant, 347 (who considers it to be for the portrait of Maddalena Doni); F. 80; exhibition cat., Paris, 1965-66, no. 37.

[73] London, British Museum, 1895.9.15.613: Bust of a woman. Black pencil, 259 × 183. F. 33; Pouncey-Gere, 13. It is attributed to Viti by Morelli.

[74] Oxford, Ashmolean Museum, 535: Two studies of heads and two of hands and a sketch from the *Battle of Anghiari* by Leonardo. Silver point on prepared paper, 211 × 274. Passavant 532. F. 210; exhibition cat., London, 1930, no. 132; Middeldorf, 45; Parker, 535.
It should be compared with folio no. 477 in Lille (F. 211) which represents a head with the pose of a young head in this drawing and the type of that of the old one. Two studies of hands for the same fresco were in the Helsetine Collection (F. 208-9).

[75] Oxford, Ashmolean Museum, 523: (r.), Four soldiers; (v.), figure studies. Ink, with some retouches. 271 × 216. Passavant, 541; F. 87; Middeldorf, 28; Parker, 523.
For other drawings derived from sculpture, see the drawing in Oxford, 522 (F. 82-83), which on the recto represents a nude inspired by the Michelangelo's *David* (as seems to be the case at least in part for the figure at the right in our drawing), and on the verso it has a study for a standing St. Paul, which is inspired partly by the Prophets of the Campanile and in part by the *St. George* of Donatello. We do not have any reason for considering this drawing as a preparatory work for a façade decoration, as proposed by Fischel.

[76] Florence, Gabinetto Disegni, Uffizi, 529 E: St. George on horseback, killing the dragon. Ink and traces of black pencil, all pin-pricked for pouncing, cartoon, 262 × 214. Passavant, 126; F. 78; exhibition cat., London, 1930, no. 121; exhibition cat., Uffizi, 1960, no. 57.

[77] Florence, Gabinetto Disegni, Uffizi, 505 E: Half-length figure of Madonna and Child in an oval frame. Black pencil and traces of stylus; white paper slightly tinted, 213 × 214. F. 105; exhibition cat., Uffizi, 1960, no. 59.
The sheet is not recorded by Passavant but it is in Crowe-Cavalcaselle (I, pp. 252-3); there is a copy in the British Museum (Pouncey-Gere, 289) attributed to Timoteo Viti.

[78] Oxford, Ashmolean Museum, 517: Sketch for the *Madonna del Cardellino*. Ink over traces of metal point, 230 × 163. From the Viti-Antaldi collection and later the Lawrence collection. Passavant, 485; exhibition cat., London, 1930, no. 123; Middeldorf 23; Parker, 517.

Also usually connected to the *Madonna del Cardellino* are the drawings of Oxford and Chatsworth (F. 112, 113), but their connection with the painting is not too convincing.

[79] a) Vienna, Albertina, 207: (r.), Four sketches with Madonna and Child; (v.), other various sketches for the same Madonna. Ink, 245 × 362. Passavant, 189; F. 115-116; exhibition cat., Stix-Fröhlich Bum, 50; Bean, 1964 (cf. note 80).

b) Chatsworth, Duke of Devonshire collection: Studies of the Madonna and Child with the Infant St. John, for the *Belvedere Madonna*. Ink, 250 × 194. Passavant, 564; F. 117, exhibition cat., London, 1930, no. 124; Bean, 1964 (cf. note 80).

[80] New York, Metropolitan Museum, Rogers Foundation, 64-47: (r.), finished study for the *Belvedere Madonna*; (v.), study for a nude half-figure. Sanguine (r.), pen (v.), 224 × 154.

Already known to Crowe-Cavalcaselle (I, p. 271), the sheet had been lost (cf. J. Bean, " A Rediscovered Drawing by Raphael, " *Metropolitan Museum of Art Bulletin*, Summer, 1964; cf. also Bean-Stampfle, *op. cit.*, 1965, no. 49). The recto shows few variations from the painting, and is almost a small cartoon. The verso is definitely for one of the thieves of a *Crucifixion* or *Deposition*, to be compared with other studies by Raphael of the same period for analogous themes, as in the verso of the Albertina for a *Deposition* (Stix-Fröhlich Bum, 51; F. 181, 182; on the recto there is a study for the *Charity* in the Vatican predella of the *Borghese Deposition*), or the drawing in the Biblioteca Marucelliana in Florence, with a Crucifix, probably derived from the Michelangelesque one in Santo Spirito, cf. A. E. Popham, " An unknown Drawing by Raphael, " *Festschrift Friedrich Wincler*, Berlin, 1959, pp. 239 ff., and A. Parronchi, " Il Crocifisso di Michelangelo già in Santo Spirito, " *Antichità Viva*, nos. 5-6, 1965, p. 41. The drawing in the Louvre is a derivation from the one in the Metropolitan Museum or from an analogous Raphaelesque original, no. 3880 (F. 183), exhibited in Paris in 1965-66, no. 39, as an original by Raphael, which is rather dry and with all probability was made by a copyist.

[81] a) Vienna, Albertina, 250; (r.), study of a standing nude with hands together; (v.), nude studies derived from the cartoons for the *Battle of Cascina* by Michelangelo. Ink and stylus, 244 × 163. F. 94; cat. Stix-Fröhlich Bum, 67.

For other Raphaelesque drawings or on analogous theme, since this mourning figure is without doubt for a *Crucifixion* or a *Deposition*, cf. note 80.

b) Vienna, Albertina, 166: three studies for a Holy Woman and a Crucifix. Ink, 271 × 212. F. 185; Cat. Stix-Fröhlich Bum, 59. Cf. note 80. It is connected by Fischel to the studies for the *Borghese Deposition*.

[82] Florence, Gabinetto Disegni, Uffizi, 539 E; Madonna and Child with the Infant St. John in a landscape, for the *Esterházy Madonna*. Ink and traces of black pencil; paper squared with stylus, pin-pricked. 285 × 191. Passavant, 114; F. 126; exhibition cat., London, 1930, no. 126; exhibition cat., Uffizi, 1960, no. 60.

[83] Paris, Cabinet des Dessins, Louvre, 3861: Madonna and Child and male head. Metal point, pink-tinted, squared paper, 226 × 152. Passavant, 328; F. 139; Middeldorf, 32.

[84] a) Vienna, Albertina, 209: (r.), study for a Madonna and Child; (v.), six diverse studies for a Madonna and Child. Metal point, prepared paper (r.), ink (v.), 256 × 184. From the Antaldi collection. Passavant, 188; F. 110-111; Middeldorf, 26; cat. Stix-Fröhlich Bum, 53.

On the verso there are several motifs for the *Colonna Madonna* and the large *Cowper Madonna* and for the *Holy Family with the Beardless St. Joseph*.

b) London, British Museum, Ff. 1-36; Sketches of a Madonna and Child. Ink and traces of sanguine. 254 × 184. F. 109; Pouncey-Gere, 19 (with a precise description of the various studies of the sheet).

[85] London, British Museum, 1895.9.15.637: Madonna and Child with an angel. Ink, 206 × 227. From the Antaldi, Crozat, Mariette and Lawrence collections. F. 134; Middeldorf, 30; Pouncey-Gere, 18.

As these later scholars carefully noticed, there is no relationship with the large *Cowper Madonna*, contrary to what Fischel had seen in it.

[86] Paris, Cabinet des Dessins, Louvre. R. F. 1066: Madonna and Child with the Infant St. John for *La Belle Jardinière*. Ink, paper ruled in squares in sanguine and black pencil, 300 × 208. From the Viti-Antaldi, Crozat, and Mariette collections. Passavant, 537; F. 120; Middeldorf, 27; exhibition cat., Paris, 1965-66; no. 40.

[87] Oxford, Ashmolean Museum, 521: (r.), study for the Child in *La Belle Jardinière*; (v.), study of a seated skeleton, ink with stylus, 283 × 160. Passavant, 457 (as in the Chambers Hall collection); F. 121; Parker, 521.

For the skeleton on the verso cf. note 23.

[88] Florence, Gabinetto Disegni, Uffizi, 1477 E: Bust of a young girl in profile. Ink, 262 × 189. F. 176; exhibition cat., London, 1930, no. 128; exhibition cat., Uffizi, 1960, no. 64.

In the notes by Guasti to the Italian edition of Passavant, the drawing is considered a study for the Magdalene in the *Borghese Deposition*.

[89] a) Oxford, Ashmolean Museum, 528: (r.), young girl in right profile; (v.), Cupids playing. Ink, 273 × 194. Passavant, 550; F. 100-101; Middeldorf, 39; Parker, 528.

b) Oxford, Ashmolean Museum, 527: Standing Woman (St. Catherine ?). Ink, 259 × 171. Passavant, 544; F. 99; Parker, 527.

[90] Oxford, Ashmolean Museum, 536: (r.), Head of St. Catherine and studies of *putti*; (v.), various studies of figures. Ink and traces of stylus, 279 × 169. Passavant, 499; F. 204-205; Middeldorf, 37; Parker, 536.

For the putti on the recto there are no precise references, only for the one at the right could one attempt to make a comparison with the *putti* of which we speak in note 136; Crowe-Cavalcaselle thought they were studies for a fountain. For the figure on the verso, which varies slightly the definitive composition of St. Catherine, there is a copy in Chatsworth (F. 206).

[91] Paris. Cabinet des Dessins, Louvre, 3871: Half-length figure of St. Catherine, cartoon for the picture in the National Gallery in London. Black pencil, white lead, grey-tinted paper made of several added sheets, pin-pricked for pouncing. 587 × 436. From the Jabach collection. Passavant, 335; F. 207; exhibition cat., Paris, 1965-66, no. 38.

[92] Besides Fischel, see the considerations by I. A. Richter (" The Drawings for the Entombment, " *Gazette des Beaux-Arts*, 2, 1945) and C. L. Ragghianti (*La Deposizione di Raffaello Sanzio*, Milan, 1947). From the series of Fischel, nos. 164-186, are to be excluded no. 176 (cf. note 88), no. 179 in the British Museum which Pouncey-Gere justly considers a copy (*op. cit.*, no. 39), and the group 182-186, not directly connected with the *Borghese Deposition*, but only generically with its theme (cf. notes 80, 94). Some doubts of attribution are left by the other drawing in the British Museum, F. 178, of which we speak in note 23.

[93] a) Oxford, Ashmolean Museum, 529: *Deposition*, study of the entire composition. Ink, 179 × 206. Passavant, 475; F. 164; Middeldorf, 38; Parker, 529.

The folio in the Louvre is a more minutely drawn replica and perhaps in parts retraced by another hand (F. 168).

b) London, British Museum, 1895.9.15.636: study for the right portion of the *Deposition*. Ink, 250 × 169. F. 165; Pouncey-Gere, 10.

It is a study for the right portion, as it appears in the sheet cited in Oxford and in the Louvre. Studies for other details are also on folio no. 530 in Oxford (F. 166-167).

⁹⁴ a) London, British Museum, 1963.12.16.1: (r.), over-all study for the *Deposition;* (v.), studies of three *putti* and of a figure lifting a corpse which is wrapped in a shroud, as other two corpses are lying on the ground. Ink, 213 × 320. From the Crozat and later the Rotwell collection.

The drawing, considered lost by Fischel (no. 170), which he published from a facsimile in the print collection of Crozat which was assembled by Caylus, was recently offered for sale at Sotheby's (cf. sale cat., October 21, 1963, no. 63) and bought for the British Museum (information and photographs were provided by J. Gere). The drawing seems to precede the following one, also in the British Museum, given its great variations with regard to the painting. Unknown is the destination of the verso, perhaps it was a life study by Raphael, done during a funeral.

b) London, British Museum, 1895.2.14.1: (r.), complete study of the *Deposition;* (v.), standing nude. Ink and traces of black pencil, 230 × 319. From the Crozat, later the Lawrence collection. Passavant, 458; F. 171-172; Pouncey-Gere, 12.

According to the identification of Gronau, the verso is a copy of St. Matthew begun by Michelangelo for the *Opera del Duomo* in Florence which in 1505 was located in the courtyard of the *Opera* building, and therefore was easy for Raphael to copy during his Florentine sojourn.

⁹⁵ a) Oxford, Ashmolean Museum, 525; (r.), group of three musicians; (v.), Christ carried to the tomb. Ink, the verso is pin-pricked, 232 × 185 (maximum measurements). Passavant, 542; F. 89, 174; Parker, 525.

For the recto there are no precise references, if not the probability that we are dealing with a copy or at least with a revival from an ancient low relief; there is a copy in the Christ Church Library, with an inscription attributable to Timoteo Viti. The verso is a rather precise study for the Christ in the *Borghese Deposition*, to be compared with another drawing more complete than the one in Oxford (F. 169; Parker, 531) which bears a significant mark from the drawing in the Louvre for *La Belle Jardinière* (F. 120): they both were sheets from the Viti-Antaldi collection.

b) Paris, F. Lugt collection: Woman walking toward the left, for the Magdalene in the *Borghese Deposition*. Ink, 269 × 187. F. 177; Middeldorf, 40; exhibition cat., *Le dessin italien dans les collections Hollandaises*. Paris, Rotterdam, Haarlem, 1962, no. 62. Other detailed studies are in the British Museum (F. 178-179; Pouncey-Gere, 11, 39).

⁹⁶ Florence, Gabinetto Disegni, Uffizi, 538 E: Study for the *Deposition*. Ink and traces of black pencil, white paper ruled in squares in sanguine and stylus; partly pin-pricked, 289 × 298. On the verso there is an old inscription in ink: " Raphael Urbinas in ecclesia divi Francisci di . . . pinxit tabula haec . . . " Passavant, 108; F. 175; exhibition cat., London, 1930, no. 127.

⁹⁷ a) Windsor, Royal Library, 12738: Madonna and Child, with the Infant St. John and St. Elizabeth: study for the *Canigiani Madonna*. Ink, traces of black pencil on lightly prepared paper, 234 × 180. Formerly in the Bonfiglioli and Sagredo collections. Passavant, 427; F. 130; Popham-Wilde, 790. The copy in Chantilly (F. 132) is more complete.

b) Lille, Wicar Museum, 458: Holy Family with St. Ann and St. Joachim. Ink, ruled in squares in sanguine, partly retraced. Folded sheet. 355 × 235. On the verso is a long inscribed autograph by Raphael, full of grammatical errors, directed to Domenico Alfani (cf. Camesasca, *op. cit.*, p. 13). From the Della Penna (Perugia) and A. Fedi (Florence) collections. Passavant, 378; F. 161-162; exhibition cat., Paris, 1965-66, 237.

⁹⁸ Florence, Gabinetto Disegni, Uffizi, 1328 F: Study of a standing friar, for the S. Bruno in the *Madonna del Baldacchino*. Ink, bistre watercolor, white lead, on background tinted with black pencil, ruled in squares with black pencil and stylus, 217 × 132. F. 148; Middeldorf, 35; Riedl, *op. cit.*, fig. 5.

One must keep in mind that in these years Fra Bartolommeo is also beginning to use a sort of charcoal pencil on the background of his drawings, which he shades around the figures.

Other studies for the same altarpiece, the *Madonna del Baldacchino*, are, besides the complete one in Chatsworth (F. 143), the drawing in the École des Beaux Arts for the drapery of the Madonna (F. 145), on the recto, and for the Child on the verso (F. 146) and also the drawing in Lille for the head of S. Bruno (F. 147).

⁹⁹ a) Bayonne, Bonnat Museum, 651: Two standing nudes, one of which holds a lamb. Ink, grey paper. From the Mariette collection. F. 199; J. Bean, *Les Dessins italiens de la collection Bonnat*, Paris, 1960, no. 130.

b) London, British Museum, 1895.9.15.624: (r.), Five studies of male nudes; (v.), Madonna. Ink and traces of stylus (r.), sanguine (v.), 269 × 197. Passavant, 451; F. 91-92; Middeldorf, 22 (v.); Pouncey-Gere, 20.

The gestures for these nudes are truly inspired by those of the *Battle of Cascina* by Michelangelo and will be repeated in the executioners in the *Massacre of the Innocents* (cf. note 107). According to Fischel this sheet should have been part of the " large Florentine notebook " (cf. note 70).

c) Oxford, Ashmolean Museum, 538: (r.), Scene of a battle with prisoners; (v.), another version of the same subject. Ink on traces of black pencil. 268 × 417. From the Viti-Antaldi, Crozat, Mariette and Lawrence collections. Passavant, 517; F. 194-195; exhibition cat., London, 1930, no. 130; Parker, 538.

According to Shearman (" Giulio Romano, " review to F. Hartt, *The Burlington Magazine*, 1959, p. 458), it would be the first idea for the group of prisoners in the *Battle of Ostia*, as Passavant already had hinted; but the approach appears somewhat arbitrary. For the influence of the Signorellian and Pollaiolesque motifs on the this kind of drawing, see also the sheet in Cambridge (F. 196) and the note below.

¹⁰⁰ Oxford, Ashmolean Museum, 539: (r.), Figures carrying a wounded person; (v.), Adam tempted by the demon. Ink, on the verso traces of lead point. 265 × 330. From the Viti-Antaldi, Crozat, and Mariette collections; Passavant, 462; F. 200-201; exhibition cat., London, 1930, no. 129; Middeldorf, 44; Parker, 539.

The recto seems to be vaguely inspired by the *Deposition* of Signorelli which is frescoed in monochrome in the Cappella Nuova of the Orvieto Duomo. The verso has certainly been used for the engraving with the *Temptation of Adam and Eve* by Marcantonio Raimondi (B. XIV, 1), but the figure of Eve alluded to here, is different from that in the engraving.

¹⁰¹ For a recent specification on this subject, see J. Shearman, *op. cit.*, 1965, p. 160, note 13.

¹⁰² Paris, Cabinet des Dessins, Louvre, 3847: Five male studies with analogous poses. Ink, and traces of sanguine. 432 × 285. From the Viti-Antaldi collection. Passavant, 351; F. 224; exhibition cat., Paris, 1965-66, no. 41.

The idea that we are dealing here with studies for a St. John the Baptist, is already found in the Inventory of the Viti-Antaldi collection, where the sheet was signed with the number 20 according to the identification made by Pouncey-Gere (*op. cit.*, pp. 46-47): " Other bigger drawings with two motifs, for *St. John Preaching in the Desert* . . . made in ink. " The figure of the Tempted Adam in the fresco of the Vatican ceiling has the same pose of the legs and head that we find in the two sketches at the right of our sketch; but the inclination of the torso (which according to Crowe-Cavalcaselle, II, p. 19, is derived from the torso of the Belvedere) is similar to the sketch at the sides of the standing figure: for this figure one should keep in mind the relationship with the standing figure in the drawing in Frankfurt for the *Disputa* (cf. note 114).

¹⁰³ Oxford, Ashmolean Museum, 554: (r.), Study for *Theology* in the ceiling of the Stanza della Segnatura; (v.), *Assumption of the Virgin*. Ink with traces of stylus, 201 × 143. From the Viti-Antaldi and Lawrence collections. Passavant, 548; F. 225, 280; Middeldorf, 47; Parker, 554.

For the destination of the study of the Assumption on the verso, cf. note 146.

[104] Lille, Wicar Museum, 433: Standing *putto* with a " cartiglio, " for the *Theology* on the ceiling of the Stanza della Segnatura. Black pencil, white lead, reddish-tinted paper, 222 × 159. Passavant, 391; F. 226; Middeldorf, 48; exhibition cat., Lille, 1961, no. 39.

The drawing is directly parallel to the other also in Lille, intended, perhaps, for the *putti* of *Astronomy*.

[105] Windsor, Royal Library, 12734: Study for *Poetry*, on the ceiling of the Stanza della Segnatura. Black pencil on stylus traces, lightly prepared paper, ruled in squares with black pencil. 360 × 227. Passavant, 430; F. 228; exhibition cat., London, 1930, no. 133; Popham-Wilde, 792.

In comparison with the fresco, in the drawing the head is slightly raised, as it is in Eve of the *Temptation*, on the same ceiling (cf. Crowe-Cavalcaselle, II, p. 20).

[106] Oxford, Ashmolean Museum, 555: (r.), Study for the *Judgment of Solomon* for the ceiling of the Stanza della Segnatura; (v.), decorative interlacing. Silver point, ink (v.); grey-green-tinted paper, 100 × 137. From the Viti-Antaldi (?) and Lawrence collections. Passavant, 470; F. 230; Middeldorf, 49; Parker, 555.

Notwithstanding the format, in proportion to the one of the fresco. the drawing has many variations from that mentioned; the executioner has the pose of the one appearing in the Albertina sheet (cf. note 107, b).

[107] a) Vienna, Albertina, 188: (r.), Study for the executioner at the left and the fleeing mother in the *Massacre of the Innocents;* (v.), Study for *Astronomy* on the ceiling of the Stanza della Segnatura. Sanguine (r.), ink (v.), 235 × 408. From the Crozat and Mariette collections. Passavant, 171 and 205; F. 236-237; cat. Stix-Fröhlich Bum, 63; exhibition cat., London, 1930, no. 135.

b) Vienna, Albertina, 189: (r.), Study of an executioner for the *Judgment of Solomon* on the ceiling of Stanza della Segnatura; (v.), Study for the false mother in the *Judgment of Solomon* and for the left executioner in the *Massacre of the Innocents*. Black pencil and white lead (r.), ink and stylus (v.), 264 × 287. From the Viti-Antaldi and Crozat collections. Passavant, 172; F. 231-232; cat. Stix-Fröhlich Bum, 64; Middeldorf, 50 (r.).

For the figure of the executioner on the right, found on the recto, see the variation in Oxford (note 106). The figure on the verso corresponds exactly with the respective one in the fresco and engraving.

[108] Windsor, Royal Library, 12737: (r.), *The Massacre of the Innocents;* (v.), Study of plate with the battle of sea gods, sanguine on traces of pencil and stylus (r.); the section in black pencil derives from a drawing in the British Museum of which we speak in the preceding note. 248 × 411. From the Bonfiglioli, Sagredo and Smith collections. Passavant, 421; F. 234-235; exhibition cat., London, 1930, no. 134; Middeldorf, 51 (r.); Popham-Wilde, 793.

The drawing on the verso has been compared with the plates made by Cesarino da Perugia for Agostino Chigi from a drawing by Raphael. It has a certain affinity of subject with a drawing of Raphaelesque school in Oxford, Parker no. 577.

[109] a) Florence, Gabinetto Disegni Uffizi, 496 E: (r.), Sketches of a Madonna and Child; (v.), Standing Venus, studies of a standing figure, of a head and a male torso. Ink, traces of black pencil, 248 × 270 (max. measurements). Passavant, 119 and 132; F. 264, 358; exhibition cat., London, 1930, no. 137; exhibition cat., Uffizi, 1960, no. 62.

The sketches of a Madonna on the recto, have to be compared partly with the *Bridgewater Madonna;* the study of Venus is in close relation with the cited drawing in the British Museum (Pouncey-Gere, 27) and with the engraving by Marcantonio (B. XIV, 311) with which it has in common the gesture and the movement of the legs, while the bust is in counterpart. See also note 136.

b) Lille, Wicar Museum, 447-448: (r.), Studies of an old man and of a young nude; (v.), studies of nudes, heads and draped nude. Ink, 275 × 205. From the A. Fedi collection. Passavant, 396; F. 265-266; Middeldorf, 67; exhibition cat., Paris, 1965-66, 241.

Crowe-Cavalcaselle, II, p. 80, put forth some doubts about the authenticity of the drawing which nevertheless appears quite typical among the more rapid sketches by Raphael; on the recto the type of the old man, who is often identified as being Aristotle in the *School of Athens* (although he is here reversed and varied with regard to it) has the same characteristics of the hooded old man on the third plane at the left, speaking with the Bishop and a friar, in the *Disputa;* while on the verso the first figure on the left must be compared with the Francesco Maria della Rovere in the *School of Athens*, the second one, instead, is to be compared with the Francesco Maria in the *Disputa;* on the other hand the figure at the center, almost a faun, has some rapport with the sketches of the plate mentioned in note 108.

[110] Such an hypothesis seems confirmed by the argumentation by Shearman, *op. cit.*, 1965, p. 165, in whose opinion the walls of the various Stanze had a unified conception, at least as a general, thematic and compositional idea.

[111] Windsor, Royal Library, 12732: Study for the left half of the *Disputa*. Brownish water color, raised with white lead on a stylus sketch, with traces of ruling in squares by stylus, 280 × 285. Passavant, 429; F. 258; Popham-Wilde, 794.

Passavant expressed some doubts about the quality of this drawing, but Crowe-Cavalcaselle (II, pp. 27-28) restored its exceptional importance as a documentation of the original, compositional idea of Sanzio for the scene. A copy in the Louvre, no. 3890, identified by Shearman, *op. cit.*, 1965, p. 158, note 2, seems derived from another lost version with a few variations in regard to this one.

[112] Oxford, Ashmolean Museum, 542: Study for the upper portion of the *Disputa*. Brownish water color, white lead and subsequent touches of color, 233 × 400. From the Crozat, Mariette and Lawrence collections. Passavant, 501; F. 259; Parker, 542.

The drawing is not ruled in squares but bears marks of auxiliary directional lines; it has been considered often as an original portion of the same sheet and the analogous drawing in Chantilly should be its fragment (F. 260), representing the lower portion of the same scene; but Parker has correctly excluded such a possibility, although the stylistic and technical rapport of this drawing with those in Chantilly and in Windsor, remains valid, as we read in the preceding note.

[113] Windsor, Royal Library, 12733: Study for the lower portion of the *Disputa*. Black pencil, prepared paper with white tempera, 204 × 410. F. 261; Popham-Wilde, 795; Shearman, 1965, p. 158, fig. 1.

The drawing is not recorded by Passavant; it is quite similar also in scale to the sheet on the same subject in Chantilly (F. 260), and could be a first sketch, or a variation for the sake of study.

[114] a) London, British Museum, 1900.8.24.108: Study for the lower portion of the *Disputa*. Ink and light water color on traces of stylus, white lead. 247 × 401. F. 267; Pouncey-Gere, 33.

Compared with the fresco, here the group of figures at the extreme left is absent and there are noticeable variations in the other figures. There are many replicas of it.

b) Frankfurt, Städelsches Institut, 379: Study for the lower part of the *Disputa*, with nude figures. Ink pin-pricked in many parts for the transferal. 280 × 415. From the Viti-Antaldi, Crozat, Mariette, Lagoy, Dimsdale, Lawrence and William of Orange collections. Passavant, 280; F. 269.

The sheet, which has not won great critical acclaim, was well evaluated by Crowe-Cavalcaselle (II, pp. 37-40), who among other things noticed the similarity of the standing figure seen from behind in this drawing with one of those in the preliminary sketch for the Tempted Adam in the ceiling of the Stanza della Segnatura; cf. note 102.

[115] a) London, British Museum, Ff. 1-35: Studies for the right portion of the *Disputa*, and the sonnet " Un pensier dolce " (cf. Camesasca, *op. cit.*, III, p. 83). Ink, 250 × 390. Passavant, 449; F. 286; Middeldorf, 58; Pouncey-Gere, 32

The group of sketches at the center is certainly for the standing figure at the extreme right in the *Disputa*, as one can deduce from the study of the foot, which is for that figure, while the other studies are of more uncertain destination. The same sonnet is found again in a drawing in the Albertina (F. 283), also made for a figure in the *Disputa* (cf. note 130).

b) Montpellier, Fabre Museum: (r.), Study of a man leaning on a balustrade, and a sonnet " Fello pensier" (see Camesasca, *op. cit.*, V, p. 87); (v.), Study of the same figure of the recto, and of the head of same. Ink and traces of stylus, 360 × 235. Passavant, 416; F. 287-288; Middeldorf, 59; exhibition cat., Paris, 1965-66, no. 243.

In the fresco, the variation of the isolated study of a head appearing on the verso has been used.

[116] London, British Museum, 1895.9.15.621: (r.), Studies of flying angels for the upper portion of the *Disputa*; (v.), another version of the same studies. Black pencil and traces of white lead, 263 × 357. From the Lawrence collection. F. 297-298; Pouncey-Gere, 31.

Of the various studies on the recto only the one on the left side is found in the fresco; the group on the verso seems instead to have been created as a whole, but it was changed during the execution.

[117] Paris, Cabinet des Dessins, Louvre, 3869: Study of heads and hands for the so-called Bramante in the *Disputa*. Metal point, prepared paper, 400 × 271. From the Ottley, Lawrence and William of Orange collections. Passavant, 345. F. 282.

While Passavant denies that it is Bramante, Crowe-Cavalcaselle (II, p. 58) confirm the traditional identification of the figure.

[118] a) Florence, Gabinetto Disegni, Uffizi, 541 E: (r.), Study of a seated nude for the Adam in the *Disputa*; (v.), sketch of seated nude in profile and of a leg. Black pencil and white lead, white paper lightly tinted, 357 × 210. F. 293-294; Middeldorf, 61; exhibition cat., London, 1930, no. 139; exhibition cat., Uffizi, 1960, no. 66; Forlani, *op. cit.* (1962), no. 13.

The figure on the verso is not easily identifiable, while the study of the leg is supposed to have been derived from the *Belvedere Apollo* as proposed by Fischel.

b) Florence, Gabinetto Disegni, Uffizi, 1342 F: Study for the St. Stephen in the *Disputa* and, below, sketches of heads. Black pencil, white lead, brownish paper lightly tinted, 320 × 193. F. 295; exhibition cat., Uffizi, 1960, no. 65. Neither drawing has been catalogued by Passavant.

[119] Among these, the drawing in Windsor is particularly interesting; Popham-Wilde, 589, attributed it to Parmigianino (F. fig. 258; published by Parker, *op. cit.*, 1939-40, plate 38) which shows the entire *School of Athens* without the figure of the so-called Heraclitus: this demonstrates that the drawing does not derive directly from the fresco, but rather from a lost drawing by Raphael for the entire scene, where the figure of the philosopher was not yet included. Also the engraving by Marcantonio for the *Apollo* in the niche, and for the *Virtue* in the false low relief (B. XIV, 334, 381) show that they came from lost drawings by Raphael, rather than directly from the fresco (Fischel: cf. also note 121).

[120] a) Frankfurt, Städelsches Institut: Study for Diogenes in the *School of Athens*. Silver point or pink-tinted paper, 245 × 285. Passavant, 281; F. 306. The figure has been sketched without the beard.

b) Oxford, Ashmolean Museum, 550: Studies of figures climbing stairs and head of Medusa for the shield of Minerva, in the *School of Athens*. Silver point, body color, pink-tinted paper. 278 × 200. Passavant, 505; F. 307; Middeldorf, 68; Parker, 550. Morelli did not attribute the drawing to Raphael.

c) Oxford, Ashmolean Museum, 551: Study for the statute of Minerva and for the other statues in the niches of the *School of Athens*. Silver point, body color, pink-tinted paper. 274 × 201. Passavant 509; F. 308; Parker 551. This drawing, too, was dubious according to Morelli.

All these drawings have been in the Wicar, Ottley and Lawrence collections.

[121] Oxford, Ashmolean Museum, 552: Group of fighting nudes, for the low relief of the *School of Athens*. Sanguine and traces of stylus, 379 × 281. Wicar, Ottley and Lawrence collections. Passavant, 508; F. 309; Middeldorf, 69; Parker, 552.

As Parker has demonstrated (*op. cit.*, 1939-40) the drawing must have been cut in the lower portion, according to what one can deduce from an engraving of the *Bacchanal* by the " Maestro H. F. E," (B. XV, 5) and from the copies of the Klinkosch Collection and from Chatsworth, which show the entire fallen figure in the lower part, which is not seen in the fresco, where it is concealed behind the heads of the figures standing in front of the low relief. Also this drawing, as the three preceding ones, was denied to Raphael by Morelli and belonged to the same collections.

[122] Milan, Pinacoteca Ambrosiana, Cartoon of the *School of Athens*. Chalk, black pencil, white lead, pricked for pouncing, 2.80 × 8 meters. Passavant, 424-425; F. 313 (313-344); Middeldorf, 70-71.

The cartoon was in the Cardinal Federico Borromeo Collection; also it is not cited in the Act of donation of the same in 1618; it is, in fact, indicated in the Inventory of the Ambrosiana of 1610, as deposited there by Count Fabio Borromeo Visconti di Brebbia (" Two pieces of drawing by Raphael of Urbino in charcoal, they are big ... done on paper glued over fabric"); in 1625, it was acquired by the Pinacoteca Ambrosiana and divided in two parts (cf. L. Beltrami, *Il cartone di Raffaello Sanzio per l'affresco della Scuola di Atene nella Camera della Segnatura in Vaticano*, Milan, 1920).

[123] That the Heraclitus was not present in the first execution of the *School of Athens* seems confirmed both by the cartoon, where there is no proof that such a figure has been erased, as Fischel instead maintains, and by the cited drawing in Windsor (Popham-Wilde, 589; cf. note 119). Heraclitus, instead, appears in a drawing in Leipzig (F. fig. 258) perhaps derived from a Raphaelesque idea or directly from the fresco. For a good justification of the subsequent insertion of Heraclitus, cf. D. Redig de Campos, " Il ' pensieroso' della Segnatura," *Raffaello e Michelangelo*, Rome, 1946, V.

[124] The hypothesis was advanced by Fischel (pp. 255 ff.) and it has been recently confuted by Shearman (*op. cit.*, 1965, p. 158). The only drawing, probably an autograph for an entire group of figures for the *Parnassus* is the one in the British Museum for the lower left side, which (although it has been denied by Pouncey-Gere as a Raphael), Oberhuber in his review restores it to Sanzio (cf. K. Oberhuber, " Ph. Pouncey-J. A. Gere, Raphael and his circle," *Master Drawings*, I, 3, 1963, p. 47).

[125] a) London, British Museum, Pp. 1-74: (r.), Standing man; (v.), Studies of draperies and hands for Horace and of hands for Tibullus in the *School of Athens*. Ink and black pencil. 343 × 242. Passavant, 443; F. 240-241; Pouncey-Gere, 29.

The identification of the various poets in the *Parnassus* was uncertain since the time of Bellori; for the same figure of Horace there is another sheet in Lille (F. 242), that sketched the advancing foot (cf. the copy in the Uffizi and note 126). The recto was not used in the fresco, even though it appears to have been executed for some of its figures.

b) Windsor, Royal Library, 12760: (r.), Studies of heads for Homer, Dante and another poet in the *Parnassus*; (v.), Study of the drapery for Dante in the *Parnassus*. Ink, white paper with traces of preparation, 265 × 182. Passavant, 431; F. 246-247; Popham-Wilde, 796.

At the Albertina there is an ancient copy (F. fig. 223) which combines the head of the recto with the drapery of the verso, presenting, therefore, a complete view of the figure, as perhaps it appeared in some lost sketch by Raphael himself.

[126] a) Oxford, Ashmolean Museum, 541: (r.), Study for the Muse Melpomene in the *Parnassus*; (v.), Study of Vergil in the *Parnassus*. Ink and stylus. 330 × 219; exhibition cat., London, 1930, no. 136; Middeldorf, 57; Parker, 541.

There is a copy in the Uffizi of the drawing on the recto, no. 1220 E, which bears on its recto a true copy of the Melpomene and on the verso a copy of the study of feet for Horace in Lille (F. 242) with an interesting inscription of the fifteenth century in ink: " This sheet was very dear to Monsù Nicolò Pussino. I obtained it from Signor Pietro Santi, pupil of Monsù La Mar, his disciple, 1699."

b) Vienna, Albertina, 219: (r.), Study for the Muse Calliope in the *Parnassus*; (v.), study of draperies for the same figure. Ink, 244 × 217. From the Viti-Antaldi, Crozat, Gouvernet, Giuliano da Parma, and the Prince of Ligne collections. Passavant 202; F. 250 (as a study for Euterpe); cat. Stix-Fröhlich Bum, 65. There is also a copy in the Uffizi, no. 1252 F.

c) Vienna, Albertina, 220: Study for the Muse Erato (?) in the *Parnassus*. Ink, 245 × 217. Also from the Viti and Crozat collections. Passavant, 203 (also for Urania); F. 251; cat. Stix-Fröhlich Bum, 66.

[127] London, Norman Colville collection: Head of a Muse for the *Parnassus*, cartoon. Black pencil, 304 × 222. From the Lawrence collection. F. 253; Middeldorf, 55. The drawing, published earlier as lost by Fischel, was later claimed as an original by A. E. Popham ("The Drawings at the Burlington Fine Arts Club," *The Burlington Magazine*, LXX, 1937, p. 87), and again by Fischel himself (*op. cit.*, 1937, p. 167), who, as he was observing the pricking (although there were no signs of holes in it), deduced after the examination that it was a typical "auxiliary cartoon." Also the analogous drawing of the Horne collection, no. 5643 (F. 254), seems an auxiliary cartoon, although it does not bear any sign of pricking or holes.

[128] Frankfurt, Städelsches Institut, 382: Study of the section for the picture with Gregory IX giving the Decretals in the Stanza della Segnatura. Ink, 385 × 250. Formerly in the Crozat collection. Passavant, 283; F. 256.
The sheet, critically not very fortunate, has been accepted by Popham-Wilde (*op. cit.*, 1949, p. 312) as a Raphael. The drawing for the picture parallel with the one of the Justinian receiving the Pandects, also in Frankfurt (F. 255), rather facile and uncertain in lighting does not seem to be Raphael. For the head of Julius II, already with a beard and therefore made after 1511, there is a cartoon in Chatsworth (F. 257).

[129] Windsor, Royal Library, 3720: (r.), The parable of the two swords; (v.), the Oath of Zaleucus. Sanguine (r.). Ink and black pencil (v.), 262 × 363. Popham-Wilde, 797.
The sheet was recognized by Popham as a Raphaelesque study for the two *grisailles* of a relative subject near a window in the Stanza della Segnatura; the scarce probability that the two *grisailles* had been made by Sanzio, does detract from the probability of attribution to him of the two drawings (the one on the verso appears a bit weaker in quality), because it is possible that Raphael could have made the drawings of the decorative parts of the Stanza della Segnatura, leaving the actual executions to his pupils.

[130] Vienna, Albertina, 205: (r.), Reading Madonna with Child, seated in a landscape; (v.), Studies for St. Ambrose and other sketches for the *Disputa* and a sonnet, "Un pensier dolce" (Camesasca, *op. cit.*, III, p. 83). Ink, 186 × 146. From the Viti-Antaldi collection. Passavant, 187; F. 283, 366; cat. Stix-Fröhlich Bum, 56. For another drawing bearing the same sonnet of the verso, cf. note 115.

[131] London, British Museum, Pp. 1.72: Various studies of the Child. Metal point, prepared paper, 168 × 119. Passavant, 445; F. 350; Middeldorf, 75; Pouncey-Gere, 23.
According to Fischel, the drawing had been part of his "Das rosa Skizzenbuch," including nos. 345-354 of his corpus (cf. also Fischel, *op. cit.*, 1939, p. 187), of those sheets, especially the folios in Lille appear doubtful (F. 346-347, 353) and especially the one in the Boymans Museum, J 110 (F. 355), supposed for the Infant St. John of the *Alba Madonna*, which almost looks like an eighteenth century forgery.

[132] London, British Museum, 1866.7.14.79: Head of Madonna and Child. Metal point, pink-tinted paper, 143 × 110. Passavant, 159 (as again in the Camuccini collection in Rome); F. 349; Middeldorf, 74; Pouncey-Gere, 24.
It has also been part (according to Fischel) of the "pink Sketch-book"; it has been considered from time to time in relation to the *Garvagh* (also known as *Aldobrandini*) *Madonna, Cowper Madonna, Madonna dell'Impannata*, and *Madonna dei Candelabri*, but all these different references demonstrated its substantial independence from each of the known Madonnas; more than the others, however, this one demonstrates similar motifs with the *Mackintosh* and *Garvagh Madonnas*.

[133] London, British Museum, 1894.7.21.1: Madonna and Child, cartoon for the *Mackintosh Madonna*. Black pencil, traces of white lead, pricked (on two added sheets). 710 × 535. Passavant, 164 (as again in the Ceccomanni collection in Perugia); F. 362-363; Pouncey-Gere, 26.
In the sections of the cartoon where there are more variations than in the painting, the pricking corresponds with the painted variations.

[134] London, British Museum, 1900.8.24.107: Madonna and Child, half-seated on clouds, for the *Foligno Madonna*. Black pencil, grey-green treated paper with traces of ruling in squares with black pencil, 402 × 268. F. 370; Pouncey-Gere, 25.
The doubts of Passavant (II, p. 538) and of Crowe-Cavalcaselle (II, p. 189) perhaps originated directly from the exceptional technique of this drawing. For the *Foligno Madonna* there is another drawing in Chatsworth (F. 369) and another quite summary sketch in Frankfurt (F. 368).

[135] Lille, Wicar Museum, 456-457: (r.), Study for the *Alba Madonna* and other sketches; (v.), Study of a male model for a Madonna alone. Sanguine and ink (r.), sanguine (v.), 422 × 272. Passavant 376; F. 364-365; Middeldorf, 53; exhibition cat., Paris, 1965-66, no. 240; exhibition cat., Lille, 1968, no. 87.
As for the date of about 1511 for the *Alba Madonna*, Fischel and Ortolani and, recently, Oberhuber agree. Among the other drawings connected with the picture, the one in the Boymans Museum seems to me a forgery (cf. note 131), while the one in the Albertina is a copy (F. fig. 289). Two sketches of a Madonna and Child, above at the left, are perhaps the first thoughts for the *Madonna della Seggiola* whose motifs will show up again in the *Madonna della Tenda* though without any hint of a round frame. The architectural sketches above have no clear reference but allude to the knowledge that Raphael had about the architecture of Bramante and also Peruzzi.

[136] Among the drawings that hypothetically could be compared with the *Galatea*, there is one in the Uffizi, no. 1474 E: it represents, on the recto, studies of *putti* on dolphins which correspond partly to certain variations in the sketches of the Child of which we read in note 109 a, and, on the verso, a plan that Oberhuber has identified as the one for the "Stalle" in the Farnesina (cf. Pouncey-Gere, *op. cit.*, 1962, addenda, no. 35, and K. Oberhuber, *op. cit.*, 1963, p. 46. plates 32, 33); also the Venus of note 109 could be connected with the marine themes of *Galatea*.

[137] The most recent attempts in that direction have been made by White-Shearman (*op. cit.*, 1958), and by Shearman (*op. cit.*, 1965), after considering copies from projects or presumed Raphaelesque projects; as for the others, in the drawing of the Louvre no. 3874, with Julius II carried by bearers (which has been considered as a study for the left part of the *Expulsion of Heliodorus* and which was also attributed to Giulio Romano) the hand of Raphael appears quite doubtful (cf. Hartt, *op. cit.*, 1958, no. 32).

[138] Oxford, Ashmolean Museum, 557: (r.), Two studies of a kneeling woman, from the rear, for the *Expulsion of Heliodorus*; (v.), Study of a woman and two children, c. s. and sketch of Prophets for Santa Maria della Pace. Black pencil, 395 × 259. From the Reynolds and Ottley collections. Passavant, 512; F. (1898), 169; Middeldorf, 73; Parker. 557.
The sketch of Prophets near an arch on the verso, has been identified as the study for the Chigi Chapel in Santa Maria della Pace by M. Hirst (cf. note 147).

[139] The drawing, at the Art Society in Zurich, was published by Fischel as a study for a woman at the left side of the *Expulsion of Heliodorus* (cf. O. Fischel, "An unknown Drawing by Raphael in Zurich," *The Burlington Magazine*, XLVI. 1925, p. 134); Shearman, who at first had supposed that this was a study for the women on the second plane of the *Fire in the Borgo*, went back to the exact references of Fischel (cf. Shearman, *op. cit.*, 1959, p. 457 and 1965, p. 168).

[140] Paris, Louvre, 3853: Head of angel, fragment of the cartoon for he *Expulsion of Heliodorus*. Black pencil, pricked for pouncing, 265 × 327. From the Crozat and Mariette collections. Passavant, 346; F. (1898), 168; exhibition cat., Mariette, Paris, 1967, no. 121.

An analogous fragment for the head of another angel is also in the Louvre, no. 3852; both the fragments are described as such by Mariette in the catalogue for the sale of the Crozat collection: " Deux merveilleux cartons des deux têtes d'anges du sujet de l'Héliodore sur lesquels Raphaël a peint son tableaux. " In Oxford there is another fragment of the cartoon, with the head of a horse driving off Heliodorus (Parker, 556).

[141] Florence, Gabinetto Disegni, Uffizi, 536 E: Study of the *Liberation of St. Peter*. Ink, bistre wash, black pencil, white lead partly oxidated, tinted paper, 257 × 417 (original measurements of the sheet). Passavant, 129; F. (1898), 178.

Morelli and, in the earliest stage, also Fischel had supposed the hand of Perino del Vaga, but later Fischel himself gave it to Raphael (Shearman and Oberhuber do the same, *op. cit.*, 1965 and 1966 respectively). There is another copy quite faithful, from Raphael's immediate circle, in Rio de Janeiro (cf. D. Redig de Campos, " Un disegno raffaellesco per la Liberazione di San Pietro a Rio de Janeiro, " *Raffaello e Michelangelo*, 1946, IV, fig. 31).

[142] This dating was first proposed by Shearman, *op. cit.*, 1965, p. 173, and it has been accepted and enlarged with additional arguments by Oberhuber (see following note).

[143] Florence, Gabinetto Disegni, Uffizi, 1973 F: (r.), Studies of a sleeping woman and of architecture; (v.), various architectural sketches. Ink and bistre water color with light touches of black pencil, 264 × 345 (maximum measurements).

Formerly attributed to Parmigianino, this drawing has been recognized and published by K. Oberhuber (" Eine unbekannte Zeichnung Raffaels in den Uffizien, " *Mitteilungen des Kunsthistorischen Institutes in Florenz*, December 1966, pp. 225 ff.) and must be compared with the drawing in Oxford, Parker 462 (in the group of the drawings of the Lawrence collection, formerly Wicar, attributed to Peruzzi by Dollmayr and Fischel in 1898) which Oberhuber does not consider so much an original by Raphael as, rather, a copy from the fresco or from a lost drawing. The sheet in Oxford, Parker 583, which Shearman refers to the *Sacrifice of Isaac* on the same ceiling, does not appear to be by Raphael.

[144] See, for example, the painting of Stradano made known by L. Berti (*Il Principe dello Studiolo*, Florence, 1967, fig. 173), representing S. Nicola da Bari throwing apples to young girls, in which one of the sleeping girls has the same identical gesture of our figure, almost certainly inspired by the engraving of Marcantonio; the drawing preparatory to the painting, with the same figure, was exhibited in the show *Handzeichnungen alter Meister aus Schweizer Privatbesitz*, Zurich, 1957, cat. no. 62, attributed there to an anonymous Emilian.

[145] Naples, Capodimonte Museum, 86653: Moses kneeling, cartoon for the ceiling of the Stanza di Eliodoro. Black pencil, water color and white lead, cartoon on cloth, 183 × 140. From the Farnese Collection. Passavant, 151; Molajoli, *Notizie su Capodimonte*, Naples, 1958, p. 49.

Accepted by Oberhuber and Shearman, *op. cit.*, 1962 and 1966, 1965 (respectively). There is a drawing in the Venice Accademia, no. XXV-6 (F. 1898, 185), which seems more a copy from the fresco than the cartoon, because of the position the figure is in.

[146] Stockholm, National Museum, 292: *Assumption of the Virgin*. Ink, 235 × 324. From the Antaldi and Crozat collections. F. 381; cat. Siren, 1917, no. 302 (as Penni); Shearman, *op. cit.*, 1961, pp. 143-44, 155-56.

[147] Oxford, Ashmolean Museum, 553: (r.), Euclid and his disciples for the *School of Athens*; (v.), Sketch with two plans for the Chigi Chapel in Santa Maria della Pace. Silver point on grey-green tinted paper (r.); ink (v.), 247 × 326. Passavant, 506; F. 311-12; Parker, 553.

The identification of the drawing's verso, which interests us here, with the plans for Santa Maria della Pace are due to M. Hirst (" The Chigi Chapel in S. Maria della Pace, " *Journal of the Warburg and Courtauld Institutes*, XXIV, 1961, pp. 161 ff.), who was the first to make the drawing known. In Stockholm there is a copy from a lost Raphaelesque project, which recaptures precisely the motifs of the sketch (cf. Fischel, *op. cit.*, 1948, II, 193). Other drawings for the Chigi Chapel are, besides those for the Sibyls in Oxford, London, and Vienna, of which we read in the following note, the one in the Uffizi, no. 544 E, for the Prophet Daniel, rather worn out (Fischel, 1948, 165), and the one in Oxford, 557 v., for the Prophets (cf. note 138).

[148] a) Oxford, Ashmolean Museum, 562: Young Phrygian Sibyl for Santa Maria della Pace. Sanguine and stylus with traces of black pencil, 363 × 189. From the Richardson and Reynolds collections. Passavant, 500; F. (1898), 284 (as the Phrygian Sibyl); Parker, 562.

Morelli attributed the sheet to Giulio Romano. The figure of the Phrygian (?) Sibyl from the beginning was thought of as seated at the right of the arch with the head turned to the left, as you can see in the general sketch (cf. note 147); but afterwards Raphael conceived the bust differently, with the head turned to the right and the left arm outstretched across the figure, as it is seen precisely in this drawing, with a motif that afterwards was to be given to the Persian Sibyl while, for the Phrygian (?) Sibyl, Raphael was to return to a calmer pose, with the head turned to the left, as is seen in the painting and also in another preparatory drawing in the British Museum (Pouncey-Gere, 36).

b) Vienna, Albertina, 181: Study of an old Sibyl for Santa Maria della Pace. Sanguine, and traces of stylus 279 × 172. Passavant, 196; F. (1898), 282; cat. Stix-Fröhlich Bum, 72.

Usually considered as the Tiburtine Sibyl while it is probably the Cumaean, Sibyl for her old age and the close similarity with the Michelangelesque Cumaean Sibyl of the Sistine Vault (cf. L. D. Ettlinger, " A note on Raphael's Sibyls in Santa Maria della Pace, " *Journal of the Warburg and Courtauld Institutes*, XXIV, 1961, p. 322).

[149] Florence, Gabinetto Disegni, Uffizi, 1475 E: (r.), *Descent of Christ to Limbo*, a tondo for the Chigi Chapel; (v.), study of a male torso. Ink, stylus tracing the *tondo*. 209 × 205. Passavant, 110; Hartt, *op. cit.*, 1958, no. 22 (as Giulio Romano); Hirst, *op. cit.*, 1961, plate 31 b, p. 175.

Hirst returns the sheet to Raphael together with the companion drawing in the Clark collection representing the *Doubting of St. Thomas* for the opposite *tondo* scheme, which is known from the copy of the Raphaelesque project conserved in Stockholm (cf. note 147). The two bronze *tondos* by Lorenzetto, now in Chiaravalle, have also been published by Hirst.

[150] See Hirst, *op. cit.*, 1961, p. 172. The group of drawings for the *Resurrection* already reconstructed by Fischel (" Raphaels Auferstehung Christi, " *Jahrbuch der Preussischen Kunstsammlungen*, XLVI, 1925, pp. 191 ff.).

[151] a) Bayonne, Bonnat Museum, 683: (r.), Sketch for the *Resurrection*; (v.), Study of four male torsos. Ink, 406 × 275. From the Duca d'Alba, Lawrence, and William of Orange collections. F. 387; cat. Bean, 1960, no. 132.

Identified as for the Chigi Chapel in Santa Maria della Pace, by Hirst (*op. cit.*, 1961, p. 171) it was considered a copy by Passavant, Crowe-Cavalcaselle and Fischel (1898). The verso appears truly a work of the shop, notwithstanding the certain autograph of the recto, subsequently recognized by Fischel (*op. cit.*, 1925).

b) Oxford, Ashmolean Museum, 559: (r.), Man seated on a stone; (v.), sketches for the *Resurrection*. Black pencil (r.), ink (v.). 345 × 265. Passavant, 520; F. 389-390; Middeldorf, 80; Parker, 559.

The study on the recto is a precise elaboration of the figure alluded to in the following sketch, also in Oxford, for the lower portion of the *Resurrection*, while the sketches on the verso allude only to some types of figures which appear in the same sheet in Oxford, no. 558, and in the more complete one in Bayonne. The type of soldier with the flag in the center, also on the verso, was to be recaptured in an engraving by Marcantonio (B. XIV, 481), inspired perhaps from some other study by Raphael himself.

c) Oxford, Ashmolean Museum, 558: Sketch for the lower section of a Resurrection. Ink, 208 × 262. Passavant, 111, p. 213 (as the School); F. 388; Parker, 558. Probably the sheet was originally longer and included the upper part of the scene, as in the analogous drawing in Bayonne.

[152] a) Windsor, Royal Library, 12735: (r.), Standing nude with an axe; (v.), group of cows. Black pencil (r.), ink (v.), 322 × 256. Passavant, 437 (for the *Battle of Constantine* with recollections of the *Liberation of St. Peter*); F. 392; Popham-Wilde, 799.
According to Crowe-Cavalcaselle (II, p. 159) this and the other study of soldiers are for the *Liberation of St. Peter*, where this figure actually appears, but in counterpart. The verso seems the work of the workshop.

b) Windsor, Royal Library, 12736: Two nude figures with shields: Black pencil, 266 × 223. Passavant, 436; F. 392; Popham-Wilde, 798.

[153] London, British Museum, 1854.5.13.11: Study of a nude sitting on the ground with raised arms. Black pencil, 293 × 327. From the Mariette collection (in its catalogue it is indicated as a study for the *Battle of Ostia*). F. 395; Pouncey-Gere, 34; exhibition cat., Paris, 1967, no. 122.
It was attributed by Morelli to the school of Michelangelo and connected with the other studies by Raphael for the *Resurrection* by Ruland. Such a figure appears in the engraving of the *Bacchanal* by the " Maestro H. F. E., " (B, XV, 5) published by Parker (*op. cit.*, 1939-40, p. 41).

[154] Windsor, Royal Library, 12742; Madonna and Child with St. Elizabeth, for the *Madonna dell'Impannata*. Metal point, white lead, prepared paper, 210 × 145. From the Bonfiglioli and Sagredo collections. Passavant, 426; F. 373; Popham-Wilde, 800; Forlani, *op. cit.* (1962), no. 14.
According to Fischel, it was part of the brown notebook to which the sheets mentioned in notes 115 and 156 also belonged.

[155] Oxford, Ashmolean Museum, 561: Seated Madonna, embracing the Child. Silver point, white lead, grey paper, 161 × 128. Passavant, 489; F. 376; Parker, 561.
Morelli considered it a copy, while Fischel in 1818 attributed it to Penni; it should have been part of the notebook of the preceding sheet together with the drawings in Munich for the soldiers in the *Battle of Constantine*, in Frankfurt for a soldier in the *Repulse of Attila* and in Chatsworth for a Reading Madonna with Child (F. 375), quite similar to this (cf. Fischel, *op. cit.*, 1939). This study has been engraved in the same direction and with few variations by an anonymous artist close to Marcantonio (B. XV, II); Reynolds was inspired by it for his portrait of the *Duchess Spencer with son* (Huntingdon Collection).

[156] Windsor, Royal Library, 0117: Landscape with ancient ruins. Metal point, white lead, prepared paper. 210 × 141. Fischel, *op. cit.*, 1939, p. 181; Middeldorf, 76; Popham-Wilde, 801.
The landscape corresponds to the one in the background of the so-called Morbetto engraving (B. XIV, 417), for which there is a preparatory drawing in the Uffizi, in a poor state of preservation, perhaps from Raphael's workshop, no. 525. It would have been part of the notebook constructed by Fischel, which is mentioned in note 155.

[157] Florence, Gabinetto Disegni, Uffizi, 524 E: Study for the *Madonna of the Fish*. Sanguine and traces of black pencil and white lead, 268 × 264. Passavant, 120; F. 371; exhibition cat., U.S.A.-Uffizi, 1960-61, no. 33.
There is a painterly sketch of it, perhaps from the Raphael's workshop, in the Norman Colville collection (F. 372) and a fragment of the preparatory cartoon is in Berlin (F. fig. 293 a).

[158] Florence, Gabinetto Disegni, Uffizi, 534 E: Study of a standing *putto* for the *Madonna of Francis I*. Sanguine and stylus, 270 × 209. Passavant, 113; F. 378; Hartt, *op. cit.*, 1958, no. 19 (as Giulio Romano).
Oberhuber (*op. cit.*, 1962, p. 63) attributes to Raphael, besides this drawing and that of the Madonna of the Louvre (F. 378 a), also the other study for the Madonna in the Uffizi (F. 377), which elsewhere I have tried to justify as by Giulio Romano, according to the indications of Hartt (cf. Forlani, *op cit*. [1962], no. 63). See also Marabottini in this volume.

[159] Among the drawings for the Stanza dell'Incendio attributed to Raphael by Oberhuber (cf. *op. cit.*, 1962, to which we refer the reader as the largest and most recent discussion on the subject), the drawing for Aeneas and Anchises in the Albertina, no. 4881 (Oberhuber, fig. 37), does not seem to be by Raphael, because the variations made by the draftsman in regard to the corresponding portion of the fresco lack a certain luministic fineness which is instead one the greatest merits of the painting and is autographic for that section. Especially weak is the drawing in the Louvre, no. 4011 (Oberhuber, fig. 44), which should be for one of the prisoners in the *Battle of Ostia*, but it is only a later copy of it; the drawing in Chantilly, F. R. 48 bis (Oberhuber, fig. 58) from the *Coronation of Charlemagne*, is evidently also a copy.

[160] Vienna, Albertina, S. R. 282: Two standing nudes for the *Battle of Ostia*. Sanguine, 401 × 281. The drawing bears the date of 1515 and an inscription in old German, recorded in full by Golzio (*op. cit.*, p. 36), by the hand of Albert Dürer, who attests that the drawing had been sent to him by Raphael as his own work. From the collection of Willibald Imhof, heir of Dürer. Passavant, 225; F. (1898), 199; Hartt, *op. cit.*, 1958, no. 9 (as Giulio Romano).
Accepted as a sure work by Shearman (*op. cit.*, 1959, 1964) and by Oberhuber (*op. cit.*, 1962, fig. 43). As we said in the introduction, the drawing has an unquestionable *pedigree*, even though doubts have risen about the autograph of Dürer for the old inscription; it was acquired from the widow of Dürer's heir, Willibald Imhof, for the Emperor Rudolf II, as is attested by the list made for Rudolf II by Mrs. Imhof. It passed then to the Treasury in Vienna, together with the other drawings of the Emperor, then to the National Library and from there, as an exchange, into the collection of Albert von Saxe-Teschen (I thank E. Knabb and K. Oberhuber for having kindly given me the information). There are, therefore, only reasons of style (a certain harshness, especially in the lines of the leg and in the type of the figures, quite ungraceful, a rarity in Raphael) to justify the many doubts advanced by the critics, from Morelli to Hartt, regarding the Raphaelesque autograph of the drawing (cf. also Marabottini in this work).

[161] a) Lille, Wicar Museum, 428: The planet Mars and an angel, for one of the mosaics of the dome of the Chigi Chapel in Santa Maria del Popolo. Sanguine, 255 × 240. Passavant, 397; F. (1898), 285; Middeldorf, 82; exhibition cat., Paris, 1965-66, no. 244; exhibition cat., Lille, 1968, no. 90. In the mosaic the figures are dressed and appear in the same orientation as in the drawing.

b) Oxford, Ashmolean Museum, 567: Study for the angel and the planet Jupiter in the mosaic for the Chigi Chapel in Santa Maria del Popolo. It is in counterpart with regard to the mosaic and has some variations in the wings. Sanguine, 197 × 168. From the Wicar and Lawrence collections. Passavant 461; F. (1898), 286; exhibition cat., London, 1930, no. 140; Parker, 567.
The sheet, after having been condemned as a forgery by Morelli, did not have a very good reception from the critics, and it has been considered both a forgery or a copy until the most recent literature, which tends to re-evaluate this entire group of drawings for the Chigi Chapel dome; this group includes the two drawings described here and also the Oxford sheet (Parker, 566), which bears on its recto and on its verso studies for God the Father creating the planets, at the center of the dome (the recto in the same sense as the figure in the mosaic, the verso in counterpart and with some variations).

[162] See, for a recent and careful reconstruction of the decoration of the entire Chigi Chapel in Santa Maria del Popolo and the relative drawings, J. Shearman, " The Chigi Chapel in Santa Maria del Popolo, " *Journal of the Warburg and Courtauld Institutes*, XXV, 1961, pp. 124 ff., where, among other things, the originality and historical importance of the entire decorative scheme (the first involving architecture, sculpture, and painting by the same artist) is well characterized.

[163] Vasari is quite eloquent in regard to: "cloth for rich tapestries of gold and silk thread; for these Raphael made large colored cartoons of the proper size, all with his own hand, which were sent to weavers in Flanders. The work is so marvelously executed that it excites the wonder of those who see it that such things as hair and beards and delicate flesh-coloring can be woven work: it is certainly a miracle rather than a product of human art... it cost 70,000 scudi." (Vasari-Milanesi, IV, p. 370). A long study on cartoons and the relative drawings and projects is the work of J. White-J. Shearman (op. cit., 1958). Among the preserved drawings, the one which can be considered as an autograph, besides the ones described in notes 165-167, is the sheet in the Uffizi, no. 540 E. (F., 1898, 255, then considered by Andrea del Sarto) which, however, has a certain flatness in the tracing.

[164] For example, for the *Miraculous Draught of Fishes*, there is in the Albertina a drawing by Giulio Romano (no. 192, Hartt, op. cit., 1958, no. 3) which has on the recto a "model" and on the verso an ink sketch, of the type which Raphael made, with the detail of the boat (cf. Oberhuber, op. cit., 1962, fig. 23).

[165] a) Paris, Cabinet des Dessins, Louvre, 3854; Study of a standing male figure for the Christ in the cartoon "Pasce oves meas." Sanguine and stylus, cut at the right side, with old additions, 252 × 134. Passavant, 350 (he does not recognize the destination); F. (1898), 244; Middeldorf, 84; Popham-Wilde, no. 802.

Hartt (op. cit., 1958, no 1) attributes it to Giulio Romano, but this attribution has no following. It is not easy to establish if the drawing, with traces of cutting at the right margin, was a single study or a fragment of a drawing with the entire scene, the same one from which the copy in Windsor was traced; this is a probable assumption, since the figure corresponds exactly with the relative one of the copy, but in counterpart.

b) Windsor, Royal Library, 12751: Study for the cartoon "Pasce oves meas"; tracing. Sanguine, with traces of stylus from the original, 257 × 375. From the Bonfiglioli (?) collection. Passavant, 425; F. (1898), 243; Popham-Wilde, 802.

This sheet, too, is given to Giulio Romano, with retouches by Raphael, according to Hartt (op. cit., 1958, no. 1 a). With all probability the tracing must have been made by Raphael from one of his originals (the same one perhaps already seen in the Louvre for Christ alone) and then greatly retouched by Raphael himself; the purpose was to see from the tracing which was in reverse with respect to the original drawing, the final effect of the tapestry, which, in turn, would be in reverse with regard to the cartoon. In the Louvre, no. 3863, there is the original "model," believed to be Raphael's by Oberhuber, but more probably by Giulio Romano (cf. Hartt, op. cit., 1958, no. 2); there is a replica of inferior quality of this drawing, but certainly it is from Raphael's workshop (Uffizi, no. 1216 E).

[166] Chatsworth, Devonshire collection, 730: Study for St. Paul in the cartoon of the *Sacrifice at Lystra*. Metal point, white lead, grey prepared paper, 228 × 103. From the Lely collection. Passavant, 563; exhibition cat., U.S.A., 1962-1963, no. 58.

Fischel, who does not record the sheet in 1898, maintains instead that it is an authentic Raphael in his posthumous monograph of 1948, p. 365; it shows only a few variations with respect to the definite figure.

[167] Windsor, Royal Library, 12750: Model for the cartoon with the *Blinding of Elymas*. Metal point, white lead, touches of ink, grey prepared paper, 270 × 355. The sheet must have been bought in Rome, according to the inventory of George III. F. (1898) 253; Popham-Wilde, 803.

Shearman (op. cit., 1959) considers it to be perhaps by Raphael, but destined for the engraving of Agostino Veneziano (B., XIV, 48), while Hartt (op. cit., 1958, no. 5) gives it to Giulio Romano.

[168] See J. Shearman (op. cit., 1964); this scholar has been perhaps too generous with regard to certain drawings. The recto of the drawing in the Louvre, no. 1120 (Shearman, fig. 85), for the group with Cupid and Jupiter (cf. note 170) does not seem to be a Raphael, but a copy from the workshop, while the drawing in the Albertina, no. 122 (Shearman, fig. 92) formerly attributed to Viti, for the group of Cupid and Psyche in the *Wedding*, appears to be a free derivation from the middle of the sixteenth century, like certain ink drawings by Naldini.

[169] Paris, Cabinet des Dessins, Louvre, 3875: Psyche offers a Vessel to Venus, for the Loggia of the Farnesina. Sanguine, 263 × 197. From the Malvasia, Crozat and Mariette collections. Passavant, 336; F. (1898), 271; exhibition cat., Mariette, 1967, no. 124.

A first hint of the composition, which is inserted in one of the corbels of the Loggia is a brilliant sketch in Oxford (Shearman, op. cit., 1964, fig. 79) which is of the same type as the one for the wall of the Chigi Chapel in Santa Maria della Pace (cf. note 147).

[170] a) Chatsworth, Devonshire collection, 53: Venus on the clouds, tracing. Sanguine, 330 × 246. This is a tracing, quite certainly reworked by Raphael himself. J. A. Gere, "Some Italian Drawings in the Chatsworth Exhibition," *The Burlington Magazine*, 1949, pp. 169 ff.; exhibition cat., U.S.A., 1962-63, no. 61.

b) Chatsworth, Devonshire collection, 56: Study of a nude girl, kneeling. Sanguine, 278 × 186. F. (1898), 197; Middeldorf, 83; exhibition cat., U.S.A., 1962-63, no. 62.

The sheet has from time to time been considered a study for one of the women in the *Mass at Bolsena* or for one in the *Fire in the Borgo*, or, more generally, for the Farnesina; Shearman (op. cit., 1964, p. 70, fig. 72) was reasonable in supposing that it is a study for the handmaid of Cupid kneeling in the scene with the Toilet of Psyche, one of the scenes which he believes conceived by Raphael himself for the lunette, but never executed; the composition has reached us through the engraving by Bonasone representing the Toilet of Psyche (B. XV, 167), which helps us to recognize another drawing for the same scene, the one in the Louvre, no. 1120, which bears on the verso a study that is a probable autograph for the standing handmaid (while on the recto the study with Jupiter and Cupid seems to be a copy; cf. note 168).

[171] See Oberhuber (op. cit., figs. 6-9, respectively). Probably the only autograph sheet of the whole is, as we have said, the one in Chatsworth, 904 (Oberhuber, fig. 6) which studies the nude figures, in sanguine, for the upper part of the *Transfiguration*, with few variations with regard to the painting. Another recent contribution to the study of this painting, with a particular interest in the drawings, was made by A. Bertini, "La Trasfigurazione e l'ultima evoluzione della pittura di Raffaello," *Critica d'arte*, 8, 1961, pp. 1 ff.

[172] Paris, Cabinet des Dessins, Louvre, 3864: Study of two standing Apostles, for the *Transfiguration*. Sanguine and stylus, 340 × 221. Passavant 321; F. (1898), 339.

Hartt (op. cit., 1959, no. 28) attributes it to Giulio Romano, while Oberhuber (op. cit., 1962, fig. 11) insists on the traditional attribution to Raphael. With the exception of the Albertina drawing, 237 (Oberhuber, fig. 8), which sketches the figure of St. Andrew and which seems to be an autograph, none of the sheets connected by the critics to the *Transfiguration* seems to be by the hand of the master, and it is extremely difficult to know to whom, among his assistants and followers (especially considering Giulio Romano and Penni), the single sheets are attributable. The drawing in the Louvre, no. 4118, recently published by Oberhuber as an autograph (op. cit., fig. 14) does not clarify the problem, since we are certainly dealing here with an eighteenth-century copy from the painting.

[173] Oxford, Ashmolean Museum, 568: Studies of two heads of Apostles, for the *Transfiguration*. Black pencil and white lead, grey paper, pin-pricked, 499 × 364. Passavant, 473; F. (1898), 341; Parker, 568.

Fischel (op. cit., 1937, p. 168, plate I c) made known this and other drawings of the same series (two in the British Museum, Pouncey-Gere, 37 and 38, and one in the Albertina, 242) as "auxiliary cartoons" and Raphaelesque autographs for the *Transfiguration*, and Hartt ("Raphael and Giulio Romano," *Art Bulletin*, 26, 1944, pp. 67 ff.) added to the series the two beautiful drawings in Chatsworth, nos. 61 and 67, which together with the one in Oxford, are perhaps the only ones revealing the true hand of Sanzio.

Bibliography

Below are listed the bibliographic citations which are most frequently used in the text and in the notes (the indicated bibliography for each drawing is only the essential one: Passavant, Fischel and, when possible, one or more entries of the catalogues or recent articles to which we refer for a more complete bibliography). The order is chronological according to the cited edition; the abbreviations in parentheses at the end of each citation are those with which the entry appears in the text or notes.

A. Bartsch, *Le peintre graveur*, Vienna, 1803-21. (B.).

Vasari-Milanesi, *Le vite de' più eccellenti pittori, scrittori e architettori*, Florence, 1878-85. (Vasari-Milanesi).

J. A. Crowe-G. B. Cavalcaselle, *Raffaello, la sua vita e le sue opere*. Florence, 1884-91.

J. D. Passavant, *Raffaello d'Urbino e il padre suo Giovanni Santi.* Notes and translation by G. Guasti. Florence, 1891.

O. Fischel, *Raphael Zeichnungen. Versuch einer Kritik der bisher veröffentlichten Blätter*, Strasbourg, 1898. (Fischel, 1898).

O. Fischel, *Raphaels Zeichnungen* (8 sections). Berlin, 1913-41. (F.).

A. Venturi, " Disegni di Raffaello (avanti la venuta in Roma)," *L'Arte*, 1916, pp. 315 ff.

A. Venturi, *Raffaello*, Rome, 1920.

A. Venturi, " Raffaello," *Storia dell'Arte Italiana.* IX-II, Milan, 1926.

A. Venturi, *Choix de cinquante dessins de Raphaël Santi*, Paris, 1927.

(Popham), *Italian Drawings exhibited at the Royal Academy, Burlington House*, London, 1930 (exhibition cat., London, 1930).

A. Stix-L. Fröhlich Bum, *Die Zeichnungen der Toskanischen Umbrischen und Römischen Schulen, in der Graphischen Sammlung Albertina*, Vienna, 1932 (cat. Stix-Fröhlich Bum).

V. Golzio, *Raffaello nei documenti del suo secolo*, Vatican City, 1936.

O. Fischel, " Raphael's auxiliary cartoons," *The Burlington Magazine*, 71 (2), 1937, pp. 167-168.

A. E. Popham, " An Unnoticed Drawing by Raphael," *Old Master Drawings*, 1937-38, p. 45.

O. Fischel, " Raphael's pink sketch-book," *The Burlington Magazine*, April, 1939, pp. 182 ff.

K. T. Parker, " Some observations on Oxford Raphaels," *Old Master Drawings*, September-March, 1939-40, pp. 34 ff.

S. Ortolani, *Raffaello*, Bergamo, 1942.

F. Hartt, " Raphael and Giulio Romano," *Art Bulletin*, 26, 1944, pp. 67 ff.

U. Middeldorf, *Raphael's Drawings*, New York, 1945.

O. Fischel, *Raphael*, London, 1948; 2d ed., Berlin, 1962.

A. E. Popham-J. Wilde, *The Italian Drawings of the XV and XVI centuries at Windsor Castle.* London, 1949.

R. Longhi, " Percorso di Raffaello giovine," *Paragone*, no. 65, 1955.

K. T. Parker, *Catalogue of the collection of drawings in the Ashmolean Museum*, Oxford, 1956.

F. Hartt, *Giulio Romano*, Yale University, 1958.

J. Shearman, " Giulio Romano " (review to F. Hartt), *The Burlington Magazine*, 1959, pp. 451-460.

J. Bean, *Les dessins italiens de la Collection Bonnat (Bayonne)*, Paris, 1960.

(M. G. Ciardi-Dupré), *Mostra di disegni dei Grandi Maestri – Gabinetto Disegni e Stampe degli Uffizi*, Florence, 1960 (exhibition cat., Uffizi).

Disegni italiani di cinque secoli, U.S.A., 1960 – Florence, 1961 (exhibition cat., U.S.A. - Florence, 1960-61).

(P. Mourois), *Raphaël – Dessins*, Lille, 1961 (exhibition cat., Lille).

M. Hirst, " The Chigi Chapel in Santa Maria della Pace," *Journal of the Warburg and Courtauld Institutes*, 1961, XXIV, pp. 161-85.

J. Shearman, " The Chigi Chapel in Santa Maria del Popolo," *Journal of the Warburg and Courtauld Institutes*, XXV, 1961, nos. 3-4, pp. 129 ff.

G. Castelfranco, " Raffaello," *I grandi maestri del disegno*, Milan, 1962.

Ph. Pouncey-J. A. Gere, *Italian Drawings in the Department of Prints and Drawings in the British Museum – Raphael and his circle*, London, 1962.

K. Oberhuber, " Vorzeichnungen zu Raffaels Transfiguration," *Jahrbuch der Berliner Museen*, IV, 1962, pp. 116-49.

K. Oberhuber, " Die Fresken der Stanza dell'Incendio im Werk Raffaels," *Jahrbuch der Kunsthistorischen Sammlungen in Wien*, 58, 1962, pp. 23-72.

Old Master Drawings from Chatsworth – loan exhibition, U.S.A., 1962-63 (exhibition cat., U.S.A.).

J. Shearman, " Die Loggia der Psyche in der Villa Farnesina und die Probleme der lätzen Phase von Raffaels graphischen Stil," *Jahrbuch der Kunsthistorischen Sammlungen in Wien*, 60, XXIV, 1964, pp. 58-100.

J. Bean-F. Stampfle, *Drawings from New York Collections; I, The Italian Renaissance*, New York, 1965.

J. Shearman, " Raphael's Unexecuted Projects for the Stanze," *Walter Friedländer zum 90. Geburtstag*, Berlin, 1965, pp. 158-180.

Le Seizième Siècle Européen. Dessins du Louvre – Peintures et Dessins dans les Collections Publiques Françaises. Paris, 1965-66 (exhibition cat., Paris).

K. Oberhuber, " Eine unbekannte Zeichnung Raffaels in den Uffizien," *Mitteilungen des Kunsthistorischen Institutes in Florenz*, December, 1966, pp. 225 ff.

Le Cabinet d'un Grand Amateur, P. J. Mariette (1694-1774), Paris-Louvre, 1967 (exhibition cat., Mariette).

Italianse Tekeningen uit Het Museen te Rijssel – Dessins Italiens du Musée de Lille, Amsterdam, Bruxelles, Lille, 1967-68 (exhibition cat., Lille).

PLATES

64/65	An Angel. Pinacoteca Tosio-Martinengo, Brescia	I
	Marriage of the Virgin. Brera, Milan	II
	Three Graces. Condé Museum, Chantilly	III
	Madonna and Child, called the "Granduca Madonna." Galleria Palatina, Florence	IV
	Madonna and Child with the Infant St. John, called the "Belle Jardinière." Louvre, Paris	V
	The Deposition. Galleria Borghese, Rome	VI
	Portrait of a Woman, called "La Muta." Galleria Nazionale delle Marche, Urbino	VII
	Madonna and Child, called the "Tempi Madonna." Alte Pinakothek, Munich	VIII
96/97	Stanza della Segnatura: la Disputa del Sacramento, the School of Athens, the Parnassus, and the Cardinal Virtues. Vatican	IX–XX
144/145	Stanza di Eliodoro: the Expulsion of Heliodorus from the Temple, the Mass at Bolsena, the Liberation of St. Peter, the Enconter of Attila and Leo the Great. Vatican	XXI–XXXII
176/177	Madonna and Child with the Infant St. John, called "della Seggiola." Galleria Palatina, Florence	XXXIII
	Sistine Madonna. Gemäldegalerie, Dresden	XXXIV
	Stanza dell'Incendio: the Fire in the Borgo. Vatican	XXXV–XXXVII
	Portrait of a Woman, called "The Veiled Woman" or "The Fornarina." Galleria Palatina, Florence	XXXVIII
	Portrait of Leo X with two Cardinals. Uffizi, Florence	XXXIX
	The Transfiguration. Pinacoteca Vaticana	XL
304/305	Study of Madonna and Child, perhaps for the Bridgewater Madonna. Albertina, Vienna	XLI
	Study for the Statue of Minerva and other Statues, for the School of Athens. Ashmolean Museum, Oxford	XLII
	Study of the Alba Madonna. Wicar Museum, Lille	XLIII
	Study of Heads for the Madonna and the Child. British Museum, London; Madonna embracing the Child. Ashmolean Museum, Oxford;	XLIV
	Study of Landscapes with Ruins, for the Morbetto. Royal Library, Windsor	XLV

CONTENTS

MARIO SALMI

Introduction

I - LUISA BECHERUCCI

Raphael and Painting

9   The paintings
10   Urbino
12   Florence
16   Perugia
27   Città di Castello
30   Siena
39   Bologna
49   Urbino and Florence

79   The language
87   Julius II
91   The Stanza della Segnatura
134   Madonnas and portraits
139   The Stanza of Heliodorus
160   Agostino Chigi "il Magnifico"
173   Leo X
180   The Tapestries
182   Santa Maria del Popolo
185   The last works

II - ALESSANDRO MARABOTTINI

Raphael's Collaborators

199   Premise
208   Raphael and his workshop
290   Epilogue
295   Appendix (bibliographical notes and biographies of the principal pupils of Raphael)

III - ANNA FORLANI TEMPESTI

The drawings

309   The Umbrian Period
309   The first drawings: the S. Niccolò da Tolentino and the Library in Siena
315   The Coronation of the Virgin and other drawings

325   The Florentine Period
325   The drawings about 1504
332   The Florentine period
348   Drawings for the Deposition and final Florentine period

354   The Roman Period
354   The beginning of the Roman sojourn
358   The ceiling of the Stanza della Segnatura
368   The Disputa del Sacramento
377   The School of Athens
380   Drawings for the Parnassus
385   Various drawings of the first Roman period
391   Drawings for the Stanza of Heliodorus
397   Drawings for Santa Maria della Pace
403   Drawings for the late Madonnas and for the Stanza dell'Incendio
408   Drawings for the mosaics of Santa Maria del Popolo and for the Vaticans tapestries
412   Drawings for the Farnesina and for the Transfiguration

427   Bibliography

Acknowledgments

The photographs illustrating the volume have been kindly furnished by:

A.C.L., Bruxelles – Albertina, Vienna – Alinari-Anderson, Florence – Annan, Glasgow – Arborio Mella, Milan – Archives Photographiques, Paris – Archivio fotografico Gallerie e Musei Vaticani – Ashmolean Museum, Oxford – Aubert, Bayonne – Bayerische Staatsbibliothek, Munich – Belli, Pesaro – C. Bevilacqua, Milan – Biblioteca Hertziana, Rome – Borchi, Faenza – British Museum, London – Brogi, Florence – Bulloz, Paris – Ciccione, Paris – Courtauld Institute of Art, Hampton Court – De Cesare, Milan – Deutsches Archaeologisches Institut, Rome – Duke of Devonshire, Chatsworth – DIMT, Milan – Erbé, Montpellier – Ferruzzi, Venice – Fiorentini, Venice – Fotofast, Bologna – Gabinetto dei disegni degli Uffizi, Florence – Gabinetto Fotografico Nazionale, Rome – Gabinetto fotografico della Soprintendenza alle Gallerie, Florence – Gaggiotti, Rome – Galleria Nazionale d'Arte Moderna e Contemporanea, Rome – Gérondal, Lille – Giordani, Rome – Giraudon, Paris – Kunstinstitut, Zurich – Istituto Geografico De Agostini, Novara – Kunsthistorisches Institut, Florence – Kunsthistorisches Museum, Vienna – Landesbildstelle Rheinland, Düsseldorf – Laniepce, Sèvres – Laverton, Rueil-Malmaison – Collection Lugt, Paris – Marré, Urbino – Metropolitan Museum of Art, Washington – Musées de la Ville of Strasbourg – Musei Comunali, Rome – Museo del Castello Sforzesco, Milan – Museo del Prado, Madrid – Museu Nacional de Arte Antiga, Lisbon – National Gallery, London – National Gallery of Art, Washington – Nationalmuseum, Stockholm – Nimatallah, Milan – Novosti, Rome – Pedicini, Naples – Pierpont Morgan Library, New York – Publifoto, Milan – Pucciarelli, Rome – Réunion des Musées Nationaux, Paris – Rheinisches Bildarchiv, Cologne – Royal Library, Windsor – Savio, Rome – Scala, Florence – Soprintendenza ai Monumenti del Lazio – Soprintendenza alle Antichità della Campania – Soprintendenza alle Gallerie, Naples – Staatsgemäldesammlungen, Munich – Städelsches Kunstinstitut, Frankfort on the Main – Steinkopf, Berlin – Szépmüvészeti Múseum, Budapest – Tacchini, Città di Castello – Tavanti, Arezzo – Teylersmuseum, Haarlem – Vasari, Rome – Victoria and Albert Museum, London – Vivarelli e Gullo, Rome – Walters Art Gallery, Baltimore – Worcester Art Museum, Worcester (Massachusetts).